THE WORLD OF THOUGHT IN ANCIENT CHINA

# THE WORLD
# OF THOUGHT
# IN ANCIENT CHINA

BENJAMIN I. SCHWARTZ

THE BELKNAP PRESS OF
HARVARD UNIVERSITY PRESS
CAMBRIDGE, MASSACHUSETTS
AND LONDON, ENGLAND
1985

This book is printed on acid-free paper, and its binding materials
have been chosen for strength and durability.

Library of Congress Cataloging in Publication Data

Schwartz, Benjamin Isadore, 1916–
The world of thought in ancient China.

Bibliography: p.
Includes index.
1. Philosophy, Chinese—To 221 B.C.    2. China
—Intellectual life—To 221 B.C.    I. Title.
B126.S345    1985        181'.11        85-833
ISBN 0-674-96190-0 (alk. paper)

*To my beloved children*
*Jonathan and Sara-Ann*
*and to Maya*

# ACKNOWLEDGMENTS

I should first of all like to express my gratitude to the American Council of Learned Societies for its generous grant, which made it possible for me to devote my undivided attention to this book.

My deepest thanks go to my devoted wife, Bunny, for her encouragement and support. I very much appreciate the help of Sylvia Appleton in organizing my manuscript and the long hours my daughter, Sara-Ann, devoted to putting it into legible shape. Finally, I am grateful to all the colleagues and friends at Harvard and elsewhere from whose observations I have gained so much.

# CONTENTS

THE WORLD OF THOUGHT IN ANCIENT CHINA

# INTRODUCTION

M Y OBJECT in this volume is to examine once again some major themes and issues in the history of ancient Chinese thought.[1] The enterprise is hazardous. Not only do we have the vast hermeneutical literature of the Chinese past but we are dealing with an area which has been and continues to be intensively studied by a host of modern Chinese, Japanese, Korean, and Western scholars. The question naturally arises—is there anything more to be said about Confucius?

Yet as in the case of ancient Greek thought, basic issues remain open and unresolved. Newly discovered materials such as the silk scrolls of the Ma Wang-tui tomb or the remnants of Ch'in law constantly come to light and the philological analysis of ancient texts continues unabated. New controversies develop that reflect the late-twentieth-century preoccupations of both Chinese and foreign scholars. As always the history of the past inevitably continues to be the history of the present.

## Why the History of Thought?

The question nevertheless remains—why should we reconsider the history of ancient Chinese thought? Or indeed, why the history of thought? The contention that the period which we are here considering is crucial to the understanding of the entire subsequent history of China in every area of life is hardly new. There has, in fact, been a sharp and even justified reaction against the excessive focus on this period by an older generation of sinologists. Few historians of China now believe that this is the only "creative" period of Chinese cultural history and that the centuries which lie between this period and the coming of the "Western impact" represent nothing but a silent, "ahistorical," and—in terms of our historicist biases—sterile stasis. Younger scholars of modern China even reject the notion of dealing with modern China wholly in terms of Western impact and emphasize the internal tendencies to change within every aspect of Chinese society during the later centuries of "traditional China."

Yet, if one wholeheartedly accepts, as I do, the premise of significant change in every area—economic, political, religious—these changes must be studied within the framework of a civilization in which the modern Western premise of a total qualitative rupture with the "traditional" past has not occurred. For example, however new the actual content of Sung or Ming thought may be, it is a thought which continues to operate within a hermeneutical tradition that takes most seriously the texts of the ancient past. It may indeed be our own judgment that vastly changed conditions and new sensibilities have led to genuine new departures, but the Ming and Ch'ing thinkers are themselves by no means bent on proving this point. They are probably quite convinced that their views simply make luminously clear the real and pure meaning of the original sources and that they have achieved a clear understanding of which sources are crucial. They by no means share the doctrine currently fashionable in the West that in all interpretation of texts, the texts are mere pretexts for the creative endeavors of the interpreter.

I hold that this doctrine is not necessarily true. The original texts may, after all, impose definite outer constraints on the thought of their interpreters, and the whole body of canonical texts within a given self-conscious tradition (such as Confucianism) may decisively shape the problematique in terms of which later thinkers confront the world, just as the traditions of statecraft may continue to shape the "practical" attitudes of the statesmen. There is a constant dialectical interaction between text and interpreter. Thus, any honest effort to deal with interpretation must include a keen concern with the texts themselves. It is only in this way that one can make judgments about the degree and nature of change. In the end, we must wrestle with our own understanding of the original sources. A concern with the texts in turn necessarily involves a concern with the milieu within which the texts emerge.

Beyond the significance of this period for the entire subsequent history of Chinese thought, I must confess that my own interest in ancient Chinese thought has also been much stimulated by the type of "world-historical" observations which we find in the chapter on the "axial age" in Karl Jaspers' book *The Origin and End of History*. In this small volume Jaspers highlights the fact that in many of the high civilizations of the ancient world—the civilizations of the ancient Near East, Greece, India, and China—we witness over the period of our "first millennium B.C." the emergence of certain "creative minorities" who relate themselves in reflective, critical, and what one might even call "transcendental" ways to the civilizations from which they emerge.[2] Whether one deals with the Upanishads, Buddhism, or Jainism in India, with the rise of biblical Judaism, with the emergence of Greek philosophy or with the emergence of Confucianism, Taoism, and Mohism in China—one finds a kind of standing back and looking beyond; of questioning and reflectivity as well as the emergence of new positive perspectives and visions. These "minorities" are no longer "cultural specialists" who simply expound the established "rules" of their cultures. Even when they continue to accept the "rules," they often see them in an entirely new light.

As with most historic change, there is, of course, no absolute beginning point of these "breakthroughs." The "discontents of civilization" no doubt have very early beginnings. Thorkild Jakobsen has stressed the beginnings of transcendental religious attitudes in the earlier literature of Mesopotamia, and in Egypt we have the wisdom literature. In China the kind of questioning and reaching beyond which we find in the *Book of Poetry* may have much earlier roots. Yet it is in the centuries which we are considering here that such tendencies, now often associated with specific individuals, truly emerge into the foreground.

The interest of these observations does not lie primarily in the very rough "contemporaneity" of these developments or in speculations about mutual influences or in any presumption of the identity of modes of thought.[3] What one rather senses are areas of common concern and dissatisfaction with prevailing states of affairs. Yet the search for new meanings in all these civilizations continues to be refracted through preexistent cultural orientations. What is suggested is thus not identities but the possibility of meaningful comparison. What is also suggested is that the movements of thought which emerged during the axial age were profoundly to shape, both directly and indirectly, the entire subsequent history of all these cultures. The problematiques posed by the axial age were in intricate and often unanticipated ways to enter into the subsequent history of human culture in all the higher civilizations.

Yet the question remains—why the history of thought? particularly when, as in this volume, I shall deal mainly not with the anonymous "mentalities" of whole populations but with the deliberations of the small minorities whose thoughts are recorded in texts. The enterprise seems not only unfashionable; it may even be called elitist.

The notion that the products of the conscious life in other times and places may have affected reality or that they merit consideration as truth-seeking efforts has long been under sustained attack from all quarters. On the one side are the claims of "depth" and behaviorist psychology, and on the other, the claims of all the social sciences, linguistic determinisms, Foucaultian doctrines of the dominance of "discourse," and so on. To emphasize the role of thought in human affairs (thought conceived of as an active process of thinking rather than as established attitudes or "mentalities") is to expose oneself to suspicions of tender-mindedness, elitism, "nonscientific" attitudes, and idealistic indifference to the commanding role of interests (however defined) in human affairs. Even cultural anthropology, which is so deeply concerned with the objective structures of collective consciousness, often has little taste for the "study of men thinking."[4]

I shall not attempt to dispose of these vast matters in this brief introduction. I shall certainly not attempt to solve the "mind-body" problem or attempt here to resolve the philosophical question of what the term "mental" means or whether the truth claims of human thought can be taken seriously. Gilbert Ryle in his *Concept of Mind* attempts to treat all "mental phenomena" either as modes of publicly observable behavior or as dispositions to behavior (it is not however made clear what a disposition is), but the question remains unresolved whether the "dispositions" to behavior which we call conscious can affect other areas of behavior. The possibility still remains in Ryle that mind even thus defined plays a crucial role as a determinant in human affairs.

The main assault against the significance of human consciousness in human affairs thus comes not so much from "materialistic" metaphysics as from those social and psychological disciplines which crave the presumed mastery and apodictic certainty of the natural sciences. The success of the natural sciences, it is felt, stems from their capacity to view the behavior of all particular events and entities as simple instantiations of general laws, systems, structures, or models. Unless the behaviors of human individuals can be totally explained as predictable instantiations of the laws, structures, and models postulated by the social scientist, his model will disintegrate. Hence the scandalous notion that the deliberations or reflections of individuals or groups may influence their own behavior or the behavior of others or the even more scandalous proposition that the truth-seeking claims of such individuals must be treated as seriously as the truth-seeking claims of the social scientist himself is simply unthinkable. Such truth claims must always be explained genetically and never "argued with" as truth-seeking claims.

What then are the grounds for asserting that the conscious verbal utterances of some modern thinkers must be treated not as reflections of culture, social system, constellations of interests, or the "discourse" to which they belong but as statements that tell us something about "the way things are" or even as theories that may conceivably affect behavior? The answer one generally finds is what might be called the doctrine of the privileged or transcendental vantage point. Here we have the notion that human history has somehow reached a point at which certain individuals can suddenly use mental capacities which in the past simply reflected the limited social, cultural, or temporal locus of the thinker to attain Truth or at least "warranted assertability." Hegel lived at a historic point when World Reason was about to become fully actualized in history and he was the voice of that Reason. Marx's views reflected the outlook of a new class which could now look at reality without "false consciousness," while Mannheim's lifetime corresponded to a moment in history and the march of science when it finally became possible for a "free-floating intelligentsia" to liberate itself from the trammels of all conditioning interests.

Some allege that the "methods of science" play the same role as a lever of transcendence in the social sciences that they presumably do in the natural sciences. Thus Clifford Geertz, after dealing with modern "ideologies" as "cultural systems," acknowledges the enormous difficulty of distinguishing between "ideology" and "science" in human affairs, particularly in Mannheim's treatment of the subject. "Where if anywhere, ideology leaves off and science begins has been the Sphinx's Riddle of much of modern sociological thought and the rustless weapon of its enemies." His own solution, which I think leaves the weapons of the enemies as rustless as ever, is to suggest "that science names the structure of situations in such a way that the attitude contained toward them is one of disinterestedness. Its style is restrained, spare, resolutely analytic. By shunning the semantic devices that most effectively formulate moral sentiment, it seeks to maximize intellectual clarity."[5] How is this disinterestedness achieved? By the determination to be disinterested? If the thought of human beings is determined by the symbolic systems that dominate their cultures, how can there be a culture in which the cultural "values" and the disinterested search for truth are so easily detached from each other? In almost all his writings about other cultures Geertz simply seems to assume that "ethos" and "world view" go together. Does the "restrained, spare analytic" style prove the absence of value assumptions? In the infinite sea of human facts, why does one choose to analyze one set of facts rather than another? In a society where the scientific posture enjoys infinite prestige, does it not pay even in terms of interest factors to assume the "scientific style"? Is Geertz in the end not simply asserting with Mannheim that at a certain point in the history of the modern West, it suddenly becomes possible for certain spirits to lift themselves onto the "plane of disinterestedness"?[6]

I do not propose to resolve here the ultimate riddle of how the same human beings who are bound to their cultures, to their places in time, to their social strata, and to their personal psychological histories simultaneously allow themselves to believe that their own behavior and outlook can be based on a view of the way things actually are or ought to be. In our ordinary experience we observe humans as creatures who make truth claims, claims to transcend interest or claims that in their case there is no contradiction between interest and truth, and yet as creatures who are bound by interests, culture, or history. Ideas may transcend interests and yet may come to serve interests and even to enhance interests, while the history of conflicting interests at times comes to be conceived of in certain modern ideologies as instrumental to the ultimate realization of the "truth." All I would urge at this point is that none of us occupies any privileged sanctuary. We are all involved. Jürgen Habermas seems to talk to us from the vantage point of some future "emancipated society" where free communication untrammeled by interests is possible. Yet he himself remains anchored in present history and in the social structure of contemporary West Germany. Like Confucius and Plato, Hegel, Marx, Habermas, and Foucault still live in an ongoing untranscended history (or in a specific discourse) and in the bounded locus of a society in which interests have not been transcended.

What of the claims of science? To be sure, we have solid and real advantages over Aristotle and Mencius. We have available to us vast stores of empirical knowledge not available to them. We also have certain relatively reliable, received canons for testing the validity of various types of concrete empirical data. To assume that any adult person is therefore free of ultimate assumptions which are by no means simply based on "empirical generalizations" derived from the data is, nevertheless, to cultivate an illusion. The very question of what data are "important" or what causal weight is to be assigned to the area of experience we regard as important—whether it be economy, language, or culture—is a question to which no preestablished "scientific method" provides an answer.

The point here is not to prove the nihilist proposition that all thought—past, present, or future—is simply a reflection of interest or simply "subjective." It is rather to indicate that if we ascribe to ourselves the capacity to concern ourselves with the validity of the ideas we espouse, despite our lack of a privileged vantage point, we have no way of totally denying this precarious capacity to others within the short span of recorded human history. Geertz, in fact, makes this point in dealing with modern ideologies, which he takes quite seriously as determinants of action if not as truth. However much we may be repelled or attracted by various ideologies, he contends, a "dispassionate" study of ideologies must not be based on a frenetic effort to reduce them to their presumed psychological or social causes.[7] On the contrary we must first take most seriously the degree to which adherents *believe in* the truth of the symbolic systems to which they adhere and even the degree to which this belief may shape their behavior. There is nothing "tender-minded" in the view that the Nazis' conscious belief about Jews may have decisively determined their behavior.

While sharing Geertz's faith in the possibility of a Weberian "understanding" of the belief systems of others, I see this disinterestedness, if at all possible, as itself based on a moral attitude. Geertz, however, insists that the disinterestedness of science is based on a disjuncture between the strategy of science and "moral sentiments." This idea presumes that although "world views" in both modern ideologies and in "traditional" cultures are indissolubly bound up with the "defense of belief and value," within modern Western culture it has suddenly become possible for some, in dealing with human affairs, to adopt a strategy of entirely disassociating scientific endeavor from other human concerns. The doctrine of the possibility of the complete disassociation of science and "value" may or may not be an "ideology." It is certainly a particular philosophy of the modern Western world. It is not science in itself.

## Culture and the History of Thought

Because cultural anthropology and the history of thought share a concern for the conscious life, something more should be said at this point concerning the relations between the two. There are to be sure many varieties of cultural anthropology. Lévi-Strauss thinks of cultures in terms of structures based on the analogue of structural linguistics while Geertz stresses symbols and symbol systems. They both, however, treat "cultures" as superordinate realities which operate, as it were, from "behind" and "through" the conscious life of human persons who again emerge as instantiations of general schemata. Lévi-Strauss, in discussing myth, states that "we do not claim to show how men think in myths but how myths think themselves out in men without their knowing it."[8] Geertz focuses on the determinative role of symbols and symbol systems. At one point he furnishes a speculative account of the emergence of *Homo sapiens* from the primate state. What shapes primates into men over vast stretches of time is the "extrinsic" force called culture. The beaver is programmed to build structures as intricate as beaver dams. Emergent man, however—considered apart from culture—is a peculiarly disoriented, unfinished, behaviorally indeterminate creature. Somehow man "loses" parts of his biological program and new behaviors come to be shaped by "extrinsic" signs and symbols. "Men build dams and shelters, locate food, organize their social groups or find sexual partners under the guidance of instructions encoded in flow charts and blueprints, hunting lore, moral systems and aesthetic judgments."[9] As we read this account, we are suddenly confronted with the image of blueprints somehow internalizing themselves in formless and inchoate organisms.

Geertz reinforces the notion of symbolic entities as dynamic forces with an existence of their own by drawing the analogy between such cultural "templates" and the biological gene. Now a blueprint as we meet it in our ordinary experience is a totally inert symbolic object brought into being by previously existing human powers of foresight, imagination, reasoning, deliberation, and the other capacities. A gene is not simply an inert blueprint. It is a dynamic organic structure which has its own power to actualize its "information" in the organism, while a blueprint possesses absolutely no dynamic capacity to build a building. Religious systems, rites, and blueprints arise out of preexisting human dispositions. Instead of describing humans as they emerge from the primate state in negatives such as "unfinished" and "indeterminate," we could describe them as developing new dispositions to foresight, imagination, and a certain range of indeterminacy (in a positive rather than negative sense) which make *possible* the existence of cultural symbols. What emerges is a strange animal who must *produce* culture in order to cope with his newly perceived environment. He is even a creature who, because he is somewhat of a mystery and problem to himself, will produce quite different cultural answers to the same "existential" questions. In Geertz's own apt words, "The orientational requirements they [cultural patterns] serve are generically human. The problems being existential are universal; their solutions being human are diverse."[10]

Thus instead of speaking in terms of reified symbol systems as preexistent structures, one might well speak of culture in terms of certain dominant orientations which came to prevail in communities and even in large collections of communities. These orientations give rise to symbols. Thus, in neolithic China we do seem to find evidences for certain widespread common religious orientations among the populations of the north China plain. Other shared orientations, however, probably come into being gradually only at later times. If one thus speaks of certain attitudes toward the political order as constituting a widely shared orientation of Chinese culture, it seems to be an orientation which may have actually arisen only within historical time.

Some cultural orientations clearly reflect the constraints of geographic and climatic environment. Yet leaving such truly extrinsic factors aside, even when we deal with cultural orientations whose origins are lost in the mists of time, and orientations which come to be accepted by communities as implicit shared assumptions, this does not mean that they simply arise out of some "collective subconscious" without any relation to the conscious ponderings, reflections, and imaginings of innumerable actual human beings living over long stretches of time.

It is quite true that a good part of human conscious life is habitual and unreflective and based on implicit assumptions consisting of "ancient opinions and rules of life" or "untaught feelings," in Edmund Burke's terms. This may be true not only of opinions that arise out of primordial cultural orientations but even of attitudes that arise out of doctrines which have quite explicit and highly conscious historic origins within the stream of recorded history.

In China dominant cultural orientations do exist which, as indicated, may find their origins in the prehistoric past. There may be others which only emerge with the rise of civilization and even some which may emerge quite consciously within the elite culture.

In the period considered in this volume these orientations are, at least in some circles, no longer simple implicit "traditional" assumptions which "think themselves through men" or untaught feelings which do *not* leave men "hesitating in the moment of decision, sceptical, puzzled and unresolved."[11] On the contrary, in the texts examined here these assumptions are either *consciously* supported or consciously questioned and above all subject to quite varying interpretations. The shared orientations themselves are most often vague and general, and in a time of trouble they lend themselves to diverse interpretations or even to "countercultural" attack. The interpretations of the shared orientations themselves become divergent—even "uncertain and unresolved." In much cultural anthropological literature the entire universal sense of an abyss between the shared norms of the culture and the actuality of behavior hardly seems to emerge as a problem. In the texts considered here it is an ever-present problem. Indeed we even find views which seem to step beyond the boundaries of what may be conceived to be the dominant cultural orientations. In sum, we are dealing here not only with cultural orientations but with a history of thought which decisively shapes the evolution of the cultural orientations.

Are the issues which divide divergent modes of thought in ancient China necessarily less significant than the shared cultural orientations? This depends on the questions one asks. Indeed it is on this level of divergence that some of the most interesting issues of a more universal comparative thought arise.

It may, of course, be argued that these varieties of thought are wholly part of the problematique of the elite "high culture" while the popular culture of China continues to abide in the "primordial" culture based on "untaught feelings."[12] Much of the invaluable literature on the popular culture of China based on the investigations of anthropologists and others does, to be sure, reveal widespread common themes but also enormous variety. Despite the work which has been done, the study of the history of Chinese popular culture over time is an undertaking which has hardly begun. What we know already suggests neither homogeneity nor lack of change over time nor even the absence of conscious reflection. It also points to constant and shifting interactions between "high culture" and "popular culture." The whole history of the penetration of Buddhism on the level of popular culture, the rise of sects and of that vast complex development known as "Taoist religion" (tao-chiao), which is difficult to class as either "high" or "popular" culture, points to the possibility that "Chinese culture" on the popular culture level may not be much more a matter of simple "untaught feelings" than it is on the high cultural level.

What one hopes will be the growing concern with the history of popular culture by no means requires an apology for a continued interest in the texts of the ancient "high culture." The writers of these texts may have belonged to the ruling "elite," much as the "intellectuals" of the modern Western world may be considered to be involved in the "elite" institutions of our own society. This connection neither makes it easy for us to predict their opinions nor necessarily diminishes the interest of what they have to say. The streams of thought which they represent were in fact to have a profound influence—both direct and indirect—on the ruling class as a whole and on the popular culture of subsequent ages. And, like their contemporaries in the other ancient high civilizations, they were neither less nor more truth-seekers concerned with general problems of life and

reality than are modern academicians and intellectuals. The
thought has its own intrinsic comparative value and even some of
the larger substantive questions addressed remain of universal
human concern. They are by no means obsolete.

Another limitation of this enterprise, is, of course, the problem of
language itself. The texts we deal with are not only in Chinese but in
variants of ancient "classical" Chinese. The philological interpretation of these ancient texts became a formidable problem even within
"traditional" Chinese culture itself. Any modern Western translation is necessarily an interpretation which cannot avoid the use of
modern Western categories of language and thought. I have thus
decided in this volume to rely mainly on my own translations even
while drawing heavily on the translations of others.

Indeed, if we accept the doctrines of linguistic determinism, we
might question whether the entire enterprise is possible. The linguistic determinism I refer to is not the Chomskyan doctrine of the
innate universal deep structure of all languages but the doctrines
which imply that different languages (or language families?) embody entirely separate images of reality. Not only explicit thought
but even culture are shaped by basic characteristics of the pre-given
language.

The very notion of a preestablished language itself raises problems. Can we presume that the ancestral forms of Chinese in the
fourth or third millennium B.C. had the same syntactic and semantic
properties as they did in the first millennium? To what extent were
the cultural orientations necessarily formed by language? May not
cultural orientations have helped to shape the language?

Again, I shall not pretend to dispose of these vast issues here. Yet,
one cannot avoid the subject. Some generalizations about the cultural consequences of languages are based on the presence or absence in the syntactic systems or the semiotic reservoirs of language
of explicit devices for expressing or not expressing certain distinctions. The English speaker can say either "a book is on the table" or
"the book is on the table." The Russian must say "book on table"
even though his language is rich in other explicit devices which are
absent in English. Are we to assume that the Russian bereft of a
language possessing the definite and indefinite articles cannot possibly grasp in his universe the abstract distinction to which these articles refer? Or can it be that where such explicit linguistic devices are
absent, the speech act simply relies heavily on the situational context? The Russian knows quite well the differences between a putative question "what is on table?" and the question "where is book?"
The *written* language of ancient Chinese texts is extremely parsimo-

nious, lacking, for example, number, articles, and suffixes of abstraction. It relies heavily on situational context or the context of shared understandings. How much can be therefore deduced from the absence of these explicit linguistic devices?

To take one example, I am inclined to deny that Chinese classical language lacks abstractions despite the lack of suffixes of abstraction[13] and even despite the observation of Chad Hansen that Chinese thought is not much concerned with "theories of abstract entities."[14] I agree that Chinese thought may not on the whole focus intellectual attention on the theory of abstractions as such (neither did *most* of the ancient cultures in which Indo-European languages were spoken). Yet terms such as those we translate as "humanity" (*jen*) or "righteousness" are indeed abstract in the basic sense that they are discussed in abstraction from any concrete instantiations.[15]

It may, of course, be plausible to argue that some languages "lend themselves" more easily than others to certain types of philosophic reasoning when the disposition for such reasoning arises, as in ancient Greece. I would nevertheless contend that when in China of the fourth and third centuries B.C. certain Chinese became concerned with questions which we would call logical and epistemological, they did succeed in groping toward a terminology for dealing with such questions. As in all cases of this variety of linguistic determinism, the Western analyst never seems for a moment to doubt his own ability to use the categories of his own language to comprehend the "inner principle" of the languages he is describing.

Whatever one's attitude to this mode of linguistic determinism, however, the problem of translatability across the barrier of culture and time remains formidable. When we unreflectively apply our modern Western categories to ancient Chinese texts, we certainly cannot assume the existence of lexical word-for-word equivalents. Words such as nature, reason, science, religion, and freedom, which are deeply encrusted with countless layers of meaning on our own past, meet Chinese terms such as *tao, li,* and *ch'i,* which have as complex a history of their own within the Chinese tradition. The notion that such words can simply be used unreflectively without a concern for the complexity of their long and turbulent history in the West or in China can only be an impediment to the enterprise of comparative thought. Yet the opposite notion that they cannot be used at all may be equally "culture-bound." The semantic range of a Chinese term may in fact overlap at many points with the semantic range of a Western term. Instead of arguing whether a term like "religion" applies to China or whether a word like *tao* may apply to the West, one must be as conscious as possible of one's particular use of such words within particular contexts. The Western categories themselves are inescapable even though we shall in this volume occasionally resort to the practice of keeping the Chinese terms intact as we do when we appropriate words such as *physis* and *logos* from ancient Greek thought. The faith which must animate an enterprise of this sort is the faith that comparative thought, reaching across the barriers of language, history, culture, and Foucault's "discourse," is possible. It is a faith that assumes a common world of human experience.

## Civilization, Culture, and Thought

I have mentioned the transition from the neolithic age to the rise of "civilization." This is a transition which can be discussed in an entirely "unilinear" and cross-cultural way in terms of a common world-historic "development." The factors of civilization seem to be *more or less* the same everywhere. With the passage from the Stone Age to the Bronze Age, we see the rise of states and class divisions, the emergence of cities, the invention of writings and vast advances in the technologies of irrigation and war, the beginnings of the use of money, the rise of religious and scribal specialists, and so on.

The passage to civilization does not, of course, take place everywhere, and one may entirely agree with Lévi-Strauss that human communities which did not enter into this path remain just as human in their ways of confronting human destiny as those that did. Why a considerable portion of mankind did not "move ahead" to civilization remains a matter of uncertainty, although in some cases one can clearly perceive the obvious constraining role of geography and climate. In other cases the reasons are not obvious. Culture, nevertheless, remains a category which transcends the "primitive"/"civilized" divide.

If the important "story" of civilization is the unilinear passage, however, why stress cultural difference? On this question the historian of thought must, I think, make common cause with the cultural anthropologist, who stresses the difference of culture *within* civilizations. If we go no further than to contemplate the artistic monuments of ancient Egypt, Mesopotamia, China, and India, we are palpably struck by the irreducible religious and aesthetic differences among them. Yet even if we turn to what some consider the "harder" areas of social, technological, and political developments, we find that the "civilizational" factors listed above do not all develop at an equal pace or in a similar way in all these civilizations, nor do they all necessarily play the same roles within the cultural orientations which

pervade these civilizations. The role of the city in China does not
seem to be the same as its role in Mesopotamia, and the emergence
of a universal "empire" seems to take place much later in India than
in China and to play a much less crucial role. K. C. Chang has suggested that writing in its origins in China may have served quite different functions from those it served in Mesopotamia. If we assume
that the pottery inscriptions of Pan P'o, which may go back to the
fifth millennium B.C., do indeed prefigure later writing systems,
Chang suggests that they may have been "markers and emblems" of
families, lineages, and clans or some division of one of these.[16] He
observes that using symbols for social group identification contrasts
markedly with the "roots of Near Eastern writing in an accounting
system."[17] Whether this hypothesis is true or not, the central point
remains valid. The "factors" of civilization may play quite different
roles within different sociocultural complexes.

The historian of thought, unlike some cultural anthropologists,
must, however, remain deeply suspicious of all efforts to provide the
timeless unproblematic "keys" to total cultures, keys leading to
crude, global propositions of the form "Western culture is x and
Chinese culture is y." The thought of ancient China does *not* provide
single responses to the problems of ancient civilization any more
than does the thought of ancient Greece. What emerge from the
common cultural orientations of these civilizations in the axial age
are not univocal responses but rather shared problematiques. When
one descends from the level of total cultural orientations to the level
of these problematiques, intercultural comparison becomes most exciting and most suggestive. The truth lies more often in the nuances
than in the crude generalizations about global features of x culture
or y culture. It is on this level that, despite the unquestioned distance created by divergent larger cultural orientations, one discerns
again the possibility of a kind of universal human discourse.

In conclusion, I would again stress the limits of this enterprise. In
dealing with the world of thought in ancient China, I shall not aim
for comprehensive coverage, nor shall I deal with all the issues or
themes raised in the modern Chinese, Japanese, and Western literature. I shall rather concentrate on issues and themes which seem to
me to be of particular significance.

While trying to keep abreast of current work in philological scholarship concerning the authenticity, dating, and philological reconstruction of texts, I shall not attempt to summarize this scholarship
nor to provide lengthy justifications for the views on these matters
which I have chosen to support. Nor shall I pretend that these matters are not relevant to thought. If it should be proven that the

thought of the Lao-tzu text had crystallized before the thought of Confucius, this would indeed affect some of the ideas and hypotheses put forth in this volume even while not affecting others. The history of thought is thus a most risky enterprise but risks must not be avoided.

Finally, since the available writings on ancient Chinese thought are vast, I will not attempt to provide a comprehensive survey of them. My bibliography will refer mainly to works mentioned in the text as well as some other major items.

# CHAPTER 1

# EARLY CULTURAL ORIENTATIONS
## Issues and Speculations

---

IN DEALING WITH evidences of the conscious life in early China we immediately confront the question—what is Chinese? Even if one assumes that a large part of the neolithic population of what is now the heartland of China was Mongoloid in its physical characteristics, that it spoke variants of the "Sino-Tibetan" language group and shared common cultural traits over wide areas, this provides no warrant for the notion of a preexistent "Chinese people" with its own closed cultural "ecosystem." The questions of where or when agriculture or metallurgy arose or how widespread was the orientation to ancestor worship remain matters of ongoing dispute.[1] To the extent that one can speak of the emergence of a relatively integrated Chinese civilization in the second and first millennia B.C., this civilization may have emerged from the confluence of developments over wide areas rather than as a radiation from one "nuclear area." Even if one accepts the view that the essential factors of this civilization are probably indigenous to the vast area of continental China east of the Central Asian plains, the question of whether specific material, social technologies, and even religious or aesthetic motifs may have been absorbed from other areas loses its passionate edge once one abandons the dogmatic notion of the nuclear center.

K. C. Chang has recently made the same point with regard to the formation of the state.[2] He strongly suggests that the traditional "three dynasties"—the Hsia, the Shang, and the Chou—may not have simply been sequential in time, but may have existed for long periods as "overlapping polities." Here, again, there may have been no one pristine state originating at one center but the simultaneous evolution of several more or less developed "state formations" over a wide area. Ancient texts such as the *Book of Poetry* and *Book of Documents* do emphasize the predynastic development of the Chou polity.[3] Chang does not, however, deal with the strong evidence found in the very ancient texts cited by him that the rulers of these polities had already claimed universal dominion or kingship, although he does refer to the "relative political eminence" of each of these polities at different points of time. The question here as with similar claims in other ancient civilizations is twofold—When was the claim first asserted? and to what extent was the claim accepted by other groups? Even a "relative eminence" might have provided sufficient incentive for asserting the claim and for establishing the concept of the supreme king. The texts cited by Chang strongly suggest that the predynastic Chou rulers had, in fact, accepted the Shang dynasty's claim of authority whatever the actual power relations between them. Furthermore, whatever may have been the case in the Hsia polity, it is quite clear from the oracle bone inscriptions of the latter half of the second millennium B.C. that the Shang rulers had claimed such supreme authority within the ecumene of the "high civilization."[4] The question of the multicentered origins of state formation must thus be considered apart from the question of the origins of the notion of universal kingship.

In speaking of the rise of a common civilization we must make all the qualifications in the Chinese case which we would apply to other ancient civilizations. In the period considered in these pages, to what extent was the civilization able to impose common social-political patterns and common cultural orientations over far-flung areas? To what extent did these common features affect the lives of the masses and to what extent were they concentrated in the elite culture? To what extent did they flatten out the regional differences which had existed in neolithic times? We know, of course, that "barbarian" populations which resisted the imposition of the common civilization lived within various areas of the heartland of the "civilized world" and along its periphery.[5] Some of these peoples were slowly absorbed into the heartland and in many cases their cultures, which were often not much less "advanced" than those of the "civilized world" (e.g., the Ch'u civilization of the Yang-tze valley), were greatly to enrich the cultural content of the common civilization. The effects of the high civilization on the masses were undoubtedly highly differential and certainly grew over time. Yet many of the neolithic orientations remained intact and even became ingredient to the "high culture" itself.

The texts I have considered in this book largely represent "high culture." Yet these texts themselves are very conscious of regional differences even in the realm of high cultural thought. The state of Lu was often depicted as the heartland of the old Chou "classical" tradition. The northern seaboard areas of Yen and Ch'i were the homeland of magical and shamanistic modes of thought. Ch'u was the homeland of an extravagantly exuberant religious fantasy (and according to some of "Taoism"), while the simple and tough inhabitants of the semibarbarian state of Ch'in in the northwest, we are told, provided an ideal "mass basis" for legalist modes of thought. There is, in the texts, an acute consciousness of the cultural difference between the older established states of the central plain and the new "semibarbarian" states on the northern, western, and southern peripheries. Yet even if this attribution of modes of thought to regional origins is entirely valid, they become a common civilization in the first millennium B.C. because they gradually come to interact within the framework of a common discourse. What is more, many of these modes of thought do share common premises derived from shared older cultural orientations.

The explosion of archaeological exploration in China during the last century and particularly in recent decades and the constant new discoveries have enormously enriched our stores of information on the prehistoric and early historic period. Much of this information is based on material artifacts and material data and thus can shed only the most indirect light on the conscious life. Yet some of it—notably the oracle bone and bronze inscriptions of Shang and Chou and the silk scroll manuscripts of the Ma Wang-tui, as well as recently recovered materials on Ch'in law—has immensely broadened our horizons without necessarily solving all our problems. Above all, the corpus of Shang oracle bone inscriptions has virtually created a new science.

Stated briefly, the term "oracle bone inscriptions" refers to the practice of divination by scapulimancy and plastromancy which emerged very early in ancient China. It involves interpreting the cracks produced by heating pieces of animal bone (often shoulder blades of cattle) or plastrons and carapaces of turtles. The patterns of cracks are interpreted by diviners, and the questions posed by the diviners to ancestral spirits or nature divinities along with the prognostications and verifications are often inscribed on the bone or turtle shell. While the practice may have been widespread among various segments of Shang society and while scapulimancy seems to have existed even in the neolithic period, the main collection of inscriptions available to us from the royal archive of the Shang dynasty was found at Anyang in Honan Province in the ancient Shang city of Cheng-chou.[6] According to Keightley's recent estimate, these inscriptions cover a period from "circa 1200 to circa 1050–1040 B.C.," encompassing the reigns of nine Shang kings.[7] When taken together with the testimony of later texts they also throw new light on a period stretching back to circa 1460–1441 B.C., the period of the dynastic founder T'ang. Due to the labors of numerous resourceful and imaginative scholars including, among others, Tung Tso-p'in, Ch'en Meng-chia, Chang Ping-ch'üan, Shima Kunio, Shirakawa Shizuka, Akatsuka Kiyoshi, and David Keightley, enormous progress has been made in deciphering and interpreting these inscriptions which shed so much light in the areas of religion, political thought and practice, social organization, calendrical science, the etymology of ancient graphs, etc.

The corpus of inscriptions is, to be sure, a source with severe limitations. It presents us with a view of the religious and political orders as seen from the political pinnacle of the society. If what we are dealing with is the religion of the ruling class, there is the added constraint that it is religion as viewed through the perspectives of the particular preoccupations of the diviner. If there were shamans, ritualists, liturgists, and other religious specialists, we have no ready access to their perspectives. If there was a voluminous literature of myth written on highly perishable materials such as bamboo slips, it has not survived. Mesopotamia with its clay tablets and Egypt with its stone inscriptions and well preserved papyri offer a much longer and more varied record of the evolution of their civilizations.

On the other side, there is no reason whatsoever to deprecate the testimony of the oracle bone inscriptions. The religion of the ruling class may not have been totally exclusive to that class and may reflect widely shared orientations of the neolithic past. The view of the sociopolitical order from the top and the self-image of the rulers provide perspectives which are crucial to the entire subsequent evolution of Chinese civilization.

Since my major concern here is with the history of thought, I shall concentrate on those inscriptions that shed light on religion or sociopolitical attitudes and the interaction between these two areas of experience.

Because the word *religion* is of Western origin, I shall have to consider the question of its semantic boundaries in my discussion below. Yet most would probably concede that a good portion of the oracle bone literature is concerned with religious matters. Divinatory inquiries are addressed to ancestral spirits and nature divinities, and there is an overwhelming preoccupation with the rituals of sacrifice (both animal and human). Lévi-Strauss, in his constant concern with the "archaic mind," sharply distinguishes between the realm of science and religion. Science builds structures of thought based on homologies and correlations among various phenomena of nature and human social life—kinship relations, colors, animals (all presumably based on experienced fact)—while religion establishes a relationship between two classes of entities (men and deities) "between which there is initially no homology nor even any sort of relation."[8] Magic, in his view, relies on applying the "science" of homologies while religion, through such practices as sacrifice, tries to create a relationship to external "non-existent" entities. Whatever one may think of Lévi-Strauss's definitions, in this view the relevant oracle bone material would certainly belong to the realm of religion.[9] While a science of homologies and correlations may have existed in "archaic" China (it did come to play a significant role in post-"archaic" Chinese thought), the data of the oracle bone inscriptions definitely point to religious orientations.

In using the term "religious orientation" one notes that the domain of the "religious" (which I shall for the moment simply designate phenomenologically as the realm of the divine, the numinous, the sacred, or even the demonic) tends to be strongly associated with quite disparate areas of human experience. At times the "religious" focuses on the entities and powers of nature; at times on the spirits of the dead; at times, as in ancestor worship, not simply on the world of the departed as such but on a numinous "biological" continuity through kinship flowing from the world of the ancestral spirits to the world of those yet to be born. At times it even becomes closely linked with the mystery of human authority and may even come to be embodied in the sacred rituals themselves. At times, as in the monotheisms and mysticisms of the axial age, there arises an impulse to seek the divine mystery beyond any incarnation in specific areas of nature or human experience. None of the orientations are, of course, mutually exclusive and yet the differences of emphasis are often quite marked and fraught with significance.

I will not attempt here to provide "explanations" of religion in general or of specific religious orientations in particular. Sometimes there are obvious, discernable connections between certain expressions of religion and specific features of the physical environment, but at other times such connections are by no means obvious. Rather than seeking explanations, one may more profitably reflect on implications.

When one examines the oracle bone inscriptions one is immediately struck by the pervasiveness of what we call ancestor worship. It is not an exclusive religious orientation and is in constant interplay with a concern with spirits of rivers, mountains, earth, wind, rain, heavenly bodies, and the "high god" (*Ti* or *Shang-ti*). Yet the orientation to ancestor worship is so omnipresent and so central to the

entire development of Chinese civilization that it warrants some separate reflection on its possible implications.

In the oracle bone inscriptions, ancestor worship is treated as the
cult of the royal clan with all its sacrificial rituals, all the elaborate
paraphernalia of the ritual vessels and the other appurtenances of
sacred royal power. The ancestral tombs are dominant features of
the royal capitals, suggesting perhaps that the royal ancestral cult
was a primary function of the royal urban settlement itself. Paul
Wheatley has suggested in his *Pivot of the Four Quarters* that the rise of
the city in all the ancient civilizations was connected with cultic
practice.[10] Yet if the city in Mesopotamia was centered on the city
god or goddess who was a nature-related deity, in China it would
seem to have been centered on the ancestral cults of the royal lineage
and the lineages of the associated nobility. This has led some to speculate that the rulers deliberately cultivated the religion of ancestor
worship as the foundation of royal legitimacy. Here I must point out
that ancestor worship as a religious orientation can be found among
many peoples in Africa and elsewhere which never produced "high
civilizations" with their sharp differentiation of classes. In China itself Chang notes that the burial practices in the "Lungshan" phase
of neolithic culture provide "good evidence of the worship of the
male ancestor."[11] Ancestor worship may indeed have contributed to
an extraordinarily powerful conception of political order in China.
This does not prove that it had not previously been a pervasive orientation of neolithic culture. Its continuing strong hold on the religion of the people in China hardly seems to be an imposition from
above.

Our first mental association with ancestor worship is after all not
with kingship but with kinship. Ancestor worship is not simply the
worship of the dead as such. In his "Fathers, Elders, and Ghosts in
Edo Religion," R. E. Bradbury points to the difference between the
worship of the dead and the worship of ancestors. In the religion of
the Edo in Africa, the "incorporated dead" are not simply the lineage ancestors but the elders, the chiefs, and the sacred kings who
are the object of a communal worship which transcends lineage.[12]
Ancestors, however, are not simply spirits who reside in the numinous realm of the dead. They are spirits who continue to maintain an organic relationship with their living descendants. As
members of a familial community across the barrier of life and
death, they continue to play a familial role in that community and
their kinship status retains its importance. In the "logical" chapters
of the book of Mo-tzu we find the following assertion: "The spirit of
a man is not a man, yet the spirit of your elder brother is your elder

brother. Sacrificing to a man's spirit is not sacrificing to a man; sacrificing to your elder brother's spirit is sacrificing to your elder brother."[13] The essential difference between a living man and his departed shade is here being emphasized, and yet the kinship status crosses the divide between life and death and incorporates the living and dead in a common society. The ritual sacrifices to ancestors discussed in the oracle bone inscriptions are in fact highly differentiated in terms of the specific kinship statuses of the consanguinal or affinal ancestors.

What we have here may be considered an almost banal sociological observation. The religious orientation to ancestor worship simply reflects the extraordinary strength of kinship in ancient Chinese social structure. In the words of Geertz, we are asked once again to observe that "ancestor worship supports the jural authority of elders."[14] We are invited to consider this social fact as somehow an ultimate datum requiring no further explanation. Kinship is, of course, a prominent fact in most ancient societies and as Edmund Leach observes, "Most of the individuals under study [in primitive societies] spend their whole lives within a few miles of the locality in which they were born and in such circumstances most neighbors are biological kin. This does not mean that the people concerned will always recognize one another as kin or that they must inevitably attach special value to the ties of kinship, but they may do so."[15] Even Lévi-Strauss, who is by no means indifferent to the factor of kinship, concedes that the kinship system does not have the same importance in all cultures.[16] The functional role of kinship in the ancient Chinese agrarian economy is not demonstrably different from its role in most ancient agrarian societies. Thus the centrality of the social fact of kinship can hardly be separated from the intensity of the religious focus on this area of human experience. The social fact is not necessarily a more ultimate datum than the religious focus.

In exploring the wide implications of ancestor worship, we first of all find that the relations which bind the living to the dead relatives, despite the distinctly numinous aura which hedges about the latter, belong to the same category as the relations among living relatives even though the forms of behavior toward them are quite distinctive. Here we already discern the germ of the later category of *li* which bridges a gamut of prescriptions, ranging from religious ritual to proper social behavior and even etiquette, to use our terms. The ancestors can confer benefits or inflict woe on descendants who do not abide by the rituals. They in turn are much dependent for their sustenance and welfare on the proper ritual behavior of the lineages to which they belong.

As a religious orientation ancestor worship highlights the kinship group as a paradigm of social order—that is, as a network of intimately related roles. The fact that these role relationships span the divide between the world of the living and the numinous world of the dead may indeed enormously reinforce the sense of the "ontic" reality of role and status and of the order in which they are embedded. Since the kinship roles are inevitably and "naturally" hierarchic, based as they are on ascriptive biological differences between the old and the young and the male and the female (in a patriarchal family), hierarchy and role on this level are an integral aspect of the ultimate frame of things, although I must point out that by its very nature kinship hierarchy is not fixed and unchangeable. Sons become fathers; daughters become mothers and mothers-in-law; and all become ancestors. There certainly remains room here for the thought that an individual is more than the sum of the roles he plays without in any way diminishing the centrality of the imperative to play one's role correctly.

It perhaps belongs to the nature of ancestor worship that one is—as in the observation of the book of Mo-tzu—mainly concerned with the role performance of the ancestral spirit and not with any separate "life-story" of the individual spirit within the world of the spirits. In later ages with the coming of Mahayana Buddhism with its heavens and hells and with its concept of the metempsychosis (*samsara*) one does occasionally find in literature a concern with the odysseys of the ancestral spirits in the world beyond. Also, spirits of ghosts who are effectively cut off from any relation to living descendants or who have met a foul death may continue to play a malevolent individual "narrative" role in the lives of the living. We also find in the texts the notion that the august dynastic ancestors play a mediating role at the "court" of the high god, Shang-ti (later Heaven). On the whole, it seems to me that the "mythic" potential of ancestor worship is very small even on the level of popular religion. This prompts the speculation that the relative paucity of myth (as opposed to legend) in the "high cultural" religion of China remarked on by so many foreign observers may have something to do with the dominance of the "spirit" of ancestor worship. In the essay on Edo religion Bradbury observes, "When gods are made by men out of men who have died and been re-incorporated into society by virtue of the status positions they occupied before death (and not by virtue of any supposed unique personal qualities) severe limits are set, I suggest, upon the imaginative capacities of the religious thinker."[17] In a sense the ancestral spirit tends to be absorbed into his role almost like the living family member who simply fulfills his familial ritual and ethical duties.

The observation made by many—either in a laudatory or deprecatory spirit—that myth in China remained fragmentary and marginal and that it did not come to be embodied in literary classics of the high culture is generally not based on the view of myth so central to the work of Lévi-Strauss—namely, myth as a code embodying the "deep structures" of particular sociocultural formations, but precisely on the opposite view of myth as preeminently story—stories in which actors, divine or human, relate to each other as separate somewhat unpredictable beings involved in dramas laden with the contingent, the unexpected, and the unresolved and pointing toward an unknown future.[18] Myth in this sense may relate to perennial human "structural" themes, but it does not merely exist to illustrate "structures." On the whole, however, the ancestral spirits, incorporated as they are into the ordered society of the lineage, do not participate in stories. They perform their functions in the ritual order.

The contrast that immediately comes to mind is with the religious mythology of other ancient civilizations, such as Mesopotamia, Egypt, Vedic India, and Greece. Here the more or less fully anthropomorphized (also theriomorphized) nature deities confront each other as independent and to some extent unpredictable personalities. While these civilizations were certainly aware of the ordered and cyclical aspects of nature, the mythology often seems more impressed with the unpredictable yet divine power and variety of the forces and phenomena of the natural world as well as of the human world. On both the human and divine level, attention is called to those aspects of life in which gods and humans confront each other as somewhat unpredictable individuals and groups rather than in terms of fixed "role behavior." They lend themselves to stories.

The gods of the Sumerian-Akkadian creation myth, *Enuma Elish,* have their own temperaments and personalities (not unrelated to the protean natural phenomena with which they are associated), and their behavior in the assembly of the gods is quite often unpredictable. The assembly in which they participate (like the assemblies of the city-states themselves) may attain consensus or be riven by dissension. The relations of the gods to their primordial divine mother Tiamat, the goddess of the primeval waters, is hostile; in the Babylonian version of the myth it is only under the leadership of Marduk, the city god of Babylon, that they finally prevail against her and all her minions and succeed in establishing a precarious order among themselves and in the cosmos as a whole. It is Marduk who "created stations for the great gods; the stars—their likeness, the signs of the Zodiac he set up; he determined the year, defined the

divisions; for each of the twelve months he set up three constellations, etc."[19] Even if these myths are laden with latent Lévi-Straus-
sian structures, they do not project the image of a preexistent
immanent order in any way parallel to the familial order of ancestor
worship which incorporates and defines the roles of both living and
dead. To be sure, I am generalizing about the syndrome of ancestor
worship and these reflections may not apply to the entire range of
Shang religion recorded in the oracle bone inscriptions. Yet the
strength of this syndrome encourages the speculation that the spirit
of ancestor worship, with its clear model of the kinship group as an
ordered society, may have in time influenced all other aspects of the
"high cultural" religion.

Another possible implication of ancestor worship for the religious
and even "philosophic" development of China involves the relation
between the divine-numinous realm and the human world. The ancestral spirits dwell in the world of the divine or numinous. In the
ancient texts, the ancestors of the royal lineage (who may, to be
sure, descend from nature spirits) are in direct communication with
the high god and can be the objects of supplications concerning
droughts, floods, and other natural events. Yet even in the ancestor
worship of commoners, the ancestors possess numinous qualities, as
many modern accounts of Chinese popular religion indicate.[20] Thus
the line dividing the "divine" from the human is not sharply drawn,
and it seems that humans may possess or take on qualities which are
truly numinous. The common practice later prevalent in both popular and "state religion" of elevating spirits of men of exceptional
powers and accomplishments to the status of functional deities
clearly supports this idea. Unlike ordinary ancestors, these heroes
and great men have in the course of their lives manifested extraordinary individual spiritual powers and seem to retain this individuated divine afflatus in the world beyond. There is, for instance,
the case of the historic yet semilegendary General Kuan Yü of the
Three Kingdoms who has emerged in recent centuries as a popular
god of both loyalty and wealth and who was also to be granted canonical status as an apotheosized spirit in the authorized state pantheon. Erecting shrines to apotheosized spirits of exceptional men
and women became a practice readily accepted on all levels of society.

The absence of a qualitative abyss between the two realms may
have also facilitated the reverse process, which has often erroneously
been called euhemerization, as Derk Bodde has pointed out. Euhe-
merus maintained that all the gods and demigods of ancient Greece
had once been human beings. The phenomenon we are dealing with

here is, as Bodde indicates, the very opposite—"The transformation of what were once myths and gods into seemingly authentic history and into human beings."[21] In China, as Maspero observes with some asperity, "They eliminate those elements of the marvelous which seem to them improbable and preserve only a colorless residue in which gods and heroes are transformed into sage emperors and sage ministers."[22] While this is generally true, it seems to me that something godlike and superhuman still clings to legendary figures such as Yao, Shun, and Yü and even to later "sage-kings." If they are human beings, they are human beings with the difference made possible by the absence of clearly drawn boundaries between the divine and the human. They maintain a divine afflatus.

Carrying the implications of this observation further, I am tempted to speculate that this absence of boundary affects not only the realm of religion narrowly defined, but the entire realm of ontological thinking. Does the fact that in later Chinese high-cultural accounts of the origins of mankind or of the cosmos, the dominant metaphor is that of procreation or "giving birth" (seng), rather than that of fashioning or creating, have anything to do with the centrality of ancestor worship with its dominance of the biological metaphor? Does this in turn have something to do with the predominance of what some have called "monistic" and "organismic" orientations of later high-cultural thought? At this point, I shall simply pose these questions.

Ancestor worship and the related centrality of kinship in the emerging social order may have also shaped the political order in many direct and decisive ways. As already indicated, Chang has pointed to the crucial role of lineage organization in the entire development of ancient Chinese society.[23]

Chang points to the striking fact that the graph tsu which refers to a patrilineal lineage is composed of an arrow beneath a flag.[24] This seems to refer to a military unit and would indicate that kinship ties formed a major basis for military organization. A tsu may have been formed of some hundred households belonging (or presumed to belong) to the same lineage and held together by common ancestral cults. Lineage may have thus become the base not only for military organization, but even for the mobilization of agricultural labor organized from above. This becomes highly plausible if one accepts Chang's view that the "tsu by virtue of the incessant ramifications of its member units was the seed of social stratification within itself and among one another. Within each tsu there were high and lowly members and among the various tsu there were high and lowly tsu."[25]

Such lineage groups probably played a leading role in establishing the foundations of state structure in China. As Chang points out, this view of the formation of the state runs directly counter to many modern Western modes of defining the origins of the state. "The state," in the words of Flannery, "is a type of very strong, highly centralized government with a professional ruling class largely divorced from the bonds of kinship which characterize simple societies."[26] In his view, these characteristics together with "legitimized force" define the state.

The contrast drawn here between the characteristics associated with kinship and the requirements of true "state" power has a long history in Western thought and may in fact represent some dominant trends in the history of Western civilization. It finds a recent expression in Max Weber's sharply drawn antitheses between the universalistic achievement-oriented nature of bureaucracy and the particularistic, ascription-oriented nature of family. Ultimately, it may even go back to the Platonic-Aristotelian contrast between the obscure "private" realm of family and the public realm of the life of citizens in the polis. The question is not whether such "ideal types" and antitheses are totally valid or totally invalid, but whether they can be applied in any absolute ways to other cultural experiences.[27]

The Chinese lineage with its powerful religious base may actually have become the focal point of "achievement-oriented" organization (*Gesellschaft* as well as *Gemeinschaft!*), and military organizations composed of lineage or partially pseudolineage groups may have provided a most effective base of "legitimate force." Indeed, given the extensive ramification of lineages (together with the incorporation of non-kin allies), they may have provided an unusually powerful base for early stages of state formation in China. Indeed, given the size of the lineage formations, there may have even been considerable room for stress on achievement within lineages.

Finally, it seems entirely possible that ancestor worship as an orientation helped shape the nature of the city in early Chinese civilization. I am assuming that Max Weber's view that the city's role in ancient China was substantially different from its role in the Greco-Roman world (or for that matter, in the ancient Mesopotamian and Near Eastern world) remains valid despite the efforts of some scholars to discern "city-states" in ancient China.[28] While the rise of urban settlements seems to coincide with the rise of civilization everywhere, and while there may be great merit in Paul Wheatley's assumption that urban settlements were everywhere linked to religious cult, to the extent that this is true, the particular nature of the religious orientation in question may have played a decisive role in shaping the subsequent role of cities as discrete entities. Although cities in ancient China were prominent not only as cult centers but also as military strongholds and political centers extending their control over agrarian hinterlands, there is little clear evidence in the ancient period of an inner political life of the urban community as such. Central to the royal capital and to the settlements of the lesser nobility are the ancestral tombs and the palace of the ruler, with perhaps shrines of nature deities as well. However, these ancestral shrines probably did not become the focus of an "urban cult" for the masses of artisans and others who dwelt within the city walls. One does not have the Mesopotamian patron-city gods, whose destinies were intimately linked to the destinies of their cities. The city gods of Mesopotamia were, to be sure, not gods of the masses, yet they provided concrete symbolic foci for the loyalty to cities as discrete sociopolitical entities. It seems to me that ancestor worship as a religious orientation on both the popular and upper-class level did little to develop cities as foci of identity. Even in modern China where lineage organizations have been important, they have often been more important than identity with the city or even the village as such.

Rather than speculate further on the implications of ancestor worship as a separate orientation, let us turn at this point to the interplay between ancestor worship and natural or "cosmic" religion. Here we find some intriguing questions concerning the religious basis of political authority in China. The oracle bone inscriptions as well as later texts make quite clear the overwhelming importance of this interplay. Whether ancestor worship was dominant during the neolithic period in some regions, while "nature religion" was dominant in others, in the earliest written record a confluence between the two has taken place. The two religious orientations may, in fact, have never been mutually exclusive.

In the impressive survey of early Chinese religion recently written by the eminent oracle bone scholar Akatsuka Kiyoshi, the author contends that many of the so-called nature deities were in fact tutelary deities of tribes—thus, tribal ancestors.[29] Leaving aside the obscurities of the word "tribe," it seems to me that the case is by no means proven.[30] It is by no means proven that the various surrounding polities to which reference is made in the oracle bones were simply kinship organizations, and if they had "tutelary gods" it is by no means proven by Akatsuka's etymologies that the graphs which refer to these gods *do not* designate spirits of mountains or streams rather than simply "totemic" or symbolic representations of the tribe. One would think that the leading groups of these tribes, like the Shang royal lineage itself, might have had every possible incentive to link their ancestral lines to the higher powers of nature spirits. In the case of the royal lineage, the inscriptions of the earlier period abound with reference to remote predynastic ancestors who seem to constitute a kind of bridge between the spirits of nature and human ancestors. Thus one has the Shang ancestor Wang Hai, who is depicted by a graph representing a four-footed animal (perhaps a boar) with a birdlike head. The birdlike head seems to relate to the prominence of the bird motif in the Shang royal myth, while certain surviving tales link Wang Hai to the god of the river, who is indeed addressed in the inscriptions as "High Ancestor River."[31] Thus, both the nature deities—spirits of rivers, mountains, and earth—and the mythic predynastic ancestors who are closely linked to these deities are at times the joint objects of lavish sacrifices.[32]

The ancestral cult as an ultimate source of political legitimation has its limitations. To be sure, the success of the royal lineage (and perhaps of other chieftains) in pursuing and obtaining power may itself prove the particular numinous efficacy of the royal ancestors. Yet in the end everyone has ancestors. Ancestor worship is, in a sense, an egalitarian religion, since all people have kin. Without naively attributing conscious political motives to the leaders of the royal lineage, one can readily discern the reasons to seek the lineage's ultimate source of legitimation in the numinous powers of nature, whose concerns go well beyond the particularistic concerns of ancestors. While there seems to be evidence that even non-kin subordinate power-holders occasionally participate in royal ancestral rites, in the end the ultimate source of the king's authority is, above all, its connection with the high god, Ti, and the entire company of nature spirits over whom Ti presides. This does not preclude the notion that many of these spirits may have been "tutelary gods" of other groups later incorporated into the royal pantheon. Even when incorporated, these spirits continue to share in some of the functions which ultimately belong to the high god. One may sacrifice to them for rain and other blessings. Keightley suggests that the difference between the powers of the high god and of some of the nature spirits was not always a difference in function but a difference based on the "restricted geographic influence of the local spirits."[33] Again, in both the popular and state religion of later centuries, local deities and ancestors share in functions often assigned ultimately to Heaven, and even in late-traditional China local authorities will remain responsible to the gods of mountains, rivers, and of "earth and grain" which seem to share in the functions of Heaven within their own territorial jurisdictions.

I think it is significant that Akatsuka, Keightley, Shirakawa, and

Chang seem to share the view that the emergence of Ti as the high god "coincides with the supremacy of Shang and its ruling clan."[34] The king's (*wang*) claim of universal supremacy within the "civilized" world parallels the emergence of a supreme ruler within the divine world. Even if we assume that this is a true account, I think we must again avoid the crudely "rationalistic" notion of Ti as conscious political "invention." The emergence of Ti as a supreme god may be associated with the theological meditations of shamans and other religious specialists who were in the royal entourage. But if it is true that in China his emergence is intimately associated with the emergence of universal kingship, that connection would shed light on the peculiarly close relation between the two and would make much more plausible the king's claim to a monopoly of access to Ti. Indeed, in certain myths which later appear in the *Book of Poetry*, there are claims that Ti or Heaven in some manner directly gave birth to the founders of both the Shang and Chou dynasties. "Heaven bade the dark bird to come down and bear the Shang who dwelt in the lands of Yin so wide."[35] In the case of the Chou, we find it asserted that "She who in the beginning gave birth to our people, was Chiang-yuan. How did she give birth to the people? She sacrificed and prayed that she might no longer be childless. She trod on the big toe of the God's [Ti] footprint; was accepted and got what she desired. Then in reverence, then in awe she gave birth, she nurtured—and this child was Hou Chi."[36] Most scholars now agree that Ti is not a deified ancestor, but the nonhuman high god who engendered the dynasty.

The graph *ti* unfortunately sheds no obvious light on its original meaning and remains highly controversial. According to some scholars, it represents the sacred altar-stand which, as it were, embodies the presence of Ti. In Akatsuka's imaginative interpretation, the graph represents a shamanistic symbolic structure in which a central tree trunk is bound by supporting logs and suggests that this symbolic altar-structure played a prominent role in worshipping the spirits of the four quarters and of the four winds. Since this rite was linked with the power to control the unstable meteorological forces, it may have become associated in the minds of the presiding shamans or priests with a higher power which ruled over all these forces—the power of Ti.

Whatever the origins of Ti, he remains awesome, transcendent, and supremely powerful. In Keightley's summary, he had "dominion over rain, wind and other atmospheric phenomena, harvests, the fate of urban settlements, warfare, sickness, and the king's person. He may share some of his functions with other spirits, but his ultimate sovereignty is indisputable."[37]

The presence of "high gods" does not always coincide with the rise of centralized polities in all ancient civilizations (and certainly not in primitive cultures). In ancient Mesopotamian myth and in Hesiod's *Theogony*, we find high gods associated with the primal natural realities of earth, heaven, and the primeval waters. We find the dyadic pairs Apsu/Tiamat and Anu/Enlil—and later the high gods such as Cronos, Zeus, and Indra whose emergence does not necessarily coincide with the emergence of centralized kingships.[38] Yet in the written testimony available to us about China, the high god Ti (later *t'ien,* or Heaven) does seem to live in close association with his earthly counterpart, the universal king. If the *t'ien* of the Chou people (whatever may have been his ultimate origins) was conceived of by the Chou founders as identical with the *ti* of the Shang, then one is profoundly impressed by the early emergence and relative stability of the idea of the high god as the heavenly counterpart in the cosmic order to the universal king in the human order and of the unique relation between the two. This relationship remained intact in China's state religion until the revolution of 1911.

In Mesopotamia, Enlil and other high gods, while representing sky and the atmosphere and other all-encompassing phenomena of nature, nevertheless come to be linked to specific city-states, and their supremacy seems to fluctuate with the fortunes of the city-state. With the rise of Babylon, we have the ascendancy of Marduk in the assembly of the gods.[39] With the rise of Assyria, we have the preeminence of Ashur. None of them become unchallenged transcendent high gods permanently linked to the universal kingship. In India, the rise of the Mauryan empire and of Indian universal kingship occurs after the birth of Buddhism and under Ashoka. It becomes legitimized within a Buddhist framework, in which one can hardly speak at all of the role of a high god.

Here I would again suggest that the powerful model of social order which we find in ancestor worship may have profoundly colored the entire "elite cultural" religious view of both the sociopolitical and cosmic orders. Within the family, the kin members both here and in the world beyond are held together in a network of role relationships ideally governed by a spirit of peace, harmony, and ritual decorum. Here the value of order is central. As a metaphor for the cosmos, it suggests a world of entities and energies held together in familial harmony under the authority of the high god. As a model for the sociopolitical order, it projects the picture of an immanent order based on networks of clearly defined roles and statuses and ideally held together by a system of sacred ritual.[40] This does not necessarily mean, however, that in terms of the relations between the cosmic and the human orders, the high god remains "ascriptively" tied to the fortunes of the royal lineage. Indeed, this was to become a central issue of early Chou royal theology. If the late Shang dynasty had intended—as some evidence seems to indicate— to link the high god irrevocably to the fate of its own lineage, the early Chou founders were particularly bent on asserting the high god's transcendence of all such ascriptive relations. Only on the most general level is the family model presented here as a paradigm of cosmic and political order.

The sense of order suggested by ancestral worship may indeed focus attention precisely on the more obviously ordered aspects of nature as well—such as the four seasons, the fixed cardinal directions, the ordered movements of heavenly bodies—rather than on nature as a realm of the unpredictable and contingent interaction of autonomous and "free" powers and entities. Within such a framework, the indwelling spirits of earth, mountains, rivers, heavenly bodies, and other divine beings come to be associated primarily with their assigned functional roles within the larger order under the aegis of the high god. This conception may account for the inhibition of the full-bodied "anthropomorphization" of such spirits within the emerging high cultural religion. There are, to be sure, hints in the literature which point to notions of dark mythic struggles between what may have been aggressive mythic beings such as Kung Kung (depicted as late as the Han dynasty as a horned monster with a serpent's body) and the mythic ruler Chuan-hsü, but in the *Book of Documents* this assumes the guise of a contest between a sage emperor and a rebellious minister.[41] As a mythic being, Kung Kung collides with Mount P'u-chou, one of the mountain "pillars" of heaven located in the Northwest. He causes the mountain to crumble, thus bringing about a sloping of heaven and earth toward each other in the northwest quadrant and producing an enormous gap in the southeast quadrant. As an aetiological myth, this explains the westward movement of the astral bodies and the eastward flow of rivers into the sea. Yet such myths culled from various sources run counter to the dominant spirit of works such as the *Book of Poetry* which envision the high god as the sovereign of an orderly universe in which nature spirits and ancestral spirits simply enact their duly prescribed roles in the larger frame of things.

When one speaks here of the early emergence in the high culture of a concept of all-embracing order, one must be extremely cautious about certain Western notions triggered by terms such as "order" or "structure." "Order" immediately suggests "rationality" and rationality immediately suggests a reductionist rationalism which drives gods and spirits out of nature and deals only with abstract "entities of reason" (*entes rationis*). What I am suggesting here, however, is a holistic englobing conception of order which embraces and incorporates every aspect of human experience—including numinous and magical aspects—rather than excluding or eliminating them on the basis of modern Western reductionist criteria of rationalism. The conception of order which seems to emerge in ancient China can embrace, subsume, and even preserve spirits, gods, and all sorts of "supernatural" (in our sense) phenomena even while reducing their mythic potential. When I speak of the very limited development of anthropomorphism, I am referring to our own tendency to identify "manlike" behavior with highly individualized "creative" and nonroutine aspects of behavior rather than with "ritualized" or "routinized" activities. We thus speak of factory work as turning the worker into a machine. Yet the ritualized, routine, and repetitive transactions that take place in families and other institutions are still performances of living human beings. The patriarch of a family is in some sense himself subsumed under the category of the familial order as one of the "role-performers" in that order. Yet in the Confucian conception, *the particular manner* in which he plays that role remains crucial to maintenance of the familial order. The father and ruler bring the "creative" power of their persons to bear precisely by acting wholeheartedly in ways which correspond to preordained sacred prescriptions rather than by acting in ways which make them the "interesting" protagonists of stories. Similarly, even if one assumes that nature spirits and ancestral spirits have no option but to act as they do, this does not necessarily diminish their reality or even significance. Spirits do not become otiose simply because their behavior corresponds to the norms of a preestablished order.

I am not suggesting that the emerging conception of cosmic order or political order in ancient China was simply a case of the "family writ large." Throughout the later history of Chinese thought we do find repeated references to "heaven and earth as the mother and father of the ten thousand things," to the emperor as "father and mother of the people," and to local magistrates as "father-mother officials." Yet while the lineage may have played an actual and crucial role in the formation of the state, and while the model of family in some of its most general features may have (as I have suggested) deeply influenced the general Chinese conception of sociopolitical order, still the Shang royal lineage certainly knew it needed the allegiance and support of groups and individuals not related by ties of blood. As the Shang sway expands, in greater or lesser depth, over wider areas, it relies not only on its ramified lineage but on allied groups and even on "officials" and "ministers" who are not all bound to the dynasty by ties of blood but by ties of interest and, hopefully, by ties of loyalty, not based on sacred kinship ties.

The king, in turn, makes every effort to identify his authority with the "tutelary gods" of nonrelated, dependent tribal groups. The king himself, as well as the ritual emissaries (*shih*) sent by him for the purpose, travels throughout the territories under royal control and participates in sacrifices to the local spirits, thus confirming the royal hegemony over the local cults.[42] In thus extending the sphere of his sacred power, the king probably draws his ultimate legitimation not so much from his ancestors as from the all-encompassing authority of Ti who rules over the entire cosmic kingdom of spirits. Thus the "religion of the state" finds a basis in the numinous realm which far transcends the religion of the kin.

The oracle bones abound in inscriptions referring to various groups of specialized functionaries associated with the royal organization. While many members of these groups may belong to the royal lineage, many apparently do not. There are the diviners, the keepers of documents or "archivists" (*shih*), military groupings of various types, and religious specialists.[43] There is a persistent tradition in later times that many of the more famous ministers such as the almost legendary Yi Yin were not of the royal line and that the whole "bureaucratic" apparatus may have included many non-kin members. The term "protobureaucratic" has been used in this connection and seems to be admissible if one does not have in mind Weberian notions of the "ideal type" of bureaucracy. The term refers simply to the power of the kingship to create an administrative division of labor sufficient for mobilizing resources and men for agricultural production, public undertakings of a religious or nonreligious nature, or military campaigns in territories under its more or less direct control. These groups whose members may or may not belong to the royal lineage are organized along hierarchic lines. At least the lower ranks of these "bureaucratic" organizations seem to be, in the words of Keightley, made up of "full-time specialists," and thus the term "bureaucracy" in this early period may describe not simply a distribution of functions among specialized "bureaux" but more precisely a specialization of men.[44] Whatever the role of kinship in these organizations, I think we can identify the faint beginnings of the principle of administrative division of labor. It is interesting that the vocabulary used in the inscriptions about the relations between the high god and the divine forces of nature is the vocabulary not of kinship but of "protobureaucracy." Ti sends forth the winds as his emissaries (*shih*) and the rains and clouds as the "ministers."

The authority of the bureaucratic organization may have been limited geographically to the area under the king's immediate control. There is evidence that the king, in establishing settlements as bases of power within newly subjugated territories, continued to rely heavily on the princes of the royal lineage as representatives of royal authority even while using a combination of coercive, religious, and "feudal" methods to establish a kind of suzerainty over non-kin power-holders in the surrounding polities. Indeed, instead of treating kinship and non-kinship ties as irreconcilable antitheses, it might be more fruitful to say that to the extent that the Shang state was successful in establishing its "universal" authority, this "success" was based on a judicious combination of both principles, and that in terms of religious legitimation, the ability to combine both principles was related to the particular combination of ancestor worship and nature religion within the religious orientation of the ruling group.

Something should be said at this point about the relationship between the "religious" and the "political" orders in general. I have referred to "religious specialists" as one of the groups "in the state organization." Chang describes this group as a category of "priests."[45] While Akatsuka very much stresses the prominent role of shamans (and shamanesses) during the Shang period, the word "priest" in the West often suggests a separate, independent stratum within a society. A cursory reading of the immense literature on the millennial histories of ancient Mesopotamia and ancient Egypt does not encourage easy generalization. Yet from the writings of Oppenheim and others, it seems that at least in the earliest period, temple establishments in the Sumerian-Akkadian city-states were separate from the royal household and may well have preceded it in time.[46] In Egypt, also, despite the centrality of the religious status of the pharaoh, there was a growing power of priestly groups and of individuals who could claim independent and direct access to powerful leading deities. There can, of course, be no doubt about the independent authority and power of the Brahman caste in India and the separate—albeit changing—role of the hereditary priestly and Levitical group in ancient Israel depicted in the Bible as having been established well before the rise of monarchy.

In the Chinese case, I am again inclined to stress, at this point, the weight of the paradigm of ancestor worship within the entire complex of ruling class religion. The king is naturally the "high priest" of his lineage's ancestral cult, as is the patriarch of any patrilineal-based kin group. Beyond this, by dint of his monopoly of access to the high god, he certainly is also in some sense the "high priest" of the worship of Ti as well. Indeed, through his special relationship to Ti, he claims hegemony over all the "tutelary deities" throughout his realm. All religious specialists seem to be directly subordinated to the king, as are the diviners, the keepers of documents, scribes, and military specialists. This subordination became even more obvious in later ages when a stratum of nonspecialized officials was expected to perform what we would call "religious" and "secular" functions interchangeably. It is in this subordination that I think we find the origins of the principle that dominated the Chinese political order ever after—"the union of governing and teaching (or doctrine)" (*cheng chiao ho-i*).[47] The sacred office (*wei*) of the kingship is ideally both the source of social order and the source of normative truth.

Shamans may still play an important role in the "state religion" of the Shang dynasty, but it is striking that their role declines markedly during the following period, suggesting that the shamanist perspective in religion was not easily reconciled in the long run with the merging "political culture" of the Chinese kingship. Mircea Eliade defines the shaman in terms of his or her power to release his soul from his bodily frame in order to communicate directly with the divine powers through direct ecstatic experience. The shaman may wander in the realm of the spirits or he may by trancelike procedures undergo possession by the spirits.[48] Maspero contends, correctly, I believe, that shamanism was in the long run not compatible with the emerging religion of the state in China.[49] This religion could not regard with favor a form of individual religious power that by claiming direct access to the divine through ecstatic experience presumed to bypass the officially sanctioned ritual channels for communicating with divine spirits. He also suggests that the entire pathos of shamanism was by the same token to become alien to the culture of the later literati so heavily based on an "Apollonian" spirit of decorum. Shamans, mediums, and sorcerers were, of course, to remain an important part of the diffuse popular religion of China down to our own times. Here the impulse for direct unmediated communication with the spirits bypassing the political order never disappears. As has also been pointed out, modes of the religious imagination associated with shamanism remain in some areas of the Chinese cultural world an important element even of the aristocratic culture. In the famous *Songs of Ch'u,* attributed to the Ch'u statesman and poet Ch'ü Yuan of the fourth century B.C., we find strong elements of something like the shamanistic outlook—particularly in the famous "spirit journey" which we find in his famous *Li Sao* elegy.[50]

On the high cultural level, however, shamanism, like myth, runs counter to the growing predominance of the idea and ideal of order—both cosmic and sociopolitical. It is an order in which one expects ancestral spirits, nature spirits, and human beings to enact the modes of behavior appropriate to their roles. The power of the shaman or religious ecstatic of any type to bypass the channels of this order to invoke the incalculable powers of spirits is thus dangerous, subversive, and inimical to the spirit of order and decorum which maintains the harmony of society.

In sum, I would argue that certain dominant religious orientations whose beginnings may have already been present in the Lungshanoid culture of the Neolithic Age may have exercised a profound influence on the direction of early Chinese culture. They seem to have created, in the first instance, a religious base for an extraordinary, powerful conception of universal kingship and, by extension, for the early emergence within the high culture of the concept of a total all-embracing social and cosmic order. This does not mean that the gods or ancestors or Heaven were ever regarded as completely "scrutable." On the contrary, the prominence of divination would at least in the earlier period indicate an enormous sense of uncertainty and anxiety concerning the intentions of the divine powers. Tung Tso-pin's division of Shang history (from 1200 to 1050) into five periods on the basis of his painstaking analysis of the entire corpus of oracle bone inscriptions suggests an evolution from an outlook which stressed a heavy reliance on divination, an enormous emphasis on sacrifices to nature deities and the mythic or semimythic predynastic ancestors, irregularity and "ad hoc arrangements" in the performance of ancestral sacrifices, and the reliance on a vast group of diviners to an outlook in which the volume of divinations is markedly diminished, sacrifices to nature deities and remote ancestors cease, the king becomes the main diviner, and the sacrificial rites to ancestors are regularized in an annual five-phase cycle of sacrifices.[51] Keightley has argued that these changes may reflect the growing efficacy of state power. Matters which had been divined before were now routinely in the power of the king to control. Much of what had been regarded as subject to forces beyond human control was now thought of as subject to royal control. Keightley tentatively sees this as a shift from a religious or "theocratic" outlook to a more secular outlook.

While it may indeed be the case that the Shang state had made considerable "progress" in establishing the techniques of coercive and noncoercive control, Keightley's language seems to me misleading. The identification of the "religious" with man's sense of dependence on forces beyond his control and of "secularity" with man's sense of his ability to shape his own destiny is one of the more simple-minded clichés of modern Western thought. Let us remember that the heavy reliance on divination in the earlier period corresponds to a time of enormous explosion in the growth of civilization. This is not a period of passive dependency. It is a period of settlement building, vast hunting expeditions, organized military campaigns, agricultural expansion, and other such promethean undertakings. It is precisely in the process of undertaking such ventures that the ruling group becomes most acutely aware of the degree to which success depends on all sorts of precarious forces beyond its control. Here one has—as has been the case in the modern world—a subtle dialectic and not a zero-sum game. Modern technology has simultaneously immensely increased man's powers as well as his acute sense of subjugation to "forces" (not, to be sure, religiously conceived in this case) beyond his control. Studies in comparative religion reveal that in all cultures, craftsmen and artisans, often in full control of their crafts (technology is, of course, the very epitome of "secular" efficacy), constantly seek divine blessings and support for the success of their labors. Tutelary gods of the crafts can be found in all parts of the world, including China.

One might indeed argue that Tung's "Period V" witnesses a shift in the nature of the royal religion rather than a process of "secularization." The growing "efficacy" of the kingship may have led to a major shift of emphasis to the cult of the royal ancestors themselves. Again, we must remind ourselves that in ancestor worship, the line between the divine and the human is not sharply drawn. Hence the last Shang kings may have indeed been confident that their growing power above all had confirmed the particular numinous power of their own lineage ancestors. It is interesting to note that it is precisely the last two kings Ti Yi and Ti Hsin who come to have the title Ti prefixed to their temple names, as if to assert that they ascribe to themselves the powers of the high god himself. And despite the diminished number of inscriptions during Period V, many inscriptions are devoted to inquiries concerning the annual cycle of ancestral sacrifices. We could interpret this change not as an evolution to "secularism" but rather as a particular overweening claim for the unique divine powers of the royal lineage. Akatsuka has indeed seen in this development a move to absolutize the divine status of the royal lineage.[52]

If this hypothesis is justified, it may throw new light on the vehement reassertion of the transcendental power of the high god (whether called *Shang-ti* or *T'ien*) by the founders of the Chou dynasty. The "wickedness" ascribed to the "last bad king" of the Shang may well be found in his "impious" religious orientation. In a section of the *Book of Documents* regarded by most scholars as genuinely early ("The Numerous Officers," *to shih*), we find the Duke of Chou attempting to convince the rebellious officers of the fallen dynasty that while all the virtuous rulers of the Shang from T'ang to Ti Yi "did not dare to lose Ti and strove to equal Heaven in the benefits which they conferred," this was by no means the case with the "later successor kings" who "did not make themselves manifest to Heaven."[53] At the core of the whole notion of the "Heavenly Mandate," which is to figure so centrally in the religious ideology of the early Chou, lies the centrality of Heaven itself. The high god's transcendent powers are by no means inextricably tied to the claims of any lineage. Thus, if the late Shang represents a tendency toward "secularization," the founding of the Chou witnesses a resounding reaffirmation of or an unprecedented new exaltation of the religious centrality of the high god. Whatever transformation the concept of Heaven was to undergo in the history of Chinese thought within what might be called the state religion, Heaven and not the ancestors was to remain the supreme source of legitimation for the occupants of the imperial office.

# CHAPTER 2

# EARLY CHOU THOUGHT
## Continuity and Breakthrough

DESPITE THE OBSCURITY which still envelops the history of China during the early centuries of the Chou dynasty, this period was to have peculiar symbolic importance. Here we find the period to which China's unique sage Confucius looked from the turmoils of his own era, seeking his image of the good society.[1] What he saw—and how that relates to what was actually there—remains a question of ongoing interest.

What Confucius saw was, of course, mediated through written sources of the intervening period, parts of which are still available to us. As limited as those sources are, they provide us with much more substantial food for thought than the extremely confined testimony of the oracle bone inscriptions. We have, first of all, the two collections of prose documents and poetry to be found in our present versions of the *Book of Documents* and the *Book of Poetry*. Most scholars now agree that only a part of the *Book of Documents* is genuinely pre-Confucian in its present form but that most of the content of the *Book of Poetry* is of pre-Confucian origin.[2] The poems are generally believed to have been composed in a period stretching from the founding of the dynasty to about 600 B.C. For the "Spring and Autumn" period (770–464), a period which presumably marks the rapid decay of the dynasty, we have in particular the marvelously circumstantial accounts (some of which, to be sure, contain a considerable admixture of legend) of the *Tso-chuan* or the Narratives of Tso, which may have been put together in its present form as late as the third century B.C. but which may nevertheless constitute a rich source for the history of pre-Confucian thought. Many scholars emphasize that many texts of the post-Confucian era (including the post-Confucian texts of the *Book of Documents*) contain materials which are probably of extremely early origin. There is, finally, the corpus of inscriptions on bronze vessels which, despite the difficulties they present, are shedding new light on the social and political circumstances of the early Chou period.

The *Book of Poetry* and the *Book of Documents* are themselves limited in scope and content. We might say that they reflect a "proto-Confucian" outlook, or perhaps more accurately, that they reflect earlier attitudes with which Confucius and his disciples strongly identified. There may be some reason for accepting the tradition that the collections may have been "edited" by persons close to a Confucian outlook. This may not seem obvious in the case of the *Book of Poetry*, which contains lyrical love songs, hunting and feasting songs, and other themes that on the surface do not seem to suggest a Confucian outlook. These may have later been incorporated because they were already subject to the kind of allegorical ethicopolitical interpretation which later became common. Examples of such interpretation can be found even in the *Analects*. On the other hand, the *Book of Documents* with its set speeches of kings and ministers seems clearly proto-Confucian in outlook.

Selective as those sources may be as a guide to the culture of early Chou, they probably genuinely reflect certain dominant attitudes in the elite culture of the period and they lend much flesh and blood to the cultural orientations which I have thus far discussed in a disembodied and abstract way. Here we have actual individual human voices—often anonymous to be sure—reflecting upon the common cultural assumptions and even bringing to them what might be called a fresh perspective.

Before considering those texts more closely, however, something should be said about the actualities of the sociopolitical order of the early Chou dynasty, which was regarded by the Confucius of the *Analects* as a model society.[3] In the words of Herrlee Creel, "The tradition that Western Chou was a period of relative tranquility and even goodwill is so general and so persistent and agrees with so much of the evidence that it cannot be wholly false."[4] And yet skepticism remains strong. When Creel informs us "that after the opening years of the dynasty there was a period of some two centuries in which—insofar as our sources indicate—Chinese armies did not fight other 'Chinese' at all and even in the final century of Western Chou, they did so only on three occasions," many would impugn the defects of the sources rather than accept the proposition.[5] Is it indeed possible that in the primitive state of technology and communication which prevailed at the time, the Chou dynasty was able to bring about a state of peace over such a vast territory for two centuries?

Some have suggested that the predynastic Chou polity of the northwest, which had probably not developed the relatively sophisticated administrative techniques of the Shang state, could hardly have imposed such effective control over such wide areas. Here, however, let me again cite Chang's hypothesis, so strongly suggested by sources in the *Book of Poetry* that the early Chou polity had undergone considerable development *alongside* the late Shang state long before achieving royal power. Archaeological finds indicate that the Chou people had internalized many aspects of Shang culture (or participated in what might already have been a shared Chinese culture). Certainly the literature we have underlines their eagerness to identify with the universal claims of the late Shang conception of political order. To the extent that their "political culture" may have differed from that of the Shang, it may have maintained a certain flexibility and lack of rigidity which may have enhanced its ability to create new institutions. Here I am reminded of the Aztec imposition of order onto the Meso-American civilization and Macedonia's unification of Greece.

Yet the larger question remains—did the Chou dynasty "system" make it possible to achieve such a degree of pacification? The fact that many Western scholars have described the major features of the system as "feudal" encourages doubt.[6] Our own associations with this troublesome word is generally that of the disintegration of power rather than of stability and order. It suggests fragmentation and strife. It conjures up an image of the Roman Empire gradually sinking into feudal "chaos." Yet I agree with Creel that if we define the term in a minimalist sense as a "system of government in which a ruler delegates limited sovereignty over portions of his territory to vassals," we may well apply it to the early Chou situation.[7] We must simply add the commentary that feudalism presupposes the notion of an inclusive political framework in which a superior ruler confers power from above and that if the term is applied to China, we must stress that the "vassals" on whom the power is conferred are very often members of the royal lineage. Conceiving of feudalism (*feng-chien*) in this simple way, one may disassociate it completely from the notion of a preexistent highly centralized state in disintegration. Under primitive technological conditions, this "feudal" strategy may have effectively extended the emerging state's authority over areas previously not under its control. This would be particularly true if—as Creel suggests—the Chou rulers (and perhaps the Shang before them) controlled a truly effective military organization relatively more powerful than anything available to their vassals.[8]

The effectiveness of the Chinese "feudalism" may, however, have also reflected the relative strength of the religious basis of the ruler's authority. To the extent that the Chou founders "parcelled out sovereignty" among their kinsmen they were, of course, leaning very heavily on the intensely religious aspect of kinship ties rooted in ancestor worship. The "vassal" members of the royal house were, in this view, to constitute "the fence and protecting wall for the Chou" in some of the key territories of the Empire. To the extent that the Chou enfeoffed nonrelated allies and local power-holders, they may have relied heavily on the vassal's sense that his own material and spiritual interests were best identified with the system. Here again, the religious foundations of the king's authority—his claim to a special relation to Heaven—may have come to win general acceptance at least so long as the royal house was able to present credible evidence of its dynastic charisma.

The religious orientations discussed above—as modified in the religious doctrine of the Chou founders—may have supported "feudalism" as a relatively stable system much more effectively than medieval Catholicism supported the feudalism of the medieval West. Marcel Bloch, like others, has pointed in the case of the West to the link between the European lord-vassal ethos and the old relations between German war-band retainers (*gisind*) to their chiefs. Its origins are clearly pre-Christian. Catholic Christianity, on the other hand, was not inherently related to feudalism in either its origins, its ecclesiastic organization, or its essential doctrine, although it did become closely enmeshed with it. The degree to which it strengthened the bonds of the feudal hierarchy to either emperor or national kings was strictly limited. In China the kingship as the apex of both "political" and "religious" order provided a formidable symbolic basis for both a feudal and later a bureaucratic system.

Another aspect of this feudalism which differentiates it clearly from medieval Western feudalism is that the protobureaucratic elements which we have discussed in the Shang are also very much present in the literature of the Chou. Here again the stark antithesis in Western thought between feudalism and bureaucracy may derive not only from the absolutization of ideal types but also from a genuine historic experience. The bureaucratic structures of the modern absolute states of Europe arose out of a clear struggle against a feudalism in which the Carolingian ghost of late Roman bureaucracy had effectively disappeared.[9] To be sure, in the Chinese case, the use of the term "bureaucracy" should perhaps be avoided, and one wonders whether Balazs's term "officialism" might not be appropriate for this period.[10] Creel has carefully presented all the reservations and cautions against using the word "bureaucracy" in anything approaching its full Western sense.[11] The high officials of the royal court are often "feudal lords." The names of offices are vague and fluctuating. The holders of office do not necessarily perform the functions associated with their titles. Offices usually are hereditary within what might be called the lower official nobility, both on the level of the royal court at the center and on the level of the courts of the "feudal states." The remuneration of office holders was the reward of appanages, which while not necessarily hereditary in principle often became hereditary in practice.

Nevertheless, throughout the system a segment of the ruling class remained closely linked by office to the royal court as well as to the courts of the local feudal princes. In a strange way, the accounts of these local courts with their own "Directors of Works" or "Directors of Crime" remind us of the petty courts of the eighteenth-century German princelings modeling their states on Versailles rather than of the feudal manors of medieval Europe. Although the titles of high office may have been conferred on high officials who were trusted by the ruler in their capacity as "generalists" and advisors, apparently on the lower rungs of this official nobility a stratum emerged which actually composed and handled an impressive array of documents, were experts in the protocols of ritual, ceremonial, and penal law, and manned the lower ranks of the military organization. The word *shih* later applied to this stratum is obscure in its etymology, but the original graph may have meant nothing more than a man engaged in agricultural labor—and perhaps by extension, a man engaged in some kind of service.[12] Clearly, however, on this level there did exist some kind of administrative machinery and personnel which operated this machinery. There is even evidence that during its period of greatest strength, Chou officials were actually able to intervene sporadically in the affairs of the subordinate feudal principalities.

Thus in the Chinese case these strategies which we have labelled "feudal" and "bureaucratic" may well have emerged simultaneously even though the former may have been the dominant strategy in asserting claims over the "world" as a whole. To the extent that the dynasty was able to establish control in any depth over areas under its immediate control, it gradually developed the rudiments of an administrative apparatus although the occupants of this apparatus may have been, in the first instance, a hereditary stratum. To the extent that it was able to extend authority over areas not immediately controllable, it relied basically on the feudal strategy.

This does not mean that a conflict between the feudal and bureaucratic principles was not to emerge during the centuries I shall be discussing. It does suggest that lines between the two "systems" may never have been as sharply drawn as they appear to be in our Western terms of reference.

My purpose in this brief discussion has not been to settle arguments about the applicability of terms such as feudalism and bureaucracy but to suggest some plausibility to Creel's bold hypothesis that the early Chou dynasty may have brought about a measure of relative order and stability within a large part of the "civilized" world over an appreciable period of time and that much of the military activity of this period may, in fact, have been directed against those called "barbarians." If this is indeed the case, it would indicate that the mix of reliance on the sacred ties of kinship among those "feudal lords" who belonged to the royal lineage, on feudal strategies toward nonrelated lords, and on protobureaucratic organization (a mix which may have already existed in the late Shang dynasty) may have plausibly created conditions favorable to a fairly prolonged "pax Chou-ica," and made it possible for the ruling stratum as a whole to identify its interests with the "system." The new ideas which we find enunciated in the literature of the early Chou may have even reinforced the hold of the system.

None of this, of course, is meant to suggest the actual existence of Confucius' "ideal" society, although one can readily imagine how the existence of a long period of "relative tranquility" might have encouraged later idealizations. We know very little about the lives of the masses during these centuries, although the *Book of Poetry* provides us with idyllic glimpses of a happy rural life "when things went well." Mencius was later to attempt a schematic reconstruction of its "ideal" agrarian system in his descriptions of the "well-field system." Oddly enough his very description has been used as evidence by mainland scholars that early Chou China was a "slave society." The peasants were obviously subject to labor service on the fields of their lords and were under the supervision of the stewards of their lords. They were obviously "unfree" in this sense, as is clear from Mencius' own account. This does not inform us about how onerous the exploitation was, or whether, in Marxist terms, agricultural workers were or were not in possession of their own "means of production." The book of Mencius, like some of the more idyllic passages in the *Book of Poetry*, which no doubt reflected a view from above, tends to suggest that the exploitation of labor power and labor time in "good times" was strictly limited and that the peasants enjoyed ample time for labor on their land allotments. What Mencius emphasizes is the essential equality *among the peasants*, their mutual cooperation and ritual solidarity. It is doubtful whether we shall ever know much more than we do now about the degree of exploitation or the harshness and effectiveness of the penal law over this long period of time.

When we turn to the area of thought we must, of course, be cautious about claiming novelty for the early Chou period. The oracle inscriptions are, after all, extremely limited as sources of Shang thought. If the highly moralistic thrust of the *Book of Documents* and the *Book of Poetry* and the grand idea of the "Mandate of Heaven" seem strikingly new, Keightley and others warn us that the idea of a "Mandate of Ti" may have already existed in the Shang dynasty. The fact that the ethical vocabulary of the inscriptions is so limited may, after all, be mainly a function of the medium itself.

Whatever may be the case, I shall nevertheless dwell here on the implications of this grand idea which dominates the more reliable pre-Confucian texts of the *Book of Documents* and which is prominent in the dynastic hymns of the *Book of Poetry*. Its manner of presentation does suggest a certain presumption of novelty.

What strikes one first of all is the extreme anxiety of the spokesmen of the new dynasty to identify with the political and religious system of their predecessors. Much has been made of the fact that the high god of the Chou people is called T'ien rather than Shang-ti and the suggestion has been made that this deity represented by a graph which seems to depict a manlike figure with a large head ( 夨 ) may have been of quite distinct origins from the Shang high god. For my purposes here what is of most importance is the enormous eagerness of the dynastic founders to conflate T'ien, who is clearly associated with the physical heavens, with Shang-ti. This message is clear. We, the Chou people, worship the same high god as our predecessors and the high god Shang-ti–T'ien has made it abundantly clear that he is in no way bound to any royal lineage. "The Mandate of Heaven is not forever."[13] In the long run the will of Heaven is not bound to any dynasty. Heavenly attitudes toward the kings are based on objective, "universalistic" criteria of behavior. The Shang dynasty has lost the mandate because of its gross ritual and moral failings.

The possibility that this idea may indeed be new is suggested by the context in which it is uttered. The Conqueror, King Wu, has just died and his heir, the future King Ch'eng, is in his minority. King Wu's brother, the famous Duke of Chou, holds the reins of power and is immediately confronted with a threat of revolt by members of the old Shang ruling class supported by his own royal brothers. Even the officials of the Chou dynasty are unenthusiastic about taking military action.[14] Yet the young king is made to say "I, the little one, dare not disregard the Mandate of Shang-ti."[15] Elsewhere the

Duke of Chou speaking in the name of the king declares "it was not that our small state dared to aspire to the mandate of Yin [the Shang dynasty] but that Heaven was not with Yin. It would not strengthen its misrule. It helped us. Was it we who dared to seek the royal throne [*wei*]? Shang-ti was not for them."[16]

In the "Announcement of Duke Shao" the latter points out to the Yin (Shang) people that, "When Heaven put an end to the mandate of the great state Yin, the many wise former kings of Yin were in Heaven."[17] He goes on to intimate that the Shang royal ancestors were either unwilling or unable to intervene on behalf of their descendants. All of this is supported by long accounts in both *Books* of how the "small state" of Chou and its worthy rulers had, by their virtuous behavior, won the favor of Heaven. Finally, the Duke of Chou argues that it was by the same display of virtue that T'ang, the founder of the Shang, had in his time overthrown the Hsia.

All of this can be treated quite transparently as a rationalization of the seizure of power, and it is certainly that among other things. Yet there is no reason to think that the Chou founders did not have intrinsic faith in the religious base of their rationalization. The Duke of Chou, it would appear, even had a perfectly clear understanding of the potentially dangerous future implications of the doctrine. In an address to his fellow regent, the Duke of Shao, he declares, "Implacable Heaven sent down ruin on Yin. Yin has lost the mandate and Chou has received it. Yet I do not dare to say whether our foundations will always abide in prosperity . . . or whether it will end in misfortune . . . Heaven's mandate is not easily preserved. Heaven is hard to rely upon."[18] This particular aspect of the idea which was to touch all imperial dynasties with the taint of mortality made it throughout Chinese history a far more problematic doctrine for both emperors and officials than any of the textbooks would lead us to believe.

I shall not linger here on the "democratic" implications of the doctrine. If what is meant by the term "democracy" is constant reference to the responsibility of rulers for the welfare of the people as a major criterion for the possession of the Mandate this is, to be sure, a very striking theme, although by no means unique to China. In most of the universal kingships of the ancient world, it is the ruler's duty to promote the welfare of his people. Perhaps more can be said for the "right to revolt" and the decisive negation of any notion of an "eternal dynastic line." The Chou conquest does not, however, suggest the image of a "rise of the masses" but rather of the rise of a new center of power which proves through fact its entitlement to the Heavenly Mandate.

What I shall rather emphasize are certain religious, ethical, and political implications of the doctrine which may well be of deeper significance. What strikes one is the clear elevation of Heaven or the high god to a central and transcendent position in the cosmos and in the ethical life of society. This may have been, as suggested, in direct reaction against a late Shang reassertion of the centrality of the royal ancestral cult. The attribution to the high god of the ultimate powers of judgment for the ethical and ritual performance of those who rule the human order seems to introduce a truly new dimension of transcendence. It is of course possible that even in the Shang dynasty Shang-ti's unfavorable responses to the divinatory inquiry of the kings were deemed to be a manifestation of moral disapproval. Here, however, Heaven–Shang-ti stands in supreme judgment of the entire dynastic line. Heaven is the supreme moral will on which the endurance of the dynasty depends. Heaven is the God of History.

This does not mean that ancestors and nature spirits have disappeared. The Chou dynasty is clearly most anxious to prove that its own illustrious ancestors enjoy the same access to Heaven as the illustrious ancestors of the Shang dynasty. The Chou, as we have seen, have a founding myth which runs parallel to the founding myth attributed to the Shang. Chiang-yuan gives birth to Hou Chi-"Lord Millet" after stepping *on the footprint* of Ti. Lord Millet is the divine-human ancestor of the dynasty as well as the culture-hero inventor of agriculture.[19] Nevertheless, while the illustrious ancestors are crucial we now know that even ancestors who have immediate access to the presence of Heaven may no longer be capable of saving from Heaven's wrath the dynasty with which they are associated. The special relationship of the universal kingship *as an institution* to Heaven has been maintained. Indeed one might say it has even been reinforced by making it less dependent on the capacities of individuals or even dynasties, but the power even of royal ancestors is, in effect, diminished.

Yet the correct performance of the rituals to all spirits—natural and ancestral—remains crucial. The scrupulous and pious performance of sacrifices and rites remains one of the criteria in terms of which the ruler's virtue is measured and he must be equally concerned with the ritual performances of his vassals. When the Marquis of Han receives his "investiture" (*ming*) from the king, the king's first admonition is, "Continue the service of your ancestors. Do not ignore my charge."[20] King Wu, like the Shang kings before him, makes a royal progress throughout the realm performing the proper sacrifices to mountains, rivers, and all the "hundred spirits" (*pai shen*).[21] The powers of the ancestral and nature spirits have not faded away. At the solemn ancestral ceremonies of the upper classes, one still looks to the ancestors to confer happiness and long life on their living descendants and the spirits lend their collective support to Heaven's overarching purposes.

Some of the most reverential hymns of the *Book of Poetry* describe in loving detail the ancestral festivals of the nobles where all the living descendants and noble guests play their assigned ritual roles in the elaborate and solemn pageant where

> Every custom and rite is observed
> Every smile, every word is in place.[22]

A young member of the family assumes the role of the "dead" ancestor making himself the "medium" of the ancestral spirit, and the master of the liturgy announces the ancestral message conveyed through him.

> Very hard have we striven
> that the rites may be without mistake.
> The skillful recitant conveys the message
> Goes and gives it to the pious son:
> 'The spirits enjoyed their drink and food.
> They assign to you a hundred blessing.
> According to their hopes, to their rules
> All was orderly and swift.
> All was straight and sure.
> Forever they will bestow on you good store.'[23]

There is music and decorous feasting and everyone plays his role with utmost decorum. The festival seems almost like a symbolic epiphany of the sacred order of society. One cannot help but feel that when Confucius read the accounts of these noble occasions he may have seen in them a beatific vision of sacramental social harmony. Yet what strikes me here is the emphasis on the sacred ceremony itself. The ancestors participate in the ceremony and confer their blessings. Yet, one feels that they, like their descendants, are somehow all subordinated to the sacred performances in which they all participate as actors. According to the striking observation of the *Record of Ceremonies* (*Li chi*), a late text of perhaps the third or second centuries B.C., the Shang people had put the spirits in the first place and the rites second, while the Chou put the rites first and the spirits in second place.

With all the profound difference in the two traditions, I am reminded here of certain observations which have been made concerning the evolution of Vedic religion in India. Zaehner has observed that with the passage from the Vedas through the Brahmanas to the Upanishads "the actual ritual became more important than the gods to whom it was offered. The sacrifice ceased to be a propitiatory act but came to be regarded as having cosmic importance in itself, and the gods, so far from being the object to which the sacrifice was offered, became mere celebrants along with men in this vital work."[24] The fact that the rituals "control" the behavior of the gods leads the Brahman priests to the reflection that the very rites and sacred formulas (Brahmanas) which they employed embody a more transcendent power than that of the gods themselves, and this leads to the ultimate realization that the power which is imbedded in all these rituals and utterances is itself the eternal Brahman beyond all forms and entities.

Heaven, of course, is not Brahman and the ancestors remain the objects of propitiation, but the notion that ancestral spirits and local spirits of nature are themselves, as it were, governed by the rituals in which they participate seems already present in these texts. Heaven, itself, however, remains transcendent. There is, to be sure, no suggestion that Heaven ordained the rules of the ritual—as in the case of the God of the Hebrew Bible, who explicitly ordains his own ritual sacrifices and thus stands in a sense ever beyond them—but clearly the will of Heaven is in no sense "controlled" by rituals. Heaven rather stands free in transcendent judgment of how the rulers of men perform both their ritual and moral duties. The rituals may emanate from Heaven but Heaven is not governed by them.

A striking confirmation of the qualitative difference between Heaven and the other spirits is to be found in the declaration, which can be found in two places in the *Book of Poetry*, that Heaven, or the high god, "gave birth to the multitudinous people."[25] While we find no statement in the *Book of Poetry* or in the pre-Confucian texts of the *Book of Documents* concerning any theogony or cosmogony, I see no reason for not taking these assertions concerning anthropogony or the origins of the human race at face value. In the line following the line in the poem above, we also find the assertion which I would tentatively translate "for every aspect of human life, there is its indwelling law."[26] Here we already have the thought that Heaven in giving birth to human beings also implants in them the patterns of order which ought to govern their behavior in their relations with each other and with the spirits. Thus the patterns of ritual and other modes of behavior which govern the human order, and perhaps also the cosmic order beyond, themselves emanate, as it were, from Heaven.

Yet if we find as early as the *Book of Poetry* the groping toward the identification of Heaven with the ultimate order of things, we also find passages which lend support to the seventeenth-century Jesuit missionaries' interpretation of Heaven in theistic terms. Heaven is a supreme, active, but not arbitrary will. We must remind ourselves that the word we have translated as "mandate" (*ming*), like the English word itself, is closely related to the word (*ling*), which means an express *command*. It is entirely clear that Heaven wills the collapse of the Shang dynasty and expressly chooses the kingdom of Chou to inherit the mandate.

> God on high in sovereign might
> Looked down majestically
> Gazed down upon the four quarters
> Examining the ills of the people . . .
> Every land he tested and surveyed
> God on high examined them
> and hated the laxity of their rule
> So he turned his gaze to the West
> and here made his dwelling place.[27]

In the same hymn, Heaven directly speaks to King Wen and advises him to crush a revolt and later praises his virtue. Here we already seem to confront the problem arising out of our own clear antithesis between "conscious will" and "impersonal order." How does one apply this antithesis which looms so large in the history of Western thought to Chinese early views of Heaven? At this point it will suffice to say that Heaven, whether as active conscious will or as the source of universal order, is quite clearly in a category which sets "him" far beyond the ancestral and natural spirits.

In neither of these texts do we have any discussion of Heaven's role in the nonhuman cosmos. Most of it concerns Heaven's relations to mankind and the human order, and it is precisely within this context that the "theistic" side of Heaven makes itself most manifest. The heavenly mandate is mainly about the moral ritual condition of mankind, and Heaven already relates to man largely in terms of the moral question. The moral question itself is not Socrates' question—What is the good?—but rather the question—Why man's departure from the good? If Socrates spends his life seeking the definition of the essence of the good, clearly he is convinced that mankind does not yet truly possess the knowledge of what it is. If in China there already exists the belief that the pattern of the good order has in some sense been "revealed" in the past, the question which arises is why are men incapable of maintaining it? The lack of man's ability to maintain the pattern is indeed explicitly stated in the very hymn which attributes to him an "indwelling law" (*tse*).

> Heaven gave birth to the multitudinous people
> but what it ordained is not to be relied on
> There are none who do not have the beginnings (of virtue)
> but few are capable of carrying it to an end.[28]

In this hymn we find not only the problem of the yawning abyss between what is and what ought to be in human affairs but an immediate link between this observation and the need for an all-embracing normative sociopolitical order in which the king and the ruling class must assume the primary responsibility for bridging the gap. Putting these opening lines into the context of the entire hymn, we find that it is by no means possible for "every-man" to bridge the gap between the beginnings and the end. The responsibility for the failure to bridge the gap, states the founder of the Chou dynasty King Wen, lies with the evil rulers of the Shang dynasty with their oppressive ministers and corrupt officials. Thus from the very outset the crucial task of the political order in realizing man's ethical destiny is clearly posited.

My concern at this point, however, is not so much with the linkage between the "moral" and the "political" as with the nature of the moral problem itself. If the responsibility for maintaining the moral order rests with the universal king and those who rule with him, why do they go astray? The mystery of why Heaven engenders man as a being whose ability to achieve his moral end is so uncertain is, of course, not solved. Yet it is clearly obvious that Heaven *wills* that man should conform to His order. Even if one should assume that there already existed the notion that Heaven's order in the nonhuman world operated immanently, unproblematically, and without obstacle the texts we have, like the Hebrew Bible, are mainly concerned with Heaven's relations to the human world. Here the difference between Needham's Judeo-Christian divine legislator and China's immanent "organismic" order may not be as absolute as he makes out.[29] Whether the order which ought to govern human affairs is regarded as revealed legislation or as in some sense an "immanent" order, the plain fact is that man can flout it. Reverting again to the metaphor of the family, one may say that the rules which *ought* to govern the relations among the family members *ought* to be rooted immanently in the sacred biological ties. Yet in fact family members disobey the rules of family life. The rules are *not* instinctual or innate self-enforcing "patterns of behavior" and the harmony of the family depends on the conscious moral attitudes of its members—particularly of the father who is, as it were, the ruler of the family. If we insist as does Needham on applying the word "organismic" to the Chinese view of both the natural and human order, it might be much more appropriate to think of the family rather than of a biological organism as the paradigm of organism.[30]

A human family like society as a whole does not instinctively obey its "immanent" laws. Thus even if Heaven is the "emanator" rather than the "legislator" of the normative order even in the human case, Heaven must nevertheless be deeply concerned with the actualization of the order. In neither case do the norms necessarily actualize themselves in the human sphere. Heaven had deliberately thrown His support to the house of Chou, which had in its predynastic period by its virtue proven its right to rule the "world" (*t'ien hsia*). The Mandate of Heaven is Heaven's strategy for assuring that good men will finally come to power and it is only through the mediation of good rulers that the normative order can be realized.

The possibility will emerge in later Chinese thought that the entire notion of the Mandate will come to be thought of in terms of an impersonal cycle of order and disorder—a kind of "law of history" and the rise of this type of "historic determinism" will in fact become a problem for Confucian thought. Yet in the *Book of Documents* and the *Book of Poetry* this is obviously not yet the case. What we have is a moral encounter between a Heaven obviously capable of being consciously concerned with the welfare of mankind and the maintenance of the ritual and moral order (whether legislated or unlegislated) on which it presumably rests and with the ruling vanguard of society which bears the responsibility for realizing that order.

At its deepest level, the idea of Heaven's Mandate presents us with a clear apprehension of the gap between the human order as it ought to be and as it actually is. Here we find clear evidence of that religious-ethical transcendence—that critical spirit toward the anterior development of high civilization which seems to be the earmark of the axial age in all the high civilizations.

The content of the *Book of Poetry* spans a period from the dynasty's founding to the seventh century B.C., which is depicted as a period of the Chou dynasty's sad decline. Thus the poems included by the anthologist reflect not only the time of Chou splendor but also the period of what is regarded as the Chou dynasty's gradual falling away from what is conceived of as the ideal pattern of its early years. Here we have, side by side, idyllic and reverential descriptions of the period when the kings, officials, and feudal lords lived in close harmony with the will of Heaven, starkly contrasted to the corruptions and anomy of the period of decline. Here we have the sufferings of soldiers sent on prolonged and apparently unnecessary campaigns in pursuit of the king's affairs; the pernicious influence of femmes fatales in the royal harem; the unbridled hybris of rulers and corrupt officials; the slander of the virtuous and the devastation wrought by sweet and deceitful words. Idyllic scenes of the happy life of peasants eager to work on the "public fields" of their lords, because their own needs have been so well taken care of, alternate with bitter complaints about the merciless exploitation of the oppressors.

> Big rat, big rat
> Do not gobble our millet
> Three years we have slaved for you
> Yet you take no notice of us.[31]

Whether such poems represent peasant ballads which actually directly reflect the sentiments of the people, as has been suggested, or whether they represent the voice of upper-class moralists, the general picture which emerges is clear.

We have referred above to the hymns which reverently describe the exalted spirit of the ancestral sacrificial ceremonies as providing an almost symbolic representation of the sacred order of society. In one particular poem we find the description of such an occasion involving the practice of ceremonial archery.[32] "The guests are taking their seats. To left and right they range themselves ... The wine is soft and good. It is drunk very peaceably. The bells and drums are set, the brimming pledge-cup is raised" ... and the archery contest takes place. "When all the rites are perfect, grandly and royally done; the ancestors bestow great blessings ... When the guests first take their seats how decorous they are, how reverent. While they are sober their manner is dignified and correct." Then, however, the immoderate drinking begins and everything falls apart. When they are drunk their behavior is utterly transformed. They leave their seats and roam, cut capers, throw themselves about; they become unseemly and rude. It is ironic that in the *Book of Documents* we find an entire text, "The Admonition on Wine," in which the Chou spokesman dwells at length on the devastating effects of the drunken excesses of the late Shang aristocracy.[33] While all this deals quite literally with the problem of drunkenness, I think we can see in drunkenness a symbol of all those unbridled passions which dissolve the forms of that sacred ritual order which make the good society possible.

To some the "urge to transcendence" which we find in these texts may seem quite modest. Here we have an aristocracy which lovingly cherishes all the trappings of rank and all the luxuries of high position. External beauty of form and dignity of appearance loom very large. Yet we also have the description of the paragon officer Chung Shan-fu whom Heaven, in the poet's view, specifically designated to aid the Son of Heaven in actualizing the "indwelling laws" of the human order. "Striving only for dignity and good deportment ... he neither oppresses the solitary man nor the widow nor does he fear the powerful and the oppressive . . . He is tireless in fulfilling his duties, clear-sighted and wise."[34]

> In his nature Chung Shan-Fu
> is a pattern [tse] of mildness and blessedness
> Good is his every attitude and air
> So cautious, so composed!
> Following none but the ancient teachings
> Striving only for dignity and good deportment
> Obedient to the Son of Heaven
> whose glorious commandments he spreads abroad.[35]

Whatever change Confucius will introduce into the vision which we find adumbrated in these texts, he already finds a full exposition of the fundamental problem—Why does the human reality fall away from Heaven's norms? How is the normative order to be restored?

# CHAPTER 3

# CONFUCIUS
## The Vision of the *Analects*

---

THE CENTURIES preceding and including the life of Confucius, conventionally known in Chinese history as the Spring and Autumn period, are generally treated as the centuries of dynastic decay.[1] The house of Chou now survived only as a wraithlike source of ultimate authority in a world where all the states and principalities had freely entered into a struggle for survival within a multistate arena. The sacred bonds of lineage, which may have bound some of the local princes to the dynasty, had largely lost their hold, as had the bonds of loyalty on the part of the unrelated princes. In some ways, the situation more closely fits our Western notion of feudalism than does the earlier state of affairs as described in the literature, but it also resembles the period of the conflicts of nascent nation-states in the early modern West. Some states were also subject to violent internal strife among the local lineages of the subnobility, leading to quite diverse and contradictory results. In some of the larger states, the rulers gradually strengthened the "bureaucratic" base of their rule by undermining the power of the local hereditary nobility and relying on "new men" drawn from various sources. In other states, as in Confucius' own state of Lu, powerful local lineages had usurped the power of the princes, creating virtual substates of their own. On the periphery of the "civilized world," the new powerful "semibarbarian" states of Ch'u, Ch'in, Wu, and Yüeh had emerged, states often not as committed to the traditions of the heartland as the older states of the central plain. It is the ruler of Ch'u who first commits the sacrilege in 880 B.C. of arrogating to himself the title king (*wang*)—a deplorable practice soon followed by others.

Yet the Spring and Autumn period remains significantly different from the following Warring States period (463–222 B.C.), when the tenuous hold of the ethicoreligious authority of the dynasty had completely receded. Confucius himself clings to the fading authority of his dynasty and in this he may be very much a man of his generation. One might well wonder why one of the powerful rulers of the time did not lay claim to Heaven's Mandate and the answer may be quite mundane—given the complex "international" situation, none of them could make a claim that would have been credible in either ethicoreligious or "real power" terms. The more powerful states were now much more effectively organized internally and could not easily win ascendancy over each other, and even some of the smaller states could now struggle for survival in the sophisticated game of "power politics." In the corrupt world of his times Confucius could not find any state that he might have regarded as the equivalent of the predynastic Chou state of old as described in the sacred record.

We do have in the seventh century the institution of the so-called hegemonic (*pa*) system. Under the leadership of Duke Huan and his famous minister Kuan Chung, the state of Ch'i in the Shantung Peninsula had established a kind of league of states ratified by the sacred authority of the Chou king (during the years 649–639). This was a kind of collective security system whereby the general peace of the Chinese world was maintained by an overwhelming preponderance of power. Later, the presidency of the league passed to the state of Chin, and gradually the effectiveness of even this limited security system simply faded away. By the time of Confucius, it had largely collapsed; all that remained was the utterly ineffective spiritual authority of the dynasty. No alternative was in sight. Yet the model of the hegemonic system, which had maintained relative peace in the world through a reliance on force with some feeble support of royal authority, became a major problem in Confucian ethicopolitical thought.

The account I have presented thus far might well be called an account from a Confucian perspective. When viewed from the point of view of a modern "developmental" perspective, quite a different picture emerges. A distinct advance in effective central organization and control was taking place in many of the states. The more capable rulers, in attempting to weaken the power of the local hereditary nobility, were like the kings of late medieval Europe—anxious to recruit talent from outside the circles of the local hereditary aristocracy. Mobility was increasing and new opportunities had emerged in both the administrative and military spheres. There is a notable rise in the prominence of the stratum of the *shih*.[2]

We have already seen that even in the early Chou, this term may have referred to a whole stratum (which probably enjoyed a hereditary rank status) of lower functionaries in the growing administrative structures of various states as well as in the royal organization itself. Their functions would be ceremonial, military, scribal, divinatory, as well as fiscal. The Chinese dictionary definition of the term as both "scholar" and "warrior" indicates that it was a cover term for both civil and military functionaries. Initially, most of these functionaries may have been drawn from the growing progeny of the noble lineages—particularly the cadet branches of such lineages. But quite possibly, as a class involved on a day-to-day basis with the actual business of government, it developed a class ethos of its own. I am tempted to suggest that the term connotes something like "men of service." Whether and to what degree there was much specialization within the class is not known, but I suspect that a natural differentiation between "civil" and "military" types existed from the outset. Running against this, however, is the later tradition of the six arts or disciplines (*liu i*)—rites, music, writing, mathematics (arithmetic?), archery, and chariot driving—which are presumably the arts mastered by any noble man or *shih*. This idea of the training of the well-rounded noble man may have existed, but the degree to which it was able to override the growing cleavage between the military and the civilian may well be questioned. In the case of Confucius himself, the *Analects* speak of his participation in the highly ceremonial archery contests of his time. Yet when attacked for his lack of proficiency in any specific art, he sarcastically replies, "What shall I practice, shall I practice charioteering or shall I practice archery? I will practice archery."[3] While this may be construed as a general attack on specialization, it is significant that the Master singles out the military arts as peculiarly ridiculous examples in his own case. Confucius himself apparently belonged to the scribal wing of the service class, which probably had become the custodian of all the cultural traditions preserved in the state archival documents.

While most of the *shih* of Confucius' time may have been of aristocratic origin, it is quite likely that enterprising commoners were beginning to find opportunities for drifting into both the civilian and military stream of this expanding service class. At least one element in this class, along with some members of the higher nobility, was becoming a kind of intellectual stratum.[4] The relations of intellectuals to social locus and interest remain as complex in our times as it is for the *shih* in ancient China. In neither age is one referring to a group which in Mannheim's terms simply "floats free" of involvement with social or personal interest. What is characteristic of intellectuals is that the relations of interests to ideas and ideals becomes highly problematic. Confucius, like the larger part of the *shih* stratum of "wandering intellectuals" of the following period for whom he becomes almost a prototype, remains committed to the "class vocation" of government service and even to the notion of privileges that rightly belong to government service, as in the case of the Western medieval clerisy or the modern academic intelligentsia. Yet it is precisely within this stratum that all the conflicts of the "hundred schools" emerge. If, as Mannheim states, the intelligentsia is marked by the fact that learning is its only capital, I must add that learning or know-how in the period I am considering may have been a form of fungible capital and that reflection arising out of learning could lead men, in ancient China as in the modern West, to diametrically opposed views of the world, whatever may have been their shared interests as a stratum.[5]

Here again, the emergence of the intellectuals out of the *shih* class, which leads to the pluralism and intellectual conflict of the Warring States period, may signify intellectual progress and creativity. But to Confucius, and indeed to most participants in the intellectual conflicts of the "hundred schools" themselves, this pluralism was a dismaying symptom of chaos and disarray. It proved that the Way had either been lost or not yet found. Yet both the pluralism and intellectual creativity do emerge. There were many other signs during this period of what we would now call development. The crucial point is that they are not particularly germane to the concerns of the Master.

I shall not attempt to recount the life of Confucius, which must be reconstructed from a vast accretion of historic and legendary materials.[6] According to tradition, he was a member of a *shih* family of declining fortunes. His youth was spent in a genteel poverty and he was forced to hold menial jobs involving some knowledge of financial matters and accounting. For the larger part of his life, he remained in the private domain, although he was firmly committed—both on the basis of family heritage and personal accomplishment—to his vocation for public service. The accounts of the offices he held over his lifetime vary widely, but one can safely assume that he never attained any great power or high position and that he never, in his own view, truly fulfilled his public vocation.

His own state of Lu in present-day Shantung province was a small, weak state, but since its ruling house descended from the great Duke of Chou, it remained closely linked to the Chou cultural heritage. This had not, however, prevented its sad degeneration. The power of the Duke had been completely usurped by the three noble families of the ducal lineage—Meng, Chi, and Shu. Later the powers of two of these families were usurped by their own family "stewards." Thus Confucius found within his own state all the violations of the normative order which so agitated his soul. He spent much time in the neighboring ancient states of Cheng, Ch'en, Ts'ai, and Ch'i, seeking opportunities for public service and was everywhere frustrated. While loyal to his state, his professed "ideal" ambition, like that of many of the wandering intellectuals of the Warring States period which followed, was to advise princes on how to establish order within their own states as well as within the entire civilized world (*tien-hsia*). However enfeebled the actual dynasty became, the tradition of the universal ecumene did not fade away.

Confucius' main vocation, like that of Socrates, becomes that of teacher—the transmitter of the *tao*—who attracts to himself a host of disciples as diverse as Plato and Alcibiades among the disciples of Socrates. He communicated a vision which, however differently it may have been perceived, must have seemed both fresh and exciting. To the Master himself, this seems to have been his ultimate solace for his failure to achieve his highest mission of shaping the world through the political order. It is undoubtedly his role as teacher that establishes his unique position in the history of Chinese civilization.

Confucius' unique dominance as a "culture hero" is truly exceptional, since there are no exact parallels in any other ancient civilization, although one can find parallels in specific religious traditions, such as Buddhism and Christianity. Unlike Socrates, who was preceded by all the imposing figures of pre-Socratic thought, Confucius is often presented as China's "first private thinker," who conveyed his vision directly to his disciples, effectively bypassing the structure of the political order. If this was the reason for his success, it would be most ironic, since it ran directly counter to the concept of "union of the political and doctrinal orders," which Confucius himself exalted. Yet many modern "tradition"-oriented Chinese, who seek wisdom in the Chinese past, continue to regard Confucius as the quintessential embodiment of the "Chinese mind" or of the basic orientations of Chinese culture. It may indeed be true that as a private thinker, unlike predecessors such as Kuan Chung and Tzuch'an who were active statesmen, he had the leisure to form his thought into a coherent and integrated vision. It was a sufficiently coherent and articulated vision to become the focus of attack of many who no longer shared his premises. It may also be true that as the self-avowed transmitter of the established truth of the past, he may indeed have more truly represented some of the *dominant* cultural orientations of the past than did some of his later rivals.

Yet the striking fact remains that in the centuries I am considering, Confucius' unique position in China's culture was hardly established. Indeed, it is not at all predictable during these centuries that his doctrines will become the "official philosophy" of China. If Confucius is the embodiment of the "essence" of Chinese culture, it took time to establish that fact.

## The *Analects* as Text

As in the case of the Gautama Buddha and Socrates, it is not easy to separate the founder's vision from the interpretations of his disciples. The corpus of statements attributed to Confucius in the literature of the following centuries is large but often suspect. The consensus among modern scholars is that our most reliable source for the early Confucian school, if not for the vision of the Master himself, is the collection of brief dialogues and gnomic utterances in the collection called in Chinese the *Lun-yü,* translated by Legge as *Analects,* and by Waley as "Selected Sayings."

The *Analects* themselves, however, remain the focus of fierce controversy. It is obviously a compilation put together in somewhat variant versions long after the Master's death. It contains not only the Master's sayings, but many of the utterances of disciples as well. Of the twenty "books" now extant, linguistic analysis indicates that some may belong to a much later period. Waley and others find many passages which they call non-Confucian and even anti-Confucian.[7] He thus finds that the professed concern with how language relates to reality must be a later addition, since the "language crisis" in ancient China belongs, in his view, to a much later development of thought. Tsuda Sokichi, a radical and iconoclastic critic of the text, finds the work so shot through with contradictions and anachronisms that it is unusable as a source of the thought of Confucius.[8]

While textual criticism based on rigorous philological and historic analysis is crucial, and while the later sections do contain late materials, the type of textual criticism that is based on considerations of alleged logical inconsistencies and incompatibilities of thought must be viewed with great suspicion. The contradictions and inconsistencies of thought alleged by Tsuda, Waley, Creel, and others are often based on the unexamined intellectual assumptions of the translators and interpreters themselves. While none of us comes to such an enterprise without deep-laid assumptions about necessary logical relations and compatibilities, we should at least hold before ourselves the constant injunction to mistrust all our unexamined preconceptions on these matters when dealing with comparative thought. One of the liberating functions of comparative thought lies in its ability to challenge precisely such unexamined assumptions concerning logical consistency and doctrinal compatibility.

My effort to present one account of the underlying vision of the *Analects* is based on my belief that the text, *taken as a whole,* does actually convey a coherent vision of reality despite the lack of surface organization in the text. I use the term vision rather than doctrine advisedly. Like a chiaroscuro painting, or indeed a Chinese landscape painting, highly economical in its use of the brush, a vision may encompass spaces full of unresolved problems and fruitful ambiguities. Even carefully articulated doctrines ostensibly based on sustained logical discourse, such as the thought of Plato or Karl Marx, remain full of unresolved problems. This will, of course, be the case *a fortiori* in a text such as the *Analects.* The very effort to translate this vision into modern Western discourse may inevitably involve the kind of distortion that would result from filling the empty spaces of a sparse Chinese landscape painting with the details of a Dutch landscape painter. If the nature of thought depends, in part, on the economy of language, something may well be lost with many words. Yet the risk must be taken.

The disjointed and laconic nature of the text may not be entirely a function of the classical Chinese language or of the "Chinese mind." Many texts discussed below are far more discursive than the *Analects.* As Waley suggests by his title "Selected Sayings," the nature of the text is peculiar because it was meant to be a compilation of particularly significant utterances and brief summations of the essence of various dialogue.

One might well begin a consideration of the vision by focusing on a central preoccupation that pervades the text. "The *tao* does not prevail in the world."[9] "The *tao* is not practiced."[10] The *Analects* seems to be one of the earliest texts available to us in which the term *tao* or way or road takes on its extended abstract and encompassing meaning. The metaphor of the way occurs in many civilizations. It is very much present in the Bible with its paths of righteousness and ways of the Lord. In the Bible, it most often refers to the course of individual moral life. In the *Analects,* in its most extended meaning, it refers to nothing less than the total normative sociopolitical order with its networks of proper familial and proper sociopolitical roles, statuses, and ranks, as well as to the "objective" prescriptions of proper behavior—ritual, ceremonial, and ethical—that govern the relationships among these roles. On the other side, it obviously and emphatically also embraces the "inner" moral life of the living individual. One might indeed say that a central problematique of the *Analects* involves the relations between the two. There is also one use of the term *tao* in the expression "Tao of Heaven," where it seems to refer to Heaven's way in the nonhuman universe as well, perhaps, as to all those aspects of Heaven in history over which men exercise no control.[11]

The word *tao* would thus be Confucius' inclusive name for the all-embracing normative human order which we have already discerned in the *Book of Documents* and the *Book of Poetry* and of which we find intimations even in the earliest orientations of Shang religion. What is clear from these statements is both the powerful perception of Confucius, as well as of others mentioned in the *Analects*, that this good order does not prevail in the world of his time and a deep sense of alienation from the way things are. If the word "conservative" means a satisfied approval of a prevailing state of affairs, Confucius is anything but a conservative.

Some, however, might be inclined to label him "reactionary" if by reactionary one means the belief that the good order has actually been realized in the historic past. According to the text, the Way had indeed existed not only in the early Chou dynasty but also at the beginning of the two preceding dynasties, the Shang and Hsia. In all three cases, the *tao* had been realized within the stream of human history and then been lost. We thus have the remarkable doctrine that the highest possibilities of human experience had already been achieved within the known human past and that the hope of the future was to recapture this lost splendor.

Leaving aside modern political labels, such as conservative or reactionary, we must ask how Confucius came to believe this doctrine. There is a common belief that most ancient civilizations believed in lost golden ages, but a closer examination of the thought of the creative minorities in all the high civilizations during the first millennium B.C. reveals that this belief, to the extent that it exists at all, is marginal and often different in kind. Socrates, Plato, and Aristotle show little evidence of any belief that the truly good society had been achieved in the Hellenic past; they are, in fact, critical of that past as described in the Homeric epic of the heroic age. Plato, in the *Timaeus* and *Critias,* does recreate an antediluvian Athens that embodied some of the vision of his *Republic,* but he makes it clear that here he is creating a myth in the narrowest sense of that term.[12] The same seems to be true of his account of cosmic cycles and cosmic golden age in the *Statesman*.[13] In the carefully constructed plan of the *Republic* there is no hint that this clear ideal model had ever existed in the known historic past. It is a pattern to be found, if anywhere, in the realm of eternal forms and not in the flux of time past.

In the Hebrew scripture, there is, of course, the idyllic state of Eden, but this is not a whole society but a state involving the interpersonal relations of two individual human beings. This is not an accidental feature of the story; the depiction of a presocial state of man is central to the meaning of the whole mythos. Adam and Eve are not only physically naked. They are, as yet, naked of social roles, status, and all the machinery of a complex society. The focus is on persons in their interpersonal relations. The gradual post-Adamic emergence of human society is a story of strife, conflict, and painful gropings toward an unknown future in a diverse and unstructured world. When the people of Israel emerge as a society at the foot of Sinai, the Law that is revealed to it will hopefully govern its life when it reaches the promised land. It does not describe any existing social order of the past and certainly does not represent a return to the idyll of Eden.

In India, there are references to cosmic cycles and past golden ages in the *Mahabharata* and in some of the Buddhist scriptures, but these are marginal. On the whole there is no sense of a society of peace and harmony discoverable in any accessible past.[14] To be sure, the "dharma" of the social order which emerges with caste society does prescribe an eternal social order, an "organic" society held together by a strict division of labor among rigidly separated castes and a karmically based law. But within the framework of Upanishadic Brahman thought, this society is presented without utopian implications as the realm of stern social duty. The political order exists in order to support the societal order with sanctions of force. As Louis Dumont suggests, the emergence of the caste system as a kind of everlasting social order based on stern duty and the law of karma takes place in a period when the ideal of renunciation had already become dominant within the elite culture. "It may be doubted," he states, "whether the caste system could have existed and endured independently of its contradictory-renunciation."[15]

Confucius, however, does not look back to a vague primordial golden age. Although living several centuries after the early Chou, through sources available to him he believes that he has access to tangible, empirical knowledge of a society in which the *tao* had actually been realized. Beyond this, he is willing to accept the word of his texts that the *tao* had also been realized in the two previous dynasties—Hsia and Shang—although he admits that he does not know as much about the concrete prescriptions and institutions of these two dynasties. He even suggests that the Chou represented a "higher" realization of the Way than its two predecessors. "Chou could survey the two preceding dynasties. How rich the pattern of its culture. We follow Chou!"[16]

Yet the question remains—why this serene confidence that the highest values of human civilization had already been realized in a past that was accessible to him? Creel's description of the relatively prolonged state of domestic tranquility achieved by the early Chou suggests that the Chinese universal kingship of the early Chou had in fact achieved a degree of pacification probably without parallel in any of the other ancient high civilizations, with the possible exception of Egypt.

Confucius' conviction seems to be based, however, not only on this shared memory but on a blending of this memory with a *conception* of the good socio-politico-cultural order which he already finds envisioned in the *Book of Documents* and the *Book of Poetry*. When positive memories based on experience are fused with conceptions of an achieved normative order found in the sacred literature, one can readily understand the all-inclusive idealization to which this may lead. If the word *tao* refers to some total state of affairs, it becomes something like the word "system" in much current Western social discourse. If the "good system" has been realized in the past, it must have been good as a whole and therefore basically in all its parts.

The notion that the *tao* had actually been realized in past experience may have been strengthened in the Chinese case by the notable absence of anything perceived as a challenging or relativizing model. The numerous Greek city-states, with their extraordinary variety of sociopolitical organization and changes over time, encouraged the relativistic questions of the sophists. For Socrates, Plato, and Aristotle, experience offered little guidance in the search for universal principles of ethical and political order. The Hebrews were not inclined to find saving truth in the experience of the Mesopotamian and Egyptian empires or in the Syrio-Canaanitish world. Revelation of the true Law came from the Lord. Confucius, by contrast, certainly would not have found anywhere in the known world of his time anything equivalent to the model of the Chou dynasty. Its very uniqueness may have established its universality as the true order of civilization as well as its cosmic relation to Heaven.

This does not mean that Confucius conceives of the *tao* as a primordial condition of men in the "state of nature." In speaking of the past, Confucius begins with the Hsia dynasty; there is no discussion of the original "precivilized" state of mankind.[17] To judge from the writings of both Mencius and Hsün-tzu, it would appear likely that like them, he believed that there had been a primitive state of mankind before civilization, and like them, he is profoundly committed to the project of civilization. The *tao* is the *tao* of an achieved universal, all-embracing, ethicopolitical order. I would guess that he fully supports the statement in the *Book of Poetry* that few men in the state of nature were capable of realizing their full potentialities. It was

only when the sage-kings had actualized the patterns of the normative culture that it became possible for all human beings to achieve
their full humanity. This would indicate belief in an initial progress
from the primitive state of mankind to the actualization of the *tao* in
the Hsia dynasty. Once the *tao* had been made manifest as an entire
gestalt, however, it was already basically present because, in a logical sense, the whole always "precedes" the parts.

This did not mean that changes and improvements in matters of
concrete detail were not possible. We have already seen that the
Chou order was, in some sense, superior to the Hsia and Shang because of its ability to draw on the experience of its predecessors.
When Confucius' favorite disciple, Yen Hui, asks about how to rule
a state, Confucius replies, "One would go by the seasons of Hsia [in
calendar-making]; one would use the ruler's coach of the Yin
[Shang]; the ceremonial head-gear of the Chou and the music of the
Shao."[18] There does seem to be the tacit assumption here that even
in matters of detail, the history of the "three dynasties" provides a
full gamut of possibilities. Confucius' examples might seem to many
moderns to refer to trivial forms of ceremony rather than to "fundamental" institutional matters.[19] Yet the question of which concrete
parts of the good order are organically ingredient and vital to the
whole and which are adventitious detail subject to change will be
debated over the ages. There is a text of the late Warring States or
Early Han period called the "Rites of Chou" (*Chou-li*) that purports
to provide a detailed blueprint of the entire early Chou system in all
its institutional and ceremonial detail.[20] The *Analects* provides no
such blueprint and yet the examples used by the Master indicate
that the *tao* of the three dynasties included concrete systems and
forms of human organization and was not simply a matter of general
principles abstracted from the prescription within which they were
embedded. It would be possible, within the framework of Confucianism, to admit legitimate variations of local customs into the
framework of the *tao,* but in dealing with prescriptions of proper behavior (*li*) involving the public and the religious life of rulers or vital
matters of family life, the Greek distinction between what is "convention" or mere "conventional" custom (*nomos*) and what is natural
and based on universal "nature" (*physis*) is not so easily drawn. A
"mere ritual form" may be an essential and enduring ingredient of
the universal *tao.*

In all of this, one can accept without reservation, Confucius' assertion that he is a "transmitter" and not "one who makes up anything on his own."[21] If the *tao* of the good order has, in fact, been
realized within the human experience of the past; if the power-

holders in his own time are totally incapable of transmitting the essence of this *tao*, he—even as commoner—is prepared to assume the awesome responsibility for the *tao*. He does not transmit the ancient, however, simply because it is ancient. He transmits it because the ancient embodies the good and the memory of this good has been preserved in records that embody the saving truth. Although we shall indeed question his assertion that he is not in some sense a "creator" or "maker," a good case can be made that the fundamentals of much of what he transmits can be discerned in the older texts.

Yet even as a transmitter, he may be an innovator. He transmits his *tao* as a private teacher to an assortment of disciples who are also, for the large part, commoners (not in government). Unlike the Duke of Chou, he is not a minister admonishing his subordinates. Even in his capacity as transmitter, he manages to win the voluntary adherence of his disciples who are somehow attracted by the reflectivity and fresh insight that he brings to bear on that which is transmitted.

## The Realm of *Li*

This freshness may have been particularly true of his reflections on the idea of *li*. If the word *tao* seems to refer to an all-encompassing state of affairs embracing the "outer" sociopolitical order and the "inner" moral life of the individual, the word *li* on the most concrete level refers to all those "objective" prescriptions of behavior, whether involving rite, ceremony, manners, or general deportment, that bind human beings and the spirits together in networks of interacting roles within the family, within human society, and with the numinous realm beyond. The graph, with its religious classifier, seems to have referred originally to religious ritual. We are reminded again of the shadowy boundary between proper ritual to ancestors and proper behavior toward living kin members. The question of Confucius' attitude to the entire realm of religion will be considered below, but there can be no doubt that rites that we would call religious, even in the narrowest definition of that term, are integral to the whole corpus of *li*. One can, in fact, go further to agree with Herbert Fingarette that the entire body of *li* itself, even when it involves strictly human transactions, somehow involves a sacred dimension and that it may be entirely appropriate to use terms such as "holy rite" or "sacred ceremony" in referring to it.[22]

Yet what makes *li* the cement of the entire normative sociopolitical order is that it largely involves the behavior of persons related to each other in terms of role, status, rank, and position within a structured society. It does not simply refer to general behavior of unconnected human beings in certain universal categories of human situations. Within the family, it involves proper behavior of father to son, husband to wife, elder brother to younger (and vice versa), just as in religious ritual in the narrow sense it involves proper rituals toward ancestral and nature spirits. The Chinese commentaries stress again and again the function of *li* in teaching human beings to perform their *separate* roles well in a society whose harmony is maintained by the fact that every one plays his part as he should within the larger whole. This may be a "sacred community" in Fingarette's sense, but it is a sacred community that accepts unblinkingly what it regards as the need for hierarchy, status, and authority within a universal world order. While the ultimate end of *li* may be to humanize hierarchy and authority, it certainly also is meant to maintain and clarify its foundations.

The order that the *li* ought to bind together is not simply a ceremonial order—it is a sociopolitical order in the full sense of the term, involving hierarchies, authority, and power. Within the family, the *li* of family life is not self-actualizing. It requires the father to be a living source of authority and power. The *li* must themselves support this authority and power. This is true *a fortiori* of the sociopolitical order as a whole. Without the universal kingship through which virtuous kings may influence an entire society, the separate *li* cannot be ultimately realized. Thus the *li* must in every way support the institution of kingship. The system of *li* within the *Analects* presupposes and reinforces the proper networks of hierarchy and authority.

To many modern sensibilities, this frank acceptance of hierarchy and authority as a necessary and even good aspect of a civilized and harmonious society creates an enormous barrier to any effort at "understanding" (*verstehen*) Confucianism in the Weberian sense. The enraged rush to explanations in terms of Confucius' obvious class interests becomes overwhelmingly tempting. My aim in this account is by no means apologetic, but I think an effort should be made to understand this aspect of the vision in terms of its own implicit logic.

Confucius, in fact, seems to be well aware of all the pathologies of hierarchy and authority, although he is just as aware in his own time of the pathologies of the subversion of authority. History teaches him that both are fatal. The decay of the Shang dynasty had begun at the top, while the decay in the Chou dynasty had come both from the profligate and unwise behavior of the later Chou king as well as from the assault on the sacred bases of royal authority by unscrupulous "feudal lords."

The fact that the extended territorial states of ancient civilizations necessarily involved an unequal division of power, hierarchy, and authority was, of course, taken for granted not only in China, but in all the ancient civilizations which came under the control of large territorial states. In China, the model of the natural and sacred hierarchy of the patrilinear family may have lent its own coloration to the concepts of hierarchy and authority, but we must again remember that even in the history of the West, with its memories of Athenian "democracy," the notion that democracy cannot be implemented in large territorial states requiring highly centralized power remained accepted wisdom as late as Montesquieu and Rousseau.

The rise of the Athenian conception of democracy (in the original literal sense of direct democracy) involving the active and equal participation of all citizens in public affairs did presuppose the scale of the city-state polity although it was not a necessary consequence of such a polity. It rested very much on what Ernest Barker calls the "tangible" and "visible" nature of the city-state, where "Athenians lived very much in the agora" where constant face-to-face encounters of "citizens" (who themselves were a small part of the whole population) took place. It also presupposed a situation in which the citizen "would naturally feel himself more of a citizen and less of a householder."[23] Within such a setting, group conflict becomes most tangible and intense, and the notion of tangible technique of control of a minority by a majority becomes plausible. One even has the sense that the older tradition of the solidarity of the companion warriors, who had founded the city-states, may have remained alive and become a factor in the concept of equal citizenship itself.

Aristotle, who is by no means an unreserved democrat in his "constitutional" thinking, is committed to participation in political life as representing the highest goal of the practical life. Like Plato before him, but in a much more moderate way, he draws a sharp contrast between the private life of the household, basically concerned with economic production and inevitably organized on lines of "natural" hierarchy, and the public life of the polis, based on the "constitutional rule of freemen and equals."[24] The family is anything but the ideal model for the polity even in Aristotle, who otherwise consciously rejects the extreme antifamilism of Plato's *Republic*.

Here, the contrast with the Confucian view of the family could hardly be more stark. Aristotle and Confucius are both agreed that the family is inevitably based on hierarchy and Confucius would perhaps have acknowledged the economic role of the family. To one who associated the family with the transfiguring rites of ancestral worship, however, the ideal family is the ultimate source of all those values which humanize the relations of authority and hierarchy which must exist in any civilized society. To Plato, the obscure life of the family, devoted to pursuing its own particularistic economic goals and with its limited familial morality, is a world in which the adult male citizen is encompassed by the narrow environment of those who are not his equals—wives, slaves, and children. As we also see in Plato's case, however, democracy is by no means the inevitable reverse side of antifamilism. The *Republic* is fanatically elitist, but its elite is an elite which can draw no spiritual or moral lessons from the model of familial life. To Confucius, it is precisely in the family that humans learn those virtues which redeem the society, for the family is precisely the domain within which authority comes to be accepted and exercised not through reliance on physical coercion but through the binding power of religious, moral sentiments based on kinship ties. It is within the family that we find the root of *public* virtue. The choice is not between a "government of freemen and equals" and a government of hierarchy and authority, but between a government which is suffused with the spirit that maintains the harmony of an ideal family life and a government in which hierarchy and authority are based on brute force or mere interest without any sense of spiritual-moral constraint.

We remind ourselves at this point that Aristotle did not believe that the virtues of the polity of "freemen and equals" could have possibly been realized in large empires. And with the emergence of the Alexandrian Empire and the Roman Empire, the role of city-states with their politics of citizenship did become much reduced. Whether the Athenians would have regarded our modern bureaucratized, representative democracy as the embodiment of the political virtues to which they were committed remains a highly moot point. There was, of course, little in the history of medieval Europe or early modern Europe which would have shaken Confucius' implicit belief that hierarchy and authority were the necessary bases of social order in any type of polity extended over wide territories.

We must candidly note that despite the widespread triumph of modern ideologies which posit the notion that hierarchy and authority are transient vestiges of an evil past about to be eliminated from the human scene, it remains unproven that complex civilizations can dispense with them even though there have been some successes in creating methods for confining their scope and rendering them accountable. Confucius' problem of how one humanizes the exercise of authority and inequalities of social power remains with us whatever we may think of his solutions.

There are, however, those who, when dealing with Confucius' conception of *li*, would very much stress the reciprocal rather than the hierarchical aspects. There are relations of *li* where *equal* reciprocity may indeed be dominant, as in the relations among friends. Hierarchy itself, to be sure, does not preclude reciprocity. The child owes his parents filial piety and the parents owe their children parental love. The minister owes his ruler obedience and loyalty and the ruler, in dealing with his ministers, "should be guided by the rules of *li*."[25]

Still there is relatively more stress in the *Analects* on the proper behavior of subordinates than on the behavior of those above. Most of the subordinates discussed—I hasten to add—are also members of the elite broadly conceived. Confucius seems even more conscious, at least in his generation, of the danger of subversion of the frail surviving structure of sacred authority than he is of the abuse of authority by those above. When thinking of "filial piety," we conjure up the image of parents in their prime repressing helpless youngsters. Confucius' attention seems riveted on children in their prime neglecting and betraying aged parents. There are also ambitious nobles usurping the legitimate authority of their princes, scheming concubines displacing legitimate successors, and all sorts of upstart adventurers. At bottom, the issue is not the abuse of authority by those above versus the subversion of authority by those below, but the universal violation of the spirit of the *li* on all sides giving free vent to unbridled lust, arbitrariness, caprice, cruelty, ambition, and greed. The issue is obedience to *li*. When asked to clarify the meaning of filial piety he replies, "When they are alive, serve them according to *li;* when they die, bury them according to *li;* sacrifice to them according to *li*."[26] The obedience is not simply to parents but to the entire system of *li* which is the foundation of human society.

I have thus far emphasized the inextricable relationship of the concept of *li* to the whole network of hierarchy and authority on which the normative sociopolitical order is based. In the stimulating and highly suggestive work of Fingarette mentioned above, the focus is rather on the nature of *li* as such.

To Fingarette, *li* is the heart of Confucius' teachings and it is the Master's conception of *li* which marks him as an innovator.[27]

I do not deny that Confucius' concept of *li, when considered within the context of his ethical doctrine,* does represent innovation, but one must not cavalierly dismiss his own repeated claims that he is a transmitter of past traditions in this area. A good case can be made that the concept has deep roots in older orientations; that in the *Book of Poetry,* holy rite (whatever name is used for it) already plays a key role as a binding force of the sociopolitical and religious order; and that the narratives of the *Tso-chuan* abound in accounts of performances of *li* and discussions of the vital importance of *li* during the centuries of the Spring and Autumn periods.

The *li*, in Fingarette's view, are not simply established patterns of customary behavior which shape people in a crudely behavioristic fashion. They are sacred, "concrete acts of human intercourse" which have the power to shape and humanize those who participate in them by dint of their "magical" quality.[28] They are thus not bare patterns of behavior, but patterns of behavior which are, as it were, the bearers of religious, moral, and aesthetic meanings. They are, above all, acts ideally based not on physical coercion or threat of coercion, but on a kind of "magical" assent such as we find in the numerous spontaneous and voluntary acts of courtesy in our ordinary daily human interactions.

This valuable insight into what the *li ought to be* is, however, immediately linked in Fingarette to a resounding negation. Since these qualities and meanings are rooted in the acts themselves, they are, as it were, properties of the acts themselves. They have nothing to do with any inner, psychological, or subjective nature of the individual. Our tendency to read such notions into the text simply reflects our Western "psychological bias."[29] What I shall here contend, however, is that the view which Fingarette harshly attacks—namely that Confucius is vitally concerned with qualities, capacities, and inner mental dispositions which we associate not simply with concrete acts but with living persons as persons—is a correct view, and that Confucius' emphasis on these inner qualities is one of his true innovations. Further, I contend that even the metaphor of the "inner" as a way of referring to these realities is by no means alien to Chinese thought in general or even to Confucius in particular. Whether Confucius is an individualist in any modern Western sense is not the point. The question is whether he is concerned with the inner life of individuals.

One does not derive from the *Analects* the impression that the performance of *li* as ceremonial forms of behavior had entirely disappeared in the world of Confucius. There was, to be sure, widespread ignorance of the *li* and inappropriate performance of *li*, as when the usurping Chi family of Lu had the sacred dance of the eight rows performed at its court—a dance which was the hereditary prerogative of the ducal family or of the Chou lineage to which it belonged.[30] Yet there are numerous passages that describe performance of the *li* which may be quite "correct" and yet which are full of outrage against the discrepancy observed between form and spirit. "If a man is without *jen* [for the moment, I shall translate this as the true inner virtue] what can he have to do with *li*? If a man is without *jen*, what can he have to do with music?"[31] "*Li* performed without reverence, the forms of mourning observed without grief— how can I bear to look on these things?"[32] "Talking of *li*, talking of *li*—Does it mean no more than presents of silks and gems?"[33] There is here a clear and ringing assertion that these sacramental "concrete acts" can easily become totally separated from all the meanings and qualities which are supposed to diffuse them. They can easily lose all their sacredness. Nowhere does Confucius imply that the aristocratic performers of these acts were not "skillful" performers.

Fingarette himself acknowledges this. "The ceremony may have a surface slickness but yet be dull, mechanical for lack of serious purpose and commitment. Beautiful and effective ceremony requires the personal 'presence' to be fused with learned ceremonial skill."[34] His major contention, however, supported by reference to linguistic philosophy is that dispositional terms such as commitment, purpose, "personal presence," and will, as well as terms referring to virtues and emotions such as "grief" in the above passage, are somehow always "aspects of action."[35] "*Jen* and its associated 'virtues' and *li* too are not connected in the original text with the language of 'will,' 'emotion' and 'inner state.' " They are always associated with the "unique context of the particular action."[36] Even where the text implies, generally, that the man of *jen* is without anxiety, Fingarette insists that the anxiety must always refer to some specific "observable condition." Somehow we are to suppose that when an emotion is a specific reaction to a specific act, it is no longer "subjective" in our usual sense of the term but rather a predicate of the act as such.

One of Confucius' most original utterances concerning *li* is to be found in a statement which I translate as follows: "If one is able to rule a state by *li* and the spirit of yielding [*jang*] [appropriate to it] what difficulty will there be? If one is not able to rule a state by *li* and the spirit of yielding, of what use is *li*?"[37] The spirit of yielding to others involves precisely the capacity to overcome such passions as "the love of mastery, self-aggrandizement, resentment and covetousness" of which he speaks elsewhere.[38] What Confucius seems to be saying is that in this disposition toward yielding, we find the underlying "spirit of *li*" which *ought to be* intimately associated with every "concrete act" of *li*.

Where, then, is the locus of this spirit of yielding and of all those dispositions which we would describe as virtues, emotions, and passions? It seems to me that they are not necessarily associated with specific performances of *li* or related to "specific conditions." The amount of space devoted to specific *li* in the *Analects* is comparatively small. Waley is entirely correct in his assertion that the *Analects* is not much concerned with the details of ritual. "The actual text of the *Analects* is concerned with the general principles of morality."[39] The virtues and dispositions, however closely related to *li*, are inextricably associated not with specific acts but with specific living persons. The "locus of the person" is, in short, the person (this is the title of chapter 3 of Fingarette's *Confucius*).

None of this implies the stark dichotomy of "individual versus society" against which Fingarette inveighs. Confucius' individual is indeed a thoroughly social being and thoroughly oriented toward action. Yet the notion that this social nature and action-orientation are incompatible with a sustained inner life of the person reflects Fingarette's own involvement with the modern Western psychology/sociology antithesis rather than anything found in the *Analects*. The notion that the person's involvement in various self-subsisting "systems of action" "out there" means that he has no "inner" autonomous life as an individual or that this inner life can have no effect on behavior is a notion which Fingarette brings to the *Analects*. Something like this point of view may indeed be discerned as one position in the later problematique of Confucianism and Fingarette's stance may actually resemble certain later Confucian positions, but it is, I submit, not present in the text of the *Analects*.

Lexical equivalents of words such as "psychic state," psychology, and subjectivity are, of course, not to be found in the *Analects,* which is certainly not a psychological treatise. For that matter, they are not to be found in the overwhelming bulk of Western ethical writings before modern times. They are not even to be found in the intensely inward-looking sermons of the Puritan divines. Ethical self-scrutiny is not "psychological" analysis. The term "inner" as referring to mind or spirit has long been known even in the West to be a physicalist metaphor and it is actually a physicalist metaphor used by Confucius himself when he says that "in the presence of an unworthy man, one should turn *inward* and examine oneself."[40] Later, Mencius will quite consciously use the terms "inner" and "outer" (*nei-wai*) to refer to the inner life of the individual and the outer ethicosocial order.[41] Unmentioned by Fingarette are Confucius' references to the heart, as in his remarks "that at the age of seventy he could follow what his heart desired without going astray."[42] These references do not prove that Confucius had arrived at a solution of the problem of the mental and the physical similar to that which was to arise out of certain modes of Greek thought. He may, like the

Hebrew scriptures, have drawn no line between the physical organs and the feelings, thoughts, and intentions which he attributed to them. The question here is not whether Confucius conceived of the mind-body problem in any dualistic Western way, but whether he attributes emotions, virtues, intentions, and attitudes to living individuals or somehow sees these mental phenomena as embedded only in concrete acts of *li* and whether he believes that the "heart," with all its capacities, has an autonomous, dynamic life of its own apart from specific responses to specific situations. Fingarette almost comes close to acknowledging that the person does indeed possess an autonomous existence apart from action when he admits that *"jen* is often directly associated with a person and suggested to be a possession of a person" and that "in the case of *jen* we should conceive of a directed force operating in actions in public space and time and having a person *as initial point-source* [italics my own]."[43] All that need be added here is that Confucius is, in fact, enormously interested in the inner state of the person even when he is not operating in the public space and regards these sustained inner states as of utmost relevance to public behavior.

Avoiding words like "psychology" and "psychic states," I shall thus allow myself here to define *jen* as referring to the inner moral life of the individual person that includes a capacity of self-awareness and reflection.

## On *Jen*

What, then, is *jen* and what is its relation to *li?* The word in itself, as a key term of the ethical life, seems to be not much older among our texts than the *Analects* itself. Its earliest occurrence can probably be found in two "hunting" poems of the *Book of Poetry* in which we catch a glimpse of two lusty noble huntsmen who are presented as "handsome and *jen.*" Lin Yü-sheng has suggested that the meaning of the *jen* in this context may have been something like manly or virile.[44] If this is the case, one can readily see how it may eventually have come to be used by Confucius in the moralized sense of the "true manhood" or "perfect virtue" of Legge's translation. Here, one would see something of a parallel to the evolution of *virtus* and virtue from the Latin *vir*. What it seems to encompass in Confucius is something as broad and even as ultimately mysterious as Socrates' idea of the good as applied to the moral life of the individual. It is an attainment of a human excellence which—where it exists—is a whole embracing all the separate virtues. Thus it certainly also embraces all the social virtues and the capacity to perform the *li* in

the proper spirit. It is this social aspect which has led to the translation of the term as love, benevolence, and humanity.[45] It must nevertheless be acknowledged that in much later Chinese thought it is
this side of *jen*—its capacity to make the individual act well in all the
encounters of social life—which is emphasized. New terms will come
to the fore to deal with the inner aspects.

A good case can thus be made that it is, above all, in his focus on
the concept of *jen* that Confucius is an innovator rather than a
transmitter.[46] Yet even here, one must be careful in one's formulation. The notion that the normative "objective" sociopolitical order
depends on the inner virtues of kings and officials is already fully
present in the *Book of Poetry*, the *Book of Documents*, and the *Tso-chuan*.
The vocabulary of personal "virtues" in these books is already very
rich and there is already the inclusive notion of *te*. This term may
have originally been associated with an inner spiritual-magical
power which makes it possible for kings or shamans to influence the
behavior of others,[47] but in these works it already possesses an un-
mistakably ethical meaning. The message is already clear. The normative order can be maintained only by rulers who possess this
spiritual-ethical power. Given these pre-Confucian texts, Fingarette's assertion that "it is not a distinct power we happen to use
in ceremony; it is the power of ceremony" does not at all fit the spirit
of the passages in question where *te* seems to be quite definitely a
distinct power inherent in the individuals concerned.[48]

It has been suggested that what is new in Confucius' conception
of *jen* is precisely the notion that moral power is not the prerogative
of those in authority—that commoners like himself may possess virtue. Yet even here, one can find in the pre-Confucian literature an
adumbration of the idea that men of virtue, such as the ancestors of
the Chou dynasty or noble ministers, prove their right to authority
by the possession of virtue.

What may well be new, however, is the notion that commoners
such as Confucius may *teach* other commoners *how* to achieve *jen*—
how to become "noble men" (*chün-tzu*). The term I translate here as
"noble man," like our own terms "noble man" and "gentleman"
was, of course, initially social rather than ethical in meaning.[49] Like
*"gens"* or *"nobilis,"* it referred to high birth and high rank. Yet in the
*Analects* it has unquestionably acquired its moral meaning. This does
not mean that Confucius has rejected hereditary rank. On the contrary, he still cherishes the fond hope that those of noble birth may
be influenced to become true noble men. He also makes it quite
plain that "when the *tao* prevails" those in authority—the son of
Heaven in particular and not commoners like himself—are the ulti-

mate source of the moralization of society.[50] Because the "son of Heaven" stands at the objective locus of sacred authority (*wei*) from which society as a whole must effectively be transformed by action and teaching, it is only when the ruler is a sage or at least allows himself to be influenced by sage ministers that the *tao* as a total state of affairs can be realized.

Nevertheless, in teaching his disciples virtue, Confucius is making the statement that the teaching of virtue can be sundered from political authority and yet ultimately become a force for transforming society. Above all, however, the most strikingly novel aspect of *jen* is that it does not refer to moral power which is simply latently present in men. It is an existential goal which Confucius attempts to achieve for himself through his own self-cultivation. It is the result of a self-effort which he believes can be taught to others. Again, like Socrates, he poses the simple question, "how can I make myself good [*jen*]?"

His concept of goodness and of how to achieve it are, to be sure, in many ways markedly different from those of Socrates. Among his numerous and constantly varied replies to the question "what is *jen*?" there is indeed one much appreciated by Fingarette. Yen Hui asks, "What is *jen*?" Confucius replies with a sentence that has received differing translations. One is, "Curb your ego and submit to *li*." One is Waley's "He who can submit himself to ritual is good."[51] Fingarette opts for "self-disciplined and ever turning to *li*."[52] In all these versions it is obvious that the man of *jen* in all his behavior never deviates from the prescriptions of *li*—from a body of "objective" prescriptions of behavior which has, with modifications, been transmitted by a long sacred tradition. One simply notes that Fingarette's version very much stresses the absolute simultaneity and inseparability of the two halves of the statement, implying that the self-discipline and the performance of *li* are two sides of the same coin. The first translation, supported by a majority of Chinese commentators, suggests that the correct performance of the *li* presupposes a sustained inner effort to overcome those evil impulses which prevent the performance of *li* in the spirit appropriate to *li*. Nevertheless, only through the established channels of *li* can one's inner self-mastery make itself manifest to society and lead within to the higher moral excellence of *jen*. The *li* are thus Janus-like. Acting according to the civilized practices of the normative tradition is a necessary ingredient of *jen*, and making one's *jen* manifest through the *li* is the only way in which *li* can be brought to life.

Here, of course, we have a sharp divergence from Socrates. To the extent that Socrates is seeking to establish the good by a method of dialectic inquiry, he places this dialectic reason above all tradition and custom. This does not mean that he necessarily rejects all established morality as wrong. In the words of Barker, "He sought to elicit from the ordinary conduct of men a clear conception of the rules by which they already acted," just as grammar teaches men the "true rules" of the language which they are already speaking "unknowingly and imperfectly."[53] The confusing history of the infinitely varied customs and practices of the Greek past in the Socratic view offered no true guide. No established belief or practice could be considered right or wrong till it had withstood the test of his clarifying dialectic and his search for true definitions. For Confucius, on the other hand, there had emerged within the history of the civilized world a universal and tested body of what might be called in Hegelian terms an "objective ethical order" embodied in the rites, practices, and basic institutions of the *tao* of the three dynasties. While in Hegel's world the subjective morality of individuals (*Moralität*) and the historically realized objective ethical order (*Sittlichkeit*) would be harmonized only in the final epiphany of the modern state, in Confucius what might be called the normative objective sociopolitical order, including the system of *li*, had, in its broad outlines, already been realized in human experience and had also been lost.

It is probably this notion of a preestablished ethical system which leads Fingarette to assert that the entire Western concept of ethical choice is lacking in Confucius.[54] Confucius already knows what his *tao* is. It is "out there" embodied in the *li*. What is there to choose? Here again, we are asked to believe that because there are no discussions of words which are the lexical equivalents of foreign terms such as "ethical choice" and "responsibility," the realities to which these terms refer are completely absent in the *Analects*. Yet the lack of any exact Western lexical equivalent of *li* does not deter Fingarette from discussing Western analogues to *li* and Western experiences corresponding to it.

When he speaks of ethical options, Fingarette most often speaks of conflicts of values or perplexities about "what is right" and it is, of course, true that discussions about such questions can be found in the "Platonic" Socratic dialogues in which Socrates finds himself in the process of working out his ethical ideas. Yet when Socrates knows the good, he seems to believe much more firmly than Confucius that knowledge *necessarily* leads to goodness. For vast stretches of Western history, there have been Stoics, religious Jews, Christians, and others who have believed as firmly as Confucius that they are in actual possession of a true substantive ethical code (*Sittlichkeit*)—a true *tao* which on the whole established definite answers to questions of right and wrong. To both the Jesus of the parables and a Torah-true Jew, the question of "moral choice" does not involve choosing among "value systems" or creating one's own values. It means choosing *between the known good and evil*. Many medieval Jewish and Christian moralists who staunchly believed in "freedom of the will" meant by it freedom to choose between the known good and the known evil. This is in no way different from Confucius' choice between following the way and straying from it. Confucius, like a vast host of Western moralists, did not believe that he was creating a new way. Like all these traditional moralists he was constantly preoccupied with the *choice* between following the way and straying from it.

In all these traditions, knowing the preestablished value system was not, to be sure, conceived of as solving all of life's complex moral problems and all of them were aware of tensions among values all good in themselves. The same is true of Confucius. The prescriptions of *li* are rules of life which, despite their extreme importance, hardly "cover" all life situations. In the *Analects,* we thus find the crucial concept of *i,* often translated as "righteousness" or "appropriateness," completely ignored by Fingarette, a concept which seems to refer specifically to right behavior in the vast sea of unique life situations where more often than not there is no simple "covering" rule of *li.* There is thus no reason to doubt the sincerity of the Master's self-assessment, when he tells us that he is unable to attain the noble man's ideal of being "wise without perplexity."[55] There are, indeed, examples in the text of such perplexity. In Fingarette we find no allusion to such inner states of perplexity or dilemmas involved in the choice of lesser evils. Confucius and his disciples constantly confront choices.

At one point, Fingarette argues that man is not, in the *Analects,* "ultimately an autonomous being who has inner and decisive power intrinsic to him, a power to select among real alternatives," on the ground that man is born as a "raw material who must be civilized by education and become a truly human man."[56] What we have here is a kind of educational determinism. Education is, of course, emphasized in most of the ethical traditions mentioned above, but clearly Confucius is convinced that the education of his young disciples who are already self-aware adults is wholly dependent on what the disciples bring to the educational encounter. "Only one who bursts with eagerness do I instruct."[57] The appropriate inner disposition must be there in the disciple before Confucius can hope to help him in his search for the *tao.* He himself provides us with an account of his own spiritual progress which he begins at the already self-aware age of fifteen when he is no longer the passive object of education by others. "At fifteen my will [*chih*] was bent on learning. At thirty, I stood firm; at forty I had no perplexities."[58] The terms here used are clearly expressive of inner dispositions and in the context, bear no relation to concrete acts of *li*. In the end, at the age of seventy, he claims that he has arrived at a point where he can follow his heart without transgressing what is right (the term "right" is here literally "the carpenter's square"). Yet the whole account suggests inner struggles and constant confrontation with moral choice in the sense suggested above.

Despite the single definition of *jen* in terms of "submission to *li*," it is clear throughout that *jen* has many other dimensions. It is constantly tested in all the troubling circumstances of what the Master regards as a world in disarray. The prescriptions of *li* do not always clarify what is right (*i*) in the infinite variety of life situations, and "righteousness" is just as essential an attribute of *jen* as is a submissiveness to *li*. *Jen*, in fact, relates to a host of virtues and there is more discussion of these virtuous dispositions than there is of *li*. It is quite true, as Fingarette asserts, that most of these virtues are social and can be regarded as dispositions to modes of action in the world. Righteousness (*i*), truthfulness (*chung*), faithfulness (*hsin*) in dealing with others, seriousness in work and a spirit of reverence, dignity, gravity—these are all discussed again and again. Yet even though they are dispositions to action, they are often discussed quite apart from the *li*. A disposition is itself not an action. At times they are discussed quite abstractly in terms of their relations to each other, as when Confucius remarks that faithfulness in keeping promises is a virtue only when the promise made accords with righteousness. *Li* does not enter this discussion.

Much of the discussion of *jen* even relates to dispositions which have no obvious relation to public action whatsoever. *Jen* is marked above all by an inner serenity, equanimity, and indifference to creaturely matters of fortune and misfortune over which one has no direct control. One may indeed say that *jen* relates to the happiness of its possessor, but that this happiness is based wholly on a "virtue ethic." Virtue is happiness. One may say that the two sides of *jen* are two sides of the same coin. It comprehends all the outer-directed virtues and "dispositions of soul" (*hsin*) which enable men to have harmonious relations with others. It is also the capacity that infuses the *li* with their appropriate spirit and that brings alive their potential spiritual power. At the same time, it endows the individual with the "inner dispositions" of equanimity, equilibrium, and self-sufficiency that make these outer manifestations possible.

The equanimity, to be sure, is not as imperturbable as that of an Epictetus. Full happiness is not completely possible because the man of *jen*'s ultimate mission is to bring peace to other men and to society in general.[59] In a world where the *tao* does not prevail, anxiety and frustration are not completely avoidable. Thus, while asserting quite flatly that "a man of *jen* is without anxiety" (or distress?), he states elsewhere that he himself can attain neither a complete absence of anxiety nor, as we have seen, an absence of perplexity.[60] Elsewhere, he informs us that a man of *jen* always possesses courage, although a man of courage is not necessarily a man of *jen*.[61] He speaks also of the noble man's lack of resentment of the fact that no one knows him.[62] He tells of his enormous admiration for his favorite disciple, Yen Hui. "A handful of rice to eat, a gourdful of water to drink, living in a mean street. Others could not have endured this distress— but Yen Hui's joy remained unaltered."[63] Of himself, he says, "With coarse food to eat, water to drink and a bent arm as a pillow—joy can be found even in these circumstances. Riches and honor acquired unrighteously are to me as a floating cloud."[64] Notice that Confucius speaks not only of equanimity, but even of joy. There is thus the joy of studying the mysteries of the *tao*. Confucius would have himself described as follows: "He is simply a man so eager [to learn] that he forgets to eat; in his joy he forgets his sorrow and does not perceive that old age is at hand."[65] Here, it is not the practice of *li,* but the joys of learning which nourish his inner life.

All of these passages refer to certain sustained attitudes. Whether one calls them "inner dispositions" or "subjective states" matters not at all. The fact is that they refer to living individuals and not to "performances of *li.*" Confucius, in speaking of anxiety or sorrow, does not always refer to some "observable condition," and the same is true of his references to joy. I submit here that Confucius' discussion of this inner contentment differs in no respect from similar discussions in the ordinary discourse of Western moralists (not ethical theoreticians).

I do not mean to imply that all the problems of the relation of *jen* to *li* are resolved in the *Analects.* There are, in fact, areas of ambiguity and obscurity which will become apparent in my discussion of later disciples revolving about the problem of "human nature" (*hsing*). Confucius provides us with no exhaustive definition of the term *jen.* Depending on the occasion, he will define it in terms of the inner qualities of equanimity and moral self-sufficiency, in terms of its manifestation in behavior toward others both within the framework of *li* and outside of it, or as an almost ineffable, mysterious reality which in its upper reaches is beyond the Master himself.

Yet Confucius is, of course, deeply committed to the indissoluble bond between *jen* and *li,* particularly if we interpret *li* as referring not only to concrete performances, but to the entire normative socio-political order of which the *li* are a part. The virtues may exist apart from *li*, but unless they are governed and contained by the sacred forms of *li*, they will go astray. "Respect without *li* becomes tiresome; caution without *li* becomes timidity; courage without *li* becomes disorderly conduct; straightforwardness without *li* becomes rudeness."[66] The *li* enlighten men about how and on what occasion these virtues are to be applied. A brave man unrestrained by the *li* may simply become insubordinate and wild, and the respectful man may simply overdo it falling into punctilio. The *li* provide the constraining pattern. Without the constant presence of the will to attain *jen* and all its associated virtues, the *li* will remain empty form. Without the structuring and educative effects of *li*, *jen* as the highest ideal of personal excellence can not be attained. Like the sacred literature of the *Poetry* and *Documents*, *li* can be internalized only through learning. They are not innate. Hence, *li* and learning are intimately linked. The implication follows that the unlearned cannot themselves achieve the highest realization of *jen*.

There is, to be sure, something like the possibility of an untaught virtue. Among the dyadic pairs which we find in the text, we find a term which seems to refer in the first instance to a simple, undifferentiated stuff (*chih*) contrasted to a term which seems to refer in the first instance to something like a differentiated articulated pattern (*wen*).[67] The dyad is used in many different semantic contexts referring to attributes of both individuals and societies as a whole (later it will even be used in metaphysical contexts). The latter term has come to refer to the extensive cultivation of a person, to literary composition, and to the "pattern of culture" as a whole. In the *Analects*, we find it in the individual context. "When simple goodness [*chih*] prevails over cultivation [*wen*] you get the boorishness of the rustic. When cultivation prevails over simple goodness, you get the [slick smoothness] of the clerk. Only when simple goodness and cultivation are duly blended do you get the noble man."[68] Simple goodness can be found among those unfavored with learning and *li* but it can only be a disoriented goodness. Yet without this goodness as an ever-present foundation, one will only have the fraudulent player of the cultural game.

It is interesting to note that in the case of all these dyads—such as *jen* and *li*, *wen* and *chih*—both terms should be organically linked. Yet, in fact, they can easily be disassociated. This situation was to leave open considerable room for later debates concerning the actual dynamic causal relations between the two. One might conceive of the *li* as the crystallized external expression of the *jen* of sages or noble men or, in a more Fingarette-like spirit, conceive of the *jen* of good men as an internalization of the essence of *li*. The Confucius of the *Analects* does not ultimately solve such problems of causation, but if he leans in any direction, it is toward the assertion that the *li* can be brought to life, like Ezekiel's dry bones, only by noble men who infuse it with the spirit of *jen*.

Before leaving the theme of *jen* and *li*, which is at the heart of the *Analects*, I should say a word about Confucius' image of moral evil. In fact the description of those evil tendencies which impede the achievement of the good is striking similar to the diagnoses made by prophets, wise men, and philosophers in all the high civilizations of this period.[69] The unbridled pursuit of wealth, power, fame, sensual passion, arrogance and pride—these themes figure centrally as the source of "the difficulty." The language of the vices lends itself comparatively easily to translation into the vocabulary of Gautama Buddha, Plato, and the Hebrew prophets. The material development of all the high civilizations had enormously increased the opportunities—at least for certain strata—for aggrandizement of power, increase of luxury, and pursuit of status and prestige. If, by civilization, one refers above all to the "revolution" in material and social technology, Freud's description of civilization in terms of the inhibitory superego may be the exact opposite of the truth. Civilization had, at least for some, vastly expanded the horizons of the libidinous imagination. It is precisely in the moral orientations of the creative minorities of the first millennium that we find a resounding no to certain characteristic modes of human self-affirmation which had emerged with the progress of civilization. For them the divine no longer dwelt in the manifestations of power, wealth, and external glory.

Confucius' critique of the pathologies of civilization remains, to be sure, moderate and "this worldly." Yet the same is the case for Socrates, Plato, Aristotle, and the Hebrew scriptures. One has to look to India for Gautama Buddha's truly radical diagnosis of the root of evil as lying not only in the manifest ills of civilization, but in the very nature of individual existence. The Buddha, of course, relates himself not only to moral evil but to the question of suffering as such. For Confucius, as for the "classical" thinkers of Greece and the Hebrew Bible, worldly goods, including honor and respect of others, remain good *within their proper limits*. Wealth and honor are what men desire. If one cannot obtain them by the proper *tao*, they should be relinquished. Poverty and disrespect are what men hate, but if they can be avoided to the detriment of the *tao*, one should not reject them. The noble man "who abandons *jen* does not deserve the name. The noble man does not go contrary to *jen* even for the space of a meal. He cleaves to it in times of harassment. He cleaves to it in times of utter confusion."[70] While the fundamental motive of the truly noble man in aspiring for office is public service, he may enjoy the emoluments and honors of office so long as they are consonant *with the tao.* The emoluments and honors are indeed necessary to public office, although the Master hastens to add that in ritual "spare simplicity is to be preferred to luxury."[71] The noble man will, however, be ever prepared to "take it or leave it." All the "worldly goods" are totally subordinate to the higher goal of *jen.* One cannot help but believe that these are sentiments which, when appropriately restated, would have been heartily endorsed by Socrates, Aristotle, Moses, and the prophets despite their enormously different positive visions of the good.

Where Confucius' ethic may, in fact, seem most specifically and exotically Chinese is in his attitude toward the *li* as holy rite as depicted in Book 10 of the *Analects.* This section has been rejected as an "inauthentic" later interpolation by many scholars, both Western and Chinese. Waley, after observing that the *Analects* are after all not concerned with "the details of ritual," concludes that this section was inserted "to meet the demands of a later Confucianism that was preoccupied above all with the details of ritual."[72] Legge's observation that "it hardly heightens our veneration for the sage" is shared by many modern Chinese scholars, who would prefer its inauthenticity.[73] The book, which provides us with a description of Confucius' ceremonial behavior, is in a particular style and is obviously based on the observations by others of his behavior. We can have no way of knowing when it became part of the whole compilation. I would nevertheless venture the view that there is nothing in the section which may not be perfectly consistent with the entire vision of the *Analects.* Here we find a Confucius who is devoted to the punctilious observance of what some may regard as trivial and pedantic practices, even involving matters of facial expression and body language. "On entering the palace gate he seems to shrink into himself."[74] "When carrying the jade tablet he seems to double up as if not able to bear the weight."[75] "With a black robe he wears a black lambskin."[76] "If his mat is not straight he will not sit on it."[77] Some of these gestures which involve a deep reverence for the symbols of legitimate authority are, of course, particularly trying to many moderns and perhaps even to some of the Master's contemporaries, as seems evident from his complaint that "the full observance of *li* in serving a prince is regarded as flattery."[78] It is, in fact, possible that the same Confucius who shrinks on entering the palace gate has very little regard for the current occupant of the princely throne. What he is honoring is that structure of sacred authority which is an indispensable aspect of the entire normative sociopolitical order.

In dealing with our own strong feeling that a truly "sincere" and "spontaneous" morality may be incompatible with the deliberate adoption of a specific external demeanor and a specific language of gestures, Fingarette's analysis becomes most relevant. Despite his acute awareness that form may exist without the authentic inner attitude, Confucius obviously believes that true attitudes must find public expression in observable, appropriate forms. No doubt, he also has a deep faith that persistent, "sincere" performance will become a spontaneous "second habit," as in the case of Fingarette's example of the handshake in our culture which is a trivial gesture, but a gesture whose absence may change the total tone of a human encounter. As in the case of a mitzvah for an Orthodox Jew, the so-called weighty and trivial are inseparable parts of a total web.

## Learning

In dealing with the value of learning (hsüeh) in the Analects, I must again refer to the Master's belief that the tao had, in its essential features, been realized in the Chinese past and that concrete knowledge of the tao in its last embodiment during the early Chou period was available. The Chou's superiority to its predecessors was found not only in its absorption of their experience but because one knew so much more about the Chou—about the actualities of its li, its institutions and its literature.[79] Hence, on one level, to know the tao of the Chou was to be in possession of a given body of "empirical data" about a known past.[80] One immediately notes the sharp contrast with the Plato of the Republic, who essentially finds no such embodied model of the good society anywhere in the Greek past, although he does draw piecemeal on that past.

In dealing with the concrete content of this learning, many of the traditional commentators stress the four disciplines of the li, music, the Documents, and the Poetry.[81] These headings do seem to cover much of what the Master has to say about concrete matters. Two of them—li and music—are elements of what was later to be called the "six arts" of the well-rounded shih mentioned above. While writing (perhaps including calligraphy) was certainly also crucial, it is not clear that Confucius believed in any professional study of archery or chariot-driving for his noble man, and as I have noted, he was even sarcastic about the notion that he should seriously study the martial arts. There are references to his participation in the highly ceremonialized archery contests of the nobility, but what he obviously appreciates is not the skill of archery, but the fact that even on an occasion as obviously conducive to a spirit of rivalry and desire for mastery over others as an archery contest, the noble man, restrained by ceremonies, remains a noble man.[82] Even in archery, it is the victory of moral power which is celebrated. All of this suggests that Confucius is not only a *shih* but also a member of that subgroup already referred to in the *Analects* as the *ju*[83] who were experts in and teachers of the civil aspects of the cultural heritage. One is reminded here that Socrates, despite his condemnation of those teachers of culture known as the Sophists, was considered by many in his time to belong to their number. While there is no evidence of any condemnation by the Master of those called *ju* (there is only one reference to them) as a group, we find Confucius admonishing one of his most "scholarly" disciples, Tzu-hsia, "to be a *ju* who is a noble man and not a *ju* who is a mean man."[84] The latter, I assume, is the pedantic expert in the cultural heritage who utterly fails to grasp its deeper meaning. Later, the word *ju* is used to refer to all those who consider themselves followers of Confucius. And yet an ambiguity seems to persist into the Han dynasty about whether it refers simply to the stratum of cultural and ritual experts as such or to "genuine" followers of the Master.

In dealing with the learning of *li,* one would surmise that it involved not merely the study of concrete rituals and ceremonial prescription, but also embraced what we would call a knowledge of the institutional settings of these practices. Confucius constantly refers to the strictures and prerogatives of rank, the protocols of "international" relations, and the functions of various offices which he seems to regard as part of the "traditional constitution" of the empire handed down by Chou. What is called the *Documents* or the *Book* (*shu*) may refer not only to the present parts of the *Book of Documents,* which are genuinely pre-Confucian, but to other documents not available to us which may deal with matters of ethics and also with matters of "policy" and political organization. Beyond this, even if one does not accept the long tradition that Confucius authored the present chronicle called the *Spring and Autumn Annals* (see Chapter 10), there is every reason to believe that he was deeply concerned with the *history* of his dynasty. The *Analects* are full of references to historic facts (or alleged facts) as well as to historic personalities. It is only by plunging into the reservoir of historic experience that one knows how mankind abides in the *tao* or falls away from it. "There may be those," he states, "who can act without knowledge. I am not one of them. Having heard about many things, I select that which is good and follow it."[85]

If the knowledge of *li,* history, and "documents" refers to the objective sociopolitical order, poetry and music seem—with all due deference to Fingarette—to apply mainly to the inner states of the heart (*hsin*). Music and poetry seem closely related, since one gathers from the *Tso-chuan* that the poetry was also sung. The poetry, by its powerful affective imagery, appeals directly to the sentiments. "It can arouse to proper sentiments; it can arouse one's [justified] indignation as well as a deep sense of solidarity with others [*ch'ün*]."[86]

To the extent that music involves instrumental performance, it refers to a skill which must be mastered. It also involves teaching the listener how to discriminate between lofty, elevating music and the depraved "popular" music of the times. Confucius believes as staunchly as does Plato that music (including perhaps dance as well) can directly and powerfully mold man's affective life, lifting the heart to a plane where it is open to the most elevated thoughts and inspired to the noblest actions. Since music, as performed, is a mode of action like *li*, I would again object to Fingarette's assertion that the emotion which music arouses lies wholly in "the performance." "Whether played sensitively, dully, or authentically, it is a 'public' act and therefore not in the psyche and personality of the performer."[87] Although Confucius seems as much interested in the listener as in the performer, there is no reason for saying that because something is "public" it is not an expression of something originating in the person, or that something which is "inner" may not find expression in the "outer" without losing its reference to the "inner." The Chinese commentators, in fact, very much stress the "expressive" function of the poetry and music as an outpouring of what is "in the heart."

Yet even though the poetry and music are essentially relevant to the cultivation of *jen* within, both involve skills and bodies of cultural material that must be "learned." They cannot be mastered by pure contemplation. Here again we note a sharp contrast with Plato who, while admiring the beauty of Homer's epic, finds in him no guidelines for the building of the ideal city. In the words of Voegelin, "the discoverer of the psyche and its order is at war against the disorder of which the traditional education through the poets is an important causal factor."[88] To be sure, some of the material in the *Book of Poetry* can be fitted to Confucius' ends only through heavy use of allegorical interpretation.[89] Yet, most of the poetry, in his view, lends itself directly to the exaltation of goodness and to indignant rejection of depravity. As indicated above, much of the poetry truly represents a kind of "proto-Confucian" orientation quite distant from the mythic, seductively "interesting" drama of the *Iliad*. Yet this does not mean that Confucius does not appreciate the aesthetic dimension of the *Poetry*.

On one level, then, learning is cumulative, empirical learning.

While it may embrace the kind of dialogic discussions we find in the *Analects,* it is not in the first instance concerned with eliciting truth simply by sustained dialectic reasoning as in the Socratic dialogues. And yet, there are constant references to the existence of a kind of knowing which can be called a capacity for holistic, intuitive apprehension—for the synoptic glance which encompasses the entire landscape of the *tao.* "Those who are born knowing it are the highest. Those who know it through learning are next. Those who toil painfully to learn are next and those who toil painfully but can not learn it make up [the bulk of] the people."[90] In the superman sage this knowledge seems to be both intuitive and innate. In some of the post-Confucian texts of our present *Book of Documents* we actually are shown how the godlike sage-kings of old Yao, Shun, and Yü are by their synoptic vision able to make manifest the normative human order.

Confucius himself, however, hastens to inform us that he is not "one who knows it from birth. I love antiquity and am diligent in seeking it out."[91] Again, his love of antiquity is not a sentimental antiquarianism. Confucius is convinced that the *tao* can be found realized in the past. Despite his disclaimer of any preestablished knowledge, however, he seems to have a fervent faith that cumulative, empirical learning, if pursued in the correct spirit, will call forth a vision of the whole, and one has the impression that without this initial faith and without at least some anticipatory intuitions of the whole, the entire enterprise is pointless. To his disciple Tzu-Kung the Master puts the question: "You think, I believe, that my aim is to learn many things and retain them in my memory?" Tzu-Kung replies: "Is that not so?" The Master replies: "No, there is a unity which binds it all together."[92] Among Confucius' disciples the one most capable of grasping this underlying unity most immediately is Yen Hui, whom his fellow disciple Tzu-Kung describes as a person "who has but to hear one part in ten in order to understand all ten parts."[93] One need not assume that the other nine are reconstructed by some formal process of deductive reasoning. It is probably by intuitive insight that he is able to locate the parts within the whole.

The question must lead, however, to a consideration of the concept of "thought" in the *Analects.* Does the emphasis on empirical learning preclude what we call thought? At one point Confucius says, "He who learns without thought is utterly confused. He who thinks without learning is in great danger."[94] Elsewhere he says, "I have spent a whole day without food and a whole night without sleep, thinking. It was of no use. It is better to learn."[95] Waley asks whether the Chinese *ssu* refers to what in the West we call thought. "Never," he says, "is there any suggestion of a long interior process of cogitation or ratiocination in which a whole series of thoughts are evolved out of each other producing on the physical plane a head-ache and on the intellectual an abstract theory. We must think of *ssu* rather as fixing attention on an impression recently imbibed from without and destined to be immediately re-exteriorized in action."[96] Whether the term "thought" as defined by Waley really defines all our own ways of using the term in ordinary English discourse is a question I shall put aside. We use phrases like "thinking of," "think-ing that," and "giving the matter some thought" in ways which do not correspond to his definition. There is absolutely no reason for thinking that when Confucius speaks of "thinking for a whole day" he is referring to mystical meditation.[97] There is also no reason, how-ever, to doubt that it involves "thinking about" the content of his learning and trying to relate it to the larger whole. The *Analects,* as indicated above, abound in abstract terms and even in propositions which directly relate abstract terms to each other as well as to con-crete illustrations, as in the discussion of the relations of knowledge to *jen.* Furthermore, if Yen Hui's ability to relate one part to ten is something in the way of "an insight," the fact is that we certainly include insights in our ordinary discourse about thought. I would conclude that much of the "extension" of the word *ssu* corresponds well to much of the extension of the word "thought" in Western languages. It may not be a specific "method" of thought in the Socratic mode. It does involve much of what we refer to as "think-ing."

As in moral discourse elsewhere, there is an emphasis on the prior-ity of action over words, but this does not mean that action does not require thought. As we have seen, the prescriptions of *li* do not cover the infinite variety of life situations nor do they solve all sorts of moral dilemmas in which one has a conflict of principles. The virtue of "righteousness" (*i*) certainly demands thought in the ordinary Western sense, and Confucius, as we have seen, can be perplexed—a state of mind which certainly suggests the presence of thought. There may be, to be sure, a discernable difference between "thought" in Confucius and the "method" of thought in the early Socratic dialogues. To Confucius knowledge does begin with the empirical cumulative knowledge of masses of particulars (particu-lars which may, however, include such items as the meaning of a poem) and then includes the ability to link these particulars first to one's own experiences and ultimately with the underlying "unity" that binds this thought together. The ability to link this knowledge either to concrete experience or to the higher unity is not automatic, but Confucius provides us with no specific *method* for achieving the goal. To Socrates, however, there is attributed the emerging belief in a specific dialectic, logical method for attaining truth. By his dialectic analysis of the limited confused views of his hearers, he is able to lift them above their limited and conventional understanding. He is not merely an imparter of factual knowledge (even though the discussion certainly involves constant reference to experience) but a "midwife" who by his method leads his disciples to the birth of a "higher" truth already potentially present in them. Aristotle defines Socrates' method as involving "inductive argument and general definition," even though Socrates himself used no such terminology.[98] Guthrie points out, however, that much of Socrates' "defining" is based on the *elenchus*.[99] When confronted with faulty definitions of various virtues and vices, he refutes these limited and one-sided definitions often without providing any final definition of his own. Yet by rigorously clarifying the fallacies of their limited views, he is pointing his disciples (and himself) on the road to the true knowledge of an encompassing goodness which, oddly enough almost like Confucius' *jen,* is, in its inner essence, beyond definition. It is essentially *this* knowledge of the supreme good that, once attained, is inseparable from virtue. Confucius presents his disciples with all the "materials" which illustrate the good *tao* of the past both as an "order of the soul" and an "order of the society," and hopes that they will be able to grasp the whole in which this knowledge is embedded. He has, in fact, many separate thoughts about many aspects of the moral and spiritual life but there is here no discrete inductive-deductive "method" which will necessarily attain the saving truth. Guthrie has speculated that Socrates' confidence in his method may have reflected the "scientific" debates of the pre-Socratic natural philosophers who had already adumbrated the idea of a "rigorous scientific method."[100] It was, of course, Plato and Aristotle with their emphasis on the paradigm of mathematics, the realm of forms, and the "science" of logic who were to carry this particular conception of a method of "thought" to its culmination.

What, however, are some of the forms which thought assumes in the *Analects?* We have some cases in which the thought is clearly embedded in concrete illustrations. When Confucius tells us that he cannot bear to see the head of the clan of Chi have the dance of eight rows performed at his court, he is saying something equivalent to the assertion that the usurpation of sacred authority is intolerable, and we are confident from reading the *Analects* that it is eminently possible to explain this proposition in terms of Confucius' whole "system."

Yet the thought is not always tied to concrete illustration. On the matter of *jen* there is, of course, no one definition which provides the exhaustive "essential attributes" of *jen*, yet in his diverse replies to a variety of disciples who ask—What is *jen?*—we find a variety of definitions. Some Chinese commentators have suggested that his answers were expressly devised to point up the particular ethical limitations of the interlocutors and hence to some extent serve the same function as Socrates' critique of the defective definitions of his disciples. The answers present a variety of perspectives, yet none of them claims to be exhaustive. *Jen* involves the submission to *li*. Only men of *jen* are without anxiety. *Jen* is loving men. *Jen* subsumes all the other virtues. It is again as if Confucius is clarifying the essential nature of *jen* by looking at it from an indeterminate variety of perspectives but constantly implying that at its heart there is something beyond all grasp. When his disciples suggest various modes of meritorious behavior as exemplifications of *jen*, the Master will praise the behavior but not be willing to equate it with *jen*. In the end he says of himself that he does not dare to claim the status of a "sage or man of *jen*."[101] It is, curiously, precisely on this level that *jen* reminds one of the Socratic good and beautiful described in Plato's *Symposium* in terms of ultimate ineffability.

As for the separate virtues, while they are discussed abstractly in their relations to each other, we find no effort made to arrive at "exhaustive definitions." To the extent that they are concretized they are done so in terms of concrete exemplifications drawn from personalities or events and the Master seems quite confident that these concrete examples epitomize the nature of the virtues in question. Yet such reliance on concrete examples, like the parables of Jesus, does not suggest the absence of thought.

Another significant aspect of the *Analects'* "Theory of Knowledge" is its concern with language and the relation of language to reality. It is a preoccupation that marked the entire subsequent development of pre-Ch'in Chinese thought.

In dealing with this question we must, however, first consider Waley's claim that the entire discussion of language in the text must be an anachronistic interpolation since the "language crisis" in China was a much later development. I would argue that his grounds for this assertion are not valid and that the concern with language is entirely compatible with the text as a whole.[102] The concern with language may well have preceded the full "language crisis."

If "ancient Chinese philosophers shared modern Western philosophy's intense interest in language" in the case of Confucius, this has little to do with any mistrust of language.[103] His confidence that he belongs to a universal civilization governed by a truly normative *tao* that has already been realized in human experience leads to a further confidence that the established language used to describe the prescriptions of *li,* the institutions and the normative roles of the good society accurately reflects the normative nature of things. Language carries its own imbedded reflection of the true order. The crisis is not a crisis of language but of the human abuse and distortion of language. Thus the language of familial and social roles—words that refer to father, ruler, son, or minister—do not refer simply to bare biologic or political facts but, as in the doctrine of certain varieties of modern sociology, every role is the bearer of its own role-norms. The word "father" carries the implication that the father will "act like a father" as well as the assumption that the language will provide information on how to do so. Thus when Duke Ching of Ch'i asks Confucius about government he simply says, "Let the prince be a prince, the minister a minister, and the son a son." Duke Ching, whose rule was being threatened by the rising menace of the Ch'en (T'ien) family, exclaims, "How true. When the prince is not a prince, when the minister is not a minister . . . one may have a dish of millet in front of one and yet not know if one will live to eat it."[104] The knowledge of how one ought to behave in one's role was already available. One did not have to engage in a painful process of dialectic reasoning in order to discover the true meaning of the uses of the word "minister." The literature provided ample examples of model ministers and ample illustrations of the acts of good ministers. Hence when Tzu-lu asks the Master what he would do if the ruler of the state of Wei[1] were to ask him to participate in government, he replies:

> Would it not be necessary to correct names? . . . If names are not correct then one's words will not be in accord [with one's actions]. If words are not in accord, then what is to be done cannot be [correctly] implemented! If what is to be done cannot be correctly implemented [*ch'eng*] then *li* and music will not flourish. If *li* and music do not flourish punishments will not be appropriate. When punishments are not appropriate the people will not know where to put its hands and feet [how to behave]. Therefore a noble man uses names only in their appropriate way, so that what he says can be appropriately put into effect. A noble man in his speech leaves nothing to chance.[105]

If the language is not used in ways which conform to its correct imbedded meanings, the entire human order will become disjointed. In the state of Wei[1] where there was an enormously entangled succession crisis, a worthy prince had taken on the duties of his unworthy father. Although he deserved to rule he should not have usurped his father's title, since an heir apparent does not usurp a father's title while the latter is still alive. He was not behaving according to the true norms of filiality. He was thus destroying the link between name and behavior and this breach of normative order could only upset the entire fabric of *li* which rested on action in accordance with the language descriptive of *li.* Since a good society is basically held together by the moral force of *li* and music, when the *li* loses its moral power, the reliance on the physical sanctions of penal law must necessarily extend beyond its appropriate boundaries.

Notice that Confucius does not simply speak of terms as such but of terms as used in speech. The locus of the trouble lies in how living human beings, particularly among the vanguard of society, use words in speech. The misuse of language in the speech of men driven by ulterior motives is the ultimate source of the disconnection of language from reality. While Socrates accuses the Sophists of using speech rhetorically to promote their own careers as masters of public relations, he basically believes that the confusion of moral vocabulary is in the end due to intellectual confusion.[106] Confucius sees the cause as mainly moral. There is a distortion of both the terms that refer to objective behavior and the terms that refer to inner dispositions. Hence the repeated attack on "clever talk" which provides men with that fatal capacity for disguising real feelings and embellishing ulterior motives by the abuse of words. "Clever talk and a pretentious manner are seldom associated with *jen.*"[107] When his disciple Tzu-lu, while holding an office with the Chi family, appoints someone to a position for which the Master thinks he is insufficiently educated, Tzu-lu replies, "Why can one only be considered learned when one has read books?"[108] Tzu-lu knows as well as the Master that learning certainly involves reading books, among other things, but it serves his immediate purpose to redefine "learning" in a way which he finds expedient. Hence Confucius' outburst that he "hates glib people."[109] The constant admonition to reticence and caution in speech, on stressing action rather than speech relates to this mistrust not of language but of the perverse misuse of language in a corrupt world.

All of this seems to suggest something like a "Platonic" element in Confucius' view of language. Is correct language a kind of "ideal language" which describes an eternal world of "ideal forms" which somehow subsists in a realm of its own? Here one is inclined to share the views of Graham, Hansen, and others that, on the whole, Chinese thought beginning with Confucius does not treat abstractions (which quite clearly exist) as "eternal forms" or self-subsistent universals, although this does not mean that one should dogmatically deny the possibility of gropings toward such ideas in the "logical" discussions of the fourth and third centuries B.C. Yet the question of exactly how the ideal relates to the actual is not easily solved.

The belief that the *tao* had been realized in the past seems to suggest that it is not "far off." One might say that it is "there," just below the surface. Yet there is no clear answer to the question, Where is the *tao* when men depart from it?, and this became an element of future debates even though none of these debates led to precisely Platonic solutions. The problem, however, is not unreal even for Confucius. Since he is no sociological behaviorist, he does not believe that playing a certain role will automatically "internalize" its norms nor that going through the motions of *li* will "internalize" the spirit of *li*. Hansen states that "the rectification of names operates on the presupposition that the primary function of language is to instill attitudes guiding choice and action."[110] Yet Confucius' central problem is that this "regulative function" of language by no means works automatically. He is thus as much agitated by the gap between the ideal and the real in the realm of "regulative" language as is Plato when he deals with true justice and the way states and individuals actually behave. Many of Plato's "eternal ideas" are, in fact, "regulative" moral terms rather than descriptions of "entities." The fact that Confucian language refers to modes of behavior rather than to observed entities does not solve the Platonic problem.

One might perhaps say that the locus of the "ideal" is to be found in the persons of sage-kings, sages, noble men, past and present, and in the will of Heaven, just as in the Hebrew Bible the locus of the ideal is the spirit of God. Ancient Hebrew is just as lacking in a term for "self-subsisting universals" as is the *Analects*. (When Philo attempts to reconcile the Bible with the Platonic concept of eternal forms, he insists that in some sense the ideas are themselves created or caused by God.)[111] What one discerns above all in the *Analects* is not so much an ideal world corresponding to an ideal language as the beginning of a tendency to see the ideal as either realized in concrete actuality or else as associated with a "reality" which goes beyond all language, as in the case of Taoist mysticism.

In Plato we find a yawning abyss between a truth arrived at through the apodictic necessity of the dialectic and of mathematical reasoning and a world of "opinion" derived haphazardly from an observation of the chaos of ordinary human experience. Confucius does not rise from the chaos of the world of particulars to a realm of eternal forms since, in his view, the *tao* remains indissolubly linked to the empirical world. He does, however, suggest an ascent to an ultimate unity which is beyond all words. And yet, for him too, empirical knowledge can also turn into the mere accumulation of senseless particulars. While Confucius may thus provide no explicit "metaphysical" explanation for the gap between the ideal reality and the corrupt actuality and no notion of an apodictic "rational method" for bridging the gap, the gap exists for him as much as for Socrates and Plato.

One is thus struck by Confucius' constant stress on the prior moral dispositions which the self-aware adult learner must bring to his learning. Not only must he be full of eagerness, but the progress of learning itself depends on the simultaneous cultivation of certain moral dispositions. "A noble man who broadly studies culture *and* [italics my own] restrains himself with *li* is not likely to go wrong."[112] The sincere observance of *li* does not automatically flow from learning, and learning without a concern for the constant practice of *li* may become completely divorced from the moral life. The "will to be good" must be a constant precondition of the proper pursuit of learning, thus leaving considerable room for debate through the ages concerning what we would call in the West the problem of the priority of will or reason.

Yet in the end, while learning like other values can become separated from the whole, it remains central to the cultivation of the individual and the ordering of society. Without properly motivated learning, the virtues are blind and *li* is mechanical. To Tzu-lu, the disciple who was most skeptical of "book-learning," he states: "Love of *jen* without love of learning is beclouded by ignorance. Love of knowledge without a love of learning is beclouded by a dissipation of the mind; love of sincerity without learning is beclouded by harmful actions; love of straightforwardness without a love of learning is beclouded by rudeness; love of courage without a love of learning is beclouded by recklessness; love of firmness without learning is beclouded by cruelty."[113] The virtues when unenlightened carry with them no information about how they apply to the complexities of civilization and even *jen,* here perhaps meaning "benevolence," can lead to disastrous results. What is meant here by knowledge (as opposed to learning) is not clear. It may mean a knowledge of insignificant facts without constant probing of the meaning of the facts, or it may refer to some who were so convinced that they had "grasped the whole" that they required no further cumulative study of the tradition. This indeed became a profound problem in later Chinese thought. It remains clear, however, that learning is an absolutely central aspect of the noble man's program of self-cultivation.

A striking implication of Confucius' concept of learning and knowledge is its implication for sociopolitical life. In dealing with the nature and content of knowledge, we have noted the contrast with the Socratic-Platonic view, but here we notice some significant resemblances. Civilized society can be governed only by the wise and virtuous, and virtue depends in some ultimate sense on knowledge. In the *Analects*, most men, whether because of circumstances or inherent limitations or a combination of both, cannot fully acquire the true learning required for the establishment of the *tao*. The fact that the vast masses of peasants have neither the time nor the energy to devote to the enterprise of learning is very central to the Master's outlook. Clearly not all men with learning are fit to govern; clearly many of the hereditary holders of power have no taste for learning; and clearly some individuals who have come up from below may become "noble men"; nevertheless, Confucius never doubts that those who govern must acquire true knowledge and that only those who acquire true knowledge ought to participate in government. Without this learning and knowledge the *tao* cannot be restored. There must be an elite of learning.

As noted, in China there was, of course, nothing in the experience of the past to suggest the possibility of a "democratically" organized polity in which all citizens were presumed to possess the capacities necessary to political participation. Socrates and Plato, however, were directly acquainted with Athenian participatory democracy (however narrow its base); they thought in terms of the city-state framework which had rendered the whole idea conceivable. Yet their critique of democracy is most vehement. Despite the incommensurability in the Chinese and Greek concepts of the polity, there is a shared assumption that the polity bears a maximum responsibility as the moralizing agent of the society. "The polis," states Ernest Barker, "was an ethical society."[114] It is the polis as a "political" community which sets and establishes the moral purpose of the entire society. Hence the severe judgment of Athenian democracy by Socrates and Plato was based on its presumed failure to achieve this supreme ethical goal of the state. "Both to Plato and Aristotle," continues Barker, "the positive inculcation of goodness is regarded as the mission of the state."[115] Having observed the participation of artisans and craftsmen in the business of the assembly; having observed how easily swayed they were by what they regarded as the self-interested rhetoric of smooth demagogues, Socrates and Plato were as convinced as Confucius that the life of these commoners did not prepare them to participate in state affairs, however much they were to be respected in the practice of their own crafts. Like Confucius, both Socrates and Plato believed that only men who have made themselves wise and virtuous are truly prepared to govern. If Plato did not find in the past any preexistent paradigm for a perfect man and a normative social order, his aim was to construct such a paradigm by a process of dialectic reasoning. Plato's vision of the whole was initially as inaccessible to the average Athenian citizen as was Confucius' vision of the whole to the Chinese peasant despite the enormous differences in their conception of the content of knowledge.

In both the *Republic* and in Confucius, what brings about the good society is a government of the best men. Again what Barker says of Aristotle's view of "political science" is most applicable to both Plato and Confucius. This "science" gives direction in two ways. "Some men it teaches to realize for themselves the ends of life . . . but most men it aids indirectly and by means of the few it has taught."[116]

Yet when we turn to the methods for producing the "best men" in the *Republic* and in the *Analects* we are again struck by enormous differences. We have the radical rigorism of Plato and what looks like the more relaxed moral optimism of Confucius. There is no question in Plato of any inherited system of *li* which, when performed in the spirit proper to it, can lead men to a life of *jen.* Nothing less than a prolonged arduous study of philosophic dialectic can lead the guardians to the higher vision of the good. In the interim they must be sealed off against all the insidious selfish particularisms of society by being cut off from the economic sphere and familial life through a system of communistic isolation. Confucius' noble men, few as they may be, live in the midst of corrupt society yet, by dint of their unremitting pursuit of *jen,* are still able to achieve an autonomous inner equanimity as well as outer integrity. Their moral attainments, far from being inhibited, are actually enhanced by their particularistic familial commitments, all of which they are able to treat in a spirit perfectly appropriate to their general integrity. It is precisely in the proper practice of family commitments that they manifest virtue. The traditions of the past which in a distorted and fragmented form are still present in the society do not represent an "irrelevant" traditionalism but the very source of wisdom.

Confucius' noble man has much more individual autonomy than the guardian of Plato's *Republic.* He can, like Yen Hui and perhaps like Aristotle's virtuous man, achieve a high level of moral perfection even when the *tao* does not prevail in the world; the *Republic,* the virtue of the guardians in itself depends on the whole system. The *Republic* does not, of course, represent the whole of Plato and certainly not "Greek thought" in general. It is interesting, however, to contrast a view in which the "good society" must be constructed by sheer power of "reason" and set in opposition to all that is and has been, and a view which rests on the serene faith that the good has been achieved within the experience of the past and that the cultural tradition has preserved the essential pattern of that goodness. In Athens, it was, perhaps paradoxically, the democrats who had faith in tradition because of their conviction that the average citizen could be a bearer of the genuine wisdom embodied in tradition. Socrates' enemies believe that they are defending the wholesome religious traditions of the Athenian past. To Confucius, a learned vanguard is essential. Yet the learning itself is much more humanly accessible than is Plato's science.

The enormous role assigned to learning helps us to appreciate Confucius' enthusiasm for learning in itself as expressed in the opening remark of the *Analects:* "To learn and at appropriate times to repeat what one has learned—is that not also a pleasure?"[117] Despite the Master's failure to achieve his highest vocation in government, learning lends deep meaning to his life. "In a hamlet of ten families there may be some as faithful and truthful as I but no one who so loves learning."[118] Learning, in its broadest reach, embraces nothing less than the mastery of significant empirical knowledge of the human past, the apprehension of the vision of unity embedded in this empirical knowledge, and the ability to apply this knowledge to the judgment of contemporary life. If it does not involve any notion of a distinct method of dialectic discourse or of mathematics as a paradigm of true knowledge, it certainly involves constant exchange of thoughts with disciples and others which allow the Master and occasionally the disciples to illuminate various aspects of the larger pattern. These illuminations need not, however, be the outcome of the laborious midwifery of dialectic argument. Yen Hui, the disciple most noted for his love of learning, will often listen to the Master for a whole day without ever disagreeing "as if he were stupid."[119] This means that he always "catches the point," as is proven by his exemplary conduct. It is in Yen Hui in particular that one perceives the fusion of the intuitive grasp or comprehension of the "whole truth" with the quality of ultimate goodness embodied in *jen.*

The generalization that Confucius in particular and Chinese thought in general are not concerned with the "disinterested" pursuit of truth or with sheer intellectual curiosity as such but only with "saving truth" may be largely true. Sheer intellectual curiosity as a major passion, some believe, is a unique Greek contribution, although it is perfectly obvious that curiosity about the infinite variety of the world is a universal human trait for which there is ample evidence in China as elsewhere. The degree to which this intellectual passion was dominant in Greek culture itself is a very real question. It may have applied to some of the pre-Socratics and perhaps to the value of contemplation in Aristotle, and yet it hardly seems to apply to Socrates and Plato despite their spectacular contributions to the scientific enterprise.[120] In the case of Confucius the generalization that his love of learning is not "disinterested" certainly holds true for the most part but not absolutely. To a certain degree, Confucius' pleasure in learning may reflect his sense of delight in the mastery of a body of significant knowledge as such. In fact, a love of "scholarship for scholarship's sake," if not of intellectual dialectic for dialectic's sake, became a motif within the history of Confucian thought even though it was never accepted as an ultimate value in its own right.

## The Family

The discussion of *jen, li,* and learning cannot, finally, be considered apart from the "objective" orders of the family and polity with which they are intimately involved. In his attention to the family, Confucius is directly relating himself to an orientation whose roots we have already found in ancestor worship. The question of how "religious" Confucius' attitude toward the family really is, will, again, depend on one's definition of religion. Whatever his attitude toward ancestral spirits, apparently his attitude toward the virtues and *li* of familial life does not primarily center on the departed spirits themselves. (I have suggested above that this shift away from an orientation on the ancestral spirits may already be discernable in the *Book of Poetry*.) He concentrates on sentiments associated with the nuclear family and with the immediately departed. Gratitude toward parents for their nurturing love, responsibility of adult children for aged and feeble parents, and a prolonged sense of loss when they depart—these sentiments can be found in all cultures. The particular intensity of Confucius' focus on these dispositions nevertheless indicates an ongoing cultural stress on them which makes them something much more than simple universal "natural sentiments." It is basically in the family that one first finds the emergence of rules of behavior based on spiritual-moral assent rather than on physical coercion. The sentiments of gratitude and self-abnegation that dominate the prolonged mourning rites for parents may be considered the ultimate basis of that power of yielding (*jang*) on which all *li* are based. It is first of all in the family that *li* and *jen* are ideally fused. Confucius, no doubt, fully agrees with Master Yu. "Filial piety and fraternal feeling—are they not the bases of *jen*?"[121] It is in the family that one learns how to exercise authority and how to submit to authority, and it is only the man of *jen* who can do both. The family is ideally the first school of virtue and the source of those values which make possible the good society. Plato, in contrast, provides us with all the reasons why the family is not the source of virtue. It is a particularistic "private" group within the polis bent primarily on the promotion of its own economic interests. Instead of focusing men's minds on large public matters, it locks men into an overwhelming concern with the petty joys and sorrows of other family members. The company of wives and children provides little room for intellectual enlargement. Hence the "public" virtues can only be developed in the public arena. Aristotle's view—in reaction to Plato—is much more favorable to the family. The family is an arena for the development of certain virtues and bonds of affection. Indeed in his remarks on love of parents we hear familiar echoes, "The affection of children for their parents (like man's love of God) is the sort of feeling one has for what is good and superior. For their parents have bestowed on them the greatest blessings—they have given them life, nursed them and provided for their education when they reached school age."[122] Aristotle discusses family virtues and affection under the general category of *philia*, which is something between love and friendship among humans in a wide variety of forms of association, and his point—as against Plato—seems to be that a good state must be made up of a wide variety of human modes of association formed for various reasons but held together by *philia*. In the end, however, when Aristotle asks himself how a good society is brought into being, he turns to the polity and to those masters of "political science" who are capable of framing systems of good laws. The family, like all other human associations, is one source of the good but all these separate goods can be secured only by attention to that study "which has most authority and control over the rest"—namely, the science of politics.[123]

Now in considering the differences between Aristotle and Confucius we must exercise great care. Confucius does not assert that all actual families are the source of the moralization of society. He freely admits that in a society where the *tao* is absent, the families of the masses who suffer deprivation and oppression cannot be expected to realize the moral potentialities of family life. The family life of the ruling class was sadly deficient in his time. He would thus probably admit that a good part of the ruling class did not learn virtue in the bosom of the family. He would, in fact, also agree that the situation could only be remedied through the political order and that the task must be undertaken by the good and the wise. The

crucial question is—how are those with a vocation for authority
made good? Whatever flexibility one can find in Confucius concerning the actual structures of hierarchy and authority, concerning the
question of heredity versus merit and concerning the scope of state
power, the centrality of the moral quality of those who rule remains
a given. In the end, the formation of this moral quality cannot be
disassociated from its base in the family.

In the *Politics,* Aristotle is preoccupied with the idea of distribut-
ing power and authority within a system of "constitutional" law to
maximize its good effects and minimize its evil effects. This does not
make him a democrat or even a believer in any one "constitutional"
solution but it does deal, within the city-state framework, with the
whole notion of controlling power and authority by a structural
"constitutional law." Aristotle's good and wise men are the "legislators" who plan the best constitutions possible on the basis of their
"science of politics." While they are undoubtedly men of virtue, it is
their intellect above all which they employ in creating a wise structure of laws. To Confucius, however, the question is—how does one
obtain a ruling class governed by *jen* and *li?* As in the case of Plato of
the *Republic* with his government of the best, the *personal* cultivation
of those with a vocation to rule is of the essence. To Confucius, however, in contrast to Plato, the first proving ground of those dispositions and habits which lead men to handle power and authority
correctly are the immediate relations of the sacred institution of the
family.

Again, we are not dealing here primarily with socialization of the
very young. We are dealing with the question of how persons who
have reached the age of self-awareness handle their family role relationships. When the "Great Learning" will later assert that anciently "he who wished to bring order to the state first harmonized
his family and wishing to harmonize his family he cultivated his
person," it is presumably speaking of an adult family patriarch.[124]
The plausibility of this doctrine in Confucius' eyes is much enhanced by his observation that the "feudal" structure of the Chou
had rested on the moral cement of abiding kinship loyalties of the
dynastic lineage, just as the disintegration of such loyalties coincided
with the disintegration of the entire Chou political system. At one
point we find Confucius answering an interlocutor who asks him,
"Why are you not serving in government?" as follows: "What do the
*Documents* say about filial piety? Filial piety—nothing but filial piety
and devotion to your brothers—this is being active in government.
This is also serving in government. Why must what you call 'serving
in government' be the only form of governing?"[125] The tone of this

reply is one of exasperation. Confucius obviously *does* desire to affect the larger society through "serving in government." Yet the point he makes is probably genuinely felt. The same fundamental qualities which are required to restore the moral bases of authority in government are to be found in family relations. To the extent that there is a genuine Confucian belief in the exemplary "demonstration effect" of good behavior, the example of a harmonious family may radiate some of its effects onto the surrounding environment even when one is not in government.

## On Government: The Realm of the "Political" in the *Analects*

There are ways of understanding the *Analects* which would raise the question of whether there is anything at all "political" in the Master's vision in our usual ways of defining that term. While Fingarette does concede that Confucius has a "political vision," he assumes that Confucius' basic concern with government is a "call for political-social unity to be ceremonial."[126] Hence the lack of any separate discussion of the political in his book.

Hannah Arendt would argue that the "political" presupposes a state of affairs in which citizens participate fully as peers in the life of "public freedom" and "public happiness." Administration is, in this sense, not political but technical. Hence Chinese "serving in government" would hardly deserve the august designation "political." The fact remains that, pace Hannah Arendt, in a world of large states where the government's administrative functions play a paramount role, we continue to use the word to embrace all the operation of administrative functions. Rightly or wrongly, we include the functioning of bureaucracy in our study of political science.

It would indeed seem possible to argue that in the ideal Confucian society the ruling vanguard is basically not a "political class" even in the administrative sense but a kind of priesthood which holds society together by "holy rite" and the spirit of *jen* which suffuses its enactment. The exemplary family relations of such a ruling class would simply radiate their magical *te* over the society as a whole. This is the textbook view of Confucianism as advocating nothing but a "government by example."

Indeed, when the Duke of She boasts that in his country "there was a man called upright Kung. His father stole a sheep and Kung bore witness against him," Confucius responds: "In my country the upright are different from this. A father will screen his son and a son will screen his father."[127] One feels that Confucius places family above polity. It is not that he approves of stealing. It is that the sacred familial ties are so overriding in importance that even in a case as painful as this they must be preserved. The entire sacred fabric of *li* and *jen* depend upon it, and it is this fabric which sustains society.

*Li,* however, do not only involve the family and some of the most important *li* apply only to the king, to lords, and to all those involved in the political order. Yet perhaps it is precisely the ceremony itself which is the essence of the political order? When Confucius says of the ancient royal ancestral sacrifice, the *ti,* that " 'if one knew its explanation, it would be as easy to rule the world as to point to this'—he thereupon pointed to the palm of his hand," one indeed does feel that certain august ceremonies are laden with an almost esoteric magical meaning which takes us far from any association with what we usually mean when we use the word "political."[128]

And yet, although etymological explanations are enormously hazardous, when we turn to the etymology of the graph that we translate as governing or government (*cheng*), we find that it relates to many more mundane associations with which we are familiar and which we tend to call "political" in our ordinary colloquial usage. The word *cheng* relates to the homonymous word meaning "right" or "correct" (正). In the oracle bone inscriptions the latter is often used as a verb. What it depicts is foot-soldiers attacking a settlement (𤘈). It is assumed by Wang Kuo-wei and others that its meaning is the same as that of the verb *cheng* (征), meaning something like "punitive attack." What is depicted is a punitive attack on a rebellious or perhaps foreign settlement designed to "correct" the settlement by force of arms. Even in the *Analects* there is one singular occurrence of the term now used for governing, *cheng* (政), meaning something like "penal laws." "Govern the people by penal laws [*cheng*] and order them with punishments and they will try to evade [the punishments] and lose their sense of shame. Lead them by moral power [*te*] and keep order by *li*. They will have a sense of shame and correct themselves."[129] The entire thrust of this passage, to be sure, strongly supports the notion of a government based on spiritual-moral force. Yet this singular, perhaps archaic use of the term *cheng* points to an older meaning which tends to suggest that the rise of polity was initially as much associated with force and coercion in China as in other civilizations. Thus even in the *Analects,* the graph *cheng*—governing or government—retains its association with the control of the instruments of punitive force. Even in the *Analects,* this older layer of meaning survives and, indeed, remains operative. All of this suggests a familiar view of government as the ultimate instance of legitimate force.

While Confucius's highest aspiration may indeed be a government based on *jen* and *li,* there is evidence that he does not envisage a situation in which recourse to force is completely dispensable. He is certainly aware that King Wu established the Chou dynasty by the sword, and he clearly informs us that when the *tao* prevails, the son of Heaven is responsible not only for *li* and music but for just "punitive expeditions" as well. Only he has the legitimate authority to punish unprincipled "feudal" rulers as well as to quell the barbarians within and outside the civilized world.

One of the tragic facts of Confucius' world is that completely unauthorized wars are waged among the states of that world and yet in an age without the *tao,* there are circumstances in which even the "feudal" princes are morally obliged to undertake just wars. When a high official of the neighboring state of Ch'i actually kills his rightful ruler, Confucius calls upon the Duke of Lu to carry out a punitive expedition to punish the perpetrator of this monstrous act of regicide. However, the three usurping families who control the Lu state prudently refuse.[130] The Master seems to take for granted the need for a military establishment as one of three requirements of any government—food, weapons, and the faith of the people—although he gives it lowest priority.[131] The noble man is in fact not free of the necessity to make judgments about the justified use of arms in certain circumstances.

Similarly, despite the clear emphasis on minimizing the role of penal law, and despite the insistence, as in the passage cited above, that a government is judged good when it can cause the people to behave on the basis of internalized moral sentiments, it remains clear that "punishments and penalties," like armies, remain part of the necessary apparatus of governing even in the good society. Presumably there will always remain an element of society not accessible to control by moral force. This probably accounts for the statement in the passage on rectification of names that "when *li* and music do not flourish, punishments and penalties will not be appropriate."[132] Where *li* do not flourish, one cannot expect most men to be guided by inner moral sentiments; hence even people with a potential for behaving on the basis of an "inner moral pilot" behave in ways that "target" (*chung*) them for punishment. Punishments will apply "appropriately" only to those who are clearly not amenable to the influence of *li* and music. One can extrapolate a Confucian utopia, in which sanctions of force as an instrument of government disappear completely. Yet one does not find such an extrapolation in the *Analects.*

Beyond the question of the legitimate role of force in governing, it is quite clear in other respects as well that government is by no means simply a matter of ceremony and example. Despite Confucius' exasperated assertion that he provides a model or example of governing simply by fulfilling his proper family role, clearly his aim is to serve in government and serving in government means more than performing a ceremonial role. Ceremony and example will influence the people only when certain environmental preconditions have been established—and these preconditions can only be established by what might be called correct "social policy."

Noble men may succeed in maintaining their own moral integrity even in highly adverse circumstances, but the same is not true for the vast mass of mankind which has neither the opportunity nor in many cases the capacity to achieve full self-cultivation. One might add that so long as the people must endure an environment of oppression and suffering, they cannot respond to the "example" of their superiors. One should hasten to add that those elements of the ruling class which also proves incapable of "learning" may also be said to be objects of an unwholesome environment.

In the case of the masses there is thus a clear recognition, which will become much more explicit in the book of Mencius, that the assurance of an economic livelihood is an indispensable precondition for the moralization of the masses. Thus we find in China the clear development of a "sociological" approach to the lives of the masses. Their behavior is fundamentally shaped by their socioeconomic environment, and the shaping of their social environment is the responsibility of those who rule.

When we seek in ancient civilizations outlooks that run in a direction somewhat contrary to this sociological view, we might again point to the city-state democracies of Greece that operated on the assumption that the average citizen possesses sufficient wisdom derived from customs and traditions of the past to shape his own moral life as well as to participate in the decision-making activities of the polis.[133] Again the vision projected in the Hebrew Bible of a divine code of laws wholly within the range of the people's understanding, which they (the people) may ideally internalize and be led to practice because of their love and fear of God, also suggests a community life not wholly dependent on the wisdom of a ruling elite.

Plato, however, on the basis of his experience, believes that the average citizen does not possess sufficient wisdom to achieve the true virtue and happiness of the polis, and like Confucius he is convinced that only an ethical-intellectual vanguard operating from the pinnacle of the sociopolitical order can achieve this aim. The Plato of the *Republic* is, in effect, more consistently and thoroughly sociological than Confucius. In the *Republic* he creates an entire system that shapes all levels of the population, including the ideal ruling class itself. It is not only the masses and the military stratum whose lives must be shaped and determined by the impersonal operation of the system, but even the guardian class itself. The communistic organization of the guardians and the rigid system of education imposed on them suggests much less reliance, at least initially, on their own individual powers of self-cultivation.

Confucius does not, of course, create a new system, and he relies heavily on the capacities of an ethical vanguard to achieve control within a normative system which in his view had already been actualized in past human experience. This observation may help us to reconcile two views of Confucianism which seem contradictory: that Confucianism conservatively stresses that good societies are made by "good men" and not by institutional or social conditioning; and that Confucianism developed an early appreciation of the decisive, deterministic power of social environment. If one conceives of the "good men" as belonging to a kind of transcendent, creative minority which employs its virtue and wisdom to shape the society and of the masses as capable of developing a degree or moral autonomy only when those above have created a favorable environment, the two views seem complementary rather than contradictory. These two aspects will later be clearly epitomized in Mencius' maxim that "Only the noble men can maintain a stable mind without a stable livelihood."[134]

When asked by a disciple what to do for the people, Confucius replies, " 'Enrich them,' and when asked about what should be done next he replies, 'Instruct them.' "[135] How then does one go about enriching the people? One begins by ceasing to impoverish them. The sage-kings of old had not only made manifest the rule of *li,* they had, like Yü the legendary founder of the Hsia dynasty, created the very infrastructures of civilization. Yü spent all his energy "draining and ditching" and helping to create the foundations of agriculture even while carrying out the holy sacrificial rites with all appropriate ceremony.[136] Now in a time of decadence and oppression the ruling class could begin by refraining from imposing burdens on the people. To the extent that the people's distress is due not to natural disasters, it is primarily due to exploitation. "A country of a thousand chariots can only be ruled properly if the ruler tends strictly to business and is truthful, is economical in expenditures and uses the labor of the people only at the proper times."[137] The peasant family left at peace to cultivate its own fields can produce its own livelihood. Removing the peasants from their productive activities for corvee labor or for producing ever more surplus in labor or kind for their superiors is a major cause of their poverty.

Thus at the heart of Confucius' conception of socioeconomic "policy" is the notion of optimum noninterference—what might be called a policy of "light government." When we look more closely at this view of policy, however, we find that it is closely linked to the values of *jen* and *li*. Since the exactions from the people and the arbitrary intervention in their lives is primarily due to greed, to desire for ostentatious display, love of luxury, wanton vainglory, and ambitions leading to constant warfare, it is the ruling class's incapacity for self-control, its incapacity for "yielding," that lies at the heart of the pathology of hybris and greed. It is a sickness that can be cured only by *jen* and *li*, just as Plato is convinced in the *Republic* that it can be cured only by creating a ruling vanguard constantly educated to the higher truth and subjected to a life of true communist austerity. A system of *li* and learning which would, however, not have these "policy consequences" would be a hollow mockery.

The people can become open to moral influence only when the heavy burden of oppression has been lifted from their shoulders. However passive a factor the people may seem to be in this whole picture, however exasperating we may find the implicit family analogy with its image of rulers as parents and people as children, it nevertheless remains a fact that the people can be "instructed." Mencius, who is much more voluble than Confucius on institutional matters, implies that institutions of popular instruction had actually existed in the "good old days," and there is an implication in the *Analects* that this instruction must take some tangible form. It ought to inculcate at the very least a knowledge of the *li* that govern family and village life and the virtues with which they are associated. The people may be brought to a point, as we have seen, where their moral life is governed by a "sense of shame" (*ch'ih*). The "sense of shame" in Confucius is not simply the "shame ethic" so often referred to in dealing with Chinese culture. It is, on the contrary, a deep inner sense of self-respect. To the extent that it involves one's image in the eyes of others, it presupposes a society in which only truly virtuous men are respected.[138]

Thus, with the removal of a negative environment, it becomes possible to foster a sense of moral autonomy in the people. A government that can rely on the autonomous moral sense of the people would not basically rely on punishments and coercion. To the extent that it eschews such means, it reinforces the trust and faith of the people. When Confucius discusses the three prerequisites of good government—food, weapons, and the trust of the people—the latter is deemed the most important. The assumption no doubt is that a people which has faith in the rulers' deep and sincere concern for its welfare will be prepared to endure economic distress when truly convinced that the cause of the distress does not lie with its rulers.

Within this context it becomes clear that the noble man's task in government is not simply to provide an example of the ideal performance of *li*. He must convince his lord to refrain from imposing excessive burdens on those below and must then in some unspecified way see to it that the people are educated to live up to the moral norms which should govern their lives within their families and communities. This does not mean that they must achieve the highest levels of knowledge or achieve the highest realization of *jen*. For although the "people can be made to follow they can not be made to understand."[139] One assumes that what they cannot be expected to understand, given the necessary limitations of their perspective, is the "whole picture" of the *tao*. Nor can one readily expect them to achieve that stoic dimension of *jen* which lifts the noble man above a concern with creaturely vicissitudes. A government that can satisfy the basic elemental needs of the people and assure order through "moral power" rather than by penal laws will win the people's trust and support even in times of war and famine. The true "man of service" (*shih*) in government devotes himself to these ends.

Beyond the concern with "policy," there is every reason to believe that when Confucius speaks of "serious devotion to business" (*ching shih*) he is again speaking of much more than ceremonies and music. He knows full well that within the bureaucratic structures of the state administration, different offices involve different functions, some of them rather specialized. In the menial offices which he had held as a youth, he himself had learned many special skills and he certainly does not deprecate skills of government which may not be directly related to ceremonies and *li*. He praises Jan Ch'iu for his "many skills."[140] Tzu-lu is decisive, Tzu-kung is penetrating in judgment, and Jan Ch'iu is versatile in his skills.[141] Elsewhere he even praises certain famous officials of the state of Cheng for their consummate skill in drafting diplomatic documents.[142] His disciples Tsai-yü and Tzu-kung are praised for "speaking well" despite the Master's aversion to glib talk.[143] These skills are not necessarily matters of either ceremony or morals, and when separated from *jen* and *li* they may easily serve evil purposes. Yet they are all necessary appurtenances of effective government.

Thus the Master's famous remark that the "noble man is no tool" does not mean that he may not have particular skills and talents which might be called technical in the broad sense of the term.[144]

The noble man in government may be called upon to serve many specific functions. He is not so much an amateur as a man in the apt words of Legge "ad omnia paratus" (prepared for everything), although with unequal degrees of aptitude.[145] The heart of the matter, however, is that all of these skills are beside the point when the essential spiritual moral problem has not been solved. In reply to Tzu-lu's question about the "complete" or "perfect" (*ch'eng*) man, Confucius mentions knowledge, courage, a lack of greed, a variety of skills, and a mastery of *li* and music but goes on to add, "But today we need not require all these things of a complete man. He who when he sees a chance of gain, acts in terms of what is right; who is prepared to give his life in the face of danger and who never forgets his promises even over a lifetime—he can also be deemed a complete man."[146] This is the core of the matter; even *li* and music are irrelevant when they do not foster or reflect such inner virtues. The other side of the coin, however, is that purely "political/administrative" skills are by no means despised as such.

One can indeed even find in the *Analects* a tension between "pure ethics" and the ethics of the political life which often involves the typical political choice between the greater and lesser evil. There is thus the difficult problem of the great statesman Kuan Chung (conventional dates 683–642) of the state of Ch'i who through his genius had managed to create the "hegemonic" collective security system (*pa*) which had brought some temporary peace and stability to the civilized world and managed to stem the total disintegration of the Chou dynasty.

As an individual Kuan Chung's morality left much to be desired. Having supported one claimant to the ducal throne, when that one was murdered he then threw his support to the later Duke Huan. As a minister he was extravagant, given to excess and luxury, and was presumptuous enough to build a screen before his gate—a practice which was the ritual prerogative only of rulers of states. Confucius is prompted to say: "If Kuan Chung knew *li* who does not know *li?*"[147] Yet despite these grave moral defects acknowledged by the Master himself; despite the fact that the strategy he devised for maintaining peace was ultimately based on the sanction of force and diplomatic guile rather than on moral force, Confucius cannot refrain from defending him against his more simple-minded and puzzled disciples. When Tzu-lu asks: "Was Kuan Chung not lacking in *jen?*" the Master's reply is that by dint of his statesmanship he had been able to "convene the rulers of the states without the use of war-chariots."[148] To Tzu-kung he continues: "When Kuan Chung was the minister of Duke Huan, he became leader [*pa*] of all the feudal princes uniting and bringing order to the world. Even now we enjoy the benefit [of his rule]. Were it not for Kuan Chung we might be wearing our hair loose and our clothes buttoned on the left [like the barbarians]," and in what seems like an outburst of exasperation he adds: "What do you expect from him—the petty fidelity of ordinary people who go off and drown themselves in ditches and drains without anyone knowing about it?"[149] This is the stock outcry against judging great statesmen in terms of the petty moral standards which govern ordinary mortals in their obscure interpersonal relations.

Here we seem to have a deep tension between a concept of personal morality based on purity of motive and intent and a concern with the good sociopolitical "results" achieved by a statesman of great talent but little personal virtue. Confucius is, of course, not Hegel and his general doctrine seems to be that the social goal of bringing peace and harmony to the world can only be achieved by a government of men of *jen.* Yet here he seems to lean heavily toward "raison d'état."

In examining this puzzle, I would suggest that much becomes clear if we assume that, despite the sad state of the house of Chou, Confucius remains fundamentally loyal to his dynasty and would do anything possible to prevent the further disintegration of its sacred authority. This would explain not only his attitude to Kuan Chung but also his attitude toward hereditary authority in general. The term *t'ien ming* is never used in the *Analects* in the sense of "the Mandate of Heaven." Confucius no doubt believed the accounts in the *Documents* and the *Poetry* concerning the proven virtues of the ancient predynastic rulers of the Chou before the Mandate was confirmed upon their state, but there is no evidence of any belief that any of the contemporary feudal houses were in any way deserving of Heaven's Mandate or of any belief that a "change of Mandate" was imminent.

The use of the sword to overthrow or establish a dynasty was indeed a problem for Confucius, as it was for his highly purist later disciple Mencius who was no longer loyal to the house of Chou. The notion of the Heavenly Mandate is, after all, predicated on the inescapable fact that the victory of a new dynasty ultimately depends on the sword, and both Confucius and Mencius, in terms of their fervent faith in government by virtue rather than by force, seem bent on muffling and minimizing the moment of force in the "change of Mandate" (*ko ming*). They focus maximum stress on the *virtue* of the new dynastic house. Confucius himself states that before the final assault on the Shang, the Chou rulers had already held sway over two-thirds of the realm and still remained submissive to the au-

thority of the Shang dynasty.[150] It was only the monstrous outrages
of the last ruler which finally led to the recourse to the sword.

There are hints that Confucius may have thought of the possibility of a new dispensation. If he could only have exercised some sustained influence over one of the rulers of the Chinese world, might
he not have created a model on a small scale of an ideal polity whose
influence might have spread?[151] We even find the lament, "The
phoenix does not appear, the river does not give forth its chart. It is
all over with me."[152] These omens (and we have no reason to believe
that Confucius does not believe in omens) were evidently believed to
presage the rise of a new dynasty.[153] The point of all this is that
Confucius did not, in fact, come to exercise such influence and no
favorable omens appear. Inscrutable Heaven gave no signs of the
imminence of a new dispensation and all Confucius could hope for
was to prevent the full disintegration of the royal authority of the
dynasty to which he remained loyal.

When viewed in this context, Kuan Chung's success in creating
some precarious order in the Chinese world with the official sanction of dynastic authority was an instance of achieving the desired
"outcomes of virtue" even without the full possession of virtue. In
commenting on the passage on "petty fidelity of ordinary people,"
the eighteenth-century commentator Liu Pao-nan observes that the
ordinary man is "a *shih* who is concerned with his own conduct and
anxious about his own personal integrity without regard to the
world."[154] Kuan Chung was concerned with the world and served
the dynasty and the preservation of its culture through his prudence
and sagacity. Mencius, who lived in an age of the Warring States
when all thought of preserving the Chou dynasty had faded, was
much more absolutist and uncompromising in his relentless attack
on Kuan Chung and all his works. Only the rise of a new True King
could save the world. While Confucius undoubtedly shares Mencius'
view that Kuan Chung's strategies do not represent the "Way
of the King," he seems to have felt that he must be grateful for any
success in preserving the remaining fabric of the authority of the
Chou dynasty from further decay.

Similar dilemmas help to explain certain stories in Book 17 of the
*Analects* that Waley believes to be of non-Confucian origin because,
in his view, they tend to reflect badly on the Master. While the
stories themselves may well be apocryphal, they are entirely compatible with the problematique of the relation of the ethical and the political we have just considered.

Under what conditions may the noble man serve in government?
The problem pervades the *Analects* and remains a Confucian prob-

lem ever after. In general, the noble man assumes office only when
he can hope to influence the rulers. To accept office with an unsavory ruler whom one cannot possibly influence to the good is to justify the suspicion that one is motivated by a desire for emoluments
and fame and not by the ideal of service. And yet, in a world where
the *tao* does not prevail, it is most difficult to find established rulers
whose life histories suggest an openness to virtue. Is it not the duty of
the *shih* to *attempt* to influence them? Perhaps they may show a
change of heart. Confucius informs us quite clearly that he has no
fixed view on this problem. On the one hand there are those like the
famous Po Yi and Shu Chi who finally retired from office rather
than fall away from their inflexible resolve and rather than suffer
any humiliation. There were those like Liu-hsia Hui who continued
to accept office even though they did suffer humiliation but who did
not depart an iota from correct behavior and proper advice. There
were those who "opted out" entirely and kept their silence, such as
Yü Chung and Yi Yi. Confucius had, he informs us, no fixed posture
on this matter and decided what was right on the basis of his judgment of the situation.[155] His desire to serve is based on almost mystical confidence in the rightness of his views. "If only someone were to
make use of me even for a single year, I could accomplish something.
In three years I could carry the work to completion."[156] Yet unless
he can prevail on some ruler to submit to his influence for a sustained period of time, he can accomplish nothing. Might even a
power-holder of doubtful legitimacy and no great promise possibly
prove accessible to his influence? His attitude here seems not very
different from that of Plato, who again goes off at the age of sixty to
Syracuse in an effort to influence the unpromising young Dionysius
II.

In the stories to which Waley refers, Confucius seems tempted to
serve with upstarts and usurpers who have seized power by "illegitimate" means. Kung-shan Fu-jao, a subordinate official of the noble
family of Chi, which itself was one of the three families which had
usurped the power of the Duke of Lu, asks Confucius to visit him.
The Master wished to go.[157] Tzu-lu, his disciple, was most displeased
and said, " 'You can not go. How can you go to Kung-shan of all
people?' The Master said: 'It can not be for nothing that he has
summoned me. If any one were to employ me, might I not create a
Chou in the  East?' "[158] Again the usurping dictator Yang Huo
shrewdly asks him: " 'Can he be called a man of *jen* who hides his
jewel in his bosom and allows his country to go astray? No! Can he
be called a man of wisdom who longs to take part in affairs yet is
continually missing the opportunity? No! The days and months go

by. The years do not wait for us!' Confucius replied: 'Yes, I shall
serve.' "[159] Tradition informs us, however, that in the end he did not
accept any of these offers.

Here we find a Confucius vulnerable to temptation, deeply frustrated and exasperated by censorious disciples who attempt to use
his own words against him. Should a man like Confucius not seize
any opportunity which presents itself to him to make some impact
on the world of power? Even power-holders whose authority will not
bear scrutiny in terms of legitimacy and whose lives will not bear
scrutiny in terms of *jen* might conceivably open a door to Confucius'
influence, whatever their motivations. As in the case of Kuan
Chung, the mere possibility of achieving some beneficial impact on
society as a whole must be considered even if it endangers some of
the most rigorous standards of self-cultivation.

Another area of Confucius' sociopolitical thought, which cannot
be simply explained in terms of the concepts of *jen* and *li,* is his attitude toward the question of merit versus heredity or ascription.
Leaving aside troublesome questions of semantics, we have already
discerned some of the aspects of Confucius' vision which have led
some to see "liberal," "democratic," or "individualistic" tendencies
in the *Analects*. On the "democratic" side, it is first of all clear that
good government exists to serve the needs of the people, especially
the economic needs. The people should be "taught," and a ruling
class which does not enjoy the trust of the people will not endure. A
good state refrains from extensive intervention in the lives of the
people. In a good society the people will enjoy a living space of their
own in which there will be scope for moral autonomy. All these
themes are further developed in the book of Mencius, but they are
already present in the *Analects*.

On the side of "individualism," we have the fact that while an individual is linked to his social roles, his behavior is not simply a
function of these roles. He has a potential moral autonomy which
makes it possible at least for some individuals to realize the full
moral potentialities of their roles and to convey to others their full
humanity, whether through the framework of the "role structure" or
outside of it. Such individuals possess a spiritual self-sufficiency
which renders them independent of "popularity" or dependence on
the powerful. Even the "people" taken as a whole—when a proper
environment is created for them—enjoy a degree of moral autonomy
which governs them in their familial and community relations.[160] If
"individualism" refers to something like Kantian moral autonomy,
something of it can certainly be found here.

Beyond this, however, there has been much emphasis on the role of merit in the *Analects*. Unquestionably the word "noble man" now refers to moral and intellectual qualities, and commentators have emphasized the statement "that in teaching there should be no distinction" and the further remark of Confucius that "from the man who brings his bundle of dried flesh [as tuition] upward, I have never refused to teach anyone."[161] In teaching his disciples, he certainly envisages the possibility of a public career for them. Thus to the extent that there is already a tendency underway for rulers—for reasons of their own—to seek out able men of all origins as officials rather than members of the official nobility or their own kinsmen, Confucius could not help but favor this tendency. We also already find enormous stress on the idea of "ministerial initiative," which is to play such a large role in Confucian thought. Confucius' great model is, of course, the Duke of Chou who, while himself a member of the royal family, served in a ministerial capacity to the young King Cheng and was in effect his teacher. The image of the hereditary holder of authority acting as the passive recipient of the advice of his wise ministers is suggested throughout.[162] The notion of the dignity of the *shih* stratum is amply illustrated throughout the *Analects* despite the complete absence of any notion of institutional protection against the wrath of the power-holder.

None of this, however, involves any diminution of the strong emphasis on the symbols of hierarchy and authority inherent in the entire system of the *li*. There is, in fact, no contradiction. One can certainly imagine a society (which was, indeed, later realized up to a point in China) in which the only truly "ascriptive" hereditary ranks and statuses are familial statuses and the hereditary status of the royal or imperial clan; in which the symbols of hierarchy, rank, and authority do not lose an iota of their sacred significance. It must constantly be reiterated that even a totally meritocratic ruling stratum may be fiercely devoted to rank and hierarchy.

Yet running quite counter to the emphasis on true merit we also find in the *Analects* an ongoing *positive* stress on hereditary prerogative. This has confirmed for many the essentially "reactionary" nature of Confucius' vision. Plato's *Republic* is after all also based on a rigid division of classes yet it remains—despite its recommendation of a eugenics program—a strict meritocracy.

In the case of the *Analects* we have already noted how indignant the Master is at the scandalous usurpation of hereditary ritual authority by the Chi clan in the state of Lu. Such usurpations are symbolic of all usurpations by noble families, concubines and children of concubines, and adventurists careerists. Old principalities are wiped out and their legitimate ruling houses disinherited. Confucius

attacks his own disciples Jan Ch'iu and Tzu–lu for abetting an attack on the small state of Chuan–yü whose rulers had been appointed by the Chou dynasty to "preside over the sacrifices to Mt.
Tung-meng."[163] The rulers of such principalities are disinherited
not only of their lands but of their sacred family graves. To be sure,
the shameless and incompetent hereditary rulers are themselves as
responsible as anyone for these disasters but this does not diminish
the evil consequences of the decay of legitimate hereditary authority.[164]

If we seek for intellectual reasons for the Master's defense of hereditary authority, based on the implicit "logic" of his vision, one
might again begin with the ethicoreligious status of the family.
Whatever Confucius' beliefs about ancestral spirits, he obviously
maintained the belief that families "owed it to their ancestors" to do
everything possible to maintain family prosperity and family honor.
It was thus entirely in accordance with *li* that the Chou dynasty
should have "enfeoffed" the survivors of the Shang dynasty with the
state of Sung so that they could perpetuate their ancestral rites with
due dignity. The blasphemous element in the wiping out of old
principalities lies precisely in the cutting off of the rites to their
noble ancestors. When we turn to the ethicosocial level, *where the
family ethic is truly practiced,* the ties of lineage are still deemed to provide the most potent base for social order and harmony. Here again
one must point to the concrete belief that the kin ties of many of the
Chou feudal lords to the Chou house had, in Confucius' view, been
an important factor in the good order of the early Chou period.

The hereditary principle is taken for granted in its application to
the supreme instance of authority in the state, the universal king.[165]
To be sure, this hereditary claim is not eternal and dynasties are
overthrown. Yet the notion that the true bearer of the kingly power
is a family and not an individual seems to be assumed. Curiously
enough, it will later be assumed even by the "Legalists," who will be
China's most radical advocates of the meritocratic principle. Without considering all the theoretical reasons that have been offered
through the centuries for hereditary monarchy, it would appear that
even the Legalist Han Fei-tzu assumes that any other method of
choosing the successor to supreme authority would inevitably create
anarchy and derogate from the mystery of authority. If this is true in
the case of the "rationalistic" Legalists, one can assume that it is *a
fortiori* so in the case of the Confucius of the *Analects*. Only in Mencius do we find an alternative possibility suggested (see Chapter 7).
It is possible indeed to conceive of one very specific negative moral
reason why the vision of the *Analects* may resist the idea of the use of

force even to remove evil hereditary rulers. The resort to force can be conceived of as justified only when all the signs point to the conditions in which a change of mandate seems justified. The noble man does not achieve his ends through the application of force or through the creation of organized power designed to overthrow established authority. He either succeeds in bringing his influence to bear on the rulers of the time or he does not. The fact that most of the hereditary rulers prove unworthy in part belongs to the mystery of Heaven's role in history. Even the force employed *in extremis* by the founder of a dynasty must be justified by an array of mitigating circumstances and by the mysteries of Heaven's Will.

Above all, however, in dealing with Confucius' respect for hereditary authority we must again mention his ongoing loyalty to the Chou dynasty. The loyalty to the shadowy authority of the king meant the maintenance—to the extent possible— of whatever fabric of legitimate authority still remained in a decaying society. There did not seem to exist in the China of Confucius' time any credible alternative focus of support which had, by its virtuous behavior, proven its readiness to inherit the mandate of the Chou. The only alternative to maintaining the Chou must have seemed something like an all-out anarchic struggle for power among states no longer constrained by the sacred principles of *li*. This clinging to the remnants of legitimate authority may account for both the defense of Kuan Chung who was not a truly "virtuous" man and the call for a "just war" by Lu against the usurping Ch'en family in the State of Ch'i, which had overthrown the legitimate ducal house.

To put Confucius' sociopolitical doctrine in terms of a conventional modern sociopolitical analysis, one might say that Confucius continued to support the feudal component of the system in which sacred authority was distributed widely among a host of hereditary power-holders while at the same time looking favorably on the widening opportunities within the bureaucratic component of the structure for men of true merit. What he may have envisioned as an ideal was the emergence of a state of affairs in which hereditary rulers would scrupulously exercise their ritual-ceremonial functions while relying heavily in "policy matters" on wise and virtuous ministers.

There is an impression that the positive attitude toward aspects of the hereditary principle which we find in the *Analects* was completely rejected particularly in later centuries when centralized bureaucratic organization and the examination system were fully in place. The ideal, we are led to believe, now was completely that of "careers open to talents," however much reality may have diverged from the ideal. It is, of course, acknowledged that Chinese bureaucrats and gentry of later ages were as anxious to pass on their privileges and advantages to their children as ruling privileged strata elsewhere but in this the Chinese were hardly unique. In fact, however, I would suggest that the ideal of respect for inherited prestige and authority was not totally rejected even as a norm. Thus the notion of loyalty to the dynasty "in which one is born" continued to be invoked in later centuries, however mixed the reasons may have been for invoking it. The notion that illustrious lineages, which had acquired "the fragrance of books," ought to make conscious efforts to preserve themselves as organized entities which would carry on the family heritage was held as a positive ideal that even the state dared not challenge. It continued to be widely believed that while such families were not immune to corruption, on the whole their survival strengthened the moral foundation of the society.

Throughout this section I have necessarily treated Confucius' thought as both sociopolitical and ethicoritual. The two are, as we have seen, inextricably intertwined. In the end, however, there is truth in Fingarette's assertion that Confucius' vision "is certainly not merely a political vision."[166] On its most exalted level we have the vision of a society which not only enjoys harmony and welfare but a society transfigured by a life of sacred and beautiful ritual in which all classes would participate.

## The Religious Dimension and the Role of "Fate" (*ming*)

Much has been made of Confucius' religion or lack thereof. Most of the discussions revolve around certain Western definitions of a Western term. Since most Western definitions of religion point to man's relations to the numinous dimension of the nonhuman universe (rather than simply to subjective states or holy rites), I shall here consider the question of Confucius' attitude toward the nonhuman realm.

Confucius, it is asserted, is "this-worldly" and "humanistic." In a sense both statements are true, and yet neither statement differentiates his thought from that of many of the leading figures of the other high civilizations of the time. "This-worldly" and "religious" are by no means antithetical categories. The religions of ancient Mesopotamia, Egypt, Aryan India, Greece, and China are all eminently this-worldly. I include Egypt here despite or because of the Egyptian passion for transporting this world into the next. The gods and spirits of all these civilizations are intimately tied to this-worldly concerns. They embody and preside over the forces of nature and civilization. The same is true of the religion of Shang in China. In all these civilizations the axial age is in fact marked by a kind of transcendental ethical reaction against the total world involvement of the religion of previous centuries, but in most cases this reaction does not necessarily assume an extreme other-worldly form. The God of the Bible is transcendental, but what He reveals to Moses is a decidedly this-worldly law. Plato's philosophy may have other-worldly potentialities, but he himself remains devoted in varying degrees to his this-worldly mission. Even in India, the Brahmanism of the Upanishads is still deeply committed to the worldly duties of the householder despite the proliferation of individual ascetics. Only primitive Buddhism seems to call for radical renunciation for those prepared for the monk's vocation.

The assertion that Confucius is a "humanist" may, however, be more informative. There can be no doubt that he would have the noble man concentrate his attention on ethical self-cultivation and on restoring the harmony of human society. When Tzu-kung informs us that one of the matters which he did not hear the Master discuss was the *"tao* of Heaven" (as opposed to the "patterns of culture"), we assume that he means the ways of Heaven in the nonhuman world or in all those areas of reality over which man has no control. It may thus cover dimensions we might call "scientific" as well as dimensions we call "religious." It is noteworthy that the same passage also refers to the famous question of "human nature" (*hsing*) as another problem which he never heard the Master discuss.[167] A difficulty we encounter here is the view shared by Angus Graham that the entire concept of "human nature" had not yet arisen and that this must therefore be a later interpolation. Yet even if we assume that the concept may have already existed, it is quite true that the Master does not dwell on "what man is" in his inner nature but on "how man makes himself good," and this pragmatism may indeed be the connecting element between his attitude toward the *tao* of Heaven and his views on human nature.[168] It is interesting to note that elsewhere we are told that he also did not discuss strange happenings, feats of strength, disorders, or the affairs of spirits (or supernatural phenomena).[169] While this list certainly includes natural phenomena, it also includes many strictly human "interests," such as idle chatter about scandals, myths, and other matters all of which are a useless diversion from the noble man's moral vocation. Even as a humanist, Confucius is above all oriented to the ethical dimension of human life. He does not seem to approve benignly of "everything human."

Again, this pragmatism does not differentiate him notably from great religious figures and wise men of the other contemporary civilizations. While Moses and the prophets may be "god-centered," they are not theologians, and the diverse revelations which they receive all direct their attention back to the concern with the salvation of man. The historic Buddha himself, we are often told in the literature, was a "humanistic" pragmatist whose main and overwhelming concern was with saving humans from the sea of suffering. His "eight-fold path" certainly dwelt above all on the human ethical-spiritual prerequisites for achieving this goal. In one sutra, he is made to dwell at length on a whole series of speculative metaphysical problems which do not "tend to edification" and should be avoided. In the case of Socrates we find, of course, a constant discussion of his "humanistic revolt" against the whole tradition of pre-Socratic natural philosophy and his turn to human concerns—a revolt which he shared with the "Sophists."[170] We may even call Socrates pragmatic because his entire intellectual method is focused on his ethical concerns and not on any theoretical "psychology" as such.

If all these figures are, in a sense, pragmatists bent on achieving human ends, it would appear that there really is no such thing as "humanistic pragmatism" in a vacuum and that all pragmatisms tacitly presuppose certain images of the larger frame of things in terms of which pragmatic goals are set and pursued. Can praxis be abstracted from certain implicit notions of the nature of things? I would thus question Hansen's assertion that a "moral pragmatism" is concerned only with "action" or regulation and not at all with "truth." The pragmatic teacher is constantly expounding what he considers to be truths about the correctness or incorrectness of modes of behavior in terms of the assumed ends of behavior. The ends themselves presuppose a certain vision of the world in which they are pursued. The many statements in the *Analects* about the relations of various moral dispositions to each other may not be concerned with "disinterested" truths about facts of nature, but they are meant to imply that something true has been said about the ethical state of affairs in question. It is an ironic fact that to the extent that Socrates did indeed develop a "method" for arriving at true definitions most of the truths he himself is concerned with are not truths concerning the neutral observation of facts but truths concerning the analysis of ethical ideas meant to eventuate in praxis.

The assertion that Confucius did not discuss the *"tao* of Heaven" does not mean that he had no beliefs about the *tao*. We of course know that the historic Buddha makes many tacit assumptions about notions such as karma, metempsychosis, and a whole series of matters which he refuses to discuss in a speculative metaphysical way, because such talk would be a diversion from his essential soteriological task. Later disciples, whether of Buddha, Confucius, or Socrates, will, however, often feel obliged to discuss precisely those "metaphysical" matters which the masters refuse to discuss in the very course of defending the tacit assumptions of their masters against hostile challenge.

A highly problematic aspect of the word "humanism" is, of course, its strong association with the whole trend of what has been called humanism in the post-Cartesian West. The notion of a radical breach and even antagonism between a human world centered on the human subject as the sole source of meaning and an indifferent, "valueless" or even hostile universe does not seem to be suggested anywhere in the *Analects*.

Much of the discussion of the theme of religion in the *Analects* has centered on passages which deal with ancestral spirits and nature spirits. Some of these are most difficult to interpret and modern translations often reflect the translator's view of Confucius' attitude toward "religion." Among the simpler assertions, we find the following: "If one does not know about life [or the living] what can one know about death [or the dead]?" "If one does not know how to serve the living how can one serve the spirits?"[171] The Chinese commentaries down through the ages, not aware of our sharp dichotomies between the realm of religion and nonreligion, are themselves enormously varied in interpretation of even these apparently simple passages. Since the *Analects* devote so much attention to the *li* of mourning and the ancestral sacrifice, some are puzzled by the second assertion. There is thus one interpretation that only those who know how to nourish the living in a true spirit can sacrifice to the ancestral and natural spirits in a true spirit. Some interpret the first statement to mean that only a man who truly knows "how to live" truly knows "how to die."[172] Yet it may also refer to an obsessive concern with the state of the dead in the world beyond and the claims of shamans and necromancers to possess information on these matters. Here the absence of what we call parts of speech in classical Chinese may have a most telling effect on the interpretation of these passages.

Whatever light these statements may or may not throw on the question of Confucius' beliefs in the matter of the spirits, they unambiguously do carry the humanist message that humans must concern themselves in the first instance with the affairs of living human beings. Elsewhere Fan Ch'ih is told "reverence the spirits" and—depending on the translation—"keep one's distance from them," or "and keep them at a distance."[173] By some, the first has been taken to mean the cultivation of overfamiliar "shamanistic" relations with the spirits or to mean that only by performing the proper ceremonies to the spirits does one keep the spirits from inflicting harm. The spirits who are themselves subsumed under the larger order of things will perform as they should when the relations with them are governed wholly through the decorous rituals of *li*, which both clarify the relations of humans to the spirits and yet make clear the separation between them.

Some have taken all this to mean that Confucius either did not believe in "spirits," was an "agnostic," or really believed only in the sacred efficacy of the rites themselves. That much of his attention is focused on the rites themselves may indeed be quite true and one need not deny Fingarette's insistence on the religious dimensions of the *li* as such. The beginnings of this attitude, as I have suggested, can already be discerned in the *Book of Poetry*. The idea explicitly proclaimed in the book of Hsün-tzu that the system of *li* is part of the whole fabric of the cosmic order—"that heaven and earth are harmonized by it; that the sun and moon are illuminated by it; that the four seasons are ordered by it, etc."—it already latent in the *Analects*.[174] Yet as we have also seen, to Confucius the *li* which govern the relations of human actors concern actual transactions among actors, and unless those involved in the transaction infuse the *li* with the proper spirit—with the proper intentionality toward all the actors involved—they remain empty form. In the human sphere, it is not at all possible for the *li* to be actualized without the proper attitudes of those involved. It is not merely a "pattern of behavior" in which people participate. It must also represent a vital relationship. Thus, the injunction to "reverence the spirits" suggests an attitude toward them rather than simply a performance. The modern Chinese Confucian thinker, T'ang Chün-i, has, therefore, suggested that Confucius believed that rituals directed toward the spirits necessarily involved some sense of intercommunication (*kan-t'ung*) with spirits however the spirits are conceived and that, to Confucius, the spirits in some undefined sense were there to participate in the communication.[175]

Nevertheless, in the next generation we will find in the book of Mo-tzu reference to Confucianists (*ju*) who seem to deny the existence of ancestral and natural spirits or at least their capacity to influence events. Yet this by no means necessarily represented the dominant trend of the Confucian literati in the long history of Confucianism. The Sung philosopher Chu Hsi, often considered highly "rationalistic" in his approach, finds an ontological niche for ancestral and nature spirits in his cosmic system and in his doctrine supports the intercommunication idea suggested by T'ang Chün-i.[176]

Quite apart, however, from the question of the Master's belief in the existence of such spirits, they are certainly not at the heart of his religious outlook. If there is any central religious term in the *Analects,* it is the term "Heaven," and here again Confucius is to a degree a transmitter. It has already been noted that the shift to the centrality of Heaven has already occurred in the *Poetry* and in the *Documents.* Heaven above all is the source of the moral order. Whatever else can be said of Heaven in those works, it represents a cosmic moral will concerned to protect and sustain the normative human order. Even in these pre-Confucian texts it would appear that Heaven, in its relation to the enduring and cyclical patterns of nature, is—to use our philosophic terminology—already thought of as immanent in the natural order. Yet in its relations to the human order which has the fatal capacity for falling away from the norms which govern it, Heaven will in fact intervene in the course of human affairs and will even make specific decisions, such as the decision that the Chou state will inherit the Heavenly Mandate.

When we turn to the concept of Heaven in the *Analects* and consider the entire body of references to Heaven in the text, the question will almost immediately occur to the Westerner: Is Heaven a "personal" god or is Heaven an "impersonal order"? The supposition is that these terms necessarily represent a clearly exclusive antithesis and that we should have available to us a clear affirmative or negative answer. In fact, the text is quite inconclusive. In various passages, Heaven is treated as a conscious being concerned not only with the human order in general, but even with the Master's own mission in particular. "The Master said—'there is no one who truly knows me.' Tzu-kung asked, 'Why is there no one who knows you?' The Master replied, 'I am not resentful against Heaven nor do I blame men. In my studies, I deal with [mundane affairs of men] below and reach up to an understanding of that which is above. Is it not Heaven that knows me!' "[177] When he finds himself in a dangerous situation in the state of Sung where the hostile minister Huan T'ui threatens his life, he states, "Heaven produced this power in me—what can Huan T'ui do to me?"[178] When the Master was imperiled in K'uang, he said, "When King Wen perished, was not the pattern of truth [*wen*] lodged here in me? If Heaven had intended that this pattern should die, a latter-day mortal [like myself] would not have been able to link up to this pattern. If Heaven does not intend to destroy this pattern, what can the people of K'uang do to me?"[179] In another place he speaks of not deceiving Heaven.[180] If one takes all these assertions at face value, they seem to suggest a conscious Heaven to whom Confucius "relates" and even a Heaven which, Confucius feels, has endowed him with a particular mission in the world. He is, to be sure, puzzled by the inscrutable ways of Heaven. Why did Heaven deprive him of his favorite disciple, Yen Hui, at an early age? If Heaven has placed this "pattern" in him, why has Heaven not made it possible for him to make it manifest in the world? Why is it that no one in the world of power truly "knows" him? Yet he is not resentful, since there is that in Heaven's designs which is beyond human comprehension. Perhaps he accepts the comfort of the frontier guardian I, who says to the Master's disciples, "you must not be disheartened by his failure. It is now a long time that the *tao* has not prevailed in the world. Heaven intends to use your Master as a wooden clapper [of an alarm bell]."[181]

Those who are convinced that, in Confucius, Heaven has simply become an "impersonal order" of nature must on the basis of their *a priori* assumptions dismiss all the above as simply a concession to popular speech or a "manner of speaking." This is a most dangerous presumption based on the *a priori* antithesis mentioned above. There is, however, one utterance in which the name of Heaven is indeed clearly linked to the order of nature and it is an utterance which bears close scrutiny. "I would prefer not to speak," says the Master. Tzu-kung then says, "If our Master did not speak, what would your little ones have to hand down about him?" The Master says, "What does Heaven say? Yet the four seasons run their course through it and the hundred creatures are born through it. What does Heaven say?"[182] Here Heaven is indeed associated with the "impersonal processes" and cycles of nature as well as with the generative processes which do not suggest deliberate thought or discrete, finite "decisions." The passage does, in fact, seem to suggest that nature is, as it were, an "emanation" of Heaven. Unlike the God of the Hebrew Bible, Heaven does not speak.

What nevertheless strikes one most about the passage is the fact that it is not fundamentally focused on Heaven but on Confucius himself. Confucius compares himself to Heaven. He would prefer to act as Heaven acts. One might say that in a sense the passage is profoundly anthropomorphic or, perhaps more accurately cosmomorphic. Confucius aspires as a human to model himself on Heaven.

The Master's preference for not speaking immediately reminds us of the entire discussion of language referred to above. Language is precisely the area where the discrepancy between what is and what ought to be manifests itself both in the individual and in the social order as a whole. The attitude toward the natural world here may in a sense emphasize impersonal order but it certainly does not remove value from nature. Confucius might, in fact, have said with the author of the first chapter of Genesis, "and behold it was good!" The fact of natural order is a wonderful and mysterious fact. Heaven has in the past also made manifest to man the normative order that should govern human society, but the task of "completing" or actualizing this order devolves upon human beings who must actualize it. The order is not immanent in the society in the sense that human beings are not preprogrammed to realize it. Here deliberate thought, foresight, and discrete decisions of a finite-temporal nature must be made and language must be used. If the *tao*, however, *did* prevail in the world, the routines, habits, and patterns of behavior that govern the good society would be so pervasive that the need for using speech would be much diminished. Confucius could provide his disciples with a living example of moral behavior without having to dwell on the treacheries and perversities of a world in disorder.

On the human side of this analogy, a world governed by the unspoken routines, rituals, and habits of good behavior would decidedly not be a mindless or spiritless world. The fact that Confucius at the age of seventy could follow his impulses without going astray does not prove that he had become a mindless automaton. Here again we must suspend all our Western associations with phrases like "mere ritual," "lifeless routine," or "mechanical habit." Where the term "spirit" is primarily associated with "creativity," "freshness," or "originality" as in our culture, or with the constant exercise of "free choices," any repetitious routine is naturally "soulless." Yet obviously Confucius did not consider the repetitive cycles of nature or of ceremonial life "soulless," nor is he suggesting that if he were in a position where he did not need to speak, his existence as a living presence would be superfluous. He would indeed make manifest his presence through the way he led his life and the example he would provide to others.

In a world where the *tao* prevailed, it would still not be true that there would be no "crossroads" of choice in Fingarette's sense but men, for the most part, always would make the right turn. What is to be cherished is not so much the freedom to make a choice, but choosing the good without constant need for deliberation, perplexity, and highly goal-oriented behavior. The "freedom of the will" exists but it is by no means the ultimate good in itself.

At this point let me suggest, however, that this analogy between Heaven and the sage or noble man may also be applied to the side of Heaven as well. The spirit of Heaven is still very much present in the regularities, routines, and generative processes of nature, even though Heaven does not speak. The contrast here with the transcendent God of the Bible should not be absolutized. In the Creation account in Genesis, it is true that the rich manifold variety of the natural world is as much stressed as its order. It is certainly not implied that God must constantly "speak" to maintain the regular course of nature. God is also praised as the author of the ordered and regular aspects of the world even though he may not be immanent in that order, and in his supreme transcendence he can, in fact, destroy it. Yet there is no reason whatsoever to believe, in the case of Confucius, that a Heaven which is immanent in the regularities, routines, and generative processes of nature may not also possess attributes of consciousness and spirit. Such a notion may be La Place's "superfluous hypothesis" from the point of view of the theoretical and technical concerns of modern science but not from the point of view of a Confucius eager to find in Heaven's way in the cosmos a model for human behavior.

To be sure, the attributes of Heaven's mind or spirit within nature seem more like the attributes of intellect and will in Spinoza's God than like the deliberative, creative, and purposive consciousness of the God of the Bible in his relations to the finite and temporal world. In Spinoza's words, one might say of Heaven in its relation to nature "that all the decrees of God have been appointed by him through and from all eternity, for otherwise it would argue mutability and imperfection in God."[183] Yet Confucius' apprehension of Heaven's relations *to the indeterminate human world* may, in fact, have been substantially different, and much more in accord with the Heaven of the *Book of Poetry* and the *Book of Documents*. Using the "cosmomorphic" analogy of the passage just quoted, Confucius would himself prefer not to speak. Yet in relating to the human world, he must speak. In the human world the *tao* ought to prevail but does not prevail. Hence the Master must rely on his ordinary reflective, deliberative, purposive, and highly engaged consciousness in order to cope with the reality of a disordered world. Similarly, Heaven, in its relations to the world of man, also still seems to manifest a mode of "theistic" concern with human destiny for Heaven is basically "on man's side." Heaven supports sages and noble men in their redemptive efforts and even deliberately intervenes in the course of human history, although its behavior in human affairs is often inscrutable. Within this framework, it is entirely possible to believe that the same Heaven which silently manifests itself in the course of the four seasons also knows Confucius and endows him with a historic mission. When one glances briefly ahead over the long history of Confucian thought, one finds that while the specifically "theistic" component of this view of Heaven often recedes, the rigid antithesis between Heaven as "order of nature" and Heaven as cosmic consciousness never does become firmly established.

The discussion of Heaven must, however, be broadened here to include a related category which plays a prominent role in the *Analects*—the category of *ming* or "fate" and "destiny." As we have seen, this word initially meant a "command." It then may have been extended to the meaning of "mandate" as in the "Mandate of Heaven." Without losing its relation to its original meaning, it also seems to come to mean all those aspects of human life over which, in the Confucian view, humans either do not exercise or need not seek to exercise control. In this context, it might be translated as "that which is ordained." Yet curiously enough, it also comes to refer to precisely those areas of life which are the proper domain of human action—what might be called the proper vocation of man or the enduring life task which Heaven has imposed on man. If *ming* as applied to a dynasty may mean its ongoing mandate to exercise its kingly authority, as applied to humans in general—and to the noble man in the first instance—it refers above all to his "personal mandate" to fulfill his moral-political vocation. In seeking a kind of covering phrase, one might well translate it as "that which is ordained" whether as fate or as a life vocation to be fulfilled.

When Confucius tells us that at the age of fifty he knew the *"ming* of Heaven" or that which Heaven has ordained for him, he may mean that he has a clear understanding of what it is that is not in his control as well as of what is his true sphere of autonomous action. Whether one lives long or dies young is beyond one's control. Whether one will attain a comfortable material existence so long as this is morally attainable or will remain poor is beyond one's control, as are many of the circumstances of life. Whether one will be happy in the conventional sense of that term is itself beyond one's control.

Even within the area which is his particular area of concern—the area of his ethicopolitical vocation—the noble man is still confronted by fatality on all sides. If he is born "into the wrong time," as is the case of Confucius, he will find few, if any, rulers who will be responsive to his message and he must, as we have seen, be infinitely scrupulous about attempting to influence those who are beyond redeeming influence. While Confucianism is often deemed to be an outlook which has an extravagant faith in the moral power of good men, we see that there is, after all, an element of historic fatality which severely constricts the scope of moral influence. The noble man, like Confucius, may raise up a host of disciples. Yet even here, some of the disciples themselves fall short of the Master's hopes and may be contaminated by a corrupt world. In the end, his only truly inviolable area of autonomy lies in his ability to cultivate his own person in the hope of influencing others. Judging from Mo-tzu's later attacks on the "fatalism" of the Confucianists of his time, it would appear that the concept of *ming* as referring to those areas of reality over which the noble man exercises little or no control was to become even further extended after the Master's death.

Yet in the face of all this, Confucius informs us that he does not "resent Heaven" and his unvarying goal in life is to fulfill his mission to the extent that that which is ordained by Heaven or immanent in the nature of Heaven will allow him to do so. The questions of theodicy—of why Heaven allows noble men and other men to suffer—is not raised. Here again, we must look very much to the "stoical" inner aspect of *jen*. Confucius may be occasionally puzzled, pained, and perplexed by Heaven's inscrutability, but he rejoices that he can participate in the moral mission imposed by Heaven on noble men. While there is no evidence that he actually as yet completely identifies sages and noble men with Heaven in any pantheistic sense, there is, after all, something heavenly about the noble man who can look at the world, to a degree, from Heaven's standpoint *sub specie aeternitatis*.

Thus, though Heaven is in many ways inscrutable, though the precincts of fate are vast and the area of human power limited, the order of Heaven in nature and the order prescribed for man is affirmed. Heaven has endowed at least some men with a knowledge of that order which should prevail in human affairs and which has actually been realized in the past. It has endowed some men with the capacity to initiate the actualization of that order even though it has not always made it possible for them to do so. Once the good order is actualized, all men can in their own life spheres participate in its implementation. It has, also, made it possible for noble men to achieve through *jen* a deep equanimity and serenity in the face of misfortune and frustration. There is still the hope that the restoration of the *tao* in its essential features may occur in the future and then the masses of mankind whose sufferings are real and tangible may also be restored to the peace, harmony, and beatitude of Fingarette's "ceremonial community."

## Responses to Critics

Although Confucius has been called China's "first private thinker," the *Analects* themselves furnish us with evidence of certain contemporary figures who sharply dissent from his vision. In Book

18, we find a cluster of stories in which certain shadowy personalities challenge some of his fundamental premises. They have been called "proto-Taoists" by some, and Waley asserts that these stories are "anti-Confucian" and they were "naively accepted by the compilers" who did not seem to realize the fact.[184] This statement is puzzling since the stories are marked above all by the Master's trenchant replies to his challengers. The stories may, of course, be apocryphal but the message seems genuinely Confucian.

These figures may be "proto-Taoist." Some of them are referred to in the book of Chuang-tzu. Yet the tradition of "escapism" represented by them may not have been new, even in Confucius' time. The common point made by all is that Confucius' tireless and unremitting efforts to find a place in government is a colossal waste of time and that the disorder of the world cannot be remedied by "righteous men." Confucius himself occasionally expresses a temptation to drop the entire futile enterprise, but in the end he remains committed to his mission to "keep trying."

Two men, Ch'ang Chü and Chieh-ni, plowing in a field (thus committed to supporting themselves by their own labor) converse with Tzu-lu about his Master. Chieh-ni says, " 'The entire world is being engulfed in a flood. Who can change this state of affairs? Rather than following a man who withdraws now from this one [one of the rulers of the time] and then from that one, why not follow a man who withdraws from the entire generation?' and with this he went on covering the seed."[185] Here and elsewhere we find a simple disbelief that the "course of history" as an aspect of *ming* can be deflected by the feeble efforts of a single individual. When the Master hears a report of this interchange, he observes, "One cannot go off to live with birds and beasts. Am I not a man among men? If the *tao* prevailed in the world, I would not be involved in trying to change things."[186]

A somewhat different point is made in the story of another aged gentleman whom Tzu-lu meets on the road, carrying a basket slung over his shoulder. Like the previous recluses, he is actively engaged in farming. Tzu-lu inquires if he had seen the Master who had gone on ahead. The old man contemptuously replies, "With your four limbs you do not toil. You cannot distinguish the five grains—who is your Master?" He then, however, provides Tzu-lu with lodgings for the night and introduces him to his sons. Tzu-lu notes that the old man's family life is exemplary. The old man obviously believes in maintaining both interpersonal and familial values in a corrupt world. He has, however, rejected the notion of any political vocation and obviously believes that the only honest way of supporting oneself in such a world is by one's own physical labor. To the old man, the very fact that Tzu-lu and his Master obviously derived their income from some other sources was in itself an indictment of them. Tzu-lu goes on to observe (and his observation obviously reflects the Master's view): "It is not right not to [attempt] to serve in office. If the proper prescriptions governing the relations of young and old cannot be set aside, how can one set aside the right relations between lord and minister? In desiring to maintain one's own personal integrity, one upsets the whole larger pattern of relationships [ta-lun]. A noble man in [attempting] to serve does what is right. He knows well enough that the *tao* does not prevail."[187]

The old man has challenged not only Confucius but even one of the larger shared implicit orientations of the cultural elite that the social order is an "integrated system" which must in the end be dealt with from the center. The vast majority of men will not by their own efforts succeed in living exemplary personal and family lives until the society as a whole, represented by the ruling elite, is able to create a favorable social environment for them. The attack on Confucius in China in recent years has dwelt lovingly on the old man's charge that Confucius and his disciples could not "distinguish the five grains." Yet the point made by Tzu-lu has not been entirely refuted. So long as one assumes that society must be transformed through the political order, one is not likely to rid oneself of a political class which does *not* derive its income from "cultivating the five grains" even when it is capable of distinguishing them. Whether the old man is simply a kind of historic determinist who believes that the cycles of order and disorder cannot be affected by human effort but who might be willing "to serve" in a period of order, or whether he is a kind of advocate of an autonomous personal and familial morality which can dispense with the mediating role of the political order is, of course, not made clear.

There is mention in the *Analects* of other "deviant" strands of thought. I use this term advisedly since there is an implication throughout the *Analects* that the Master's own vision is based on a synoptic *balanced* vision of the whole. There is one passage in the *Analects* which Waley translates as follows: "A gentleman can see a question from all sides without bias [chou]. The small man is biased and sees a question from only one side."[188] This interpretation, of course, emphasizes the intellectual side. Yet it is interesting to note that many of the Chinese commentaries deal with it in terms of moral dispositions. The *chou* or "all-round" image refers to the man of fundamental integrity—fidelity, sincerity, and truthfulness (*chung-hsin*)—who will always see matters from the point of view of the larger public (*kung*) interest. The mean man will always see things from the lopsided view of partisan and selfish interests. In both interpretations, however, we have the opposition of comprehensiveness versus one-sidedness. This is, I suggest, one of the ongoing problems not only of Confucian thought but of Chinese thought in general. Does lack of comprehensive insight lead to the distortions of moral disposition or does an unbalanced moral disposition lead to a beclouded view of reality? The problem is not specifically Confucian or Chinese. What is particularly striking in the Confucian case is the high confidence that in the noble man or sage, the higher knowledge and the ethical perfection coincide, as in the case of Yen Hui who could always see the "whole picture" and seldom deviated from *jen*.

This passage is closely followed by another passage which deals with the question of deviancy itself. The term used (*i-tuan*) has in later texts often been translated as "heresy" or "heterodoxy." The term *tuan* seems to refer to the beginning point (as in the "four beginnings" of Mencius) of a thread or line and by extension to the starting point of a road or even of a process. *I-tuan* would then refer to a "diverging or deviating thread or line." One of the Chinese commentaries is most enlightening on this point. In any human society, men are involved in different walks of life, and Mencius says that even noble men must pursue different courses, but in the end because "the true *tao* is marked by unity, all paths converge [*kuei*] on it." "Divergent threads are those which beginning at different points end up at different points."[189] The threads are separated and do not merge into the total fabric. Thus, Waley's translation, "He who sets out to work on one strand destroys the fabric," seems most suggestive. The deviant perspectives which Confucius finds in his world do not originate from completely divergent apprehensions of the whole picture. They originate in the absolutization of certain one-sided tendencies which arise out of differing and limited life experiences. They are again based on a failure to see limited perspectives as limited perspectives within the balanced framework of the whole, and the question of whether such "deviancy" arises out of moral limitations or out of intellectual one-sidedness remains part of the problematique of Chinese thought.

## Disciples

The *Analects* are, finally, much occupied with the relations between the Master and his disciples and here we meet the universal dialectic of Master-disciple relationships. Whether we deal with Confucius, Gautama Buddha, Socrates, or even Sigmund Freud, there is always the Master's apprehension that his disciples have only a limited or one-sided grasp of his total vision. Whether due to limitations of temperament or personality or to the moral and intellectual limitations discussed above, they seldom seem to grasp the vision in its wholeness. From an outsider's point of view there is, to be sure, a word to be said on behalf of the disciples. The Master's vision may not be as totally coherent as he believes. It may, in fact, contain many unresolved ambiguities and obscurities with which the disciples are forced to contend in meeting the attack of unfriendly opponents, and reality itself may prove richer than the Master's vision.

In Confucius' vision individual virtue, spiritual equanimity, the sincere authentic performance of *li,* the enthusiastic devotion to learning both as accumulation of empirical knowledge and the achievement of higher insight, and unflagging concern with all matters effecting the sociopolitical order (not simply "holy rites") are all as it were Hegelian "moments" in a higher unity. Yet in the course of time, the different perspectives of his disciples on "what is most important" and how the moments relate to each other were to lead to quite divergent perspectives. In the third century, the great Legalist thinker Han Fei-tzu would refer to eight schools of Confucian thought. One can even say that some of the "divergent threads" themselves even contributed to the rise of hostile modes of thought.

Here let me mention some characterizations of the Master's immediate disciples which seem to emerge from the *Analects* as well as from descriptions in other sources, such as Ssu-ma Ch'ien and Hsün-tzu. There is, first of all, the saintly and somewhat mysterious personality of Yen Hui. He seems to be the Master's favorite disciple and his early death deeply affects him. Of all the disciples he seems to have come closest both to the intuitive grasp of the "underlying unity" and the achievement of *jen,* and Confucius' ardent admiration for him helps establish the centrality of *jen* in Confucius' total vision. His own appreciation of the Master's *tao* gives us some inkling of his grasp of the mysterious element in Confucius' outlook. "The more I strain to gaze at it, the higher it soars. The deeper I dive into it, the harder it becomes. I see it in front of me and it is suddenly behind me. Step by step, the Master skillfully leads one on. He has broadened me with culture [*wen*] and restrained me with *li.* Even if I wanted to stop, I cannot. Even when I strain all my capacities, something lofty still looms ahead."[190] It is not clear that he ever serves in public office even though he desires to do so. It is thus no wonder that the Chuang-tzu, who uses both Confucius and Yen Hui for his own purposes, makes him a recipient of his own mystic gnosis.

In Tzu-lu we find an entirely different personality. A bold young man of ardent temper, he may have been a professional warrior before becoming the Master's disciple. He is almost the embodiment of martial courage and it is to him that the Master particularly stresses the limitations of courage and daring as isolated virtues in themselves. He is not an intellectual or scholar and must be convinced of the need for learning; yet he is deeply committed to "righteousness" and seems to be almost a prototype of the warrior hero (*yu-hsia*) who would defend the right with his broad sword. He does not, indeed, appreciate subtleties and ambiguities. He seems, however, to be a man of real administrative ability and Confucius deeply appreciates both his practical abilities, his activistic courage and his enthusiasm for doing the right.

At one point, Tzu-lu reveals to the Master his life dream, " 'Give me a country of a thousand chariots hemmed in by powerful states or invaded by powerful armies, plagued with drought and starvation and in the space of three years, I could endow the people with courage and teach them right conduct.' At this, the Master smiled."[191] In his critique of this dream, the Master says, "in governing a state, one must rely on *li*. His words showed no evidence of a concern for 'yielding' [*jang*]. That is why I smiled at him."[192] Tzu-lu's confidence in his ability to do good completely overlooks the fact that the insidious lust for power and glory can overcome all aspirations to goodness and all ability to control these passions. The ability to yield—which is associated with the sincere practice of *li*—is more fundamental to good government than anything else. Elsewhere, indeed, we find Tzu-lu being criticized when in office for supporting a questionable undertaking of the Chi clan. Yet we nevertheless are left with the impression that the Master appreciates his courage, his eagerness to do good, and his practical abilities.

Tzu-chang, one would gather, is also not addicted to the formalities of *li*; Hsün-tzu will later rebuke him for his lofty disregard for all external appearances. He adopts a lofty moral posture of openness to all men and great magnanimity. He is prepared to associate with all men. To the finicky and ceremonious Tzu-hsia, who says that "one should associate only with those with whom it is proper to associate and keep away from those with whom it is not proper to associate," Tzu-chang replies, "what I have heard is different. A noble man honors men of worth, but is open to all men. He praises the good and pities the incapable. Am I a man of outstanding worth? Why should I not be open to other men? Am I not a man of worth? Then others will keep away from me. Why should I keep away from others?"[193] Tzu-chang has great confidence in his own moral attainment. He cannot be tainted by his associations. Yet Confucius himself is not so self-confident in this matter and his extremely earnest young disciple, Tseng-tzu, seems to imply that Tzu-chang makes too easy a show of his own lofty idealism.[194] When the Master accuses him of "going beyond" one would assume that he goes beyond in that he has an excessive trust in his own moral elevation and does not feel the need to submit to the control of *li* and scrupulous self-examination.

Tzu-hsia and Tzu-yu represent other tendencies. They are both masters in their knowledge of the cultural heritage.[195] In the later tradition, they are even credited with preserving the knowledge of the four basic disciples of *"Documents, Poetry, li,* and music." Tzu-hsia and Tzu-yu are associated with the scrupulous accumulation of learning. Tzu-hsia thus says, "He who from day to day is conscious of what he lacks and from month to month does not forget what he has mastered can be said to love learning."[196] Tzu-hsia is even more closely associated with the scrupulous attention to the practice of *li* in particular. He does, to be sure, insist that one must constantly think of what one has learned.[197] One would gather, however, that the Master does not think that he has fully realized the inner spirit of either learning or *li.* If Tzu-chang goes beyond, Tzu-hsia with his unimaginative diligence falls short.[198] It is Tzu-hsia who is admonished by the Master not to be a small-minded type of *ju.* Tzu-yu, while deeply committed to learning, does not share what he regards as Tzu-hsia's scrupulous overpreoccupation with the practice of the minor *li.* He, in fact, attacks the latter's petty ritualism. "When it comes to sprinkling and sweeping, answering summons, and replying to questions coming forward and retiring, Tzu-hsia's disciples are quite acceptable, but these are minor matters. When it comes to the essential, they are at a loss."[199] Tzu-hsia indignantly replies in essence that, in learning, there is a logical order and that one teaches people step by step according to their capacities. Only the sage sees the beginning and end in one embracing glance. It is interesting to note that Hsün-tzu later delivers a stinging attack on the disciples of both Tzu-hsia and Tzu-yu. Despite his own devotion to both learning and *li,* he describes them as groups in which both *li* and learning have become detached from all connection to the higher concerns of Confucianism and from significant engagement in the moral tasks of the age.

I have here provided selected impressionistic sketches of some of the Master's disciples based on the most ancient textual material available.[200] Most of them are attracted to the Master because of the power of the vision which he projects and undoubtedly most wish to absorb the vision, yet each inevitably sees the whole from his own particular perspective. This perspective often assumes hardened and even exaggerated forms, particularly as they come to be linked in complex ways with vested interests among the disciples of the disciples. The vision thus turns into a problematique and yet in some way it continues to exercise its hold as a total vision, calling for every renewed hermeneutical effort.

At the time of the Master's death in 479 B.C., he had every reason to be profoundly discouraged concerning his public hopes. If he had lived longer, his discouragement would probably have increased. From his point of view, the entire evolution from the Spring and Autumn period to the period of Warring States would have appeared as a further descent into darkness. It is thus not surprising that in the centuries which followed there would emerge tendencies which, instead of attributing the failure of the vision to the inscrutability of Heaven's ways, would challenge the very premises of the vision itself.

# CHAPTER 4

# MO-TZU'S CHALLENGE

S CHOLARS AGREE that the three centuries following the death of Confucius mark a decisive period of transition in the course of Chinese history. The decadent tendencies deplored by Confucius accelerate. The ghostlike authority of the Chou house gradually fades, giving way completely to an uninhibited struggle for survival and domination among the states of the Chinese world and finally leading to the dominance of a few large "superstates." Within those states there is a steady decline of the old upper aristocratic families and the steady march toward a more bureaucratic organization of power. Many of the offices of these states are filled by elements of the new "floating stratum" emerging between the peasantry and the older aristocracy.

One element within this stratum is a new merchant class which reflects the rise of a money economy and growth in production, improvement in communications, and the growing tastes for luxury of the princes and their establishments.[1] How significant this commercial sector became in the economy as a whole is still an unresolved question. The word *shih*, which had been applied to the stratum of lower service nobility, is now applied to that whole new "intelligentsia" that wanders about from state to state offering its wisdom and expertise to the princes of the time. As in the case of Confucius and his own disciples, members of this group may have been drawn in large part from the older political stratum of *shih*, but also from déclassé upper nobility or even from below. The princes of the time are eager to staff their governments with "men of merit" wholly dependent on the princely power, although it is by no means easy in an age of utter confusion to determine where true merit lies. Some princes even become patrons of learning—who for varying motives are prepared to support clienteles of wandering *shih* who do not necessarily serve in office. Indeed as the "hundred schools" proliferate, some were willing to sponsor open intellectual debates and even developed a taste for them.

The great prototype of such "enlightened" princes is Duke Wen of the newly risen state of Wei (446–395 B.C.).[2] Duke Wen illustrates the profoundly conflicting intellectual currents to which such patrons were exposed. If, as recorded, he began by being a true follower of Confucius' disciple Tzu-hsia, in his actual political practice he was soon won over to the "new realism" of the "proto-Legalists" Li K'o and Wu Ch'i.[3] It should be added that one additional element in this new floating stratum are the wandering free-floating professional warriors who also managed to gain the patronage of the princely class.

As far as the lives of the masses are concerned, there must have been growing distress and dislocation, due to the unending wars, ruthless exploitation, and the loss of whatever economic security existed under the older systems of boundedness to the soil. At the same time, however, there is a new development in agriculture—the emergence of what has been called "private property." I use the term advisedly, because in the modern West it suggests a kind of Lockean, legally defined absolute dominion that is not all suggested by the Chinese texts, which link the growth of individual tenure to the growing power of the princes to control the output of agricultural producers, to assign lands directly to peasants, and to tax them directly. This all coincides with the weakening of the older nobility, which had in the past enjoyed the income provided by corvée labor on various tracts of land. Contemporary discussions of this period in the People's Republic put these issues under the rubric of the "rise of the landlord class." If the notion of a landlord class suggests that with the rise of "private property" a whole element within the peasantry can now become large landed proprietors through strictly economic methods, it seems to me that the evidence for the widespread existence of such a new class initially separated from the evolution of the political order seems largely absent in the literature we presently have. The evidence rather indicates that the new private property was subject to heavy control and heavy exactions by the holders of political power and that the fate of whatever new ruling class was emerging, whatever its sources of income, was closely tied to the developing bureaucratic political order. It hardly resembles either the class of what we call feudal lords in medieval Europe or the gentry of seventeenth-century England. At the same time, there may have also existed the possibility for some elements of the peasantry and the growing class of craftsmen and merchants to release themselves from the land and to take advantage of new opportunities for upward mobility.

The historic Mo-tzu (Mo ti), whose dates have been calculated as lying somewhere between the early fifth century and the beginning of the fourth century (circa 480–390 B.C., according to the calculations of Ch'ien Mu), lives at the beginning of this major transition.[4] The paucity of information about him encourages much speculation about who he was and what class or stratum he "represented." Even his surname is a matter of dispute—some arguing that it is not a surname at all but a designation which refers to some aspect of his life, such as the possibility that he had been a convict or a craftsman. He may well have been of plebeian origins, but his education in the traditional culture was certainly broad and impressive. Whatever his origin, he identifies himself wholeheartedly with the *shih* and "men of worth" (*hsien*) who aspire to state service. This fact has led some scholars in modern China who have regarded his philosophy as reactionary rather than progressive (such as Kuo Mo-jo) to identify him as a member of the *shih* class. But the ponderous and clumsy style of his book does suggest the "solemn self-educated man," as Graham suggests.[5] It lacks the aristocratic grace of the *Analects*.

While there may be some ground for suspecting a plebeian background, the claim that he is an artisan seems hardly proven, based as it is on assumptions about what craftsmen as such thought. His concern with military technology and with the arts and crafts does not prove that he is a craftsman any more than the fact that his movement is organized along military lines proves that he is a member of the professional warrior stratum. His movement may have attracted many commoners, but it may also have attracted déclassé nobles and disillusioned Confucianists. The later Mohist "logicians" who became caught up in the task of creating what might be called a true scientific language were certainly "intellectuals" who could easily lose themselves in the implicit logic of the intellectual enterprise despite the utilitarian teachings of their master.

The text itself, we are told, originally consisted of seventy-one chapters, of which fifty-three survive. Of these, some eleven deal with the arts of war and military technology, while six deal with an area which Graham calls "logic, ethics, and science." These latter chapters are patently a later development of the school perhaps dating from the third century, and the chapters on military science may also represent a later development. The remaining chapters, which either directly quote Mo-tzu or directly pass on his words, are generally thought to represent his doctrines quite adequately. Among the original chapters one finds ten large themes, including "Rejecting Fatalism," "Heaven's Will," "Universal Love," etc., which are treated in triads of three chapters apiece (although several of the chapters are missing) that seem to represent three different versions of the Master's doctrine, thought by some to belong to the variant traditions of different groups in the movement. Yet the doctrine as a whole seems remarkably coherent.

Mohism, in striking contrast to Confucianism, is a movement with its own religious military organization headed by a kind of Supreme Master (*chu-tzu*). This urge to organize is, I think, entirely consistent with the entire Mohist outlook.

Let us approach Mo-tzu's doctrine by looking at the assumptions which he shares with the Confucius of the *Analects*. We are, in fact, informed by the *Huai-nan-tzu* book of the early Han period that "Mo-tzu studied the teachings of the Confucianists and accepted [or received] the methods of Confucius."[6] The supreme public goal of Confucius is to "bring peace to the world"—to create a society in which all men will enjoy peace, economic security, and harmony. The noble man's self-realization may, of course, be considered a parallel goal, yet in the Master's vision it is clearly subordinate to the universal social goal. There can be no doubt whatsoever of Mo-tzu's profound commitment to this ultimate goal. Like Confucius—and here both simply share a common cultural orientation—he is convinced that the achievement of this goal must be a total sociopolitical enterprise which can be realized only by an elite vanguard operating through the political order. "Only the ruler of the state can unite and make uniform the state's standards of morality" (*kuo chih i*).[7] The concept of the pyramidal order in which the ultimate responsibility for the entire social order is to be found at the top remains intact although the concept of "order" itself undergoes a radical change. At one point Mo-tzu explicitly separates Confucius from his latter day disciples. Ch'eng-tzu asks: "If you attack the Confucian literati [*ju*], why do you praise Confucius?" Mo-tzu replies, "What I approve is that which is true and cannot be changed."[8]

Yet it is the burning conviction of Mo-tzu that there is much that is not true and that the latter-day Confucianists embody this untruth. What he notes in them first of all is their enormous passivity in the face of fate (*ming*)—a passivity which he cannot disassociate from their entire attitude toward the universe, toward the whole area which we call religion. Despite the indisputably activist, mundane, and utilitarian bent of Mo-tzu's thought, it seems appropriate to consider his attack on Confucius by beginning with his views on religion and fate.

## Fate, Heaven, and Spirits

We have already noted in the *Analects* how vast are the areas of experience over which humans do not exercise control and over which they do not aspire to exercise control. Even in the *Analects*, however much Confucius yearns to transform the human world and to influence his environment, the only area he can ultimately claim to control is that of his own self-cultivation and his capacity to exercise influence over his disciples. Yet he never ceases to look for signs that the actualization of Heaven's goals for mankind may become possible. Among the *ju* whom we encounter in the book of Mo-tzu, one would gather that their discouragement with Heaven's inscrutable ways has gone much further and is closely related to their "irreligion"—in some cases to an outright denial of belief in the ancestral spirits and nature deities and even to doubts that Heaven is concerned with man's historic fate. They are nevertheless described as clinging convulsively to the cultivation of *li*, music, and the study of the sacred literature. It is possible that most of the *ju* whom Mo-tzu meets belong to the Tzu-hsia/Tzu-yu strain of Confucianism described above and, if we assume that the word *ju* originally referred to the entire group of cultural experts in rites and in the knowledge of the sacred literature, it may be that the majority of the Confucianists (*ju*) described belonged to this larger group.[9] If they are indeed disciples of Tzu-hsia and Tzu-yu, they give the impression of embitterment, disillusionment, and, in the eyes of Mo-tzu, even of cynicism. As cultural experts their services are still "saleable." Mo-tzu strongly implies that their major concern is with their own emoluments and with a life of ease.

To Mo-tzu there is a profound connection between their general life attitudes and their views on fate, Heaven, and the spirits. At one point he speaks of the four policies or tenets of the Confucianists which are bringing ruin to the world: (1) they claim that Heaven does not make itself manifest (*wu ming*), that the spirits do not display divine powers (*pu shen*), and that neither Heaven nor spirits speak; (2) they indulge in excessive and wasteful rites of mourning; (3) they indulge in the luxurious extravagances of music and dance; and (4) they believe that length of life, poverty and wealth, order and disorder, and safety and danger are all governed by fate.[10] The combination of these attitudes may indeed seem incongruous. Yet in fact it reminds us of Fingarette's total concentration of the "religious" impulse of Confucianism on the practice of holy rite and music. Man can remain in contact with the *tao* of an inscrutable universe precisely through music and the practice of rites. Here indeed we find religious rites totally detached from the objects of worship. The *li*, including religious rites, have themselves become the center of religious-cultural meaning. At one point in a dialogue of Mo-tzu with the Confucianist Kung Meng, the latter says, "There are no spirits," and he also says that "one must study the sacrificial rites."

Mo-tzu replies: "To maintain that there are no spirits and to study the sacrificial rites is like studying the ceremonies for treating guests without having any guests."[11] Kung Meng's lack of faith in the spirits seems to be closely linked to a deep despair concerning any kind of Heavenly concern for human fate arising out of the contemplation of the fate of Confucius himself. Kung Meng-tzu says: "In ancient times those who achieved the rank of the Son of Heaven were the supreme sages. Those next to them [in wisdom] became prime ministers and high officials. Now Confucius mastered the *Poetry* and the *Documents,* was deeply versed in rites and music, and knew all things in detail. If we assume that Confucius should have been a sage-king why did he not become a Son of Heaven?"[12] Here we have an early expression of the notion, which later played a large role, that Confucius should have become the sage-king founder of a new dynasty. The *Analects* provide no evidence that the Master himself believed this or that his own faith in Heaven's ultimate providence was shaken by his failure to become a sage-king. Yet if this belief had become widespread among some disciples, this may be one reason for the collapse of a belief based on a very particular version of providentialism. Kung Meng-tzu's statement seems to suggest that such Heavenly providence may have been operative in the past but that Heaven, for inscrutable reasons, no longer manifested its concerns with the human world. Mo-tzu himself is not shaken in his own religious beliefs by this assertion. He simply denies the premise and brusquely dismisses Confucius' qualifications. "The sage must revere Heaven and serve the spirits, love men universally and stress frugality. Herein lies knowledge. Now you say Confucius had mastered the *Documents* and *Poetry,* [etc.] . . . and was therefore fit to be a Son of Heaven. This is like counting a man's teeth to prove his wealth."[13] The defect lay in the limits of Confucius' own vision.

Fatalism, lack of faith in Heaven's providence and the efficacy or even existence of the spirits, heavy emphasis on ritual and music, and passivity in all other areas of life are—at least in Mo-tzu's eyes—organically related. The same Kung Meng who rejects the spirits and the providence of Heaven is obsessively concerned with the "preservation of ancient words and ancient dress" and the meticulous observation of the three-year mourning rites. Indeed, in dealing with the problem of the relationship of *jen* and *li,* he leans very heavily to the priority of *li* and says quite boldly that "One must use ancient dress and ancient language—after that there will be *jen.*"[14] The proper and narrow domain of the noble man's behavior is the assiduous practice of rites, ceremonies, and music including, of course, maintaining the proper external demeanor. "The noble man maintains his dignity and waits."[15] Here Kung Meng's faith is in what Fingarette calls the "magical" power of *li* and his belief in it seems genuine. "If he is truly a good man who will not know him?"[16] He goes on to compare the power of a good man who has achieved his goodness by unflagging cultivation of the *li* to a beautiful woman for whom men will fight even though she remains in seclusion. Mo-tzu in reply rudely points out that in a disordered age men will still fight for a beautiful woman but few will seek out a "good man." "Unless he forces them to listen no one will know him."[17] To Mo-tzu, who has no faith in the magic power of *li* and music, Kung Meng's absorption in this futile realm of activity represents a total surrender to the forces of fate.

The crux of the matter is that Mo-tzu perceives a direct relationship between the notion of the passive indifference of Heaven and the passivity or even nonexistence of the spirits, and the passivity and impotence of the Confucianists of his time. He attacks the movement toward the concept of an impersonal order, immanent in nature and society, from which the power of conscious will has been banished. Far from perceiving the problem in terms of the modern Western antithesis between a world in which the will of God or the gods governs all and a world in which men control their own destiny, he perceives an antithesis between the concept of a world—*both* cosmic *and* human—as an inscrutable, impersonal order (which may nevertheless embody magical and mysterious properties) beyond the control of any conscious will and a world in which order itself is the achievement of the strenuous efforts of the wills of both gods and men. What the advocates of "fate" deny is the active, intentional will of *both* gods and men. In a world engulfed by aggressive wars of strong states against weak states, by the extravagant luxuries of the rich and powerful, and by the grinding poverty of the masses, the paralyzing belief in fate undermines the will of all.

What Mo-tzu defiantly projects is a radically different vision of the foundations of order, both cosmic and human, which he firmly believes is based on the true nature of the older religious tradition. There is no preexistent, immanent order of things. The order of human society (and, one would presume, of the cosmos) is produced and maintained by the purposeful cooperation of Heaven, spirits, and men of good will in the face of what seems to be the inherently centrifugal tendencies of the pluralistic, recalcitrant world of the "ten thousand things." This cooperation must be sustained and unremitting. Order must be imposed on chaos. Unless men believe that Heaven, the spirits, and they themselves can exert themselves constantly and without relaxation against the disintegrating tendencies, disorder and chaos will prevail. One thus perceives that the three triads of chapters on "Heaven's Will," "Throwing Light on the Spirits," and "Rejection of Fate" are all organically related.

As in the case of Confucius, Mo-tzu remains, however, essentially preoccupied with the human world and his religion is totally related to his human concerns. There are no cosmogonic accounts and not much discussion of how Heaven and the spirits maintain the order of nature, except for a constant implication that the disorders of nature which effect men are due to Heaven's displeasure.

While we find no cosmogony in the Mo-tzu, we do find an account of the origins of human order which, for the first time in the texts available to us, provides us with an account of men in a "state of nature." This theme of how order is created out of chaos accords, in fact, very well with the entire religious outlook outlined above. Order is wrested from chaos:

> In ancient times when the people were first engendered at a time when there was no government it is said that men all had their own views of what was right. For one man there was one view of what was right and for two men two views, for ten men, ten views . . . Every man affirmed his own view and negated the views of others, hence in their intercourse there was constant strife. Within the family, fathers, sons, and brothers resented and hated each other . . . isolated and scattered they could achieve no harmony or cooperation . . . the masses were as hostile to each other as fire and water . . . the disorder in the world was like that of birds and beasts. It was then understood that the cause of the disorder in the world was the lack of a ruler . . . Therefore the wisest and most capable was selected as the Son of Heaven. Once the Son of Heaven was established, since his strength was insufficient, there was again a selection of the wisest and most capable and they were appointed as the three ministers . . .[18]

Now this astonishing account of the origins of the state so reminiscent of Hobbes begins with a world of self-regarding individuals. There is no mention of an immanent tendency toward morality, since the people's "view of what was right" (i) was simply that they should serve their own individual interests. Most shocking of all is the denial that the sacred ties of family rooted in ancestor worship are in any way able to restrain the war of man against man—this despite Mo-tzu's reaffirmation of the divine powers of the spirits. Here one might say that two preoccupations of Mo-tzu are in sharp tension with each other. On the one hand he wishes to stress the central importance of the active *will* of and intelligence of Heaven, spirits, and men. At the same time he is anxious to deny any notion of an immanent good in individuals or any latent good order of society. The notion of any immanent propensity toward harmony within the biological family must be rejected along with all other sorts of immanence, although it is also possible that his views of the family may also reflect his own life experiences. Above all, however, the good is nothing pregiven. The good must be achieved! With all this, however, there is still the overriding assumption which relates Mo-tzu, despite his uncharacteristic views, to a major cultural orientation—his tendency to look at the situation wholly from the point of view of a total sociopolitical order.

There is no necessary relation between Mo-tzu's belief in the effective will of Heaven and the spirits and his further belief that Heaven and the spirits relate to mankind only through the mediation of the political order. Hobbes must devote a considerable portion of his *Leviathan* (parts 3 and 4) to refute Judeo-Christian notions that God relates to humans through prophets, churches, individual inspiration, and other ways which totally by-pass the political order. In Mo-tzu's case the notion already adumbrated in the oracle bone inscriptions that the high god's channel of communication with humanity is through the universal king remains assumed and unchallenged. Indeed one can say that the role of the Son of Heaven is in fact enhanced. While Confucianism posits the individual family as an alternative source of moral authority within society alongside that of the Son of Heaven, Mo-tzu's image of a "state of nature" as a state of atomized individuals in all-out conflict with each other seems to lead, by a logic similar to that of Hobbes, to the notion that only by the concentration of an undivided authority or "sovereignty" in one ruler can conflicts among individuals or even groups be overcome.[19] There must be a universal conformity to the will of those above, culminating in the person of the Son of Heaven, who must, however, conform his own will to the will of Heaven. This notion is closely related to the larger notion that in dealing with the common good of society (*tien-hsia chih li*) one must begin with the general interest of the whole of society and regard all particular interests, whether of individuals or groups, only from the point of view of the whole. This can be done, however, only when one has a situation "where everyone approves of what is approved by the Son of Heaven and everyone rejects what is rejected by the Son of Heaven."[20] A Son of Heaven who truly fears the active will of Heaven and of the spirits who loves mankind and desire its welfare will necessarily strive for the common good.

It is a curious fact that in two of the accounts of the origins of the state, it is simply stated that "the wisest and most able was chosen as Son of Heaven." In the third variant, however, it is stated that "the world wishing to unify the ideas of what was right [*i*] chose the wisest man."[21] It has been suggested that here we have almost something like the notion of a social contract. It is indeed striking that Mo-tzu does not, in the text as we now have it, say that Heaven chose the wise man. Is it possible that Mo-tzu keeps Heaven out of this entire account of the origins of mankind because he is troubled by the question of why a good Heaven created such a disordered creature? Whatever may be the answer one should nevertheless hesitate to see a parallel to Hobbes's social contract in which putatively equal individuals "covenant" with each other to establish a sovereign power. What Mo-tzu emphasizes above all is the choice of the "wisest and ablest" as the Son of Heaven, and one must assume that it is the wisest and ablest among men who by their comprehension of the situation are prompted to do the choosing. Those who have no wisdom are not likely to understand that "the reason why disorder exists in the world is due to the fact that there is no ruler."[22] Hobbes's concept of the contract is, however, based squarely on the assumption "that nature hath made men so equal in the faculties of body and mind; as that though there be found one man sometimes manifestly stronger in body or of quicker mind than another; yet when all is reckoned together the difference between man and man is not so considerable."[23] There is even no necessary implication that the man or men to whom all agree to surrender their common power are necessarily wiser or more sagacious than the rest. In effect, what they have surrendered to is the abstract entity of the "Sovereign Power." Hobbes explicitly attacks Aristotle because "for the foundation of his doctrine, he maketh men by Nature, some more worthy to Command meaning the wiser sort (such as he thought himself to be for his Philosophy); others to serve (meaning those that had strong bodies, but were no Philosopher as he) as if Master and Servant were not introduced by consent of men, but by difference of Wit."[24] While both Confucius and Mo-tzu have a conception of an ongoing structure of government (the "kingship" is again not a person but an institution), the view of both remains very much focused on the quality of the men who occupy these institutions and not simply on any "sovereign power" in abstracto. At least in the case of the founding sage-king, his wisdom and ability are crucial.

To Mo-tzu, while men in a "state of nature" may be equal in their lamentable self-regard, they obviously differ from each other enormously in their intellectual capacities and we shall indeed find that in some ways the "plebeian" Mo-tzu seems much more committed to intellect as a value than is Confucius, since it is above all through his own skill in reasoning (*pien-hui*) that he undermines the false assumptions of the Confucianists and establishes the truth of his own doctrine.[25] It is precisely through their superior "wit" that the wise and able men in the "state of nature" were able to attain a true understanding of the human and divine worlds. One is not relying on simple, external abstract mechanisms of control.

Not only did the sages understand that if men continued to pursue their own self-interest all would be miserable but they also understood that Heaven and the spirits love men and wish to benefit them. They understood that Heaven wishes them to bring into being a system in which those who act well will be rewarded and those who act wickedly will be punished. Above all they understood that Heaven provides the ultimate model (*fa i*) for men. Since all men and women, whether they be fathers, mothers, teachers, or rulers, tend to be nonloving and self-interested, only Heaven, in its transcendental impartiality, sets the pattern for men. "Heaven is all-embracing and not selfish, Heaven is generous and ungrudging; Heaven's understanding is eternal and never declines. Therefore the sage-kings make Heaven their standard . . . Heaven displays its love of all men by giving them all life and sustaining them. If one flouts Heaven, Heaven will inflict calamities. Because the sages made Heaven their standard all their actions were effective [*yu-wei*]."[26] Thus the sage-kings were the active collaborators of Heaven in "constructing" an ideal pattern of human society. I use the Western word "constructing" here in relation to the metaphor of order because, in this case, it eminently seems to apply.

## The Utilitarian Ethic

What Heaven and the spirits desire is for men to be prosperous, to be secure, and to live in peace. Sages and worthy men who model themselves on Heaven have no other aim than to benefit mankind. The word I have here used for "benefit" is a translation of the word *lì*, which also appears in the *Analects* in an entirely pejorative sense. In the *Analects* it means a concern with personal interest and it is the opposite of the motive of *i*, or righteousness. Mo-tzu's use of the term in his own way thus almost suggests a gesture of defiance.

The issue should, however, be made more precise. Confucius, as we have seen, is certainly interested in benefitting society. He wishes the people to be "enriched," to enjoy peace and security. One might say that he wishes even more for them. He would have them participate in the religious and aesthetic satisfactions associated with *li* and music. It is, however, his point of view that such benefits can be achieved only in a society in which the vanguard of society has been able to conquer within itself all those individual passions for gain and self-aggrandizement which make the realization of such social goals unattainable. Hence the noble man's constant and scrupulous scrutiny of his own motives is crucial to the achievement of the social goals themselves. Mo-tzu, as we have seen, has, however, set out from the assumption that men in a "state of nature" are all overwhelmingly bent on benefitting themselves. It is a situation which cannot be remedied by extolling "virtue" as an end in itself. One must somehow—by every means possible—bring the self-enclosed egoists which we find in the state of nature to the conviction that their own self-interest is entirely dependent on the general interest of all of mankind. The "dialectical" logical chapters of the Mo-tzu written at a much later date and representing new developments nevertheless greatly illuminate the original doctrine. At one point we find a precise and clear-cut definition of the term righteousness (*i*). "Righteousness is benefitting" (*li*), followed by an explanation describing the righteous man. "In intent, he takes the whole world as his field. In ability, he is able to benefit it. He is not necessarily employed."[27] Man inevitably "loves himself" or is basically concerned with his own vital interests. The man of righteousness is the man who clearly *understands* that his own interests and the interests of all can be served *only* when "the greatest happiness of the greatest number" is achieved. He understands that one's "object" of benefitting must, in the first instance, be the whole (human) world. Only when the "general interest" of the world (*tien-hsia chih li*) has been served can the genuine interests of individuals be met.[28] The essence of the matter is that the Mohist truly "righteous man's" attention is totally and undeviatingly fixed on the world "out there." He is totally oriented toward "doing good" and not preoccupied with "being good." This attitude is made clear in the Mohist discussions of the other ethical virtues and especially in the dialectic chapters. In dealing with *jen* in the *Analects* we have seen that it is a kind of total inner excellence of soul from which all the other virtues flow. It is this inner quality that makes it possible for men to "love" all other men in due degree ("graded love"). Here again the Mohist definition is direct and unambiguously outer-oriented. "*Jen* is to love [others] as individuals." In the appended explanation we find it stated "The love of oneself is not for the sake of using oneself [not like loving a horse]."[29] The point here is very subtle. To the later Mohists, love by no means excludes love of oneself. Just as one, in loving oneself, does not think of oneself as a means to other ends, one should have the same attitude toward other human beings. Here love is defined almost in terms of Kant's principle of treating all men as ends in themselves. The ultimate beneficiaries of all love are the majority of individuals who make up mankind, although we shall find that this theoretical equal love of all may demand the conferral of quite unequal benefits (as with fairness in the case of Rawls) and also may require the sacrifice of some individuals. Interesting as this point is, however, what I would here emphasize is the definition of *jen* wholly in terms of love—an outwardly oriented disposition of mind which focuses wholly on achieving the benefit of others. This outward orientation is made even more clear in another late Mohist proposition which reflects a debate echoes of which we shall later encounter in the book of Mencius. "It is a fallacy to suppose that *jen* is 'inner' and righteousness [*i*] is 'outer.' *Jen* is love. To be righteous is to benefit. Loving and benefitting are on this side; the loved and the benefitted are on that side."[30]

All the virtues are, in effect, outer-oriented dispositions oriented toward achieving results in the world "out there" and never, as Graham points out, "directed toward the subjective side of experience." This does not mean that there is no affective side of experience or that feelings do not affect the world, but the Confucian focus on the inner—the entire brooding on purity of motivation—is a useless diversion from the overwhelming task. Mo-tzu here seems to share the pathos of both the modern radical and the modern technocrat.

States of feeling are in fact crucial—particularly the feeling of "love," however that term is defined.[31] Unless men can be induced to love all men universally, the general interests of mankind as a whole will never be realized. In the end, only universal love can enable individuals to identify their own interests with the interests of others. The universality or indivisibility of love for all men must be the starting point, and here we shall find that Mo-tzu is, in one sense, more radical in his point of departure than Hobbes. While Hobbes very much stresses the "warre of every man against every man," he admits that even "among the savage people in many places of America" there is "the government of small Families, that concord whereof dependeth on naturall lust."[32] Whether lust here simply means sex or instinctive family affection it is possible even in a state of nature for some sort of "we group" feeling to exist. Even more significantly, Hobbes is convinced that in the "warring states" world of seventeenth-century Europe, it is quite possible for an individual nation-state to establish a true "commonwealth" within its borders. The savage state of nature in the international arena of his time seems to bother him not at all.

In Mo-tzu's universal state of nature, the war of every man against every other exists even within the bosom of the family. Only

when the wisest man was chosen as the *universal* king of all civilization was he able to bring about by various means a state of universal
indivisible love for and the universal benefit of mankind. Without
universal love of all (civilized?) mankind, even the partial loves of
family group and of separate states are inconceivable. Only when
universal love is in place do the various loves which pertain to particular groups and individuals become possible. One can proceed
only from the whole to the parts. "If we could cause all men to love
each other universally, to love others as they love themselves would
there any longer be any unfiliality? One would regard one's father,
elder brother and ruler as one regards oneself."[33] It is only with *universal* love that partial loves become possible and yet remain within
their proper limits. Otherwise all these groups become, as it were,
particular collective egos in constant conflict with each other and
the interest of society as a whole.

Implicit in all this is the assumption that when the founding sages
established the state they did in fact create a kingdom of universal
love which had since degenerated, leaving behind not necessarily a
total collapse into a state of nature but rather a collapse into the
fragmented loyalties to particularistic entities, such as families and
individual egos.[34] Like Confucius, Mo-tzu shares the assumption
that the good order had arisen in past history although it had not
existed in the state of nature.

At this point his attack on the Confucian conception of the family
becomes most trenchant. A family in a total disordered society is
simply a special interest group. Robbers love their own families:
"They steal from other families in order to benefit their own."[35] The
notion of the family as a primary school of virtue which radiates its
influence over the environment is here completely negated. This is
the closest Chinese equivalent of Plato's view of the family as a focus
of narrow interests. Similarly, however, "the rulers of states love only
their own states. They attack other states in order to benefit their
own."[36] Love must be extended to the whole civilized world (or even
to all mankind) or it is nonexistent. Mo-tzu would have been astonished by Hobbes's notion that rulers who acted with unbridled ra-
pacity in the European international arena could have established
harmonious "commonwealths" within the boundaries of their own
states.

This, however, reminds us that in Hobbes's creation of the social
contract the sentiment of love—however love may be defined—plays
no role whatsoever. The individuals involved who are approximately equal in their mental powers all achieve a dispassionate understanding that peace and security are in the end preferable to the

miseries and "brutish state" of constant strife and insecurity and thus arrive at a reasoned decision to surrender their liberties to the sovereign power. After the establishment of the "civill estate," what mainly holds the state together are the criminal and civil laws which rest heavily on the coercive sanctions of the sovereign (even when these are held in reserve). Why then the emphasis on "universal love" in Mo-tzu? I must point out that he does not overlook "rewards and punishments." He still realizes that men will continue to love themselves. Even Heaven and the spirits do not simply love mankind. They are ever ready to punish the doers of evil and to reward the doers of good on all levels of society from the Son of Heaven down. Punishing and rewarding are also necessary instruments of rulers. What is more, it is made amply clear that the ultimate reason for universal love is that it is only through universal love that the general interests of mankind can be served. What the man of righteousness takes as his business is to actualize that which benefits the world (*t'ien-hsia chih li*) and to remove that which harms the world. What harms the world is universal strife. And what is the cause of this universal strife? "It arises from lack of mutual love."[37] Both rulers and people must be made to understand that only through universal love can they achieve the welfare of all.

It may be argued that a kind of love which is wholly the result of utilitarian reasoning hardly resembles the outpouring of either eros or agape. Graham asserts it is not an emotion at all.[38] Yet if it is not an emotion, it is certainly an abiding moral disposition and Mo-tzu seems to believe that it is both possible and necessary to cultivate this disposition. The word love (*ai*) might perhaps be translated more accurately by a much less charged word, such as universal fairness or sense of equity. In the later logical chapters we indeed find the assertion "that one may learn not to be concerned for oneself alone."[39] Another way of translating "love" might perhaps be "an impartial reasoned concern for all men as ends in themselves." There can be no doubt, however, that as an attitude it is indispensable to the achievement of the more tangible ends of welfare, peace, and security.

Clearly, Mo-tzu believes that the same human beings who must be controlled by rewards and punishments can also be impelled by the sentiment of love as he defines the word. His general appeal to the rulers of his time can be summarized as follows. Their own interests in wealth, security, and peace can be served only if they realize that they can enjoy these goods only in a world where universal love prevails. The rulers of large states who carry out aggressions against small states cause enormous sufferings to their own people as well as to others, and in the end they will incur the wrath of Heaven and the spirits. Heaven and the spirits love mankind impartially and will punish rulers who inflict suffering on men. Here we find a simultaneous appeal to ultimate self-interest, to fear of punishment, and the exhortations to love all combined in the same argument. The righteous man of worth uses every argument possible to persuade and cajole the rulers into "loving universally and benefitting all men." They must above all be persuaded that belief in fate should have nothing to do with their behavior. The cycle of "order and disorder" is not a matter of fate. Disorder is due to the misbehavior of evil rulers. Aggressive rulers who carry out needless wars against small states must be persuaded that, since war is not in the general interest of the world as a whole, it is not in their own interests. They must be reminded of the horrible economic costs to their own state and of the fact that their victories will stir up the jealousies of other states. Finally, if they display their own love for others, they will win the love of Heaven, of their own people, and of mankind, and they will reap the benefits of this love. They must above all realize that they, like their weaker subjects, stand beneath the stern judgment of Heaven.

As in the case of Confucius, the initiative for enabling all men to "love each other and benefit each other" lies with those above.[40] The authority which resides in the political order is still overwhelming. In the chapter on universal love, in order to prove the extraordinary charismatic power of those who possess political authority over their subjects, Mo-tzu invokes such stock example as that of King Ling of Ch'u who, because he loved his officials to have small waists, actually induced his courtiers to eat only one meal a day and to hold in their breath when tightening their belts.[41] Rulers can, after all, induce ordinary men to die for them in battle. Obviously, only those who can avail themselves of the aura of sacred political authority can induce people to love each other and benefit each other. The rulers must first of all rid the people's minds of the idea of fate. The insidious Confucian fatalists maintain that "if it is one's fate to be rich one will be rich. If it is one's fate to be poor one will be poor."[42] They thus persuade the people that it is futile for them to attempt to improve their own lot. While this is not the only cause of poverty, it plays a powerful negative role. Such doctrines as the doctrine that "respectful behavior is of no benefit and crime does no harm" undermine all efforts to establish a system of rewards for good behavior and punishment for evil behavior.[43] The people must also be imbued with the faith that Heaven and the spirits desire nothing more than mutual love among them. On the other side, getting rid of the waste of substance and energy involved in useless rites and music and bringing an end to wars of aggrandizement will enormously lighten the burdens of the people and convince them of the love and care of their rulers. They will gratefully respond to this love. By all these means, the masses will also learn to appreciate the benefits of mutual love and only then will their more particularistic relations also be illumined by love. If in the logical chapters "righteousness" takes the whole world as its "field," filiality takes parents as its "field."[44] Thus filiality and the other more particularistic commitments do not cease to exist. They simply become a smaller field within a larger total field and the righteousness which pervades the whole field is bound to pervade the smaller subdivisions.

## Utility, *Li*, and Music

Some elements in this program continue to remind us of the *Analects*. Despite the enormous differences in the attitude toward the family, we must remind ourselves that Confucius also does not expect the familial virtues to flourish among the people in a negative "total" environment. In Mo-tzu there is a much greater sense of urgency—one might almost say desperation—concerning the task of meeting the elemental needs of the people for food, shelter, clothing, security, and peace. Nothing less than a total and sustained concentration of all the energies of the society are required to attain this goal. Any diversion of society's resources for needless activities is a subtraction from what is required for subsistence. In the three chapters on "frugality" or "economy" (20, 21, 22), we are reminded at first of the *Analects*. The people are impoverished by corvée labor, by the exaction of taxes in kind by being dragged off to useless wars, and by the unconscionable luxuries of the powerful. It is interesting to note that despite Mo-tzu's alleged affiliation with the artisan class, he stresses very much that in ancient times the talents of artisans were used only to meet man's elemental needs.[45] To the extent that a segment of the class of craftsman was now involved in catering to the taste for sophisticated luxuries and ritual objects, Mo-tzu can hardly be said to have approved of their arts.

Where the confrontation with Confucius and Confucianists becomes most apparent is in the matter of *li* and music. It concerns not only the question of frugality but almost every issue that divides the two outlooks.

Let me begin, however, with all the necessary qualifications. Mo-tzu does not negate the notion of *li* (ceremony) entirely. He is, in fact, no egalitarian; he believes that initiative must begin in the political order and that the political order as well as the familial order must be hierarchically articulated according to rank, role, and status; consequently he accepts the view that social behavior should confirm this hierarchy. If men of worth are to be encouraged to work in government, they have every right to expect the material rewards and the *honors* which come with office. The ample remuneration of capable and worthy men is one of the necessary expenditures of government as are the signs of deference and respect which go with honor. The dialectic chapters define *li* as follows: "*Li* is respect [or reverence]." The appended explanation then states: "The nobles are addressed as 'sir' and the commoners by their given names . . . because modes of behavior are different for different ranks."[46] Here, again, *li* is basically a disposition to behavior in the public world. To the extent that the word *li* covers the sphere of respectful manners, it seems that Mo-tzu believes in *li*. It is also clear that he believes in the performance of all those religious rites of sacrifice which express men's respect for and gratitude toward Heaven and the spirits. In fact, one lamentable result of the extravagant mourning rites of the ruling class is that the impoverished masses do not even have sufficient surplus to carry out decent sacrifices to the spirits.[47]

The assumption seems to be that the truly necessary expression of proper modes of behavior, whether in the realm of manners or religious ritual, should require no great expenditure of substance or waste of energy. Mo-tzu's animus is directed particularly against the mourning rites of the ruling class with their ever more extravagant coffins, funerary goods, and tombs, as well as the lamentable notion of three-year abstention from all sorts of useful activity (chapter 25). They sap the time and energy so necessary to the tasks of government. The same applies for the realm of music.

The vehement attack on the "dysfunctionality" of *li* and music is, of course, based on Mo-tzu's total disbelief in their "magical" spiritual-ethical function. "Holy rite" as such and music in particular have nothing to do with the elevation of the soul. The virtues as Mo-tzu defines them are not at all reinforced by the practice of *li*. The righteous man simply understands the social need for deferential, differential behavior in dealing with people in different ranks and statuses. Beyond this, he understands the need for loving and serving all men despite their differences in statuses and has the will and energy to act appropriately in all life situations. Thus the enactment of *li* in no way fosters his own "excellence of soul" (*jen* in the Confucian sense) or, for that matter, of the souls of those to whom his ritual enactments are addressed. In carrying on religious sacrifices, he does so out of gratitude to the spirits and in order to please the spirits, not because he believes that the ritual makes him a nobler person. In this sense, ritual is not "magic" in Fingarette's sense.

If this is true of ritual and ceremony, it is true *a fortiori* of music. Music neither helps self-cultivation nor harmonizes society. Mo-tzu does not deny that the sounds of lutes, bells, and drums produce pleasure and, in fact, he sees nothing more than sensual pleasure in the Confucianists' enjoyment of music. "One does not deprive the people of their clothing and food in order to obtain that which pleases the eye, brings joy to the ear, is sweet to the mouth and brings ease to the body. The Man of *jen* does not do this."[48] The elevation of soul produced by noble music may have escaped him and even if he himself experienced it he would have denied that such "states of mind" in themselves produce moral results. In one rather remarkable dialogue with a Confucianist he asks: "Why does one perform music?" The latter replies: "One performs music for music's sake."[49] Mo-tzu replies: "You have not answered me. If someone asked you why does one need a house you would reply 'in order to avoid the cold in winter, the heat in summer and in order to separate man and woman' . . . Your answer is equivalent to saying that a house exists for a house's sake."[50] While Mo-tzu's reply is predictable, the Confucianist's assertion is somewhat arresting. It exemplifies the constricted "fatalistic" attitude of the circle of Confucianists with which Mo-tzu was in contact. Their conception of their roles has shrunk to that of custodians of rites and music in a disordered age. They still may believe that rites and music embody higher spiritual values, but they are profoundly convinced that order and disorder are largely in the hands of fate. They seem to have no great hope that they can have any immediate impact on the world of their time. They also, of course, may simply themselves take comfort in the solace which music provides. To Mo-tzu, this confirms their selfishness.

In sum, I think that Mo-tzu, having rejected all the positive grounds on the basis of which Confucianism exalts *li* and music, is free to see them as contributing nothing to the real needs of society and as a wasteful and harmful diversion from the "business of sage-kings above and the interests of the myriad people below."[51]

The reference to sensual pleasures, however, raises the question of Mo-tzu's attitude toward pleasure. He does not dismiss "wealth and status" as incentives, as is made quite apparent in the chapters on "Advancing Worthy Men" (8–10). If rulers wish to attract worthy and virtuous men to government they must "enrich them, respect them, honor them, and praise them."[52] However much Mo-tzu may lean to the side of meritocracy, there is no call whatever for economic equality or status equality. What then is to prevent the worthy men who attain wealth from indulging in all the luxuries of the flesh? To what extent is it legitimate for them to cultivate the more refined pleasures so long as they show wisdom in government? Somehow the prospect of the corruption of worthy men by wealth and power does not arise. There are, of course, no answers to any of those questions in the text. Yet one has the overall impression that in Mo-tzu's view these worthy men would live lives of the greatest simplicity and sobriety. Their luminous intelligence, righteousness, and fear and love of Heaven and the spirits would presumably shield them from temptation, and their understanding that the satisfaction of the people's basic needs in their most unadorned "utilitarian" form requires nothing less than the total commitment of all their energies would lead them to refrain from useless luxuries. Mo-tzu's greatest hero among the sage-kings of yore is the great Yü, who spent his life in unremitting toil in vast water control projects despite his high position and presumed wealth. Mo-tzu actually provides us at one point with a glimpse of his ideal society. It is not the primitive situation in which men lived in holes in the ground and wore animal skins. It is the unadorned purely functional culture created by the first sage-kings. They built houses high enough above the ground to avoid the damp, with walls sturdy enough to keep out the wind and cold, roofs solid enough to keep out the snow, sleet, and rain, and inner walls high enough to separate the sexes.[53] They made houses convenient for living and not for show. They invented textiles to keep people warm in winter and cool in summer, and not for display. There was an abundance of necessities and complete absence of frills. The presumption is that both people and rulers lived in this plain fashion. The message is clear throughout—the rulers' cultivation of luxury and display can be attained only through the impoverishment of the people.

One is nevertheless more inclined in the case of Mo-tzu than in the case of Confucius to ask why does not something like a notion of technico-economic progress emerge here? As we shall see, we have an outlook which will prove favorable to innovations in logic, optics, mechanics, and physics and will even conceive the project of forging a new more accurate "scientific" language. The book often does speak admiringly of the craftsman's mastery of his craft and does, in fact, favor certain *specific* kinds of technological innovation. Graham states that "the Mohists submit all traditional morality to the test of social utility and explicitly defend innovation."[54]

We must, however, scrutinize more closely this defense of innovation. A Confucianist repeats Confucius' sentiment that "the noble man transmits and does not invent." Mo-tzu replies: "Anciently, Yi invented the bow. Chu invented armor. Hsi Chung invented the cart [or chariot], Ch'iao Chui invented the boat. Are we to suppose that our present day armorers, tanners, wheelwrights, and carpenters are all noble men and those were all mean men?"[55] Yet this argument when examined closely does not necessarily imply any need for further invention in these areas. These inventors, as culture heroes, like the sage-kings themselves who first established the entire basic infrastructure of civilization, invented the basic and essential material tools of civilization. While Mo-tzu does maintain that the great inventors of essential artifacts were greater than their followers (as Confucius would no doubt admit in the case of the sage-kings), he does not imply that further innovations are necessary. In fact, as we have just seen, he would prefer to return to this eminently useful technology in its pristine, unelaborated state.

Yet where innovation is deemed *necessary,* Mo-tzu will favor it, as in the area of military technology. One of his main strategies for stopping the aggression of large powers against small powers is to do everything possible to improve the arts of defensive warfare, particularly in such matters as siege and defense. This interest is clearly spelled out in the military chapters, which no doubt reflect the expertise of his followers in matters of military engineering and military tactics.[56]

Mo-tzu's attitude toward innovation is wholly pragmatic. Where innovation seems necessary for the benefit of mankind, whether in military technology or in methods of argument, he favors innovation. On the other hand, as far as certain basic truths about society are concerned, he is eager to present himself as a transmitter. At one point he taunts his protagonist, Kung Meng, with the assertion: "You model yourself on *Chou* and do not model yourself on the *Hsia.* The 'ancient' that you look to is not ancient enough!"[57] Mo-tzu's hero is Yü, the founder of the Hsia dynasty, and one may assume that the ideal, unadorned civilization which he describes in Chapter 6 was his depiction of the Hsia, although he actually respects the sage-kings of all the "three dynasties." Mo-tzu's appeal to an ideal past may be the kind of conscious device which became widespread throughout the whole Warring States period. Since the notion that the good society had been realized in the past was deeply engrained in the dominant cultural orientation which had been so emphatically confirmed by Confucius, there was enormous ongoing pressure to ascribe one's ideas to ancient sages and sage-kings. If such ideas could be ascribed to figures of the truly unknown mythic past, the thinker was freer in his power of invention. Ku Chieh-kang, the eminent Chinese historian, has indeed proposed a view well summarized by Bodde as follows: "that the historical age of a myth (the period of history to which it purports to belong) usually stands in inverse ratio to its 'literary age' (the period when it is first actually recorded in the literature)."[58] Whatever may be the case with later myths about figures such as the "Yellow Emperor" and Fu Hsi, I would nevertheless suggest that Mo-tzu probably quite sincerely believes in his attributions. His very account of the origins of the state implies his profound belief in the wisdom of the founders. The fact that he obviously genuinely prefers civilization in its simple unadorned state suggests that there was nothing wildly implausible from his point of view in believing that the Hsia had been closer to his ideal than the Chou. He also no doubt believed that his conception of religion was closer to the true beliefs of the ancients.

In explaining Mo-tzu's failure to conceive of any idea of "economic development" through improvement in the technology of production, I suggest that Mo-tzu shares with Confucius and with many of the "creative minorities" in other contemporary civilizations, such as the Hebrew prophets and even Aristotle, a diagnosis of civilization which may associate a concern with technological innovation (including the social inventions of trade and money) not so much with "progress" as with war and immoderate luxury and display—with what were regarded as the pathologies of civilization. The existent economic technology and the existent traditions of the useful crafts were considered adequate to assure for the masses of mankind what was considered an adequate livelihood. It was, of course, a conception of adequacy which accepted natural disasters, plagues, and other hazards as part of the natural order of things. While Confucius would accept luxuries and amenities which were a necessary aspect of *li* and music (and even here he advocates economy rather than luxury), he certainly accepts this diagnosis. The fact that Mo-tzu so much stresses material needs does not dissuade him from the view that these needs are best satisfied in their most elemental forms. The problem is thus not that of the "growth of the forces of production" but the task of distribution.

In sum I would argue that Mo-tzu's utilitarian orientation favored neither innovation nor ancient practice as absolutes. Where innovation is necessary to benefit the world it should be pursued. Where ancient practice provided the basic principles of a happy society, it should be preserved.

## Men of Worth (*hsien*)

Nothing more clearly differentiates Confucius from Mo-tzu than their conceptions of the model of man required to transform society.

While Mo-tzu will occasionally use the term "noble man" and while Confucianists will frequently use the term *hsien,* I shall here use the terms to differentiate the two ideals of manhood. *Hsien* is Mo-tzu's preferred term.

Beginning on the side of man's intellectual capacity, we find an extraordinarily different emphasis in the concept of the intellect. One would of course expect Mo-tzu to reject much of the Confucian *content* of learning as useless, but one finds that there is also a decidedly different view of the function of the intellect. The notion of the larger truth somehow emerging intuitively—for the perceptive man—out of the gradual accumulation of significant empirical knowledge is not found here. While I have argued that "thinking" is certainly present as a value in the *Analects* in all the separate thoughts and reflections of the Master and his disciples, argument is rare. Mo-tzu, to be sure, will also set out from the "empirical facts" to support his arguments. Two of his three "tests of verification" (see below) rest on "facts." Yet the facts—or alleged facts—are always used in support of arguments. The evidence of Mo-tzu's overwhelming concern with dialectic and disputation (*pien*) as a primary way of attaining truth is evident throughout. Some of the arguments seem quite crude, but as Graham asserts, this is, indeed, the first textual evidence of "rational discourse."[59] If by "rational discourse" one means the reliance on reasoned argument and even the beginnings of a notion of a "science of argument," Mo-tzu, in attacking the premises of a view which presents itself as a "total vision" of order, must dismantle it piecemeal by argument and must "construct," as it were, his own alternative conception of order. Beginning not with an immanent order but with a plural, unorganized world, the sages who were the first rulers fought their way through to an understanding of how the human world was to be organized. "The sages who made it their business to bring order to the world had to know what were the causes of disorder and how they could bring about order."[60]

We are thus not surprised to find that the "men of worth" are described as men who excelled "in their virtuous behavior, their skill in argument and their knowledge of methods."[61] While all of this presupposes various forms of learning, it is not the learning which is stressed. No doubt the men of worth would learn whatever specialized knowledge was required and there would be absolutely no prejudice against specialized expertise. Mo-tzu, we are told, made himself an expert in the technology and tactics of siege warfare. Having decided that the art of defense against siege warfare was essential in helping small, weak states to resist the aggressions of large, powerful states, he made himself an expert in this area and would have encouraged his followers to acquire any "methods" or "techniques" that were necessary to their task.

Skill in argument, however, was probably of supreme importance. The rulers must be forced to realize the errors of their ways. Argument is, after all, a mode of combat. The man of worth is an intellectual warrior who forces the ruler to submit to the force of argument. On any given clear-cut issue, there is a wrong answer and a right answer. In the dialectical chapters, disputation is defined as "contending over converse (mutually exclusive) claims. Winning a dispute is fitting the facts."[62] While Confucius could treat error as one-sidedness, as the thread deviating from the whole fabric (which, of course, still left it in its status as error), in Mo-tzu's world where particular issues must be confronted separately and head on, answers to disputes as here defined must be decisive, precise, and conclusive. It is through solving a host of separate problems and finding separate causes that one constructs a structure of truth.

The man of worth is not, however, simply an intellectual warrior who argues relentlessly for his cause but an aggressive activist in every sense. Mo-tzu speaks not only of his dialectic skill and knowledge of methods but also of his "virtuous behavior." There is a definite Mohist view of the moral man. Indeed we find in the book an entire chapter on "self-cultivation" (chapter 2, which some scholars, however, deem to be inauthentic). It is a morality whose chief term may be said to be the will (*chih*) constantly seeking expression in action. This is evident in all the definitions of ethical virtues in the dialectic chapters. There must be the unflagging will *and* ability to benefit the world, even though it is often pointed out that "success is not necessarily achieved," but this lack of success must never be an excuse for inaction.[63] Confucius deliberates on whether entering the service of a given ruler can possibly have any effect, given the nature of the ruler. As we have seen, this was not an easy question for him. However, to do so in the clear knowledge that the enterprise was futile was to open the door immediately to question about one's motives for accepting office. To Mo-tzu, this is an immoral surrender to fatality. The question of motive or the opinion of others concerning one's motives is irrelevant. To focus on motive is again to focus attention on some supposed source of goodness within and to avoid the overriding necessity of *doing* good. The Confucianists in Mo-tzu's book are, of course, depicted as much more unambiguously passive than the Confucius of the *Analects*. Kung Meng states: "The noble man maintains his dignity and waits. When asked, he replies; when not asked, he abstains. He is like a bell. When struck it rings and when not struck remains silent." Mo-tzu replies that a noble man who refrains from remonstrating with his ruler or warning him of dangers—whether his advice is solicited or not—is a disloyal subject. A truly noble man is a "bell which rings even when not struck."[64] The man of worth cares nothing for the appearance of dignity or for the feelings with which such "mind sets" are associated. We find in fact that the Mohist sage is as detached from his passing emotions as the Confucian man of *jen* (or even more so). The sage is "sure to rid himself of pleasure, anger, joy, sadness and love and employ *jen* and righteousness."[65] (Love here seems to refer to love as an unreasoning passion or attachment and not the love of "universal love.") He evidently achieves this detachment from the emotions not by attaining an inner state of serenity and equanimity but by committing his total will and all his energies to the task of "doing good." Since he does not at all share the belief that the purity of his motives or the aura which radiates from the dignity of his person can influence those about him, he does not brood on his own motives or on his own dignity either. What he relies on is the power of his argument, his expertise in government, and his indomitable will to achieve the good.

There are, to be sure, still troubling questions which emerge about the springs of the *hsien's* motivation. How does he achieve this selflessness and this detachment from emotions and how does he reconcile this mastery with an uncompromising utilitarianism? Mo-tzu's utilitarianism, like all utilitarianism as described by John Rawls, involves the satisfaction of desires precisely associated with individual "agreeable feelings" which constitute Bentham's pleasure principle.[66] Whence, then, this indifference to pleasure, joy and love (in the emotional sense)? We have already seen Mo-tzu's own insistence that if rulers wish to attract men of worth they must reward them with wealth and honors, and while we have suggested that this can be explained in terms of the effects of these rewards on the attitudes of the people, mysteries concerning the motivations of the man of worth remain.

How do the men of worth or even the founding sages achieve their transcendence of the "state of nature"? As already hinted, the ultimate source of their transcendence seems to lie in their superior intelligence, for in the state of nature they certainly love themselves as exclusively as other men. They simply understand that they, like all men, will continue to abide in a state of utter misery if human beings in general cannot be brought to the realization that their interests will be served only by submitting to the general interest. They can be brought to this understanding only if they come to realize through universal love that all men are, like themselves, "ends in themselves." Whether Heaven's grace aides them to achieve this understanding is not evident, but they do understand that Heaven impartially loves all mankind and must want men to love each other. This understanding does not derive from the all-encompassing intuition of Confucius but is an achievement of ceaseless reasoning.

Having understood the causes of disorder and the causes of order, the sage and man of worth begins (quite unlike Hobbes's sovereign) by developing within himself all those virtuous dispositions which are required in order to serve the general interests of mankind and at the same time manages to free himself from all those useless emotional diversions which interfere with his stern life's task. The correct disposition of the will thus seems to be a consequence of superior intelligence. In the dialectic chapters we find a definition of all the sources of knowledge and of the content of knowledge. The sources are "hearsay [wen], explanation (logical) and immediate experience," but one of the many contents of knowledge is the knowledge of "how to act" (wei), which is then explained as "willing and doing."[67] The entire implication is that the correct disposition of the will is entirely an outcome of "knowing."

None of this, however, solves all the problems. No matter how convincingly the "altruistic" utilitarian may argue that in the end all human beings will reap the tangible benefits of the moral individual's behavior, it can never be demonstrated that he himself as a concrete living individual will reap any of these tangible benefits. Hence the question of his motivation—of his detachment from individual "feelings"—retains its mysteries.

One of the questions which indeed is raised in Mo-tzu's own case is why Heaven and the spirits do not reward him for his service to mankind. When he feels sick he is asked: "Your excellency maintains that the spirits make themselves manifest . . . they can reward the good man with happiness and punish the evil with misfortune. Now your excellency is a sage. Why have you fallen sick? I believe your doctrines are incorrect and that the spirits are not conscious." Mo-tzu replies: "Although I am sick how does that prove that the spirits are not conscious? There are many ways in which men get sick. There is cold, heat or overwork. If one has a home with hundred doors and closes one, how can one keep out a thief?"[68] An old man says to Mo-tzu: "No one is righteous these days. You alone torture yourself to do the right. Wouldn't it be best to give up?" Mo-tzu replies: "Here we have ten men. One man tills and nine are idle. The one who tills must work all the harder because those who eat are many and the tillers few. Why do you exhort me to stop?"[69] Whatever one may think of his replies, they seem to have nothing to do with expectations of any kind of material reward from either men or spirits. The springs of his actions seem to lie deeper. However much the answers may illumine his dedication, they do not solve the questions raised by his doctrine.

Another aspect of the doctrine of the man of worth is its enormous stress on the principle of merit. Here we seem to see an almost radical lurch to the side of meritocracy. Mo-tzu preaches quite openly to the rulers that if they continue to lean on incompetent relatives and aristocrats they face disaster. "The ancient sage-kings were not partisan toward fathers and brothers; did not lean toward the noble and the rich and did not favor beauty. If there were men of worth they promoted them."[70] We also find references to the fact that the emperors Yao and Shun chose their own successors on the basis of merit, thus launching a discussion of the possibility of the rule of merit even on the level of the universal kingship, which continued through the whole Warring States period. It would indeed appear that none of the considerations which continued to dispose Confucius toward abiding respect for the hereditary principle are operative here. There is no loyalty to the house of Chou. However much the ancestral spirits are honored as part of the world of spirits, there is no religion of the family or feeling that family prerogatives must be maintained. The anguish which Confucius experienced when the Chi clan usurps the sacred rituals of the Chou family would leave Mo-tzu unmoved.

A final aspect of Mo-tzu's doctrine which would directly affect the role of men of worth is its stress on organization. The Mohist organization, which had its military as well, perhaps, as its religious side, was in the scene throughout the Warring States period. Here we find the manifestation of the Mohist's willingness to rely on pressure and force. While we cannot estimate how strong the organization became or how large its mass basis, its formation was obviously based on the maxim that in organization there is strength. Graham cites the instance in the *Lü-shih Ch'un-ch'iu* in which the Grand Master of the Mohist organization contracts with a local lord to undertake the defense of his city.[71] There were undoubtedly other unrecorded interventions of this type. The organization, one would presume, not only created a base of power but also coordinated activities and served as a training ground for the various types of experts required by the movement. While the *Analects* does not directly discuss the subject, we can surmise that the Confucius of the *Analects* would never think of such organizational devices. What the noble man brings to bear on the ruler is his moral power (*te*) and nothing else. The creation of organized power—particularly of an organization with a military cast—can have as an aim only the express use of coercive power. Despite Confucius' ambivalence toward Kuan Chung's reliance on the instruments of coercion to obtain "good results," the truly noble man does not rely on organized pressure or coercion.

Yet despite the radical emphasis on merit, despite the positive appreciation of the power of organization, and despite the aggressive-activist approach to the achievement of righteous goals, we find actually no evidence of any effort to "change the system" as such or any hint of turning the Mohist movement into a movement of rebellion. On the contrary, Mo-tzu seems to accept the multistate system of his time as a given. His fierce campaign to defend small, weak states against large aggressive states is, one might say, precisely aimed at keeping the international status quo intact. He begins with the situation at hand.

Paradoxically, Mo-tzu's total rejection of *ming* or "fate" also leads him to reject those aspects of the Confucian concept of *ming* which might encourage a hope for the future based on Heaven's presence in the patterns of history. The notion that cycles of order and disorder are governed by Heaven's presence in the larger impersonal patterns of history makes it possible in a time of disorder to hope for the rise of a new Heavenly dispensation. Yet despite Mo-tzu's emphasis on the will of Heaven, he does not indulge in reflections on the "laws of history." Heaven acts in the world by inspiring sages and men of worth to follow the model of Heaven and not by manifesting itself in the impersonal patterns of history. The overthrow of the Shang dynasty by kings Wen and Wu was wholly due to their efforts and had nothing to do with any patterns of history. Paradoxically again, Mo-tzu's Heaven plays a far smaller role in human affairs than does the Heaven of the contemporary Confucianists with whom he was in contact. Mo-tzu does not attempt to descry any future trajectory of history. While Mo-tzu's "theism" has been compared to that of the Bible, the subtle mysterious dialectic of the interplay between divine plan and human action which we find in the Hebrew Bible cannot be found here. The Mohist operates within the situation as he finds it in the firm belief that human actors basing themselves on Heaven as a "model" will play the decisive role in shaping the future.

This brutally consistent emphasis on the primacy of the human will does not, however, shake in the slightest Mo-tzu's conviction that the masses must be led by the vanguard of those who know. His concept of knowledge probably places his "men of discernment" at an even further remove from the masses in general than does the "learning" of Confucius, although he does have high respect for the

skills of craftsmen and persons skilled in the arts of war. Righteousness is not attained "when those below rule those above but when
those above rule those below." Heaven can bring its will to bear on
men only through the pyramidal political order in which every level
conforms to those above and those on top conform to Heaven. In
Mo-tzu's mind the idea of a unified "general interest" of mankind
can thus not be disassociated from the idea of the central unified
source of political authority. In the absence of such a center one will
again relapse into the war of particular interests. The pinnacle may
certainly be occupied by ignorant and unworthy rulers, but even
sages and men of worth can enlighten and mold the people only
through the structure of the political order. Universal love (a universal concern for the interests of all men) cannot mean universal economic or political equality. According to a passage in the later
logical chapters, since achievement of the general interests requires
an ordered and ranked political structure (*lun-lieh*), it follows that
one must treat persons quite unequally in terms of the roles which
they perform in the structure as a whole.[72]

In principle none of this seems to preclude the overthrow by sages
and worthy men of established hereditary authority. Is this not in
effect what King Wu did in overthrowing the Shang? Neither fatalism nor any inherent respect for the hereditary principle nor any reluctance to use force in a good cause should stand in the way.
Perhaps the absence of any doctrine of revolt in the Mo-tzu simply
reflects the thoroughly realistic assumption that in the world of his
time there were no prospects of success for a "Change of Mandate"
(*ko ming*). The historic records of the pre-China period, while
recording local uprisings, do not record anything resembling em-
pirewide revolts from below before the rising of Ch'en She at the end
of the Ch'in dynasty. The only alternative, therefore, was to deal
with the prevailing state of affairs and aggressively hammer home to
the rulers the necessity of accepting the true doctrines of Mo-tzu.
There is, however, also the possibility that Mo-tzu's Hobbes-like
conviction that strong political authority is the primary sine qua
non for avoiding chaos—his deep conviction that the general interest can be obtained only by bringing about "conformity with superiors and uniting opinions" leads him to believe that commoners like
himself and the members of his organization should not dream of
striving for state power.[73] When Yao conferred his kingship on the
commoner Shun, it was the case of a commoner being chosen by a
ruler. When King Wu defeated the Shang, he was already the head
of state. Perhaps the indiscriminate seizure of power by commoners
(many of whom would not be sages or men of worth) would simply

bring about total disintegration of the fabric of authority as such. It was a fabric as necessary to Mo-tzu's universe as it was to the universe of the *Analects*.

## "Logic and Science"

Angus Graham has titled his masterly reconstruction of what he calls the "dialectic chapters" of the Mo-tzu book (40–44) "Later Mohist Logic, Ethics and Science," thus indicating the difficulty of pinning down their contents in terms of specific Western categories.

I shall not attempt here to deal with all the issues raised by this monumental study because of limits of both technical competence and space. Furthermore, to treat these chapters at this point may seem anachronistic, since much of their content belongs to a period as late as the third century. They reflect the response of later Mohists not only to Taoism, Confucianism, "Correlative Cosmology," and other later doctrines but also to the entire "language crisis" of the fourth and third centuries represented by such "sophists" as Hui Shih and Kung-sun Lung-tzu. Yet a close study of these texts indicates that however different the quality of the reasoning in these chapters from the original text, they strengthen the view that the later development is organically linked to both the spirit and even the content of the original doctrine. It seems obvious that these dialecticians regard themselves as defenders of the original faith, although one would gather from the last chapter of the book of Chuang-tzu, which is a late survey of trends of thought of the third or perhaps second century B.C., that they themselves were already split into three sects. If one can presume a direct evolution from Mo-tzu to the later Mohists it would seem that early Mohism itself played a leading role in giving rise to the entire discussion of language, logic, and epistemology which we find in the "school of names or terms" (*ming-chia*).

Mo-tzu, as we have seen, is aggressively bent on demonstrating that his doctrines are right and that those of his opponents are wrong, and one classical albeit crude concept of a "method of argument" can be found in his "three tests of verification" or "three standards."[74] In verifying a proposition, one bases oneself first of all on the actions of the sage-kings. Secondly one relies on the consensus of mankind drawn from their own experience, and thirdly one relies on the "pragmatic" consequences (*yung*) of a given mode of belief (e.g., fatalism leads to disaster). Thus applied to the question of the existence of spirits, it is obvious from the sacred texts that the sages

of old believed in the reality of the spirits—that men have everywhere had actual experiences of the presence of spirits and that the
belief in the spirits is necessary for the establishment of the good society.[75] In the first argument Mo-tzu aligns himself solidly with
Confucius' belief in the higher wisdom of the sage-kings. The second
"empirical" test is dismissed by Hansen as not being a case of British
"philosophical empiricism" but a kind of reliance on "poll-tak-
ing."[76] Yet the notion of relying on the consensus of men based on
ordinary experience is not as unrespectable in Western thought as
Hansen implies. The "pragmatic" test may also not be as unrelated
to Western pragmatism as he implies. It seems quite obvious that in
Mo-tzu's mind the good consequences of these beliefs have something to do with their "truth" and that the third standard is very
much related to the first two.[77]

Here, again, without in any way attempting to compare the quality of Mo-tzu's dialectic with that of Socrates, I must point out that
Socrates' dialectic method also arises within a context of ethical and
political concerns and not in the context of a concern with "descriptive functions." Guthrie indeed even goes so far as to call him a
"utilitarian."[78]

The three tests are by no means the only evidence in the oldest
layer of the text of Mo-tzu's concern with dialectic and logic. He is
concerned throughout with the question of the particular causes or
reasons for things—particularly of the causes of disorder in the
world. It is thus interesting that the dialectic chapters begin with a
precise definition of "causes" (ku). "The cause of something is what
it must get before it will come about." The explanation (shuo) then
goes on to distinguish between "minor cause or reason and major
cause or reason." The minor cause is explained as follows: "Having
this it will not necessarily be so. Lacking this it will necessarily not
be so." Major cause or reason is explained as follows: "Having this it
will necessarily be so. Lacking this it will necessarily not be so (like
the appearing of something bringing about the seeing).[79] This example not only illustrates the continuity of concerns with the original text; it also illustrates how the resources of the Chinese language
can be used to elucidate the difference between two notions as abstract as necessary condition and sufficient cause or condition (in
Graham's terminology). It finally makes it amply clear that even if
we accept Needham's view that the major orientation of Chinese
thought is "organismic" in some sense, it was quite possible for *some
Chinese* using the Chinese language to conceive of a pluralistic universe in which the separate realities had quite separate "particulate"
causes or reasons due to "prior actions or impulses of other things"

and not due to the fact that "their positions in the ever moving cyclical universe was such that they were endowed with intrinsic natures which made that behavior inevitable for them."[80]

We also find in the oldest layer of the text a constant discussion of "models" or "standards" (*fa, fa yi*) for both entities and modes of behavior-concepts which receive considerable attention in the dialectic chapter. In chapter 4, called "Standards and Models," as in the case of Socrates and Plato, there is a direct reference to the crafts which rely not only on carpenter's squares, compasses, and plumb-lines but also on certain ideal techniques of work. In the dialectic chapters, the concept of "standard" is, to be sure, rendered much more precise and a standard (*fa*) is defined as "that in being like which something is so."[81] This almost reminds one of Plato's view that particulars "copy forms." Thus the question which was raised with regard to the status of "names" in Confucius (e.g., the ideal father) seems to rise again. Is the "standard" a kind of Platonic form? At first glance, our reluctance to find Platonism in Chinese thought is reconfirmed when we find that the standard for a circle can be found either by having an "idea" (*i*) of a circle in one's head, by a compass, or by a physical example (or a drawing) of a circle.[82] All of these "standards" are particular objects or are based on particular subjective experiences. However, we also have a definition of a circle as having "the same lengths from a single center."[83] This is a purely geometric definition, and presumably the compass and the drawn circle are only standards to the extent that they correspond to this definition. Thus a compass is probably only a standard to the extent that it fits the definition.[84] One can say that to the extent that a compass falls short of the definition, it can be said to fall short of the ideal. Indeed it is quite clear in the oldest layer of the text that standards do provide images of the ideal in the ethical sphere.

In the original Mo-tzu text it is, however, soon made clear that the true ultimate analogue of the craftsman's "standards" is nothing less than Heaven itself, which is a conscious, willing being. "There is nothing like taking Heaven as one's 'standard.' Heaven's actions are all-encompassing and unselfish . . . Thus the sage-kings took Heaven as their standard and their actions were effective."[85] Thus the "locus of being" of the "standard," here as perhaps in Confucius, is not a "realm of eternal forms" but either Heaven or ideal living human beings such as the sage-kings. When one turns to the definitions of the ethical virtues in the dialectic chapters, which in effect provide the standards of ethical behavior, one finds that here too they are discussed in the "explanations" in terms of the actions of living exemplars.[86] Where this leaves logical forms, circles, and squares in terms of their ontological status we have no way of knowing.[87] While agreeing that there is here no Platonic realm of eternal forms, Graham's own final designation of the Mohists as "nominalists" is as much based on the Western realistic/nominalist dichotomy as is any explanation in terms of Plato. The standards are, it is clear, not "mere names."

Graham's summary of the world-picture of the late Mohists is "that it is a cosmos of concrete and particular objects each with its mutually pervasive properties located in space changing through time, interconnected by necessary relations like the logical relation between their names."[88] I would submit that the picture thus described may not be so far removed from the world-picture of the "early" Mohists, however great the difference in sophistication.

It is true that the original text does not discuss "necessary relations." Yet to the extent that the wills of Heaven and of the sages are concerned with ethical goals, the concept of will here is not arbitrary and may in fact be quite compatible with notions of a calculable world in which necessary logical and mathematical relations obtain. To the extent that Heaven's will is a will to the good, it acts through the constraints of those necessary structures through which the good is achieved. As Kierkegaard insists, the ethical must relate to the general and the universal. "Heaven necessarily wishes men to love each other and to benefit each other."[89] Thus the late Mohist interest in logical and necessary relations may be no more incompatible with the spirit of early Mohism than was the burning interest of medieval theistic Jewish, Christian, and Moslem thinkers in Aristotelian logic and in mathematics. In the Mohist case, the metaphor of the craftsman frequently comes to mind. Like the good craftsman, the Mohist is an active, goal-oriented individual bent on realizing his project in the world. He is confident in his powers to use his tools and shape his materials, but in order to do so he must intimately know the "laws" and necessary relations which govern the tools he uses and are inherent in the materials he handles.

What the later Mohist dialecticians strive to create is a kind of "scientific" language for dealing with the world. Unlike Confucius, they do not believe that such a language is already available within the tradition. On the other side, they strongly defend what is essentially a "common sense" view of experience based on the human "life-world" (Husserl's *Lebenswelt*) against the attacks of later "sophists" and Taoists, such as Chuang-tzu, who have lost all faith in the power of human language to provide a true view of reality.

If one raises the question of which modes of thought in ancient China may have contained elements potentially favorable to a subsequent emergence of natural science in the modern Western sense, late Mohism would occupy, I submit, a much more central place than the "Taoism" which Needham seems to prefer. At one point Needham himself states: "The Mohists not mistrusting human reason at all clearly laid down what could have become the fundamental basic conception of natural science in Asia."[90] There are the actual explorations of optics, mechanics, and physics. There is the concern with geometric definition and the mathematical treatment of optic phenomena. In the words of Graham, "They confine themselves to solutions which are geometrically visualized and experimentally testable."[91] They are deeply committed to seeking out separate particular causes for separate effects. There was, however, as Needham points out, "no equivalent of the Epicurean atomic theory."[92] There is no "reductionist" impulse to posit some ultimate "stuff" of minimal properties of mass and motion in terms of which all the variety of the world may be explained. If they are not reductionists, however, they remain resolute pluralists rather than "organismic" holists. Despite the presence of all these elements potentially favorable to science, even the Mohists "logicians" were probably not basically preoccupied with either the "dispassionate" study of nature nor with any notion of an overall technological revolution, however much they may have favored certain specific technologies. Their overwhelming goal remained the achievement of a society of peace, security, and the satisfaction of man's "basic" economic needs. Yet, despite Hansen, I find no evidence that they believed that their effort to "regulate" the world could be completed detached from an effort to "describe" it. Their ability to use the resources of the Chinese language to cope with some of the same logical epistemological and mathematical problems which preoccupied ancient Greek and even modern Western thought remains an ongoing challenge to all linguistic determinisms.

## The Fate of Mohism

Much thought has been given to the question of why Mohism as a total doctrine fades away in China after the early Han period and why it seems to exercise, with some exceptions, little influence on the later course of Chinese thought (until the nineteenth and twentieth centuries).

The two questions should be considered separately, since a strong case can be made that in the centuries of the Warring States period, when the *Ju* (the Confucianists) and the *Mo* are always juxtaposed as the two main rival schools of thought, Mohism was a major school of thought.[93] Mohism exercised a considerable influence on emerging trends of thought during that period either directly or as a kind of catalyst. As I have suggested, its attitude toward language, dialectic, and logic may have provided one strong impetus to the entire "language crisis" of the fourth and third centuries—a crisis which profoundly affected not only the "logicians" or "sophists"of rival points of view but the Taoism of Lao-tzu and Chuang-tzu as well. Graham has done pioneer work in demonstrating the extent to which the technical vocabulary of the later Mohists as well as of the "sophists" permeates the entire book of Chuang-tzu. I would further suggest that the entire preoccupation in Taoism with the antithesis between spontaneous, nonpurposive, and "natural" modes of behavior (*wu-wei*) and deliberate, calculating, and purposive modes of action (*yu-wei*) may at least in part have represented a sharp reaction against the extraordinary highlighting of the latter within Mohist thought. Again, the entire "egoistic" approach associated with the name of Yang Chu may well have arisen out of a direct "dialectic" confrontation with early Mohism. The fact that Mencius later attempts to define his own outlook by seeing it, at least in one perspective, as a rejection of both Yang Chu and his own account of Mohism certainly played some role in the formation of his thought, and I think it likely that the emphasis on both "legitimate" force and "punishments and rewards" as well as the implicit Mohist conception of the original "nature" of man may have helped to prepare the soil for certain aspects of Legalism. Hence the strong influence of this quite pervasive outlook on the shape of Warring States thought in general can hardly be denied.

In accounting for the decline of Mohism, some have pointed to the collapse of its organization. To the extent that Mohism was based on an organized movement operating outside the framework of the established political order, it could not survive the establishment of the centralized bureaucratic state which, in line with an already long-established tradition, could not tolerate the notion of such "external" organizations. It could only survive within the loose and open conditions of the Warring States period, where it operated alongside the other "wandering" warrior bands offering their services to rulers of the time.

Whether the survival of the doctrine depended wholly on the survival of the organization, we cannot, of course, know. One might presume that the "scientific" pursuits of the late Mohist dialecticians might have continued apart from any organization. Yet their demise must be viewed in conjunction with the fading away of the entire "school of names" with its particular interest in problems of logic and "linguistic analysis."

Perhaps more crucial is the movement's lack of success in convincing its intended audience. Mo-tzu is certainly portrayed as a man who did not succeed in his mission even though he wandered tirelessly from ruler to ruler employing all his powers of dialectic. In attempting to imagine the effects of the Mohist arguments on the rulers of his time, one can appreciate why his long-term utilitarian arguments were not very likely to influence them. In addition to the difficulty already mentioned, the possibility that a cessation of aggressive wars might lead to some long-term benefit to all was probably as unpersuasive for them as it is to governments in the twentieth century. The question was how they would benefit here and now, particularly when, like later rulers, they probably viewed these wars as part of a general "balance of power" game in which they could easily persuade themselves that what was at stake was not simply state expansion but security and survival. The same would hold true for arguments concerning "benefitting the people." There was no assurance that the benefits which would accrue to all in the future would lead to any more satisfactory pay-offs in terms of concrete immediate goals. Thus, Mo-tzu's "utilitarianism" was probably not a whit more convincing to the average ruler than Confucius' stress on a morality of motives.

As for the religious component of Mohism, whatever the subjective attitudes of those in the movement, it is true that it is presented in the texts as a kind of stateman's view emphasizing the sociopolitical need for a belief in the living will of Heaven and the spirits.[94] The cool Mohist arguments were hardly likely to sweep the adherents of fatalism off their feet by their religious fervor. While Mo-tzu speaks much of Heaven's love for mankind, he does not speak of loving Heaven "with all one's heart and all one's soul." On the contrary, he would probably find such an attitude disrespectful to the high authority of Heaven. The stock expression which prevails throughout is "honor Heaven [tsun-t'ien] and serve the spirits." This lack of any apparent devotional element, when combined with the inability to prove that Heaven or the spirits deliver immediate rewards and punishments, probably left his upper-class hearers indifferent to his particular religious message. To the extent that Mo-tzu's religion shared much in common with the "religion of the masses," the form which he gave to this religion emphasizes above all the mediating role of the political order.[95] Unlike the Hebrew prophets who addressed both kings and masses, his preachments largely concentrate on rulers. To the extent that the diffuse popular religion provided the people with a sense of immediate communication with spirits and divine powers by-passing the entire sociopolitical order, Mo-tzu's tendency to link the will of Heaven and the spirits primarily to the realm of the political order would indicate that the religious aspect of the Mohist movement may have had little mass appeal. Unlike some of the "religions of rebellion" of later periods, it would certainly seem to have had no millenarian appeal.

Yet if the message of Mohism probably had limited contemporary appeal, contemporary Confucianism was hardly more successful. Yet we know that in the long run its lack of success proved more fatal than the similar lack of success of the Confucianists. To be sure, even at the time, the Confucianists or the *ju* stratum as a whole (whose relations to the doctrine of the Master remain problematic) continued to act as experts in ritual and in the sacred traditional literature, and continued to enjoy the emoluments of the rulers, as we can see from Mo-tzu's diatribes against their indolence and hypocrisy. I must, of course, point out that, as is usually the case in the history of human thought, Mo-tzu's image of the *ju* probably does little justice to the entire range of contemporary Confucian thought. We thus know that Confucius' grandson Tzu-ssu, who was probably a contemporary of Mo-tzu, is traditionally considered to be the fountainhead of those tendencies in Confucian thought which culminated in the book of Mencius, the "Great Learning" and the "Doctrine of the Mean." If this is indeed the case, he would have represented tendencies quite different from those of the Confucianists depicted in the Mo-tzu text. The same would be true of that vein of Confucian thought which finally culminated in Hsün-tzu.

Yet the fact that the *ju* did, after all, find access to government, whatever the nature of their outlook, points to what some consider to be the fundamental factor in Mohism's ultimate failure—its radical deviation from certain deep-laid, widely shared orientations of the elite culture. Lavish mourning rites, ceremonial music, and the concern with ceremonial dress and all the refinements of etiquette, however formalized and detached from meaning they may have become, were indeed part of the traditional elite culture. The author of the last chapter (33) of the Chuang-tzu text, who attempts to provide a balanced account of the various doctrines which he criticizes, simply finds the "Mohists of later ages who 'dress in skins and coarse cloth, wear wooden clogs or hempen sandals never resting day or night driving themselves on to the bitterest exertions' " incomprehensible.[96] The author of this chapter is no Confucianist, yet the Mohist interdiction of singing in life and mourning in death, the notion that all should bury their dead in "coffins of pawlonia wood three inches thick without outer shell" no matter what their status or rank, is simply an affront to all "natural" human feelings.[97] The "logic chopping" of the later Mohists with their constant debates about "sameness and difference," "hard and white" would have as little to do with discovering the larger synoptic truth as their needless and ostentatiously "inhuman" "practicality" had to do with attaining the *tao*. It is precisely in such powerful perceptions of what belongs to the "natural human feelings" that one can sometimes perceive the power of certain dominant cultural orientations (in this case, particularly on the elite cultural level). Here one must again affirm the inertial power of general, deeply rooted cultural orientations. Mohism proves decisively that such orientations could *not* prevent the emergence of countercultural tendencies. Yet at least in some areas of experience, they could prove massively resistant to any long-term impact of such tendencies.

# CHAPTER 5

# THE EMERGENCE OF
# A COMMON DISCOURSE
## Some Key Terms

---

I HAVE THUS FAR treated Confucianism and Mohism as two quite separate schools (*chia*) and this conventional treatment may be entirely justified. What we call Confucianism is not in Chinese named after the founding father but designated by the term the "teachings of the *Ju*," which would indicate the extent that that particular group may have become the main bearers of the Master's vision. Mohism derives its name from its founder (assuming that Mo is indeed a surname). Both doctrines, however, remain very much linked to the founding father.

When we turn to the "hundred schools" of the fourth and third centuries, we soon find that the method of dealing with the history of thought solely by aligning discrete schools of thought (as in the case of certain types of modern Western intellectual history) in serried array becomes a problematic enterprise, particularly when used as an exclusive approach. Much of the traditional Chinese view of this period derives from the doxographers of the early Han dynasty, who were very much addicted to this method.[1] They retrospectively imposed terms such as Taoism (*tao-chia*), Legalism (*fa-chia*), and Eclecticism (*tsa-chia*) on the complex currents of the age. While one can indeed distinguish broad streams of thought which seem to share certain large assumptions, they often draw on quite disparate sources and embrace what might be called diverse substreams from beginning to end. They seem, in some ways, more comparable to vague terms such as liberalism, conservatism, and socialism than to terms such as Marxism or Hegelianism.

Some of the thinkers of the Warring States period themselves attempt to furnish us with their own accounts of contemporary winds
of doctrine. When we examine the writings of Mencius, Hsün-tzu,
Han Fei-tzu, and chapter 33 of the book of Chuang-tzu, all of which
provide such accounts, we find that they know nothing of Taoism,
Legalism, or Eclecticism, and they treat separate individual figures
who are later subsumed under these large categories as representatives of quite diverse modes of thought. The entire category of
"eclectic" (*tsa*) applied to a large group of personalities, who have
unfortunately left us with only small fragments of their oeuvre, is a
highly suspect, residual category. Thus, to describe the thought of
figure X as a "mixture of Taoism and Legalism" at a time when
these streams of thought were themselves not perceived as coherent
wholes may be entirely unjustified. X may indeed combine themes,
concepts, and even problematiques which were later assigned to
these separate "schools," but his way of combining them may in fact
have been quite as logical and coherent as that of the main protagonists of the major schools. This does not mean that the Han doxographers were entirely mistaken when they retrospectively referred
to Taoism and Legalism. These may indeed be discussed as at least
partially distinguishable general streams but the enterprise now becomes problematic and highly hazardous.

I have just mentioned themes and concepts which enter into a
common discourse.[2] There is in fact a whole vocabulary of terms
which comes to be shared by a wide diversity of modes of thought.
The terms themselves are such that while they may contain a certain
common range of meaning, they nevertheless lend themselves to extraordinarily differing interpretation and emphasis. We have already noted how the term *jen*, so rich in its semantic extension in
Confucius, seems to become much reduced in Mo-tzu without, however, losing all connection with its meanings in the *Analects*. In Mo-
tzu, it is wholly the "other-regarding" "benevolent" aspect of the
term which becomes dominant. On the other hand, the term "righteousness" (*i*), which is indeed extremely important in the *Analects*,
becomes quite central in the Mo-tzu where it refers to the unflagging determination to *act* in a way which will benefit mankind as a
whole.[3]

What I shall consider below are three terms chosen among others
which, it seems to me, come to play a considerable role within the
entire discourse of the Warring States period. They belong to a
common fund of shared notions which enter into the discourse of the
"schools."

## *Hsing:* Nature or Human Nature

The term *"hsing,"* often translated as "human nature" or "nature" (since in later texts its reference is by no means exclusively human), becomes crucial in the emerging debates within Confucianism, although it also figures to some extent in other schools as well.

Angus Graham has suggested that the term comes into currency as an active term of controversy only with the emergence of the views that have been attributed to the shadowy figure of Yang Chu the "egoist."[4]

In dealing with the original meaning of the term, Graham points to the striking affinities of the etymology of the term with the etymologies of the Greek *physis* and the Latin *natura*. The word *hsing* is derived from the word *sheng*, whose original meaning as a verb is "to be born" and "to grow," and whose nominal meaning is "life."[5] The resemblance to the Greek *phuo* (to grow) and the Latin *nascor* (to be born) is most striking. Out of this meaning there emerges the derived meaning of an innate tendency toward growth or development in a given, predetermined direction. In Chinese the matter is complicated by the fact that in early Chinese writing, the entire practice of distinguishing different meanings of related terms by adding "classifiers" to graphs was not yet well established. It would thus appear that the graph *sheng* without the classifier ( 生 ) may itself have come to be used quite early to mean "human nature" in this sense rather than simply "life." Graham does not absolutely deny that the problem of "human nature" may have been posed at a very early point, but he contends that its first reliable recorded usages is found in statements describing the doctrine of Yang Chu and that in Yang Chu it did not simply refer to innate "natural" propensities in general but to the particular propensity of human beings to pursue their own natural "desires" for health, long life, and freedom from anxiety. The only instruction which Heaven inscribes in us is the instruction to seek our own individual creaturely well-being. Yet in posing this very specific proposition, Yang Chu opened the entire discussion concerning the basic "inborn" predispositions inherent in all human beings.

Without dwelling on the fact that the graph actually occurs in a section of the *Book of Documents* that is considered by many scholars to be genuinely pre-Confucian,[6] we must consider the more important point made by the late distinguished historian of Chinese thought, Hsü Fu-kuan, in his *History of the Chinese Philosophy of Human Nature*, that in dealing with this question one must go beyond the limited evidences of philology.[7] The history of an idea may be more than the history of the term with which the idea ultimately comes to be identified. A case can be made that the problem of human nature is present in early Chinese thought apart from the use of the term. To the extent that we have at a very early point the emergence of the concept of a normative sociopolitical order with its prescribed codes of behavior, the problem of why individuals do or do not conform to that order is already posed. More precisely, the question of the general relationship of this order to "innate" human propensities is already latently present. We thus have the poem in the *Book of Poetry* which states that when "Heaven gave birth to the multitude of people," what it ordained (*ming*) was "not to be relied upon. They [humans] all had the beginnings but few could carry through to the end."[8] In effect, it already poses the problem of human nature even though the term is nowhere to be found. Here we have something like the theory of an innate tendency to the good which is, however, a weak potentiality easily overcome by adverse forces.

   If we follow the evolution of the word *hsing* itself, we find it used in the chronicle *Tso-chuan* with a distinctly moralistic flavor. Given the uncertainties concerning the dating of this text, we cannot prove that these passages are older than the few references we have to Yang Chu, but the dates of Yang Chu himself are themselves obscure. The famous statesman Tzu-ch'an is quoted at length on the subject of *li* (ceremony), which, in the course of a long speech, he erects into the very principle of both cosmic and human order. At one point, he states, "the six *ch'i* produces the five tastes, gives rise to the five colors and displays the five notes. When any of these are in excess, there ensues confusion and disorder and we lose our proper nature [*hsing*]."[9] Graham, commenting on this passage, points out that the aim of maintaining the balance among the various constituents of human life is to "maintain a long life."[10] While the aim may still be a long life, there is the notion that only moral means and a heavy reliance on *li* can achieve this aim and there is even the implication that the *hsing* which is lost is a *hsing* with inherent moral tendencies. This becomes even more apparent in another passage quoted by Graham which asks "how can heaven allow one man to run riot over the people and so by his licentious indulgence abandon the *hsing* of heaven and earth."[11] Here the *hsing* has nothing to do with the ruler's own health but with the devastating effects on others occasioned by the departure from the inherent "nature" of heaven and earth. It would thus appear that in a period roughly contemporaneous with Confucius, the word *hsing* may already have been used in certain circles to refer to inborn moral propensities or even to the "nature" of the cosmos and did not belong exclusively to the "ordinary language of everyone who worries about his health and hopes to live out his natural span."[12]

The word *hsing* occurs twice in the *Analects,* once in a statement in which Confucius says that "men are close in nature but far apart in practice," and in another in which Tzu-kung observes that "I have never gotten to hear what the Master says about 'human nature' and 'the Way of Heaven.' "[13] Tzu-kung's statement would imply that the concept was already current but that the Master simply did not regard the discussion of it as profitable. The only other possibility is that both passages are much later interpolations. If we assume, for a moment, that the concept was already current, how would we explain the contents of these remarks? They might both indicate that Confucius as a "pragmatic" moralist much prefers to discuss the "existential" question—how can we make ourselves good?—rather than to "theorize" about innate propensities. His focus remains steadfastly fixed on what men can do with whatever *hsing* they may have. This view of the matter would be very much in accord with the one substantive statement in the *Analects* about the nature of *hsing*.[14] Assuming that the statement is authentic rather than a late interpolation, what it asserts is that men are close to each other in their original propensities but that their practice of life tends to draw them apart. The focus here is wholly on "making oneself good" rather than on the "ontological" discussions of the original nature.

It must again be stated, however, that this moral "pragmatism" or existentialism does not preclude a stress on "inwardness." The man who seeks to achieve *jen* must be concerned with his inner moral state of being, but this kind of moral introspection does not require the creation of theories about human nature or focusing of attention on how human nature relates to the Way of Heaven. The long discourse of Tzu-ch'an, cited in the *Tso-chuan,* assuming that it is early, is precisely an example of how the question of human nature can be related to questions concerning the Way of Heaven. It correlates all sorts of natural phenomena to human phenomena in numerical categories, and seems in fact to anticipate the "correlative cosmology" of the Warring States period. If the concept was already in existence, then Confucius was not so much ignoring questions that no one had as yet raised as consciously refraining from entering into matters that were already under discussion in the world of his time. Tzu-kung's wonder over why his Master did not discuss *hsing* and the Way of Heaven (and possibly the relations between the two) would thus be entirely comprehensible.

Yet Graham's case that *hsing* did not emerge as a subject of "philosophic" discussion until the emergence of Yang Chu may seem to be strengthened by the absence of the term in the text of the Book of Mo-tzu. Yet Mo-tzu may in fact provide a vivid illustration of Hsü Fu-kuan's stress on the need for separating ideas from terms. The vivid description of man in a state of nature as a creature bent on pursuing his own self-interest almost seems to provide a classic case of "human nature" theory akin to its use in the modern contract theories of Hobbes and Rousseau. It is nevertheless true that the word *hsing* itself is sedulously avoided. Here again, the word with its suggestion of innateness, of forces at work within human beings which lie beyond their control may have implied precisely the kind of immanence and fatality that Mo-tzu was bent on resisting. Mo-tzu may provide no satisfactory answer to the question of why the will of Heaven has created humans as creatures initially bent only on their self-assertion, but he is certainly anxious to absolve Heaven of responsibility for this state of affairs. Again it is not the original propensity which is important. What is important is what human effort can do to direct and change this propensity.

It is remarkable that the conscious resistance to the term *hsing* carries over even into the later dialectic chapters of the Mo-tzu, which were completed at a time when the Confucian debates on human nature were already in full swing. The word *hsing* does not appear in the logical canons as a word to be defined. It is mentioned once in an obscure discussion which simply confirms the Mohist objection to the term. If the pernicious doctrine is proclaimed that criminal behavior of criminals is due to a *hsing* imposed by the will of Heaven, "the criminal will think that 'every man for himself' is the will of Heaven."[15]

The extremely odd definition of "life" (*sheng*) (it would seem to be mainly human life) in the Mohist canons (chapters 40 and 41) as "a body being located with 'intelligence' or 'knowledge' [*chih*]" would seem to focus attention squarely not on the initial innate tendency to self-interest but on the human capacity through the power of intelligence and will to overcome such initial innate propensities.[16]

It is possible that the views of Yang Chu rose out of a dialectic encounter with Mohism, as Graham suggests.[17] Yang Chu may have seized upon Mo-tzu's description of man in a state of nature as a creature seeking to maximize his own welfare and, in defiance of Mo-tzu, accepted this state as a description of man's heaven-endowed *hsing*. Man's only innate propensity is the propensity for self-preservation in health, security, ease, and as long a life as possible. Yang Chu would thus have "seen through" the weaknesses in Mo-tzu's "altruistic" theory of utilitarianism with its irrational stress on the ultimate general interest of all men. To be sure, the egoism of Yang Chu as it is portrayed in such sources as the *Lü-shih Ch'un-ch'iu* does not seem to share the insatiable aggressiveness of Mo-tzu's man before the rise of the state. The "natural" tendency implanted in man by Heaven is the tendency to live out one's own life in health, in the absence of anxiety, and in the moderate satisfaction of one's sensual desires. This involves as little entanglement as possible with the social order, whether such entanglement takes the form of seeking honors or "doing good." As described in the most ancient texts, it may also involve avoidance of hedonist excesses. Thus, Yang Chu's contribution to the entire discussion of *hsing* may not at all have been the invention of the notion as a "philosophic term" but rather his particular self-consciously "egoistic" interpretation of it.[18]

As Graham himself points out, the late Han thinker Wang Ch'ung mentions vigorous discussions of the problem of *hsing* by such early Confucianists as Shih Shih, Fu Tzu-chien, Ch'i Tiao-k'ai, and others, some of whom may have actually preceded Yang Chu.[19] Mencius seems to be well aware of his forerunners in the enterprise of dealing with this theme.

I would suggest that the notion of a "heavenly endowed" or "heavenly ordained" tendency, directionality, or potentiality of growth in the individual may have arisen quite early and that the problem of the relation of this *hsing*, however conceived, to the normative social order may have been posed even before Confucius. Despite the "pragmatic" or "existential" reluctance of the Master to dwell on these matters, his disciples felt impelled to do so. The provocative views of Mo-tzu and Yang Chu may indeed have contributed to the vigor of the debate, but they probably were not the first to pose the issues involved.

## Ch'i

Another term which enters prominently into the discourse of the Warring States period is the term *ch'i*. When we turn our attention to the origin of the term and the graph which represents it, we find little tangible evidence in the earliest sources.[20] If any concept of *ch'i* existed in the Shang or early Chou periods, it does not find expression in the sources available to us. The effort to find the original graph in the oracle bones and bronze inscription has so far proven fruitless. Instead, what we find is an effort to reconstruct the origins of the term by tracing back from later usages.[21] The latter Han dynasty etymological dictionary of graphs, the *Shuo-wen* of Hsü Shen speaks of the "vapor of clouds," and Akatsuka has suggested that clouds and winds do, of course, point to the formless powers of the universe. Even if the winds and clouds were divine, their manifestations suggest the formless and unindividualized "substance" and "energy." When we meet the term in the *Analects*, one of its meanings is indeed "breath." As Kurita Naomi has pointed out, we are here immediately reminded of the association of mists, air, and breath as well as the association of these with the soullike or spiritlike in the early cosmologies of other cultures.[22]

Another gloss of the graph (also supported by the *Shuo-wen*) emphasizes its rice (*mi*) component. According to this view, the graph represents the nourishing vapors of boiling rice or grain. These vapors represent the nourishing powers of food that maintain life and human energy. The image of food even suggests the interchange of energy and substance between humans and their surrounding environment. This interpretation would emphasize the association of *ch'i* with human life.[23]

All of this seems to suggest that here we finally may have the closest Chinese approximation of the Western concept of "matter." I must, of course, immediately point out that in most of the cultures where the wind-air-breath association arises, it does not necessarily lead to the notion of it as the primordial stuff out of which "everything is made," nor is there any evidence that it did so in early China. It is, in fact, mainly in the Milesian strain of pre-Socratic thought of Greece that we find any clear evidence of the notion of a primordial stuff and it is only in Anaximenes that the notion of *aer* is identified as the stuff "from which the things that are becoming and that are and that shall be and gods and things divine, all come into being."[24]

Even if the word *ch'i* later comes to be conceived in China as some pervasive stuff/energy, it emerges in the literature much later than the terms referring to *order* both human and cosmic which have been discussed above. If one can indeed make the generalization that Greek "philosophy" begins in Miletus with notions of a "primordial stuff/energy," one would have to say that Chinese "philosophy"—if one is allowed to use the term—begins with reflections on an all-embracing primal order and the notion of an order which does not require the reduction of its multiple components and relations to any preexistent "stuff."

What may be a comparatively early reference to *ch'i* in the *Tso-chuan* refers to the six *ch'i* of heaven which give rise to the five tastes, manifest themselves as the five colors, and display themselves in the five notes, and, when disordered, produce the "six diseases." It is then specified that the six *ch'i* are *yin, yang,* wind, rain, darkness, and lights.[25] Here *ch'i* is not considered apart from the specific constituents in which it is imbedded. It is by no means clear that the six *ch'i* are conceived of as one pervasive stuff/energy. In one passage of the *Tso-chuan,* Tzu-ch'an also discusses *ch'i* in an unspecified way in referring to the individual organism. In rebuking the Marquis of Chin for his dissolute life (particularly his indulgence in sexual excesses), he maintains that a regular life devoted to the honest conduct of business with adequate periods of rest allows one's inner *ch'i* to be properly regulated and to circulate freely. The Marquis's irregular mode of life leads his *ch'i* to be "stopped up, become congested, and thus become reduced and attenuated."[26]

We find here a kind of physicalist language which seems to refer to a sort of circulating fluidum that has the Cartesian attribute of matter as the spatially extended, and *ch'i* may certainly have properties which are in later Western thought attributed to matter. At the same time, because of its unquestioned dynamic qualities, some have insisted on calling it energy rather than matter on the basis of the constantly repeated cliché that in the West matter is static while *ch'i* is dynamic. But consider the primal stuff of Thales and Anaximenes. There is nothing static about their "water" and "air," which seem to move eternally.[27] The notion of a matter which is simply inert and moves only when impelled from without represents one small development within the Greek discussion of the primal stuff. Yet one may nevertheless agree that *ch'i* comes to have properties of both energy and matter, as is clearly proven by the application to it of the notion of condensation and rarefaction in later Chinese thought.

It is also clear, however, that *ch'i* comes to embrace properties which we would call psychic, emotional, spiritual, numinous, and even "mystical." It is precisely at this point that Western definitions of "matter" and the physical which systematically exclude these properties from their definition do not at all correspond to *ch'i.* There seems to be absolutely no dogma that all these properties may not simultaneously inhere in the same "substance." To the extent that the word "energy" is used in the West to apply exclusively to a force that relates only entities described in terms of physical mass, it is as misleading as matter, I think, as an over-all name for *ch'i.*

In much of its modern colloquial usage in both Chinese and Japanese, *ch'i* usually refers to terms which describe states of emotion, dispositions of sentiment, and attitudes. It thus refers to all kinds of states of "high spirits" (whether of anger or exaltation), to morale, zeal, courage, and arrogance. It applies to moods, tastes, and even nuances of outer bearing as they reflect these inner dispositions. If there is any commonality in all these meanings, it is that they refer to some pervasive "state" of some entity or state of affairs rather than to entities as such. If anger is a state of *ch'i* within a human person, the weather may equally be said to be a certain state of the heavenly *ch'i* (*t'ien ch'i*).

To be sure, even in the case of Thales and Anaximenes, one can by no means dogmatically say that the "primordial stuff" excludes the psychic, the spiritual, or the numinous any more than the dynamic. Anaximenes's air, like Thales's water, is "full of gods."[28] Viewed in hindsight, however, one can see how the direction taken by these thinkers later reinforced by the atomism of Leucippus and Democritus could lead to a clearly "reductionist" conception of matter. This would give rise to the possibility of explaining the diversity of the physical world as we perceive it as combinations of or "constructions" out of some simple homogeneous stuff of minimal properties by employing such principles as the principle of condensation and rarefaction or the principle of compounding and construction. Thus, Anaximenes did indeed provide an account, in these terms, of how fire arises out of finer air and how water and earth are condensed out of denser air.

Whether the impulse which lay behind this kind of "reductionism" was a spirit of "disinterested" scientific curiosity we cannot, of course, know. Cornford, like some Marxist historians, speculates that it relates to the practical "positive" spirit which pervaded the Ionian commercial city of Miletus and mentions the practical technological interests which are attributed to Thales in some of the early literature.[29] Whatever its origins, it represented a sharp reaction against Homeric mythos. This approach would see reductionist impulses rising out of an "interested" orientation toward the practical and the technological rather than the orientation to the contemplative and theoretical which we find in Aristotle.

Kirk and Raven, in a chapter on "Forerunners of Philosophic Cosmogony," however, point to another dimension which relates the Milesian search for a primordial stuff to the nature of Greek and even Middle Eastern religion already discussed above.[30] Both Mesopotamian and Greek religion, represented in Hesiod, associate divinity not so much with order as with the primal power and constituents of nature—the heavens, the ocean, the earth, eros—and stress the mythic encounters among these forces. Thus the *Enuma Elish*'s stress on Tiamat and Apsu as the upper and lower waters which together engender the other constituents of the world, as well as similar Egyptian accounts, may have indeed strongly affected the world picture of a man like Thales who lived on the coast of Asia Minor. Here the dominance of the divine powers associated with the element of water, when translated into a nonmythic language, suggests the notion of water as the ultimate stuff of being.

Whatever may have lain behind this "reductionist" tendency, it did not, as we know, necessarily become the dominant principle even among those called the pre-Socratic philosophers, while Socrates, Plato, and Aristotle were to move in quite different directions. And yet one might say that it remained a latent presence within the subsequent history of Western thought and was to be "reactivated" in the scientific revolution of the seventeenth century—placing its indelible stamp on most modern Western definitions of the word matter. It is this reductionist definition which effectively links the word matter to the physical sciences.

To the extent that the notion *ch'i* in its more philosophic development resembles anything in early Ionian thought, it seems to be closest to Anaximander's *apeiron* or "boundless." While Anaximander was himself a Milesian, he refused to derive the world from any of its "warring constituents."[31] He instead posits a "boundless" indefinite and indeterminate reality from which all the separate elements and entities of the world emerge. Anaximander's *apeiron* is thus not a "reductionist" matter but a boundless indescribable encompassing reality from which all limited things "emerge." Similarly, in the case of China, one finds no impulse to identify *ch'i*, whatever its original meaning, with any specific constituent of reality such as water, earth, or air, which are somehow all there in "their own right" in the encompassing order of the world. It is significant that Anaximander's *apeiron* is also associated with the notion of a primary world order, which emerges in its wholeness out of the *apeiron*. In this order, opposing elements are held in harmony by a kind of "justice" in which things "pay penalty and retribution to each other for their injustices according to the assessment of time."[32] They are not "reduced" to each other. To the extent that *ch'i* comes to play a dominant role in some later modes of Chinese thought (as in Chang Tsai of the Sung dynasty), it certainly is much closer to Anaximander's "boundless" and "indefinable" than to any concept of matter in terms reducible to minimal, physical properties, such as can be assigned to water and air or the properties of "mass" and "movement" which we find in modern physics.

It is also quite clear that the concept of *ch'i* as a pervasive and continuous stuff/energy endowed with properties which are both "physical" and "nonphysical" is far less central in pre-Ch'in Chinese thought than the concept of a total cosmic and social order often referred to by the word *tao*. In many texts it emerges only as a kind of connective substance of the all-encompassing order and is more often discussed in its differentiated aspects than as a homogeneous substance.

In the *Analects*, we find it used to refer on one occasion to breath,[33] on another occasion to something like the vital energy blood-*ch'i* (*hsüeh-ch'i*) of a man in his full vigor,[34] and in another case Master Tseng even uses it to refer to the proper tone of voice used when speaking.[35] All these references are to human phenomena, as one might expect given Confucius' concerns. When we turn to Mo-tzu's original text, we find that the human application is dominant as well. It is used to refer to life energy and health. In the righteous society of the past food was sufficient "to increase their *ch'i* and satisfy their hunger."[36] The sages built houses so that the rigors of the seasons would not harm the *ch'i* of men, and in another place he speaks of digging graves deeply enough to prevent the oozing up of what was presumably *ch'i* as a noxious emanation from the dead.[37] Again, all these references are to human phenomena although there is discussion in the "military" chapters of lucky and unlucky emanations (*ch'i*) from the four cardinal directions. It is most striking that the term *ch'i* occurs only once in the dialectic chapters.[38] The entire discussion of logical, mathematical, and scientific (optics, mechanics, physics) ideas takes place without any reference to the notion of *ch'i* as a kind of "underlying matter," just as Pythagorean mathematics and Aristotelian logic are not particularly related to the "reductionist" matter of Thales, Anaximenes, or the atomists in ancient Greece. In Lao-tzu and Chuang-tzu *ch'i* indeed assumes highly mystical dimensions.

The fact that neither Confucius nor Mo-tzu dwell on the cosmic aspects of *ch'i* may simply reflect their largely "humanist" concerns. During the Warring States and early Han periods, it is quite clear, however, that it comes to refer to aspects of the human, the cosmic, and even the mystical, and thus becomes deeply involved in the entire discourse concerning the relations between the two, but at no point does it become a "reductionist" matter in the Western sense.

## *Hsin* (Heart/Mind)

I shall finally briefly consider here one other category which plays a crucial role in the discourse of the Warring States period and the subsequent development of Chinese thought—the category of *hsin*, or heart/mind. Its origins seem to be both ancient and unambiguous. The graph as it appears in the bronze inscriptions is a picture of the physical organ, and it figures prominently throughout the *Book of Poetry* as the center of emotions and sentiments. The heart

continually expresses grief, sorrow, disappointment, and occasionally there is mention of the king's heart as tranquil or calm. The
sentiment of love is attributed to the heart and it is the source of
moral exertion as well. King Ch'eng, we are told, "exerted his heart
to secure the peace of the realm."[39] Elsewhere it is made clear that
the *hsin* is also the source of intellect and understanding. "This King
Chi–Shang-ti filled his mind/heart with discrimination."[40] Thus as
early as the *Book of Poetry* the heart/mind already seems the center of
all those expressions of the conscious life which we attribute to both
heart and mind in the West. Its range is equally broad in the *Analects*. At one point, it refers to desires, when Confucius informs us
that at seventy he could follow his heart's desires without going astray.[41] At another it is the seat of *jen*. We are told that in the case of
Yen Hui, "His heart would not stray from *jen* for three months."[42]
At another point, it clearly applies to intellectual effort, when Confucius asserts that it would be better to use one's mind (*hsin*) on
"Chinese" chess rather than waste it in idleness.[43] It is striking in view
of all this that the category of *hsin*, which lends itself so easily to the
metaphor of the "inner," is so notably absent in Fingarette's book.

In the older parts of the book of Mo-tzu, the word is used as the
ultimate reference point of emotions and thought and yet it is characteristic of the dialectic chapters that it is used mainly as the organ
of intelligence and is probably suspect because of its associations
with inwardness. There is much more emphasis on the will and intelligence as outward-facing dispositions.

The concept of *hsin* is central to some of the basic issues of Warring States thought. It relates to the crucial issues dividing Confucianism from Taoism and plays an extraordinary central role within
the entire Confucian debate on human nature. Indeed, to the extent
that we translate the term "human nature" as *hsing*, one should note
that these debates involve much more than the notion of *hsing*. They
encompass nothing less than a consideration of the entire question
"What is man?"; consequently, they are certainly as much concerned with the category of *hsin* as they are with the category of
*hsing*. Indeed, if we look forward a millennium to the Neo-Confucian
(*tao hsüeh*) debates of later centuries, we shall actually find that the
question of how *hsing* relates to *hsin* becomes central to the problematique which emerges within that stream of thought. The very fact
that the *hsin* is itself the center of will, emotion, desire, and intellect
(both "rational" and intuitive) means that it will itself become the
center of much contention in all the discussion concerning the relationship among all these "faculties."

# CHAPTER 6

# THE WAYS OF TAOISM

I N DEALING WITH the foreign term "Taoism" I shall confine my attention to the high-cultural development of the first four centuries B.C. Without denying the relationship of that vast later development which has in China been subsumed under the heading "Taoist religion" (*tao-chiao*) to this earlier stream, we shall have a sufficient task in attempting to fix the outer limits and common assumptions of the ancient "school of Tao" (*tao-chia*) as defined by the Han doxographers, as well as by modern interpreters in China, Japan, and the West.

The term *tao-chia* has come to be applied to a wide assortment of personalities and texts which on the surface seem to represent quite different tendencies. These personalities were in fact regarded by their contemporaries as representing diverse outlooks. It is indeed most difficult to trace the links of ideas among them in chronologic terms or in terms of implicit logic. To be sure, there are two names which both in China and the West loom high above all others: Lao-tzu and Chuang-tzu. Yet these are names attached primarily to texts. While there certainly was a historic Chuang-tzu, he seems to be associated basically with one strand of thought in the book which now bears his name. The effort to determine the real Lao-tzu has, on the other hand, turned into a minor industry and the controversies continue unabated. Thus it is difficult to trace influences. Some of the ideas which appear in the "inner chapters" of the Chuang-tzu (*nei p'ien*, the first seven chapters largely attributed to the historic Chuang-tzu) are also found in the fragments of some of the "Taoists," such as Shen Tao, and others who were active at the Chi-hsia "Academy" in the state of Ch'i (see the last part of this chapter). Since many of these figures were probably contemporaries of the historic Chuang-tzu and the composer of the Lao-tzu book, it becomes extremely difficult to answer the question of who influenced whom when one deals with specific ideas.[1] As indicated in Chapter 5, this is a world of shared notions subject to variant interpretations. Many sections in the Chuang-tzu text seem to be more closely affiliated with the Lao-tzu strain than they are with the historic Chuang-tzu. There is finally the added difficulty, by no means confined to ancient China, that many of the ideas labeled "Taoist" can be found in the "eclectics" who find no difficulty in wedding notions labeled Taoist with ideas which seem to be distinctively non-Taoist. This eclecticism, if such it is, can even be found in the great synthesizer of Legalism, Han Fei-tzu, as well as in the Confucian Hsün-tzu.

There seems to be considerable (but not universal) agreement that the text of the Lao-tzu, later also given the title of "the classic of the Tao and its Power" (*Tao-te ching*), represents an earlier stratum of Taoist ideas and a mode of thought which may have emerged after Confucius and Mo-tzu and probably before the historic Chuang-tzu and the various "Taoists" of the Chi-hsia Academy.[2] Some argue that many of its aphorisms and maxims may have been drawn from a common fund of well-known sayings, and D. C. Lau even calls it an anthology. Yet here again, I am inclined to remark that, however disparate the sources of the text, whoever finally molded it into one composition did succeed in projecting a remarkably unified poetic vision of the world. The recent discovery of what may be the oldest extant versions of the text—the Ma Wang-tui silk scrolls—on the whole affirm this view.

The questions of dating may, of course, never be solved, and one cannot, unfortunately, simply say that the dating of the texts is a matter of no consequence in dealing with the relations of the ideas. If the composition of the Lao-tzu book really represents a mode of thought later than that of the Chuang-tzu or of the adherents of the "Yellow Emperor and Lao-tzu" (Huang-lao) school (discussed below), this would indeed affect the picture of their relationship that I shall here propose for dealing with the main broad currents within ancient Taoism. With all the hazards involved, I shall nevertheless proceed to distinguish what seem to me to be three main currents, or "ways," of Taoism (I shall, however, accept the assumption of the Han doxographer that these currents share a sufficient basis in common premises to justify their subsumption under the "Taoist" category)—the Lao-tzu current, the Chuang-tzu current, and the Huang-lao current.

In considering the rise of what I shall without apology call the mystical Taoism of Lao-tzu and Chuang-tzu (since mysticism is what the two texts share in common, despite their significant differences), I shall attempt to relate them to the context of the Confucian and Mohist controversies that may provide its immediate background. Even if this Taoism can be called mystical, it is, of course, a mysticism which arises within a Chinese context and not in an Indian or Christian context. In asserting that this Taoism is mystical, I am not asserting that the mysticism of Taoism is Brahmanism, Mahayana Buddhism, or the mysticism of Jakob Boehme. It is a mystical outlook which remains irreducibly Chinese and entirely sui generis.

In seeking the sources of mystical Taoism, some have pointed to the shadowy recluses in the *Analects* who reject Confucius' enterprise. Indeed, one of them—the "madman of Ch'u"—appears in the pages of the Chuang-tzu, where he strongly reiterates the view that Mo-tzu was to identify as fatalism. "When the world has the Way the sage succeeds; when the world is without the Way the sage survives."[3] This reminds us of Mo-tzu's contemporary Confucianists except for the striking fact that the madman seems to care nothing for rites and music and is bent wholly on his own self-preservation in the spirit of Yang Chu. We shall indeed find that what I call the Yang Chu motif is indeed part of the vision of both Lao-tzu and Chuang-tzu. Nevertheless, the "primitivist" critique of civilization which we find in the Lao-tzu is entirely lacking. What we have instead is a kind of all-enveloping historic fatalism. Civilizations rise and fall and human effort to affect the course of events is unavailing.

Perhaps more important than these "escapists," when viewed from the Taoist perspective, are certain tendencies in Confucius himself which seem to point toward the Taoist vision.

We have already noted the Master's reluctance to speak based on his vision of Heaven's relations to the four seasons and the generative processes of the universe. Here he seems to envision a human order which might run with the unpremeditated, spontaneous regularity of the natural order. It is true that most of the *Analects* is focused on conscious, goal-directed efforts of human moral agents. Yet Confucius is also acutely aware that it is precisely in this area of conscious human purpose that humans go astray. He in fact dreams of a state of affairs where the good society would come to be embodied in unreflective habitual behavior. Human behavior would correspond to the mysterious rhythms of nature.

There is one passage in the *Analects*, which I have not yet mentioned, which seems so Taoist in its language that many suspect later interpolation. Here we actually find the term *wu-wei*, which lies at the heart of Taoist thought. The term can be interpreted literally as meaning nonaction or, more importantly, as the kind of unpremeditated, nondeliberative, noncalculating, nonpurposive action (or, more accurately, behavior) that dominates Taoist discourse. "Was it not Shun who ruled by *wu-wei?* What did he do? He simply main-

tained himself in dignity and reverently faced south" (the correct
position of the sage-ruler on his throne).[4] His correct praxis simply
flowed effortlessly and without deliberation from his spiritual power.
One might say that Shun's relationship to human society was precisely that of Heaven to the order of nature. The great power (*te*) of
his spirit permeated and sustained the order of society. Whether or
not the statement is to be attributed to Confucius, it may indeed be
entirely compatible with Confucius' dream of the truly good society.
It must immediately be added, however, that Shun, like his predecessor Yao and his own follower Yü, is nevertheless one of the founders of human civilization. Situated as he is between the more activist
first founder Yao and the more activist controller of floods and promoter of agriculture Yü, he may simply have represented a more
quiet interlude in the fashioning of civilization. He nevertheless undoubtedly manifests his *te* by acting through all the civilized forms
of high civilization. There is here, to be sure, no hint of Lao-tzu's
"primitivist" critique of high civilization. What Confucius dreams
of is a society in which civilized behavior will "just come naturally,"
as it does in his own case after the age of seventy. This may be his
dream, but he is acutely aware that this is not the actuality. The *tao*
can, in fact, be restored to the world only by the noble man's sustained conscious efforts, by painstaking self-scrutiny, scrupulous attention to behavior, unflagging devotion to the cultivation of
learning, attentive practice of *li,* and conscientious service in government.

Yet, as we have also seen, even in the Master's conception of
learning one also finds intimations of tendencies which point in the
direction of Lao-tzu and Chuang-tzu. There is that sense of an inex-
pressable underlying unity which should emerge from and inform
all ongoing learning. There is the aspiration to obtain, as it were, a
synoptic intuitive vision of the entire "landscape" of the *tao* and the
intimation in the words of Yen Hui that in this intuition there is
something "ungraspable" beyond all words.

There seems to be, in fact, a deep inner relation between the intuition of oneness and the notion of *wu-wei.* To the extent that the
noble man achieves this sense of oneness of the order of things, one
may say that he is "aligned" with the *tao* and his behavior comes to
be governed by the larger holistic pattern. Here again, however, despite these intimations of higher illumination, Confucius insists
throughout that the pursuit of learning in the ordinary sense of the
incremental accumulation of knowledge and of conscious reflection
on knowledge must continue without let-up.

When we turn our attention to Mo-tzu, we are suddenly struck by the realization that precisely those tendencies in the *Analects* which point in the direction of the Taoist "turn" seem to arouse Mo-tzu's fiercest resistance. The holistic, immanentist view of order and the concept of *wu-wei* would certainly be considered by him as aspects of that fatality which he deplores. Holism implies the immanence of Heaven in the order of things and the determination of all the parts by the whole. While the *Analects* still refer to Heaven's intentionality in its relationship to human affairs, Mo-tzu's Confucian protagonists seem to believe that the course of human history itself, the whole cycle of order and disorder, is not influenced by any conscious intentionality of either Heaven or man. Their own realm of conscious, purposive activity seems to have shrunk to the narrow domain of ceremonies and music. As against this, one might say that what Mohism represents above all else is the apotheosis of the very opposite idea and ideal of *wei* or *yu-wei*—of deliberate, analytic, and goal-oriented thought and action in a plural world—to cite Graham, "of concrete and particular objects" and of concrete and particular persons, spirits, and situations. He lives in a world where order must be "constructed."

The concept of *wei,* with all its nuances of meaning in the language, is illuminated with great lucidity in the dialectic chapters of Mo-tzu. The word may simply mean "making," as in "making a coat," or "unmaking" or "doing away with" (as in curing an illness), or engaging in various conscious activities which require not "making" but "doing," such as ruling a country or engaging in trade.[5] Since these chapters are already contemporary with the full development of Taoism, one finds in them even a concession to one concept of *wei* as natural transformation (*hua*)—a meaning which might be called Taoist. The word is thus defined as "dissolving" (as in sleet) and a "frog turning into a quail" (evidently referring to a widely held popular belief). There is thus a recognition that in some parts of nature such "built-in" transformative processes may exist.[6] Above all, however, *wei* refers to deliberate goal-directed activity. In another passage where the meaning of *wei* as "being for" or "doing something for the sake of" is expounded, the canons make it clear that all appropriate action should be based on an accurate analytic knowledge of the factors which bear on the situation at hand and on an accurate "weighing" of such factors.[7] The stress on intellectual analysis is obvious and the intuitive grasp of the whole is conspicuously absent.

My argument here is that the Lao-tzu and the Chuang-tzu not only draw on strains whose beginning can be discerned in the *Analects,* but may also represent a sharp reaction against the exaltation of conscious, purposive action *wei* so explicitly and vehemently espoused by the Mohists. There are specific allusions in the Lao-tzu to a rejection of Mohist ideas. One particularly clear passage states that "not advancing men of worth will lead people not to contend."[8] Lao-tzu's point is that the desire for goods and fame are the root cause of that human strife and conflict which lie at the heart of the social tragedy. The aggressive efforts of the "men of worth" to achieve office and Mo-tzu's injunction to reward such men of worth with wealth and honors can only have one result—that all others will desire to do likewise, thus spreading the diseases of a competitive higher civilization throughout the society. Mohism forcefully calls attention to the *yu-wei* foundation of the project of civilization.

One of the effects of Mohism which becomes particularly apparent in the Chuang-tzu book is that it actually leads both Lao-tzu and Chuang-tzu to see Confucius or the Confucianists wholly from the point of view of those features which they share with Mo-tzu. In the end, both Mo-tzu and Confucius are, after all, convinced that the achievement of the norms of civilization require both knowledge and deliberate unremitting moral efforts of sages, noble men, and men of worth. In the Lao-tzu–Chuang-tzu perspective, both Confucian noble men and Mohist men of worth are busybodies who wander about the world deceiving themselves in the belief that they can transform the human world by *yu-wei* activity. One might also add that, from the point of view of the third century Taoists, both schools had spectacularly failed to achieve their professed goals.

Before I turn to the mystical core of the Lao-tzu vision, however, there is one other motif in both the Lao-tzu and Chuang-tzu books which deserves some attention—what might be called the Yang Chu strain. Here again, our ignorance of the dates of all three makes it impossible to resolve the question of mutual influence. There is actually one tradition which makes Yang Chu a disciple of or contemporary of Lao-tzu.[9] If this were indeed the case, it would indicate that the Yang Chu motif was already an integral part of the Lao-tzu vision and that Yang Chu simply extracted from the vision what suited his purposes. On the other hand, we have the view represented by Graham that Yang Chu's point of view really emerged out of his dialectic encounters with the Mohists and that it is precisely his particular view of human nature which may have influenced both Lao-tzu and Chuang-tzu.

Without attempting to resolve the question of influence, it is nevertheless possible to discern both within the Lao-tzu and the historic Chuang-tzu what Lau calls this particular "mundane" strain. Summarizing this tendency once more in the words of the *Huai-nan-tzu*, one's life aim should be "to fulfill one's *hsing,* preserve what is authentic [in oneself], and not allow one's body to be placed at risk by external things."[10] This in turn means maintaining one's health, avoiding anxiety, satisfying one's physical desires without, however, injuring one's health or becoming entangled in needless passions. Here there is no mysticism but rather a deep appreciation of the value of "just living" in as comfortable and anxiety-free a manner as possible. Living this way is the only obligation which our Heavenly nature imposes upon us. To the extent that participating in fulfilling social obligations or pursuing social honors, power, and wealth interfere with these aims, one should not "sacrifice one hair of one's body" to serve society. It is indeed in this rejection of the notion that social goals are in any way necessary to one's felicity that one sees the most obvious affinities between two outlooks. It is thus quite possible that the reason why Mencius, who may have been a contemporary of Chuang-tzu, is not at all aware of "Taoism" is because, when viewed from his particular perspective, people such as Chuang-tzu might have indeed been viewed as representing the outlook of Yang Chu, who advocated "everyone for himself" which amounted to a "denial of one's ruler."[11] In fact, we have no reason to suppose that Yang Chu at all shared Lao-tzu's primitivistic critique of higher civilization and his real social doctrine—if he had any at all—may have been that one should make oneself as safe and comfortable as possible in whatever social circumstances one found oneself.

And yet, it is in fact true that the Yang Chu stress on the value of "mere living" is shared by both Lao-tzu and Chuang-tzu, and both will offer down-to-earth prudential advice on how to avoid risking one's life. It is this, indeed, which leads Lau to raise the question of whether a term like "mysticism" is at all applicable particularly to the commonsensically "Chinese" outlook of the Lao-tzu.

## 1. Lao-tzu and the Ineffable Tao

In dealing with the text of the Lao-tzu—one of the most frequently translated and yet one of the most difficult and problematic texts in all of Chinese literature—I shall nevertheless begin precisely with its mystical dimension in the face of the constant assertion that it is nothing but a handbook of a prudential mundane life philosophy, a treatise on political strategy, an esoteric treatise on military strategy, a utopian tract, or a text which advocates "a scientific naturalistic" attitude toward the cosmos. This is not to assert that elements suggestive of all of these may not be present. To the extent that they are, however, they have their locus within a vision which I would maintain is as mystical as any orientation to which that term has been applied in any other culture.

Among students of comparative religion, there seems to be some consensus concerning the earmarks of mystical orientations in religion.[12] One will find considerable common ground in the writings of authors as diverse as Underhill, Stace, Jones, and Scholem, and among authorities on Indian thought. In all of them we find some notion of "ground of reality" or ultimate aspect of reality or a dimension of "nonbeing" (naturally all metaphors when applied to the ineffable are suspect) which cannot be discussed in the categories of human language. It is a reality or dimension of reality beyond all determinations, relations, and processes which can be described in human language. Yet the mere assertion of the existence of such a reality does not in itself constitute mysticism. It is rather the profound faith or "knowledge" in the sense of gnosis that this reality—incommunicable in words—is nevertheless the source of all meaning for human beings which makes mysticism in some sense a religious outlook. The "mystery" is not an absence of "knowledge" but a kind of higher direct knowledge of the ineffable source of all that which lends existence meaning. It thus refers to a plenitude rather than to an absence, but a plenitude beyond the grasp of language.

Yet even this seems insufficient to characterize mysticism. The fact is that medieval religious philosophy in the West and in Islam—whether Jewish, Christian, or Islamic—is equally insistent that God in his essence is unknowable and inaccessible to human language. He can only be known by the *via negativa*—by the language which tells us what he is not. Finite man in his incorrigible finitude can never "know" the inner essence of God, who remains the irreducibly Other who can only be known through his manifestations within the finite world. Thus, the concept of the unknowable reality may be monotheistic, as well as mystical. It is only in God's relatedness to finite reality that one applies to him the attributes of personality. In most orientations which have been called mystical, however, there is the assumption that finite humans or some finite humans can achieve oneness or some kind of mystic union with the ultimate ground of reality, and more often than not this doctrine has immanentist or pantheistic implications (perhaps not in early Buddhism).[13] I hasten to add that the presence or absence of mysticism has nothing to do with the term used to symbolize the "ultimate" or "higher" reality or aspect of reality.

All the above factors are, I think, present in and even central to the visions of the Lao-tzu and the sections of the Chuang-tzu book which belong to the "historic" Chuang-tzu. Yet again, there is no such thing as mysticism in general. Taoism is obviously as sui generis as is Mahayana Buddhism, Brahmanism, Sufism, and Christian and Jewish mysticism. The ineffable reality itself cannot, in principle, be differentiated, since it is by definition beyond all differentiation, but the paradoxical fact remains that most mysticisms have, of course, attempted to use language to convey their truth. To the extent that they do so, their dominant metaphors and the ways in which they relate their mysticism to all aspects of their cultural heritage and historical situation profoundly color their entire vision. Here the orientations of the culture become fully operative.

Beginning, however, with the mystical dimension of Taoism, we are immediately struck by the use of the word *tao* as the dominant term of this Chinese mysticism. How does a term which seems to refer in Confucianism mainly to social and natural *order* come to refer to a mystic reality? Let me make two observations at the outset. As a mystic, like mystics elsewhere, the Lao-tzu is not deeply committed to the term itself: "I know not its name so I style it the *tao*. If forced to name it, I would call it the *great*."[14] And yet when the Lao-tzu uses the term to refer to the world of "determinate being" to the word of the "ten thousand things," it retains its meaning of encompassing order.

How may a word which refers to *order* come to have a mystical meaning? In the modern West, words which refer to "impersonal order," or "structure" to use the most common contemporary metaphor, seem to suggest the very antithesis of the mystical. A structure is something totally transparent to our analysis. We know what it is made of and how it is put together. Ideally, it should contain no mysteries. As has already been suggested, however, the concept of order which we have found in China is not a structure in this sense. It is the total organic pattern, not at all "built-up" out of the parts. I am, of course, well aware that even in the modern West, the literal sense of the word "structure" as "something which has been built" has been largely abandoned. We thus speak of "emerging structures," and this seems to imply a total gestalt emerging as a totality. And yet there is the ongoing sense of something which can—at least in thought—be taken apart and put together again. So long as one thinks of an order, whether spatial or temporal, as an immanent whole, one notes that it is composed of a multitude of separate components and relations and yet what holds the whole together is not in the parts. It is the elusive whole which holds the parts together. To the extent that there is an order, there is some kind of ungraspable principle of unity at its heart. Indeed, in a dynamic order, the elements and the relations may undergo great change, as in the processes of biological growth, and yet the principle of unity will remain.

Much of what I have said here immediately reminds us of Needham's conception of the dominance of "organismic philosophy" in China. Again, however, one must ask—what does the word "organism" mean? What is the nature of the whole which envelops and determines the parts? At one point, in fact, Needham flatly states that one would not wish to deny that ancient Taoist thought had strong elements of mysticism.[15] On the whole, however, he is painfully anxious to disassociate his conception of organism from mystical implications. He thus states that in the Chinese conception of organism, "the parts, in their organizational relations whether of a living body or the universe were sufficient to account by a kind of harmony of wills, for the observed phenomena."[16] He then, however, adds, "the cooperation of the component parts of the organism is not forced but absolutely spontaneous even involuntary." Now "harmony of wills" and "cooperation" are a language which seems to suggest separate entities which "voluntarily" come together to cooperate by express design. The image suggests that the parts somehow exist as "individuals" before they come to "cooperate." Needham, however, hastens to erase this impression by implying that in fact the "organizational relations" are really logically prior to the parts, and he makes it quite clear that the cooperation of the parts is, in fact, "involuntary" and really determined by the whole. All these terms—organizational relations, organizing principle, organism, process, and so on—seem to point to some kind of determinable knowledge about something quite definite, while the Lao-tzu seems to insist that what accounts for the order as a whole as well as the "spontaneous" behavior of the parts is itself beyond language. What, indeed, is an "organizing principle" *an sich?* If a term like "organizing principle" is meant to refer to anything describable and definite, it is not the *tao* in its ineffable aspect of nonbeing (*wu*). Lao-tzu, however, prefers not to name the unnameable or to imply any knowledge of "how it works."

It is, of course, true that Lao-tzu's mysticism does not rest on a theistic metaphor. The insistence on the word *tao* represents a striking departure from the centrality of the word Heaven. As indicated earlier, the word Heaven continued to carry with it some sense of Heaven as a conscious, guiding force and Heaven remains the central term even in the *Analects.* To the extent that the word *tao* in the *Analects* is used to refer to the cosmos, the controlling term seems to be the "*tao* of heaven" and not *tao* as such. While Heaven may already be immanent in the processes of nature; while Heaven's presence in nature may manifest itself in a *wu-wei* fashion; in its relation to the human world, the term Heaven still seems to have intentional and providential associations. As for Mo-tzu, one need not dwell on his emphasis on the "theistic" dimensions of Heaven.

Thus, in generally preferring the word *tao* to the word Heaven as a term for the ultimate, the Lao-tzu may be fully aware of the *yu-wei* associations which cluster about the term Heaven. In the very first passage of the book as it is now arranged, we find the statement, "the nameless is the beginning of heaven and earth."[17] Elsewhere we find it stated with regard to the *tao* that, "I know not whose son it is; it seems that it precedes the 'High God' [*ti*]."[18] Heaven and earth are not the ultimate. One can make determinate statements about them and, like all determinate things, they are finite and perhaps not eternal. There is, in fact, a definite implication that the whole determinate universe may arise in time and disappear in time (although it may also recur in a cyclical pattern). While attributing "long life and endurance" to them, he denies them eternity. "Heaven and earth cannot go on forever."[19] In all their actions, even they are utterly dependent on the nameless Tao.

It is true that mystical views have emerged as countercurrents within predominantly monotheistic religions, just as theistic strains have emerged within predominantly mystical orientations. In Islam, Christianity, and Judaism mysticism arises largely in association with the word God and some of the major metaphors remain theistic, such as the metaphor of the love of God. Even sexual love, as we know, can become the metaphor for losing all determinate existence. These movements become mystical not because of their assumption that God's "essence" is inaccessible to human language—a doctrine which they shared with most medieval religious philosophy—but because of their assumption that finite humans can, in some sense, come to "know" the unknowable essence of God and come to be "at one" with it.

Yet Taoism may not be unique in arriving at mysticism through the metaphor of a term referring to *order*. Upanishadic mysticism in India does not seem to emerge initially from meditation on the inner being or love of the Vedic gods, as much as from the Brahmans' meditations on the meaning of sacrificial rites and the sacred priestly formulas, the Brahmanas, used in their rites. These rites which constitute a ritual order seem to embody a higher source of power than the gods whom they control. In Zimmer's formulation, the sacred magic formula is "the powerful urge and surge that rises from man's unconscious" crystallized in a charm or formula, just as by extension it comes to mean the supreme ineffable power which lies behind all the forms and structures and orders of the ordered world, including the gods themselves.[20] That which makes order an order and ritual form a form is itself unknowable. In Taoist terms, it is both *tao* and *te*. I shall not dwell on the evolution of the term "logos" in Neo-Platonic philosophy. It would appear, however, that through the contemplation of the eternal forms and the order of these forms which are, in Plato, contemplated by the intellect, one rises to the one and the unknowable, which is beyond all determinations.

The theme of the inaccessibility of the ultimate reality to language is, of course, a basic theme in the Lao-tzu and in the Chuang-tzu, and here we are again forcefully reminded of the early emergence in China of the "language" question. If Confucius deeply believes in language as providing an image of true order and if Mohism gropes toward the notion of a new, improved language which will provide a new and more precise picture of the world in all its particularities, the Lao-tzu book while not casting doubt on the language which describes the natural order (although it does indeed cast doubt on the received language descriptive of the human order) finds that that which makes the determinate *tao* possible lies beyond all language. What the Lao-tzu dwells on is the impermanent, finite nature of all the determinate realities of which one *can* speak. Hence the ringing assertion in the first line of the text as now constituted: "The *tao* of which one can speak is not the eternal [or permanent?] *tao;* the names which one can name are not the eternal name."[21] This is not Vedanta. The world of our ordinary experience does not seem to be a cosmic illusion (*maya*) projected by the absolute. In addition to the *tao* in its unnameable dimension, there is *tao* in its aspect as the "speakable" and there are the "ten thousand things," which can be named. Indeed the image of the world which can be named is in the Lao-tzu text quite "commonsensical." Yet a major characteristic of this world, however real, is its impermanence related to its determinate finitude. The *tao* in its aspect of the ineffable eternal is nondeterminate and nameless. It cannot be identified with anything nameable. It is nonbeing (*wu*). I translate this term here with a term often used in Western writings on mysticism, since it seems to correspond adequately to its use in the translation of mystical literature in other cultures.[22] *Wu* is a reality which corresponds to no determinate finite entity, relation, or process which can be named. Yet it is eminently "real" and the source of all finite reality.

The neutral belief in such a reality would not constitute mysticism, but the Lao-tzu text is indeed not neutral. There are some thirty of the eighty-one chapters of the book which deal with the mystic dimension and they are among the most poetic and rhapsodic passages in the entire text. Here, as elsewhere, in all mystical literature, we find the constant paradoxical effort to speak about the unspeakable. "Born before heaven and earth—silent and void—it stands alone and does not change. Pervading all things, it does not grow weary."[23] "Gaze on it. There is nothing to see, it is called the invisible. Listen to it, there is nothing to hear, it is called the inaudible. Grasp it, you cannot hold it. It is called the ungraspable. It is called the form of the formless, the image of the imageless."[24] "The *tao* gives birth to them and nourishes them. It brings them up and nurses them; it brings them to fruition and maturity; feeds and shelters them. It gives them life, yet does not claim possession."[25] "The *tao* is broad reaching left and right—the ten thousand things depend on it for life, yet it does not desert them. It accomplishes its task, yet claims no merit; it clothes and nourishes the ten thousand things, and does not claim to be the master. Forever without desire, one can call it small. The ten thousand things return to it and yet it lays no claim to being their lord."[26] "Heaven in virtue of the one possesses clarity. Earth in virtue of one is stable. The gods [or divine beings] in virtue of the one are numinous."[27] "You cannot keep it close. You cannot keep it far off. You cannot benefit it, nor can you name it . . . You cannot ennoble it or debase it."[28]

To those to whom mystical language in general conveys no meaning, these selections will be as obscure as Meister Eckhardt or much Indian mystical and Sufi literature. In none of these passages can the word *tao* be translated simply as "order of nature" if order of nature is meant to refer to determinable, describable forms, relations, patterns, or processes. The frequent assertion that *tao* in its dimension of namelessness and nonbeing is nothing more than the "process of nature" simply raises the obscurities of the word "process." The concept of nature may involve change and process, but what does one mean by the word process when it is detached from all describable processes? What is a contentless process? A process is something which *can* be described in its succession of stages and in terms of its concrete articulations and relations. To the extent that there is an indescribable element in process, it is no different than the unknowable aspects of the concept of order. The Lao-tzu is serious about leaving the unnameable unnamed.

Another argument used to disprove the existence of mysticism in the Lao-tzu and Chuang-tzu is the absence of accounts of specific techniques for attaining mystical experience. In fact, a good deal of mystical literature consists not of direct descriptions of meditational

techniques, but of paradoxical efforts to convey the indescribable in
words, such as we find in the above passages. Such passages abound
in the Chuang-tzu. These utterances may or may not reflect ecstatic
experiences, but they are, it is true, not descriptions of ecstatic techniques. The relationship between ecstatic and meditational techniques and mysticism is itself an enormously difficult topic. If one
simply identifies mysticism with methods designed to achieve what
Scholem calls the "tremendous uprush and soaring of the soul to its
highest plane," it is entirely possible that the ancient Shamans had
such experiences and did not interpret them in mystical terms.[29]
The yogic techniques of India were as much associated with the
Sankhya philosophy, with its conception of infinite numbers of self-
subsistent life monads, as they were with Brahmanic or Hindu mysticism, and many contemporary "transcendental meditators" are
quite prepared to account for their experiences wholly in terms of
modern Western psychology. One is, of course, free to identify the
word "mysticism" simply with these ecstatic experiences without regard to the vision of reality with which they are associated.[30] Yet in
dealing with the major mystical orientations, such as Brahmanism,
Sufism, or the mysticism of Meister Eckhardt, I find that it is the vision of reality that corresponds to mystical Taoism and not the description of technique.

  Without denying the role of the "mystical" experience in any of
them, I am nevertheless struck by the degree to which what might
be called strenuous intellectual effort enters into all of them.[31] The
role of intellect may, it is true, be negative in that it undermines
"false" views of reality. Indeed, the historic Chuang-tzu, we will
find, is an extremely enthusiastic employer of the intellect as a destructive tool (like the Buddhist philosopher Nāgārjuna). One even
suspects that the author of the Lao-tzu engaged in deep intellectual
reflection on the role of language.

  In the book of Chuang-tzu we do in fact meet individuals who are
depicted in states of mystical trance. What we do not find in either
text is any extensive technical descriptions parallel to anything that
can be found in certain varieties of Indian mystical literature providing elaborate accounts of yogic and meditative techniques. In
this, however, the Chinese texts are not significantly different from
some of the most impressive mystical literature of other cultures.

  Yet the point at which Taoism, like other mysticisms, takes on its
own specific character as Taoism is that mysterious region where the
world of nonbeing comes to relate to the world of the determinate,
the individuated and the related, or perhaps literally in Chinese, in
the world of the "there is" (yu).

  We have already noted that in the first chapter of the Lao-tzu one of the main factors which divides being from nonbeing is the eternity of nonbeing and the transience and finitude of being. There is, however, no implication that the transient and finite is either "unreal" or intrinsically "evil" as such. The dominant metaphor which emerges here, as in the case of other mystical outlooks, is crucial to the entire vision. In the Lao-tzu, we thus find the statement, "the nameless is the beginning of Heaven and Earth; the named [or nameable?] is the mother of the ten thousand things."[32] The use of the metaphor of the mother is most striking. It reminds us of the centrality of the biological-generative metaphor even in the earliest Chinese religious orientations, which I have discussed above, and of the highly positive familial, nurturing associations which surround this term. It suggests a definitely benign and affirmative view not only of the principle of individuation but of the world of entities which have been brought into being. This mysticism does not negate nature. It affirms nature.

Here we find a striking contrast with early Buddhism with its revulsion against the principle of individuation and its deep apprehension of the entire cosmos as a realm of suffering. The author of this book, like the Confucius of the *Analects* and Chuang-tzu, has for some reason been able to attain a lofty indifference to the question of creaturely suffering so dominant in early Buddhism. Such an attitude allows him to relate to nature in wholly affirmative terms.

The use of the metaphor of the mother, however, also calls our attention to another major theme of the Lao-tzu—its exaltation of the feminine as the symbol of the principles of *wu-wei* and "spontaneity" (*tzu-jan*), which link the world of nature to its source in nonbeing. "The spirit of the valley never dies. This is called the mysterious female. The gateway of the mysterious female is called the root of heaven and earth. It continues on as if ever present and in its use, it is inexhaustible."[33] Here the symbol of the valley whose nature is wholly determined by its empty space and its passive receptivity to all that flows into it seems to be related to the sexual and generative role of the female. The female role in sex is ostensibly passive. Yet the "female conquers the male by stillness; in stillness she occupies the lower position."[34] Essentially, it is the female who plays the leading role in the procreative process. She acts "by not acting" in both the sex act and in generation. She thus represents the nonassertive, the uncalculating, the nondeliberative, nonpurposive processes of generation and growth—the processes by which the "empty" gives rise to the full; the quiet gives rise to the active, and the "one" gives rise to the many. The female is the epitome of *wu-*

*wei.* While nonbeing is itself unnameable, one nevertheless has the impression throughout that the passive, the empty, the "habitual," and nonassertive aspects of nature are emblematic of and point toward the realm of "nonbeing." Since in Lao-tzu's view, the nonhuman cosmos and even "natural" aspects of human life operate in this spontaneous and *wu-wei* fashion, one can say that nature abides in the *tao* and that in nature there is no rupture between nonbeing and being. The *wu-wei* aspect of nature is the manifestation of the *tao* in its "nonbeing" aspect, and nature thus abides in the *tao*.

*Lao-tzu's Nature and "Scientific" Naturalism*    Before turning to the actual rupture with the *tao* which the Lao-tzu discerns within the human realm, I should say something further about the Lao-tzu's view of nature and what Needham regards as the text's orientation to "scientific" naturalism. One may, in fact, point to commonalities between Lao-tzu's nature and certain aspects of eighteenth- and nineteenth-century Western "scientific" naturalism. The processes of nature are not guided by a teleological consciousness and despite the pathos suggested by the use of the image of the mother with its nurturant associations, the *tao* is not consciously providential. "Heaven and earth are not *jen* [here probably benevolent] they treat the ten thousand things as straw dogs."[35] Heaven and earth do not concern themselves with the weal or woe of individual humans or of other creatures. One indeed may say that Lao-tzu's nature is an order that runs spontaneously and without deliberate planning or premeditation. This is indeed its glory and its mystery.

Can such a view of nature be mystical? Does it not rather resonate with the perspective of a "scientific" naturalism? Is it possible for a mystical view to have some affinities with a "naturalistic" view? It is in fact entirely possible. I am reminded of the early Buddhist treatise, the Milindapanha, in which the arguments used to deny the existence of an enduring ego or self are almost identical with arguments used in David Hume. What is shared is the common concern to undermine the notion of a persistent ego. Yet no two outlooks could possibly be further from each other in either basic preoccupation or total context than these two. Hume and Nagasena are both, for different reasons, bent on disproving the existence of a persisting ego.[36] Similarly, most modes of mysticism, in fact, are decidedly nonprovidential. The ultimate aim of the mystic is not the achievement of creaturely felicity as an individual in the world. There is no notion of the infinite value of individuated existence as such even though—as in the case of Taoism—it is not necessarily regarded as without value. The fact that one is reabsorbed like a drop in the ocean of the ultimate is a consummation much to be desired. Hence, all the problems of the theodicy fall away. One puts in one's appearance as one of the ten thousand things, savors it as much as one can, and then "returns to the mother." The entire pathos of the stress on the value of individuated existence which rejects as "meaningless" a nature indifferent to the fate of the individual myriad creatures which it spawns is here absent. One is indeed reminded that the Lao-tzu passage is not only a comment on nature. Like the famous passage in which Confucius says he would prefer not to speak, it seems mainly concerned with the analogue between the *tao* and the human sage-king. Lao-tzu immediately proceeds to add to his observation on Heaven and earth that the "sage is not benevolent. He treats the people as straw dogs."[37] The Taoist sage (here the sage-ruler) who somehow embodies within himself the power (*te*) of the *tao* is here depicted as a ruler who does not deliberately concern himself—in busybody fashion—with the individual fates of his subjects. In true cosmomorphic fashion the sage is himself "modelled" on the mystery of the *tao*. He is not intentionally "good." He simply makes it possible for the spontaneous *wu-wei* forces of the *tao* to work their way in human affairs. He himself sees the human world from the point of view of the *tao*. He removes the obstacles to the free operation of the *tao*.

Again, it must be stressed that the spontaneous patterns, routines, cycles, rhythms, and habits of nature do not seem to betoken "spiritlessness" or lack of wonder or mystery. On the contrary, it is the manner in which being spontaneously "emerges out of non-being and returns thereto"; the fact that "both emerge out of the same and that their names are separate" which constitutes the mystery—"the mystery within the mystery—the gate of all wonders."[38] Here again, regularity and routine do not drive out mystery. They embody it.

However does the vision of Lao-tzu (I shall treat other texts separately) provide evidence of any impulse to engage in the disinterested "observation of nature" or any concern with "scientific inquiry"? Is the Lao-tzu interested in the way in which "nature works"? It is again true that we have here an attitude of what Needham calls "ataraxy"—of serene indifference to the vicissitudes and terrors of the world and an aspiration to look at nature without value judgments. Such ataraxy can in fact be found in many mystical outlooks, and in China it is even anticipated in Confucius' attitude toward the workings of Heaven in the cosmos. Yet the fact that these outlooks may share with the scientific perspective an absence of value judgment in dealing with the world of nature does not

prove the presence of an impulse to carry on the systematic investigation of nature. It would indeed be difficult to prove that either the
motives of "scientific curiosity" or of benefitting mankind through
technological improvement would have prompted the resolutely
primitivistic Lao-tzu, whoever he was, to devote his energy to "scientific investigation."

The nature which appears in the Lao-tzu is the nature of our ordinary experience and nothing more. There are observations of natural processes in the book. There is a particular preoccupation with
the dyadic opposites of nature—the masculine and feminine, dark
and light, weak and strong, hard and soft, dynamic and passive—
which reminds us of similar concerns in Anaximander and Heraclitus. One already finds the notion of *yin* and *yang* in its abstract
meaning of the general principle of dyadic complementary and/or
opposition. These observations and ideas probably belong to the accepted current views of nature in the intellectual world of the time.
An examination of the passages involved indicates, however, that
the point is never that of simply making a "scientific observation."
There is no evidence whatsoever (such as we find in abundance in
the Mo-tzu) of any desire of the Lao-tzu's author to know the causes
of separate things and events or to use scientific knowledge for technical purposes.[39]

The treatment of dyadic opposites in the text, while having no
necessary relationship to "scientific inquiry," does, to be sure, raise
a problem from the point of view of the mystic core of the book.
While the terms of the various dyads are often treated as equal,
they are sometimes given unequal weights, indicating the presence
of an unexpected moralistic torque, which would create a problem
from both a "value-free scientific" as well as a "mystical" point of
view. Lau has pointed out the obvious and striking "assymetry" in
the Lao-tzu's view of the female versus the male, the weak versus the
strong, the soft versus the hard, and the passive versus the active.[40]
In all cases, the first term of the dyad is definitely "preferred." It
enjoys a higher "ontological" status, just as water is preferred to
stone; it seeks lowly places, and it is, in a profounder sense, stronger
than stone.[41]

When dealing with organic life, there is the powerful metaphor of
the superiority of infancy. "Man when born is soft and weak. When
he dies, he is hard and solid. The ten thousand things—grass and
trees—are born soft and supple. When they die, they are withered
and hard. Therefore, the hard and the strong are the companions of
death; the soft and weak are the companions of life."[42] Elsewhere,
the infant is portrayed as full of an unformed and undifferentiated

potency. The Lao-tzu is not asserting that the unfavored sides of these dyads are not parts of the order of nature. He does, however, seem to be asserting that things emerge from nonbeing in their soft, undefined, fluid, and therefore *truly* potent states. They are thus, at least in some sense, closer to the heart of the *tao*. As they progress to hardness, crystallization, and clear differentiation, they are more isolated and cut off from the source of being. In the end, of course, death which allows creatures to "return to the mother" releases them from their hardness and isolation.

It is, however, clear that all of this reflects the Lao-tzu's continuing overwhelming concern with human life and hence the presence of a somewhat inconsistent "moralism" and even "humanism" which he seems to share with his predecessors. Lao-tzu's mysticism is thus closely linked to the injunction in the imperative mode, "abide by the soft!" This injunction clearly indicates that the discussion of the "dialectic" of nature reflects not any concern with scientific investigation, but an abiding interest in restoring a "natural" way of life for human beings during their sojourn within the kingdom of the ten thousand things. It is, indeed, an impulse which is in deep tension not only with any alleged "scientific" propensity but with his mysticism to the extent that mysticism points to a realm "beyond good and evil." Lao-tzu had not entirely freed himself from "value judgment."

A word must also be said about the general attitude toward "learning" and "knowledge" in the Lao-tzu. In responding to passages such as the following: "He who engages in learning daily increases. He who deals with the *tao* daily decreases. He decreases and decreases further until he attains *wu-wei* [nonaction or nonpurposive action],"[43] Needham states that "what they [the Taoists] attacked was Confucian scholastic knowledge of the ranks and observances of feudal society—not the knowledge of the *tao* of nature."[44] Now one need not doubt that the Lao-tzu devalues the Confucian knowledge of ranks and observances, but there is again no evidence whatsoever that it recommends the pursuit of knowledge of nature's workings. There is, in fact, some evidence to the contrary. When the Lao-tzu attacks the "knowing the beautiful as beautiful" and further asserts that "the five colors blind the eye, the five notes deafen the ears, and the five tastes injure the palate," I suspect that, in his view, the careful observation, dissection, and analysis of the differentiated characteristics of the world of nature are closely linked to the human fixation on ever more differentiated and varied consumer pleasures and for "goods which are hard to come by."[45] The observer of nature cannot be indifferent to an accurate observation of "sense data." The Lao-tzu seems mainly concerned that the sharp discrimination of these sense qualities is intimately linked to the obsessive desire for sensual pleasure. The desire for such goods whether by feudal rulers or the masses who emulate them are as much a part of the "artificial" civilization which the Lao-tzu rejects as are "ranks and observances." Thus, when he says that the sage is "for the belly and not for the eye," we may interpret this fairly literally.[46] The belly refers to the simplest satisfaction of basic biological needs, while the eye refers to the careful discrimination of the outer sensual qualities of things so necessary to "sophisticated" pleasure. The careful and close observation of the properties of things may well have been associated with the craftsmen who created the "unnatural" luxuries of high civilization.

On the other side, there is the telling passage in which the Lao-tzu asserts "that without stepping out of one's door one knows the world. Without looking out of the window one sees the way of Heaven. The further one goes, the less one knows."[47] Here the knowledge referred to seems to be that of the mystic gnosis and it would appear that purely empirical knowledge of any kind is depreciated. The kind of careful "observation of nature" of which Needham speaks was certainly to flourish in China. Yet there seems to be little ground for assuming that it had anything to do with the vision which we find in the Lao-tzu. On the contrary, the systematic and careful "scientific" observation of nature would seem to be precisely one of those highly deliberate, calculating, and intentional projects which in no way corresponds to the spirit of *wu-wei*. Again, this does not mean that Lao-tzu and particularly the historic Chuang-tzu are not *au courant* of the ideas of nature available in their time.[48] It does mean that the notion that they were fundamentally concerned with the devotion of energy to the "scientific" observation of nature either as an end in itself or as a means to technical ends remains totally unproven.

*The Human Realm*    Lau has asserted that the Lao-tzu, like other ancient Chinese thinkers, was fundamentally interested in advocating a way of life and that in the case of this text, as in the case of other texts, "no fast line was drawn between morals and politics."[49] Although I have here begun my consideration of the book with a focus on its mystical dimension, I am not denying its fundamental concern with the human realm. It is, in fact, the relationship between these two dimensions—both of them equally important—that constitutes the heart of the vision as well as of the problematic aspects of this vision.

To the extent that human beings as creatures "abide" in the *tao*, they are part of that world of nature which Lao-tzu affirms. All the instinctual, "autonomous" aspects of man's biological life operate within the realm of *wu-wei* and one might say that human life on the simplest vegetative "programmed" level unites the human to the *tao* and may be considered good. One might also say that the urge to preserve life on this level is also good. Here is where we find the Yang Chu strain imbedded in the Lao-tzu. The ordinary, unreflective, nondiscriminating man immersed in the routines and habits of a simple life who clings to the sweetness of "mere living" is, at least on one level, at one with the *tao*. I say "on one level" because there does seem also to be the infinitely higher level of the gnosis of the Taoist sage. The emphasis on the prudential, "mundane" clinging to mere living is illustrated throughout the book. While one possesses life, one savors it, yet one is ready to leave it without regret. To the extent that threats to life come from war, political ambition, strife, and the competition for power and wealth, or even from the self-conscious pursuit of moral programs of "uplift," as in the case of both Confucianists and Mohists, these threats arise out of the pathologies of civilization and should be avoided at all cost. "Your name [in the sense of reputation] or your person—which is dearer to you? Your person or your goods—which is worth more? Know where to stop. Therefore, be content with your lot and you will not be disgraced. Know when to stop and you will meet no danger. You can then live long."[50] "Cause the people not to treat death lightly and not to wander off to distant places."[51]

As for the inevitable pains inflicted by the *tao* and the prospect of death by natural causes, the Taoist sage in Lao-tzu seems prepared to accept them with the utmost equanimity. He accepts his destiny to live and his destiny to die. Despite the appreciation of life, the Lao-tzu at one point even states that "the reason I have trouble is that I have a body. When I no longer have a body, what trouble have I?"[52] Lau finds that since "survival is assumed without question to be the supreme goal of life," this passage clearly "goes against the general tenor of the book."[53] This remark, however, strongly reflects Lau's own unwillingness to take seriously the centrality of the book's mystical dimension. Survival may be the supreme goal in life, but to the man of gnosis able to identify with nonbeing, life itself with its ever-present threat of trouble is not the supreme value. He will not sacrifice life for illusory goods, but he is quite prepared to abandon it when his time comes.

The word *hsing* (human nature) does not occur in the Lao-tzu. One suspects that as a mystic who believes that at least some have the power to become "one with the *tao*" he may shy away from any tendency to fix human capacities within any finite groove. The word *hsing* had become linked with the question of the innate capacity to conform to a normative social order which the Lao-tzu rejects. Nevertheless the entire discussion of human affairs is based on the premise that the "natural" desires of men who abide in the *tao* are in themselves limited and simple. So long as the people are not exposed to the lures of false desires and aspirations, they can be kept in their pristine natural state. "Not to value goods which are hard to come by will keep the people from theft. Not to display that which is desirable will keep the people's minds from being confused . . . the sage empties their minds [*hsü-hsin*] and fills their bellies; weakens their wills and strengthens their bones. He sees to it that they constantly remain without knowledge and without desire."[54] "Emptying the mind" (a term also applicable to the Taoist sage) means removing all the false goals and projects of higher civilization and returning minds to the pervasive sway of the *tao*. "If we are without desires, the people will themselves become simple [like the uncarved block]."[55] Again, "desires" in this context do not seem to mean the simple satisfaction of biological instinctual needs for food, sex, and shelter, but the kinds of desires and needs created by civilization. The "filling of the belly" is the very antithesis of the gourmet's calculating project of inventing ever new ways of interesting his jaded palate.

At this point, however, the inevitable question arises—how does the breach with the *tao* occur in the human sphere? The first answer seems to be that it is due to the rise of civilization. It is thus quite correct to call the Lao-tzu a "primitivist" tract—an attack on the entire project of civilization. But why does civilization arise? Here our focus shifts to the mysterious emergence within the human *hsin* (mind) of an unprecedented new kind of consciousness that seems to exist nowhere else in nature. Somehow within the Eden of the *tao*, there arises the deliberative, analytic mind which has the fatal capacity to isolate the various forms, constituents, and forces of nature from their places in the whole in which they abide, to become fixated on them, and to make them the objects of newly invented desires and aspirations. The human mind itself becomes, through this new consciousness, isolated from the flow of the *tao* and finds its meaning in asserting its separate existence against the whole. An entire new world of conscious goals is posited—goals of new sensual gratifications, pleasures, wealth, honor, power—even the goal of individual moral perfection. Thus, the "great artifice" (*ta-wei*) is born.[56]

As we have seen, the hard, the assertive, the strong, and the ugly exist in nature itself, but in nature they are not isolated from their opposites or from the whole. This new deceptive consciousness has, however, the power of isolating them and fixing them. It itself becomes an embodiment of the hard, the analytical, and the aggressive and the self-encapsulated. It brings all things into hard clear focus, removing them from the harmonious hazy state in which they naturally abide. Among the discriminations now made are the clear discriminations between the beautiful and the ugly, the good and the bad. "The world knows that the beautiful is beautiful, thus the ugly is posited. Everyone knows the good as good, thus the evil is posited."[57] In nature, all opposites are mutually dependent and yet in the sphere of ethics and aesthetics, we would absolutize one of the poles and attempt to eliminate the other. The other pole is, however, never destroyed. It simply also stands out in its isolated clarity. The true evil here is the conscious intent to pursue the "good" in isolation as an end in itself. In a state of nature, the ugly and the "not good," whatever that may be, are imbedded in the harmonious whole. While the hardness and strength are part of the "ecology" of the *tao*, they are in nature transfigured by the higher good of spontaneity and *wu-wei* in which they abide.

This fatal *yu-wei* consciousness lies at the root of the whole project of civilization. Yet we are provided with no account of why or how it emerges. The original culprits are, of course, the "culture heroes" who have brought into being the entire project of civilization.

There is a long passage which describes a declination from the highest "embodiment of the *tao*" (*te*) to a complete alienation from the *tao* (the point of reference seems to be to the sage-ruler). "The [man of] highest *te* does not manifest his *te* and, therefore, has *te; the* man of lowest *te* [is concerned] not to lose his *te* and is, therefore, without *te.*"[58] The possessor of the highest *te* is unconscious of his *te* and, one might say, without any self-consciousness. Thus, the *te* simply manifests itself in all his behavior. There then somehow emerges the self-conscious concern with the possibility of "losing *te.*" The highest *te* is *wu-wei* without deliberate consideration (*i wei*)—a term which seems to mean something like a conscious concern with specific sequences of action. The man of lower *te* is very conscious of such specific consequences and thus must be conscious of not losing his *te*. He is thus already in the realm of *yu-wei*.

The Confucian man of *jen* who may represent the highest level of the lowest *te* acts with conscious intent of becoming good but he still does not dwell on the specific consequences of his acts (*pu i wei*). In Lau's translation, he is not, however, without "ulterior motive" in the broadest sense of that term. The man of righteousness (*i*), on the other hand, is wholly oriented to the external consequences of his acts. We then make the plunge to those whose action is based on the contrived rules of *li* and who conceive of *li* as an instrument for controlling society "out there." Here we already have the kind of person who when others do not respond to the sway of *li* will "bare his arm and use force."[59] We note in all this not only a declination from *wu-wei* to *wei*, but also from the inner to the outer—from inner *te* to external machinery. From the assertion of the ego in "goodness" one descends to the assertion of the ego manifesting itself in aggression, greed, and violence. The connecting link between Confucian *jen* and wickedness is the goal-directed consciousness.

In such paradoxical statements as when the Lao-tzu proclaims "that when the six familial relations are no longer in harmony, one has filiality and parental kindness" one notes that, so long as this deliberate, deceptive consciousness had not arisen, the harmonious pattern of familial and social life as described by Confucius may have in fact existed "naturally" as it does among the programmed "social" animals.[60] Did the harmony break down because of the emergence of moral depravity, which led men to be highly conscious of the need for virtue, or was it the case that both self-conscious morality and moral depravity were both fruits of the same deliberative and purposive consciousness? Do they both derive from the same "tree of knowledge of good and evil"? It would seem that the latter was, in fact, the case. *Jen*, righteousness, skill, and the search for utility all grow from the same root. "Cut off *jen*, abandon righteousness, and the people will return to filiality and kindness; cut off skill and abandon utility and robbers and thieves will disappear."[61]

The Lao-tzu does indeed attack the more obvious evils of civilization in a prophetic spirit. "The people are hungry. It is because those above devour too much in taxes."[62] "The court is corrupt, the fields are overgrown with weeds. The granaries are empty, yet there are those dressed in finery with swords at their sides filled with food and drink."[63] "Where troops have encamped, there will brambles grow . . . in the wake of mighty armies, bad harvests follow without fail."[64] Yet these obvious social evils seem to be quintessentially part of the project of civilization as such and the false human consciousness which lies behind it. If this false consciousness originated anywhere, it would seem to have originated first among the Confucian culture heroes who dreamed of "improving on nature" by concentrating attention on the "good" and the "beautiful." It was inevitable that others would arise who would assert their egos against the *tao* in cruder and more direct ways.

The particular animus of the Lao-tzu against *li* seems to reflect the belief that these rules and prescriptions are contrived out of the

Confucian realization that *jen* and *i* as moral influences will simply not work against the more obvious evils of society. Hence the need to contrive all the external rules of *li*. While Confucius himself seems to believe that *li* are part of Heaven's order, and while he dreams of a society in which their performance becomes habitual and "spontaneous," in the view of the Lao-tzu they are, on the contrary, consciously contrived and deliberately practiced. Confucius himself insists that the practice of *li* must be based on a constant and alert attentiveness to the intentionality which accompanies their practice. They redeem neither their performers nor their recipients, and are furthermore closely associated, as Mo-tzu had already observed, with the useless luxuries of civilization.

*The Political Perspective*    Can we then say that the Lao-tzu represents a primitive anarchism and a total rejection of political order and hierarchy? In the West, we would generally associate this with any primitivism. Yet the fact remains that the text abounds in advice and exhortations addressed to rulers. Some interpreters indeed firmly believe that the entire text is primarily a treatise on statecraft and even on military strategy.

The text itself provides us with no historic account of any devolution from a state of nature to the rise of civilization, although many passages in the book of Chuang-tzu, which seem closely allied to the Lao-tzu outlook, do provide such accounts. We thus read of an ancient state of affairs in which men "lived with birds and beasts and grouped themselves with the ten thousand things . . . how would they know of noble men? How would they know of mean men?" They were all without desire, and rested in the *tao*. "However, along came the sages huffing and puffing after *jen* reaching in tiptoe toward righteousness and the world for the first time had doubts."[65] Here indeed we seem to have something like a primitive harmonious anarchy followed by the unaccountable rise of a new notion of good and evil among those called the sages. It is not implied even here that the sages were the evil conspiratorial "kings and priests" of the Western eighteenth-century enlightenment. They were bent on *jen,* righteousness, and world improvement, but it is in them that the insidious *yu-wei* consciousness emerges. It would also appear, however, that other humans, while not originating this consciousness were as vulnerable to the disease as the proto-Confucian sages themselves, just as Eve is already latently vulnerable to the blandishments of the snake. The propensity to fall seems latent in the human animal. It is also interesting to note, however, that even the author of this passage takes for granted the existence of a political order even in the state of nature. He assumes that even in the state of nature there had been the exemplary Taoist sage-ruler Ho Hsü, who had simply maintained mankind in its pristine innocence through the power of his *te*. In the text of the Lao-tzu, we find the universal kingship (*wang*) mentioned as one of the four fundamental components of the cosmos—the *tao*, heaven, earth, and the kingship.[66] Here we have a clear illustration of how the pervasive cultural orientation toward the mediating role of sage-rulers is present even in the Lao-tzu strain of Taoism with its strong "humanistic" concern. One might say that in a true Taoist society, the authority of the truly Taoist universal king may be as "natural" as the presence of the dominant male in the group life of many of the higher mammals.

However one may account for the origins of human civilization, it is suggested throughout the text that only Taoist sage-rulers can reverse the pathology of civilization. Lao-tzu, indeed, offers his advice not only to potential "universal kings" but even to the princes of states of his own time. As in the case of Confucius and Mo-tzu, he obviously does not seem to believe that the masses can save themselves, exposed as they are to both the seductions of civilization and the oppressions inflicted by civilization. Having been exposed to false consciousness, the masses participate in it fully and long to share in the goals of their masters. They can hardly transcend their environment. If civilization began with the false consciousness of the proto-Confucius sages of the past, it is now only sages who have achieved the higher mystic gnosis who can save the mass of people from the pathologies of civilization. Humankind may possibly be returned to the unreflective, innocent state of nature, but people are not, it would appear, themselves capable of achieving the higher gnosis of the sage.

It is the Taoist sage who is alone able to put an end to the artificial projects of civilization and make it possible for the majority of men to return to a state of *wu-wei*. It is possible that living as he did in the fourth or third century B.C., the author or compiler of the text may have indeed shared the faith of Mencius and others that the time was ripe for the rise of a new universal king who would transform the world through the radiating power of his gnosis, although there is no evidence in the text for the notion of any *tao* of history. The belief in the radiating, almost magical power of the Taoist sage is even present in the Chuang-tzu text, where figures such as the hideous Ai T'ai-to must fight off the people who flock about him drawn by the radiance of his spiritual power.[67] Beyond this, however, we are not told how the sage will obtain political power in the first place. Obviously, the Taoist sage does not plan or contrive to obtain

it. In the explicit words of the text, "the empire will be won by refraining from deliberate action [*wu shih*]."[68] What we have here is
the mystical hope that the "world" (*t'ien hsia*) will somehow naturally gravitate to the orbit of the sage-ruler who embodies the mystic
power (*te*) of the *tao*.

The discussions of how the Taoist sage-ruler actually rules seem to
alternate between depictions of his mystical powers (*te*) and what
might be called his "policy" orientations which are, of course, described mainly in negative terms. "As for the best ruler, they [the
people] simply know that he is there."[69] His being there is not a vac-
uous presence, however, since his self-effacing quality, his submissiveness, his utter impartiality, as well as his refusal to intervene in
the lives of his subjects in order to display his providential concern
("he treats them as straw dogs") are all qualities which come to per-
meate the lives of those he rules.

Yet in addition to these descriptions of the ruler's radiant charisma, there are many negative "policies." He does not advance men
of worth. He empties the minds of the people of the useless knowledge which leads to the multiplication of false needs. He refrains
from war to the extent possible. A large state ruled by a sage can by
its conciliatory, humble, and considerate policies (holding itself in
the lower position like the female) actually induce small states to
seek its protection. Small states ruled by sages renouncing power
and pride can win the protection of such large states without in any
way resenting it.[70] Thus, Mo-tzu's problem of the relations of the
large and small states is resolved or dissolved amicably without recourse to war.

The passage which most vividly projects the Lao-tzu's vision of
the good society is in chapter 80:

> A small settlement [community] with few inhabitants. Even though
> they have labor-saving implements, see to it that they are not used.
> See to it that they take death seriously and do not wander far off. Al-
> though they may have boats and carts, see to it that no one rides
> them; and that though they have arms and weapons, no one will drill
> with them; see to it that they return to the knotted cord [rather than
> writing], that they be content with the food they have, that they be
> pleased with the clothes they have, and satisfied with their dwellings
> and enjoy their own customs. The neighboring settlements may be so
> close that one can hear the cocks crow and the dogs bark, but the
> people may grow old and die without going back and forth.[71]

This does not seem to be the description of a utopia of the primeval
past. Clearly we are in a period when "advanced technology" is
available. The sage-ruler, however, sees to it (lit. "causes" *shih*) that
it is rejected. The sage realizes that the complexity of the civilization

is to some extent the function of size; therefore, he prescribes a "small community." What the language suggests is not a spontaneously emerging "anarchist" state of affairs but a state of affairs brought about by a sage-ruler. Presumably, the sage is able to inaugurate his policies because he has won the hearts of the people, but negative as the policies are they nevertheless seem to require some kind of intervention. The whole idea is to reduce to a minimum all the projects of civilization, making it possible for the people to sink back into the simple life in which they remain so self-sufficiently contented with their essential daily *wu-wei* routines that they require no outside stimulation. It is, in a sense, pointless to discuss the nature of the system here envisaged. If it is anarchism, it is anarchism completely lacking in dreams of individual freedom and "creativity" and not incompatible with the idea of sage-rulers. If it is collectivism, it is a collectivism which reduces dynamic collective undertaking to the vanishing point. If it is laissez-faire, it is a laissez-faire which has nothing to do with economic enterprise. Contrary to Needham's assertion that technology is only disapproved of in Taoism because it is exploited by feudalism, there seems to be the assertion here that precisely the same calculating consciousness which produces technology also produces sharp social differentiation and hence oppression. The two are indivisible. They spring out of the same contriving *yu-wei* consciousness.

It is true that the behavior of the sage-ruler seems to involve unresolved contradictions. He seems quite deliberately to create a utopia which will turn the world back to the simplicity of the *tao*. The restoration of the primitive must be a conscious project. Here again, we have the problem of the moralistic torque, which introduces a basic inconsistency into the entire vision of the Lao-tzu. There can be no human morality without preference, without rejection, and without deliberate choice. The civilization-negating "policies" of the sage-ruler seem themselves to be an example of *yu-wei*. The contradiction remains unresolved.

There is, however, another interpretation of the Lao-tzu's sociopolitical orientation which would dismiss the entire interpretation proposed above as naive and literal. Lao-tzu, in this view, is a cunning and canny would-be statesman who wraps his Machiavellian political advice in mystical verbiage. Just as Lau insists that the book is about a down-to-earth concern with individual survival as a supreme value, others insist that it is mainly an esoteric handbook of wily statecraft. And indeed the text was—up to a point—treated in this "instrumental" way by the entire stream which we have chosen to identify as Huang-lao Taoism (see below).

We have thus noted throughout that the soft is really stronger than the hard, that the feminine is ultimately more potent than the masculine, and that water will wear down a stone. Are we not dealing here with a strategy of "stooping to conquer" and with something like the spiritual antecedents of judo (the "way of softness")? The practitioner of judo is obviously "out to win." Viewed in this light, one empties the people's minds in order to make them docile instruments of the ruler's policies, which are themselves aimed at maximizing his goals of wealth and power. The large state's policy of winning over small states by kindness and humility is nothing more than a more subtle brand of imperialism. An observation which seems particularly wily is "that in order to shrink it one must purposely allow it to expand; in order to weaken it, one must purposely allow it to grow strong. To do away with it, one must first purposely allow it to establish itself firmly; in order to take away, one must first give. This is called subtle illumination. The soft and weak can overcome the hard and strong."[72] Here, indeed, one finds the cunning of the judo strategy. It is designed to bring about the fall of the proud and the mighty. In the apt words of Lau, it is a case of "giving the strong enough rope to hang themselves."[73] It is quite legitimate for the sage-rulers or Taoist adept to encourage the strong to overreach themselves. This by no means necessarily implies, however, that the soft and weak are simply bent on inheriting the place of the strong and the powerful or that they have been converted to their delusive goals.

Similarly, the contention that the Lao-tzu is basically concerned with military strategy rests on one or two passages. While the drift of the entire book is overwhelmingly pacifistic, there does seem to be recognition that even the sage-ruler may become involved in war, given the actualities of the times. In that case "he aims only to achieve results. He does not dare to intimidate. He achieves results and does not boast, does not brag, is not arrogant, he carries it out only when there is no other way."[74] In carrying on war, the true "Taoist" general does not seek a battle, knows when to retreat, does not become angry, does not lord it over his men, and knows how to use them. He never underestimates his enemies. All of this may be sound military advice and the knowledge of how to use others was to become a centerpiece of Huang-lao Taoism. Yet it is also quite compatible with the general vision of the entire text and does not in any way prove that the Lao-tzu is mainly or centrally interested in military science.

When one sees these passages in the context of the entire text, they by no means prove that the Lao-tzu's "esoteric" aim for individuals or for the sage-ruler are power, wealth, and honor. The man of true gnosis, who is the only fit ruler, is by the very nature of his mystical insight not ensnared by these goals; he sees through them. The primitivist critique of the civilization which produces these delusory and factitious goals is maintained throughout. One need not deny that isolated passages in the text will later lend themselves to be used to support such "instrumentalist" interpretations just as other passages will be used to support the Yang Chu doctrine of survival and longevity as the supreme goal. Indeed, the same passages will later be used to support the entire cult of immortality. When viewed within the context of the mystical and primitivist core of the book, however, it becomes difficult to take such interpretations seriously as interpretations of the vision of the text as a coherent whole.

## 2. The Chuang-tzu

The Lao-tzu may well draw its maxims and sayings from many sources, and many of its separate ideas may have been common currency among contemporaries, whose works have been lost, but the text as a whole does, I would maintain, embody a coherent vision of great power and originality. The much larger text of the book of Chuang-tzu, taken as a whole, certainly deserves its reputation as one of the great masterpieces of Chinese literature. It is exceedingly rich as a source of materials on Warring States thought. It would, however, appear to be an assemblage of quite disparate strains of thought. There is now a wide agreement among Japanese, Chinese, and Western scholars that the present collection consisting of thirty-three chapters represents quite separate streams of "Taoist" thought.[75] Its various sections may have been drawn from much larger bodies of material, and the more or less sustained literary quality of much of the work may be mainly a tribute to the judgment of later selectors and editors. It has been estimated that the contents may span a period running from the fourth century B.C. to the end of the third century or even beyond that period. We know that the work was first edited by the famous father and son bibliographers, Liu Hsiang and Liu Hsin of the Han dynasty, and that the present version of thirty-three chapters was put together by the work's most famous commentator, Kuo Hsiang of the third century A.D.

From a very early date, the first seven chapters were classed as the "inner chapters" and were believed to represent the authentic core of the thought of the historic Chuang-tzu, while the "outer" and "miscellaneous" chapters (wai-p'ien, tsa-p'ien) were long felt to represent other outlooks. It should be added that the whole matter is

much complicated by the fact that the chapters themselves seem to
be collections of separate passages rather than integrated wholes.
There are passages in the inner chapters which, when subjected to
stylistic analysis, seem to represent other strains not belonging to the
line of the historic Chuang-tzu, while many sections in the later
chapters seem very close in style and thought to the thought of the
historic Chuang-tzu or his disciples. Graham has, on the basis of his
own stylistic analysis, and on the basis of work by Chinese scholars,
such as Kuan Feng, identified four strains in the book: the historic
Chuang-tzu strain, which may represent the thought of the disciples,
as well as of the master; the Lao-tzu primitivist strain, very strongly
represented in chapters 8–11, as well as elsewhere; a strain which
seems to be close to Yang Chu's "egoism" (which Graham calls "individualism"); and a strain which he calls "syncretistic," but which I
would suggest may represent what was later called the "Yellow Emperor–Lao-tzu" (Huang-lao) strain discussed below.

All we have on the life of the historic Chuang-tzu are a few isolated sentences in the history of Ssu-ma Ch'ien. He is said to have
been a man of the southern, weak, and declining state of Sung and is
also said to have held a position in a place called Chi-yuan. Given
his unusual mastery of the thought currents of his time, it is obvious
that he was a member of the *shih* stratum. The effort to deduce his
class background from the "pessimism" of his vision seems to me as
treacherous an undertaking as all such efforts to deduce class background from the contents of thought in the case of original minds.
Most significant from the point of view of his total philosophy is his
friendship with his intellectual protagonist, the famous "sophist"
Hui Shih (Hui-tzu). One certainly senses here the presence of an exceptional personality endowed with both great intellectual power
and dialectic ability, a soaring poetic imagination, and bubbling
wit. Some have seen a stark contradiction between the "logic chopping" and the poetic imagination. To me both seem to reflect the
ardor of Chuang-tzu's effort to convey his vision by every means
available. Graham has demonstrated that the closer we come to an
understanding of the technical vocabulary of those engaged in the
dialectic and logical debates of the school of names (*ming-chia*—a
term used by later doxographers to embrace the Mohists, Hui Shih,
K'ung-sun Lung, Yin Wen-tzu, and others), the closer we come to
an understanding of the issues which lie behind Chuang-tzu's deep
engagement with these sophists.[76]

We shall again begin our account of the historic Chuang-tzu with
the mystical vision which he shares with the Lao-tzu. Chuang-tzu's
constant efforts to describe the indescribable in many ways simply

amplify and enrich what we have already found in the Lao-tzu, "Dark and hidden the *tao* seems not to exist and yet it is there. Fluid-like without form and yet spirit-like [numinous?]. The ten thousand things are sustained by it and do not know it. This is what is called the source and the root."[77] "Look for it, but it has no form; listen but it has no voice . . . the *tao cannot* be described. Described it is not the *tao*. What gives form to the formed is itself formless."[78] "There is a being. There is not being. There is a not yet beginning to be non-being . . . suddenly there is non-being and of 'being' and 'non-being' we know not which is and which is not. Now I have said something but I do not really know whether my saying is saying something or nothing."[79] The book teems with such passages, some of which are entirely congruent with similar passages in the Lao-tzu. However, the final passage shows Chuang-tzu wandering into dialectic waters where the Lao-tzu, on the whole, does not seem to linger. Chuang-tzu is here obviously deeply concerned with a gnostic question which may well reflect his contacts with the school of names. Can one really set up an opposition between being and nonbeing? In doing so, is one not speaking of the ineffable nonbeing as a "something"? Can one apply the notion of the opposite to the ineffable? Can there be any temporal priority between the two? And if nonbeing cannot be considered as a separate something, can we really think of the "determinate" and "separate" things as "somethings" apart from "non-being"?

Indeed, even when we turn from those passages in which Chuang-tzu speaks of the indescribable to the passages in which we deal with the world of the ten thousand things, we find ourselves in a quite different world from the "mundane" commonsensical world of the Lao-tzu. To Chuang-tzu, the achievement of the true gnosis requires nothing less than the shattering of our ordinary understanding of the world about us. It is only when our ordinary perspectives on experience are shaken to the foundation that the true gnosis becomes possible.

Before considering his efforts to achieve this gnosis, however, I must also say something about evidences of trancelike "mystic experiences" and states of mystical illumination in the Chuang-tzu text. The extremely crucial chapter 2 ("On Seeing Things as Equal") begins with the trancelike experiences of the mystic Nan-kuo-tzu. "He sat leaning on his armrest staring at the sky and breathing with a vacant look as if he had lost his opposite [his ego?]. Yen-cheng Tzu-yu, who was standing by in attendance, inquired 'what is this—can the body really be made to become like a withered tree and the mind like dead ashes? The man who sits here now is not the man who was sitting here before.' "[80] Elsewhere we find Confucius observing Lao-tzu in a state in which his "form and body seem shrunken like a withered tree." Lao-tzu then informs him that "I was letting my mind [*hsin*] wander to the beginning of things."[81]

There is another hint of the achievement of such a state in a passage where the protagonist is Confucius' disciple, Yen Hui.[82] Confucius, who is used here as elsewhere (perhaps ironically) as the spokesman of a Taoist outlook, advises Yen Hui on how to achieve the higher gnosis by "letting his mind fast." "Unify your will. Don't listen with your ears, listen with your mind—no, don't listen with your mind, but listen with the *ch'i;* hearing stops with the ears; the mind stops at signs [or concepts?], but *ch'i* is empty and yet all things depend on it; the *tao* gathers in emptiness alone. Emptiness is the fasting of the mind."[83] Here we note that the *chi'i* discussed in the previous chapter is already conceived of as a "metaphysical," mystical reality which serves, as it were, to connect the world of the manifold, determinate, and discrete to the world of nonbeing. The procedure recommended seems to involve precisely the kind of "emptying of mind" of all consciousness of the determinate which we find in so much literature on "meditational" techniques. Yen Hui, it would appear, is eminently prepared for these instructions.

One other seemingly unlikely area in which one finds discussions of "mystical" techniques is in passages dealing with skills or crafts. What we find in these passages is by no means a utilitarian exaltation of skills as such. What we are always presented with is a depiction of the skill in its full state of perfection. One such example is that of the hunchback cicada-catcher who unfailingly catches cicadas with his sticky pole. Confucius is astounded by his skill and the cicada-catcher then informs him that he is able to bring himself to a state of mind where he "is aware of nothing but cicada-wings not wavering, not dipping, not letting any of the ten thousand things take the place of cicada-wings—how can I help but succeed?" Confucius then turns to his disciples and says, "he keeps his will undivided and concentrates his vital spirits [*ch'i*]."[84] In the practice of the skill he fully surrenders to the spontaneous spirit of *wu-wei* which unites him to the *tao.* Even Needham, who longs to find in Taoism a positive attitude toward technology as such, remarks that the "Taoists probably saw in those who exhibited these skills a certain admirable self-forgetfulness arising out of an extremely close contact with the processes of nature."[85] Such states of mind, whether of cicada-catchers or of the bellstand-maker who forgets that he has "limbs, a form, and a body . . . because his skill is concentrated and all outside distractions fade away," are analogous to Yen Hui's fasting of the mind and are meant to serve as paradigms of the meditational state.[86] We find there, to be sure, no analogues to the long and scholastic Indian technical treatises on yogic or meditational techniques, but these passages do clearly point to a belief in such states.

When we turn to the world of being (*yu*), we find that Chuang-tzu, like the Lao-tzu, also affirms the world of nature but that the manner and content of the affirmation is strikingly different. In some ways, indeed, it is a more unreserved and totally consistent affirmation. There is here no moralistic torque. There is no preference for softness over hardness or for the feminine over the masculine. The metaphor of the mother does not appear. Here one indeed finds a truly value-free attitude toward the natural world. From his close friend and protagonist, the sophist Hui Shih, Chuang-tzu may have learned to doubt whether opposites are opposites at all in any absolute sense. In an infinite space, the terms large and small have no absolute meaning. "From the point of view of their difference, if we regard a thing as big because there is a certain bigness to it, then among all the ten thousand things, there are none that are not big . . . if we know that heaven and earth are grains and that the tip of a hair is a range of mountains, then we have perceived the law of difference."[87] Again, what do high and low mean in an infinite space? As we shall find, Chuang-tzu's efforts to upset our commonsense concepts of the world do not, by any means, involve a rejection of the natural world as we perceive it. It involves, however, a rejection of the absolute categories of predication which we bring to our perceptions. These relate only to the world of our ordinary perceptions. One can say that the underlying attitude is one of an "aesthetic" acceptance of the whole grand spectacle of the world as immediately perceived. I use the word aesthetic with quotation marks here because, unlike Lao-tzu's ethical bias, it does not involve preferences. It does not require a rejection of what is ordinarily considered to be the ugly or revolting in the narrow sense of the word "aesthetics." Chuang-tzu is genuinely value-free in this sphere. "Man claims that Mao Ch'iang and Lady Li are beautiful, but if fish saw them, they would dive to the bottom of the stream."[88] The *tao* is as much present in urine and excrement as in anything else. It is an aesthetic which simply rejoices in the vast and infinite variety of forms and in the inexhaustible world of protean transformations as such.

A case can indeed be made that, in the Chuang-tzu, the inexhaustible variety and "creative" ingenuity of nature is more deeply appreciated than its order and regularity, and that in his case it would be limiting indeed to translate the term *tao* in its "being" aspect as "order of nature." Much of the imagery suggests not so much order and pattern as inexhaustible grandeur and protean changeability. In the "Autumn Floods" (chapter 17), we have the enormous flooding waters of the great river flowing into the immensity of the North Sea. P'eng the roc-bird, rises into the air ten thousand *li* and surveys the vast and infinitely varied landscape below stretching into infinity. In another passage, Chuang-tzu presents us with images of the "incipient germs" (*chi*) of animal and plant life which produce entirely different creatures depending on the natural habitat in which they find themselves.[89] "In the water they become break-vines. On the edge of the water, they become frog's robes. If hill slippers get rich soil, they will turn into crow's feet. The roots of crow's feet turn into maggots and their leaves turn into butterflies which are turned into insects that live under the stove ... so all creatures come out of these incipient germs [*chi*] and return thereto."[90] Watson aptly describes this whole passage as "a romp through ancient Chinese nature lore."[91] What is celebrated here is the delightfully inexhaustible and protean transformations of nature.

All of these passages descriptive of nature make points which, in their contexts, are by no means simply concerned with observations of nature as such. The roc-bird represents the grandeur and "freedom" of the man who looks at the world from the standpoint of the higher gnosis as opposed to the cicada, the little dove, and the frog, who represent the ordinary man locked into the conventional outlook of our ordinary "little understanding." The image certainly has nothing to do with a mere contrast in physical size between the roc and the dove, since no one is more conscious than Chuang-tzu that the tip of a hair is not small and Mt. Tai is not large from the point of view of the two infinities. The contrast between the vastness of the flooding river and the immensity of the North Sea is ultimately meant to indicate that there is, in fact, no absolute large and small and that these terms make comparative sense only from the perspective of particular entities in their relations to each other. The passage about the incipient germs (*chi*) of things is a paean to the principle of infinite transformation and change—Chuang-tzu is no more fixated on the cyclical and regular patterns of change in nature than on unpredictable and unexpected change. Yet while these images never are introduced solely for their own sakes, these poetic invocations of the phenomena of nature certainly do betray an enormous delight in the spectacle of nature as such.

There are, to be sure, also passages which do indeed discuss the organized patterns and regularities of nature, and here the question which again arises is—is there here a "scientific" interest in the objective investigation of nature? Needham has in fact drawn heavily on the Chuang-tzu text. An argument can indeed be made that the Chuang-tzu is more truly "objective" than the Lao-tzu. There are truly no value judgments here and there is indeed considerable information concerning contemporary concepts of nature. This information is often interwoven, however, with a good deal of material drawn directly from the world of folklore.

There is thus one famous passage in which one of Chuang-tzu's allegorical personae "Little Understanding" (our ordinary *"shao-chih"* understanding of the world) asks Great Impartial Harmony (T'ai Kung-tiao, the higher gnosis), "Within the four cardinal directions and the six realms [heaven, earth, and the four directions] how do the ten thousand things arise?" Great Impartial Harmony goes on to delineate some of the enduring patterns and regular principles of the natural world. There are the interactions of *yin* and *yang,* the four seasons "producing and killing each other." There are the principles of attraction and repulsion which account for sex and other phenomena. There is the principle of condensation and rarefaction. There is the interaction of fast and slow processes and in human life the fluctuations of misery and happiness which seem to relate to all these principles. "There are the principles of the successive order of things and the mutual interaction and the principle of an alternation of rising to dominance and then retreating [*chiao-yün*]." Chuang-tzu then goes on to assert that "while these names and realities can be recorded and while their details and subtleties can be noted ... these are the properties which belong to things. *All that* words can exhaustively describe; all that our [ordinary] knowledge can attain to is the level of things. The man who looks to the *tao* does not try to follow what has disappeared nor to find the source whence it has arisen" (emphasis mine).[92] Needham, however, translates the final passage with a different emphasis: "words *can* describe them and knowledge *can* reach them—but not beyond the extreme limit of the natural world," thus implying a kind of positivistic injunction to confine one's knowledge to the "six realms" about which one *can* indeed have real knowledge. He then adds, "it is indeed a profession of faith in natural science."[93]

While the passage does provide valuable information about concepts of nature in the intellectual world of the time, the entire spirit of the passage seems to me to run directly contrary to the view that man's true concern lies in the area of natural knowledge. The last remark about "not following what has disappeared" is, in fact, a positive injunction against seeking the underlying, unobserved causes of things which figure so largely in the book of Mo-tzu—particularly in the dialectic chapters.

There are many interesting principles (*li*) mentioned in the passage, but they are all what might be called empirical generalization derived directly from observation of publicly perceived phenomena. There is no evidence here of any "reductionist" tendency or any tendency to seek the structure of the hidden causes behind the world of appearance. While "condensation and rarefaction" are mentioned, there is no hint that the rich variety of nature might somehow be "reduced" to this one principle. Above all, there is no evidence that Chuang-tzu derives his "peace of mind" by "formulating hypotheses and theories concerning nature." He rather seems to view all these principles, which may indeed be present in the world of the "six realms" and which were probably not formulated by him, from the higher standpoint of his mystic gnosis. Understanding these things belongs merely to the realm of Little Understanding and not to the realm of the higher gnosis. The aspirant to sagehood is not likely to spend his life in the pointless pursuit of this inferior knowledge.

A good case can be made that Chuang-tzu is much more interested in questions which might be called "epistemological" or "logical" than in natural science, although here too he is not interested in them for their own sake. We have already noted his extreme reluctance to regard being and nonbeing as dyadic opposites. Not only does treating them as separate lead to treating nonbeing as something, it also leads to treating the ten thousand things as discrete beings totally separate from nonbeing. One may enjoy the spectacle of the phenomena of nature without raising questions about the "ontological status" of such phenomena in themselves. One suspects that it is precisely Chuang-tzu's concern with man as one of the ten thousand things which leads him to be most concerned with the question—What indeed is the reality of individual entities? It is precisely at this point that the analyses of his friend Hui Shih may become most relevant, despite Chuang-tzu's mistrust of his seeming infatuation with intellectual analysis as an end in itself. It is Hui Shih who helps to demonstrate that the ordinary language which describes our ordinary experience of the world in no way provides us with an ultimate account of the world in which we live. Indeed, much of the Mohist "logic," which achieved its final form only after Hui Shih and his famous rival Kung-sun Lung, seems to contain a systematic effort to refute both of these "sophists" as well as Chuang-tzu in the name of a revindication of the commonsense view of reality.[94]

*The World of "Being"* (yu)    I shall not pretend here to provide a penetrating analysis of these "sophists" who represent the very climax of China's ancient language crisis, but I must say something about them, particularly about Hui Shih, who is by far the most important influence on Chuang-tzu, who found the issues he raised to be of the utmost relevance. Kung-sun Lung remains a subject of unresolved debate among philosophers far better trained in logic than I, and there is absolutely no agreement on how the fragments attributed to him should be translated or even any agreement on which parts of the fragments are authentic. Paradoxically, because of the unbridgeable disagreements among Western translators of Kung-sun Lung-tzu, the paradoxes of Hui Shih seem in some ways more accessible than the logic of Kung-sun Lung. The ten paradoxes of Hui Shih, which we find in chapter 33 of the Chuang-tzu and which seem to be the only remnants of the writings of Hui Shih (which, according to the testimony of that chapter of the Chuang-tzu, "would fill five carriages"), seem intent on shaking the ways in which we think about the world of determinate "things."[95] I use this language because it is by no means obvious that Hui Shih means to deny the existence of the particular things themselves. What he seems to deny is the absolute reality of many of the categorical predicates, attributes, or general properties which we assign to things—particularly, it seems, spatial, temporal, and classificatory attributes. In using terms such as "attribute" and "property," I am aware that I am using Western terms which are asserted by some to be utterly inapplicable to the Chinese language and hence to Chinese thought. Graham, to be sure, does not reject the term "property" and even acknowledges that in Chinese things "have properties." He even finds in the Mohist logic a term for "predicate" (ken).[96] Yet in dealing with Kung-sun Lung, he refuses to use these words and insists on the somewhat opaque word "meaning" to translate the key term chih which has been translated by some as "attribute." Here again, the term is rejected because it seems to suggest "universals" and there is the firm a priori conviction that universals do not exist in the Chinese language and culture. Nevertheless I would suggest that the school of names may have hovered close to something like universals even though they may have given them no Platonic or Aristotelian interpretation. Without attempting to unravel Kung-sun Lung, it seems to me that the subject/predicate, entity/property or attribute language still seems to offer more plausible results than anything else that has so far been suggested in this area, particularly Graham's vague word "meaning." I shall therefore allow myself to use the term "attribute."

The Hui Shih paradoxes, as we have seen, seem to suggest that attributes such as high and low, large and small have no meaning in an infinite space. "The largest has nothing outside it. We call it the one of largeness. The smallest has nothing within it. We call it the one of smallness."[97] One Chinese commentator comments that both "ones" are the same one. There is no absolute largeness or smallness, high or low in infinity even though things may have these qualities relative to each other.[98] Again, there is a suggestion like that of Zeno that the absolute continuity of time does not allow for such things as discrete atemporal moments, thus suggesting constant change: "the sun at noon is the sun setting—the thing born is the thing dying."[99] Relatively, of course, the sun is in a different position at noon and at sunset. Again in the matter of classification, we tend to class things according to sameness and difference (the *genus* and *differentia* of Aristotle). At times, we may focus on the identical properties, such as the common qualities of mammals. At times we focus on the differentia, such as on the different properties of oxen and horses. Thus the "ten thousand things are all the same and all different" and our insistence on defining common or differentiating qualities as being the *essential* qualities in defining the species or genus of any particular entity may be wholly a function of our perspectives.[100] It is entirely plausible that Hui Shih's relativization of high and low, big and small, his emphasis on unceasing change in time, and his doubts about classification were related not only to "logic" but also to the ethicosocial implications of the terms high and low, great and small, as well as to the constant shift in human fortunes and the meaning of the passage from youth to old age. From the point of view of the absolute, humans and all other things are indeed equivalent (of equal value) despite their differences relative to each other—hence the final injunction of Hui Shih to "love all the ten thousand things—treat Heaven and earth as one body." Again, none of this is meant to deny the existence in some sense of the ten thousand things, but to reduce to a matter of relativity and perspective the differences among them. The relativity belongs to the world of our ordinary understanding, which sees things wholly in their specific relatedness to each other. Indeed, it would appear that from Chuang-tzu's point of view, Hui Shih even assigns "things" too solid an existence. Thus to Chuang-tzu, "love" is not a supreme value. It involves the fixation of attention on other specific individual entities rather than on the union with the *tao*.[101]

Yet Chuang-tzu himself does not wish to deny all reality to "things." "Saying is not blowing breath. Saying says something."[102] If our language was not clouded over by the fixed judgments of right and wrong created by the false consciousness of our daily lives, if our language was not befuddled by our fixed *parti pris* or our tendency to absolutize relative distinctions among things, our words might give us a correct account of what is found in our unmediated experience of the world. Our language would respond to the way things present themselves without prejudice. Such an unbeclouded language would spontaneously respond appropriately to all the kaleidoscope shifts in the nature of the world and to the infinite variety of perspectives from which the world can be viewed. "If a man sleeps in a damp place his back aches, but is this true of the loach?"[103] It is quite accurate for the man to say that his back aches from the damp. This is saying "something" about man's relation to dampness. If he says that "dampness" is bad in any absolute sense, however, then his language does not "say something" or, rather, says too much. While "things" and situations may be "something," they are not self-sufficient entities which can be grasped in all their aspects from our own individual and transient perspectives. They are rather fluid somethings whose aspects and transformations depend on their relationship with a whole world of somethings, as in the case of the penumbra which upbraids the shadow. "You moved before. Now you stop. You were sitting. Now you stand. Why have you no fixed principle?"[104] The penumbra's behavior is totally dependent on the shadow's behavior. The shadow's behavior depends on the moving organism and the moving organisms's on the tao. Language can say something about their movements. It cannot speak about them in terms of absolute "rights" and "wrongs" (in either the moral or intellectual sense of those terms). Thus, all particular beings and relations have their source in nonbeing.

There is even a hint that the reality of the ten thousand things may be such stuff as "dreams are made of." Someday there may be a great awakening in which we know that this is all a great dream."[105] Yet it is probably wrong to think of this, as we might be inclined to do, as the solipsistic dream of an individual subject. When Chuang-tzu wonders whether he is Chuang-tzu who has dreamed that he is a butterfly or a butterfly who has dreamed that he is Chuang-tzu, since the "reality" of both Chuang-tzu and the butterfly is essentially dreamlike, one would have to suppose that both the dream of Chuang-tzu and of the butterfly are projections of the tao itself. Since this imagery occurs in only one or two places, we cannot, however, say that the analogue of the dream is meant to be taken entirely seriously. All we can say in the end is that—whatever the "reality" of the "ten thousand things"—they have no isolated categorically fixed "self-existence" of their own.

On the opposite side of the dream metaphor we also find a passage which rather emphasizes the relative actuality of particular things. Little Understanding asks Great Impartial Harmony, "What are administrative unit words?"[106] This seems to be a technical term which refers to administrative units made up of groups of families and to higher administrative units made up of these units.[107] The question seems to be, what is the "ontologic status" of such entities? Are they "real" entities subsuming the different subentities which they contain? It seems to be analogous to asking whether entities such as counties or political parties are "real" entities which actually subsume their human members. The reply seems to be that they *can* indeed be treated as real as the entities which compose them. "One unites the different to make the same," states Great Impartial Harmony and then turns to the image of a horse, "you can point to the hundred parts of a horse and not obtain a horse and yet the horse is tied up there in front of you. Thus, we put together the hundred parts and call it a horse."[108] The actual horse is an experienced fact (whatever ultimate "ontic" status one assigns it). The fact that all its parts can be considered separately does not detract from this experienced fact. It may be an evanescent fact; the horse may be readily dissolved into its parts, but then again its parts are also evanescent and will just as inevitably return to nonbeing. If there were available a modern notion of particle physics, Chuang-tzu might well say that the ultimate particles of which a chair are composed are no more or less "real" than the chair itself. It is thus readily understandable that when the scholastic philosophies of Mahayana Buddhism came to China several centuries later, the Chinese literati of the time immediately perceived an affinity between Chuang-tzu and the endless discourses on the wholly "conditional reality" and "ultimate emptiness" (*sunyata*) of the entities of our ordinary experience in the Prajña-paramita sutras and elsewhere.

Before turning to the troubled human realm, however, I should say something about another motif in the Chuang-tzu strain which has often been passed over—what almost might be called the quasi-theistic metaphor in Chuang-tzu. The whole matter has been generally by-passed on the ground that since Chuang-tzu is a mystic or a "naturalist" or an adherent of "organismic philosophy," the quasi-theistic metaphors can only be "poetic." To be sure, Chuang-tzu is *not* theistic in any ultimate sense any more than the Lao-tzu can be considered to be an adherent of a mother-goddess because of his use of the "mother" metaphor. Yet metaphors such as "the Creator of things" (*tsao-wu-che*), the "creative principle" (*tsao-hua*), or the "true ruler" (*chen tsai* or *chen chün*) may be not less significant to the whole Chuang-tzu vision than is the metaphor of the mother in the Lao-tzu. "If I should say that I do not want to be anything but a man— nothing but a man—the Creator would surely regard me as an inauspicious sort of person. So now if one thinks of heaven and earth as a great furnace and the Creator as the skilled smith, where could he send me that would not be all right?"[109] In another passage, after discussing all the changing moods and turbulent emotions of our restless lives he remarks, "I do not know who [or what] causes them. There must be some genuine ruler but we do not have an external sign of him. That he can form things [or act] is certain, but one does not see his form. He has identity but no form."[110] In discussing the operations of the human organism, he asks how it works as a functioning whole. Is there any favorite organ? It seems that now one organ is in control and now another but that no particular organ is in any permanent or privileged control. He concludes that basically it is the *tao* which is in control, but in talking of the *tao* in this context, he again says it would seem that "they [the parts of the organism] have a genuine ruler present in them. When we seek to identify it, whether we find it or not neither adds nor detracts from its genuineness."[111] Incidentally, I agree with Graham that the main point of this passage is that the human heart (*hsin*) does not—or ought not—to occupy any privileged position within the human organism.[112] The "true ruler" of the organism is not the heart, which is one organ among many, but the *tao* itself. Yet one again is struck by the metaphor of the ruler. Elsewhere, we find the phrase a "companion of the Creator," and Chuang-tzu's own philosophy is epitomized in chapter 33 by the phrase that "above he wandered with the Creator."[113]

The phrase "poetic metaphor" as we tend to use it in modern literary discourse does not dispose of this matter any more than it does in the case of the Lao-tzu's "mother." Like Chuang-tzu's "words," metaphors say something. The mother and the feminine are central, as we have seen, to the whole Lao-tzu vision and the metaphor is used to refer to that mysterious area where nonbeing and being interact. "Poetic" or "metaphoric" cannot in this case simply mean "subjective." In fact, the metaphor may well relate to a debate which was going on at the great intellectual center of the period, the Chi-hsia Academy, between two academicians named Chi Chen and Chieh-tzu. All we know of them is that Chi Chen was associated with the doctrine that "no one or nothing makes it" (*mo wei*), and Chieh-tzu is associated with the position that "someone or something causes it" (*huo shih*). The question seems to be—how do things come into being? The first answer seems to be the conventional Taoist answer, that they come into being by the process of *wu-wei* with no specific cause of their particular appearance other than the natural process of "birth" or growth. They simply emerge naturally and spontaneously from the *tao*. The latter view may possibly reflect a Mohist outlook. It is bent on explaining things in terms of proximate, particulate, and specific causes which, in this case, seem to take the form of some purposive shaping or fashioning power. The approach is illustrated vividly in a passage of the *Lü-shih Ch'un ch'iu*, "When the *ch'i* of spring arrives, grass and trees grow. When the *ch'i* of fall arrives, grass and trees wither. Now growing and withering are caused by 'something or someone' [*huo-shih*, the same phrase as Chieh-tzu's]. They are not spontaneous [*tzu-jan*]. When what causes them is present, everything takes place. When the cause is not present, nothing can take place."[114] Disastrous springs and unseasonable summers are indeed possible. Here again the express analogy is to the role of rulers in the state and the specific political philosophies which they adopt. The good state does not "achieve itself" spontaneously. The argument seems to involve a direct attack on the notions of *wu-wei* as applied to the political realm. The moral intent of rulers is crucial.

One might think that Chuang-tzu or his disciples would obviously opt for Chi Chen's doctrine of *mo wei*. In fact, in a passage which seems to belong to the authentic Chuang-tzu strain, he does not clearly opt for either side, although he makes it clear that the entire discussion pertains only to the realm of being (*yu*) where language can be applied. He is not entirely prepared to say that the fact that "chickens crow and dogs bark" can simply be disposed of by references to "no one made it" (*mo wei*).

The notion that nature suggests the same specific fashioning and creating activity that we associate with human artifacts is no more absent in Chinese thought than in Plato's *Timaeus* or certain modes of Indian thought. Some were evidently dissatisfied with the notion that the myriad "things" of the world, in all their irreducible and unique specificity, were simply to be accounted for by "spontaneous growth." As already indicated, things can be looked at in two ways—either in their concrete, tangible presence (*shih*), like the "horse tied up before me," or in their "emptiness," like a horse dissolved into it hundred parts which are further dissolved into emptiness (*hsü*). The perspective of "Someone causes it," Chuang-tzu seems to say, overemphasizes the tangible, concrete, contingent reality of the thing in its unique presence. "No one made it" overemphasizes its ultimate transience and "emptiness."[115] When Chuang-tzu concentrated his attention on the unique design, exuberant variety, and astonishing uniqueness of things, the metaphor of the *tao* as "Creator" or "creating power" somehow involved with the discrete particularity of things comes to mind. The fact that "chickens crow and dogs bark" seems to call for some specific creativity. One senses that it is not the "scientific" interest in "how things are made" but something like an aesthetic-artistic appreciation of the uniqueness of creativity which is operative here. Artistic creativity is a mystery which contains both an element of conscious action (*wei*) and an element of *wu wei*. It would appear that when dealing with the realm of manifold nature (*yu*), Chuang-tzu is even prepared to relativize the opposition between *wu-wei* and *wei* along with all other such dyads. This notion of a specific "creative" principle or "creator" was, in fact, to remain a qualifying feature of most "organismic" thought even of the later period. It is present even in the Neo-Confucianism of Chu-Hsi, where the term *tsao-hua* or creative principle or creator of transformations is frequently used alongside the principle of generation or spontaneous growth.

*The Human Realm*    In Chuang-tzu as in Lao-tzu, it is within the human sphere that all troubles arise. How is it that the peculiar creature called human becomes detached from the *tao*? Indeed in Chuang-tzu, the problem seems to run deeper than in the Lao-tzu. In the Lao-tzu, human beings, when released from an environment created by the distortions of high civilization, may well return to the unreflective life of the *tao*. Like the Lao-tzu, Chuang-tzu does not explain why or how the fatal *yu-wei* consciousness emerges, but in the Chuang-tzu strain one might say that the pathology of human consciousness is congenital to the entire species and that it is deeply rooted in the human heart/mind itself. We thus find that there is no "primitivistic" solution. The situation cannot be reversed by Taoist sage-rulers. While avoiding the term *hsing* (human nature), there is a term in the Chuang-tzu strain which, as Graham insists, may mean something like the "essential nature" (*ch'ing*) of the human as human (that which differentiates him from Heaven or the *tao*).[116] It is not, in fact, the feelings which separate humans from the *tao*. Joy, anger, delight, and other feelings all spring from the *tao* like "vapor condensing into mushrooms" or like the distinct sounds which issue from various natural cavities and hollows when the raging wind blows.[117] They are parts of the human organism governed by the "genuine lord" of all the cosmos.

Somehow, however, one organ in this particular organism—the human heart/mind—has the fatal capacity to arrogate to itself the attributes of a fully closed off, fully individualized entity, "the fully completed or individualized heart" (*ch'eng hsin*), which by a kind of self-encapsulation is able to establish a self-being of its own cut off from the flow of the *tao*. The word *ch'eng* as referring to the general process by which the things of nature become self-encapsulated

things or processes with a self-being of their own is used throughout
in a negative way. Any thing or process that becomes fully self-encapsulated and separated from the flow of the *tao* "injures" the
*tao*.[118] A curious example is that of the consummately perfect (*ch'eng*)
lute performance of the musician Chao, the very perfection of whose
music as a kind of self-enclosed reality cuts it off from infinitely
higher music of the *tao*.[119] The human heart asserts its own self-being
by fixing on aspects of the protean world which surrounds it, attempting to freeze them as objects of our fixed goals or thoughts,
and thus absolutizing them. Men's likes and dislikes become fixed
both by obsessive, grasping passions as well as by fixed opinions
concerning "right" and "wrong" even while he himself, like all finite, transient creatures, moves inexorably toward death. "They become entangled with everything they meet; they struggle with their
minds day after day . . . sometimes straying wildly, sometimes probing deeply, sometimes calculating . . . in their small fears they are
fretful, in their large fears they are downcast. In making judgments
about 'right' and 'wrong' their minds shoot off like a cross-bow pel-
let. They cling to their opinions as if they had taken a holy oath.
They fade, like fall and winter . . . is it not sad how we slash and jos-
tle each other and our race to extinction is like a gallop which nothing can stop. We toil away our entire life and see no success . . . is it
not sad? What's the use of saying I'm not dead yet. As the body
decays, the mind decays with it. Is this not a supreme sorrow?"[120]
Here is the life of everyman, as well as of the intellectuals. Whether
jostling for wealth, power, or the rightness of one's fixed opinions
and doctrines—all are asserting their fully individualized mind
(*ch'eng hsin*). The tragedy is not in living and dying, but in what the
Buddhists might call the clinging to and freezing of various aspects
of the world of being. There is no hint that having a "sage-king" rid
men of the external environment of higher civilization will cure this
condition and, hence, we have here a radical denial of the saving
role of political order even in Lao-tzu's sense. Civilization, one
might say, is itself a "natural" outcome of the "essential nature" of
the fully individualized man, and one feels that Chuang-tzu is
acutely aware of the contradiction in the concept of Lao-tzu's sage
who sets himself the *conscious* design of leading men away from civilization.

While the fixed goals of power, wealth, or sensual gratification
are, of course, rejected, an enormous amount of attention is also paid
to what might be called the fixations of the intellect. Chuang-tzu is
dismayed by the intellectual conflicts of his time, of which the
struggles between Confucianists and Mohists provide a paradigm.

Nature, of course, abounds in *natural* differences but humans have the capacity to have totally different opinions about the same matters simply by dismissing each other as "wrong." How can anything in the *tao* be "right" or "wrong"? The Chuang-tzu raises a problem also raised by Plato in the *Sophist*. "By what is the *tao* hidden that we have the genuine and the false? By what is language obscured that we have rightness or wrongness? How can the Way disappear and not be present? How can words be present and not be acceptable?"[121] Plato remarks that "anyone who says anything must say something and it is quite undeniable that one who says what is not something says nothing at all."[122] When Confucianists and Mohists have different judgments about the same state of affairs, what is wrong for one is right for the other. While Plato believes that there is a strictly intellectual power of dialectic which can ultimately, by reasoning, lead him to a true picture of reality, Chuang-tzu would no doubt have gleefully dwelt on the counter-claims of Aristotle, who found Plato wrong. It is not that the perspectives of Confucius or Mo-tzu may not have some truth when applied to certain situations, but their effort to encompass the infinite ocean of circumstances and perspectives with their own "rightness" and to find moral and intellectual "wrongness" everywhere is as much a manifestation of the self-assertive and isolating heart/mind as is the monomaniacal ambition of the tyrant. There is an implication throughout that those who trumpet their "rights and wrongs" have motives other than sheerly intellectual or moral motives. What they seek is a "name" in the sense of fame and reputation, either for moral rightness or intellectual prowess. Certainly debates about fixed principles or rigid antitheses cannot attain the ultimate ungraspability of the *tao*. Intellectual debates are about winning and losing and not about the truth and it is simply the more skillful dialectician who wins. "Suppose you and I have an argument. If you have beaten me instead of my beating you, then are you necessarily right and am I necessarily wrong?"[123] If another debater is brought in, he simply brings a third point of view. Only the man of gnosis can truly adapt to the myriad situations of life without a vested interest in preconceptions and *parti pris,* since he has no need for self-assertion. Adapting here does not mean adapting in order to "control" but in order to "get by." Chuang-tzu's "true man" (*chen jen*) has no need to control anything.

The historic Chuang-tzu moves further than any ancient Chinese thinker in the direction of denying any function to the political order in "correcting" things. The notion of the sage or of the political order as a power for "correction" presupposes the whole notion of fixed views on "right and wrong." He nevertheless seems to take the political order for granted as part of the furniture of ordinary human life in its hopelessly unredeemed state. Rulers "good or evil" seem to be an inescapable part of the cacophonous symphony of the human realm. In totally denying any redemptive role to the political order, however, Chuang-tzu, like Mo-tzu, also steps outside of a dominant cultural orientation, although in quite a different direction.

Even in Chuang-tzu, to be sure, there is still the notion of the enormous charismatic power of the Taoist "perfect man," which may readily become the focus of political power. The charisma created by the higher gnosis of "genuine men" attracts others like honey attracts the bees. People, like the hideous Ai T'ai-t'o, have to fend off those who crowd around them, and rulers worn down by their cares are anxious to hand over political responsibility to them. Even the famous mystic Lieh-tzu, who is treated by Chuang-tzu somewhat suspiciously as a man inclined to use his spiritual power to display himself and to control the world through his charismatic magic, is nevertheless alarmed by the effect of his powers on others. Passing a soup-stall on his way to the kingdom of Ch'i, the soup-makers drop everything and rush to serve him.[124] He suddenly turns about and cancels his trip to the court of the Duke of Ch'i. He then remarks to the recluse Po-hun Wu-jen, "If I can't dispel this inner spiritual power [nei ch'eng], it becomes a kind of radiance that once outside of one overpowers men's minds."[125] He then goes on to express the fear that if the Duke of Ch'i were exposed to it, wearied and crushed as he is by the cares of government, he might try to shift the government onto Lieh-tzu himself. Po-hun Wu-jen replies that there must be something about Lieh-tzu himself which leads him to encourage this kind of influence to manifest itself. He suspects that Lieh-tzu may, despite his protestations, crave fame and domination. The point in all such cases (and Chuang-tzu may well have truly believed in such radiant power) is that the problem for all his men of gnosis is how to avoid government. The fact that people flock around to bask in their spiritual radiance does not mean that the sage can simply redeem them through his love. Their yearnings may merely have the effect of entangling the sage himself hopelessly in the world. Yet elsewhere it is implied that if circumstances do force one to become entangled in power responsibilities, the sage may simply "go through the motions" maintaining his full inner detachment.

In chapter 3 ("The World of Men"), we have a sustained attack on the notion that Confucian "noble men" can possibly influence evil rulers, through the Confucian mode of moral persuasion. In the

world of "little understanding" in which most men live, evil rulers
are as "natural" as Confucian moralists. The protagonists are Confucius and Yen Hui.[126] Yen Hui wishes to go to Wei in an attempt to
influence the tyrannical and ruthless young ruler to better his ways.
Confucius plies him with questions about how he proposes to accomplish his purpose. He begins by pointing out that "the perfect
men of old saw that they had it in themselves before passing it on to
others," strongly implying that Yen Hui lacks this wisdom.[127] Instead, he is full of self-righteousness and probably bent on achieving
fame. For him to preach to a man like the young ruler about *jen* will
be regarded by the ruler as an effort to parade his own excellence,
and this the ruler will surely not abide. Moreover, the ruler may be
quite as good a dialectician as Yen Hui and even beat him in the
argument. Yen Hui is simply courting death. Yen Hui proposes a
whole series of alternate strategic approaches, which are all rejected
by Confucius, who is convinced that none will prove effective
against the impermeable self-assertion of the ruler.

Confucius then abruptly shifts direction and urges Yen Hui to
"fast his mind." We then have the lesson in achieving mystic gnosis
already outlined above. He effectively learns to "fast his mind." The
lesson is successful and Yen Hui reaches a level on which he is able
to say, "before I heard this, I was certain that I was Hui but now
that I have heard it, there is no more Hui."[128] He is purged of ego
and forgets all his stratagems. Confucius then seems to advise him
(the language is obscure) to go to Wei and simply make himself
available. If the ruler is prepared to listen to him, he should respond.
There is here some implication that the ruler's exposure to his silent
mystic aura may possibly affect him somehow. One is left with the
impression, however, that Yen Hui himself may now have lost interest in the entire enterprise.

On the whole, however, the general message throughout is that
the political order can not remedy the human plight, which is rooted
in the individual mind itself. The political realm itself reflects this
delusive consciousness. It remains part of the furniture of an unredeemed world. The "true man"—who is not necessarily a recluse—
may find himself in circumstances where he must play a role in government. In that case, he will simply adapt to whatever the situation
requires and "go through the motions." Chuang-tzu himself, it
would appear, avoids office like the plague. In the end, it is basically
clear that Chuang-tzu assigns no redemptive role to the political
order.

*The Enlightenment of the "True Man"*   The claim has frequently been
made that Chuang-tzu is an "individualist." This is indeed true in

the sense that, finally, every individual must find his own salvation from the miseries of a life controlled by "little understanding," and those who can save themselves are probably few.

One might well ask, however—how is a solution at all possible? If humans are imprisoned in their individualized, encapsulating minds, how can they escape? A hint is already offered in a description of the human organism, where it is maintained that the "true ruler" of the human organism is not the mind, which is really one organ among others, but the *tao* itself. It is, however, also clear from Yen Hui's mystic ascent that the individual has the latent capacity to "fast" or empty or transcend his individuated mind and thus to become one with the undifferentiated *ch'i*. But what is it that makes this possible? The answer seems to be that it is the mind itself which even while imprisoning man in the world of "little understanding" also seems to possess mysterious powers of self-transcendence. Wang-t'ai, the one-footed convict sage, has a "unique way of using his mind" to achieve the higher gnosis so that "through his knowledge he gets at his mind and through his mind he gets at the 'constant' mind."[129] There is thus a level at which the mind itself becomes the instrument of salvation. Elsewhere, an allegorical persona called the Nameless Man says, "let your mind wander in the great purity."[130] It is probably this ultimate level of indeterminacy of the mind which leads Chuang-tzu to avoid the constrictive term *hsing* (human nature) to describe human spiritual potentiality.

Yet there does not seem to be much evidence that very many are able to attain this transcendence. Nan-po k'uei-tzu asks Woman Crookback (the only feminine sage in the gallery of allegorical personae), "can the *tao* be learned?" She replies equivocally, "how can it—anyway, you are not the one to do it."[131] She then draws a distinction between herself and another sage, Pu-liang Yi. While she has the *tao* of the sage, Pu-liang Yi has the *talent or capacity* (*ts'ai*) of a sage. From the commentators, one would gather that while Pu-liang Yi has the spiritual capacities to lead him beyond the merely intellectual (like Hui Shih), the Woman Crookback has the gnosis which comes from immediate experience. One nevertheless has the impression that the vast majority of humans have neither the *tao* nor the capacity to achieve the *tao*. They seem both unable to achieve the higher gnosis or to become one with the *tao* on the simple-vegetative level envisioned in the Lao-tzu's primitivist utopia. As ordinary humans, they remain dominated by their "individualized minds." It is only the "true man" who can draw the vital distinction between that within himself which belongs to man—that which leads man to his "false consciousness" (little understanding)—and that within him which belongs to Heaven or the *tao*. "There must first be a 'true person' before there can be true knowledge."[132] Chapter 7 provides a full description of the behavior of such a person; he is indifferent to life and death. He is as "cool as autumn and warm as spring." Yet he is not necessarily a recluse and goes through all the "motions" of men who live in the world. He is after all on one level, one thing among the ten thousand things, and for him to act as if he were not attached to being would itself be to set up again the false intellectual antithesis between being and nonbeing which Chuang-tzu rejects. "He has the form of a man but not the particular nature [*ch'ing*] of a man. Since he has the form of a man, he associates with men. Since he doesn't have the particular nature of men [the individualized heart], the discrimination between right and wrong cannot touch him. Puny and small! He thus belongs to the world of man. Vast and great, he perfects his Heaven alone."[133] It would appear as suggested that "true men" may share all the emotions of ordinary people, but do not become identified with them. They adjust to any situation into which life thrusts them but remain completely uninvolved. As indicated, it is not inconceivable that they may even become involved in circumstances involving power and wealth, but here too they will go through the motions in complete detachment.

The superb serenity of the "true man" is vividly depicted in the accounts of how he faces crippling diseases. "Master Yü fell ill. Master Ssu went to see how he was. 'Amazing,' said Master Yü. 'The Creator is making me all cramped up like this. My back sticks up like a hunchback's and my vital organs are on top of me. My chin is hidden in my navel. My shoulders are above my head, and my pigtail points to the sky. It must be some dislocation in my yin and yang *ch'i*.' Yet his heart was calm and unconcerned."[134] That part of Yü which belongs to Heaven is able to regard his own body from the lofty perspective of Heaven. He is able, as it were, to participate in the joyful and playful transformative creativity of the *tao* itself.

When we compare this image with that of Job's sufferings in the Bible, we immediately become aware of a striking lacuna in this account. We are nowhere told anything about the agonizing subjective pains which must accompany the progress of this disease, while in the case of Job, we are fully aware of the maddening itches which accompany his skin disease. Job remains ever aware of the incorrigible finitude which separates him from God in this life, and his sufferings confirm his finitude. Although God does not offer an answer to his moral questions, he does reveal a vision of the grandeur of the universe that evokes a sense of the metaethical meaning of the cosmos. Yet Job himself incorrigibly remains a finite being still vulnerable to all the ills to which man is heir. He cannot become a "companion of the Creator."

Not only a biblical monotheist but a Theravada Buddhist might have found Chuang-tzu too easily comforted after his wife's death. Hui Shih is astonished to find him singing and pounding a tub. Hui Shih says, "you lived with her. She brought up your children and grew old with you."[135] Chuang-tzu replies that although he grieved at first, he realized that she had simply emerged from the *tao* as one of the ten thousand things and returned thereto. She was an episode in the grand pageant. In early Buddhism, however, "being separated from that which one loves" is one of the irreducible agonies and sufferings of individuated existence, since those one loves are not simply interchangeable "abstract" particulars, but singular and unique objects of love.

Chuang-tzu here shares the lofty serenity of Confucius in the face of creaturely suffering, although his perspective is that of a mystic rather than that of a man of *jen* secure in the sense of his moral integrity. Yet here we may well again touch a shared orientation within the high culture of ancient China. There is the supremely confident ideal of "sagehood" in which the sage partakes of a kind of "divine power" even while remaining a finite human. Chuang-tzu's "true man" is a mystic who is also able to affirm the world because of his essentially aesthetic attitude toward it. Both the persistent patterns of nature and its protean transformations—the cycles of the seasons, the raging floods, the howling winds, the darting minnows and the soaring eagles—and even what appear to most of us with our little understanding to be the conventionally ugly and painful aspects of things in nature such as the crippling transformations of Yü are part of the grandiose spectacle. To the company of these tropes one might add the useless gnarled old trees, which represent the fact that all the varied expressions of the *tao*'s creativity in nature are to be regarded as ends in themselves and need no justification as "instruments" to other ends.[136] It is by allowing oneself to become an instrument to other ends that one both endangers one's life and loses one's connections to the ineffable *tao* as one of its creative expressions.

Does Chuang-tzu prove that he has indeed moved beyond finite human perspectives or even passed completely beyond the realm of judgments of right and wrong? His great protagonist Hui Shih, who despite his rejection of commonsensical views of reality seems somehow to remain committed to the image of man's incorrigible finitude, challenges Chuang-tzu's confident assertion that one can have the form of a man without his essentially finite nature.[137] Hui Shih's question concerning how a finite creature among finite creatures can so transcend the conditions of his finitude as to be one "with Heaven" seems quite cogent. We are nevertheless left to conclude that in the argument between them, Chuang-tzu has definitely "won." This very display of superior dialectic may itself betray a trace of human pride in winning as well as a tell-tale, quite human sense of superior enlightenment.

### 3. The Teachings of Huang-lao: The Instrumental Tao

I have thus far spoken without apology of the mystical Taoism of the Lao-tzu and of the historic Chuang-tzu even while noting the marked differences between the two. Yet as we know, the doxographers and bibliographers of the Han dynasty applied the term "Tao school" (tao-chia) to a much wider assortment of Warring States figures. The *Historical Records* of Ssu-ma Ch'ien thus uses the term tao-chia interchangeably with another term, "the Teachings of the Yellow Emperor and Lao-tzu" (huang-lao) and retrospectively applies this term to the outlooks of third and fourth century figures such as Sung Hsing, T'ien P'ien, Shen Tao, Shen Pu-hai, and Han Fei-tzu. The dynastic *History of the Former Han Dynasty* applies the term to Sung Hsing and Yin Wen-tzu. Many of the same figures are elsewhere assigned to other "schools," further complicating the picture. Thus, Shen Tao, Shen Pu-hai and Han Fei-tzu are also considered three of the four pillars of Legalism, while Sung Hsing and Yin Wen-tzu are also assigned, with some reason, to the Mohists.

Several scholars in the People's Republic have in recent years defined "Huang-lao" Taoism as a fusion of Taoism and Legalism.[138] Yet some of the figures mentioned above are not Legalists and it is also most difficult to pigeonhole some of the personalities of the early Han dynasty to whom Ssu-ma Ch'ien applies the term "Huang-lao" as Legalists. What I shall propose below is that the term, which probably did not emerge before the early Han dynasty, is meant to describe an outlook much broader in scope and that the fusion of Taoism and Legalism is simply one variant of a broader outlook which Creel has called "purposive Taoism" and which I shall tentatively call instrumental Taoism.[139]

Ssu-ma Ch'ien's retrospective use of this term may, of course, tell us more about him than about many of the figures to whom he refers. Yet since Huang-lao Taoism reached the height of its sway among the officials and literati of the first half century of the Han dynasty (circa 206–140 B.C.) and since there is even some reason to think that Ssu-ma Ch'ien himself, as well as his father, Ssu-ma T'an the grand historian/astrologer, were associated with this outlook, one cannot lightly dismiss his various applications of the term to figures of the Warring States period.

It is noteworthy that the term is applied by Ssu-ma Ch'ien and Pan Ku to several personalities associated with the famous Chi-hsia Academy already mentioned above. In the fourth century and early third century, this particular institution seems to have played a central role in the intellectual life of the times. The state of Ch'i was at the time still considered one of the most powerful and prosperous of the great powers. On the one hand, it was close to the old cultural center of Lu and hence in touch with the older Chou traditions; on the other hand, its rulers seemed to be quite open to all new currents of thought. The ruling house belonged to the notorious T'ien clan, which had usurped the throne from the old established ruling house, which traced its legitimacy to the very foundations of the Chou dynasty. This usurpation, which began with the murder of the legitimate ruler by the notorious minister T'ien Wen-tzu in 481 B.C., was generally regarded as a classical example of usurpation of power achieved through the application of illegitimate force. It is thus entirely likely that the T'ien family rulers were by no means deeply committed to the older traditions and quite open to new ideas which might provide their rule with a new basis of legitimation as well as to new ways of dealing with the growing, fierce struggle for ascendancy within the world of the Warring States. One can also understand their urge simply to enhance their prestige as patrons of the wandering *shih*. Both King Wei and King Hsüan were evidently bent on following the model of the famous Duke Wen of Wei[2], mentioned above, who had made himself the patron of intellectuals at the beginning of the previous century. King Hsüan who had usurped the throne was particularly enthusiastic about attracting wandering *shih* to his capital Lin-tzu and seemed to be particularly free of "ideological" commitments. The *shih* were granted generous stipends, luxurious quarters, high rank, and large retinues, and were provided with "lecture halls" at Chi-hsia gate at the west wall of the city. The translation "academician" seems appropriate, since the prevailing principle was that "they would not engage in governing but discussed various theories," and yet we are also informed that they were "fond of discussing political affairs."[140] Whether the principle was established by the rulers or the academicians, it would appear that most of them did indeed not desire to become entangled in the dangers and responsibilities of public office. Thus, Mencius, who was in touch with all these people, may well have refused to join because of his firm principle that one should not accept endowments from a prince without serving in office.[141] On the other hand, we are told that many of the academicians are themselves quite proud of their "independence" and we may indeed have here something as close as anything we can find in Chinese history to an institution devoted to the free exchange of ideas.

It has, however, been suggested by Kuo Mo-jo that there is some connection between the fact that many of the famous members of the Academy are reputed to be adherents of Huang-lao Taoism and the peculiar position of the "Yellow Emperor" in the state cult of the T'ien ruling house.[142] The first authenticated reference we have to the shadowy figure of the Yellow Emperor actually occurs in a bronze inscription attributed to King Hsüan of Ch'i. In it, he speaks of the Yellow Emperor as the high ancestor of the T'ien family. In seeking his high ancestor in a quasi-divine, quasi-human figure of the remote past, the king was, of course, following a practice which was now widely prevalent among the ruling houses of the large powers, which had all by now appropriated the title of "king" (*wang*) for themselves. From the book of Mencius, one gathers that this usurpation of claims of descent from quasi-divine sage-emperors had something to do with the revived sense of favorable prospects for the reemergence of a new universal king within the Chinese world. Thus, the rulers of the large states were most anxious to establish the cosmic and historic prestige of their own pedigrees.

This does not mean that the Yellow Emperor was an invention of the Ch'i rulers. The whole question of the origins of this figure and of his role in the political mythology of ancient China has been much explored by modern Chinese scholars. The word we translate here as "Emperor" is, of course, the word *ti* used to refer to the high god (*Shang-ti*) of the Shang dynasty. The appropriation of the term to refer to earthly rulers seems to have already begun, as has been pointed out, by the time of the last two rulers of the Shang dynasty. In the Warring States period, the word *ti* had already been applied to the shadowy figures of Yao, Shun, and Yü, who were now also symbolically associated with Confucianism, although Yü himself, the ever-self-sacrificing, constantly toiling founder of the Hsia dynasty had also become the patron sage-emperor of the Mohists.

Yang K'uan has suggested that the name *huang-ti* (the Yellow Emperor) may have at first been confused with the homonym *huang* (meaning "august" or "great") *ti*, which had been used as a title for the "high god" himself.[143] He suggests that in the course of time, by a process already familiar to us, the "august emperor" was transformed into a quasi-divine, quasi-human ruler and that the shift from the *huang* meaning "august" to the homonym *huang* meaning "yellow" is linked to the gradual emergence of the kind of "correlative cosmology" (see Chapter 9 below) which was to become so prevalent in the elite culture of the late Warring States period. It may reflect the notion of the correlation among the five cardinal directions (east, west, north, south, center), the four seasons, and the "five colors." Within this cosmology, "yellow" as the color of the earth and the "center" would generally be in a dominant position, thus perhaps helping to explain the Yellow Emperor's abiding centrality in late Chinese political mythology (as opposed, for instance, to the "white emperor" and "black emperor" who in the end disappeared from the scene). We can thus readily understand the eagerness of the Ch'i ruling house to claim the Yellow Emperor as their ancestor. It is also quite plausible that the lack of any link between the Yellow Emperor and Confucianism and Mohism may have facilitated his appropriation as the symbolic focus of Huang-lao Taoism. In the process so well described by Ku Chieh-kang, the lateness of his emergence may be directly related to the remoteness of the period to which his rulership is assigned.

The kings of Ch'i were not, however, intellectual leaders and the linkage between the Yellow Emperor and Ch'i tells us nothing about the doctrines which come to be associated with his name. There is, in fact, no evidence that the kings tried to impose any "official" ideology on the academy.

In searching for the content of the doctrine, we might begin by asking why Sung Hsing (360–290? B.C.), who seems to have some association with the academy comes to be called an adherent of "Huang-lao." From the meager accounts of his doctrine which we have, one is at first much more inclined to identify him as a Mohist. In the final chapter of the Chuang-tzu (chapter 33), we find it stated that he and his disciple Yin Wen-tzu "desired peace for the world and the preservation of the lives of the people. In providing sustenance for themselves and others, they stopped at what was sufficient . . . they sought to save the people from strife, to suppress aggression, put an end to the use of arms and to put an end to wars."[144] It would appear that Sung Hsing completely identifies with the Mohist principle of utility (*li*). In an encounter with Mencius, we find him rushing off to Ch'in and Ch'u to persuade their rulers not to engage in war. When Mencius asks what his arguments will be, he replies that he will persuade them that "war will not be beneficial [*li*] for either of them."[145] Here we clearly find an activist in the Mohist mold. Indeed there is even the suggestion of a radical new mode of activism not to be found in the Mo-tzu. Sung Hsing is prepared to by-pass the political establishment and directly appeal to the people "with these aims in mind, they [his followers] walked the whole world over trying to persuade those above and to teach those below and though the world refused to listen, they clamored all the louder and would not give up until men both high and low were sick of seeing them and still they forced themselves to be seen."[146] It was also clear that both Sung Hsing and Yin Wen-Tzu were somehow interested in drawing clear distinctions between various realms of reality and hence also interested in the right use of language. Yin Wen-tzu is, in fact, classified as a member of the school of names in late bibliographies. What then is Taoist about these men? It would seem to be their keen feeling for the autonomy of the inner life and their ability to render their souls invulnerable to all the false notions of good and evil so prevalent in their social environment. If they were Mohists, they may have felt that Mo-tzu's grave neglect of man's inner spiritual state may have been one of the weaknesses of his outlook. Thus, one of their other favorite maxims is that "men's true desires are few and yet they believe them to be many."[147] They suffer all the insults and abuse which the world inflicts upon them because they know in their hearts that their true dignity is not touched by such insults. The Confucian noble man cannot achieve this degree of equanimity because he must worry about affronts to the dignity of his person, since the entire fabric of *li* depends on the preservation of the dignity of noble men. Confucius may be indifferent to the fact that men do not know him. As a noble man, however, he cannot be indifferent to indignities to his person. Sung Hsing, however, is able to avoid all anger and contentiousness. Thus, in his inner imperviousness to the world, he does indeed share Lao-tzu's and Chuang-tzu's profound spiritual independence.

Yet this inner equanimity, far from hampering his activist role in the world, renders him all the more resolute. One of the boundaries which he is thus able to draw clearly is the boundary between his inner quietude and contentment and his unflagging activism on behalf of mankind. His belief that man's "desires are basically few," which contrasts so sharply with Mo-tzu's view of men in a "state of nature" as completely wedded to their own self-interest, may encourage his conviction that he can appeal to the people directly by preaching and teaching. Ch'ien Mu points out that Sung Hsing is classed in Pan Ku's bibliography as a member of the school of "story tellers" (*hsiao-shuo chia*) perhaps because of the illustrative tales and parables he used in the course of "walking about the world."[148] His impervious equanimity in the face of insults would certainly help him in this endeavor.

One readily sees here the motifs which remind us of the Lao-tzu and Chuang-tzu. Sung Hsing's heart is indeed indifferent to the world and Chuang-tzu himself praises him. "As far as the world went, he was not worried by it" and yet "there was something still imperfect about him."[149] It would nevertheless appear that what Sung Hsing has of Taoism is its inner detachment although there is no hint concerning the "religious" basis of his outlook in general. Beyond this inner detachment of heart, there seems to be little else about him that would help us to define the meaning of Huang-lao Taoism in his case except for the fact that he uses his inner tranquility as an instrument to promote his social ends. This may have been what Chuang-tzu considered to be his "imperfection." His "Taoist" aspect is thus, to a point, instrumental to other goals. He can use his spiritual power to "reform" the world.

When we turn to his fellow academicians, P'eng Meng, T'ien P'ien, and particularly Shen Tao, we may be on more solid ground.[150] What they share with Sung Hsing is his inner equanimity and detachment. This detachment seems, however, not to be contradicted by any "purposive" activism in the outer world. Here the spirit of *wu-wei* pervades both the world within and the world without and there is much in the description of their outlook which actually reminds us of themes in the Chuang-tzu. "Impartial and without bias, even-minded and without preferences, they follow the tendencies of things without wavering . . . they do not calculate and do not scheme on the basis of their own knowledge . . . they do not choose among things and simply go along with them . . . their fundamental principle is to treat all things as equal."[151] Here we have again the dismissal of all value judgments, the mistrust of "subjective" opinions and all fixed perspectives on the drift of things in the outer world, and the readiness to submit without resistance to what might be called the obvious dictates of external circumstances.

It is not easy to tell whether the notion of "treating all things as equal" is derived by them from Chuang-tzu (and Hui Shih) or whether Chuang-tzu derives it from them or whether we have again one of those notions which was circulating widely in the discourse of the time and whose ultimate source remains unclear.

The idea of the *tao* as the ultimate reality which embraces all things both in the world out there and the world within and the idea of passively "drifting with the *tao*" is very much present. Conscious agency and conscious intent are eliminated from both the "objective" and "subjective" worlds, thus leaving much room for Needham's ataraxy. There is nothing which suggests the exaltation of mystic gnosis (but this may simply reflect the limits of our materials) and it may well be that in this case Taoism is not so much a deep mysticism as a kind of "life attitude" willing to submit to all the ways of the *tao* immanent in man and nature without probing further into the deeper mysteries of being and obviously without the aesthetic elan of a Chuang-tzu.

One indeed wonders whether one does not finally have here Needham's "scientifically" oriented Taoists. When they speak of the *tao*, at least in the fragments which we have, they do not become involved in the realm of nonbeing. They always see the *tao* "embodied" in its processes, situations, and patterns. Yet their stipends at the academy are presumably based on the fact that despite their spiritual passivity, they are quite interested in following the *tao* of political affairs and discerning the patterns of "order and disorder" in the human world. We thus realize that their refusal to hold office is quite consistent with their stance as unbeclouded, uncommitted, and uninvolved observers of the world. Yet they remain willing commentators on public affairs.

And yet, the extreme nature of their ataraxy or "peace of mind" leads one to reflect once more about the relationships between ataraxy and the "scientific attitude." The scientific perspective requires one to look at nature without "value judgment," to regard all phenomena of nature as instances of larger laws and patterns, and to eliminate consideration of teleology. Yet the modern scientist himself is almost an embodiment of *yu-wei*. At the most ideal level he is consumed with the project of discovering scientific truths; he relies completely on his analytic and calculating intellect and on the more "applied" level he aims to "control" nature. Nor is he at all above the aim of achieving fame. However nonteleological his view of nature, he himself remains the intensely goal-oriented Cartesian subject. Shen Tao, on the other hand, is described as follows:

> He eliminated knowledge, discarded the self and submitted to that which could not be helped ... he accepted no responsibility and laughed at the world for advancing men of worth. Following his whims and unrestrained he did not engage in [purposive] activity and repudiated the great sages of the world ... Avoiding "rights" and "wrongs" he avoided trouble. He did not take knowledge or deliberate thought as his teacher and knew nothing of past and future. He simply rested where he was. Pushed, he would move, dragged he would proceed further ... he revolved like a whirlwind, spun like a feather.[152]

He aspires to the inert passivity of a clod of earth. He aspires not to "study" things which abide in the *tao*, but to be one of them.

Yet the striking fact remains that Shen Tao also came to be regarded as one of the fathers of Legalism, and an examination of the more reliable fragments of his writings, recently assembled after a painstaking scholarly analysis by P. M. Thompson, reveals that he very much deserves this reputation.[153] As a member of the Chi-hsia Academy, one of the things he was "pushed and dragged" to do was, after all, to deliver judgments on sociopolitical affairs. He by no means shares Lao-tzu's primitivism and seems to regard the sociopolitical world of his time as just as "natural" a part of the world of the *tao* as the forces and patterns of nature. There is no thought here of rejecting high civilization. What is more, unlike Chuang-tzu, who seems to regard the political order as "natural" only insofar as it is a natural expression of man's perverted individualized mind (*ch'eng hsin*) which can be by-passed only by the "true man," he seems to accept the institutions and patterns of civilization as themselves embodied expressions of the *tao*. If he is a "scientist" he is rather like a modern social scientist who regards the structures and processes of society—considered apart from the deliberate activities of individual humans—as having a dynamic *wu-wei* life of their own as "patterns of behavior." One can translate Shen Tao's language of submitting to things and "following what cannot be helped" as referring basically to this kind of submission to the dynamic forces of the larger sociopolitical order, and it is thus only men like Shen Tao himself without *parti pris,* without value judgments, without fixed perspectives and opinions deriving from his own individual intellect, and without ambitions to participate actively in the course of affairs who can be like the quiet mirror which reflects the world as it is. He does not derive peace of mind from his scientific investigation. He rather derives his unbeclouded view of the sociopolitical order from his peace of mind and completely uncommitted existence.

From his "unbeclouded" perspective, Shen Tao seems to perceive not only the shifting circumstances of the sociopolitical world but also certain "constant" principles of sociopolitical order embedded in the *tao* itself. One of the statements attributed to him is that "today our states have no constant *tao,* our officials have no constant method [*fa*] and, therefore, the state daily falls into error."[154] It is a statement which, to be sure, raises questions about consistency of thought (how can "error" arise in the *tao?*), but it does point to Shen Tao's belief that there are certain constancies of the human sociopolitical order which, despite the flux of circumstances, correspond to the constancies of the patterns of nature. The notion of the abiding principle of sociopolitical order is, of course, not new and as I have stressed is rooted in an orientation which can be found in Confucius and even earlier. Yet, as we have seen, it is Confucius' ardent conviction that the norms of this order can be actualized and maintained only by the moral acts of human moral agents. While there is the x factor of "fatality," the noble man must ardently believe that his own moral intent and will to goodness can lead to the actualizations of these norms. Mo-tzu carries this emphasis on human agents further. The moral order itself is an artifact created by the good will of Heaven, the spirits, and man and can only be maintained by the creative will of men of worth.

In Shen Tao, on the other hand, the "constant way" and "constant *fa*" are embedded in the very fabric of the sociopolitical order itself.[155] To use the phrase of Marx, they are (or ought to be) independent of the wills of men. Thus one of his most striking principles is what might be called the principle of authority (*shih*)—that mysterious power which makes it possible for one feeble man to command the obedience of vast numbers simply by dint of his occupation of a specific societal locus.[156] "The soaring serpent hovers over the mist; the flying dragon rides the clouds; if the clouds and mist disperse, they become the same as earthworms. They have lost that on which they ride."[157] "When Yao was a commoner, he could not control his immediate neighbors; when Chieh was a Son of Heaven, he could disorder the whole world."[158] "A man of worth cannot persuade the multitude but a position of authority [*shih-wei*] can subdue a man of worth."[159] Shen Tao is quite aware of the fallibility and limits of those who hold authority. Yet the phenomenon of authority itself is a basic and indispensable constituent of the *tao,* much more important than the quality of those individuals who hold it, since it is one of the vital impersonal conditions of the possibility of civilized human society. Furthermore, authority should ultimately rest not on sages—who are, as it were, rare accidents of nature—but on all impersonal structures and mechanisms which embody the *wu-wei* of the *tao.* Shen Tao, in fact, does not have any faith in the individual minds of sages. "If a ruler abandons the *fa* and relies on his person in ruling, then rewards and punishments will proceed from the heart of the ruler."[160]

The word *fa* certainly includes penal law, but if one can accept Thompson's judgment of the authenticity of the fragments he includes in his book, it would appear that *fa* also covers an aspect of Legalism which has otherwise been attributed to that other pillar of Legalism, Shen Pu-hai (see Chapter 8 below). Here we find outlined the principle of the clear division of labor not only in the bureaucratic structure of government but in society as a whole, with the accompanying "Weberian" notion of a clear definition of the specific "functions" and tasks of various "offices" as well as of the "functional specificity" of those who assume these tasks. "In ancient times artisans did not combine different jobs and officers did not combine offices. Because the artisans did not combine different tasks, their tasks were simplified and easy to master; because the officers did not combine offices, their tasks were few and easily maintained."[161] What is envisioned is a vast social mechanism in which each part performs its clearly defined function and the whole order operates by *wu-wei*. Again, to be sure, the general image of a sociopolitical order as a network of social roles and ranks each with their prescribed modes of behavior is already inherent in the idea of *li*— but again, we note that in Confucius *li* are not objective rules of behavior which function automatically. The inner moral quality of the human agents who enact them is crucial to their fulfillment, and the noble men who perform these specialized tasks must embody a total human quality of *jen* which is itself by no means specialized.

Shen Tao's vehement rejection of the role of individual moral and intellectual judgment as a factor in the social order is vividly illustrated in his assertion that "a filial son is not born in the house of a kind parent and loyal ministers do not arise under a sage ruler."[162] Here we find a radical and total negation of the direct power of moral influence. A question nevertheless arises which does not arise in the case of the self-running machine. How are the human parts to be impelled to perform their specialized tasks? In Shen Tao's answer, we again find a theme which has generally been attributed to the other great Legalists Shang Yang and Han Fei-tzu. What is posited is a conception of man—or of most men—as creatures who simply act on the basis of self-interest—who "act for themselves" (*tzu-wei*). The way of Heaven follows the "essential nature" of men, which is simply to avoid pain and seek benefit. Here Mo-tzu's model of man in a "state of nature" actually becomes the foundation of the smoothly functioning social order. The ruler is able to use men by taking account of this fact. He relies on an objective system of rewards and punishments. It would, of course, appear that this "action for oneself" involves a view of man as a purposive actor and thus seems inconsistent with any notion of *wu-wei*. Yet the purposive action here is reduced to a simple mechanical model which almost makes of the individual himself a kind of predictable instrument of the *tao*. He is like the economic man of classical economics whose simple response to profit and loss automatically makes him the instrument of the mechanism of the free market. "If man does not obtain that for which he acts, those above cannot use him."[163] This "self-action" of the average individual is itself part of the large encompassing system which acts by *wu-wei*.

Another interesting feature of the fragments is that Shen Tao does not completely reject the role of *li*. He does not seem to believe that the *fa* of punishments and rewards—the *fa* of bureaucratic organization—cover all aspects of social reality and even finds a restricted place for *li*. *Li*, as in Mo-tzu, seem to deal with those rules of propriety which confirm the distinctions between ranks in society and the proper familial relations. What is most fascinating, however, is his effort to think of the *li* themselves as impersonal rules, not at all dependent on the sentiments or personal qualities of persons. "The state has the *li* of high and low rank but not a *li* of men of worth and those without talent. There is a *li* of age and youth, but not of courage and cowardice. There is a *li* of near and distant relatives, but no *li* of love and hate."[164]

From all this, it is quite apparent why Shen Tao "laughs at men of worth" and "rejects sages." His social order will not depend on fallible personal moral judgments or sentiments but on the *fa* of a civilized order, which is itself an expression of the *tao*. Such a world is, of course, not made up of unchanging constancies. There are also shifts and fluctuations and only those like Shen Tao, completely free of preconceptions and *partis pris,* can, like the placid mirror, correctly and intuitively comprehend the essential "drift of things."

Without claiming that Shen Tao is the "real" father of Legalism in all its aspects, it is indeed most remarkable to discern how many of the themes of Legalism are touched upon by him in these fragments. Here indeed we find a vision which does seem to fuse Taoist and Legalist themes.

Shen Tao faces a problem familiar to modern Western social scientists. His mind is not simply a passive mirror which reflects the ubiquitous *tao*. He also cannot refrain from providing prescriptive advice. Indeed his position at the Academy obliges him to furnish advice. If the impersonal mechanisms which govern human affairs have always existed, how can one speak of man's mind meddling with the course of the *tao?* Shen Tao, in fact, falls into the old Chinese habit of drawing a contrast between "ancient times" when civilization performed according to the *tao* and later ages when again the false *yu-wei* consciousness of men was somehow able to intervene and bring about chaos. Here his position is not too different from those classical economists who assert that the free market is the natural expression of man's nature and then deplore centuries of human folly for interfering with this natural propensity, or from those who have a deterministic scheme of social history and proceed to blame human error for history's failure to pursue its majestic course. Shen Tao, one might say, also has his ideal society. Yet, given his entire outlook of radical passivity, one can imagine that he is also quite prepared to resign himself to the follies of mankind as themselves an unaccountable expression of the *tao*. One cannot envision him as an activist promoter of his own ideals even though he believes that his teachings can be instrumental to the purposes of rulers.

While Shen Tao may already point to some of the main features of Huang-lao Taoism, I would suggest that the outlook as it finally emerges in the third and second centuries is much more all-encompassing in scope. The Yellow Emperor himself must be brought into the picture. While Shen Tao "rejected sages," the Yellow Emperor is the Taoist sage-king par excellence who embodies in his own person both the mystic gnosis of the Taoist sage and is simultaneously, by that very token, the source and patron of all those arts and techniques which make human civilization possible. In this, he strongly resembles certain sage-kings who appear in what Graham calls the "syncretistic"—and which I would be inclined to call the Huang-lao chapters—of the Chuang-tzu text (particularly chapters 13 and 33). As a Taoist sage-king he is able to abide in the realm of nonbeing and yet somehow to make manifest in the world those arts and methods which govern or ought to govern civilization. He is, as it were, the mediator between the *tao* and human civilization who "acts without acting." In the "Way of Heaven" chapter (13) of the Chuang-tzu, where the ancient sage-kings are treated as Taoist emperors, we read that "though their knowledge encompassed heaven and earth, they did not deliberate—they did not act . . . The emperor and kings did not act and the world was benefitted."[165] They somehow made manifest the arts of civilization but were not themselves technologists. These arts and technologies are based on the *wu-wei* patterns, which emanate from the objective *tao* of nature.

The phenomenon of the instrumental use of mystical gnosis is not peculiar to China. Lovejoy remarks with reference to both India and medieval Europe that "the otherworldly philosopher is made the ruler or secret ruler of the world. The mystic or the saint becomes the most powerful and sometimes the shrewdest of politicians. There is perhaps nothing so favorable to success in the world's business as a high degree of emotional detachment from it."[166] Edgerton observes in connection with the rise of Brahmanical mysticism in India that at least one of its aspects was the belief "that if we can only know the one principle of the whole universe—the one which is to be identified with 'all'—with everything that is—we shall be able to control all."[167]

The mystical dimension of the Yellow Emperor is vividly illustrated in the silk scroll manuscripts recently excavated from the Ma Wang-tui tomb in Hunan province. The manuscript has at least tentatively been identified by T'ang Lan as the text of an ancient lost work called the "Four Canons of the Yellow Emperor."[168] Here we find it proclaimed that "only the sage can discern the formless and hear the soundless and know the reality of emptiness . . . the sage-king uses it and the world is subdued."[169] In the "Way of Heaven" chapter of the Chuang-tzu, we have a very similar description of the sage-king: "Emptiness, stillness, purity, silence, *wu-wei* are the substance of the Way and its power, therefore the emperor, the king, the sage rest therein. In emptiness they attain fullness, in fullness they grasp the patterns of things [*lun*]. Empty they are still; still, they may rest in *wu-wei*, being *wu-wei*, then those charged with affairs fulfill their responsibilities."[170] Here we have something that might be called a mystical "cosmomorphism" in which a finite human being comes to embody the essence of nonbeing and is able to "use" his gnosis to establish the *tao-shu*, "the methods of the *tao*," which control the human world.

One of the "methods" of the sage-king mentioned in the "Way of Heaven" involves his ability to maintain his own quietude and inaction precisely by relying on the purposive activity (*yu-wei*) of his subordinates, as suggested above by Shen Tao. His great administrative art lies in delegating responsibility on the basis of a system in which the subordinate officials are assigned clear goal-oriented tasks, given proper incentives and disincentives, and continually judged on the basis of their performance.[171] The sage-king simply infuses the system with his spiritual power. His "methods," however, are not necessarily confined to the science of bureaucratic government or penal law. From his Olympian heights, he is clearly aware that civilization, which is many-sided and complex, requires other "methods" as well. States require a military base and the sage-king knows by gnostic intuition the laws and arts of "military organization," but the "details" of dealing with "the three armies and the five weapons" are again delegated to those below. Again he knows through his synoptic intuition the methods of rewards and punishments, profits and loss, and the five punishments which create, as it were, the incentive pattern of society. He also knows, however, that *li* and music are also needed to control and regulate the emotional life of the people.[172] The details again are left to the ritual specialists who abide in the realm of *yu-wei*. From their lofty view of the total landscape, the sage-emperors of the past were able to make manifest the *wu-wei* processes which govern every aspect of human civilization and were thus able to make manifest the system, infusing it with their own spiritual authority. They were able to employ the *yu-wei* consciousness of ordinary men to implement a system based on *wu-wei*.

Here we are indeed far from Chuang-tzu's efforts to smash our ordinary commonsensical understanding of the world. On the contrary, what emerges out of "nonbeing" is a clear picture of the "natural" bases of human civilization. Lao-tzu's world, of course, is also described in commonsensical terms drawn from ordinary experience but the world of higher civilization is treated as a kind of "unnatural" excrescence. When the "four canons" proclaim that the *tao* "gives birth to *fa*," the word *fa* seems to refer to nothing less than all the "natural processes" which govern both the natural world and the world of human civilization.[173] The latter had been "naturalized."

The sage-king's inner knowledge of the world derives not from "empirical investigations" but from his intuitive grasp of the whole. Those "who rush forward to speak" of "forms and names" and of "rewards and punishments" in all their empirical detail do have a function in society. "They know the instruments of order but they do not know the *tao* of order. They can be used but they are unable to use the world."[174] Imbedded in all this we even find an approach to the various "fixed" perspectives of the "hundred schools" which is strikingly different from that of Chuang-tzu. To Chuang-tzu, the conflicts among the contending schools of thought, each bent on imposing its frozen view of the world on a reality which cannot be captured in formulas, are part of the human tragedy. Here, in what I take to be the comprehensive Huang-lao approach, all of these schools simply arise out of an attempt to universalize perspectives which may have their own limited validity when applied as "methods" to specific aspects of reality. The Confucianists have discovered the method for dealing with those areas of life to which "*li* and music" apply and the Legalists, according to their varieties, have some "external" knowledge of methods of government administration and penal law. The adherents of the various schools are rightly understood, not universal thinkers but specialists in various methods or "disciplines" of the *tao* who simply try to universalize their one-sided methods.

This point of view is, I suggest, fully developed in two texts, both of which may be quite late—chapter 33 of the Chuang-tzu (the "World," *t'ien-hsia*) and the postface of the *Historical Records,* where Ssu-ma Ch'ien records the views of his father Ssu-ma T'an on the "six schools."

The first text provides a remarkable survey of the intellectual scene at the end of the Warring States period. It is interesting that the author calls all the tendencies he treats (they include Confucianism, Mohism, the doctrines of Sung Hsing, T'ien P'ien, Shen Tao, Lao-tzu, Chuang-tzu, Hui-shih, Kung-sun Lung, and others) "methods of the *tao*" (*tao-shu*). He also seems to assume that anciently, all these methods of the *tao* had contributed their own limited truths to the larger whole. Now, however, their adherents seem to believe that "nothing can be added" to their own particular points of view. The ancient harmony, however, had derived wholly from the mystical gnosis of the ancient sage-kings who had found the source of their wisdom in the "One."[175]

It is quite clear that the author has deep empathy for the mystical core of Lao-tzu and Chuang-tzu. He appreciates Lao-tzu's doctrines of the "soft" and the "feminine" but nowhere alludes to his primitivism. He even appreciates Chuang-tzu's poetic mystic flights even though he seems to admit that he does not truly comprehend him and finds him completely "impractical."[176] In the author's world, however (somewhere between the late Warring States period and early Han?), the "Way and its power are no longer one." The hundred schools "have fallen apart." The worthies and sages are confused. The world seizes upon one of the aspects of the *tao*, examines it and clings to it. "It is like the eyes, ears, the nose, and the mouth. They each have that which they perceive but they cannot inter-connect. The 'hundred schools' all have their 'skills' and strong points and they may all be used at the appropriate time, but none is wholly sufficient; none is universal." "Is it not sad—the 'hundred schools' move ever farther apart they can no longer be harmonized."[177] I shall not here attempt to follow the author's analysis of the strengths and weaknesses of the various "schools" he considers, yet the general framework may represent, I suggest, an example of Huang-lao Taoism.

The same is true, it seems to me, of Ssu-ma T'an's treatment of the six schools in the first half century of the Han dynasty (circa 206–140) when, we are told, the Huang-lao outlook attained the height of its popularity among the officials and literati of the new dynasty.

This was the period when the Chinese world had just emerged from the world-shaking experiences of the "Ch'in revolution" and the devastating civil war which followed, and the reestablishment of order under the new Han dynasty. The plebeian founder of the dynasty, Han Kao-tsu, was apparently quite innocent of doctrinal commitments although he obviously desired—to the extent possible—to preserve as much as possible of the centralized bureaucratic system introduced by the First Emperor of the Ch'in (Ch'in Shih Huang-ti). Unlike the latter, however, he seems to have been quite uninterested in the imposition of a unified state doctrine and among some of the leading literati themselves one finds an enormous revulsion against the fanatical zeal of the Ch'in founder. While the *ju* of the former Ch'i states of Ch'i and Lu were quite anxious to impose their own versions of the ancient traditions of Confucianism, many among the new ruling stratum seemed to be quite content with the undefined status quo. It is necessary here to remind ourselves that in many of the states of the late Warring States period before the Ch'in revolution, there had actually existed no official commitment of the rulers of many of the states to any specific school or doctrine. It would appear that, within this environment, the Huang-lao pluralistic attitude to the relative merits of various schools may have, for various reasons, appealed to many.

The linking of the Yellow Emperor to the figure of Lao-tzu during this period may have its own significance. The Lao-tzu book, unlike the Chuang-tzu, was, of course, concerned with the role of sage-rulers. The Lao-tzu was a putative advisor of rulers and if one overlooked his primitivism, some passages in his book, as I have indicated, could be interpreted in a "Huang-lao" spirit. Beyond this, while his radical primitivism is not accepted, it may well be that his appeal nevertheless lay in the general spirit of noninterventionism and laissez faire which permeates the book. Thus, Ssu-ma T'an was quite convinced that Legalist penal law and Legalist "administrative science" are necessary aspects of government. He nevertheless says of the Legalists that "they were harsh and little inclined to compassion—and yet their methods of defining correctly the status of those above and those below cannot be changed."[178] Ssu-ma Ch'ien strongly implies that the Huang-lao people were committed both to penal law in its proper place, and simultaneously to a mitigation of its draconic harshness.

Yü Ying-shih, in his essay on anti-intellectualism in China, has, however, stressed both the despotic and anti-intellectual nature of the Huang-lao outlook.[179] It is quite true that when the good order prevails, all spiritual authority would proceed from the mystic sage ruler who "works the handles that control the world."[180] The ritual experts, the bureaucrats and law officials, the experts on omens and astrology—all would deal with the "details" of their various competencies, but would no longer confront the emperor as autonomous "over-all thinkers" with their own private judgments.

The other side of the coin, however, is that the ideal Huang-lao emperor does delegate considerable responsibility to others and presumably does not intervene in the conduct of daily affairs nor does he necessarily favor one "school." The early Han emperors were, of course, hardly ideal Taoist sage-emperors and the advocates of Huang-lao Taoism were not so much the emperors (although the Emperor Wen-ti was presumably greatly influenced by it) as officials and literati such as Chi An, perhaps Ssu-ma T'an, and Cheng Tang-shih. Ssu-ma T'an, in fact, scolds the Confucianists for overstressing the active role of the ruler: "they believe the ruler must be the model for the world. The ruler leads and the ministers comply. The ruler is in the forefront and the ministers follow. Thus the ruler wears himself out and the ministers are at ease."[181] Ssu-ma T'an's reading of Huang-lao Taoism emphasizes the noninterventionist stance of the ruler. His central point in describing the "six schools" as he perceives them (Confucianism, Mohism, Legalism, the School of Names, the Yin-Yang School, and Taoism) seems to be a concern that none of them, aside from Taoism which encompasses them all, should be allowed to achieve dominant position as a "method" even while accepting the "legitimate" insights of all. Thus, while one may indeed say that an *ideal* Huang-lao system would in a sense reduce and perhaps eliminate the moral and intellectual autonomy of the intellectuals, in the circumstances of early Han China, it nevertheless represented an opening to a kind of intellectual and even social pluralism. One wonders if it is not this pluralism which leads Ssu-ma T'an's famous son Ssu-ma Ch'ien to defend the legitimacy of such social groups as the "Wandering Knights" (*yu-hsia*) and even successful business entrepreneurs as legitimate representations of the *tao* against the monopolizing claims of the Confucian *ju* so much favored by the Emperor Han Wu-ti.[182] Political Huang-lao Taoism was, of course, to be a passing although intriguing manifestation of what might be called Taoism as an instrumental sociopolitical philosophy.

The term "Huang-lao" itself was in the Latter Han dynasty to undergo a further semantic shift. While there is no intention here of dealing with that vast area of Chinese religious history which has come to be subsumed under the heading of "Taoist religion," the very phrase "Huang-lao" comes to be associated in the latter Han dynasty (25–220 A.D.) with the whole cult of "personal" immortality, which in itself may have become related to the earlier more modest striving for longevity.

The cult may itself have had its origins in circles quite far removed from those of Lao-tzu and Chuang-tzu. It would indeed appear that both Lao-tzu and the historic Chuang-tzu accept death and the "return to nonbeing" with the utmost equanimity. To the extent that both affirm life in this world, longevity is accepted as a desirable worldly good. One linkage between the immortality cult and Lao-tzu and Chuang-tzu, however, seems to be based on the notion that those who succeed in "embodying the *tao*" (*t'i tao*) within themselves are able to use this knowledge either to prolong their individual existences or to achieve immortality as individuals in some kind of transfigured form. Here again, as in the political Huang-lao doctrine, the mystic gnosis comes to be instrumental to preeminently creaturely concerns. The mystical yearning for ultimate dissolution into the *tao* did not, of course, appeal to all and one could argue that the world-affirming aspects of the Lao-tzu and Chuang-tzu texts may themselves encourage the craving for some sort of individual survival. Here also, as in the case of Huang-lao political philosophy, one could indeed find passages, particularly in the Chuang-tzu, which could be interpreted as favorable to this new turn. Thus, in the sixth chapter of the Chuang-tzu we read in a passage full of mythic references that the "Yellow Emperor got it [the power of the *tao*] and ascended to the cloudy heavens."[183] This myth would make the Yellow Emperor not only the originator of all the arts of civilization, but the model of the immortal who achieves immortality by "embodying the *tao*."

Similarly, we find the phenomenon of the apotheosization of Lao-tzu and the conflation of Huang-ti and Lao-tzu who, under such names as Huang-lao Chün and T'ai Shang Lao-chün, become "embodiments of the *tao*."[184] As living deities they intervene in human affairs and come to play a central role in the pantheon of the Taoist "religion," as well as in "ideologies of rebellion." The apotheosization of the great man is, of course, entirely compatible with the most ancient religious orientations, and the process of his apotheosization can be compared to the Bodhisattva ideal which emerges out of Buddhism. The mystical essence of the *tao* and of the Buddhahood become incarnate or "entified" and endowed with a salvation-bearing mission. It is not our purpose here to deliver judgments on these "instrumental" interpretations of the early Taoist texts. They seem to represent a profound human tension between the enormous attraction to the mysterious "power" of those who have achieved the mystic gnosis which lifts them above and beyond the world and all its goals and projects and the contrary urge to draw on this power in the service of entirely creaturely human aspirations and concerns.

# CHAPTER 7

# THE DEFENSE OF THE
# CONFUCIAN FAITH
## Mencius and Hsün-tzu

O UR EXPLORATIONS of Chinese thought after the death of Confucius have led us quite far from the views of the *Analects*. Its premises are attacked from every direction and the Confucian "camp" itself is in disarray. Han Fei-tzu informs us that in the third century there were some "eight schools" of Confucianism, and clearly the differences among these schools were far from trivial.[1] In the third century Hsün-tzu will attack false interpretations of the Master's vision with the same vehemence with which he attacks "external" heresies.

Still, Han Fei-tzu, while taunting the Confucianists for their disarray, makes it quite clear that Confucianism and Mohism remain the two dominant teachings of his time.[2] While the word *ju* translated here as "Confucianist" may again be taken to refer to the whole stratum of cultural experts, some of whom may have been quite "unideological," the reference to the eight schools suggests that we are indeed dealing here with explicitly Confucian modes of thought. Although Confucianism and Mohism are here treated as two established traditions of thought, the other thinkers of the Chinese world later assigned by the Han doxographers to various schools are simply attacked as individuals, as in the case of the "World" (chapter 33) chapter of the Chuang-tzu and as in Hsün-tzu's attacks on the deviations of his time. Thus, it is perhaps plausible to assume that Confucianists of various types still constituted the largest stream within the stratum of the *shih*, particularly in the states of Lu and Ch'i, which had been the Master's base and which were to constitute Mencius' (Meng-tzu) primary area of operation. Indeed when one reads the book of Mencius one has the impression of a man securely embedded in the Confucian tradition who, while he is thoroughly alert to the challenges from without and thoroughly immersed in the intellectual discourse of his time, remains superbly unshaken in his faith.

This vibrant faith is all the more remarkable when we consider the fact which also later struck Ssu-ma Ch'ien that Mencius was a contemporary of Shang Yang, the Legalist minister of the state of Ch'in who had already proclaimed the "enrichment of the state and the strengthening of the military" as the primary goals of the state as well as of the "military theorists" Sun-tzu and T'ien Chi who were bent on establishing an autonomous military science.[3] If we can accept the dates proposed by Ch'ien Mu as the *terminus a quo* and the *terminus ad quem* of Mencius' life (390–305), we find that he is probably a contemporary of Chuang-tzu, Hui-tzu, Shen Pu-hai, and some of the most illustrious figures of the Chi-hsia Academy, two of whom are, in fact, mentioned in the book of Mencius. The strength of his faith seems particularly noteworthy when we contrast it to the attitude of the Confucianists of the previous century who figure in the pages of the book of Mo-tzu. Living in the generation following the Master's death, the latter seem particularly disheartened by the failure of the Master's vision in the world of their time. Not only do they seem to have lost faith in Heaven's providential role in history, but they no longer seem to believe in the noble man's ability to influence the world through the power of his moral suasion. The noble man's function seems to have shrunken in their view to the modest role of the custodian of "holy rites," music, and learning. At least in Mo-tzu's jaundiced account, their ritualistic formalism had none of the redeeming features which elicit the enthusiasm of Fingarette.

Yet we do know that other interpretations of the Master's vision must have been present even in the world of Mo-tzu and that either Mo-tzu's contacts were limited or that he chose to stress this particular version of the Master's vision, as is often the case in intellectual controversy. One of the alternate approaches may indeed have been that of Confucius' grandson Tzu-ssu, who may well have been Mozu's contemporary.[4] According to tradition, Mencius was actually a disciple of Tzu-ssu's disciple. While we have little direct evidence of his thought, the fact that tradition attributes to him the authorship of the "Doctrine of the Mean" (see below) would indeed place his thought in a line close to that of Mencius.

One of Tzu-ssu's dominant characteristics as depicted in the literature was a fierce sense of his own autonomy and dignity as a teacher and advisor of rulers. It was a trait very much emulated by Mencius, and in both men it derives from their profound faith in the moral mission of noble men. The *li* on which Tzu-ssu insists are the *li* of proper relations between a lord and his minister (teacher-advisor in this case). When a ruler sends a gift to a *shih* in his own name, the rule is that the recipient should bow twice in receiving the gift. When Duke Mu of Lu sends such gifts to Tzu-ssu, he constantly sends them in his own name and Tzu-ssu became indignant at the humiliation of constantly being forced to bow. "The prince treats me," he asserts, "the way he treats his horses and hounds."[5] A prince who truly respects the "virtuous man" would send regular gifts of food and grain without constantly demanding such acknowledgment. The basic point here is that in honoring the bearers of virtue the duke is honoring virtue, and the man of virtue in defending his virtue is essentially defending virtue itself as the ultimate source of all social harmony. When Duke Mu asks about whether he, as a ruler, can be the friend of noble men, Tzu-ssu replies, "From the point of view of position you are a ruler and I am a subject. How dare I be friends with you? From the point of view of virtue it is you who should serve me. How can you be friends with me?"[6] The principle which presumably lies behind this seemingly pedantic punctilio is that the noble man must protect his dignity because it is the virtue of the noble man which is the ultimate and only hope of the restoration of the *tao*.

Indeed, the reassertion of this theme is at the very heart of the whole book of Mencius. To assert and defend this theme in the world of the brutal power politics of the fourth century—the world of Shen Pu-hai, Shen Tao, Shang Yang, and Chuang-tzu—was a bold and one might even say a quixotic enterprise.

## Mencius

The hard facts of Mencius' biography are few. Born in the tiny principality of Tsou, which was a dependency of Lu, he is close to the heartland of Confucianism. In later years he would serve at the court of King Hsüan of Ch'i, who may have been the founder of the Chi-hsia Academy. The king was evidently prepared to listen with curiosity if not with great conviction to any of the intellectuals of his time, as is apparent from Mencius' lengthy dialogues with him. As in the case of the academicians at Chi-hsia, King Hsüan as the magnanimous patron of *shih* is prepared to provide him with rank and generous emoluments. Mencius himself, one gathers, was able to participate in the high life-style of the successful *shih* of his day. Yet it is apparent from the dialogues that the king is not even remotely prepared to take his message seriously. Neither is King Hui, the ruler of the relatively newly established state of Liang,[7] who is obsessed with his lifelong effort to preserve his territory against the encroachments of the surrounding great powers. (The only ruler who seems prepared to take his message seriously is Duke Wen of the tiny principality of T'eng.) Basically, as Ssu-ma Ch'ien succinctly remarks, "He never secured a sympathetic hearing no matter where he went."[8]

The present book of Mencius is undoubtedly a compilation of his disciples, but unlike the *Analects* it provides us not only with the isolated aphorisms and sayings of the Master but with a wealth of sustained discourse, including dialogues with rulers and with intellectual protagonists such as Kao-tzu and Sung Hsing. There are many passages which may be taken as a faithful commentary on and elucidation of ideas which are simply touched on in the *Analects*. Throughout one is aware that Mencius is not making manifest a new vision but defending a faith and that he is prepared to use every tool available to him to defend the faith. Thus, in the Mencius one finds actual concrete applications of some of the dialectic and logical categories employed by the Mohist logicians and other teachers in the school of names. Mencius uses these tools because he must—not because he believes that they provide the true method for arriving at truth. He would much prefer to propound the way rather than defend it by logic-chopping and dialectic. "Outsiders all say," says Kung Tu-tzu his disciple, "that you are fond of argument [or dialectic—*pien*]. I venture to ask why." "I am not fond of argument," announces Mencius, "I simply have no alternative."[9] In a world of disorder he must defend the all-embracing vision of the Master by employing the very methods which others have used to lead men's minds astray. If in a disordered world it is easy to use "logic" and dialectic to lead men astray, the fact is that the same tools have at least the merit, when skillfully employed, of providing correctives. If the state of the world were such that the vision of the Master would win ready assent, such methods would not be necessary.

Mencius' views on "heresy" and deviation from the truth are based on a clear philosophy of history. It is one of the inscrutable mysteries of Heaven that human history has always alternated in cycles of order and disorder. "The way of the sages declines."[10] Wrong views and heresy are not the original cause of disorder. They are the symptoms of a disorder already in being. The source of disorder is the evil deeds of evil rulers. "Tyrants arose one after another.

They pulled down houses in order to make ponds and the people had nowhere to rest. They turned fields into hunting parks depriving the people of their livelihood. Heresies and violence arose."[11] Intellectual confusion and violence were themselves symptoms and consequences. Distorted ideas simply reinforce and confirm preexistent moral distortions. If men are to be disentangled from their wrong ideas, however, they must be met with intellectual argument. Perverse propositions (*yin-tz'u*) must be corrected with true propositions. Like Mo-tzu, and unlike Chuang-tzu, Mencius clearly believes that arguments can be won.

Mencius ostensibly has a clear and simple picture of the main feature of the intellectual situation of his time. "The words of Yang Chu and Mo-tzu fill the world. Those who do not turn to Yang Chu turn to Mo-tzu."[12] This simple account is highly puzzling, for while it is clear that Mohism constituted a powerful movement, the notion that the doctrines of Yang Chu the egoist enjoyed equal support in the intellectual world of the times is, as Ch'ien Mu has pointed out, not supported by any evidence whatsoever.[13] What we find here in Mencius is, I would suggest, a phenomenon in the history of thought which can be found in all times and places. Mencius structures the intellectual situation of his times wholly in terms of certain particular perspectives arising out of his own preoccupations. The way in which a convinced evangelical Christian would structure the doctrinal configuration of the modern world would certainly be markedly different from that of various schools of Marxists or secular liberals. In terms of certain issues which he finds central, Mencius finds that Confucianism represents the true mean between the deviant extremes epitomized by Mo-tzu and Yang Chu. Mencius seems to be saying that Confucianism represents the sensible medium between total self-love and total indiscriminate "altruism." Yet, in fact, when he says that Mohism undermines parental authority and Yang Chu undermines the authority of rulers, he seems to be saying something much more complex. It is indeed natural to "love" one's family more than mankind as a whole, but actually Mencius believes that the very love of mankind in general is only possible as a result of the irradiation—in diminishing strength, to be sure—of that love which naturally has its source in the bosom of the family. On the other side, Yang Chu's concentrated self-love (which is perhaps not incompatible with his love of his own family) undermines the role of the political order. "He denies the ruler" and thus will create universal chaos leading to a state of misery for most individuals. Essentially then, Mo-tzu and Yang Chu between them undermine the foundations of the familial and political order which are so necessary for the well-being of both self and society. In a society where the moral authority of both the family and the political order are undermined by false doctrine, the tendencies to immorality are given free rein.

A careful examination of the entire text reveals that the simple Yang Chu/Mo-tzu antithesis does not do full justice to Mencius' actual relationship to all the intellectual tendencies of his time. The text indicates that even in the case of Mohism, Mencius' most fundamental objection does not revolve about the question of "universal love" but rather about the question of the utilitarian basis of Mohist morality. As we have already seen, Mo-tzu's "universal love" is clearly instrumental to the further end of serving the general *interest* of mankind and it is this emphasis on "interest" which becomes a crucial point of attack for Mencius.

Indeed in providing an account of Mencius' battles against the errors of his time, we might well begin with his attack on the principle of utility or interest (*li*) since it touches the very heart of his moral philosophy. I should note at the very outset that Mencius is well aware that Mohism is primarily concerned not with self-interest of individuals but with the universal, general interest of mankind. Thus, in the dialogue with Sung Hsing (already discussed in the previous chapter), who was a Mohist in his social ethic, Mencius seems to approve of Sung Hsing's aim of preventing a murderous war between the states of Ch'u and Ch'in. "Your purpose," he states, "is lofty indeed."[14] He then, however, vehemently objects to the arguments which Sung Hsing proposes to use to persuade the kings of Ch'u and Ch'in to refrain from war. Sung Hsing would attempt to persuade both that war would not be "in their interest" (*li*). He would no doubt argue that the war would greatly impoverish and weaken their people and that this would in the end weaken their states and diminish their own wealth and prestige. When actions detrimental to the general interests of mankind are taken, the more particular interests are in the end bound to suffer. Mencius' reply seems to be that so long as human attention is focused wholly on presumed "utilitarian" results—on the outcomes which are supposed to eventuate from given courses of action—the nature of the satisfactions achieved (security, wealth, power, or honor) are such that persons will tend to desire these outcomes for themselves here and now. The argument that the particular interests of individuals or particular groups will be best served when the general interest "of the greatest number" is served is in fact not true for any given individual here and now. Hence, to the extent that the mind is fixed on goods such as security, wealth, ambition, or honor, the pursuit of the general interest will constantly disintegrate into the pursuit of particular interests. The message will simply pervade society that action should be predicated on considerations of interest, and particular individuals and groups will never be convinced that the satisfaction of their immediate concrete desires will be served by the satisfaction of the long-term general interest.

Mencius' argument becomes particularly effective when he uses it against King Hui of Liang (Wei[2]), whose first statement to him when he arrives at his court is, "You must surely have some way of serving the interest of my state."[15] Obviously the war-obsessed king is thinking not of the exalted goal of peace but of the frank pursuit of the state's security, wealth, and power. Mencius immediately points to the disintegrative effects of focusing on these results. If it is legitimate for Hui to sacrifice the state to this goal, why should the great ministers not say, "How can I serve the interests of my family?" and why should the *shih* and commoners not say, "How can I serve my own interests?"[16] There is no escape from the fact that if wealth and honor are goods, they are, first of all, goods for me or for those whom I consider to belong to my own "reference group." To Mo-tzu, selfishness is the commitment to a regard for my own interest or the interests of my immediate group, while justice is the commitment to the common interest of mankind as a whole. To Mencius, however, the dichotomy is between the commitment to *interests* or to "humanity and righteousness" as motives of action—to the sense of "what ought to be done," whoever or whatever may be the object of the action. The notion that in basing morality on the pursuit of interests men can be led to support the "universal" interest over particular interests is a chimera. Mo-tzu himself, let us recall, feels obliged to introduce the mediating principle of universal love to induce men to sacrifice individual interest for general interests, and Rawls points out that even Western utilitarians feel obliged to introduce an unaccountable principle of "sympathy and benevolence."[17] King Hui, no doubt, simply assumes that he should be able to rely on the loyalty of his ministers and soldiers even though they themselves may reap no benefits from his wars. Why should they not instead be interested in their own welfare? Thus, Mencius' fundamental answer to Mo-tzu's insistence that the family itself represents a particular self-interest would be that, *ideally speaking,* it is in the bosom of the family that the individual learns to act in terms of virtuous motives as ends in themselves rather than as means to ulterior ends.[18] It is only this capacity of mankind to act in terms of "what is right" without regard for consequences which makes the dream of a good society possible. As a Confucianist, Mencius of course by no means dismisses the goal of the general welfare of mankind. His argument essentially is that good social consequence can be achieved only if we assume a human capacity for acting in terms of *"jen* and righteousness" as ends in themselves. It is only men wholly motivated by the right who can in any long run produce a good society, even though there may occasionally be people like the famous Kuan Chung who were able to achieve certain results of *jen* even while their motives were highly mixed and even while they relied on the instrument of coercion. They were, as it were, able to "borrow" the consequence of *jen*.[19] Yet, as we shall see, such consequences of *jen* without the presence of the motives of *jen* are likely to be evanescent and superficial.

Mencius' central task is to prove in the face of a doubting world that the achievement of a good society depends wholly on the inherent moral intentionality of good men. In his case, however, this must be more than a simple reiteration of the message of the Master. While all those within the Confucian tradition might accept this proposition, two questions became matters of raging dispute: how humans—particularly those who must constitute the ethical vanguard of society—become good men, and how their ethical quality can transform the society. The Confucianists depicted in the pages of Mo-tzu, who may have been close to the views of Tzu-hsia, were clinging to the practice of "rites and music" as the only way of internalizing *jen*, despite the Master's teaching that rites and music without any inner disposition of soul were futile formalisms. They also seem to have had little faith that the inner disposition of soul would necessarily influence the world of their time. The Mohists, of course, were entirely reluctant to look "within" and, indeed, had posited a kind of "state of nature" in which individual human organisms were conceived initially as wholly self-regarding creatures. There is no "inner" source of moral behavior and men have to be taught the utilitarian necessity of universal love. Thus the question of *hsing*, which poses the question of where one is to seek the source of moral action, could not be avoided. Confucianists might generally accept a common code of morality—a common conception of what the nature of the noble man is—but one could no longer avoid the question of the ontological source of this morality.

Clearly, then, by the time of Mencius the question of *hsing* was already raging in Confucian circles. Kao-tzu believed that human nature was neither good nor bad. Others believed that there are those who are good by nature and those who are bad. Others believed that with the "rise of King Wen and Wu the people were given to goodness, while with the rise of King Ku and King Li they were given to cruelty ... Others believed that there are those who are good by nature and those who are bad."[20] Here we have views running a gamut from the notion that moral categories do not even apply to the individual organism and are wholly a creation of "society," to views which simply see different moral propensities as a result of different hereditary endowments. The latter view, incidentally, even while it may be compatible with a Confucian's traditional conception of the substance of morality, would seem to effectively negate any belief in "Confucianizing" society as a whole.

While the entire debate seems to revolve about the "goodness or badness" of the nature, the word *hsing* is only one category in what comes to be a much more complex multicategorical debate on the nature of the human reality, both in its social and individual aspects.

*Mencius' "Philosophic Anthropology"* It is evidently Mencius' burning conviction that human beings can be led to act from pure moral motives only if they realize that the sources of, and capacity for, such behavior lie latent within their own individual selves—that is, within an inborn "natural" tendency or *hsing* of the human organism. This point becomes clear in his famous debate with Kao-tzu.

Kao-tzu is a shadowy personality about whom little is known, although efforts have been made to link him with a person of the same name in the book of Mo-tzu. In Neo-Confucian literature, for reasons discussed below, he is often identified as a Taoist. Yet if we confine our attention to the contents of the debate itself there is no reason to think that the content of his "objective" value system is anything other than Confucian. Mencius and he seem to differ not at all on the question of what proper behavior is in the concrete circumstances discussed in debate. What is at stake is wholly the question of the source of morality.

The interpretation of this debate remains extraordinarily difficult, although much light has been cast on it by Lau and others.[21] The passage is fascinating as an example of an effort to apply concepts current in the logical-dialectic discussions of the time to questions of truly profound significance. I shall here attempt to convey my own understanding of the debate.

Kao-tzu maintains that human nature (*hsing*) is that "which is inborn [and common to all living things]" (*sheng chih*).[22] He then specifies that the only "inborn" common propensities of living things are the appetites for food and sex. Presumably all else is shaped by environment. Only these common properties of all living things are "internal" (*nei*) to humans at birth.[23] All else, one might say in our terminology, is internalized by culture "out there" (*wai*). He goes on, however, to say that while *"jen* is internal, righteousness is external."[24] The word *jen* here is somewhat puzzling if we attribute to it the full exalted meaning of the *Analects*. In the context, however, it seems to mean little more than the natural affections, which may be closely associated with sexual attraction but which may also extend to the kinship bonds which we may, after all, also find in other animals. "Righteousness," which is the capacity to act correctly in all the complex circumstances of civilized human life, cannot possibly derive from any inner instinct or innate, intuitive capacity. It is based wholly on learned rules of behavior, which the individual internalizes "from outside." We may thus have a "natural affection" for elders who are our kin because they are kin, but we have no inborn propensity to respect elders as a class even though Confucian morality prescribes such respect. "There is an elderly man and I treat him as an elder [with respect]. It is not that I have the propensity within myself to treat him as an elder just as my recognition of the fact that he is white is due to my power to perceive whiteness in him. It is because the whiteness [like the rule of treating elders as elders] comes from without that I recognize him as white."[25] The rule "treat elders with respect" derives from no inner impulse. It is acquired only from without (whether through coercion or education is not made clear). Kao-tzu does not deny the moral code but is proposing, I submit, something much like Clifford Geertz's assertion that "cultural patterns . . . are *extrinsic* [emphasis mine] sources of information. By extrinsic I mean only that—unlike genes for example—they lie outside the boundaries of the individual organism as such in that intersubjective world of common understanding in which all human individuals are born."[26] Like Geertz, Kao-tzu believes that "culture" is a separate autonomous realm that transforms the unformed individual organism which is man at birth into a human being. Since he probably believes in the universality of the Confucian traditional moral code, however, he does not share Geertz's cultural relativism. He can talk about the rules of the culture in universal terms.

As a Confucian, Mencius also believes in the "objective" prescriptions of *li*. He even seems to believe that they must be learned. Yet he has a burning faith that what is learned is really ours to begin with because the *li* are ultimately the external expressions of a capacity for "humanity and righteousness" as intrinsic to the human organism as is his whole physical organization. He obviously also believes that only if humans understand that what is right is inherent in their "natures" can they be brought to exercise their responsibility as moral agents. He must therefore refute Kao-tzu with every weapon possible. He asks Kao-tzu if his concept of "nature" as that which is inborn in all living things—the common property shared by all living things—is the same as the assertion that all white things are white. Upon receiving an affirmative answer he asks whether saying that all white things are white is the same as saying that because man shares certain properties with animals therefore man is "nothing but" an animal. When Kao-tzu answers affirmatively he presses on with the question, "Is the whiteness of a white feather the same as the whiteness of white snow and the whiteness of white jade?"[27] The answer is, in his view, obvious. Here we have a common property shared by objects which we would all agree are as different from each other as one can imagine. All they share is a single predicate. Mencius proceeds to ask, "Is then the nature of a hound the same as the nature of an ox, and the nature of an ox the same as the nature of a man?" And his point is clear. They may all belong to the class of animals in terms of certain common properties but their differentiating properties may be the crucial properties.

Here I would urge against Graham an analysis which can very well be discussed in terms of something like our concept of the logic of classes. Should the fact that several classes share certain common properties serve as a sufficient basis for a class definition? Kao-tzu may, of course, urge that sex and food appetites are essential inborn attributes because they are shared. But why must one assume that only shared attributes are inborn? Why may the differentiating attributes not also be inborn? The enormous difference between an ox and a hound which lead us to assign them to different species are differentiating attributes. Can we say that the inborn differences ($i$) here are less important than the inborn identities ($t'ung$)? Since differences are important in defining "the nature" of animals and since we recognize these differences as inborn, what reason is there for asserting that that which differentiates humans from other animals (particularly given the spectacular nature of these differences) is not inborn? Indeed what reason is there for saying that those attributes which man shares with other animals are more important or essential than those which differentiate him?

This whole discussion forcefully calls to mind all those passages in the Mohist logic dealing with the species classification of horses and oxen, the Hui Shih reference to "great differences" ($ta\ i$) and "little differences" ($hsiao\ i$), great identities and small identities, and even Kung-sun Lung-tzu's concern with the proposition that a "white horse is not a horse." One suddenly has the sense that if we had available to us the whole literature of which those propositions and "sophisms" are fragments, we would soon discover their real relevance to the actual questions of the age.

Kao-tzu and his disciples, however, continue to challenge the view that the prescriptions of right behavior could possibly have their source in any innate moral propensity. "If a man from the village is a year older than your elder brother, whom do you respect?" asks a disciple of Kao-tzu. "My elder brother," replies Mencius' disciple Kung Tu-tzu. "In filling the cups of wine [at ceremonial village occasions] which do you give precedence to?' 'To the man from the village.' 'The one you truly respect is the former—the one you treat as an elder is the latter. This shows that it [correct action] is external not internal.' "[28] The respect for one's elder brother is, one might say, an extension of natural familial affection (*jen*). It is thus "internal." The rule that on certain village occasions the fact of age itself takes precedence over kinship ties is based on no internal moral impulse. It is simply obedience to a "learned" external rule.

Mencius' reply is in essence that feelings of respect are not only directed to persons in their fixed roles and statuses. There are solemn occasions and special circumstances in which one's sense of respect is elicited by the nature of the occasion itself. At a village ceremony one's attention is focused on the village elders as a group and on this occasion, one's sense of respect is concentrated on the fact of age as such. Mencius' morality—in fact his emphasis on "righteousness" as such—can be very "situation-oriented" and by no means simply fixed on the unchanging rules of *li*. In all moral action one is not simply learning the preestablished "rules of the game." The rules of the game themselves arise out of deep innate propensities involving not only a feeling for persons but also for the meanings of specific situations. All the rules have their ultimate root in some natural propensity.

The debate with Kao-tzu, however, by no means begins to exhaust the many dimensions of Mencius' "philosophic anthropology." All it does is establish the "logical" foundations for his belief in the innateness of the latent tendency toward the good within the individual human organism.

For a description of this innate good we must look to other passages. When we do, we soon discover that the category of the heart/mind (*hsin*) is certainly as important as the category of the "nature" (*hsing*) itself. *Hsing*, it turns out, is only one term in the vocabulary required to establish Mencius' complex image of the human being. The *hsin* is, in fact, the ultimate "locus" of that part of man's nature which differentiates him from other animals. The *hsing* is, rightly understood, the innate tendency of the heart to grow toward the full actualization of its moral capacities. Indeed, the center of Mencius' problematique in dealing with man is really *not* the nature (*hsing*) but the heart/mind (*hsin*).

In dealing with the inborn moral capacity, Mencius describes it in terms of four parts or aspects. The capacity itself may be thought of as a kind of Aristotelian entelechy since the final goal of full moral realization is already present as a *potentiality* from the beginning. In the actual growing individual, however, this four fold potentiality first manifests itself as the so-called four beginnings (*ssu-tuan*)—the four spontaneous dispositions of feeling which are present in the child from the beginning and which remain latently present even in the corrupted adult. If properly "nourished" and if unblocked by impediments, such feelings will grow plantlike into the full maturity of the four cardinal moral sentiments which together constitute the fully actualized human nature (*hsing*).[29] These sentiments, when not impeded, are spontaneous and intuitive, unreflective and uncalculating. They may be said to belong to what may be called the *wu-wei* level of the heart. There is thus the sentiment of compassion (the inability to bear the suffering of others), the sentiment of shame, a kind of innate sense of courtesy and of deference (*jang*), and a kind of intuitive judgment of what is right and wrong in given life situations.[30] If all these dispositions are allowed to achieve their full development, they eventuate in the full realization of the four cardinal virtues. Compassion matures into humanity or *jen;* the sense of shame matures into the virtue of righteousness (*i*) in all life situations.[31] The sense of courtesy and deference matures into the "spirit" of *li,* and the ability to make intuitive moral judgments leads to true moral knowledge (*chih*). Just as in Socrates all virtues are manifestations of one high good, the four virtues are ultimately one, though one can think of them separately as intimately related aspects of the good. It is also interesting to note that while *li* is mentioned, the term seems to refer more to the inner attitude appropriate to *li* rather than to *li* as a body of prescriptions, even though Mencius always remains punctilious in his own practice of *li* as rules. There is nevertheless a clear implication that the prescriptions of *li* as an aspect of objective morality by no means cover the total arena of human ethical action. The concept of "doing right" (*i*), which covers the infinitely varied circumstances of private and public life, seems much more central and seems to subsume *li.*

The primacy of the first virtue of humanity is clearly illustrated in the famous example of the infant on the brink of falling into a well. Any human being—in Mencius' view—no matter how corrupted or dulled by the habits of an unworthy life, will feel a spontaneous, uncalculating impulse to snatch the child away from the well. "Not because he wants to get into the good graces of the parents; not because he wishes to win the praises of his fellow villagers or friends, nor because he dislikes the cry of the child."[32] There arise exceptional circumstances in life which can at times pierce through the accumulated layers of evil habit and calculating behavior to make contact with the underlying spontaneous impulse to the good, particularly the impulse of compassion. When such an occasion arises, one does the good spontaneously and without premeditation. Here one suddenly witnesses the eruption into our lives of pure moral motivation unsullied by utilitarian calculus. This very example, however, points to the reverse side of the coin. In most humans, for the larger part of their lives, this original impulse to the good is effectively buried under the accumulated weight of a benumbing callous, and evil practice.

Mencius is acutely aware of the fact of moral evil and is bent on providing a theory of man which will account for it. To do so he explores questions which lead him far beyond the simple proposition that "man's nature is good." This proposition is indeed essential, but to get at the larger picture of the human being we must attempt to understand some of the densest and most difficult passages in the entire text.

At first approximation one is inclined to say that, like some believers in the goodness of human nature in the West, Mencius believes that what deflects or blocks the nature from its natural trajectory is an evil sociopolitical environment. The impressive parable of "Ox Mountain" seems to illustrate this point. The trees on Ox Mountain are constantly being cut down by axes and new shoots are constantly being devoured by sheep and oxen. Yet the shoots continue to sprout and the mountain continues to be bald and desolate.[33] For most people, the shoots of virtue in their hearts are constantly being cut down by the economic sufferings, heartless exactions, and constant warfare inflicted upon them by harsh and ruthless rulers. Why, however, are the shoots of goodness so effectively blocked in the rulers themselves who, after all, enjoy all the creature comforts? It is not clear that the entire parable of Ox Mountain is meant to refer in the first instance to the groaning masses, since the passage is followed very closely by a reference not to the masses but to rulers. "Do not be puzzled by the king's lack of wisdom. Even a plant that grows most readily will not survive if it is placed in the sun for one day and exposed to the cold for ten."[34] The cold winds to which the king is exposed are his sycophant courtiers and evil advisors while Mencius himself represents the one day of warm sun. Yet the propensity to expose himself to evil and avoid the good must in the end originate with the king himself. He, after all, chooses his advisors. The explicit analogue of the trees and the axes is the man who "lets go of his true heart" not because of unfavorable external circumstances but because of a perversity at work within himself.[35] While the people's potential for goodness is indeed crushed by the failure to satisfy their elemental needs, there is no assurance that a comfortable material environment will be sufficient to release even their potential for goodness. The ancient sage-kings, on the contrary, found that "if they are well fed and have warm clothing and are comfortably lodged and are not taught, then they are close to beasts."[36] Thus, the impediments to the growth of the plant of goodness are not simply external to the organism. There somehow resides within the human organism itself a disordering principle sufficiently powerful in most men to block the inertial tendency to the good. What then is the nature of this principle and how is it overcome?

In attempting to answer the question we must turn to what is perhaps the most difficult passage in the book (bk. 2, pt. 1, chap. 2). Mencius is here participating in a wide-ranging and many-dimensional contemporary discussion of "philosophic anthropology" which is no longer easily comprehended. It is reflected in a variety of texts, some of which are found in later collected works such as the *Kuan-tzu* and *Huai-nan-tzu*, which were assembled as late as the early Han dynasty. While Mencius and Chuang-tzu were probably completely unaware of each other, they both seem to have been participants in the larger discussion since they share a common terminology. Recent intertextual studies by Chinese and Western scholars have thrown much light on various aspects of this discourse, but much remains obscure.

The crucial dialogue in the Mencian text opens with a discussion of the "unmoved heart." Mencius, like Confucius and like many of his own contemporaries—both Confucian and non-Confucian—remains profoundly concerned with the attainment of an attitude of inner peace, serene courage, and equanimity in the face of the anxiety-ridden world in which he lives. His disciple, Kung-sun Ch'ou, thus asks him if he could maintain his "unmoved heart" if he were suddenly elevated to high office in the state of Ch'i facing all the anxieties, perils, and spiritual temptations of such a position.[37] Mencius replies that he had already attained an "unmoved heart" by the age of forty. He also points out, however, that his antagonist Kao-tzu had also attained this state. Indeed, there were even some men who had achieved a posture of stoic indifference to the vicissitudes of the outer world simply by cultivating within themselves a constant disposition of physical courage, and it is in connection with this disposition that the term *ch'i* is first introduced as a crucial category alongside "nature" and "heart." Meng Shih-she, one of the virtuosi of physical valor mentioned, had maintained his courage by "holding fast to his *ch'i*." Courage belongs to *ch'i* because it is fundamentally an emotional disposition, and emotional dispositions, as we have seen, belong to the category of *ch'i* as a kind of psychophysical energy/substance. It seems possible for some men to cultivate this emotional disposition within themselves just as others may build up aspects of their physique by physical exercise. Mencius, however, immediately points out the narrow limitations of an "unmoved heart," which is maintained simply by this cultivation of physical courage in a passage which already points to his own central doctrine. Courage may serve any ends and since it simply belongs to the realm of the passions and emotions it may, in fact, become subservient to unworthy purposes. Courage may serve ignoble purposes. The man of *moral* courage, however, is courageous only when he is right. Confucius is quoted as saying, "If in looking within, one finds oneself to be in the wrong, then even though one's adversary be a coarsely clad commoner, should we not tremble with fear? If on looking within, one finds that one is right, one should move forward against men in the thousands."[38] Thus, an "unmoved heart" can be achieved by all sorts of methods, and simply cultivating the *ch'i* of courage is one such method. The Confucian man of "unmoved heart" obviously requires courage. His courage is, however, firmly based on unswerving righteousness. In Mencius as in Confucius, inner equanimity and virtue are inseparable.

The discussion of courage as an emotional disposition introduces us to the crucial category of *ch'i*. The *ch'i* is not the heart, although it is intimately related to the heart. It is rather a kind of energy/stuff (sometimes associated with the blood, as in Confucius' *hsüeh-ch'i*) which circulates throughout the body and its organs and which embraces all vitalities associated with the emotions, the passions, the appetites, and the desires. When embodied in the organism it seems to correspond roughly to Aristotle's "irrational part of the soul."[39] The constantly circulating and ever-changing passions, emotions, and appetites are—as in much ancient thought—the arena in which the disorders and perversions of the human person make themselves manifest within the organism and it is, in effect, the turbulence and disorders of the *ch'i* which most directly obstruct the growth of the "shoots" of goodness in the human heart.

Yet clearly Mencius does not regard the vital energy of the *ch'i* in itself as the ultimate cause of moral evil. As we have seen, it is associated with courage, which is in itself good. Indeed, when he speaks of the disorders of the *ch'i*—using distinctly physicalist imagery—he speaks not of an excess of *ch'i* but of a deficiency of *ch'i*! One might say that *ch'i* when viewed from the cosmic perspective may well be in Mencius as in Chuang-tzu a mysterious vital substance/energy which binds the individual to the ultimate source of being. As we have seen, Yen Hui is advised by Confucius in the book of Chuang-tzu that, in making his mystical ascent, he should listen not with his heart but with his *ch'i*, which is empty and unites all things to the *tao*.[40] Mencius would of course emphatically reject Chuang-tzu's view of the heart, but we can by no means be sure that he would not accept his exalted view of the *ch'i* when viewed from a cosmic perspective.[41]

How is it then that *ch'i* within the individual can become the source of perversity and disharmony? If we place the text alongside texts which may be roughly contemporaneous, we begin to discern the rough outlines of an account of the operations of *ch'i* in the human organism which Mencius seems to share with many contemporaries. The account is highly physicalist in its imagery and yet one can draw absolutely no line here between physical, psychic, or even numinous aspects.

When the *ch'i* "fills the body," all the senses and physical organs, with all their affective and perceptive properties, function precisely as they should within their proper domains.[42] One might say that when all parts of the organism are full of *ch'i*—distended, as it were, to their proper limits but no further—there is a harmonious and just balance among them. It is when *ch'i* drains out of the body and becomes depleted that imbalances occur which relate directly to imbalances and disorders in the emotions and passions.[43] In a passage of the Chuang-tzu which is not easily identified with any particular stream of Taoism we find it stated that, "If the *ch'i* that is stored up in a man becomes dispersed, then he suffers a deficiency. If it ascends and does not descend, it causes him to be constantly irritable. If it descends and does not ascend, it causes him to be chronically forgetful. If it neither ascends nor descends but gathers in the middle of the body in the region of the heart, he becomes ill."[44] In the *Huai-nan-tzu* we find the following highly revealing passage:

> If the blood-*ch'i* can be concentrated in the five organs without drifting away then the chest and stomach can be replenished and the lustful desires diminish. When the chest and stomach are full and the desires are diminished, the ears and eyes are clear and the sense of hearing and sight are penetrating we call this clarity. The five organs are then subject to the heart and there is no deviation. The will dominates and behavior does not go astray. When the will dominates and behavior does not go astray, the spirit [*shen*] flourishes and the *ch'i* does not dissipate.[45]

The entire discussion here corresponds exactly to Mencius' assertion that "the will commands the *ch'i*, while the *ch'i* fills the body."

What, however, is the causal relationship among all these categories? What causes the depletion of *ch'i* and what causes its replenishment? The men of mere physical courage try to "maintain their *ch'i*" by cultivating a dominant emotional disposition which can perhaps control certain forms of depletion, particularly loss of *ch'i* through fear. In the Chuang-tzu passage referred to above, King Huan of Ch'i has been transfixed with fear after seing a ghost. If he had maintained a steadfast courage he might have avoided the illness resulting from his loss of *ch'i*. Yet connected with the *ch'i*, there are many other irrational passions which physical courage cannot control and which may overwhelm physical courage, which is itself an organically based emotion. Thus, Mencius, in comparing his own "unmoved heart" to that of his rival Kao-tzu, points out that both he and Kao-tzu agree that "what is not to be gotten from the heart is not to be sought in the *ch'i*."[46] The spiritual basis of the "unmoved heart" should rest on something much more solid than anything derived from the emotions or passions.

What is it, then, that causes the dispersion of the *ch'i* and the disorder of the passions which, in Mencius' view, is sufficient to block the actualization of the heart's potential for achieving the promise of its nature (*hsing*)? The *ch'i*, it would appear, is very much affected by its interaction with the outer world and this interaction occurs in the realm of the senses which provide men with their channels of communication with the outer world. Kung Tu-tzu asks, "Though men are equally human, why are some great men and some small men?"[47] The answer is "that the organs of hearing and thinking are unable to think and can be misled by outer things. The organ of the heart/mind can think. If it thinks it will obtain [the right view]; if it does not think, it will not obtain it."[48] Again, it is not the senses themselves that are the locus of evil. On the contrary, the senses as such also belong to our "heavenly" nature. They are part of that nature which we do indeed share with the animals. It is entirely natural for the palate to love good tastes, the ear to love good sounds, and the eyes beautiful sights. Evil somehow arises in the area of the interaction between the *ch'i* and the senses and the objects of the outer world. There is something in the nature of the *ch'i* and the senses as they operate within the human being which leads them to become fixated on and obsessed with or excessively repelled by various aspects of the outer world. The epicurean glutton does not simply enjoy good tastes, he becomes fixated on a limitless quantity and variety of good tastes. In human beings the "unthinking" senses can trigger either vast excesses of desire or repulsion which completely upset the balance of the emotions and dissipate man's vital *ch'i*.

Where the vital *ch'i* is not drained off by these external obsessions, then the vital *ch'i* is maintained in balance. It also is clear in Mencius that while, as in Greek thought, the senses are the channels of communication with the outer world, he does not mean to imply that the only forms of evil temptation in the outer world are excessive sensual delights. More "abstract" vices, such as the lust for power, fame, and worldly honor can, it would appear, also be communicated through the senses.

Finally, however, how are the senses and the *ch'i* controlled? What strikes one above all in this passage is the reference to the capacity of the heart/mind as the "organ of thinking" and the will of the heart/mind to think or the absence of the will to think. Here we are confronted with a dimension of the heart/mind whose existence we would not have suspected if we had simply focused on the "nature" innate in the heart. The spontaneous tendency toward goodness is embedded in an unreflective, almost Taoist-level of the heart. Yet when we speak of thought and of will (*chih*) we are dealing with the distinctly un-Taoist *yu-wei* realm of deliberate goal-oriented judgment and conscious decision.[49] In concrete situations one must make a choice between good and evil and this is a deliberate act of the intentional will. It is not the heart as the spontaneous vehicle of the "good nature" which brings order to the senses and harmony and replenishment to the *ch'i*. It is the heart as the intentional organ of willing and thinking. Mencius does not simply assert that it is the "heart" which rules over the *ch'i*. He asserts that it is "the will [*chih*] which rules over the *ch'i*," and his Han commentator Chao Ch'i indeed says that the "will is what the mind intends and consciously considers" (*nien-lü*).[50] Mencius' view of the heart may be very close to the passage in the *Kuan-tzu* which reads, "When our hearts are well-ordered our senses are also well-ordered. When our hearts are at rest then our senses are also at rest. What orders them is the heart/mind. What sets them at rest is the heart/mind. The heart thus contains another heart. Within the heart there is another heart."[51] It is this "inner" intentional heart which ultimately determines whether the "natural heart of goodness" will be retained (*ts'un-hsin*) or lost (*fang-hsin*). It is difficult to say which "level" of the heart is the lower and which the higher. It is the major task of the conscious-willing heart never to lose contact with the inertial tendency toward goodness embedded in the spontaneous level of the heart—a contact which is in fact easily lost when the conscious mind confronts the overwhelming attractions and repulsions, perils and lures of the outer world. It is only the conscious level of man's mind which can by its unceasing, ever-renewed moral effort lead most humans to salvation. There is, to be sure, the shadowy ideal figure of the sage-king who by dint of some mysterious inner grace never loses contact with his "true heart" (*liang-hsin*). Here one might say that it is the total trajectory of his good nature finding its source in the "four beginnings" which determines the entire course of his life without diversions or obstructions. He never departs from the norm and lives in the world without facing the necessity for choice between good and evil. All his discrete judgments flow from his unfailing totalistic *wu-wei* intuition like the correct notes of a melody.

We find here one clue to why "freedom"—the freedom to choose between good and evil, which is certainly an implicit attribute of the conscious mind in Mencius—never seems to be put forth, in most Chinese thought, as a supreme value. The sages live in a world of harmony with the universe on every level of their being. Their conscious hearts are always at one with their spontaneous hearts. Their senses are under the complete control of their hearts and the fully nourished vital energies of *ch'i* are fully in balance within the body and in harmony with the cosmic *ch'i*. Such sages are beyond the need for the indeterminacies of freedom. The ultimate value, after all, is the good itself, not the freedom to seek the good.

And yet, Mencius, whose concern is with the majority of struggling mankind and not with the ideal sages, obviously places enormous stress on the conscious *yu-wei* level of the heart/mind, which is the center of the moral drama. It is only by the unceasing discrete acts of the moral will that the senses can be controlled and the *ch'i* can be nourished. The senses and the *ch'i* can be ultimately controlled only by the determination to act rightly—to "accumulate righteousness" (*chi i*) in all the complex circumstances of life.[52] A man who concentrates his whole mind on acting rightly will have found the loftiest and truest method of achieving an "unmoved heart" because he will be in full control of his appetites, emotions, and passions and will thus constantly nourish his *ch'i*. The *ch'i* can then become a "flood-like *ch'i*" which, as in the *Huai-nan-tzu* passage, becomes in its turn by a kind of "feedback process" a vital energy which nourishes and strengthens the innate propensity to goodness. One might say that goodness becomes embedded in character. A man who can thus "realize all the potentialities of the heart" (*chin-hsin*) will obviously share the totally unmoved heart of the Confucius of the *Analects* and will also be a man capable of saving the world.[53]

How then does Mencius' true method of achieving an unmoved heart through righteousness differ from that of Kao-tzu? Kao-tzu states that "what one does not obtain in words he does not seek in his heart."[54] Kao-tzu, we will recall, does not believe at all in any

inner propensity (*hsing*) in the heart inclining humans toward goodness. He thus cannot possibly believe in achieving equanimity by the
unremitting effort to accumulate acts of righteousness. On the contrary, he may believe that Mencius' constant, unremitting acts of
self-scrutiny may in fact be incompatible with the achievement of
inner equanimity. Later generations even see in him a Taoist or
proto-Buddhist bent on detaching his heart from all external concerns. He submits to the rules of *li* but does not see these rules as rising out of inner propensities of the heart.

What, however, does he mean when he says that he obtains his
equanimity through "words"? Language is again the repository of
both false opinions and of true doctrine. If we assume that Kao-tzu's
conception of a true code of behavior is essentially Confucian, he
finds the locus of this code in the external rules which make up the
code, and since the rules are made up of words, he simply submits to
the rules without in any way worrying about the relations of these
external rules to any internal state of heart. Culture is held together
by the rules and does not involve any inner commitment of the
heart/mind. One might say that he realizes that peace and order
must be maintained in the society by the normative rules of the culture but perhaps, as in the case of Shen Tao, the maintenance of the
normative rules requires no subjective moral involvement. He is detached both from his turbulent emotional life (*ch'i*) and from all the
painful stresses of a sense of inner moral responsibility. Mencius, on
the other hand, stresses that he also "understands words." He can
understand both the difference between false and true doctrine as
well as the states of mind which are reflected in such doctrines.[55] He
understands that these tendencies of language arise out of the deeper
moral tendencies embedded in the heart. Through words he can
read the heart. The realization of the true way cannot come simply
by submission to external rules embedded in language but arises out
of an undeviating commitment of the will to do the right. Only he
who rests in such a determination can achieve an unmovable heart,
a true mastery of his own emotional life, a true relationship to the
social world out there, and a true comprehension of what is true and
false in the "words" of others.

Let me speak further about "thinking" and "knowledge." One
might be inclined to say that Mencius emphasizes the moral will
above all else and that he would agree with Kant that the only thing
which can be called good without qualification is the good will.[56]
Yet it is also obvious that moral action (as in Kant) involves knowledge. We have seen that even the unreflective heart has a kind of intuitive power of judgment (*shih-fei*) unmarred by corruption which

is the beginning of true moral knowledge. "What a man is able to do without learning is his true ability; what he is able to know without reflection is his true [intuitive] knowledge."[57] Yet despite this assertion, the total context suggests that when he speaks of the function of the heart as "thinking" he is not referring to this nondeliberate intuitive knowledge but precisely to the "non-Taoist" deliberate level of the mind which is determined to think in the ordinary meaning of that term. "If one thinks [a deliberate act] one obtains it. If one does not think one does not obtain it."[58] The whole question of the relationship between the intuitive dimension of knowledge and the role of deliberate discrete acts of will and acts of conscious reflection centuries later became a major complex issue of "Neo-Confucian" thought. My own reading of the original text would suggest that the potentialities of the intuitive mind can be realized in most men (leaving aside the sage "supermen") only by deliberate decisions to do the right in all concrete situations and by a willingness to learn (in a highly conscious way) whatever is required to make a proper moral judgment. Only a human of this type can himself master the disorders of his own *ch'i* and thus set free his own inherent capacities. Otherwise the inherent intuitive capacity remains in most men utterly passive and "weak"—completely vulnerable to all the disordering forces of both the external environment and the internal environment of the depleted and imbalanced *ch'i*. Knowledge and thought are thus crucial but they are a kind of knowledge and thought which are constantly linked to the moral acts of the individual. The accumulation of acts of righteousness may require the acquisition of a considerable amount of empirical knowledge, for moral judgments of noble men do not involve only the encounters of personal life but the larger affairs of society as a whole. While learning as a value seems to occupy much less space in the Mencius than in the *Analects,* one need not doubt for a moment that Mencius takes for granted the necessity to learn. He himself is obviously highly learned in the cultural heritage. There is, however, an implication that to the man bent on realizing his potentialities of goodness, learning comes "easily." In learning the prescriptions of *li*, the meaning of the *Poetry,* and the knowledge of the institutions of the past, he immediately recognizes in these traditions the outer expressions of impulses deeply embedded in his heart.

To recapitulate my own understanding of this quite complex view of man: The human is born with an innate propensity (*hsing*) to achieve the full moral life. This unreflective spontaneous propensity reveals itself first in the form of certain natural moral sentiments embedded in the human heart (the four beginnings) which already contain the potentiality for the highest moral attainment embodied in the "four virtues." If unimpeded, the evolution toward actualization of these capacities will be realized. There are, however, powerful forces both within the individual and outside of him which obstruct this evolution. The vital psychophysical energy of *ch'i*, which expresses itself in man's emotions, passions, and appetites (which are quite "natural" in themselves), can easily become disordered, unbalanced, and depleted and this imbalance itself blocks and enfeebles the heart's inertial tendency toward goodness. The main arena of this disorder is the realm of man's transactions with the outer world through the channel of his senses. There is something about man's relations with his environment which creates within his *ch'i* enormous imbalances, excesses, and obsessions. For the masses of men it is, of course, the harshness of the sociopolitical environment which completely disorders their *ch'i*. In the privileged it is the environment's seductive promise of infinite sensual delight, power, fame, and honor. Yet if one probes more deeply, one finds that this account is still inadequate. Heaven has in fact endowed humans with a kind of transcendental "heart within the heart" which is capable, through arduous moral effort expressing itself in moral decisions based on reflection and deliberate thought, of preserving the spontaneous heart of goodness and not losing contact with it through all the vicissitudes and assaults of our ordinary life. Here one cannot merely talk of an inertial tendency to the good but of unceasing existential moral decisions. Those who actually make such existential decisions are able to gain mastery and control over the vital *ch'i* of their emotional and appetitive life, which, when well ordered, themselves sustain and support their moral efforts. They are able to understand the world in which they live, to feel at one with it and at one with Heaven. With Heaven's help, the noble man can help create a world "out there" in which all men will be able to reestablish contact with the inherent sources of their own natures.

If we contrast Mencius with his contemporary, Chuang-tzu, we find here almost a defiant Confucian reply to Chuang-tzu's view that the distinctly human consciousness—with its tendency to fix the human on his own "individualized" heart (*ch'eng hsin*)—is precisely what alienates him from the *tao*. Mencius' reply is that leaving aside the supermen sages, the peculiar human, *yu-wei* moral consciousness is the transcendental instrument of human salvation which unites man to Heaven. Through his moral consciousness man is at one with the *tao* and is able to harmonize his own *ch'i* with the cosmic *ch'i*. No doubt, Mencius would have appeared to Chuang-tzu to be the exact counterpart of Yen Hui before his mystic enlightenment—a busybody full of stratagems and schemes for reforming the totally unresponsive rulers of the time and at bottom bent on making his own name in the world. Mencius would of course have rejected the motive attributed to him and maintained that he had fulfilled his Heaven-assigned mission of "realizing the potentialities of his heart" and nourishing his "floodlike *ch'i*" by living a life based on an unbending moral will. As for his success or failure, that would be an aspect of the inscrutable dispensation of Heaven.

*Society and the Political Order*   In much modern discussion of Mencius in China and the West, he has often been taken on the one hand as the representative of democratic, populist, or "socialist" tendencies within ancient Confucianism, and, on the other hand, as the representative of some of its most "reactionary" maxims. I need not dwell here on the vagaries of these terms, but the use of these terms by modern Chinese interpreters may in fact point to certain aspects of the Mencian sociopolitical vision. I should therefore like to consider the aspects of his thought to which these modern tags have been applied.

In his "social" philosophy Mencius displays an acute consciousness of the ordinary material needs of men. In this matter, as in many others, there is no reason to think that his thought differs from that of the *Analects* but the detailed nature of his discussion certainly highlights this theme. The people, unlike the *shih*, cannot be expected to maintain a "steadfast heart" without a "stable livelihood."[59] In his dialogue with Kao-tzu, Mencius certainly does not deny that the need for food and sex are an authentic part of the "nature." The nourishment of *ch'i* would certainly include adequate physical nourishment and the satisfaction of all basic material needs. Mencius does not despise the sense desires as such and says explicitly that they also belong to the "nature" (*hsing*), even though it is in the area of the interaction of the senses with the outer world that human perversity first seems to arise. It is not only "natural" to satisfy one's physical needs, but all men naturally love good tastes, good sounds, and physical beauty. Mencius' commitment to civilization is amply proven by the fact that he accepts as the standard of good tastes the cooking of the paragon cook Yi Ya as well as the standards set by other culture heroes.[60]

There is evidence that Mencius does not negate what might be called the "civilized" satisfaction of men's physical needs rather than simply their most rudimentary, brute satisfaction. His attitude toward merchants who by now must have been a prominent feature of the social scene is not overly negative. Merchants who bring goods

from areas where they are abundant to areas where they are scarce
have a legitimate role in society and we find him calling upon rulers
to protect the rights of merchants in the marketplace. He urges King
Hsüan not to levy excessive taxes on them so that they "will enjoy
the refuge of your marketplace"[61] and also defends the notion that
prices should be determined by the free market.[62] In his defense of
the division of labor against Hsü Hsing, he stresses the fact that even
in the society of his time peasants depend on pots, pans, plows, and
caps produced by others and that this is an eminently desirable state
of affairs. This does not indicate that he at all envisions a society in
which merchants or trade would play a dominant role but it does illustrate the point that he envisions the possibility of a livelihood for
the people which would include an unspecified standard of "civilized" comfort and amenities.

In his dialogues with King Hui and King Hsüan, Mencius even
seems to be condoning the extravagant luxuries of those princes.
Here, however, I suspect that Mencius is using a persuasive rhetoric
tailored for the moral limitations of his audience. The two princes in
question are not likely to give up their huge hunting parks, expen-
sive concubines, and lavish palaces. While Mencius no doubt believes that there is a certain level of luxury which is a necessary
appurtenance of the ceremonial life of rulers, when they ask him if it
is legitimate for them to enjoy these ostentatious luxuries he argues
that such luxuries are legitimate only if the people can also enjoy
something of the good life. When King Wen of old had a hunting
park, the park was open to woodcutters and hunters and, more fundamentally, he enjoyed these perquisites only after he had seen to
it that the people's livelihood had been assured.[63] Obviously King
Hui and King Hsüan would not be able to maintain the kinds of establishments they had if they were truly concerned with the people's
livelihood.

Neither sense pleasures nor even honors are dismissed as evils in
themselves and in this Mencius' "this-worldliness" differs in no
marked respect from Confucius or indeed from contemporary moralists in Greece and Israel. These goods are evil only when they are
not subordinated to the higher good, however conceived, and are inevitably constrained by the higher goods. In Mencius the senses "do
not think" and thus lead to fantasies of limitless gratification not
only of the senses but also of the desires for fame and honor. "All
men have the common desire for honor and all men have in themselves that which is worthy of honor, but all men do not think of
it."[64] "Those who are satiated with humanity and righteousness do
not desire the fat meat and fine millet of others and, enjoying true

fame and wide praise, they do not desire the elegant clothes of others."[65] Here the honor is the kind of honor elicited solely by excellence of soul. Thus the highest good is the deep inner satisfaction and the tranquillity which comes from a life devoted to "humanity and righteousness" and other goods are good only to the extent that they are subordinate to and limited by this supreme good. Thus while not denying that sense pleasures and reputation are goods, this view is not incompatible with his assertion that "in nourishing the mind there is nothing better than to reduce the desires."[66] The depletion of emotional and appetitive *ch'i* that results from a fixation on limitless satisfaction and the wrong kind of fame, which can only be satisfied by constant aggrandizement (with the inevitable accompanying fear of loss of power), are not compatible with the nature of the heart. The same Mencius who expediently argues to King Hsüan that his excessive luxuries might be justified if he took care of the needs of the people, elsewhere expresses his obvious contempt for contemporary rulers with "their halls tens of feet in height . . . their tables laden with food measuring ten feet across . . . and their female attendants numbering in the hundreds."[67] To be sure, there are no sharp lines drawn between the legitimate satisfaction of creaturely needs and excess, but the general implication is that desires should be limited not only because Mencius shares Mo-tzu's assumption that there are maximum constraints imposed by the limits on economic productivity but because, even if he could have imagined something like a consumer society based on limitless growth, he would probably in terms of his own premises have rejected it.

A life spent in the limitless expenditure of vital energy in obtaining an infinite variety of goods would certainly lead to a starvation of the *ch'i* and of the "heart of humanity and righteousness." In dealing with the people, Mencius talks of a situation in which the aged wear silk and eat meat and the masses are neither cold nor hungry. The notion that the nonproductive aged will enjoy this surplus implies a society which is certainly above bare subsistence and one in which the masses can no doubt participate in the life of festival and familial and communal "holy ritual." All this may still be quite compatible with his admonition to "reduce the desires."

At the heart of Mencius' "social policy" we find Confucius' emphasis on a ruling class which *refrains* from imposing excessive demands on the people by allowing the people to make its own livelihood. There is, however, much more discussion here of the kind of institutional arrangements which will make the implementation of such a policy possible. Thus the same Mencius who so much stresses the roots of goodness within the human heart also turns out

to be much more explicit than the Master in the *Analects* in providing a picture of the specific institutional setting—presumably
derived from the ideal institutions of the past—through which this
goodness is to be realized. It is thus by no means anomalous that
during the Sung dynasty the famous statesman Wang An-shih, basically preoccupied with creating a kind of "outer" institutional blueprint of the good society, and Chu Hsi, basically preoccupied with
cultivating the sources of moral excellence in the individual, should
have both found inspiration in Mencius. We cannot know from the
*Analects* whether Confucius was interested in the details of land systems. Even if he was he may not have shared, in his own time, Mencius' apocalyptic expectation that the time for reinstituting the ideal
land system of the past was at hand. His remarks, as we have seen,
seem to concentrate on very general statements concerning the general policies which should guide the ruling class.

Mencius is quite clear, however, that "benevolent government"
requires its appropriate "institutional expression." A carpenter requires the compass and the square, a musician requires the pitch
pipes, and the sages of the past made manifest institutions *through*
which the virtues of ideal rulers are realized in the world. "Goodness
alone is not sufficient for governing while the laws [institutions] cannot implement themselves."[68] While Mencius is aware that there
had been changes in land systems in the past, he particularly praises
the model of the nine-unit system (the "well field" system) which
had presumably existed in the Chou.[69] Leaving aside details of the
system which may never have existed in this schematic form, it
seems in Mencius' presentation to be based on a plan of equal
lots distributed among eight families and the cooperative cultivation
of the ninth plot, which would provide revenue for the lord. To
modern interpreters eager to detect a "socialistic" strain in Mencius,
the concept of equal distribution of the means of production among
the peasants, the lack of "private property" and the limits set on
revenue for those above suggest a strain toward "primitive socialism." On the other hand, those who regard him as reactionary stress
the fact that the peasants are bound in serflike fashion to their villages, that the whole system is imposed from above, and that the
peasants are engaged in compulsory "exploitative" labor. In the
perception of Mencius himself, there is, of course, no incompatibility
between the equal distribution of the means of production among
the peasants and the absolute need for a ruling class and social hierarchy—while the system is conceivable only if the peasants "do not
leave the village."[70] The collective cultivation of the lord's field provides the most humane and least arbitrary method of providing a

specified revenue for the rulers above. Presumably, this mode of meeting the needs of the rulers will provide ample time and resources for the eight families to provide for their own livelihood. If, in addition, the people are "taught" the basic rules of "human relationships" this institutional arrangement will provide an atmosphere in which the peasants will live in peace and harmony. While Mencius furnishes no information concerning land relations in his own times, there is frequent attack on the oppressive, arbitrary exaction of surplus by the rulers of the time.

While Mencius obviously believes that benevolent government "must begin with land demarcation," some of the most strikingly "radical" assertions in the sphere of political philosophy involve the emphasis on the principle of merit in government. The ambivalence which we noted in the *Analects* on the question of merit and hereditary prerogative has not completely disappeared, but the weight is now very much on the side of merit.

Here again we must begin with the new historic environment. To the extent that Confucius' defense of hereditary prerogative was still related to his determination to preserve whatever remained of the legitimacy of the Chou dynasty, this motive has completely disappeared in Mencius' case. The survival of the Chou house is no longer a live question for Mencius, whose mind is keenly alert to the possibilities of a new dispensation. The stratum of wandering *shih* to which he belonged had greatly increased in numbers and prestige. The old local hereditary nobility had greatly declined and both King Hui of Liang and King Hsüan of Ch'i, while belonging to the aristocracy, were the scions of houses which had usurped the power of the older ruling lineages which had traced their legitimacy to the Chou revolution.

On the other side, the ancient ideal of the universal polity and the universal kingship had not disappeared. It was, in fact, now a widely discussed theme. The emergence of the states of Ch'i, Ch'u, and Ch'in as supreme superpowers again brought within the range of possibility the establishment by one power of a "hegemonic" supremacy in the Chinese world or even the establishment of a new universal king. Within this context, Mencius' discussion with rulers such as King Hsüan of the criteria of true kingship (*wang*) may no longer have seemed farfetched. When King Hsiang of Liang asks, "How can the world be settled?" Mencius replies without hesitation, "By unification" and one presumes that this was by now a view widely shared by the politically articulate elite of the times.[71] Within this context, Mencius' uninhibited emphasis on merit as opposed to hereditary prerogative was by now widely shared. It was no longer necessary to preach even to the ruler of the time that pedigree would neither save them nor lead them to ascendancy in the all-out struggles of the late Warring States world.

What distinguishes Mencius is thus not the emphasis on merit and achievement, but the uncompromisingly moral cast of his conception of merit. His doctrine of true kingship is, of course, that only a ruler prepared to establish a "benevolent government" within his domain will be worthy of true kingship, or will indeed prove worthy to survive in the new order which is about to dawn.

It is in his defense of the latter proposition that we find some of his boldest utterances. In a world in which hereditary legitimacy is threatened from all sides, King Hsüan of Ch'i asks a question no doubt in the minds of many contemporary rulers in spite of, or perhaps because of, the questionable origins of their own pedigrees. "Was it permissible for King Wu of Chou to kill his lord Chou [the infamous last ruler of the Shang dynasty]?" Mencius, directly applying Confucius' doctrine of "names and realities," replies, "I have heard of punishment of the common fellow Chou but not of the killing of a king."[72] Given his abandonment of all the norms of kingship, Chou obviously no longer deserved the title of king. This answer, which must have thoroughly shocked King Hsüan, apparently completely negates the bases of hereditary authority.

Yet, in fact, Mencius' doctrine is somewhat more nuanced than this statement suggests, as is clear from his long discourse on the history of royal legitimation which again seems to reflect a general debate of the times. The famous Emperor Yao of old had chosen his own successor Shun on the basis of Shun's merit and passed over his own son. The same was true of Shun's choice Yü. Yü, however, passed on the throne to his own son, thus inaugurating the first hereditary dynasty.

Mencius' disciple Wan Chang asks, "There are some who say that when it came to Yü his virtue was inferior. He did not pass on his throne to the worthiest but to his own son."[73] Mencius' doctrine, which must, of course, justify the sacred canonical history to which he is committed, is based on a complex doctrine of the operation of Heaven. He first of all rejects the notion that the sage-kings simply had the right to elect their own successors. This form of election might have resulted in a rule no better than the results of the hereditary system since it would depend on the arbitrary choice of the ruler. "Yao could not give the world to another." Yao proposed Shun to Heaven and Heaven indicated its acceptance in two ways. When Shun made sacrifices to the gods, the gods "accepted" his sacrifices (perhaps through the favorable conjunctions of natural

forces) and when he carried on administration, the people were obviously content. The latter assertion provides the ground for the frequent contention that Mencius conceived of legitimacy as being
based on "popular sovereignty." The people's contentment is one of
the indispensable criteria for Heaven's choice of the ruler "since
Heaven sees with the eyes of the people."[74] Whether this conception
constitutes the basis for a conception of popular sovereignty will, of
course, very much depend on one's interpretation of the term "sovereignty." To dismiss the role which Mencius assigns to Heaven as a
"manner of speaking" again represents an arbitrary imposition of
certain modern Western notions on Mencius' world view. It seems,
on the whole, entirely compatible with the Mandate of Heaven doctrine as we find it in the *Book of Poetry* and the *Book of Documents*.

When Mencius speaks of the succession of Yü's son, he is again
able to point to the latter's intrinsic virtue, but when he deals with
the adoption of the hereditary principle for the remainder of the dynasty, he must appeal to the inscrutable and unfathomable will of
Heaven which had in its wisdom determined that at least for a time
its mandate would be transmitted through a lineage. Under such
circumstances, mediocre rulers may prevail for a time although
Mencius points out that even in times of mediocre rulers, worthy
ministers exercised enormous powers, as when Yi Yin banished the
king T'ai-chia who had "upset the laws of T'ang [the first ruler of
Shang]."[75] Here we have a clear illustration of Mencius' exalted
conception of the role which ought to be enjoyed by virtuous ministers. In a period when the hereditary principle prevails only the
most evil kings can bring the dynasty to an end. It is thus quite clear
that whatever Mencius' predilections, he is prepared to agree that
by Heaven's dispensation in such a period even relatively unworthy
rulers who may not deserve the name of king may nevertheless enjoy
legitimate authority. For commoners such as Confucius (and perhaps himself), however, to obtain the kingly mantle they must, like
Shun and Yü, receive the recommendation of a reigning sage-king.
In all this, it is quite clear that Mencius seems to regard the situation
in which the "worthiest" rule as the ideal state of affairs but piously
accepts the inscrutable will of Heaven in history. It is a will which
does not always move in ways corresponding to the more obvious
pattern which virtuous men might prefer. The fact that Heaven confers the Mandate on lineages as well as on sages points to the unfathomable aspects of Heaven's will.

In explaining what may seem to be Mencius' extravagantly optimistic hopes for the reunification of the world through the establishment of a "true kingship" in the brutal world of his times, the above

passage as well as other views on Heaven's role in history must be given full weight. Despite Heaven's inscrutability, Mencius thought he could discern a general pattern in the operations of Heaven in history. "Every five hundred years a true king should arise and in the interim there should be men renowned in their generation. Over seven hundred years have now passed since the rise of Chou and the five hundred year period has passed. The time would seem to be ripe. It must be that Heaven does not desire to bring peace to the world. If it did, who is there in this generation other than myself [to bring it about]? How can I not be discontent?"[76] Elsewhere he states, "The appearance of a true king has never been longer overdue than today and the people have never suffered more under tyrannical government than today. It is easy to provide food for the hungry and drink for the thirsty."[77]

We first of all note Mencius' almost religious sense of his own vocation and mission in the world of his time, although we must also note that given the doctrine that a commoner can be recommended for the true kingship only by a reigning sage-king, none of this means that he himself cherishes pretensions to the universal kingship. Yet it does indicate that in some sense he regards himself as Heaven's apostle to the rulers of his time. Secondly, we note that in the background of his dialogues with the rulers of his time there is an apocalyptic expectation that the time is ripe for a restoration of the *tao*. The people are thirsting for salvation. To be sure, the pattern of history cannot be reduced to a mechanical chronology and Heaven's design retains its inscrutable aspects but the very bleakness of the time suggested—as in messianic doctrines elsewhere—that the age of Mencius represented the darkness before the dawn.

It is, I would suggest, within the context of this apocalyptic mood that we may view Mencius' advice to rulers as unpromising as King Hsüan of Ch'i. The appearance of the model of "benevolent government" anywhere in the world would prove such a magnet to the people throughout the world "hungry and thirsty" for redemption that they would readily repudiate their own unworthy rulers and welcome conquest by a righteous king with open arms as in the days of Wu Wang of old.

Mencius is aware that King Hsüan of Ch'i is anything but a promising candidate for true kingship and he approaches him from "where he is." He tries to persuade him at one point that he possesses within himself the spontaneous impulses which could be expanded into a "heart of humanity and righteousness" but on the whole he uses rhetorical devices more suited to the limitation of his beclouded nature, such as the argument concerning the circum-

stances under which the King's extravagant luxuries might be justified. He even employs the strictly "realistic" argument that King
Hsüan cannot possibly prevail by force of arms against all the armed
might of the powers in a world in which there are at least eight
powers all as powerful as Ch'i. If one power becomes too powerful
the others will certainly unite against it.[78] In the end neither the appeal to his better nature nor rhetorical arguments succeeded in
turning such weak-willed rulers as Hui of Liang and Hsüan of Ch'i
from their greedy habits and "conventional" political views. To
judge from the book as a whole, however, none of this seems to shake
Mencius' faith that the reunification of the world when it does occur
will be achieved only by a "true king."

If Mencius is less ambivalent than the *Analects* on the question of
merit versus hereditary prerogative, the same is true of his much
more purist attitude toward the hegemonic (*pa*) system of Kuan
Chung with its emphasis on peace through power and collective security. Looking back on the old hegemonic systems of the late
Spring and Autumn period, Mencius feels that he can stand in final
judgment on them. In the end they did nothing to reverse the decline of the Chou dynasty. He is more convinced than ever that the
*tao* will be restored only by a total reliance on the four cardinal virtues embedded in the heart of a righteous ruler.

Such then is the soaring and defiant idealism of Mencius. It is,
nevertheless, also the same Mencius who provides us with the classical justification of the principle of hierarchy and authority in society
in terms of the social division of labor. It is also the same Mencius
who makes clear the utter helplessness of the people without virtuous rulers. Here we have the "reactionary" Mencius. He is speed-
ily able to prove to Hsü Hsing, the southern "agrarian utopian"
(*nung-chia*) who believes that all men should sustain themselves by
their own labor in the fields, that he himself is utterly dependent on
the labor of others for his clothes, his pots, and his plows. If the civilized world depends upon the division of labor among the hundred
crafts, why, Mencius asks with Socrates and Plato, is the most crucial craft of governing a less valuable form of specialization than
farming? There must be those who "work with their [physical]
strength" and "those who work with their minds [*hsin*]."[79]

What then of the equal innate capacity for goodness of all
humans? I have translated the word *hsin* in this passage as "mind"
since it seems to focus on the capacities of the *hsin* which are patently
intellectual. The account which Mencius proceeds to give of the civilizing activities of the early sage-kings seems to stress not so much
their "heart of goodness" but what might almost be called their

"technical intelligence." Knowledge (*chih*) is, to be sure, one of the four cardinal virtues, yet in the context of the discussion of the four virtues it seemed to be basically a knowledge tied to moral judgment. In the passage concerning the establishment of civilization, however, we are told of Yi's use of fire to clear the forests and even of the "Education Minister" Hsieh who "taught the people basic human relations."[80] Here, suddenly the sages seem to become social engineers who create the basic infrastructure of civilization.

On the other side one is struck by the extraordinary passivity of the people. Without the sages, they are completely at the mercy of nature and totally unable to cope with their most rudimentary needs. Rousseau's man in a state of nature is isolated and primitive, and lives wholly "in the immediate." Yet somehow he seems quite capable of taking care of himself almost like the solitary orangutan. On his primitive level he is autonomous and self-sufficient. Mencius' humans, however, seem to require civilization even to meet their basic needs. They are creatures made for civilization. Yet the vast majority seem incapable of initiative even, it would appear, in the realm of proper family relations!

Taking the text as a whole, it may nevertheless be possible to reconcile this picture with Mencius' more general view of man. On the question of moral knowledge versus technical intelligence, one need merely assume that the superior man who is able to exert his will (his "heart of hearts") to the utmost, is easily able to extend his innate moral knowledge to acquire whatever technical mastery is required. What the sage is able to do in the first instance is to overcome his self-involvement and to extend his concerns to mankind as a whole. What thus distinguishes him at the outset is his ability to worry about the needs of others. "Yao alone was filled with anxiety."[81] His moral concern then leads him to do whatever is required to deal with the situation. The mastery of the technical requirements follows almost intuitively from the moral determination. Thus, Yü, having grasped the need for flood control, soon grasps the almost Taoist principle that in carrying on flood control one follows the "natural tendency of water" and relies wholly on the natural contours of the land.[82] Learning as empirical knowledge is required but the man who is able to activate his "intuitive capacity" (*liang-neng*) soon masters the essential.[83]

Conversely, the potential of the masses in general for goodness is soon overwhelmed by the disabling effects of their primitive environment and leaves both their moral capacities and their intellectual capacities completely inoperative. The accent thus falls not on the equality of their nature but on the inertness of this potential—on what David Nivison has called the "weakness of will." Here one might say that if Mencius' "people" cannot be compared to Rousseau's humans in a state of nature they can perhaps be compared to Rousseau's people once they have entered "civil society." Once the people are exposed to the disorders of emerging civilization they can realize their "general will" only through the mediation of great legislators such as Lycurgus and Solon. "There is needed a superior intelligence which can survey all the passions of mankind though itself exposed to none."[84] There are, of course, significant differences between Rousseau's legislators and Mencius' sages, but in both a moral-intellectual vanguard must play a crucial role in actualizing the dormant potentialities of the people. Taking into account the full complexity of Mencius' view of the human reality, there is in fact no contradiction between his emphasis on the *potential* equality and innate goodness of all men and his extraordinary emphasis on the notion that this potential can be realized only through the mediation of a moral-intellectual elite which can exert the "mind within the mind." History proves that such individuals are few in number.

*Religion*   Mencius' view of Heaven is as many-sided as his concept of the human reality although it coincides in many ways with the Heaven of the *Analects*. It is often stated that in Mencius Heaven has become quite explicitly conceived of as immanent in the cosmos and particularly as immanent in the nature (*hsing*) of man. The concept of "human nature" (*hsing*) is as much an embodiment of Heaven as the movements of the heavenly bodies.

Yet as we have already seen, the concept of *hsing* forms only one element in Mencius' complex view of the total human being. Again, leaving aside the case of the sage whose "nature" never deviates from its proper trajectory, how does Heaven relate to the "heart" on both its levels as well as to the indeterminacies of the *ch'i?* The famous text, "He who fully realizes the potentialities of his heart [*chin-hsin*] knows his nature. He who knows his nature knows Heaven" has often been cited as the proof-text of the notion of Heaven's immanence in man.[85] In fact, leaving aside the mythic sages, whose heart is the "spontaneous heart," only a human being who can operate on the level of conscious and unremitting moral effort is capable of truly realizing the potentialities of the mind. It is in fact only the human being who has the ability to realize that the spontaneous level of his heart is easily lost; who realizes that he can easily lose contact with his nature and his unproblematic relationship with Heaven who can truly know Heaven. "Knowing" on this very crucial level involves human reflective knowledge and deliberate decision.[86] The sociobiologist's ants never fail to fulfill their program of "altruism" embedded in their DNA. Man, however, possesses, as it were, the "supernatural" power to stray from his "program" and must therefore possess the supernatural power to live up to his program and to know what his program "ought to be." To know his program is to stand outside of it. That in man which is able to "know" the nature stands outside of the nature and outside of Heaven.

It is thus no accident that when Mencius speaks of "knowing Heaven" on this level he falls into a quasi-theistic language. "By maintaining a firm hold of his heart [ts'un-hsin] and nurturing his nature he serves Heaven."[87] On this level man seems to relate to Heaven as the "other" who must be served, and the term "serving" in the sense of fulfilling a task which Heaven has imposed upon him may here be no more "metaphorical" than it is in Judeo-Christian tradition. Here again, as in the Analects, the notion that Mencius must opt for an immanentist, naturalistic (in the quasi-Taoist sense) view of Heaven or a view of Heaven as a "separate moral will" is an antithesis which we impose on the text.

There are many other passages in which Heaven itself emerges as an active will. We have already discussed the passages in which it is Heaven which ultimately *decides* that Shun will be Yao's successor and that after Yü, the hereditary principle will prevail. Mencius even shares with Confucius the faith that within his generation he himself bears a Heaven-endowed mission. One might, to be sure, say that within the historic order, Heaven is already conceived of as immanent in the impersonal pattern of history—in the rhythm of its cycles of order and disorder. Yet for some inscrutable reason, Heaven has chosen to depart from the five-hundred-year cycle which Mencius discerns as the pattern of the past. Heaven itself is evidently not bound to the pattern. One cannot yet speak of a self-sufficient "law of history." All one can say is that when Mencius speaks of man in terms of the "spontaneous" aspects of his being—of his physical and sensory capacities as well as of his innate spontaneous moral propensities—Mencius' view of Heaven is treated in a quasi-Taoist *wu-wei* language. When speaking of man as a conscious, willing being, Heaven itself seems to relate to man as transcendent moral will.

In an ideal world the "heavenly" would be totally immanent and actual and man would simply be "continuous" with Heaven. All men would be sages. In the actual world, however, the human may easily lose his "infant's heart." Nevertheless, he is endowed with the marvelous power to "perfect his own person" and on this level Heaven itself relates to man as the "other" which has endowed him with this capacity for the realization of the good. At times, one even senses that Mencius treasures this conscious *yu-wei* self-effort as much as he does the ideal *wu-wei* spontaneity.

In a world in which the faith in the promise of the salvation of the world through the moral will of noble men was under attack from every quarter—even within the Confucian camp—Mencius defiantly, almost quixotically, reaffirms this faith. Without referring to the Taoism of Chuang-tzu and Lao-tzu, of which he seems to have been unaware as a separate tendency, he defiantly asserts that the intentional *yu-wei* moral consciousness is man's only instrument of salvation. Far from being an anomaly in nature, it is itself a power conferred by Heaven. On the other side, to the extent that Shen Tao, Shen Pu-hai, and the emerging tendencies toward Legalism were strongly arguing that the establishment of peace and order in the world had nothing to do with the subjective intentionality of noble men, Mencius continues to believe that it is only through the actions of noble men that salvation can be attained. This belief seems to be fortified and enhanced, in this case, by an apocalyptic reading of Heaven's intentions in the world of his time.

One reason for the relatively small impact of Mencius on the Confucianism of the centuries which immediately followed him may well be the failure of these apocalyptic expectations. Heaven's way in history continued to remain inscrutable. The "world" was in fact to achieve reunification by the reliance on brute power, despite Mencius' assurance that "there are cases of gaining control of a state without humanity but there is no case of the world being won without humanity."[88] Mencius' dominant position within the world of Confucian thought was not won until well over a millennium later in the Neo-Confucianism of the Sung dynasty. When it finally did win ascendancy it was not Mencius' apocalyptic hopes but the metaphysics of the individual's moral life which were to be the central focus of attention.

## Hsün-tzu: The Defense of the Faith

If Mencius operates from deep within the fortress of his faith, his later protagonist Hsün-tzu is in the thick of the battle against enemies from all sides. Hsün-tzu is thoroughly familiar with the intellectual currents of his time. Far from disdaining the activities of the Chi-hsia Academy, he is an active member and participant in its intellectual debates.[89] He is keenly responsive to other currents of thought and certainly does not hesitate to learn from them. What is more, as the defender of what he regards as the true conception of Confucianism, he turns his sharp intellectual weapons not only against the external enemies but also against those within the Confucian camp who in his view weaken and pervert the Master's true message.

Born in the northern "peripheral" state of Chao, he may have been exposed to non-Confucian modes of thought from an early age. According to the calculation of Ch'ien Mu, his life falls somewhere between the years 340 and 245 B.C. Otherwise, the meager accounts of his life abound in discrepancies. He seems to have spent periods of time as a member of the Chi-hsia Academy, even holding at one time the rank of libationer. He is also said to have fled the kingdom of Ch'i when the tyrannous King Min forced many academicians into exile. For a time he was in the service of the powerful leader of the state of Ch'u, Lord Ch'un Shen. He is also recorded as having been present in the state of Chao and a visit is mentioned to the state of Ch'in where the reforms of the famous Legalist minister Lord Shang were already in place. On the whole, it would appear that despite the "realistic" cast of his interpretation of Confucianism, he was not notably more successful than Mencius in his career as a statesman, while, according to tradition, his own two notable disciples, Li Ssu and Han Fei-tzu, were to become pillars of Legalism.

The text of Hsün-tzu seems to be largely based on the words of Hsün-tzu, although one does find passages in which the Master is quoted by name by his disciples. The style of the book is clear, eloquent, and trenchant and at times rises to poetic heights. One senses the presence of a mind of considerable intellectual power and of an unbending self-assurance. Yet despite the "tough-mindedness" of many of Hsün-tzu's intellectual positions, one senses a truly deep— almost poetic—feeling for the *li* as "holy rite" as well as a burning indignation directed against the errors and corruptions of the age.

*Human Nature*   I shall begin a consideration of Hsün-tzu's doctrine conventionally by examining the proposition which clearly distinquishes him from Mencius, his main target of attack within the Confucian camp—namely, the proposition that "human nature is evil." In sharp reaction against the usual textbook account of Hsüntzu which emphasizes this proposition, there have been scholars both in late traditional China and in modern China, as well as elsewhere, who are inclined to deny the centrality of this proposition to his entire outlook. Some have even suggested that the entire chapter which bears the title "The Nature is Evil" may even be a later interpolation into the text.[90]

It is, of course, quite true that the proposition by no means sums

292 THE WORLD OF THOUGHT IN ANCIENT CHINA

up Hsün-tzu's conception of man any more than the proposition "the nature is good" sums up Mencius' philosophic anthropology. Hsün-tzu's view is no less complex than that of Mencius and indeed includes some of the same crucial terms we have already met in Mencius—the *chi'i*, the sense organs, the heart/mind, the will (*chih*), and the emotions, as well as others not stressed in the Mencius. Yet I would submit that the terms "good" and "evil" as referring to the "nature" are entirely meaningful in both conceptions. We need not associate the word "evil" in Hsün-tzu with Augustinian views of original sin. The concept of sin itself is, after all, treated quite variously even in the Judeo-Christian tradition, and in some tendencies it is not incompatible with concepts of individual moral improvement. The only meaning we need assign to the word "evil" is the meaning which Hsün-tzu himself assigns to it. If we do this we find that what is said in this chapter is consistent with the entire text of the book. As Hsün-tzu understands the term, it is central to his outlook.

One might say that Hsün-tzu takes up and carries further the cause of Kao-tzu in his dialogue with Mencius. He negates any inborn spontaneous tendency toward "humanity and righteousness" within the human heart and denies that the "objective" structures of morality which we find embedded in the tradition of "*li* and righteousness" (*li i*) could have derived from any moral propensity innate in the human organism. One might say that his opposition to Mencius sets out from this denial. On the other hand, he does go beyond the mere assertion that man simply shares the basic "harmless" instincts of other animals. He seems to refer to something more dynamic when he speaks of man's propensity to evil. Evil, to be sure, arises in the same area in which it arises in Mencius—in the area of man's contacts through his senses with the outer world. While in Mencius the disorder arises somewhere in the area of interaction between the perceptions and the world of objects out there, in Hsün-tzu the dynamic impulse of boundless desire seems to arise from within. "When man is born he has desires. If he cannot obtain what he desires he must seek to satisfy them and in his seeking there is no measure or limit."[91] If nature has a limited capacity to satisfy human desires—and this does indeed seem to be the case—this is because the human libidinous urges have no clear limit. Hence strife must arise among men.

The difference of emphasis becomes clear in the quite different accounts of man in a "state of nature" which we find in both texts. What strikes one in Mencius is not so much the boundless libido of humans in this state, but their terror and confusion in the face of an

untamed external nature. At first their innate propensity to goodness is overwhelmed by feelings of fear and insecurity, which can
upset the inner balance of the *ch'i* quite as easily as lusts and desires.
Later when their material environment is improved by the sages,
they may still be led astray by their appetites and indolence and
may still require teaching despite their innate goodness. Hsün-tzu,
however, sets out not from the helplessness of most men in a "state of
nature," but from their unbridled and fierce desires. If there is anything in man to which the word "nature" (*hsing*) with its implication
of spontaneity and unreflective directionality applies, it is to this
realm of the passions and desires. There are differences among men
in terms of their temperamental bents and Hsün-tzu associates these
differences with the imbalances of *ch'i,* making some hard and assertive, some sluggish and indolent, but fundamentally they are all
bent by nature on satisfying their limitless desires.[92]

   This difference in the interpretation of the realm of desire is associated with an even more fundamental difference in the treatment of
the heart or mind. Mencius' "nature" may be read as the natural
tendency of the heart (that is, of the heart on its unreflective level).
In Hsün-tzu it would be far more appropriate to translate the word
*hsin* simply as "mind," since it by no means comes into the world
directed by innate moral propensities. What it does encompass,
however, is a precious intellectual capacity—a capacity which *may*
or *may not* be exercised to acquire knowledge, deliberate, reflect, and
achieve conscious goals. The mind is, at least at first approach,
quintessentially the very center of the *yu-wei* consciousness, particularly the capacity for knowledge.

   "Knowledge" is, of course, also one of Mencius' "four virtues" and
also has roots in the spontaneous tendencies of the heart. It manifests itself, however, ideally as man's intuitive ability to make correct
moral judgments. The man who has a "will to the good" on the
more deliberative level of his heart/mind will be able to "accumulate acts of righteousness" by his unflagging determination to be
just.[93] The word "capacity," which we have used in Hsün-tzu's case,
does not refer to an immediately available "intuitive" knowledge.
It is a capacity for acquiring experience and reasoning about experience and it demands constant cumulative acts of *mental* exertion. Although there is a mysterious "Taoist" dimension of the mind
of the "sage" in Hsün-tzu, it in no way removes the need for a resolute commitment to the study of the manifold world which surrounds us. The center of gravity in dealing with mind lies in the
process of "learning"—a category which receives only minimal attention in Mencius. Hsün-tzu attacks Mencius head-on for the as-

sertion that "the fact that man learns is due to the goodness of his nature."[94] On the contrary, the determination to learn can draw on no inner propensity other than the capacity to learn itself. It is a capacity which includes not only the capacity to accumulate empirical knowledge, but also the power to think and reason as well. The ancient sage-kings Yao and Shun were not a whit better in their natures than other mortals. "That wherein the sages are the same as the mass of men and not different from them is their nature; that wherein they differ from and surpass the mass of men is in their deliberate action."[95] Here, too, of course, one might say that in Mencius also what differentiates the sage is the "heart within the heart," which is actually capable of a deliberate determination to act. In the Mencian case, however, the determination is essentially the determination "to do good," a determination which, like that of a strong swimmer swimming with the current, is nevertheless able to draw immediate support from the deepest tendencies of human nature. The deliberate action of Hsün-tzu's sages and noble men, in the first instance, involves sheer intellectual effort and a determination to learn how to rescue both themselves and other human beings from the miseries of the chaos and strife which result from their insatiable and conflicting interests.[96] In using his intellect the sage is like the artisan who regards his own nature and that of others as a raw material to be shaped and constrained in order to produce the finished artifact.[97] The artisan must study both the properties of raw materials and what might be called the rules governing the practice of his art but does not for a moment suppose that the artifact grows "organically" out of its raw material. Again he is like Kao-tzu's carpenter who cuts the willow wood to make bowls. Here we have not only an attack on Mencius but what seems to be a bold and defiant attack on the whole tendency culminating in Lao-tzu to attack human civilization because it is created by the deliberate human consciousness. Civilization is indeed a "Great Artifice"(ta-wei) and that is its glory!

The ancient sages began, as it were, from their insight as social and political philosophers and what they saw was remarkably close to what had been seen by Mo-tzu's ancient sages. They clearly understood that their own intolerable wretchedness and insecurity and that of all other humans would never be overcome until external constraints were imposed on the pursuit of the limitless desires. As with Hobbes, the sages (but not the mass of mankind unable to reason their way through to this conclusion) came to the realization that all the creaturely goods and gratifications simply become hollow and without savor when the human mind is obsessed by fear and anxiety. On the other hand, the "desires cannot be made few" (contrary to Sung Hsing's assertion). Hence a choice must be made between a greater gratification for the strong (itself a gratification poisoned by anxiety) and a restricted gratification for all men but in circumstances of security. The sages realized the need of "seeking what is feasible" in terms of the available priorities. "When the mind is anxious and afraid we can eat delicious food without tasting it, listen to glorious music without hearing it, see beautiful ceremonial garments without appreciating their beauty."[98]

It is from this insight that the founding sages arrived at the realization that the only way to curb the boundless desires and confine them within proper limits was to create and impose a clear system of rules of behavior, laws, and institutions (*li i fa tu*). It is clear from the outset that the word *li* is used in its very broad extension embracing all the status and roles of familial and political order as well as all the prescriptions of behavior embedded in these institutions. It is noteworthy that Hsün-tzu's stock term for the area of moral behavior is "*li* and righteousness." The order of words is not accidental. The "internalized" habit of acting "rightly" is an end product of the habitual practice of the prescriptions of *li*, which in Kao-tzu's terms are "external." It is also noteworthy that the *fa-tu* which points to directly coercive penal law and constraining institutions seem to go hand in hand with "*li* and righteousness." Since the object is to curb and limit men's self-interest from without, and since this is a difficult undertaking, one must use every means possible to achieve the goal. Hsün-tzu ardently dreams of a society in which the rules of *li*, which are rules which can in the best of worlds be internalized by education and moral suasion, will be the primary means for creating harmony and security, but he has no prejudice against the view that these must be strongly reinforced at all times by external penal rules and institutions which rely on physical coercion.

Unlike Hobbes, Hsün-tzu does not raise the question of how the sages manage to establish their authority.[99] It would seem to be a much more difficult question for him than for Mencius, whose frightened and disoriented people easily accept the charisma of the sages. The question, however, is not addressed. There is, of course, no need to wonder why Hsün-tzu, like Confucius and Mencius before him, simply assumes the need for hierarchy and authority. The good order can be inaugurated and maintained only by a vanguard elite. In Hsün-tzu's world, while most men share with the sages a mind with the bare capacity for understanding, the fact is that the vast majority seem incapable of exerting these capacities. One can hardly picture them reasoning their way through to a Hobbesian contract.

They may nevertheless somehow be made to realize that if security and peace are to be won, there must be a clear division of social labor and that this clear division, as in the family, necessarily involves a differentiated allotment of power, authority, access to material goods, and ritual roles.

To Hobbes, with his Western legalist background, all men come to realize the need for a "common power to keep them in awe" because "prudence is but experience which time equally bestows on men."[100] In a sense what they submit to is the abstraction of "sovereign power" which, of course, in actuality comes to be embodied in a hierarchy of living men or a monarch even though it might conceivably even take the form of a democracy. In the case of both Mencius and Hsün-tzu we deal not with an abstract "sovereignty" but a vanguard elite. The ongoing quality of the vanguard elite—however this quality is conceived—remains crucial from beginning to end. Here, Hsün-tzu remains profoundly Confucian. The good social order was not only inaugurated by sages. To the extent that it is based on "*li* and righteousness" it must continue to be based on the qualities of the elite, since *li* is a kind of law which can be actualized in society only by men who are able to actualize it in their own personal lives. The so-called Legalists will indeed arrive at the notion of a social-political system which "runs itself," but the heart of Hsün-tzu's Confucianism lies in the vehement resistance to just this Legalist notion.

The contrast with Hobbes remains striking. In Hobbes, the character of the bearer of "sovereign power" is not the issue and one does not expect to find a treatise on the "moral cultivation" of rulers in the *Leviathan*. Hobbes might prefer good monarchs to bad, but the heart of social order and the law which maintains it is the strength of the "Soveraigne Power" as such. Hsün-tzu, in spite of his emphasis on an externally imposed system, is thus passionately concerned with the education or self-education of those with a vocation to rule. All depends on it. "The law [*fa*] cannot stand alone. The various categories [of *li*?] cannot implement themselves. It is only when one obtains the [right] man that they can be actualized. Without the right man, they are lost. The law is the principle of good order. The noble man is the source of the law. Thus, if one has a noble man, even if the law is rudimentary, its effects will be widespread. If one does not have a noble man even if the law is full and detailed, it will lose its proper order and will not respond properly to changes in circumstances."[101] Thus, Hsün-tzu remains overwhelmingly concerned with the cultivation of noble men.

Having determined that civilized society can exist only when the desires of men are controlled, Hsün-tzu's sages and noble men begin with themselves. They set out from a general sociopolitical "philosophy" which explains the source of misery in the human world, but this inevitably leads them to understand that the task must begin with the effort to bring their own natures under control.

Noble men are thus motivated by the burning desire to acquire a deep knowledge of the cultural heritage which makes this self-mastery possible. "Wood is straightened by aligning with a rope and bent into a wheel by aligning it with the compass, and the metal sword is sharpened with the whetstone . . . The noble man acquires broad learning and tests himself daily. He will then become enlightened and commit no transgressions."[102] The constant stress on learning refers concretely to the cultural heritage embodied in the *Book of Documents, Book of Songs,* the study of *li,* and there is also mention of the testimony of history as embodied in the *Spring and Autumn Annals.*

Hsün-tzu's conception of learning is very close to that of the *Analects* and at least in this area he seems closer to the *Analects* than does Mencius. Learning in the literal sense is elevated to the level of a sacred enterprise. It certainly involves, as with Confucius, much more than fact-gathering. Fundamentally, it involves nothing less than the herculean task of mastering the anarchic forces of one's own nature. Only by exposing oneself to the true wisdom embodied in the cultural heritage can one acquire this power. One has indeed the sense that despite Confucius' insistence on the "unity" underlying all learning he would clearly have appreciated Hsün-tzu's emphasis on unremitting, cumulative concrete learning and might have been somewhat disconcerted by Mencius' "easy" confidence in his "intuitive" insights. Knowledge must be acquired from without. "If one does not climb the mountain, one cannot know how high the heavens are and if one does not gaze into deep ravines one cannot know the thickness of the earth. If one does not listen to the words handed down by the sage, one does not understand the greatness of learning."[103] Here one realizes that one of Hsün-tzu's main grievances against Mencius is his resentment of the latter's seemingly cavalier and debonair attitude to learning and unjustified belief that learning is "easy." The individual determined to learn has a steep path to climb. He does not simply rely on "book learning." One of the particular emphases of Hsün-tzu is his almost Zen-like concern with contacts with a true teacher who has, as it were, managed to embody "*li* and righteousness" within his own person. The teacher should be a stern master who is, at the same time, able to convey directly to his disciple the spiritual, almost "Taoist" self-assurance which he has managed to attain.[104] He does not simply communicate learning. He communicates his own being as an exemplar of the results of true learning.

There is here a firm faith that with the steadfast devotion to learning and the proper guidance of a true teacher, the man of true intelligence can mold himself to virtue and to the firm control of his own recalcitrant nature. "Piled up earth becomes a mountain and winds and rain arise therefrom . . . accumulated [habits] of goodness turn into virtue and numinous enlightenment is attained. The sage-like mind can then extend its influence over a thousand *li.*"[105]

When Hsün-tzu speaks in this vein one even wonders whether his "tough-minded" stance is not an armor used to defend a "tender-minded" Confucian core against the brutal trends of the time. It is, in fact, this genuinely optimistic faith that the "internalization" of the moral-cultural heritage may in the end lead some to the attainment of virtue which has led some to doubt that Hsün-tzu genuinely believed that "the nature is evil."

It must be repeated that Hsün-tzu is not Saint Augustine. Indeed not even all Judeo-Christian modes of thought which stress man's sinfulness necessarily deny the possibility of the triumph of goodness in the individual. Faith that moral education may lead to moral victory is by no means incompatible with the view that the battle is prolonged and arduous and the victory is won against enormous resistant forces within the human person. Heaven in Hsün-tzu has not provided us with any innate propensities toward the good but it has provided us with the "heavenly mind" which possesses the intellectual capacity to understand the human condition. This understanding even makes it possible for a few to actualize their powers of reason and to apply these powers both to the task of their own self-transformation and to the further transformation of society. Without such a vanguard able to actualize the "spirit of the *li*" within itself, the transformative power of *li* will never make itself effective in the society as a whole.

Even in this most "sociological" school of Confucianism, which seems to treat the *li* almost in the manner of Fingarette's holy rite, the "inner" quality of individual sages and noble men remains a crucial ingredient of the entire vision. It is an aspect of his doctrine to which Hsün-tzu clings with enormous tenacity. Indeed, the crucial question which he addresses to Mencius is this: if the nature is truly good, "Why does one require sage-kings and why does one require '*li* and righteousness'?"[106] It is precisely because the nature is evil that "the power of rulers was established above to oversee them and '*li* and righteousness' made manifest in order to transform them."[107] To be sure, the question grossly oversimplifies the complexity of Mencius' own position. Mencius, as we have seen, very much stresses the essential inertness of the potentiality for goodness in most human beings and he finds ample grounds in his system for the need for sages and noble men. Mencius might perhaps have countered with his own question. If all men have an equal capacity for learning and reasoning, why can only a select group actualize its intellectual powers? Hsün-tzu himself, after all, repeats the adage that the "man in the street can become Yü." He goes on to state that all men have the *capacity* to realize humanity and goodness. If they only *exerted* themselves to learn; if they would concentrate their entire will on thought and study and "unceasingly accumulate habits of goodness," they could actualize their capacities. "They can do it but they cannot be made to do it."[108]

We seem to have the same problem of the "failure of will" in both Hsün-tzu and Mencius. Let me suggest, however, a real area of difference between them. In one case we have a natural, dynamic tendency to growth no matter how weak and how easily "blocked off," and in the other we have bare intellectual capacity. There is nothing "plantlike" or organic in Hsün-tzu's latent intellectual capacity. It seems much closer to the concept of intellectual capacity that we find in the Mohist logic. In the logic the word "knowledge" (*chih*) in the sense of intelligence is defined as "capacity" (*ts'ai*). As Graham points out, the word derives from a word meaning "timber," which suggests a kind of inert raw material. In the Mohists it is only by an actual decision to think or reflect (*lü*), defined by the Mohist canon as "seeking" (there is a "seeking with the intelligence"), that one actualizes one's capacity.[109] There is here no suggestion of any innate dynamic which inertially leads one to reflect. The Mencian man of good will who is resolutely determined to act rightly is soon borne along, like the swimmer riding with the current, by his "heart of goodness" and his "well-nourished" *ch'i*. The task of self-cultivation does seem much "easier" in the case of Mencius, and there is a suggestion that even those who never become learned intellectuals may achieve righteousness albeit within the narrow confines of the commoner's existence. Yet though this possibility still very much depends on whether noble men are able to create a propitious environment, one has a sense that the common man's capacity to share the intellectual attainments of Hsün-tzu's sage is considerably less than his capacity to share the moral attainments of Mencius' sage.

In sharp contrast to Mencius, Hsün-tzu's ethic seems to be essentially utilitarian. The sages realize that all men can escape from a nasty and brutish existence only by devising the system of *li* and laws. They create those rules in order to assure all humans peace, security, and the *reasonable* satisfaction of their creaturely needs and desires. Here again we must remind ourselves, however, that both Confucius and Mencius are also deeply concerned with the peace and welfare of society as a whole and that both regard the noble man as an instrument for achieving these desirable goals. Their anti-utilitarianism manifests itself mainly in dealing with the sources of moral behavior within the individual. The general goals themselves depend on the pure motives of the ethical vanguard.

Hsün-tzu, on the other hand, seems willing to speak not only of the general welfare of society but even of the crasser goals of the state, wealth, and power, which were the overwhelming preoccupation of the rulers of his time.[110] Unlike the apocalyptic Mencius, we shall find that the achievement of relative order even by the use of methods which depart from Confucian ideals seems to Hsün-tzu desirable within the desperate circumstances of his times. To this extent he may indeed be called utilitarian. Unlike Mencius, he will not turn aside questions about the power and wealth of states even though he will always add a Confucian dimension to his answers.

In the end, however, Hsün-tzu's ethic of the noble man is not utilitarian. The sages may have set out from a self-regarding impulse to escape from wretchedness, but through their enormous intellectual exertions and insights they achieved complete success in internalizing within themselves the spirit of *"li* and righteousness." Thus, their own personal motivation, in the end, becomes basically "moral-spiritual." When we read Hsün-tzu's chapters on *li* and music, we find a deep "inner" devotion to "holy rite" and music which seems to carry him well beyond his appreciation of their social function. I am reminded of T. S. Eliot's view of the cultural heritage as that which stands between us and utter brutishness. In the face of Mohist and Legalist attacks on rites and music, he dwells in poetic terms on "the *li* which is serving life adorn our joys and in departing from the dead adorn our sorrows."[111] As in Western classicism, noble form elevates and by the same token humanizes all the experiences of life. Here we do indeed find Fingarette's conception of "holy rite" at the very heart of Hsün-tzu.

To be sure, the same *li* also serves to maintain and reinforce all distinctions among the social roles, ranks, and statuses of the social order, assigning to all of them their proper functions and forms and thus serving to assure the peace and harmony of society. Yet even here, from Hsün-tzu's point of view, which is, of course, that of the ruling elite, all the distinctions of *li* which help to articulate the good social order are themselves instruments in the whole orchestra in which each player, whatever his instrument, may come to savor his participation in the symphonic whole. It is in the Hsün-tzu that we find the explicit statement that while the significance of the sacrificial rites for the noble man is that it is the "way of man," for the common people it involves "the service of the spirits."[112] This does not mean that the noble man regards the sacrifice simply as instrumental to the preservation of social order. Rather, he regards the numinous or sacred element of the rite as lying within the rite itself. In both the case of noble man and commoners, the sacrifices have an aesthetic ethical and spiritual effect since even in the case of the common man the rites "perfect their customs" (ch'eng su).[113]

The cosmic dimension of li, which emerges in the chapter on li and which seems to reinforce the view that li is much more than a "socially functional" device, is somewhat surprising. It is a dimension which seems to run against any view that interprets Hsün-tzu's notion that "Man makes culture" to mean that culture is an arbitrary "conventional" (in the Greek sense of nomos) invention. In Chinese, the word wei, perhaps even in Hsün-tzu's time, seems to have had the sense of "man-made" or artificial in the pejorative sense. Yet here we find Hsün-tzu definitely linking the li to the larger cosmic patterns. "The heaven and earth are harmonized by it [the li]; the sun and moon are illumined by it, the four seasons derive their order from it, the stars and planets move by it, the rivers and streams flow through it, the ten thousand things flourish by it, good and evil are controlled by it, and joy and anger find their proper expressions through it."[114] Here the word li is elevated to the status of a principle of order governing both the cosmos and the human order. The Western idea of convention and contrivance suggests that what has been made might have easily been made in some other fashion. The Greek sophists looking at the variety of customs, "constitutions," and sociopolitical institutions available in the city-state world of their time might easily have conceived all of them as arbitrary inventions. To Hsün-tzu, however, the good order of society which he describes is the universal order of civilization. Hence, when we speak of the sages as "making it" or "forming it," we find that what they actually do is make manifest the overall pattern appropriate to the end of harmonizing the centrifugal tendencies found in the individual human organism. It may not be innate in the individual but it seems to be latently present in the objective cosmic order. The li is in essence a kind of "natural law" in the stoic and medieval sense. Like natural law, it is not self-enacting. Yet it would appear that what the ancient sages did in bringing the order of society into existence was not invent an arbitrary system of li but "discover" it by a process of arduous reflection. Again, one need not imagine here a Platonic realm of eternal forms and yet in some sense the *li* are part of the larger cosmic pattern and as such are much more than simply utilitarian devices. They are certainly not arbitrary conventions.

*Society and the Political Order*    Sages and noble men, having internalized the spirit of *li* in themselves and having triumphed over their own blind passions, are able to "create" and maintain order in society as a whole. The task, however, is formidable and even where "kingly" government is most successful, the practice of *"li* and righteousness" as methods of "socialization" will have to be generously supported and reinforced by rewards and punishments. The qualitative difference between constraints based on force and constraints based on *li* remains. Only through *li* can one *ultimately* subdue or transform the hearts of men.[115] But both types of constraints are external—that is, they are mechanisms for directing behavior imposed from outside. One uses whatever method is required to steam the straight wood into the rim of a wheel. In dealing with society as a whole, "teaching" must be supplemented, perhaps even in the best of times, by rewards and punishments. Ample incentives, in terms of material rewards and honors, must be bestowed on worthy officials since even men of virtue continue to cherish "creaturely" desires, however much these desires are governed and constrained by *"li* and righteousness." Without these incentives, most ordinary men will not wish to assume the burden of office.

We are, thus, not at all surprised to find that in sharp contrast to Mencius, Hsün-tzu brings a degree of relativism to bear in his judgment of the "hegemonic" (*pa*) conception of government.

When King T'ang of Shang and King Wu of Chou ruled, they were able to transform society fundamentally by inculcating *"li* and righteousness." The hegemonic ruler of later times, such as King Huan of Ch'i and the famous Kuan Chung, succeeded in establishing a system of calculable and objective penal law and a system of government based on calculable and predictable incentives to which they themselves remained faithful (*hsin*).[116] They were thus able to maintain the framework of a livable society. "Even though they had an eye to profit and loss, they did not deceive their people."[117] They were sufficiently able to control their own appetites and impulses to create a viable predictable system, albeit a system ultimately based on force. They were also able to apply the same principles of long-term self-interest to the realm of interstate affairs. They were, however, never able to attain the highest principles of government and were never truly able to "win the hearts of the people."[118]

Hsün-tzu's relative appreciation of the hegemons and of the contemporary Legalistic experiments of Lord Shang in the state of
Ch'in must, however, be seen very much in contrast to a third truly
evil model which he evidently regarded as the prevalent scourge of
his time—the government based on simple "scheming and plotting"
(ch'üan-mou).[119] Here one finds the arbitrary unbridled pursuit of
short-term "petty interests" by those in power.[120] Their pursuit of
wealth, power, and luxury is ungoverned by any respect for either li
or law whether in domestic affairs or in the interstate "balance of
power" game. Unlike the kings and hegemons, they will not allow
their impulses and caprices to be curbed by any system of either li or
law. In contrast to such contemporary misrule the hegemonic (or
Legalist) model seems to represent a step toward virtue. Hsün-tzu is
particularly bent on making the Confucian point that even this less
than perfect model requires a minimal moral foundation of mutual
trust between rulers and ruled.[121] The very machinery of punishment, rewards, and predictable rules requires a "state of mind"
based on expectations of predictable behavior by the ruler.

The same point is made with regard to military force, which
Hsün-tzu accepts as an inescapable fact of the times. The military
expert Lord Lin-wu, in a dialogue in the presence of King Ch'eng of
Chao, stresses variables such as topography, accurately observing
the plans and movements of the enemy, observing weather conditions, and strategies of deception. "These are the essential techniques for employing armies." Hsün-tzu replies, "Not so! I have
heard that according to the ancient way the fundamental principle
in employing armies and carrying on warfare was to unite the people. The essential in military affairs is to remain close to the people."[122] The morale of the people is fundamental, and with a people
and army that trusts its rulers and generals, all things can be ac-
complished. Thus, the very ability of rulers to employ legitimate
force in both domestic affairs and foreign wars depends on a certain
moral cement binding rulers and ruled.

While Hsün-tzu may not entirely despair of the emergence of a
"kingly" ruler in his time, he certainly has no apocalyptic expectations based on any view of Heaven's way in history. He is thus not
loathe to proffer "legalistic" advice alongside of his Confucian vision
or even to relate himself to the rulers' overwhelming obsession with
wealth and power. I agree entirely with Leon Vandermeersch that
Hsün-tzu is by no means a precursor of Legalism, since he is either a
contemporary or successor of some of that school's most important
founding fathers—men such as Lord Shang, Shen Tao, and Shen
Pu-hai.[123] He does incorporate what he regards as "correct" in their
teachings into the body of his Confucian outlook, even while fiercely

resisting what he regards as pernicious in their views. His relative approval of hegemonism seems to reflect their influence, although I do not agree with Vandermeersch that in Hsün-tzu the "ideas close to those of the Legalists appear like insertions into the interior of Confucianism which cut a rather strange figure within it."[124] Here it seems to me that Vandermeersch underestimates the ambivalences and problematic nature of the original vision of the *Analects* and, hence, of the possible variety of interpretations to which the vision lends itself. Confucius himself, as we have seen, had not entirely rejected the role of force and penal law in human affairs and had shown a certain ambiguity in relation to the hegemons. Hsün-tzu's "system" in fact provides a fairly plausible explanation of how he is able to accommodate Legalist elements within it. One might even say that his critique of Legalism, even before his alleged disciple Han Fei-tzu had constructed his grand Legalist synthesis, is a cogent Confucian criticism and one which is by no means totally "unrealistic."

Vandermeersch discusses the remarkable passage in which Hsün-tzu reports on his visits to Ch'in, where he witnessed the results of the reforms instituted by the famous Lord Shang (whom he does not mention). The whole system of draconian penal law was presumably in place, as was the system of advancement based on merit in both state and army. Hsün-tzu finds the "backwoods" Ch'in people simple and unspoiled. They fear and obey their government. The officials all do their work with dispatch and integrity. There are no factions and no corruption. The simple people seem to have the virtues of "the men of antiquity." Indeed, part of his point seems to be that the system works so well precisely because the "semibarbaric" people are so rustically simple. They have not experienced the higher values of civilization but neither have they experienced its corruptions. "Their music is not lascivious and their dress is not frivolous."[125] Having expressed great admiration for the Ch'in "methods," however, he goes on to remark that a state which completely eliminates the moral influence of the Confucian noble man is bound to lose in the end. He has, as we shall find, absolutely no objection to the meritocratic aspects of the system and is quite prepared to admit that strong penal law and rewards for merit are probably necessary in all times and places and more necessary in some circumstances than in others. Elsewhere, however, in a passage not cited by Vandermeersch, he goes on to observe that Ch'in is in a constant state of anxiety. Due to its extraordinarily aggressive foreign policy, it is in constant dread that the "world will unite to crush it."[126] Kings T'ang and Wu, in the sacred history of the past, had with their comparatively small states as a base been able to win the trust and confidence of the surrounding states and thus created a victorious alliance by winning the confidence of others. Thus, while rewards, punishment, and other external coercive methods may create a draconian order for a time within a society, when applied to an aggressive foreign policy (and the implication is that such is the only policy which can apply, since the regime's entire outlook eschews moral factors) they can lead only to disaster.

Hsün-tzu was not, of course, an accurate prophet and the Ch'in state was in fact to reunite the empire. If he had lived, however, he might conceivably have pointed to the amoral and inept "schemings and plottings" of the other states as the cause of this disaster. He would certainly not have been surprised by the quick demise of the Ch'in dynasty under the inept second emperor of that dynasty. The latter totally lacked the kind of minimal trustworthiness and self-control required to make even a Legalist system viable. Even a Legalist system requires the sustained moral basis of "faithfulness" (*hsin*). It is not automatically self-sustaining. One has the feeling, indeed, that Hsün-tzu uses the probity of the simple Ch'in "barbarians" as a foil in a manner similar to Plato's use of Sparta in his attacks on contemporary Athenian corruption. The Ch'in people, at least, have a naive "faithfulness" which responds to the trustworthy predictability of the Ch'in laws.

In all his praise of the hegemonic or even legalistic state, Hsün-tzu never wavers for a moment in his basic commitment to the higher ideal of the "kingly" state. He probably believed to the end that only a "kingly" state could truly reunite the world. He did not expect any heavenly assistance in bringing about the restoration of the good state, but given his faith in the sacred history of the past, he probably had no doubt that the basic model could be restored in the future.

It is, to be sure, true that even his view of the ultimate kingly system seems to involve some strikingly new emphases. His almost radical emphasis on the meritocratic principle is particularly striking, as is the considerable role which rewards and punishment seem to play even in his concept of the ideal state. One certainly has the impression that Hsün-tzu fully accepts the decline of the whole hereditary subnobility within the states of his time as well as the trend toward bureaucratic mobility. "The incapable must be dismissed without hesitation. The children and grandchildren of kings, dukes and high functionaries must be returned to the ranks of commoners if they cannot identify with *li* and righteousness; the children and grandchildren of commoners, if they are able to acquire true learning to correct their conduct and act according to the dictates of *li* and righteousness, must be elevated to the position of high ministers, ministers and officials."[127] Given the natures of men, however, the prospect that most will ever fully internalize the true spirit of *li* and righteousness is, statistically speaking, not very great. Hence, coercive sanctions for bad performance must be constantly available. On the other hand, even men of the highest moral attainment still have a strong desire for rank, wealth, and power and to the extent that these can be enjoyed within the bounds of the system of *li*, they have every right to expect generous rewards. Here Hsün-tzu could after all look for support beyond Mencius and Confucius to the texts of the *Book of Documents* itself which indicates no lack of reluctance on the part of King Wu and the Duke of Chou to stress the sanction of force. Within the good society the entire "rational" system of coercive social controls works well precisely because it is maintained by a government of noble men. "Without noble men it cannot be done."[128] The laws must be discussed and, one might add, mitigated according to circumstance, by judgments based on *li* and righteousness. "There are such things as good laws [again in the extended sense] going hand in hand with disorder. I have, however, never heard of having disorder where noble men are in charge."[129] Office, ranks, laws, and *li* must all be clearly defined and articulated, leaving no room for arbitrariness. Yet, in the end, all depends on the integrity of truly noble men.

It has often been said that the adaptation of Confucianism to the centralized bureaucratic model of government in the early Han dynasty was directly influenced by Hsün-tzu's conception of the "kingly system." Whether or not this is true (and the question of his actual influence in the early Han remains a matter of controversy), his view may point in the direction which would have made such an adaptation possible. He decisively shrinks the area of the legitimacy of hereditary prerogative and also legitimizes the idea that even the best of kingly states will not succeed in completely suppressing the need for sanctions of force.

Like Mencius, he does not, of course, completely nullify the hereditary principle. We have no reason to think that he anticipated a reunified empire which would in the end completely abolish the so-called feudal (*feng-chien*) system. He probably did not anticipate a fully "bureaucratized" empire. It is noteworthy that in his discussion of the elevation of commoners he does not include the ranks of kings and lords among the ranks to which they may hope to aspire. The notion that the highest instance of authority should ordinarily remain hereditary is here maintained, as it is indeed maintained even in the Legalism of Han Fei-tzu. On the other hand, the notion that sanctions of force must play a role even in the best obtainable Confucian order provides a Confucian (and not a Legalist) rationale for the entire evolution of legitimate penal law throughout the long history of official Confucianism.

It is possible in the Mencian vein to envision a Confucian "Republic" in which society is completely harmonized by the moral force of an ideal ruling vanguard. Even in such a society, the radiation of moral force would, of course, still be mediated through the sacred *li* and, as we have seen in Mencius, through appropriate sociopolitical institutions. Yet one can somehow envision in Mencius an ideal Confucian utopia. Like Plato of the *Laws*, however, Hsün-tzu does not seem to envision such a totally "ideal" society. In the words of Plato's *Laws*, "If a man were born so divinely gifted that he could naturally apprehend the truth, he would have no need of laws to rule over him for there is no law and order which is above knowledge. But there is no such mind anywhere or at least not much; and therefore we must choose law and order which are second best."[130] In Plato this represents a retreat from the high hopes of the *Republic*. His faith in producing through education a group of truly sagelike philosopher-kings—if he had ever truly believed it—has sadly declined, and the system based on a law which incorporates a kind of "external reason" is clearly regarded by Plato as "second best." The comparison with Hsün-tzu is instructive. Hsün-tzu has by no means lost his faith in the possibility of educating noble men. Unlike Plato, he believes that the history of the past provides abundant examples of the emergence of sages and noble men who, through education and self-education, rise to the highest potentials of their being. Plato, of course, continues to believe that some men may, through their intellectual powers, achieve the highest philosophic insight. What he now doubts is whether it is possible to turn such philosophers into kings. Hsün-tzu, however, has by no means given up his faith that noble men in the future as well as in the past may become rulers or at least the respected advisors of rulers.

I must, however, point out that Plato's *Laws* are much more broadly conceived than Hsün-tzu's "punishments and rewards" with their narrow stress on incentive mechanisms based on the pleasure-pain calculus. Plato's law in the *Laws* covers most areas of civil law, laws governing education, and even "rites" which are very much the equivalent of Chinese *li* and which are designed to produce the same educational effects as *li*. Indeed, as in Hebrew law, the law itself educates.

Why then does Plato regard the polis based on his *Laws* as "second best" while Hsün-tzu is willing to describe a "kingly system" which includes a heavy reliance on the sanctions of penal law and other institutional types of coercive control? A tentative answer might be that in the *Republic* Plato envisions a truly perfect polis in which, in Voegelin's words, the ruling stratum will consist of persons "in whose souls the order of the idea can become reality so fully that they, by their very existence, will be the permanent source of order in the polis," while in the *Laws* the citizens are "unable to develop the source of order existentially in themselves."[131] With the absence of faith in the capacity of "philosophers" to internalize the ideal order through education of the souls of men, any other way of promoting the order of society is "second best." Hsün-tzu, on the other hand, continues to believe fervently not only that noble men have in the past actually fulfilled their transformative-educative role in society, but can still do so in the present and future. The vast majority of men are, to be sure, resistant to transformation but they always have been, even under the sages of old. Hence, even the sages were prepared to reinforce their efforts to transform the people through *li* by supplementing *li* with incentives relying on rewards and punishments. It was precisely in an environment in which the people had reasonable expectations that good behavior would be rewarded and evil behavior punished, that it became possible for them to open themselves to the transformative-educative effects of *li*.

The fact that the recalcitrant material of the mass of men may never be totally transformable is far less important than the fact that sages and noble men *may* in the future, as in the past, bring their powers of soul to bear on society as a whole both through *li* and laws. Their spirit is embodied not only in the *li*, but in the laws as well. The fairness of the laws themselves, based on the principles of just deserts and a reliable predictability, reflects the probity of noble rulers. Even hegemonic rulers require the achievement of this minimal integrity but in the sage and noble man, his faithfulness in administering the "objective" penal and administrative law is simply one aspect of his total moral excellence which he has been able to achieve in the course of a lifelong self-education. Society may always resist total "kingly" transformation, but philosopher-kings in the Confucian sense are still possible.

*The Human and the Cosmic*    In this account of Hsün-tzu's social and political ideas there has been little reference to Heaven. This is consistent with the view that the shaping of the human order is entirely a human enterprise, even though it has already been noted that the *li* which play such a crucial role in human culture are in fact linked to the very patterns which govern the cosmic order.

The sharp bifurcation between Heaven and man has led some to see in Hsün-tzu almost an anthropocentric humanism of the modern Western variety and a sharp contradiction between nature and culture. Indeed, one might say that humans have little reason for gratitude to the Heaven or nature from which they derive their recalcitrant and unfortunate natures (hsing). The incalculable limitless libido which they derive from Heaven leads to all the anarchy and disorders of human society. This wu-wei aspect of man—his spontaneous natural tendencies—causes all his misfortunes. In striking contrast to Lao-tzu and Chuang-tzu, it is precisely in the specifically human aspect of man that Hsün-tzu seeks man's salvation. Man's deliberating, calculating, planning goal-directed mind—his ability to make and fashion (wei)—is his glory as man, just as the yu-wei moral will is at least one part of man's glory in Mencius.

Paradoxically, however, Hsün-tzu's conception of Heaven seems profoundly Taoist. He totally accepts Chuang-tzu's distinction between "that which Heaven does" and "that which man does."[132] He simply inverts Chuang-tzu's values. Heaven is, first of all, not providential. It does not concern itself with the fate of human individuals or collectivities. "Heaven is invariable in its actions. It is not present for Yao and absent for Chieh."[133] "It does not put an end to winter because man hates the cold. The earth does not put an end to the vastness of its dimensions because man hates long distances and the noble man does not suspend his action because small men are in an uproar."[134] Here, let me again note in passing the "cosmomorphic" analogic description of the sage and the noble man which we have already found at the heart of Taoism itself. The point I would stress here, however, is that Heaven pursues its spontaneous and wu-wei course without regard for man.

Hsün-tzu's view of Heaven is directed not only against the notion of Heaven as a "theistic" providential will, but also against the type of "correlative cosmology" (see chap. 9 below) which is already very prevalent in his time. Heaven does not resonate with and react to human affairs. And it does not reveal men's fortunes through the configurations of human physiognomy.[135] The aspects of Taoism which can be compared to "scientific" naturalism in the West are fully present in Hsün-tzu.

But the "naturalism" of both Lao-tzu and Chuang-tzu run in a direction opposite to that of a "scientific humanism." They would annihilate if they could the queer and anomalous human yu-wei consciousness (Chuang-tzu's "individualized mind") which isolates man from the flow of the *tao*. If this mode of rationality represents a consciousness which "science" requires, all the worse for science. Here, surely, Hsün-tzu may indeed be said to come much closer to the spirit of scientific humanism than anything we have met thus far. Heaven has no concern for man, but man by closely and consciously studying the regularities of Heaven or nature can take full advantage of them for his own conscious purposes. If men make proper provisions for meeting all the known vicissitudes of nature— floods, droughts, calamities of all sorts, and even unaccountable prodigies—then they will be performing their proper functions as men.[136] "Heaven has its seasons; the earth has its resources, man has his power to order things and it is thus that he participates in the activities of Heaven and earth. To abandon that by which he participates and to desire to possess that within which he participates is to lead to utter confusion."[137] Elsewhere we will find that it is Chuang-tzu who wishes to possess that "within which he participates." He aspires only to "know Heaven" in itself and to be one with Heaven.

Here we seem to find the paradigm of the positivist-technological orientation toward nature uncluttered by anything like Mo-tzu's providential view of Heaven's will. To the extent that such a perspective is dominant in the project of science, Hsün-tzu is a plausible forerunner of the scientific predisposition in ancient China. Yet in Needham's view, Hsün-tzu falls well below the Taoists as a precursor of a scientific attitude. He points out that Hsün-tzu's view may be all too positivistic-technological and that "he denied the importance of theoretical investigations."[138]

It is, of course, true that Hsün-tzu's science is based totally on the concrete observation of nature as it presents itself to us in ordinary experience. Having observed the patterns and regularities of Heaven and earth, one immediately "applies" this empirical knowledge to one's practical needs. As Hsün-tzu says with regard to the movement of the Heavenly bodies, the cycle of the four seasons, the transformations of *yin* and *yang*, and the ten thousand things in general, "One does not see their causes but one sees their outcomes. This is what we mean when we call it numinous [or mysterious, *shen*]. Everyone knows about their coming into being but no one knows their formless [origins] . . . That is why we call it Heaven. The sage does not seek to know Heaven."[139] For man's purposes it is not necessary to linger on the hidden springs of things although we know that all things spring from the unknowable *tao*. There is no need to look for a more "real" reality behind our directly experienced reality. We already know the basic observable, predictable patterns which can be relied on to serve human purposes.

Needham's observation is puzzling, since there is no evidence that either Lao-tzu or Chuang-tzu had any other view of nature. All their observations of nature are as much based on concrete experience as are those mentioned by Hsün-tzu and, as indicated, they seem—quite unlike the Mohists—to have no impulse whatsoever to seek out any hidden causes of things. Like Hsün-tzu, they are totally content to view the processes and entities of nature and their repetitive patterns as emerging out of the mysterious womb of the "formless." What Hsün-tzu attacks in them is not their faulty view of nature, which he on the whole accepts, but their mystical fixation on Heaven or the formless *tao* as an end in itself. They exalt Heaven and constantly meditate on it. They constantly extol Heaven. They contemplate the mysteries of the four seasons in aesthetic rapture. They desire to be at one with that from which things arise rather than deal with things when they are actualized.[140] Their view dwells on the mystical as an end in itself and ignores the practical.

In Hsün-tzu's eyes, the disposition of the Taoists is radically anti-technological and this is what divides him from them. If by "theoretical investigations" Needham means a search for "underlying" discrete causes of things, it would appear that neither Hsün-tzu, Lao-tzu, nor Chuang-tzu is concerned with such investigations.

I should add that while Hsün-tzu seems to possess a predisposition favorable to technology, there is nevertheless no evidence in the book of any great desire for technological innovation. Here again one may find the basic conviction that the technologies required for a decent life for all are already available in the world of his time and that the real problem is to remove those disorders of society and those distorted intellectual perspectives which prevent the people from fully and single-mindedly applying the knowledge which they already possess to the improvement of their lives.

Needham also charges that Hsün-tzu strongly objects to the "efforts of the logicians and the Mohists to work out a scientific logic."[141] While this statement is generally true, the question of Hsün-tzu's relation to the "language philosophy" of his time is much more complex than the remark implies. There is ample evidence in the chapter on "Correcting Names" (chap. 22) that he is remarkably familiar with some of the main issues discussed among the "logicians" and "sophists" of the time, and a good case can be made that on some issues he even shares the preoccupations of the Mohists.

While Hsün-tzu may be aligned with the Taoists in his view of Heaven, his defiant affirmation of man's *yu-wei* consciousness and his profound faith in the power of human conscious activity places him on this issue very much on the side of the Mohists. To the extent that the Mohist logicians were bent on defending the capacity of human language to constitute the true nature of the world and to vindicate our ordinary commonsensical experience, he is all on their side against the efforts of Hui Shih, Chuang-tzu, and perhaps the Kung-sun Lung-tzu to undermine our faith in ordinary experience.

While both the Mohists and Hsün-tzu are basically confident in their faith in the language we use to refer to the world of nature, they are both aware, as was Confucius before them, that the language of human and social affairs can become highly confused and problematic. Both are convinced that a truly correct language which provides a clear and unambiguous picture of both the natural and human world is a product of conscious human activity. What divides them fundamentally is Hsün-tzu's belief that such a language has already been created by both the people and the sage-kings of old, while the Mohists are profoundly convinced in the light of their innovative doctrine that such a true language is yet to be fully fashioned. Not surprisingly, not Hsün-tzu but the Mohists are pioneer innovators in this field. Yet clearly Hsün-tzu is quite prepared to draw on their categories to provide us with a more precise defense of what he considers to be the true language of the sage-kings even while he attacks many of the Mohists' substantive doctrines.

For Hsün-tzu to treat language as a conscious human creation is consistent with his outlook. His view that it is a human creation leads him to adopt the view that there is no "inherent" relation between the sounds of words and their meanings. The names of the "ten thousand things" arose out of meanings attached by the ancients over the course of time to various sounds by a process of conventional agreement (yüeh). As for the names of categories of institutions, ranks, laws, and li, the lucid minds of the sage-kings made it possible for them to assign all these categories of experience to their proper classes, categories, and relations, and once they had done so they conventionally assigned certain meanings to certain sounds. "A name has no inherent appropriateness. One names by establishing a convention. Once the convention is fixed, the usage becomes established and we call it appropriate."[142] The sage-kings, Hsün-tzu would have us believe, not only affixed names to the objects of our common experience but also devised all the categories and classes which allowed them to assign words to their proper levels of reference. Thus when it was appropriate to refer to the features which all "ten thousand things shared in common," they used the highly abstract common name "thing" to refer, one would presume, to the highly abstract property of being a determinate something as such. Thus, the word "thing" is "a common name." When one wishes to differentiate animals and birds from things in general, one uses the term "birds and beasts" as classes which point to differentiating properties from the point of view of "things" in general, but refer to the common properties of birds and beasts (for example, the fact that they are living).[143]

Now in all this discussion of the theory of classification it is apparent that Hsün-tzu owes much more to the Mohists than he does to the sage-kings of old. Yet it remains his fundamental conviction that the establishment of a clear and unambiguous language had been primarily the work of the sage-kings and that his own doctrine based on his own definitions provides the authentic interpretation of that language. Nevertheless, the Mohists and logicians seem to have enormously enriched his awareness of logical categories.

Hsün-tzu believed not only that the sages had clearly established the fundamental logical categories and classes but that they had also solved the problem of applying them to reality so that what they had bequeathed was a complete map of social reality. The Mohist "logicians" were also striving to establish a complete coherent normative language, but the remains of their writings give the impression of a project underway and we thus have a sense of an on-going effort to create a new and "more accurate" language. Since they confront reality as a plural world of separate problems, they are very much interested in finding particulate causes for separate realities and in applying this interest to their investigations in the area of natural science. In confronting their opponents they also actively apply their logical methods. Hsün-tzu does not follow the Mohists either in their concern with optics, mechanics, or other "natural sciences," or in their enthusiastic effort to apply their logical principles to the art of argument.

Indeed one finds that in dealing with the "fallacies" of the Mohists and the "sophisms" of Hui Shih and Kung-sun Lung-tzu, Hsün-tzu does not really engage in argument. He simply indicates how their propositions diverge from the true picture of reality provided by the sage-kings. In dealing with the Mohist proposition that "to kill a robber is not to kill a man," he does not enter into the involved argument which lies behind this proposition. The Mohist proposition is based on the Mohist refutation of the objection that if one is to love all men universally, as the Mohists maintain, one should not kill robbers since robbers are men. The Mohist counterargument is that while robbers are men, the particular differential properties which make them robbers are such that one must base one's action on this differential property of being robbers rather than on the common property of their humanity if the interests of mankind in general are to be served. One must kill them precisely because they are robbers and not because they are men. To Hsün-tzu, however, who has evidently not examined the background of the proposition or refuses to consider it, this simply is a case of "using terms to confuse terms." Everyone knows that a robber is a man and in his particular view of humanity, there is absolutely no difficulty about killing someone called a man. While we have found in Mencius' debate with Kao-tzu an actual example of "applied logic," one does not find it in the chapter on "Correcting Names." Basically, Hsün-tzu applies, in this chapter, the same method for refuting wrong views which we find in many other passages. He provides an epitome of the essential heart of the view which he is attacking and points out how it diverges from the all-encompassing truth of Confucianism as he understands it. Since he is a man of remarkable intelligence, the epitomes are often shrewd and penetrating. His attitude toward "logic" is that the sages in their cogitations had not only developed whatever logic was required for their needs but had already embedded it in a language which provided a complete and comprehensive map of reality.

Although Hsün-tzu is entirely convinced that he possesses a perfect language which resolves all problems, I would suggest that there remain difficult questions yet to be considered in dealing with his doctrine of the relation of Heaven and man. Is it indeed true that he has clearly differentiated the "functions" (shih) of Heaven and the functions of man?[144]

Heaven, we have seen, is immanent in the human organism in the form of the latter's recalcitrant nature. We are, however, surprised to find that in speaking of the mind—the organ of deliberate consciousness and presumably the center of that which differentiates man from Heaven—Hsün-tzu suddenly calls it "the heavenly ruler," thus implying that in some sense Heaven is immanent in the mind itself.[145] When we look more closely, we find an extremely subtle and difficult analysis of the relation of Heaven to the human mind. What the sage ultimately attains through his powers of reason is a comprehensive, impartial, "unbeclouded" view of reality. He totally understands that the human deliberative consciousness is a frail if precious possession. Not only can it be easily drowned in passion, it can easily become obsessed with some one lopsided aspect of reality which totally "beclouds" the grasp of the whole. "The sage knows that the great calamity in the mind's pursuit of true method is that the mind will become beclouded and obstructed."[146] How does the sage maintain a transcendent overview? How does man truly know the Way?[147] The answer is "through emptiness, unity and quietude. The mind has never ceased to accumulate and yet it has what is called emptiness. It has never ceased to have different thoughts and yet it is pervaded with what is called unity. It has never ceased to be in motion and yet it has what is called quietude."[148]

All of these "Taoist" attributes somehow manifest themselves at the very heart of the sage's conscious life. The sage plunges actively into the world of reflecting, reasoning, intending, and planning. He is not like the sage-king of Huang-lao Taoism who simply sees the whole picture in a flash through his synoptic intuition. Yet somehow he manages to establish and maintain contact with the inner nature of the *tao*. Indeed, the mind of the sage "embodies the *tao*." Hsün-tzu describes a state of clear enlightenment in which "among the ten thousand things there is no form which one does not see . . . sitting in one's room one sees the four seas; located in the present one sees all eternity."[149] One presumes that this sort of gnosis is arrived at only after supreme intellectual effort and yet it is also suggested that somehow "emptiness, unity, and quietude" are a necessary precondition of a truly "objective" grasp of reality. Somehow, we find here a dimension of the mind of the sage or noble man which seems to carry him far beyond his rational intelligence. There is thus a level of the mind of sages which actually assimilates the human to the heavenly and by doing so gives a transcendental dimension to the human intelligence itself. In the mind of sagelike men, the abyss between man and Heaven, now conceived of in very Taoist terms, is somehow bridged.

Here one suddenly perceives a truly Taoist dimension of Hsün-tzu. Yet in fact he remains a Confucian. His sages and noble men do not escape the need for unremitting intellectual and moral effort and for accumulating new knowledge, as is true of Confucius in the *Analects,* who also had already had a kind of intuition of the unity which lies behind all learning. His emptiness, unity, and quietude simply assure that the "knowledge already acquired does not harm the knowledge yet to be received."[150] Because his mind is unblocked and unbeclouded—truly objective—he can fit all new knowledge into his comprehensive perspective. Indeed, Hsün-tzu is himself thus able to incorporate insights drawn from Legalism, Mohism, and all sorts of perspectives into his synoptic Confucian framework.

Hsün-tzu's sages and noble men nevertheless still have links to the frailties of their unruly, creaturely nature. The mind is called the "heavenly ruler" and in its relations to the passions and sensual lusts of its own body it must assume the role of an active earthly ruler. It issues commands which the body must obey. To be sure, one must assume that the human who achieves a state of emptiness, unity, and quietude soon achieves a complete victory over his own infirmities.

Thus, we find that, in the end, Heaven is present not only in the recalcitrant forces of human nature but also—in mysterious ways—in the human mind itself, which is the very instrument of salvation. Beyond this presence of Heaven in the mind, we have already noted that the "objective" order of society embodied in *li* and law is also on some level embedded in the order of Heaven and that in fashioning the human order the sages do not freely invent but actually make manifest a universal pattern somehow already rooted in the ultimate nature of things. Hsün-tzu's sage most definitely does not, like Nietzsche's superman, freely "create values."

Yet despite this surprising "Taoist" dimension, the original impression of the human being as an ill-adjusted organism does not disappear. Heaven is still present in the individual's human recalcitrant nature. It is immanent or potentially immanent in the human mind; it is also immanent even in the pattern of the normative order actualized by the sage, and yet one might say that the area of non-immanence is the area where all these categories interact. Within the confines of this space, the conscious mind, particularly the conscious mind of sages and noble men, must undertake their enormous *yu-wei* efforts to win control over themselves and over the human environment. Through their minds they can draw on the power of the "emptiness, unity, and quietude" of the *tao*, but their responsibility remains awesome. Hsün-tzu's noble men are less inclined than either Confucius or Mencius to rely on the mysterious and utterly inscrutable ways of Heaven in history. "Are order and disorder due to Heaven?" The answer is that "the calculations of the positions of stars, moon and planet are the same for the virtuous emperor Yü and the villainous King Chieh. Yü responded to them by creating order. Chieh responded to them by creating disorder."[151] The noble man must thus remain an indefatigable activist who does everything possible to advance the cause of order. Like the Mohist worthy man, he cannot hold back from giving advice to anyone. He must be thoroughly abreast of current affairs and much more flexible than the purist Mencius in the advice which he proffers as a statesman. Where a situation is completely unfavorable to "kingly government" he can try to persuade the ruler that, at the minimum, the only way he can achieve some headway in his narrow pursuit of wealth and power is by establishing an honest "hegemonic" government. If not "used," his ultimate solace seems to lie in the Taoist dimension of "clear enlightenment" which he can find in the inner depths of his own "heavenly" mind.

*False Doctrines*    Hsün-tzu takes seriously the responsibility of refuting false doctrine and the perversions of language which encompass

him on all sides. As in the case of Mencius, false doctrines and social
disorder are two sides of the same coin. Given his more intellectualist
bent, however, he is more prepared to see intellectual failure as a
cause of ethical perversity as well as the reverse relationship, although in his chapter on "Getting Rid of Beclouding" he does discuss the role of vicious passions in distorting the mind.

As a member of the Chi-hsia Academy, Hsün-tzu was thoroughly
familiar with the dominant tendencies of his time even though his
reading of these trends was somewhat different from that of the
"World" chapter in the Chuang-tzu. Like the author of the "World"
chapter, however, he knows nothing of the doxographic categories of
the early Han and treats the trends he discerns wholly in terms of
various individuals who are their advocates.

He generally treats these tendencies by epitomizing what he regards as their central assumptions. In dealing with aberrant trends
within the Confucian camp, however, with the exception of his
treatment of Mencius, he uses another method. He simply provides
us with acid thumbnail sketches of the "life-styles" of those who
have drastically perverted the Master's conception of the noble man.

In one chapter, however, (18, "On Correcting Falsehoods") he
does carry on a sustained argument against certain particular "vulgar ideas" widely circulating in his time.[152] Consider, for example,
the two propositions of Sung Hsing which he refutes: (1) "that if
men did not feel disgraced when insulted, there would be no strife
among men"; and (2) "that the essential desires of men are few." He
argues concerning (1) that even Sung Hsing admits that men hate to
be insulted but he believes that they can feel hate without feeling
disgraced. However, when men feel hatred, they have an impulse to
strike out against those whom they hate. Hence, anything that
arouses hatred will arouse strife. There may be those, of course, who,
for temperamental reasons, feel no such hatred, but whatever
arouses hatred will lead to strife. Since a chaotic society is full of a
multitude of occasions for hatred, the notion of eliminating strife by
not responding to insults is a delusion. What is more important, the
sage-kings do not base their conception of good order on eliminating
the passions but on the channeling and confining of passions. By establishing a normative order in which what is truly honorable is
honored and what is truly disgraceful is disgraced, the sages use the
hatred of disgrace and the love of honor to good purpose.[153]

Similarly, with regard to the notion of the paucity of human desires (2), he has Sung Hsing admitting that the human senses naturally desire gratification. To admit that the senses desire
gratification and yet to posit that there are limits to such desires is

like "loving female beauty and hating Hsi-shih [the famous paragon of feminine beauty]."[154] Again, the sages accept the insatiability of the desires in men ungoverned by *li,* and, to the extent that they rely on incentives of rewards and punishments, they channel and confine these desires in the service of higher ends. These arguments may be more or less persuasive, but they are not typical of his basic method.

His thumbnail sketches of false tendencies in the Confucian camp are devastating. How could he defend the true heritage when so many were distorting the Master's message? He thus heaps scorn on the followers of Tzu-hsia and Tzu-yu, who seem to resemble the Confucianists we have met in the book of Mo-tzu. Like them, he himself cherishes *li* and the assiduous study of the Confucian heritage yet his description is contemptuous. "Their clothes and caps are neatly arranged; their demeanor is grave. They are retiring and spend days without uttering a word such are the unworthy *ju* of the Tzu-hsia school. Shirking their duties and shamelessly gorging on food and drink—grandly proclaiming that noble men do not exert their strength, these are the unworthy *ju* of the Tzu-yu school."[155] As against these and other perversions, Hsün-tzu closely identifies with Confucius' disciple, Tzu-kung, who was profoundly versed in *li* and music but was also an active vigorous statesman immersed in the affairs of his time and well versed in the practice of government. The doubts expressed in the *Analects* about his excessive worldliness and ambition find no echo here. Here we find the true noble man who "in times of ease is not indolent and in times of urgency is completely alert. In dealing with the fundamentals and responding to changing circumstances, he always does what is appropriate."[156]

Mencius is treated more seriously in terms of his doctrinal errors. His teaching that the nature is good undermines the imperative to learn. I have already dealt with the obvious question of why, if the nature is good, are sage-kings and noble men required at all. There are, in fact, serious Mencian answers to such questions. Yet the questions do nevertheless point to significant differences of outlook fraught with practical consequences. "Learning" does not emerge in Mencius as the arduous and demanding enterprise which it is in Hsün-tzu. "The nature of man is without *li* and righteousness and man must strenuously engage in learning in order to seek to obtain them."[157] One imagines that education of children for Hsün-tzu would be based on a stern discipline which would not spare the rod. Ceremonies and punishments would go hand in hand even though the humanizing effects of *li* might, in the end, win the upper hand. It would appear that to Hsün-tzu, completely devoid of the apocalyptic strain, Mencius' preachments to the rulers of his time to contact the roots of goodness in their own hearts would seem futile—and thus would simply convince the unsympathetic that Confucianism bore little relation to reality.

His epitomization of the beclouded and one-sided views of other thinkers are shrewd if highly simplified. The hedonist, Wei-mou, simply gives intellectual sanction to his own lusts and pleasures. He is so completely beclouded that he does not realize that his mode of behavior would mean the destruction of all the principles of human civilization.[158] Mo-tzu's enormous emphasis on unadorned utility and austere frugality completely ignores the crucial role that *li* play in civilizing the human passions and establishing the symbolic base of the order of society.[159] Chuang-tzu is obsessed with Heaven, or rather with becoming one with Heaven, and does not know man. He overlooks the fact that it is only by acting as a man that one knows Heaven.[160] Hui Shih and the other "sophists" attempt to undermine our faith in the true normative language created by the sage-kings of old. They clearly insinuate that this language does not describe the world as it is and, hence, would annihilate all the categories and distinctions which make the normative social order possible.[161]

Perhaps most insidious of all, in the context of the time, is the doctrine of Shen Tao, who "is beclouded by the law and knows nothing of worthy men."[162] Shen Tao, as we have seen, dreams of a system of impersonal laws and institutions maintaining the sociopolitical order, an order which would render totally superfluous the role of moral agents—of sages and noble men—in human affairs. In Hsün-tzu's indignant words, "He exalts law and is without law."[163] The law which he seems to disdain is probably the law of *li*—a moral law which the noble man imposes in the first instance on himself. "He despises self-cultivation and has a predilection for creating [new] laws."[164] The ancient laws of *li* which Shen opposes are connected with the belief in the power of men to moralize themselves and then to moralize society. They are laws of life which depend on a belief in the vital role of human actors in creating a moral social order. Shen Tao, in the truly antitraditional spirit of Legalism, would—one presumes from the fragments—create a whole new system of impersonal criminal and administrative law which, by relying on a kind of behavioristic model of man, would make "worthy men" entirely dispensable. With such a system in place he would simply "acquiesce to that imposed from above and follow along with the prevailing customs below."[165] The fierce moral autonomy of the Confucian noble man would disappear. It is thus that Shen Tao can picture himself as the inert passive clod described in the last chapters of Chuang-tzu.

In all of his criticisms, Hsün-tzu seems to depart from an Olympian confidence in his own unbeclouded vision of reality. In part, this confidence reflects his sense of his own ability to incorporate whatever element of truth there may be in the one-sided views which he treats into his large Confucian synthesis. In dismissing them he always adds the observation "that they have reasons for what they maintain and their words seem sufficiently reasonable to deceive and confuse the ignorant mass of men."[166] He is able to absorb whatever is "reasonable" in them into his own synthesis. He thus ultimately remains supremely confident of the objective "emptiness" of his own mind.

And yet, despite this appearance of confidence, one feels a certain note of desperation in the vehemence of his defense of Confucianism against the rising tide of what was later called Legalism. Here, too, as Vandermeersch points out, he had incorporated what he could of its message but at bottom what he is really defending against them is the bastion of his belief in the capacities of noble men as moral agents and of the relevance of these capacities to social order, as opposed to a simple "behaviorist" model of man which was becoming ever more alluring. In arguing that no techniques of war will work without a basis in troop morale, that no system of penal laws and incentives will work without a basic attitude of trust, what he is defending is the very notion of the relevance of Confucian moral self-cultivation. The currents of the "men of worth" of the time were strongly against him. An anonymous disciple complains bitterly of the lack of appreciation for his wisdom in an age when "*li* and righteousness made no headway and the efforts to carry out a transformation through teaching could not succeed."[167] The fact that his disciple, Li Ssu, was to become the chief Legalist minister of Ch'in Shih Huang-ti, the founder of the Ch'in dynasty, indicates the difficulty of making even this most "realistic" defense of Confucianism plausible to intelligent young thinkers of the time. Li Ssu directs to his teacher a most challenging observation. "The Ch'in have been victorious for four generations. Their army is powerful. Within the four seas, their power over-awes the princes. They do not accomplish this by humanity and righteousness. They do it by conducting their affairs according to what is most useful and expedient [*pien*]."[168] Hsün-tzu replies that their conception of what is truly useful is narrow and short-sighted—that, in the end, only a government able to win the love of the people by benevolence and righteousness can win their unstinting allegiance. In fact, Ch'in is in constant mortal fear that the other states will unite to crush its power. Unlike King Wu, Ch'in cannot possibly win the allegiance and affections of the surrounding states, all of which cordially hate it.[169] To the ambitious young Li Ssu, the contemporary facts of history do not seem to support his Master's case.

# CHAPTER 8

# LEGALISM
## The Behavioral Science

---

THE TERM "LEGALISM" has already figured prominently in the discussion of Huang-lao Taoism and of the book of Hsün-tzu. Let me now focus attention directly on the stream of thought to which the term has been applied.

The Western term "Legalism" has become the conventional translation of the Chinese *fa-chia* (school of *fa*) and I shall continue to use it despite its misleading connotations. The use of the word is essentially based on the fact that the Chinese word *fa* is often translated as "law," although a good case can be made that in many of the ancient texts which we are considering this is often a highly misleading translation.[1]

Like the term *tao-chia* (translated as Taoism), the term *fa-chia* is a creation of the Han doxographers applied retrospectively to a variety of pre-Ch'in texts. Like the former, its first attested use is to be found in Ssu-ma T'an's "Essential Points of the Six Schools." My concern here is not with the term but with the question of the coherence of the various texts to which the term has been applied.

In dealing with the word *fa* I must, in fact, begin with a consideration of its many semantic extensions in the ancient texts, since they may all be relevant to the deepest assumptions of the Legalist outlook.

The meaning which figures most prominently in the most ancient texts—particularly in the book of Mo-tzu—is something like "model" or "standard." It is a meaning which is often closely linked to such stock metaphors as that of the carpenter's square and compass and the builder's plumb line. Yet in a characteristically Chinese fashion the model or standard is very often the model not of an object but of a pattern of behavior. It appears only twice in the *Analects*. Here too the meaning of standard or general model seems to apply in one case while law may apply to the other. When Confucius speaks of his own behavior at the age of seventy as never deviating from the carpenter's square, he is in effect describing something like the *fa* of his own behavior in this sense. Mo-tzu speaks of the ruler's behavior as providing a *fa* for the nobles and officials. From this meaning one can readily derive the verbal meaning of the word as copying, imitating, or "modeling oneself on." One can also see how the term comes to be extended to mean a prescriptive method or *techne* designed to describe the rules of a craft or political techniques designed to control social behavior.[2] In a broader extension of meaning and often compounded with other words (*fa-tu, fa-chih*), it seems to refer to complex networks of relations which probably mean something like "institutions" or "systems" of patterned behavior.

It still remains possible that in its original meaning, the word *fa* may have referred to penal law and it is often closely associated with the more specific word *hsing*, undoubtedly meaning "punishment" or penal law.[3] *Hsing*, however, also has its own intriguing etymological associations. The graph is often used in ancient texts interchangeably with its homonym *hsing* meaning "form," suggesting that the two words are somehow closely associated in origin. How then, in both cases, may words associated with penal law come to be linked with words meaning model or form? One is tempted to speculate that the penal law is here envisioned as a kind of mold forcibly imposed from above to correct the aberrant behavior. Vandermeersch ingeniously suggests that the punishments were thought of as means of "re-forming" men.[4] He interprets this quite literally, however, as referring to the famous five mutilatory punishments (cutting off noses, feet, etc.) but it might be interpreted somewhat less literally as referring to the reshaping of behavior brought about by the application of penal law. A carpenter's square, when used to shape a shapeless material, brings a form into being, reminding us of the tropes we find in both Lao-tzu and Mencius of the injury caused to natural materials by the "carving out" of artifacts ("cutting of wood to make bowls").[5] Thus from the very outset, there may cling to both words lingering connotations of patterns or models forcefully imposed from above.

To be sure, to Confucius and Mencius, compasses, squares, and *fa* are not patterns forced on men—or at least on noble men. They are standards or normative patterns to which noble men conform themselves. Confucius conforms himself to the carpenter's square. Mencius clearly states, quoting a well-known saying, that "virtue alone is insufficient for ruling; the *fa* [probably in the broadest sense of normative rules and patterns of behavior—even including the *li*] cannot carry themselves into practice."[6] In this significant passage, penal law (*hsing*) is mentioned as one of the subcategories of *fa* which cannot be implemented where the virtue of rulers does not prevail. "Noble men will violate the dictates of righteousness and small men will violate the penal laws."[7] Creel suggests that while the word *hsing* certainly meant "penal law" from the very outset, the primary meaning of the term *fa* in most texts is model or technique.[8] With the rise of Legalism, with its orientation toward the forcible imposition not only of penal law but of institutional models of all sorts, it is possible that the coercive connotation of the word *fa* is very much reinforced.

To the extent that the term *fa* comes to be associated with *hsing* or "penal law" or even techniques of control and institutional devices coercively imposed, it is difficult to believe that those below develop any strong sense of identification with *fa*. In the ancient Middle East where codes of positive law such as the Code of Hammurabi are strongly concerned with civil and commercial law, it is entirely possible that, despite the heavy penal sanctions often attached to these laws, the people who were constantly involved in civil and commercial transactions may have developed a certain appreciation of the positive role of law in their lives. Within the city-state context, the ruler such as Hammurabi might under such circumstances have gained genuine legitimation from his role as promulgator of the legal code. Han Fei-tzu will indeed argue that while "the people's nature is such that they delight in disorder and do not cherish the law," the ruler will in the end be able to prove to them that their own long-term interests will be best served by a system based on a draconian code of penal law.[9] The people do not understand their own ultimate needs any more than the wailing infant can be made to understand the pain inflicted when the parents lance the abcess on his head.[10] Given the substantive content of *fa* whether conceived of broadly as representing coercively imposed institutions or penal law, Han Fei-tzu has no illusion that the bulk of the population can immediately be persuaded to love the law or accept it willingly.

## Anticipations of Legalism

In my consideration of the *Book of Poetry* and the *Book of Documents* I have treated these texts as essentially proto-Confucian in outlook. While this remains basically true, it must nevertheless be pointed out that a certain dichotomy which emerges as central to the early Confucian vision is not as sharply drawn in these texts (particularly in the authentically pre-Confucian section of the *Book of Documents*).

The sharply drawn antithesis between a society based primarily on the spiritual-moral cement of *li* and a society based primarily on sanctions of force is, as we have seen, central to the Confucian outlook. To the extent that *li* is conceived of as a body of prescriptions *ideally* based on noncoercive bonds, to the extent that it is conceived of as finding its ultimate source in moral impulses which have their roots in living individuals, in a truly good society the need for penal sanctions and external compulsion will not be thoroughly eliminated, but will certainly be minimized. In the *Book of Documents,* however, passages attributed to King Wu and even to the Duke of Chou indicate that the use of force in a "righteous" cause is by no means deprecated. It is indeed difficult to believe that in historic fact the conqueror of the Shang and the statesman who quelled the threat of rebellion against the newly formed Chou dynasty could have been strongly averse to force as such, despite the strenuous later efforts of Confucius and Mencius to minimize and mute the positive role of "just" force in their moral outlook. Thus in the "Announcement to K'ang" we find the young prince K'ang, who has been charged with founding the new principality of Wei[1], being admonished to adhere faithfully to the penal code of the Shang dynasty and to punish severely all manner of crime and all forms of official malfeasance.[11] He is admonished to adhere strictly to the provisions of the penal code and not to follow his own "inclinations."[12] If he does so, then his punishments will be "righteous punishments" (*i hsing*). Even more significantly, he is admonished to use the full severity of law against the unfilial and the unfraternal so that penal sanctions are introduced into the very heart of the familial network where the bonds of family morality should reign supreme. Passages such as these will indeed in later ages provide canonical sanction for including in the official legal codes the most horrendous penal sanctions for violations of family morality. It is quite clear that the early Chou rulers were not at all reluctant to support the "holy rites" with heavy penal sanctions. The virtue of the rulers was manifested as much in their righteous punishments as in the power of their moral influence. The Confucian revulsion against force as such still lay in the future. While the reliance on force and penal law is, we shall find, only one aspect of Legalism, it is an aspect which is thus able to draw on a much older tradition of candidly accepting the role of force in the social order—a tradition whose traces can be found even in the canonical texts themselves.

In the history of the Spring and Autumn period so vividly depicted in the *Tso-chuan*, one notes many tendencies leading in a proto-Legalist direction. While Confucius' own outlook represents a basic rejection of the proto-Legalist "trends of the times," the pages of the *Tso-chuan* depict many pre-Confucian statesmen who seem, on the contrary, quite prepared to accept what seem to them to be the imperative demands of the times. As active state officials, they direct their attention to the problem of the survival or ascendancy of the states which they serve. I shall not dwell on the famous Kuan Chung who, as a minister of Ch'i, was clearly prepared to use the sanction of force in international affairs and was also credited with a series of proto-Legalist reforms within the borders of Ch'i itself.[13] He is, in fact, treated in much of the later literature as a forefather of Legalism and the impressive early Han compilation, the *Kuan-tzu*, which includes a strong Legalist component, was later to be attributed to him.

Something more should be said, however, concerning the image of Tzu-ch'an, who was an older contemporary of Confucius himself. Tzu-ch'an is depicted in the *Tso-chuan* as one of the wisest men of his time and also as a leading statesman in the small ancient state of Cheng, which was under constant threat of extinction by its powerful neighbors, Ch'u and Chin. He is depicted as a man who exemplifies the virtuous practice of *li* in his personal life, and as such, he enjoys the admiration of Confucius himself. Yet as an active statesman he is depicted as single-mindedly bent on assuring the survival of Cheng. While Confucius no doubt regards the preservation of ancient states as a value, he basically looks at the rise and fall of the states of his time from his more universalistic and moralistic perspective. Since they are all bereft of the *tao*, their fortunes and misfortunes seem to have little relevance to the moral task of the age. Tzu-ch'an, however, as an active statesman deeply committed to the survival of his state, no longer seems to believe that the sincere practice of *li* can alone secure the survival of his state. Within the boundaries of his state, the bonds of *li* had not prevented murderous and anarchic conflicts among the members of the dominant lineages and local nobility. Anarchy was also evidently rife among the people, and the people's productivity, one gathers, had been disrupted by a chaotic agrarian situation. The sketch of Tzu-ch'an's reform program which we find vaguely described in the *Tso-chuan* in some ways seems to anticipate the fully developed Legalist programs of later times and the entire account may reflect later embellishments of the story. The overall aim is to strengthen the authority and power of the ruler against all the centrifugal forces which were debilitating the state. While the hereditary nobles would in his program continue to act as functionaries, they would be chosen on the basis of merit and were to adhere strictly to the rules governing their offices and ranks. A greater control was to be achieved over the economic resources by "clearly demarcating the lands of the people."[14] The people were to be organized into "mutually responsible groups" and the penal laws were to be made public by being inscribed on bronze tripods, thus finally assuring law and order on the grass-roots level by a reliance on strict penal law.[15] By such measures, the state of Cheng might at least be able to survive as an entity even though remaining a satellite of the neighboring great power of Chin.

We have no record of Confucius' response to this entire program. We do, however, have a record of a response to the "making public" of the penal code by the statesman of the neighboring state of Chin, Shu Hsiang, whose views seem to parallel those of Confucius, and we also have recorded in the *Tso-chuan* a later protest by Confucius himself against a similar later reform in the state of Chin.[16]

The issue involved in the "publication" of the penal code is ostensibly the following: So long as the penal law remains in the secret archives of the state, those who administer the code are free to employ their own private judgment and their own moral discretion in applying the codes to the infinite variety of human situations. They are thus able to exercise their moral judgments. Shu Hsiang even says that "the ancient kings deliberated about the nature of particular circumstances and did not make codes of penal law."[17] However, since heinous crimes could not be prevented, they did finally create penal codes, but in relating to the people they basically relied on the power of the *li*—on humanity and righteousness. What the people relied on was the virtue of the ruling class, and the people could thus, under proper social conditions, themselves internalize proper ethical attitudes.

Tzu-ch'an's motivation in making public the code seems to be precisely to escape from this vague and arbitrary way of controlling popular behavior. If the people know that certain types of behavior considered "dysfunctional" by the rulers will inevitably lead to certain dire consequences, the need for the reliance on the woefully unreliable subjective moral judgments of a ruling stratum, which in the state of Cheng had amply proven its incompetence, would have been removed. It need not be assumed that Tzu-ch'an had already come to accept the simple "pain-pleasure" model of man which was to characterize later Legalist theory. Yet he had evidently concluded that at least in terms of his immediate political goals the general reliance on the potent incentive of fear of the law provided the most reliable method of controlling the behavior of the masses. His response to Shu Hsiang's rebuke is most revealing: "I do not have the necessary talent. I cannot plan for our children and grand-children,

I can only plan to save our present generation."[18] He may agree that ultimate salvation of the world can only be achieved by the restoration of a government based on the virtue of superior men, but in the short run—as Hsün-tzu will later acknowledge—a draconian system of penal laws can be most effective.

If we put together the views of Shu Hsiang and Confucius we find that they share two overriding premises: (1) that if the people's behavior is governed wholly by its response to an "objective" and invariant code of penal law, the raison d'être of the ruling class as an ethical vanguard will be undermined; and (2) the people after thoroughly familiarizing themselves with the provisions of the law will simply develop enormous ingenuity and resourcefulness in evading the law and finding their way around it, as Confucius states in the *Analects*. In their efforts to struggle against the oppressive system imposed on them, they will simply become crafty, cunning, contentious, and bent on defending their own self-interests against an implacable state. In Confucius' words, they will no longer "know shame."

The first thesis has been heavily relied upon by those who contend that the entire aim of Confucius' ideology was the essentially reactionary aim of preserving the prerogatives of the hereditary nobility which claimed to legitimize itself in terms of its supposed ethical function. As Confucius quite candidly states in the words of the *Tso-chuan*, "The people will study the tripods and will not honor the nobles; what function [*yeh*] will the nobles then have to preserve?"[19] There can be no doubt that Confucius profoundly believed in and identified with a ruling stratum which ideally based its claim to authority on its supposed role as the ethical vanguard of society. He indisputably believed in the functionality of such a class as fervently as modern lawyers, bureaucrats, and academicians believe in the functionality of their own vocations. Whether this means that he identified this "ethical" stratum wholly with the hereditary nobility is another matter which has already been considered above. There is, as we have found, considerable evidence that even on grounds of personal interest, he had every reason to favor the movement toward the rise of a nonhereditary stratum of functionaries. He simply continued to cling to the idea that the leading function of any ruling class—hereditary or not—was ritual-ethical. He was well aware that the ruling class was *not* performing its "class" function. It would, after all, certainly be quite misleading to think of the "publication" of the penal laws as in any sense a move toward "democracy" or to fancy that the Legalists would themselves not believe in a highly authoritarian ruling class.

The second thesis will remain one of the most interesting Confucian arguments against Legalism. It is intriguing that neither Shu Hsiang nor Confucius chooses to stress here the "benevolence" of a "government of men" or the cruel oppressiveness of the system of penal law. What they choose to attack is the simple "behaviorist" assumption that negative conditioning based mainly on fear will in fact accomplish its purpose of controlling the people. However passive the people, it does possess a capacity for a moral life of its own and the obverse side of this moral capacity is the capacity to develop cunning and ingenious ways of resisting efforts to control it by simple fear-inspiring mechanisms. While the issue here is penal law, one might say that on a deeper level one already has prefigured the fundamental issue dividing Confucianism from Legalism as a total system. In Confucianism we do have a vision in which the agency of living persons (albeit the agency of a vanguard elite) plays a dominant role in shaping society. Individual humans may achieve the highest norms of sociopolitical order or they may effectively outwit it. In Legalism we will have a vision of a society in which "objective" mechanisms of "behavioral" control become automatic instruments for achieving well-defined sociopolitical goals. When viewed from this perspective, the *Analects* can be viewed to some extent as representing an anticipatory, skeptical resistance to a tendency toward what will later be called Legalism—a tendency which was already under way in the Master's lifetime.

Tzu-ch'an's program anticipates a major aspect of Legalism—its dynamic goal-oriented nature. It is indeed almost "rationalistic" in the Weberian sense of instrumental rationalism (*Zwecksrationalität*). It is a "rationalism" designed to devise the means appropriate to the achievement of the goal later so clearly defined by Lord Shang: "The enrichment of the state and the strengthening of its military capacity."[20] To Tzu-ch'an, to be sure, this goal does not represent any romantic imperialism. In his own weak state of Cheng, it represents a strategy of survival. These goals, however, clearly correspond to the "demand of the times" as viewed from the standpoint of the rulers of the Warring States period. Unlike Mencius, the Legalists will be eminently prepared to answer the question of King Hui of Liang—What can you do to serve the interests of my state?—in the spirit in which it is asked. They are, however, it must be noted, not the only "realists" prepared to relate themselves to such pragmatic questions. The expert theorists in military strategy such as Sun-tzu and the experts on "international affairs" such as Su Ch'in and Chang I represent, as I shall later suggest, somewhat different approaches to the same goals.[21]

In the period following Confucius' death, the factors favorable to the evolution of Legalism hardly diminished despite the fact that the main immediate challenge to Confucianism would, of course, come from Mo-tzu and his followers.

A case can indeed be made that Mohism in some ways prepares the ground for a full-blown "theory" of Legalism. It is indeed entirely possible that the usual Mohist account of man "in a state of nature" bent wholly on pursuing his own self-interest did indeed strongly influence the Legalist "model of man" which we find in the books of Lord Shang and Han Fei-tzu. There is certainly a common rejection of a morality of "inner intentions" and of the role of *li*. The morality of both is clearly "utilitarian" even though there is a wide divergence in the concept of the ends to be pursued. There is, as has been noted, a healthy regard for the role of "rewards and punishments" as a motivating force throughout the book of Mo-tzu. Yet, as we have seen, the discussion of rewards and punishments is indissolubly bound up with a deep emphasis on the moral will of Heaven and the spirits who are to be both feared and loved. The ends to be achieved are universal peace and welfare. The strengthening of powerful states is by no means a terminal goal.

In the end, one is more impressed by the differences. Mo-tzu's ends continue to be universalistic in the Confucian sense.[22] His attitude toward the conflicts of the states in his times is wholly oriented toward the goal of "world peace" and the prevention of war. His utilitarianism is also by no means as resolutely "behavioristic" as that of the Legalists. His utilitarianism and his rejection of the "inner" sources of morality do not preclude a space for the role of moral sentiments. As we have seen, "universal love" in fact becomes the crucial cement binding the individual interest to the general interest. Again as Rawls points out, Western utilitarianism also seems to require a role for sympathy and benevolence as a mediating force. The utilitarian "conception of justice is threatened with instability," he asserts, "unless sympathy and benevolence can be widely and intensely cultivated."[23] Mohist universalistic utilitarianism is thus, contrary to the contention of Vandermeersch, neither more nor less inconsistent than modern Western "universalistic" utilitarianism in its introduction of a role for moral sentiments.[24]

Legalistic behaviorism, with its studious indifference to sentiments, may indeed be more rigorously logical than Mohist utilitarianism, but Legalist utilitarianism is, after all, not focused on any immediate achievement of the "greatest happiness of the greatest number." Its immediate utilitarian goal is the enhancement of state power which may have no *immediate* relation whatsoever to the "happiness of the greatest number."

Vandermeersch has pointed out that in the period following Confucius' death, the center of proto-Legalist tendencies shifted to the area of the former state of Chin. The state of Chin which, like the state of Ch'i, had been a leader of the hegemonic league of powers, had also as a result of its many conquests been a pioneer in establishing direct local bureaucratic control of many regions of its state, thus participating vigorously in the general movement toward bureaucratic "rationalization" in the Chinese world of the time.[25] On the other side, however, it was also a state in which the upper layers of government were still dominated by large "feudal" lineages. After 497, the state was actually divided into three new states by the lineages of Wei$^2$, Han, and Chao. While the rulers of the new states thus created were themselves members of the hereditary local nobility, they had managed to found their new states by overthrowing the legitimate Chin prince. This alone may have been sufficient to weaken their bonds to tradition and the history of their own rise to power probably made them justifiably suspicious of the hereditary subnobility in their own domains. This may indeed account for the enthusiasm of the young Duke Wen of Wei$^2$ for surrounding himself with members of the wandering *shih*. At first, as we have seen, he was most deferential to disciples of Confucius such as Tzu-hsia, but soon became much more responsive to the proto-Legalist advice of ambitious and realistic young *shih* such as Li K'o and Wu Ch'i, who also figure among the forefathers of Legalism.[26]

According to tradition, these men were disciples of Tzu-hsia and Tseng-tzu, but as ambitious and able young careerists living in the same world in which Mo-tzu was sharply attacking the irrelevances of the "fatalistic" Confucian *ju*, they quickly turned their attention to programs which both anticipated and influenced the Legalist program of Lord Shang. The weakening of the princely relatives and noble clans, the increase of agricultural production by opening up new lands, thus providing the rulers with direct access to the revenue from these lands, the reform of military organization, and the stress on clear codes of penal law all figure largely in the accounts we have of their programs.

## The Theoreticians

While much of the program of Legalism had thus been anticipated by these forerunners, it is only in the fourth and third centuries B.C. that we see the full emergence of the "theory" of Legalism with the figures of Shang Yang, Shen Pu-hai, Shen Tao, and Han Fei-tzu. It is, of course, the latter figure who, as the grand synthesizer of Legalist thought, treats Shang Yang, Shen Pu-hai, and Shen Tao as his "theoretical" predecessors and who presents them perhaps overschematically as the representatives of three major separate yet entirely compatible strands of his overall synthesis. Creel, in his major study of Shen Pu-hai, sharply dissents from the view of any basic compatibility between the doctrines of his hero and the doctrines of the others here labeled as Legalists.[27] I shall, nevertheless, attempt here to defend Han Fei-tzu's assumption of a "deep structure" shared by all.

Shang Yang, whose name we find attached to the text of the *Book of Lord Shang*, was, we are told, an aristocrat from the old small state of Wei[1] (not Wei[2] the successor state of Chin).[28] A man of soaring ambition, he seeks his fortune in the rising state of Wei[2] where he comes under the influence of the circle of Wu Ch'i and Li K'o. His talents not being appreciated by the ruler of Wei, he soon seizes the opportunity to become the advisor of the ruler of the adjacent "semibarbarian" state of Ch'in. Ch'in, as we have found it depicted in the account of Hsün-tzu, is a remote "frontier" state in which only the upper class has as yet been deeply affected by Chinese civilization. In Hsün-tzu's account, the masses still live in conditions of Spartan simplicity untouched by either the higher values or the subtle corruptions of civilization. Indeed, it is this state of affairs which in Hsün-tzu's view makes it possible for Shang Yang to apply his program with such success.

The present *Book of Lord Shang* is certainly not wholly the work of Shang Yang and is probably put together by later disciples. Yet the ruthless and dogmatic clarity of its style conveys the spirit of one strong personality. Here we find a completely self-assured "iron man" of action contemptuous of all the nonsense peddled by the wandering *shih* of his time. Unlike Shen Tao and Han Fei-tzu, he apparently feels no need to provide his program with a cosmological-ontological foundation. His goals are clear and he knows how to achieve them. He will turn the state of Ch'in into the wealthiest and most powerful state of the Chinese world (and perhaps in the process use it to wreak personal vengeance on the ruler of Wei who has rejected his services).

According to Han Fei-tzu, Lord Shang is preeminently the theorist of *fa*, while Shen Pu-hai is the theorist of *shu* (bureaucratic method, or "technique"), and Shen Tao is the theorist of *shih* (or authority). Does *fa* mean here an exclusive concern with penal law as the instrument of social control? A perusal of the entire book makes it quite clear that this is not the case and when Lord Shang speaks in chapter one ("On Changing *Fa*") of changing the *fa* he seems to be speaking of nothing less than a total program of social-institutional change. To be sure, penal law as well as systems of "positive incentives" do indeed play a crucial role in the entire program.

I shall not here elaborate on the entire program, which has often been described elsewhere. Its main emphasis is of course on "agriculture and war."[29] "That by which a state is advanced is agriculture and war." Agriculture is the only true source of wealth, and wealth itself, while it will satisfy the basic economic needs of the people, is mainly treated as instrumental to the achievement of state power. Land is to be assigned to peasant households whose revenues will be directly available to the state. Military service is to be encouraged by making the penalties for avoiding service more frightening than the fear of death in battle. On the other hand, outstanding performance in battle is to be richly rewarded. All useless and "dysfunctional" activities which divert men from the tasks of agriculture and war—such as commerce, useless crafts, and the cultivation of ancient erroneous "learning" which encourages people to rely on their individual moral values and private intellectual convictions—are to be eliminated. The penal laws are to be applied universally to all regardless of rank, and the noble families must prove their right to their genealogical claims by their performance on the field of battle. Rank and its accompanying privileges are to be based wholly on merit.[30]

Penal law and rewards do indeed play a central role in this entire program. Since the entire program is to be "set in motion" by reliance on the negative and positive incentives of a universal, objective, and impersonal system of penal laws and rewards, it is this simple engine of incentives which will move all human energies in the desired directions. It is a program which demands a simple behaviorist model of man based primarily on the elemental tropisms of pain and pleasure. In a strange echo of Mencius' statement that "human nature is good just as water tends to flow downward,"[31] Lord Shang proclaims that "the tendency of the people to pursue its interest is like the tendency of water to flow downward."[32] Han Feitzu will assert later that "in ruling the world one must follow the bent of man's true nature [jen ch'ing]. Man's nature is based on his likes and dislikes. Thus rewards and penalties can be effectively used, and because rewards and penalties can be effectively used prohibitions and commands can be implemented, and thus good order can be actualized. The ruler holds the handles in order to establish his authority."[33]

This model of man is not to be deplored. When properly manipulated by those who understand the true science of human behavior, it can be channelized to move the entire society in the desired direction. Those anomalous elements of society whose motives cannot be controlled, such as righteous recluses who are immune to both the fear of pain and the attraction of pleasure, are a menace to the entire Legalist program. This model of man is as necessary to the predictability of the system as is the simple model of economic man to the predictability of classical economics. I am reminded here of Michael Crozier's remarks about certain proponents of "organization theory." "If the latter do not want to see anything but the simplest economic motivations in human behavior, this is because such a simplified approach makes it possible for them to consider each human being as an interchangeable instrument whose response to organizational stimuli is entirely predictable."[34] The notion that an observation about twentieth-century "organization theory" may be applied to the thought of China in the third century B.C. may seem totally unacceptable. I again suggest, however, that despite the enormous differences in language and metaphor, we may in fact find in ancient China more anticipations of contemporary Western social sciences than of the natural sciences.

Lord Shang, of course, stresses severe punishments more than the "positive reinforcement" of rewards. The Legalist program as he conceives of it makes harsh demands. Men must be prepared to die in battle or to toil away their lives in agriculture. The natural bent of human beings is toward safety and indolence. While generous rewards are recommended for performance in battle and while economic inducements are offered for success in production, the fact is that men basically hate hard labor and physical danger. Thus the sanctions against indolence and against allowing people to be lured into the "secondary occupations" (commerce, craftsmanship) and useless activities such as the study of the irrelevant cultural heritage, the vain lucubrations of sophists, cosmologists, diviners, and all other pursuits irrelevant to the goals of state wealth and power must be severe and unrelenting. "Positive reinforcements" seem to be insufficient to prevent the seductive attraction of all these diversions. On the other hand, if punishments are made severe and implacable for even small infractions of prescribed behavior, the temptation to flout the law on more important matters will disappear.

Both Shang Yang and Han Fei-tzu even provide a kind of historic-evolutionary framework for their theories. While they are resolutely "antitraditionalist," unlike some figures of the eighteenth-century Enlightenment in the West, they do not dismiss the entire history of the past as a tale of meaningless nonsense. Rather, like progressive nineteenth-century historicists, they are prepared to concede that some of the ideas preserved in the sacred cultural heritage may have once been relevant. Both of them characteristically even stress what we would now call the importance of the demographic factor. In the beginning when human beings were few in number, the frictions among them were rare, even though they were essentially the same creatures obedient to the same tropisms of pain and pleasure as they are now. As in the accounts of Mencius, the first humans were peculiarly helpless organisms, and here too we find those exceptional human beings known as the sages intervening to create for them the infrastructures of a tolerable physical existence and the bases of an ordered political hierarchy.[35] However, since population was sparse and food supply plentiful, the early rulers could afford to exercise a lax and laissez-faire control—hence the notion of rule by "benevolence and righteousness." With the growth in population and the growing scarcity of goods, the struggle for survival gradually has grown in ferocity, and it has become more and more apparent that it is only by mechanisms of punishments and rewards that people can now be controlled. The methods of Yao, Shun, and Yü may have been quite appropriate in their time, but they are now obsolete. This is what might be called the simple overall account.

In fact, however, both Lord Shang and Han Fei-tzu are forced to account for some much more puzzling and complex by-products of the rise of civilization. Thus, Lord Shang acknowledges that alongside the simple tropisms of pain and pleasure, with the rise of social hierarchies there also arose the love of "honor," which is a somewhat intangible and complicating "gratification." Men actually seem to be willing to suffer physical hardships in order to attain honors, and even the enlightened ruler of the present must include the incentives of honor and prestige within his machinery of punishments and rewards. Beyond this, there are all the false and illusory moral, intellectual, and cultural "needs" which have been a puzzling by-product of the rise of civilization. These phenomena are just as puzzling as the false reflective and purpose-oriented *yu-wei* consciousness which emerges in Lao-tzu's account of the rise of civilization. Civilization has in fact produced all sorts of anomalous and illusory notions of individual autonomy—the Confucian notion that the realization of moral values is the private preserve of individuals; the notion that "intellectuals" can develop their own "private theories"; that men of the sword can presume to present themselves as private military condottieri and heroes arrogating to themselves the right to offer their services—and the notion that some men can make the private decision to opt out of society entirely, rendering themselves completely immune to the motivations which make it possible for the social system to work. All of these false notions of individual autonomy which are an unaccountable product of civilization must be eliminated if the social-political order required by the times is to be realized. These notions may be based on illusion but they have real, dysfunctional consequences.

They may not have been particularly harmful in the past, when the struggle for survival was not so fierce, but in the "modern" world of the late Warring States, they must be eliminated if a truly "public" behavioral science is to be established. Like Skinner, both Lord Shang and Han Fei-tzu are thoroughly convinced that the notion of the "individual initiation of behavior" is entirely incompatible with a *true* science of sociopolitical organization.

Han Fei-tzu, however, will subsequently argue that Lord Shang's presentation of the true science is not complete even though he contributes some of its major elements. What he provides, above all, is a clear vision of the historic goals to be attained—the creation of a state sufficiently wealthy and powerful to achieve a clear hegemony within the anarchy of the Chinese international arena. He provides the basic plan for creating the agricultural and military organizations which are required, and with his integrated system of penal laws and rewards, he provides the engine for effectively channeling the behavior of the people. Thus when Han Fei-tzu refers to Shang Yang as the man of *fa,* it would appear that the word *fa* refers not simply to his concept of a legal code but in fact to his whole "model" of social reorganization.

## Shen Pu-hai

What then are the missing ingredients in Lord Shang's program? At least in Han Fei-tzu's view, he overlooks the fact that the whole program must be implemented by the ruler and the ruler can implement it only through his bureaucratic apparatus. In his preoccupation with the larger social program, he has overlooked the immense problem of (1) how the ruler can *control* the officials through whom he must implement his program, and (2) how he can assure the competency of the officials who implement the program. It is here that Han Fei-tzu's fellow countryman from the state of Han, Shen Pu-hai, the Chancellor of the Marquis Chao of Han (one of the three successor states of Chin), seems to him to fill the gap.[36] If Lord Shang's program is associated with the word *fa,* Shen Pu-hai's science is associated by both Han Fei-tzu and Ssu-ma Chien with the word *shu,* usually translated as "method" or "technique."[37] The technique in question is precisely the technique of organizing and controlling a truly effective bureaucracy.

Creel, is, I think, quite correct in seeing in it nothing less than a "theory of bureaucracy" or, perhaps more broadly, a "theory of organization." This has led him to devote an entire monograph to the figure of Shen Pu-hai, despite the paucity and cryptic nature of the fragments which can be attributed to him with any degree of plausibility. Given the basic triumph of the principle of bureaucracy at least in the formal aspects of the Chinese polity in later centuries, the very early emergence of an explicit "theory" of bureaucracy is indeed a most significant event. Creel is, of course, entirely aware that the tendencies leading to the triumph of the bureaucratic principle were of long duration and were certainly not simply due to the theories of Shen Pu-hai. He has himself written a seminal article on the actual beginning of local bureaucratic government in China.[38] Yet the emergence of an explicit "theory" of bureaucracy is a most significant event in the world history of sociopolitical thought. Without entering into the question of how the Legalist notion of bureaucracy may relate to works such as the *Arthasastra* of Kautilya in India, the Legalist theory of bureaucracy certainly does not find a counterpart in ancient Greco-Roman political thought. Max Weber will, of course, assert that bureaucratic government in China remains from beginning to end a "patrimonial bureaucracy" and not a true realization of the "ideal-type" of modern bureaucracy.[39] Yet however rudimentary its details, Shen Pu-hai's "model" of bureaucratic organization is much closer in conception to Weber's modern ideal-type than to any notion of patrimonial bureaucracy. If this is indeed the case, it indicates that the Chinese practice of "patrimonial bureaucracy" in later centuries took place in a political culture which was already quite aware of the possibility of something like the pure "bureaucratic" ideal-type and which thus consciously resisted the model on grounds of both interest and doctrine.[40] One may perhaps even speak here of a conscious age-long effort to conserve the "patrimonial" element of official Confucianism against the possibility of the triumph of the Legalist ideal-type. It may also be argued that the full triumph of the "ideal-type" (if it has indeed occurred anywhere) required the instruments of modern technology.

When we turn to Shen Pu-hai's "technique" as depicted in the Shen fragments and in the interpretation of Han Fei-tzu, we find first of all an enormous concern with the problem of the ruler's control of the officialdom. While this motive is certainly present in Weber's theory of bureaucracy, it is not central. Weber seems confident that at least in imperial Germany the monarchy's control of its own bureaucracy is well established. In the state of Han in the fourth century B.C., even if we suppose that a goodly part of the

Marquis of Han's high-level entourage was made up of "salaried" officialdom rather than noble functionaries with hereditary sources of income, their desire to advance their own power and prestige by influencing the ruler or even overthrowing him was still an ever-present possibility. What is more, there was still the pernicious yet pervasive tradition of the moral autonomy of noble and worthy men which led officials to question and undermine the policies and commands of their rulers.

The rulers themselves are woefully vulnerable to flattery, to the irrational attraction of intellectual brilliance, outstanding valor, saintly virtue, or physical beauty. What is more, the average ruler's own "private knowledge" is no more infallible than that of his officials, and when he makes the effort to control his officials by a pretense of personal omniscience and the unfailing brilliance of his own analyses, his nakedness will soon be revealed.[41] What must be established are impersonal, objective mechanisms and rules for strictly limiting the powers of officials and subordinating them to the unchallenged control of the ruler. There must be mechanisms which are completely independent of the vagaries of interpersonal relations. Han Fei-tzu elaborates such methods at great length. Officials are systematically encouraged to spy on each other and to denounce each other. There are many devices for isolating functionaries from each other and preventing collusions against their ruler.[42] In the end, however, one finds a congruence between some of the main mechanisms used to assure the ruler's absolute control of his officials and the mechanisms designed to make bureaucratic government effective. In Han Fei-tzu's summation of the basic elements of Shen Pu-hai's technique, we find the following: "To bestow office on the basis of the capacity of the candidate; to demand actual performance in accordance with the title of the office held; to hold fast the handles of the power of life and death and to examine the abilities of his ministers—These are the things that the ruler keeps in his own hands."[43]

The first part of this statement involving the relations of office and officeholder has often been discussed under the category of *hsing-ming,* a term which like the term *shu* has often been linked with Shen Pu-hai. The word *ming* meaning "name" seems to link Legalism to the pervasive preoccupation with "names and realities," or the question of language. Shen Pu-hai, like Hsün-tzu and others, is most anxious to find a langauge which will provide a true and accurate description of the political reality with which he is concerned. More precisely, what the term seems to refer to in this context is a definitive and accurate description of the various functional parts of a well-run bureaucratic organization. The "name" or "title" of an office should convey an exhaustive and accurate "job description" of that office—the functions to be performed and the clear limits of its scope of action. The word *hsing,* while reflecting the confusion between the word *hsing* meaning "punishment" and the word *hsing* meaning "form" discussed above, seems to refer here to the meaning of "form." If we remind ourselves again that in the Chinese context a form may refer not only to the form of an object but also to a form or configuration of behavior, we can readily accept Creel's view that *hsing* means the actual *performance* of a functionary. When the actual performance of a functionary corresponds to the title or job description of the office, when the *hsing* corresponds to the *ming,* effective government will obtain.

The notion of "functional specificity" of office was not absolutely new, but the notion that there were objective ways of selecting officials on the basis of their capacity to perform the functions in question and the notion of instituting "objective" methods of testing their performance, was probably new. When an official's activities are strictly defined by the requirements of his job, when his promotions and demotions are objectively determined by his performance, his opportunities for threatening the power of his ruler are sharply diminished. By the same token, however, he will also effectively carry out his assigned tasks. There will be objective methods for recruiting candidates for office strictly on the basis of merit, and accurate ways of testing their ongoing performance. The officials will have discretion in administering the day-to-day details of policy, but the source of grand policy will be the ruler, who will now be relieved of the vast task of making personal decisions concerning the detailed operations of his bureaucratic apparatus. Here we have a combination of both "rational criteria of achievement" and "functional specificity."

Creel insists, however, that Shen Pu-hai's technique of bureaucracy has no necessary relation to Legalism if the latter term implies a major emphasis on a draconican system of penal law. It is indeed true that in the fragments gathered by Creel in Appendix C of his book there is no discussion of penal law. It is also true, however, that in his summation of Shen Pu-hai's doctrine, Han Fei-tzu speaks of the ruler's control of "the handles of life and death," implying that the system did not preclude capital punishment. This may have been due to Han Fei-tzu's misinterpretation. It is, of course, a fact that in a bureaucratic organization the ruler has available to him a large repertoire of formidable incentives and sanctions which do not require the immediate recourse to cruel physical punishments. Demotions, failure to promote, reductions in rank, and dismissal from office can be the cause of untold anguish to ambitious officials whose goals are wealth, honor, and prestige. The immediate recourse to harsh penal law so necessary in the case of indolent workers and reluctant soldiers may not be immediately required. Yet Creel makes it clear that Shen Pu-hai was keenly concerned with the threats to the power of the ruler. Would he then have completely disapproved of Han Fei-tzu's techniques of espionage, mutual denunciations, and various methods for "trapping" officials into acts which reveal suspicious motives? Han Fei-tzu was evidently convinced that such devices were entirely compatible with Shen Pu-hai's own ongoing concern with "power relations" and that bureaucratic "rationality" by no means precluded the motives associated with rewards and punishments.[44]

## Han Fei-tzu

Han Fei-tzu perceives that the doctrines of Shen Pu-hai and Shang Yang are not antagonistic, but are as complementary as food and clothing.[45] Lord Shang's *fa* provided the program for controlling the entire society. Shen Pu-hai's *shu* provided the organization for implementing the enlightened ruler's program. Because Lord Shang neglected the principle of proper bureaucratic organization, various powerful elements in the state were able to maintain their own bases of power and even to use Lord Shang's reforms to enhance their own power. Lord Shang's own tragic death resulted from this fatal oversight in the matter of the control of officials. Shen Pu-hai, on the other hand, failed to establish a unified program of reform and did not even integrate the legal structure of the state. Scheming officials were thus still able to take advantage of the irrationality of the laws.[46]

Han Fei-tzu seems to have sought the ultimate common foundation of Legalism at a deeper level. What penal laws and bureaucratic devices have in common is, after all, that they are all universalistic, impersonal, and objective mechanisms for controlling human behavior and are all based on a simple "behavioral" mode of man. The bureaucratic devices pay somewhat more attention to the more intangible gratification of honor and prestige, but even Lord Shang had admitted these factors into his model of man.

In Han Fei-tzu's synthesis we find a third component which in his view had been neglected by both Shang Yang and Shen Pu-hai—Shen Tao's principle of the mystery of authority. The entire system in the end rests on the authority of the ruler. Shen Tao, like Max Weber, was acutely conscious of the fact that in the end authority does not rest on coercion. The power to coerce rather rests on the acceptance of authority (*shih*). How the people, who are many, are brought to accept the commands of the ruler, who is one, remains the ultimate mystery of authority. Without authority, the ruler cannot be the ultimate source of all the impersonal codes and mechanisms of control which maintain the entire social order. It is, of course, true that when the system is functioning, the system itself enhances the mantle of mystery and the sense of remoteness which surrounds the figure of the ruler, but finally it is the symbolic aura of authority surrounding the figure of the ruler which makes possible the implementation of the system. Without the internalization of this aura in the minds of the people, the entire system may readily collapse.

There are paradoxes here. In a system which would eliminate personal initiative as the source of social behavior, everything comes to depend on a symbolic person. In a system which attempts to demystify tradition, authority to be authority must ultimately in some sense be based on a preexistent mystery. Authority in the Legalist system should ultimately be established authority and not "charismatic" authority, since "charisma" leads us back to the pernicious emphasis on the exalted role of individual persons.

Vandermeersch has pointed out that the Legalists do not arrive at the notion of an abstract entity such as the "nation" or "fatherland" as the ultimate locus of authority. Within the dominant cultural orientation with its conception of a universal sociopolitical order, the center is from the outset a universal kingship, and the locus of kingship must be in the person of a king. The abstract notion of the ancient city-state in Greece as a "polis-fatherland" which might in its history actually undergo the rule of various types of government and which could therefore be considered apart from the specific structures of polity did not emerge as an option any more than it did in the universal kingships of Egypt or the ancient Persian empire. Even in the territorial monarchies of early modern Europe the separation of the concept of the "state" from the concept of monarchy was not an easy process, although it was undoubtedly encouraged by the Greco-Roman tradition of the fatherland. Nevertheless, while Shen Tao's conception of authority assumes that authority must have its locus in individual rulers, in fact the accent falls on the abstract moment of the authority of the rulership and not on the person of the ruler. The real source of authority is the kingship (*wei*) and not the king.

The rejection of charismatic authority is quite logical. If any subject can take it into his head that because of his personal virtue or wisdom or because of the bestowal of the Mandate of Heaven he has the "right" to overturn an established ruler no matter how wicked or incompetent, then the abstract basis of authority is undermined. Obedience to authority must not be based on the accident of the personal quality of the present occupant of the seat of authority. Han Fei-tzu will not admit the legitimacy of the overthrow of either the Hsia or Shang dynasties. "Kings Tang and Wu considered themselves to be righteous and killed their lords."[47] He is perfectly well aware that dynasties have fallen and rulers overthrown and that their incompetence has something to do with these events.[48] He is also aware that in the course of time new dynasties and rulers have come to acquire the symbolic support of authority. Like Hobbes, he admits that these are facts of history, but he cannot for a moment sanction the "right" of individuals to overthrow established authority as a *principle*. The Confucianists who exalt the ascriptive authority of parents nevertheless feel free to exalt moral heroes who undermine the authority of legitimate lords.[49] This, again, is a reflection of their deplorable personalistic emphasis on the moral agency of individuals. Authority, like law and method, is ultimately an impersonal power (even though it operates through persons) rooted in the *tao* itself. One might say that in a fully realized Legalist utopia, where the ruler exercises his control of the society through the impersonal mechanisms of *fa* and *shu*, his own personal character will become a matter of little concern. Yet the vagaries of human personality in the case of the ruler himself remains an incalculable variable.

When we examine Han Fei-tzu's synthesis of the ideas of Lord Shang, Shen Pu-hai, and Shen Tao, we find a remarkably consistent vision. In the world of the third century, it is a vision which already reflects a belief in the possibility of a reunification of the Chinese world under the hegemony of a state truly dedicated to the Legalist science of wealth and power. In the book of Han Fei-tzu, one even discerns the outlines of an ultimate universal utopia lying beyond the more immediate goals of the Legalist program. Once the law and the methods of rational government have become internalized in the habits of the people, the old dysfunctional attitudes based on a belief in "private action" (*ssu-hsing*) will disappear.[50] The irrelevancies of the cultural heritage with its stress on personal morality, the proud adherence of the wandering philosophers to their own inane "private" doctrines and private values, private vendettas, and "private warriors" will have disappeared and the "public interest" (*kung-li*) will reign supreme.[51] Peace, harmony, and general welfare will prevail.

This does not mean that there is no inner tension in Han Fei-tzu's outlook. Born in the weak state of Han, Han Fei-tzu was reputedly a member of the ruling family and an aristocrat.[52] Like Li Ssu, the future Minister of Ch'in Shih Huang-ti ("the First Emperor of Ch'in"), he is also alleged to have been a disciple of Hsün-tzu and, like the former, to have been ultimately unconvinced by his teacher's efforts to defend Confucianism. One nevertheless has the impression that one is, after all, dealing here with a vulnerable "intellectual" determined to be as tough-minded as possible. He is quite capable of rage and indignation against a world unprepared to recognize his merits.[53] He certainly completely lacks the "clodlike" "Taoist" indifference of Shen Tao despite his own search for a "Taoist" basis for his own convictions. His public career is basically tragic. Having failed to influence the incompetent ruler of Han he finally gains access to the young ruler of Ch'in—the incomparable Ch'in Shih Huang-ti—whom he evidently regards as the living embodiment of his ideal of the "enlightened ruler." In the end, however, he incurs the suspicion of the future emperor and is executed. It is his fellow student, Li Ssu, by no means a powerful theoretician but evidently a much more adroit instinctive politician, who will play a large role in implementing his fellow-student's theories.

Presumably Han Fei-tzu fully shares Shen Tao's contempt for the role of "men of worth" and "enlightened rulers" in human affairs. His entire system is ultimately designed to eliminate the need for them. Yet as an ambitious activist filled with an overwhelming confidence in the validity of his science, he must, like Lord Shang, believe that, in the circumstances of his time, the true system can be brought into being only by *true* men of worth and truly enlightened rulers. The true science of behavior which will finally eliminate the need for erroneous "private theories" can be actualized only by worthy individuals such as Lord Shang and himself who possess true theory. In his essay entitled "Solitary Indignation," he posits an unbridgeable abyss between the *"shih* who possess the [true] knowledge and the [true] method" such as himself and the entire pack of self-seeking peddlers of false ideas and misleading ideals who so easily lead astray the weak-minded rulers of the time.[54] Despite his commitment to the simple behaviorist model of man, somehow *"shih* who possess true knowledge" stand beyond this model both in terms of intellectual capacity and even moral integrity. The man of true knowledge and true method is in fact also a man of deep and unbending moral strength single-mindedly devoted to the highest interests of his ruler. Historic evolution may have created a situation favorable to the introduction of the true system, but the system can in the end only be realized by sagelike men who, like other sages, possess transcendental qualities which sharply differentiate them from the generality of mankind.

Thus, despite his commitment to Shen Tao's conception of authority, we find that Han Fei-tzu also has some important reservations concerning Shen Tao's total elimination of the role of great individuals in human affairs. A sage or a "man of worth" can, it is true, do nothing without authority, just as dragons cannot soar without the support of clouds and mists. But evil and incompetent rulers may use authority to disorder the world and destroy their own authority.[55] There are also times when authority can be saved or enhanced only by the presence of sage rulers and sage ministers.[56] To be sure, exceptionally sage rulers and exceptionally evil rulers will "appear once in a thousand generations."[57] In the ordinary course of things, when mediocrity reigns supreme, the weight of authority itself is sufficient to sustain order. The strong implication is that in the circumstances of Han Fei-tzu's time individual men of exceptional worth who are able to obtain the ear of truly "enlightened rulers" may still play a crucial role in transforming the world. They will be like prescient social engineers who are able to create a world where social engineers are no longer necessary.

## Legalism and Taoism

Ssu-ma Ch'ien, as I have already indicated, classes Shen Pu-hai, Shen Tao, and Han Fei-tzu as adherents of Huang-lao Taoism. We have already examined the case of Shen Tao, who treats the impersonal structure of political authority and human society as an expression of the spontaneous process of the *tao* within the structure of human civilization.

The book of Han Fei-tzu contains two chapters which are presented as Legalist commentaries on certain passages in the Lao-tzu (chapters 6 and 7). I would myself be inclined to agree entirely with Vandermeersch that even if these chapters are not from the hand of Han Fei-tzu himself, they are consistent with the spirit of what Ssu-ma Ch'ien calls Huang-lao Taoism in its Legalist variant. Indeed, what I take to be the essential features of that outlook are discernible in many other parts of the book and are quite similar to some of the passages we have already found in what I take to be the "Huang-lao" sections of the Chuang-tzu.

Despite the element of historic "relativism" which Han Fei-tzu introduces in dealing with the past, there is nevertheless an implication throughout that once the true Legalist method of organizing society has been realized, it will somehow correspond to a truly "natural" system of human organization—a system aligned with the *tao*. Once the system of rewards and punishments has become ingrained in habitual behavior, once the methods of defining the proper relations of "names and performances" in government are in place and all the devices for controlling bureaucratic behavior are operative, once the acceptance of the authority of the ruler has been internalized in the attitudes of all men, one will finally be able to say that the processes of human society correspond to processes of the *tao* in nature. The curse of *yu-wei* behavior originating in the lamentable "false consciousness" deplored by Lao-tzu will be eliminated and the human race will behave with the *wu-wei* spontaneity of all the other objects and processes of nature.

In stunning contrast to Lao-tzu's primitivism, however, man's true nature will be realized precisely *through* the sophisticated machinery of a developed Legalist sociopolitical order. Hsün-tzu, as we have seen, had tried to combine his Confucianism with a Taoist ontology, but his ongoing reliance on the transformative role of noble men led him fiercely to defend the notion of the role of the conscious actions of purposeful moral agents. In the Legalist order, however, one had the possibility of a truly and completely *wu-wei* society.

The fact that this *wu-wei* society must be brought into being by the deliberate actions of enlightened rulers and "men of true method" presumably does not preclude its "naturalness" any more than the fact that legislators who are committed to a free market economy must first take the initiative to remove the "artificial" institutional obstacles which impede a free market economy precludes the "naturalness" of such an economy or the fact that "socialism" must be "built" by a Leninist vanguard precludes the ultimate "naturalness" of the socialist system. There are, after all, hints in the Lao-tzu himself that the creation or restoration of a truly primitivist good society depends on the initiative of Taoist sage-rulers.

Han Fei-tzu, however, is not only interested in what might be called the "objective" aspect of the *tao*. In chapter 6 ("Commentary on Lao") he also concerns himself with the Legalist-Taoist sage, and here he actually seems to lay claim to the possession of something like the mystic gnosis itself (as Hsün-tzu had before him). He glosses Lao-tzu's statement that "[he who possesses] the highest *te* [does not seek] the *te*" to mean that the Taoist sage who actually "embodies the *tao*" need no longer strive to achieve emptiness, quietude, and all the other states of gnosis.[58] Those who must continue to seek it, such as the escapist Taoists, prove thereby that they do not yet possess this higher grace.[59] The man of true Taoist gnosis, precisely because he already is in possession of this gnosis is, in fact, able to operate with unfailing insight on the level of his deliberate, analytic consciousness. Here as in the case of Hsün-tzu, instead of a mutual antithesis between a mystic gnosis and a *yu-wei* consciousness, there is a subtle dialectic relationship between the two.[60] The Legalist-Taoist sage is able to draw on his higher gnosis to achieve a clear and unbeclouded understanding of the principles and processes which should govern human civilization. Because "he embodies the *tao* his knowledge is profound."[61] Here we probably find the ultimate explanation of what divides the man of true knowledge and higher integrity from the generality of mankind. His intellectual grasp has its source in a power which transcends the ordinary intellect, and he seems to draw his moral superiority from the same source. It is a conviction from which Han Fei-tzu undoubtedly draws much spiritual comfort. Yet unlike Hsün-tzu, Han Fei-tzu can envision an ultimate good society in which the role of the conscious activity of "good men" will have become completely nugatory.

## Legalism in Practice

In the end, of course, the implementation of the entire system depends on the appearance of the truly enlightened ruler. One might say that the need for such a ruler constitutes the soft core of the whole imposing structure, for a truly Legalist enlightened ruler may be as rare a reality as Mencius' truly virtuous ruler. He must be anything but an arbitrary despot, if one means by a despot a tyrant who follows all his impulses, whims, and passions. Once the systems which maintain the entire structure are in place, he must not interfere with their operation. He may use the entire system as a means to the achievement of his national and international ambitions, but to do so he must not disrupt its impersonal workings. He must at all times be able to maintain an iron wall between his private life and public role. Concubines, friends, flatterers, and charismatic saints must have no influence whatsoever on the course of policy, and he must never relax his suspicions of the motives of those who surround him. Indeed, Han Fei-tzu's own execution may have been due to the First Emperor's overzealous commitment to his admirer's maxim. While Han Fei-tzu no doubt regarded himself as the fully objective and disinterested exception to all of his own generalizations about other officials and advisors, according to one account his advice to the First Emperor concerning the treatment of his own native state of Han led the latter to suspect that his views reflected partiality for his native land rather than an unreserved loyalty to the interests of the Emperor himself.[62]

The First Emperor of the Ch'in nevertheless seems in many ways to have approximated the image of the Legalist "enlightened ruler." His revolutionary adoption of Shen Pu-hai's "pure" model of bureaucratic government was, of course, to have permanent consequences for the entire future course of Chinese history. If we can believe Ssu-ma Ch'ien's account, he seems to have remained basically faithful to the principle that a true Legalist ruler did not interfere arbitrarily in the operation of the objective and impersonal laws, mechanisms, and procedures which were imposed on the society as a whole, and, as we are told, he extended the conception of objective standards and models to areas such as the standardization of the written language, the length of wheel axles, and weights and measures. The obvious brutalities of the regime as depicted by Ssu-ma Ch'ien do not reflect the random acts of a capricious despot, but are very much related to Legalist ideas concerning the inflexibility of the penal law and the need to purge society of "dysfunctional" attitudes and modes of behavior.

It would, of course, be intriguing to know whether Han Fei-tzu would have approved of his program of unceasing imperial expansion once the "civilized" world had been reunited. If Legalism seemed to have been vindicated as the "rational" means for pursuing state wealth and power, these goals had the disturbing potential of becoming limitless in nature. Can the limitless be pursued rationally? Might Han Fei-tzu have perceived that the limitless drain of human and material resources would have undermined the foundation of the system itself? What would he have thought of the emperor's predilection for the currently popular "correlative cosmology" which seems to have been related, in the emperor's case, to a vaulting and megalomaniac ambition to reach beyond the control of the civilized world to achieve a kind of magical control of the ruling forces of the cosmos in the interests of his own personal immortality?

The spectacular success of the Ch'in conquest seemed to have finally proven something which, after all, did not seem to require proof even in terms of the sacred accounts of past history—namely that the universal kingship could not be reestablished without recourse to military power and not simply by "spiritual-moral" influence. While both Confucius and Mencius were, in some sense, ultimately aware of this fact which was made quite clear in the ancient texts, there were many ways of minimizing and muffling it. Kings Wen and Wu had enjoyed the Mandate of Heaven and were able through the power of their virtue to attract to themselves the voluntary support of numerous allies. It was this enormous accretion of spiritual and moral power which was decisive in giving them victory on the field of battle. Yet in the end they could not deny that victory in battle had played its role. The Ch'in victory, nevertheless, seems to be the ultimate defeat of Mencian apocalyptic hopes.

The later Confucius criticism of the Ch'in revolution dwells not on the triumph of the Ch'in dynasty but on its rapid disintegration under the supposedly incompetent Second Emperor.[63] At the very least, this fact seems to have vindicated Hsün-tzu's suspicion that such a system could only work for a time. It certainly lent weight to Han Fei-tzu's observation that truly "enlightened rulers" were not likely to occur more than once in a thousand generations. He might conceivably have argued that the system had hardly had time to become implanted as a "second nature" in the behavioral pattern of the people. This in itself would have indicated, however, that the realization of the system might require a succession of charismatic "enlightened rulers" for its true implementation. The crucial role of fallible human agency could not in the end be denied.

Whatever one's attitude to the Confucian belief in the transformation of society through the virtue of ethical elites, it is nevertheless a belief which also posits a certain potential for moral and intellectual initiative in human beings. It thus, in effect, may be essentially more "realistic" than the simple behaviorist model so clearly enunciated by the Legalists. Despite its moralism, or because of it, it is able to take into account the role of human sentiment, ingenuity, cunning, and resourcefulness in frustrating and evading all institutional devices. Creel praises Legalism as an anticipation of the Weberian theory of bureaucracy and of "managerial" science. Yet as Crozier points out, it is precisely in dealing with modern bureaucracy that Weber somehow seems to have forgotten the richness of his basically complex view of man and to have somewhat neglected the difference between ideal-type and actuality. Do the methods for selecting candidates for office really work that well? Do not Byzantine patterns of personal power relations penetrate the very strongholds of bureaucratic organization? Can private sentiments and passions ever be ruled out? How does one motivate the lower ranks of bureaucracy who have the most modest chances of advancement? When the mass of men see no relationship between penal law and their own life interests will they not, in the end, prove extraordinarily ingenious in evading it?

Legalism has often been compared to Machiavellianism, and it is true that both tend to separate the question of power from all considerations of personal morality. Yet a perusal of *The Prince* and *The Discourses* indicates that Machiavelli concerns himself not with universal abstract models and systems for controlling human behavior but with *strategies* of power applied to the infinitely varied circumstances of political history. As an heir of Aristotle, he is in fact prepared to accept the possibility of a variety of sociopolitical organizations and his ideal power-holder will use a variety of strategies which fully take into account differences of "political constitutions." What is more, he is fully prepared to take into account moral attitudes, sentiments, and beliefs as real factors of power with which the statesman must deal. He deals with them, to be sure, from the point of view of power manipulation, but he does not posit any simple, predictable "behavioral" model. D'Entrèves remarks that what Machiavelli expounded was a "political art" not a political science.[64] In this, his approach seems closer to that of the "international strategists" of the Warring States period, such as Chang I and Su Ch'in, rather than to the science of the Legalists, who do indeed seem closer in spirit to certain nineteenth- and twentieth-century social scientific "model builders."

In dealing with this difference between Legalism and the Machiavellian spirit, I will focus briefly on the figure of Liu Pang, later the founder of the Han dynasty, as we find him presented in the famous biography of Ssu-ma Ch'ien.[65] The biography is, of course, richly embellished with legend, but the sense of the man's powerful personality is conveyed with great clarity. A man of commoner origins, he takes advantage of the vast new opportunities provided by the Ch'in revolution to secure a post in the new subbureaucracy by passing a "civil service" examination. When in office, he hardly becomes the faceless bureaucrat who simply implements the law. Instead, he uses his position to win as much influence as possible among his superiors on the local scene. When assigned to head a corvée labor group to work on the First Emperor's Mausoleum, he finds that many members of the corvée group manage to escape and, like the other famous rebel Ch'en She, decides that he has no alternative but to raise the flag of rebellion. Whether this was more a case of seizing a golden opportunity, as Dull alleges, is not material, since the issue here is not whether Liu Pang was a "righteous peasant leader," but how he made his way to power in a period of dynastic disintegration. In Ssu-ma Ch'ien's account, Liu Pang wins out in the carnage of the ensuing civil war not so much by dint of his military genius, but by dint of his superb judgment of men and his due regard for factors of sentiment and popular feeling. As a true Machiavellian, he acutely appreciates the importance of all these factors.

While surrounding himself with brilliant military and political strategists, Liu Pang attains power as the first Han Emperor without any commitment to any clear formula of sociopolitical organization, although his power instincts would certainly incline him to favor the centralized bureaucratic model of the Ch'in. As a thorough pragmatist, however, he thoroughly understands the need to compromise with all of his lieutenants who are quite unprepared to submit totally to this model.

The First Emperor of the Ch'in, on the other hand, is the hereditary ruler of a state which had already implemented many features of a Legalist program. By relying on the power of his own state and the disarray of the other surviving "great powers," he is able to extend his rule to the entire "civilized" world. He can thus allow himself to indulge in the dream of a Legalist "utopia" completely controlled by impersonal mechanisms of law, "technique," and the mystery of authority—a society in which the incalculable forces of private passions, sentiments, values, and convictions will have been eliminated, although it is quite clear that he placed no limits on his own fantasies of omnipotence. Liu Pang, rising to power by cunning and shrewdness, knows that in the end even the achievement and maintenance of power require an ability to cope with complex and incalculable forces of personality, passions, moral ideas, and the unpredictable resourcefulness of others.

# CORRELATIVE COSMOLOGY
## The "School of *Yin* and *Yang*"

T O THE EXTENT that Hsün-tzu, the Confucian, and Han Fei-tzu, the Legalist, seek an "ontological" ground for their doctrines, they both draw on Taoism.[1] The same, of course, would be true of all those to whom the term "Huang-lao" Taoism can legitimately be applied. Other varieties of Confucian thought and Mohism probably continued to cling to older views of Heaven. Yet as we move from the fourth into the third century B.C., we become ever more aware of the growing ascendancy of another mode of thinking about the general frame of things—a mode of thinking which was actually to survive the Ch'in revolution and achieve the height of its influence in the Former Han dynasty (roughly 200 B.C. to the first century A.D.), leaving its lasting mark on the entire subsequent development of the "philosophy of nature" in China. It is later treated in the doxography of Ssu-ma T'an as one of the "six schools" under the rubric of the "School of *Yin* and *Yang*" (*yin-yang-chia*). It is perhaps also described more precisely elsewhere as the doctrine of the "Interrelation of Heaven and Man" (*T'ien-jen chih chi*). In seeking an English term I have opted for the term "correlative cosmology," although "correlative anthropocosmology" might be more accurate. Like most of the other streams of thought we have distinguished in the previous pages, it was not hermetically sealed off from the general discourse of the times and was indeed to interact in complex ways with all the dominant tendencies of the period. To many it will undoubtedly seem more culturally remote and exotic than many of the modes of thought we have considered thus far. Yet, as Needham has already noted, in the sixteenth and seventeenth century worlds of Giordano Bruno and Nostradamus, it might not have seemed at all remote.

As in the case of the other "schools," this school was not linked to the vision of any single individual or to any single text and the question of its beginnings remains a matter of great dispute. It is, in fact, considered by some to be a primordial and quintessential expression of the "Chinese mind." Any reader of Marcel Granet might indeed regard it as the central stream of the entire Chinese "structure of thought."[2] Others have discerned in it something like the expression of the Chinese Jungian "collective subconscious." The fact of its comparatively late emergence as a total outlook in the texts available to us is, of course, no proof that it may not indeed represent a truly archaic level of the culture.

It is in fact a mode of thought which in its basic principle corresponds closely to what Lévi-Strauss has described as the primitive "science of the concrete." This is, in his view, a pervasive dominant mode of thought in most "primitive" societies and, without the slightest pejorative intent, he does not hesitate to call it "la pensée sauvage." Whether it was in fact as universal and as dominant as he asserts is a question we shall not consider here. It is a kind of anthropocosmology in which entities, processes, and classes of phenomena found in nature correspond to or "go together with" various entities, processes, and classes of phenomena in the human world.[3] He treats so-called totemism, which links human groups to natural species in mutually dependent relationships, as simply an instance of this more general "structural" principle.[4] Thus, it is entirely conceivable that such correlative thinking may have existed even in neolithic "primitive" China before the rise of high civilization and before the divergence between high and popular culture. Yet it is not present in our earlier available texts. Here we again face the problem that we have faced in the case of mythology, where the earliest texts we have are not particularly oriented to the mythic. Here too there may have existed cultural tendencies not reflected in the earliest high cultural texts, which were only to surface in later centuries. It is quite clear, however, that, unlike myth, it is a mode of thought which at a later period *does* manage to win a position of prominence within the high culture itself. If it had been "suppressed," it certainly did not remain so. Hence the problem of its *late* emergence in the high cultural texts remains a problem.

The fact is that neither the oracle bones, the bronze vessels, nor any of the earliest texts we have seem to provide strong evidence of correlative cosmology, even though some discern evidence of totemism in the iconography of the Shang bronze ritual vessels.[5] Much of the information furnished in these inscriptions sheds light not on correlative cosmology, but on what Lévi-Strauss would himself define as the realm of religion. Correlative cosmology in his view is a "science

of the concrete" because it relates concrete phenomena actually perceived in our ordinary experience to each other "horizontally." Its
materials are all drawn from the "real" world. Animals, plants, the
four cardinal directions, kinship organizations, human traits, and
celestial bodies are all "real." A religious ritual—specifically the ritual of sacrifice—which relates humans "vertically" to gods and spirits represents in this view an effort to establish "a desired connection
between two initially separate domains," of which one—the divine—is "non-existent."[6] Seen in terms of this definition of religion,
the oracle bones are, as we have found, overwhelmingly concerned
with sacrifices to spirits and divine beings and inquiries directed to
them. Hence they are eminently religious in Lévi-Strauss's sense.
Whether the prominence of divination as a practice may have eventually favored the emergence of correlative cosmology is a matter to
be considered. Yet divination, as such, was initially a communication with beings who represented Lévi-Strauss's "initially separate
domain." Divination was certainly a practice very much present in
ancient Mesopotamia where divinatory communication took place
with the highly anthropomorphized gods of the Mesopotamian pantheon. The diviners could not control the verdicts of the gods any
more than the oracle of Delphi could, in theory, control the verdicts
of Apollo.

When we turn to the *Book of Poetry* and those sections of the *Book of
Documents* generally regarded as pre-Confucian, we again find no
evidence of correlative cosmology, although there is much evidence
of religion in Lévi-Strauss's sense. The doctrine of the Mandate of
Heaven certainly initially involved the interrelation of two "separate domains," one of them divine, even though it would become
possible in later periods to set the idea within the framework of correlative cosmology. When we turn our attention to two of the central
constituent ideas of Chinese correlative cosmology—the conceptions
of *"yin* and *yang"* and of the five elements—we find that the graphs
*yin* and *yang* do indeed appear in the *Book of Poetry* but seem to refer
to concrete phenomena such as shadow and light, to the sunny or
shady slopes of hills, or to other concrete phenomena.[7] They have
not yet become the abstract principle of duality. The five elements
concept does not occur at all. On the other hand, sacrifice, prayer,
and invocation of Heaven and the spirits are central themes
throughout.

To the extent that the accounts we find in the narratives of the
*Tso-chuan* furnish a more or less credible, truly contemporary account of the period of the *Spring and Autumn Annals* (721–479 B.C.),
we do begin to discern early evidences of correlative thinking in this

text, although many scholars are convinced that many of its set speeches reflect post-Confucian thought. In the recorded discourses of those specialized functionaries and wise men called *shih*, who seem to combine the functions of astronomers, astrologers, calendar experts, and chroniclers, we do indeed find evidence of correlation of human events with the movements of the heavenly bodies. One is indeed tempted to speculate that something like a rudimentary astrology provides the first most important application of correlative cosmology in China, at least on the high cultural level.[8] There are other passages which also anticipate features of later correlative cosmology, although we cannot be sure that they are not later embroideries on the original narratives. It is thus significant that one astrologer-chronicler links certain heavenly bodies to the material elements water and fire. *Yin* and *yang* as categories of the cosmic order also appear but they are, in one account, subsumed by a court physician under the larger category of the "six *ch'i*" (*yin, yang,* wind, rain, darkness, and light).[9] The physician finds all these elements commingled in the human body and some commentators surmise that *yin* and *yang* here refer simply to cold and heat. Illness is treated as a symptom of an imbalance among all these forms of *ch'i*. Whether this should be considered an instance of correlative cosmology is doubtful, however, because there is no clear evidence of any explicit correlation or "resonance" between the movement of these elements in the human organism and in various external cosmic forces. In other passages one can also actually find references to the "five modes of action" (the "five elements").

If anticipations of correlative cosmology are already present in the pre-Confucian period, it may well be to ideas of this sort that Tzu-kung refers in the *Analects* when he asserts that the Way of Heaven was one of the matters about which he had never heard the Master discourse. Confucius, who insists so firmly that humans focus their attention on the realm of their own moral autonomy, would not spend much time reading the signs of nature even though he may well have believed in such signs (as is hinted in both the *Tso-chuan* and the *Analects*). It is interesting to note that the famous Tzu-ch'an, who does often discourse on cosmic matters in the *Tso-chuan*, nevertheless refuses to pay attention to a prediction of a destructive conflagration based on the appearance of a comet. He specifically asks concerning the diviner Tsao who had made the prediction, "How should Tsao know the Way of Heaven?"[10] In Lévi-Strauss's terms, one would have to say that Confucius relates to Heaven much more in the mode of religion than in the mode of correlative cosmology. To the extent that one can discern latent intimations of "holism" or organismic thinking in the *Analects,* it seems to point much more toward Lao-tzu and Chuang-tzu rather than toward correlative cosmology.

Mo-tzu represents, if anything, a sharp reaction against any tendency toward the notion of any kind of immanent order of nature, correlative or otherwise. His outlook is, if anything, eminently religious in Lévi-Strauss's sense and he fervently espouses the concept of "initially separate domains." He believes in omens and portents but these are not connected with any system of abstract correspondences between natural and human phenomena. They rather express the conscious will of Heaven and spirits. They are indeed literally signs from the gods.

In dealing with later Mohism, let me briefly anticipate here the discussion of Tsou Yen's theory of the dynamic cycle of the five elements (a full discussion follows below). It is most significant that the later Mohist "logicians," who live in a world where correlative cosmology is already well established, will make a frontal assault on any notion of a dynamic inner relationship among the five elements. Stated briefly, Tsou Yen's idea presupposes a dynamic cycle of water, earth, wood (vegetation), metal, and fire which corresponds to cycles of human history. Each element wins an "ascendancy" over its predecessor. The theory is evidently based on the observation of such ordinary natural phenomena as the quenching of fire by water and the melting of metal by fire. The Mohist canon bluntly points out, however, that "the five elements do not always win ascendancy over each other."[11] The variable of quantity may make all the difference. "The fact that fire melts the metal is because there is much fire."[12] A feeble fire will not melt a large volume of metal and a small quantity of water will not extinguish a large fire. There can thus be no absolute, immanent necessity governing the supposed dynamic relations of these elements or of any of their supposed correlates in the human sphere. In particular contingent situations, one must rather look for the particular discrete historic causes of such situations. This observation has momentous implications for Tsou Yen's efforts to link the "cycle of the elements" deterministically to the cyclical patterns of human history. The Mohists, in dealing with historic change, will *not* seek out immanent necessary patterns. They will seek specific proximate causes in the actions and intentions of men or, perhaps, of Heaven and the spirits. They will not rely on notions of immanent cycles in either the cosmos or in human affairs.

When we turn to our early Taoist texts, we do indeed find a holistic, or what Needham would call an "organismic" view of the world. I would nevertheless contend that the basic thrust of this holism moves in a direction fundamentally different from that of correlative cosmology even though tendencies will later emerge to fuse the two.

It is, of course, true that in the Lao-tzu text, the concept of *yin* and *yang* in the sense of an abstract dyadic principle underlying all cosmic phenomena is already present. It is not difficult to imagine how terms which may have originally referred to light and dark or heat and cold may become general abstract terms referring to all dualities. Certainly the observation of the prominence of the principle of duality in the frame of things is not unique to China, nor does it necessarily carry with it any specific notion of the exact nature of the relation between the terms of the dyad. Thus the notion that in China the dyad is always "dialectic" and dynamic is simply not true, since in many instances it seems to refer to nondynamic complementarities, opposites, or simple alternations. Furthermore, the *yin* and *yang* idea in itself does *not* necessarily imply correlative cosmology. In the Lao-tzu, as we have seen, the notion of *yin/yang* is central both in relation to natural and human affairs and is treated in the peculiarly "assymetrical" manner described above. Softness and hardness may be present in both nonhuman nature and in the human realm, but there is no hint of any "resonantial" interaction between the two spheres. The *yin* and *yang* also appears in the Chuang-tzu text's account of both the natural world and the human organism, but again there is no hint of specific correlative interactions between processes and classes of things in the natural realm and in the human realm. Instead, all the processes in both realms are constantly referred back "vertically" to their origins in the ineffable *tao*.

The essential preoccupation lying behind the correlative cosmology seems to be that of finding in the homologies between human and natural phenomena a means of controlling human civilization as well as human individual life by "aligning" them with the cycles, rhythms, and patterns of the natural realm. In contrast to Lao-tzu, the categories of higher civilization and the project of civilization are wholeheartedly accepted as part of the structure of the cosmos itself. There is above all the basic assumption that the natural world is intimately and "providentially" implicated in human affairs. Lao-tzu's "primitivism" rejects all the works of higher civilization as representing a breach with the *tao*, and his *tao* is not providential. It is not at all "involved" with the ordinary objectives of the social order or the weals or woes of individuals. Rather, the individual (and in Lao-tzu, the Taoist community) finds his salvation by reuniting with the ineffable *tao*. Finally the central emphasis on the ineffability of the *tao* seems notably absent in the supreme confidence of the correlative cosmologist in his ability to fathom all things. Here we become suddenly aware that if organismic thinking is a predominant shared orientation of Chinese thought, the differences which divide one form of organismic thought from another may be quite as significant and fundamental as their shared holism. This is certainly true of what Needham regards as the nonorganismic philosophies of the West. There is no reason why it should not be equally true of China.

In the Hsün-tzu and Han Fei-tzu we find, as noted above, no impulse whatsoever to link their outlook to correlative cosmology even though both live in the world where its influence is already pervasive. Hsün-tzu in his resolute antiprovidentialism strongly opposes the art of physiognomy, which finds a correlation between the physical organization of the human body (which may be in itself considered a "natural" factor) and the life course of the individual. He indeed regards such a correlation as a direct threat to the Confucian stress on individual intellectual and moral autonomy. Han Fei-tzu seeks his ontological support in the text of Lao-tzu.

## Tsou Yen and the "Five Elements" Theory

Ssu-ma Ch'ien's history very much identifies the emergence of correlative cosmology with the shadowy figure of Tsou Yen, a native of Ch'i, a member of the Chi-hsia Academy, and apparently a most popular and successful advisor of the rulers of his time.[13] "He went to Yen where King Chao acted as his herald . . . and asked to take the seat of a disciple so as to receive his instruction. Here a palace was built for him . . . In all his travels among the feudal rulers he received honors of this sort."[14]

Although there are solid reasons for seeking the beginnings of correlative cosmology in tendencies which emerged before Tsou Yen, without regarding these tendencies as in any sense "primordial," it is possible that it was he who first posited a vast imposing specific system of correlative categories embracing all phenomena both human and natural. He is particularly well known for his correlation of the "five elements" with the cyclical patterns of human history, and it is probably this idea above all, with its implied predictive powers, which aroused the burning interest of the rulers of the time. In the apt words of Joseph Needham, "If Tsou Yen had had the 'know-how' of the atomic bomb in his possession, he could hardly have faced the rulers of the states with a steadier eye."[15] The notion of bringing the disordered human sphere into harmony with the patterns of Heaven may indeed reflect a general Chinese cultural orientation as indicated above. Yet the particular, concrete solutions offered by correlative cosmology may have seemed excitingly new.

I shall here use the conventional term "five elements" (*wu hsing*) for the sake of simplicity, although the Chinese term itself refers not only to the material elements as such but to the entire syndrome of correlates, both natural and human, with which the elements are associated.[16]

The origin of the five elements theory remains a matter of dispute among both Chinese and foreign scholars. The Chinese term translated as five elements (*wu hsing*) does not of course refer to elements at all. The word *hsing* seems to mean actions or movements, while Tsou Yen himself uses another term—the "five powers [*te*]."[17] It is thus quite clear that by the time these terms are used, while they clearly include the material elements, they already refer to a whole set of associated factors of which the material elements represent one set. What then is the history of the linkage between these sets of five and the elements water, fire, wood, earth, and metal? Why, indeed, these particular material elements? Ku Chieh-kang has suggested that the original notion of a correlation between a set of five natural phenomena and a variety of human phenomena was initially linked to the periodic movements of the "five planets."[18] This would link the numerological set of five in the first instance to a rudimentary astrology which, as has been suggested, may have been one of the first forms of correlative cosmology. This would also help explain the "dynamic" aspect of a concept linked to the movement of the planets. Kuo Mo-jo has seen a possible linkage to the five cardinal directions (north, east, south, west, and center) and their association with the movement of the winds, thus linking the notion to a concern with metereological phenomena, which is already prominent in the oracle bones.[19] Vitaly Rubin, following the views of Granet, suggests that the crucial element is the numerological set of five itself. "The number as in all numerology," he states, "refers not to the ordinal function of numbers in counting or in quantification but to classifying sets."[20]

All of this suggests that the ideas which lay behind the correlations of the sets of five may not have first been associated with the five material elements as such. Perhaps the five material elements assume a dynamic "dialectic" relation to each other only because of their association with other truly dynamic phenomena, such as the movement of heavenly bodies. If all this is true, it would strongly suggest that the basic history lying behind the full conception had little to do with the pre-Socratic question—what are the ultimate constituent material elements of the world?

The question nevertheless remains—if the five elements in the lit-

eral sense represent the class of material substances within the correlated clusters of five, why the choice of these particular elements?
Water, fire, and earth, of course, appear as primordial elements in
the elements theory of Empedocles; in China air may have been associated from the outset with the all-absorbing substance of *ch'i*—a
category which has a history of its own quite separate from that of
the five elements. Yet, why metal and wood (or vegetation)? It has
been suggested by Hsü Fu-kuan and Li Te-yung that in fact the
grouping of these elements was not originally associated with questions concerning the primordial matter or substances of the world
but with the practical, productive activities of agriculture.[21] The
fundamental prerequisites of agriculture are earth, water, wood, and
metal, which are crucial to the fashioning of implements, and fire,
which is crucial to the melting of metal and perhaps to the clearing
of land as well. Some plausibility is lent to this view by a passage in
the *Book of Documents* which speaks not of the five elements but of the
"six storehouses." The Emperor Yü is quoted as saying, "Virtue is
seen in good government. Good government is proven by its [capac-
ity] to nourish the people. There are water, fire, metal, wood, earth,
and grain. These must be properly regulated."[22] One can readily
imagine how in attempting to align these essential elements of agricultural production with the sets of five one might eliminate grain
which is, after all, a product of agriculture rather than one of the
"factors of production."

All efforts to reconstruct the origins of the five elements theory
must remain speculative. It would nevertheless appear that the most
plausible views are those which do not see it as originally an effort to
answer the pre-Socratic question—What is the simple stuff or stuffs
of which the world is "made" or "composed"? If this is indeed the
case it may help to explain the durability of the theory. Over the
centuries, it continued to provide what was considered to be a satisfactory way of talking about nature and man even during periods
when correlative cosmology was not a dominant tendency of Chinese thought. It continued to serve its purpose adequately precisely
because it was not primarily designed to answer the pre-Socratic
question. If the pre-Socratic question had been central, the Chinese
mind would have been quite capable of conceiving of different answers. Needham has suggested that the long endurance of the five
elements theory in China ought to be compared to the stubborn
persistence of Aristotle's four elements theory in medieval Western
thought.[23] There may indeed be some parallel here in the fact that
many medieval scholastics were also not primarily preoccupied with
finding in ancient thought answers to this particular "natural scientific" question.

Nevertheless, certain modes of pre-Socratic Greek philosophy seem indeed to have been deeply concerned with answers to the question of whether the ultimate material or "stuff" of the universe was "one," as with Thales and Anaximenes, or multiple, as with Empedocles. In either case, one does indeed find here a "reductionist" notion of ultimate "material" constituents of the manifold universe of our ordinary experience. To the extent that Thales and Anaximenes posit the notion that all the diverse entities, qualities, and processes of the world are ultimately explicable as being "built-up" out of simple, homogeneous substances such as water or air (which may themselves, nevertheless, still have attributes of divinity) by principles such as those of condensation and rarefaction, we already have something like the reductionist hypothesis which is later to achieve its most sophisticated form in the atomism of Leucippus and Democritus where all the entities and qualities of the world are explained as being "built-up" out of the atoms conceived of as simple mass-point "building blocks" with minimal properties of mass and shape. In the words of Heidel, "It is not necessary to descant on the historic significance of this conception as leading to the ultimate assumption that the essential properties of things are the properties of mass."[24] This "reductionist" assumption did not necessarily become the dominant assumption of either ancient Greek thought or medieval Western thought. Yet it did not disappear from the cultural heritage of the West and it was there to be tapped when there were those ready to turn to it in the sixteenth and seventeenth centuries. It is present not only in the Ionian monists but also in the more "chemical"-minded pluralists such as Empedocles who, in discussing the four elements, states "that from these things sprang all things that were and are and shall be, trees and men and women, beasts and birds and water-bred fish and the long-lived gods too, most high in their prerogatives. For there are these things alone and running through one another they assume many a shape; so much does mixing effect."[25]

As far as we can tell from the fragments we have, Tsou Yen is not at all interested in reducing the five elements to each other or, indeed, in reducing any of the correlates of the five material elements to the five elements as such. He is not saying that the colors or the seasons or the "five dynasties" somehow "sprang from" the five material elements. All classes of phenomena maintain their own concrete existence within a nonreductionist order, which includes and embraces all. In this sense, even if correlative cosmology is a late emergent, it does indeed conform to the "holistic" concept of order which we have found in other modes of Chinese thought. It is a holism prepared to subsume and classify the manifold phenomena of the experienced world rather than to "reduce" them to some primordial "material."

By the same token, it is a "science of the concrete" which accepts wholeheartedly the testimony of our ordinary experience. Reductionism necessarily involves the notion of the kind of discrepancy between "reality" and "appearance" which one finds in Empedocles, Parmenides, and Democritus. In their universe, the world as it presents itself to us through our ordinary sense experiences is, in some sense, not the real world, just as to many modern "scientific naturalists" the world of our ordinary experience is clearly not as "real" as the world of ultimate particles.[26] It is true that, to Hui-shih and the historic Chuang-tzu, the world of ordinary human experience is also, in some sense, a world of "appearance." Chuang-tzu's ultimate world, however, is to be sought in the ineffable *tao* and not in ultimate particles and the mathematical relations among such particles. In most correlative cosmology, however, the correlated "concrete" realities of our ordinary experience remain irreducibly real aspects of our natural and human environments. Tsou Yen and later Tung Chung-shu are thus quite content to accept the world of "appearance" as they find it.

As indicated above, many interpreters have sought the equivalent of pre-Socratic reductionism in China not in the five elements theory as such but in the concept of *ch'i*. It is true that *ch'i* itself is very much present in most versions of correlative cosmology. The five elements, the four seasons, and all the phenomena of nature all come to "possess" their own *ch'i* or—to put it somewhat differently—the universal *ch'i* manifests itself through all. Again there is no implication that this in any way detracts from the irreducible reality of the diversity of the forms in which *ch'i* manifests itself. Again if *ch'i* as a "substance" relates to anything in the pre-Socratic thought, it is to Anaximander's "Boundless" (*apeiron*), which is an indeterminate substance which can manifest itself in the determinate manifold of the world rather than a homogeneous elemental stuff of minimal properties such as Anaximenes' air. *Yin* and *yang* and the five elements may in some versions of correlative cosmology emerge out of the all-encompassing *ch'i* but the *ch'i* is not the bare raw material out of which they are "constructed." When Tung Chung-shu will later talk of the *ch'i* of the five elements and of the four seasons, we cannot in fact be sure that *ch'i* is anything other than an effluent or radiating energy of all these quite separate categories of existence.

One must assume that if the Milesian pre-Socratics in Greece moved in the direction of reductionism, theeir preoccupations seem to have been markedly different from those of the Chinese theorists of correlative cosmology although we cannot be absolutely sure what they were. There is, of course, the widely held assumption that for the first time in human history we have here a manifestation of a disinterested scientific curiosity about the ultimate structure of nature unencumbered by ethical, religious, and other soteriological concerns. To the extent that the word science or philosophy which claims to be based on science has come to be defined as the "disinterested" search for scientific truth as such, it is often stated that only in Greece can we find the beginnings of philosophy. This is certainly not the case for a good part of Greek philosophy. When we read the fragments of Xenophanes, Heraclitus, Parmenides, Pythagoras, and Empedocles, it becomes difficult to maintain that these particular "pre-Socratics" were in any way detached from a deep concern with those areas we call religious, ethical, and even political. Kirk and Raven remark "that after the Milesians the old cosmogonic approach according to which the most important object was to name a single kind of material from which the whole differentiated world could have grown, was enlarged and moderated. New problems of theology and of unity in the arrangement rather than the material of things exercised Anaximenes' successors Xenophanes and Heraclitus."[27] Cornford and others (particularly some Marxist historians of philosophy) imply that the "scientific tradition" of the Milesians had something to do with a "practical" and even technical bent, which represented a decisive break with the spirit of the old mythological Homeric world in the Ionian city-states. "Science and commerce are here as elsewhere twin products of that daring spirit of exploration and adventure which voyages over strange seas with a strictly practical object in view."[28] There are, of course, many stories about the engineering feats of Thales. Others, however, would continue to stress the unique passionate search for a disinterested knowledge of how the world is "put together." There is yet another view that the single substance of the Milesians was eternal, unchanging, and divine and thus possessed in their case a definitely religious dimension which did not, of course, preclude the role of scientific curiosity.

Again I would stress that the universal human trait of disinterested curiosity concerning the natural world which surrounds us, which can be found everywhere even when it does not become a central concern of every culture, was as much present in China as elsewhere. If by the use of the term "science" we refer to the incremental accumulation of accurate observations of the natural world, China falls behind no other civilization, as has been amply demonstrated in Needham's many works, just as it was not behind others—and was in some areas ahead of others—in the empirical development of technology. Nor is there any proof that the dominance of the *yin/yang* and five elements theory necessarily impeded the advances of *this* type of premodern science any more than Aristotelian nature philosophy did in the medieval West.

The question we are concerned with here, however, is whether Chinese correlative cosmology in Tsou Yen or others was basically concerned with this sort of "disinterested" study of nature or development of technology. As we have seen, Tsou Yen's most well-known theory was his correlation of the five elements with the cyclical patterns of history. According to this theory, under the Yellow Emperor the "dominant" prevailing element had been the element of earth, together with all its concomitant homologies. Under Yü, the founder of the Hsia dynasty, there had been an ascendancy of wood (or vegetation); under the Shang dynasty, an ascendancy of metal; and under the Chou, an ascendancy of fire.[29] Presumably any new dynasty would be dominated by the principle of water. Within the material elements series, the concept of the "mutual conquest" relation among earth/wood/metal/fire/water was, as suggested, probably based on simple natural observation such as the observation that vegetation "overcomes" earth by drawing its sustenance from it; that metal overcomes wood as when a sharp ax can be used to fell trees; fire melts metal; water extinguishes fire; and earth can somehow conquer water (by drainage or absorption?).[30] The correlates in the realm of nature associated with each of the elements may include colors, seasons, or cardinal directions and in the human realm such categories as ethical qualities, departments of government, the governing principles of a dynasty, and even various aspects of individual life. Tsou Yen himself, in addition to his concern with five elemental cycles, was equally interested, we are told, in the waxings and wanings of the *yin* and *yang* dyad whose alternatives cut across the cycles of the five elements. Thus, on the historic side, alongside the five periods he posits the alternating pattern of dynasties governed by the principle of simplicity (*chih*) and other dynasties governed by the principle of cultural complexity (*wen*).[31]

There are other aspects of Tsou Yen's teachings which are mentioned. He presumably had an enormous interest in world geography and for reasons not available to us seemed to have stressed that the Middle Kingdom of his time was a very small part of the entire earth. Whether this focused attention on the cosmic scope of his vision as opposed to the limited vision of many of his contemporaries, we cannot know. His correlation of the elements with patterns of history must have mainly appealed to the rulers of his time because of its presumptive, predictive value. He offers them, in effect, advice on what modes of behavior—whether magical, administrative, or ethical—would be most effective in "aligning" their policies with the emerging historic "field of forces." Some of the advice may have involved magical ritual acts, such as the adoption as the emblematic color of one's historic epoch the color corresponding to the element in ascendance. The color would become the dominant color of ceremonies, ceremonial clothes, banners, and such. The First Emperor of the Ch'in, who was, one gathers, as much under the influence of Tsou Yen as he was under the influence of the Legalists, having logically decided that water was the ascendant element of his dynasty, adopted black as his emblematic color. Tsou Yen's advice may also have pertained, however, to questions of government organization, the relative weight to be assigned to *li* versus punishments (*fa*), and other wide-ranging matters of substantive policy.

If we can believe Ssu-ma Ch'ien's testimony, Tsou Yen's own ethical values were essentially Confucian and he used his entire system to encourage "humanity, righteousness, frugality" and basic Confucian norms of social relations. If this is indeed so, it would indicate that he was a pioneer not only in the systematization of correlative cosmology but also in the effort which finds its culmination in Tung Chung-shu's later effort to fuse correlative cosmology with Confucian values in particular. This was not, however, to prevent the First Emperor of the Ch'in from justifying his own commitment to Legalism in terms of Tsou Yen's historic doctrine. Water, we are told, which he took to be his dynasty's dominant element, was associated with *yin* and thus with the severity of winter and darkness. "Hence in affairs of government he put laws [*fa*] before everything else."[32] Here we suddenly find a correlative-cosmological rationale of Legalism which would certainly have disconcerted Han Fei-tzu. It throws an unexpected light on the nature of the First Emperor's "rationalism."

Ssu-ma Ch'ien, whose admiration for the correlative cosmology which dominated so much of the thought of his own period seems to have been strictly limited, somewhat deplores Tsou Yen's effort to support Confucian values with this vast historico-cosmological machinery and contrasts him unfavorably to Confucius and Mencius, who simply preached goodness and righteousness as ends in themselves and thus found few buyers.[33] The First Emperor's interpretation of the doctrine had clearly demonstrated how this science—based on the suggestive association of ideas—could come to be linked to quite varied ethicopolitical orientations.

Needham, in dealing with Tsou Yen's correlative cosmology, calls

his school the school of "naturalists," distinguishing it sharply and
favorably from what he calls "phenomenalism," which he tends to
relate mainly with the Confucianized cosmology of the Han period.
Tsou Yen, in fact, stands high among those whom Needham consid-
ders to have been favorable to the scientific enterprise. In the latter
category of "phenomenalists" he would include figures such as the
most famous Han Confucian synthesizer of correlative cosmology,
Tung Chung-shu. While the naturalists are associated with "proto-
science," the phenomenalists are associated with "pseudo-science."[34]
While the naturalists are basically concerned with the investigation
of nature, the phenomenalists (as Confucianists) are basically concerned with human and sociopolitical affairs. Phenomenalism is essentially the belief that "governmental and social irregularities" can
lead to vast dislocations in nature.[35] It is thus very much tied up
with the belief in omens and portents, while Tsou Yen and the naturalists, one would gather, were basically interested in the "proto-sci-
entific" application of *yin/yang* and the five elements theory to
further the understanding of nature.

Despite the fact that Ssu-ma Ch'ien's history is our only ultimate
source in this matter, despite his attribution of Confucian values to
Tsou Yen, as well as his strong implication that Tsou Yen was basically concerned with furnishing political and ethical advice, Needham simply brushes aside this testimony. That Tsou Yen was, in
fact, deeply interested in omens is perfectly obvious even from the
few fragments we have available to us. The dominance of the Yellow
Emperor is presaged by the appearance of large earthworms and the
dominance of Yü the Great by plants which did not wither. The cosmos, it is quite obvious, was in his view deeply implicated in human
affairs. Was there anything out of keeping with the logic of his correlative cosmology in the proposition that irregularities arising on
the human side (and it was precisely on the human side that irregularities would arise) might lead to "resonantial" irregularities in nature?

It is, of course, possible that in his studies of mountains, rivers,
birds, and beasts to which the Historic Records allude, Tsou Yen
drew on a large fund of natural observations. Yet, such observations
are by no means lacking in those Needham calls the "phenome-
nalist" cosmologists, and the question remains whether the *yin/yang*
and five elements doctrine into which Tsou Yen incorporates these
observations really were an "aid" to his observations. To the extent
that correlative cosmology encouraged the observation of natural
phenomena, this was as true of those called "phenomenalists" as it
was of Tsou Yen.[36]

Needham also claims that Tsou Yen was linked to the beginnings of alchemy and thus to science insofar as the latter involves the actual experimental manipulation of materials. Yet, the link between Tsou Yen and alchemy remains extraordinarily tenuous. Ssu-ma Ch'ien relates that certain shamanlike figures from the northeastern state of Yen, such as Hsien-men Kao, who were interested in magical techniques for achieving immortality, "transmitted the methods of Tsou Yen but without being able to understand them."[37] The text clearly implies that these magicians or shamans simply adopted the theories of Tsou Yen and, as stated in Ssu-ma Ch'ien's view, "did not even really understand them." Whatever may be the case, there is no implication that Tsou Yen was, himself, interested in their endeavors. Nor is it even clear that their magical techniques at all involved alchemy. Nathan Sivin, in his *Chinese Alchemy,* flatly states that he is unable to find any evidence that Tsou Yen wrote a book "on the actual turning of base metals into precious ones" or even that the techniques used by the men of Yen had anything to do with alchemy.[38] The Tsou Yen fragments strongly suggest that like all the members of the *yin/yang* school whom Needham places in the category of "phenomenalists," he was overwhelmingly preoccupied with human and even specifically sociopolitical concerns which could not, he felt, be divorced from a concern with the realm of nature.

The cycle of history *ought to* correspond to the cycle of the elements. Yet in fact it does not do so automatically. Human rulers do not "automatically" align themselves with the "historic field" within which they find themselves. The human world is constantly "out of phase." To use a metaphor of Tung Chung-shu greatly admired by Needham, the human order often *fails* to "resonate" with the natural order. "The *kung* or *shang* note when struck upon one lute will be answered by the *kung* and *shang* note struck upon other string instruments. They sound by themselves."[39] Needham contrasts this metaphor of "mysterious resonance" to notions of "mechanical impulsion or causation." Yet at closer view the matter looks more complicated. It is not merely that single notes resonate. The dynamic processes of nature are not so much discrete events like single notes as they are parts of an ongoing melody. One might say that the striking of the first lute is itself not an isolated event but a moment in an ongoing melody. Within nature, in the cycle of the elements and the cycle of the four seasons, we have the resonances of ongoing harmonious melodic themes. In the human sphere, however, human beings have the power to strike discrete dissonant notes which create dissonant resonances in the entire harmonic system. The dissonant resonance is in fact produced by the appearance of a kind of particulate causation—the disordering acts of rulers and of humans in general. Thus to Tsou Yen, no less than to Tung Chung-shu, events occurring in the human realm may set up dislocations in the entire harmony of the cosmic organism.

If Tsou Yen was the first great systematizer of correlative cosmology, his is by no means the only version of a mode of thought which we find in a large body of literature spanning the period of the Warring States and Early Han dynasty. It is, of course, a mode of thought which allows for infinite permutations. In the so-called old-text version of the *Book of Documents* we thus find the treatise on the Great Plan (*Hung fan*), which most scholars consider to be a post-Confucian work. Hsü Fu-kuan makes a somewhat persuasive case for considering it a relatively early version of correlative cosmological thinking but others place it very late.[40] The "Monthly Ordinances" (*Yüeh ling*) section of the *Record of Rites* (*Li chi*) which dates from the Warring States or Early Han period provides a quite different version of cosmology. Finally, the most imposing detailed and architectonic synthesis of what might be called "cosmological Confucianism" is to be found in the writings of Tung Chung-shu, the famous contemporary of Emperor Han Wu-ti who is thought to have played a leading role in the establishment of Confucianism as official state doctrine.

Turning to the text of the Great Plan, which was purportedly conferred by the High God on the Emperor Yü, what we find is the seriatim listing of nine numerical sets of crucial natural and human categories which are, however, not neatly coordinated in numerical terms. Thus alongside the five elements and their various correlates, both natural and human, we find categories such as the "eight [functional divisions] of government" (*pa cheng*) which include food (the control of agriculture?), public works, crime, military affairs, and so on, and the five calendric subdivisions (*wu chi*) (e.g., the year, the month).[41] A noteworthy feature is that while some of the categories are obviously meant to apply to the sociopolitical order others seem to focus on the individual. The five elements are thus associated with tastes and with the five categories of human behavior (*wu shih*), including items such as demeanor, speech, seeing, hearing, and thinking along with the normative principles governing these modes of behavior, such as respectful demeanor and correct speech.[42] Here we find a striking example of the linkage of cosmological homologies to the psychophysical life of the individual human being—a mode of correlative cosmology which was in the long run to have a more profound impact on the total culture (including the traditions of medicine) than the homologies with patterns of history and the sociopolitical order.

Nevertheless, the Great Plan is most concerned with the sociopolitical order and even some of its key categories concerning the individual really refer to the fifth category of "kingly perfection" (*huang chi*), where the individual involved is the universal king himself who is the pivot of the entire order. It is he who makes possible the "five happinesses."[43] It is he who must rely on his own judgment about how to employ in government the three virtues (*san te*) of straightforwardness, firmness, and mildness.[44] A striking feature of this entire schematism is that none of the categories including the five elements themselves seem to be marked by any notion of dynamic cyclicity. The items of the sets are simply listed seriatim and what we have is a generally static classification. The dynamic factor in the scheme seems to lie mainly in the behavior of humans, particularly of the king himself. The ideal ruler controls the system quite firmly in terms of his profound comprehension, yet even for him doubts may still remain. It is striking that the author allows in his scheme a place for indeterminate contingency. In situations of doubt, the king is exhorted to consult the instruments of divination, such as the tortoise shell and milfoil stalks.[45] The independent dynamic of the patterns of history linked in Tsou Yen to the dynamic relation of the five elements is notably absent.

Another version of the correlative cosmology which may be no older than the third century B.C. is the "Monthly Ordinances" (*Yüeh ling*) included in the canonical "classic," the *Record of Rites* (*Li chi*), which is probably a compilation of the late Warring States or Early Han period.[46] The central category here is the cycle of the year and the theme is the proper ceremonial and practical orientation of the ruler to the tasks governing each month and season of the year. Each month is related to astronomical conjunctures, to the elements, and to the correlates of taste and musical notes, as well as to certain temporary presiding deities, and so on. The ruler is admonished to see to it that the practical tasks of agriculture appropriate to the season are carried out. Thus, proper ritual and what might now be called "rational" practical admonitions are completely intertwined. The Son of Heaven must perform the appropriate sacrifices of the month, wear the proper ceremonial robes, eat the appropriate foods, and perform the proper ceremonies in the Hall of Light (*ming-t'ang*), which is a microcosmic architectural representation of the entire cosmic order.[47] At the same time, he promulgates instructions on the appropriate tasks of agriculture. By concentrating our attention on the time frame of the four seasons rather than on large historic cycles, this particular system provides us with an extraordinarily vivid and concrete image of how the ruler and his officials align themselves ritually/magically with the annual temporal cycles of the natural world.

The growing hold of correlative cosmology on the intellectual and political elite during the world-shaking and "revolutionary" period which runs from the third to the first centuries B.C. calls for further reflection. The cataclysmic convulsions of the period may have strongly reinforced feelings that events were governed by vast forces beyond the control of either individuals or states. Within the Chinese world of thought (with perhaps some exceptions—Hsün-tzu comes to mind), the modern Western sharp dichotomy between natural and social-historic forces would hardly have seemed plausible. Yet what we have is something quite different from the kind of "fatalism" of the generation which followed Confucius. Paradoxically, what correlative cosmology offers is both a sense of the human's dependence on all levels of his being on cosmic forces and yet the exhilarating promise of the capacity on the part of some minds to comprehend these forces which seem to be eminently "knowable" and the power to use this knowledge to achieve an "alignment" between the human and natural worlds.

As we have seen, even Mencius' Confucian faith seems to have been fortified by his belief that he could discern the cyclical patterns of Heaven's manifestation in history, a belief that furnished a foundation for his more apocalyptic hopes. There is indeed a tradition that Tsou Yen, who was present at the Chi-hsia Academy in the generation after Mencius, may have himself been influenced by the kind of historic speculation we find in Mencius. If this were the case, it might help to explain Hsün-tzu's puzzling attack on Tzu-ssu and Mencius as fashioners of what he calls the *wu-hsing* (translated here as the five modes of action or the five elements).[48]

Whatever one may think of the relation of correlative cosmology to the advance of "natural science" in China, there may indeed be a kind of parallel to a widespread perception of the role of science in the modern world. Science deeply reinforces the feeling that humans are fundamentally shaped by forces—natural and social—beyond human control. There is, however, the accompanying belief that those who understand these forces are somehow able to master them in the service of human ends. In Huang-lao Taoism also, the Taoist sage is able to draw on his mystic gnosis to control the world. There is nothing mystical, however, about the knowledge of the expert in correlative cosmology. He can clearly comprehend the interrelationships of natural and human forces. The world is entirely scrutable and thus entirely open to an understanding of its inner connections. The cosmologist is thus able to find the appropriate "technology" for aligning the human realm with the realm of nature. He does not "control" nature but his knowledge of how to "align" the human with the natural immeasurably enlarges his ability to control the human world.

## Correlative Cosmology and the Realm of Religion

I have thus far not attempted to relate this correlative type of thinking to various Western definitions of the word religion. Needham sees this type of thinking in relation to the category of science and of "organismic" philosophy (although drawing a sharp invidious distinction between its supposedly "naturalist" and "phenomenalistic" forms). Other scholars in contemporary China have assigned it entirely to the realm of religious superstition.[49] To the extent that the entire system is conceived of as operating through a vast network of correspondences and resonances among natural and human phenomena, its key terms do not refer to acts of spirits and gods. *Yin/yang* and the five elements are presumably abstract entities (*entes rationis*) and thus presumably not spirits or gods. Correlative cosmology would indeed seem to correspond more closely to the preferred language of Needham in discussing "organismic" philosophy than does the Taoism of Lao-tzu or Chuang-tzu. What holds the entire cosmic organism together in the latter is the ineffable, unfathomable mystery which subsumes the whole known world. Correlative cosmology, on the other hand, seems to focus on a vast horizontal network of observable processes and entities which almost seem to achieve a unity by what Needham chooses to call "a process of 'cooperation.' " It is eminently a *tao* of which one *can speak*. Nevertheless, most of the systems of correlative cosmology which we meet do have a term for the ultimate reality which is both immanent in and subsumes the parts. Tsou Yen refers in the fragments we have of his thought to Heaven: "During the rise of Yü the Great, Heaven produced trees and grass which did not wither in autumn or summer."[50] The same is true of the *Lü-shih Ch'un-ch'iu* and Tung Chung-shu. In the Great Appendix of the *Book of Changes,* the great ultimate principle (*t'ai-chi*) engenders the entire symbolic system of hexagrams and also, one presumes, the actual world which they symbolize. Whether one should think of these ultimate principles in this immanent form as mystical or religious would again depend on one's view of religion and mysticism. Heaven seems to be immanent in the system and operates only through its articulations. Given the necessary periodicity of the five elements, Heaven necessarily gives rise to all the correlative clusters. Heaven is indeed no "law-giver God" standing outside the system; Heaven is necessarily realized through the system. Yet this Heaven is neither the entirely nonprovidential *tao* of Lao-tzu or of Hsün-tzu nor Spinoza's God. From the human point of view the entire system is "providential" in that all its operations are deeply implicated with the human order, as when Heaven "naturally" produces omens to announce a new dynasty. The universe is somehow "on man's side" and even on the side of the normative human order of civilization. When irregularities and disturbances occur on the human side, Heaven will necessarily react with portents and disasters. Yet one cannot speak of heaven's transcendental "theistic" interventions, since Heaven will act only through the impersonal patterns which manifest its being. Omens and portents are thus an inherent part of the system.

Yet when we examine Tung Chung-shu's architectonic Confucianized system of correlative cosmology, a Westerner is instantly struck by the pervasive presence of heavenly attributes which would in the West be called anthropomorphic. Heaven is the ancestor and father of both the ten thousand things and of mankind.[51] Heaven shares with humans the attributes of anger, love, joy, and sorrow, which all find expression in the "moods" which govern the four seasons.[52] Heaven's emotions, however, always necessarily manifest themselves in their proper place and order. There is in fact a "mind of Heaven" (*t'ien hsin*) which permeates all its activities. The sacrifices to Heaven must be performed. "When a son does not serve a father, is this not regarded by everyone as impermissible? How can this be different from a Son of Heaven not serving Heaven?"[53] The sacrificial rite is itself a necessary part of the entire correlative order. Despite Needham's assertion to the contrary, Heaven may in this version of correlative cosmology be a ruler, a father, and a sustaining principle, and the explicit analogy between Heaven and earthly rulers is constantly maintained. Yet it is true that Heaven as ruler does not rule by "fiat" nor does he consciously "make" laws or fashion the order over which he rules any more than a true father "makes" the institution of the family or even the basic *li* which should govern the family. Indeed, an ideal human ruler, in this view, would also not make laws of his own or rule by fiat or run counter to the immanent normative order of society. In his rule he would conform to Heaven. Here again we find another instance of the "cosmomorphic" man which we have already found in the *Analects*. Here too, the conformity to order would not make the virtue (*te*) of Heaven or fathers superfluous. The feelings and intentions of rulers and fathers would simply conform to the ordered feelings and invariant intentions of Heaven. "A father is the Heaven of his son. Heaven is the Heaven of the father. Without Heaven there would be no life. Heaven is the ancestor of the ten thousand things. Without

Heaven they would not come into being."[54] Heaven sustains the world just as the good father both bears and sustains his children. The fact that they do so through the immanent order of the world and the immanent order of the family renders neither Heaven's "heart" nor father otiose.

At one point Needham acknowledges that organismic thinking, particularly in the form of the macrocosm/microcosm doctrine, actually can be found in the West and that it is a particularly important strain of sixteenth- and seventeenth-century European thought.[55] He also points to the fact that both the "universe analogy" and the "state analogy" to the human organism could be found in both the West and China. He nevertheless then insists that in the West, because of the characteristic European "schizophrenic" split between "Democritan mechanical materialism" and "Platonic theological spiritualism," there was a felt need for the organic system to be controlled by a "guiding principle"—"by entelechies, animas, archaei," and so on. We are then assured in emphatic terms that "this was exactly the path Chinese thought had *not* taken."[56]

The fact remains that in Tung Chung-shu, Heaven is the heart of the universe just as the earthly ruler is the heart of the sociopolitical order and the heart is the ruler of the body. We are even told that "the ruler of men in his method models himself on Heaven."[57] One cannot know exactly what Needham means by the term "guiding principle," but I think that the difference between the "world soul" of Western organismic thought is not as distinguishable from Tung Chung-shu's Heaven as he would have us believe. It may be true that in Lao-tzu and Chuang-tzu what sustains the organismic order is an unfathomable, ineffable mystery which cannot be described in any language—whether we use terms such as "world souls" or "natural processes." The case is somewhat different in correlative cosmology, which often comes very close to something like the metaphor of a "world soul." This world soul is not necessarily more of a "personal" god in Giordano Bruno than it is in Tung Chung-shu. Yet Tung Chung-shu's language seems to lend itself much more to this metaphor than to Needham's metaphor of cooperation of "component parts" or "harmony of wills," which even in the words of Needham is *not* a voluntary cooperation but a system subject to a "cybernetic control."[58] Is "cybernetic control" not a kind of "guiding principle"? In the end, wherever one has a "holistic" system, the whole however conceived in some sense subsumes and "controls" the parts. If the coherence of the whole is maintained by an unspeakable mystery, one no more can speak of it in terms of a "harmony of wills" than in terms of a "guiding principle." In Chinese correlative cosmology, however, Heaven seems to be as much a "world soul" as it is in "organismic" thinking in the West (although one may readily grant that this may not be a dominant orientation in the history of Western thought). The difference, if any, is a matter of nuances rather than of absolutes.

In Tung Chung-shu, as in all correlative cosmological thought, the problematic area remains the human realm. Once again, we meet the fatal human capacity to initiate actions which upset the harmony of the whole—the capacity to strike the wrong note in the resonantial symphony. Tung Chung-shu finds no difficulty in speaking of Heaven's reaction to human misbehavior in language which refers simultaneously to the dislocations of the *yin* and *yang* and the five elements and language which refers to "heavenly intent" (*t'ien i*). The "intent" of Heaven in nature never departs from its proper course but when the ruling elements of human society misbehave, it is entirely "natural" that Heaven should react through natural disorder and disasters. There is thus an enormous pressure on the rulers and elites who govern society—or on individuals, to the extent that individuals are responsible for their own individual behavior—to attend vigilantly to the correctness of their ritual and ethical behavior. On the human side, "particulate causes" in the sense of deliberate, discrete decisions must be present.

Correlative cosmology relates to the realm of religion in this sense on yet another level—on the level of the manifold numinous spirits and deities who remain very much present in nature. They do not disappear from nature. All "organismic" thinking in China remains quite capable of incorporating them. Built into the system, in fact, is the notion that the indwelling spirits of mountains and rivers and the ancestral spirits must continue to be the recipients of the ritual honors which are their due. Indeed, if they do not receive proper ritual attention, this may again disorder the harmony of the entire system. The performance of the proper sacrifice to a mountain spirit may be simultaneously regarded as "an act of religious piety" toward the spirit or as a "magical" act designed to maintain the geomantic harmony of the spatial world. By the same token, the spirits' reaction of anger at failure to perform the rites is itself an inevitable manifestation of a breakdown of an aspect of the system. Here Lévi-Strauss's sharp distinction between sacrifice and magic is no longer easily maintained.

In the "Monthly Ordinances" (*Yüeh ling*) of the *Record of Rites,* one of the essential functions of the Son of Heaven is to conduct the worship of the spirits who preside over the seasons. The god of agriculture Kou Mang, who may be of quite ancient origins, is simultaneously the god of the element wood and must be worshipped in the spring. Chu Yung, the god of fire, is naturally associated with fire as one of the five elements and must be worshipped in the summer.[59] We thus find that the five elements themselves are not simply Auguste Comte's abstract ideas totally antithetical to numinous spirits. They may in fact be associated with indwelling "presiding" numinous spirits which must continue to be the objects of proper ritual performance.

In a fascinating account in the *Tso-chuan* in which we find elements of the mythic lore of dragons interwoven with elements of correlative cosmology, we are told that each of the five elements have their presiding "officials" (*wu kuan*) (who are in this account themselves apotheosized human beings). As officials they are "in charge" of all the phenomena governed by their element. To answer the question "Why are there no dragons now?" the astrologer/historian Ts'ai Mo explains that the position of the presiding official of the element of water is now vacant. Dragons belong to the element of water and hence, like all other creatures, are very dependent on the care of the presiding official in control of the element to which they belong. In the absence of the presiding spirit of water, dragons are no longer accessible.[60]

While this tale may represent an early version of the five elements theory and while discussions of *yin/yang* and the five elements in later ages often become entirely divorced from reference to presiding spirits, the use of the "state analogy" in this account reminds us of an observation of Needham in his discussion of the *Book of Changes*. Here, he himself suggests that the *Book of Changes* with its "cosmic filing system" was strongly influenced by the paradigm of the "bureaucratic social order."[61] Indeed, one might say that the "state analogy" may be much more important as a paradigm of Chinese holism and organicism than the biological organism (elsewhere we have noted Munro's suggestion that the original paradigm may have been that of familial order). The five elements in the above tale are in effect five "departments" administered by their ministers. The implications of this type of "organicism" are again quite different from those of a biological model. Bureaus, even in a highly routinized administration, still require living bureaucrats. One may envision an ideal bureaucratic system like that of Shen Pu-hai in which the behavior of presiding officials will totally and "automatically" conform to rules of procedure and administrative regulations. Yet, once again, the functionaries must perform their duties. They are not otiose.

This "bureaucratic image" can later be found not only in the cosmological texts of the high culture but also in the diffuse popular religion of the people. Divine "offices" such as that of "god of insects" or "god of fire" can in later ages come to be occupied by a variety of spirits over time and space, including the apotheosized spirits of great heroes and magistrates.

Similarly, in the type of correlative cosmology which reaches its full development in the Han, the fact that the spirits all function within the framework of the system does not in itself render them superfluous. The behavior of natural spirits will, in fact, conform to the impersonal rhythms and regularities of nature so long as proper ritual and ethical behavior prevails in the human realm. When the good order is maintained, the spirits will not produce maleficent effects.

On the human side of the equation, one need hardly point out that those who serve in government may carry out their duties well or poorly. The functional norms of office do *not* automatically internalize themselves in those who perform the functions. The human realm remains the "part" of the organismic whole which can fatally disarrange the whole.

It is thus by no means entirely possible to separate correlative cosmology from the realm of religion as conceived of in the West. Nevertheless, one can continue to speak of the primacy of the concept of order within this outlook. Indeed, during the period spanning the Warring States and the Early Han dynasty one can, in fact, discern an ongoing tension between the kind of religion which was compatible with correlative cosmology and the religious tendencies resistant to the subordination of the vast and incalculable realm of divine power to the constraints of the system. Such resistance certainly existed on the level of the diffuse popular religion but was even to be found on the highest levels of political power. In the accounts which we find in Ssu-ma Ch'ien and the *History of the Former Han Dynasty* (*Ch'ien Han-shu*) concerning the religious proclivities of emperors such as the First Emperor of the Ch'in, Liu Pang (Kao Tsu) the Founding Emperor of the Han, and above all Han Wu-ti, there is much evidence of tension.

Ssu-ma Ch'ien's famous treatise, "The Feng and Shan Sacrifices," which may be described as a kind of history of the religion of the state from ancient times to his own day, throws particular light on the religious preoccupations of the First Emperor and of the author's contemporary, Emperor Han Wu-ti.[62]

Both of these striking personalities, who resemble each other in many ways, are enormously concerned to assure for themselves and their dynasties the support of whatever cosmic forces there may be for both their public and private aspirations. Both seem committed—up to a point—to the correlative cosmological system. Yet both seem to yearn to break out of the confining constraints of the system. In the relationship between Tung Chung-shu and the Emperor Han Wu-ti, we note that Han Wu-ti seems not at all assured that the "system" as expounded by Tung Chung-shu is necessarily "on his side." Both emperors seem extraordinarily interested in establishing direct, unmediated contacts with the vast world of numinous powers, which may not be subordinate to the constraints of the system.

Their enormous anxiety to be in contact with the entire world of numinous spirits is striking, and throughout the treatise one notes an indeterminacy about the world of spirits. New divine beings are likely to emerge to light from any quarter, as in the case of the diffuse popular religion of later ages. The possibility of the elevation of human figures to divine status no doubt encourages this tendency, but we even find that abstract entities and mystical principles may become incarnate, as it were, as living numinous spirits. The First Emperor of the Ch'in sacrifices to the "eight spirits," which include spirits called the "lord of heaven," here treated not as the ultimate source of the universe but as the partner divinity of the lord of the earth, the lord of arms, the lord of *yin*, the lord of *yang*, the lord of the moon, the lord of the sun, and the lord of the four seasons.[63] The officiants at many of these specific cults were not *ju* but the shaman/magician types who claimed direct access to these deities and to their divine power. The Emperor Han Wu-ti, who was particularly addicted to the shaman/magicians (*fang shih*—"experts on methods"), is persuaded by one of them, Miu-chi, to inaugurate a cult to "The Great Unity" (*T'ai-i*) "as the most honored of the spirits of Heaven and to his helpers the Five Emperors."[64] The term "Great Unity" seems to derive from the mystical One of the Taoists.[65] Here, however, it becomes an "honored spirit" and the object of a specific cult.

In all of these exuberant cults one discerns a distinct retreat of the role of Heaven as the supreme source of the cosmic order and the highest object of imperial religion. One can, of course, only speculate at this point. No doubt during the long period of the decline of the universal kingship, the sacred rites of worship of Heaven by the universal king had receded into the background. The word *ti* which originally referred to the high god was now attributed to the universal king himself and even pluralized to refer to the "Five Emperors" (*ti*). The word Heaven itself had in Taoism and in Confucianism come to be conflated with the *tao* of Taoism and thus to be associated with the impersonal order of the *tao*. In Tung Chung-shu, however, Heaven is restored to its position as the central source of being and also as the "heart" of the correlative cosmological order. It is thus not insignificant that Tung Chung-shu himself places an enormous stress on the ancient imperial sacrifices to Heaven, which one would gather from what he says were not, in fact, being performed. "The Son of Heaven is called the Son of Heaven. How can he receive the appellation of Son of Heaven without performing the rites appropriate for the Son of Heaven? The Son of Heaven must sacrifice to Heaven just as a man must feed his father."[66] Heaven is the "lord of the hundred spirits" and all the sacrifices to other spirits will not avail without him. Heaven sustains and informs the universe and its order and thus the very principles of Confucian morality. Thus Tung Chung-shu's emphatic insistence on Heaven and proper rites of sacrifice to Heaven is a crucial aspect of his entire system of cosmological Confucianism.

On the other hand, one cannot but feel that Han Wu-ti is most attracted to the shaman/magicians who promise immediate access to divine powers unmediated by the constraints of the correlative cosmological order. Avid to secure signs of divine legitimation for his dynasty and support for his vaulting expansionist ambitions and no doubt fully convinced that he, above all, is the most likely candidate for the attainment of the personal immortality now promised by the spreading cult of immortality, he turns to the *fang shih*, for they claim to possess the methods for drawing directly on the support of the divine powers.

In the "Feng and Shan Sacrifices" we read that "Sung Wu-ch'i, Cheng-po Chiao, Ch'ung Shang, Hsien-men Kao and Tsui Hou were all men of Yen who practiced magic [*fang*, literally "methods"] and followed the way of immortals discarding their mortal frames and relying on the spirits."[67] We shall not speculate here on the distant origins of the belief in the survival of the human individual as some kind of immortal entity. Yü Ying-shih has suggested that traces of the belief can be found as early as the eighth century B.C.[68] Certainly the belief in the survival of ancestral spirits and in the apotheosization of great men provided dispositions favorable to the belief. The notion of the development of techniques of prolonging life perhaps in the circle of Yang Chu's followers may also have encouraged the belief in the progress from longevity to immortality. In the form in which it occurs during the period we are considering, the immortal is no longer an earthbound soul but a free celestial being unburdened of all the limits and infirmities of mortality (*hsien*), and it is—one would gather—primarily the *fang shih* who by their contacts with the divine spirits are able to obtain the secrets of this state.

There is little evidence that any of this has anything to do with the texts of Lao-tzu and Chuang-tzu, however much the texts may have later been interpreted in a manner designed to support "immortality Taoism." Ssu-ma Ch'ien seems to discern no relationships between the experts on immortality and what his father Ssu-ma T'an calls the "school of *tao.*" Nor does there seem to be much evidence of a close link of these shaman/magicians to correlative cosmology. In Ssu-ma Ch'ien's own account they "claimed to transmit [Tsou Yen's] teachings but were unable to understand them."[69] When the famous *fang shih* Li Shao-chün comes to impart his teachings on immortality to Han Wu-ti, he links his dietary and "alchemical" teachings directly to the worship of the god of the fireplace (*Tsao-chün*). "If you sacrifice to the fireplace," he states, "you can transform cinnabar into gold. Using this gold you may make drinking and eating vessels which will prolong the years of your life. With prolonged life you may visit the immortals who live on the island of P'eng-lai in the middle of the sea. If you visit them and perform the Feng and Shan sacrifices you will never die."[70] Here we find no hint of correlative cosmology and all depends on direct contacts with spirits. The divine spirits as represented to the emperor by the compliant *fang shih* are ever ready to respond to his most boundless aspirations and desires. When viewed from this perspective, Tung Chung-shu's cosmological Confucianism represents a strikingly inhibitory and constraining system.

Han Wu-ti is, of course, known in Chinese history as the Constantine of Confucianism who followed the momentous advice of Tung Chung-shu and others to establish the "five classics" of Confucianism as the foundation of all official education and to proscribe all "unorthodox" doctrines (*i tuan*).

The relation of Han Wu-ti to the Confucianists nevertheless remains a most difficult matter. He obviously regarded the *ju* of his time, many of whom came from the old culture centers of Lu and Ch'i, as experts in the cultural and religious heritage of the past. He turned to them for information about sacred custom and ceremony which would help to establish the cosmic legitimacy of his dynasty. Whether the term *ju*—even at this time—necessarily implied any commitment to deeper levels of Confucian thought still remains unclear. Yet many undoubtedly regarded themselves as "Confucianists" of some sort. One of their main attractions nevertheless was that they were presumed to possess information which the emperor regarded as essential. It is also clear that most *ju* also supported the emperor in his aversion to the Huang-lao Taoism which had enjoyed such predominance during the reigns of his predecessors—and particularly of the hated Empress Dowager Tou.[71]

In Ssu-ma Ch'ien's account, Han Wu-ti was particularly obsessed with carrying out the successful performance of the so-called Feng and Shan Sacrifices on the sacred Mt. Tai in Shantung. According to a prevailing idea of the period whose origins are obscure, the "successful" performance of this most exalted sacrifice confirms the overwhelming approval of the reigning monarch by all the spirits of heaven and earth.[72] In the words of Ssu-ma Ch'ien, "When these are carried out there is none among the countless spirits who does not enjoy pure offerings."[73] Assuming that the traditions concerning the correct performance of the rites were a hoary sacred tradition, the *ju* should have been the custodians of this tradition. Yet many of the *ju* candidly admitted their lack of knowledge concerning the modalities of the sacrifice, while the less scrupulous were completely unable to reach agreement. Ssu-ma Ch'ien himself strongly implies that the emperor was in fact morally unworthy to perform it. In the end the *ju* failed to satisfy him and he proved just as ready to receive advice from the *fang shih*. Yet, he continued to regard the *ju* as the custodians and major interpreters of the sacred ancient texts.

## Cosmological Confucianism and the Imperial State

No doubt the suggestion of Tung Chung-shu that the emperor proscribe the "hundred schools" and establish an official orthodoxy must have appealed to Han Wu-ti's most authoritarian and most despotic proclivities. It has thus been urged that Tung Chung-shu's "cosmological Confucianism" proved to be an outlook peculiarly favorable to imperial despotism. By incorporating the Han dynasty into the orbit of the cosmic cycle of dynasties, this mode of Confucianism gave its blessing to the new centralized bureaucratic principle of government, which marked such a striking departure from the "feudal" model of the past. The latter had presumably been the ideal of Confucius, who had regarded it as the "Chou" model. Tung Chung-shu implies in all his writings that the Confucian ethic and the teachings of the *Spring and Autumn Annals* are as applicable to the realities of the centralized bureaucratic state (the model was itself still somewhat mitigated by the survival of "feudal" units called the *kuo*) as they had been to the dynasties of the past. The entire corpus of his writings does tend, in fact, to suppress the fact of what seems in retrospect to have been a fundamental change in polity.

Finally, in urging that the "five classics" be made the exclusive basis of elite education and in urging the proscription of other modes of thought, some think that Tung was simply reinforcing the most despotic tendencies of the imperial polity.

There is, however, much to be said on the other side. While Tung Chung-shu's cosmological Confucianism confirms the cosmic status of the universal king, in the case of Han Wu-ti, Tung also seems to have conceived of it as a weapon of inhibition and constraint. Ssu-ma Ch'ien, who treats Tung with marked respect in contrast to his contempt for some of the other leading Confucian political actors of the time, suggests that the omens and portents which play so prominent a role in Tung's cosmology are used by Tung to constrain the emperor's despotic aspirations. We are told that at one point Tung almost lost his life as a consequence of his critical interpretation of the conflagration of the mortuary temple of the Emperor Kao-tsu. He had evidently implied that it was a consequence of the emperor's misbehavior.[74]

It is also significant that in his "philosophy of history" Tung Chung-shu stresses not only Tsou Yen's five element cycle but also his doctrine of the *yin/yang* alternation from one dynasty to the next of the principle of cultural complexity (*wen*) and the principle of simplicity (*chih*). Tung implies that after the excessive overdevelopment of the machinery of culture under the Chou, the dominant principle of the Han dynasty—the true successor of Chou—ought to be that of austere simplicity. His quite unavailing recommendations in the spheres of domestic and foreign policy do indeed emphasize light government and nonintervention in the very face of the emperor's frenetic dynamism and love of pomp and luxury.

Within this context, one can well understand why the emperor may have been more inclined to look to the *fang shih* and their promise of direct access to the favors of the gods and spirits rather than to the cosmological Confucianism of Tung Chung-shu, with its stern stress on the primacy of an order which was not invariably responsive to his highest aspirations. It is striking that we find absolutely no evidence of belief in the cult of immortality in Tung Chung-shu's writings.

To be sure, Tung Chung-shu is anything but a liberal "pluralist." In his advocacy of the establishment of cosmological Confucianism as the true orthodox doctrine, he simply reconfirms the orientation to the ancient notion that the correct political order and "true teachings" must coincide (*cheng-chiao ho-i*) after the long interval of the Warring States and Early Han when this principle had been in abeyance. It was an orientation shared by most of the leading figures of the "hundred schools" even when they had been obliged to tolerate the undesirable confusion of an unwelcome intellectual diversity. A figure such as Hsün-tzu was prepared to see other modes of thought as containing grains of truth. Yet all these limited and one-sided perspectives had to find their modest place within the frame-work of an overall Confucian synthesis. The only mode of thought which may have contained something like a "pluralistic" potential-ity was Huang-lao Taoism, which achieved the height of its influ-ence during the early years of the Han dynasty.[75] If one were again to attempt a summary of the basis of this pluralism, it seemed to rest on the belief that from the point of view of the ineffable and inex-haustible *tao,* all schools of thought and "methods" (*shu*) are equally limited perspectives with equally limited insights.

It might be interesting at this point to say something about the attitude of the Huang-lao school of the early Han period toward the claims of correlative cosmology. If the assumption is correct that Ssu-ma T'an's "Essentials of the Six Schools" may accurately repre-sent the Huang-lao outlook, we find that the School of *Yin* and *Yang* is mentioned alongside the other five "schools" as providing a legiti-mate and yet limited perspective on certain areas of experience. Its defect is that "it encourages superstitious taboos; it constricts men with fears," yet simultaneously "it leads to conformity with the or-dering of the four seasons."[76] The reference here seems to be to the relative restricted type of correlative cosmology described in the "Monthly Ordinances." Rulers should act in ritual ways appropri-ate to the cycles of the seasons but the implication is strong that such acts only deal with certain limited areas of experience, just as Con-fucian prescriptions of *li* are mainly appropriate for dealing with the area of appropriate familial and political relations.

The great Taoist sage-ruler will call upon experts on *yin/yang* phe-nomena, on Confucian ritual, and on the law and bureaucratic or-ganization wherever their services are appropriate. He will leave the "details" to them. His higher gnosis leads him to understand both the limits and appropriate areas in which the limited perspectives of all the schools are applicable. Ssu-ma T'an treats the "schools" not simply as separate doctrines but almost as specialized activities re-quiring particular talents, methods or technes (*shu*). One indeed wonders whether Ssu-ma Ch'ien's own defense of varied walks of life such as those of the so-called wandering knights or private warriors (*yu hsia*) may not be a further extension of his father's Huang-lao "pluralism" against the efforts of the Emperor Han Wu-ti to estab-lish a monopoly of social power and prestige for "Confucian" scholar officials.[77] To be sure, Han Wu-ti himself, as we have seen, by no means relies exclusively on the Confucian *ju.* In matters of his "religious" concerns, some of his favorite advisors are the *fang shih* and in matters of state policy he relies heavily on undisguised Legalists, such as the famous Lord Sang Hung-yang. Yet his educational policies, which establish the Confucian curriculum of the "five classics" as the basis of all elite education, lay the foundation for the ultimate predominance of the conventional Confucian status ideal. Thus, if the Huang-lao Taoist influence of the Early Han period represented a tendency toward a kind of intellectual and social pluralism, it was to prove a passing episode even though its spirit may be preserved in Ssu-ma Ch'ien's famous historic masterpiece.

Correlative cosmology in its Confucian tendency was to emerge as a triumphant doctrine both within official Confucianism and in high cultural thought in general throughout the Former Han dynasty (206–25 B.C.) and well into the Latter Han (25 B.C.–220 A.D.), when it would come under increasing challenge.

While Ssu-ma T'an speaks of the anxieties and fears inspired by this outlook, this first expression of Confucianism as an established "official" faith reflected a high confidence in the human power to comprehend the workings of the cosmos and of its ways in human affairs. In its Confucian form it nourished the confidence that Heaven is entirely scrutable in its unambiguous support of what were considered to be the Confucian ethical norms. Neither the Confucius of the *Analects* nor Mencius nor certainly Hsün-tzu rested his faith on such a supreme confidence in his capacity to read all the designs or workings of Heaven. To Tung Chung-shu, Heaven's ways are scrutable and transparent. There is no chiaroscuro. The only mystery lies in the perverse human capacity to disrupt the harmonious workings of the entire order.

It was thus probably inevitable that with the enormous crisis which arose during a period running from the first century B.C. to the first century A.D., the confidence in this system among the more thoughtful members of the intellectual elite gradually began to wane. The story carries us well beyond the scope of this volume, but what one can discern in the Latter Han dynasty is an effort on the basis of new reading of the sacred canons to disentangle what were regarded as essential Confucian verities from the total embrace of correlative cosmology.

Correlative cosmology, in fact, comes under increasing challenge and even radical attack. Yet it never disappears entirely as an aspect of state Confucianism. Even nineteenth-century emperors feel obliged to issue penitential edicts for the occurrence of natural disasters. Yet, if we examine the "Neo-Confucian" thought which dominated the intellectual life of China after the Confucian "renaissance" of the early Sung dynasty, we find that, on the whole, it very much "marginalizes" correlative cosmology.

Nevertheless, the crucial categories associated with correlative cosmology—the concept of *yin* and *yang,* the five element categories, and others—will remain a universally accepted language for talking about nature and about many aspects of human life. They penetrate deeply into the popular culture and dominate the language of medicine, geomancy, and other accepted "sciences" without major challenge. One is thus again tempted to ask why the Chinese did not with some minor exceptions conceive of alternate categories for understanding the structure of the natural world. One would have to reply again that their basic concerns may have lain elsewhere. The famous Chu Hsi, overwhelmingly preoccupied with establishing the foundations of the moral life in the human person, seems quite content to analyze the concept of *ch'i* in terms of the five elements. These five categories seem to prove sufficient for his analytic purposes. He is not really fundamentally interested in creating a more effective science of chemistry. In the words of Nathan Sivin, anyone who rigidly imposes his own question on the thought of another culture "may never discover that the problems his sources aimed to solve lay in quite another direction."[78]

# CHAPTER 10

# THE FIVE CLASSICS

THUS FAR I have focused on one aspect of Confucianism in its first expression as established doctrine—its fusion with correlative cosmology.[1] A much more enduring aspect of this newly established Confucianism is its close association with a body of canonical texts which has come to be known in the West as the five (or six) classics (*ching*).[2]

In many early references the six classics are identified with the "six arts" or what might be called the "six sacred disciplines" (*liu i*).[3] It might indeed be more accurate to think of the whole matter in terms of ongoing disciplines. The classics are in essence particular texts within the disciplines which achieved canonical status. Throughout the Han dynasty, we will thus have different versions of texts such as the *Book of Documents* or different "commentaries" on the *Spring and Autumn Annals* (these commentaries themselves may be conceived of as texts within the discipline) which become associated in complex ways with crucial issues in the intellectual history of Confucianism.[4]

Four of the disciplines—the *Poetry*, the *Documents*, *li*, and music—are clearly present in the *Analects*. They form part of the normative *tao* transmitted by the Master although we can have no idea of what texts he refers to in teaching *li* and music. The present *Record of Rites* (*Li chi*) is probably a compilation of the late Warring States or Early Han period which includes many texts not directly concerned with *li* as such. The four disciplines themselves obviously belong to the early Confucian curriculum. They are an integral part of the normative *tao* transmitted by the Master.

The *Spring and Autumn Annals* is first mentioned by Mencius, who associates it with Confucius and who cites Confucius himself as saying, "It is the *Spring and Autumn Annals* which will make men know me. It is the *Spring and Autumn Annals* which will make men condemn me."[5] It is, however, Mencius' adversary Hsün-tzu who will already speak of the *Poetry*, the *Documents*, the *li*, and the *Spring and Autumn Annals* as a *ching*.[6]

The *Book of Changes* mentioned neither by Mencius nor Hsün-tzu thus emerges as the most problematic Confucian canonical text. At the core of text as we now have it is a divination text which, in its origins, may have had no particular relation to Confucian doctrine whatsoever. Yet both of these texts, which achieve canonical status in official Han Confucianism, remain important foci of a vast hermeneutic enterprise throughout the history of Chinese thought and must therefore receive some separate consideration despite the enormous difficulties which surround the traditions associated with them.

## The *Spring and Autumn Annals*

The *Spring and Autumn Annals* tradition is almost as difficult of access as the *Book of Changes* tradition because of the peculiar textual problems involved, and yet, because of its canonical status it was to become a central focus of much later Confucian thought in an area involving the interaction of history, ethics, and politics.

The first great puzzle is that the core text itself is made up of nothing more than a series of flat and terse notices recording certain significant historic events. These notices are ostensibly based on the official chronicle of the State of Lu during the period from 721 B.C. to 479 B.C. (the period which receives its name from the text) even though the events to which the notices refer cover not merely the state of Lu but the entire "civilized" world of the times. Mencius informs us that "when the world had declined and the *tao* had faded away, heresies and violence became prevalent. There were even instances of regicides and parricides. Confucius was filled with apprehension and composed the *Spring and Autumn Annals.*"[7] This leads one to expect a dramatic historic account. Yet, as Legge indignantly remarks, "Instead of a history of events woven artistically together we find a congerie of the briefest possible intimations of matters in which the court and state of Loo were more or less concerned."[8] The entire work is made up entirely of facts such as the following: "Chin [the state] put to death its great officer Yang Ch'u-fu." "In the summer the Duke had a meeting with the Earl of Cheng at Shih-lai." "In the second month, the first day of the moon, the sun was eclipsed," and so on. Can it be that Confucius poured his passionate concerns into these dry notices?

There is solid ground for believing that all the states of the Chinese world had their official chronicles which recorded significant official events. Mencius himself names the chronicles of other states. The chroniclers may have been the *shih*, the functionaries concerned with calendrical, astronomical, astrological, and historical affairs. It is possible that the stylistic conventions governing the official recording of significant events may have called for this bare and austere style. Perhaps the very bareness of the style underlined the sacred and public significance of the event. If this is indeed the case, Mencius' remark that Confucius composed his book in the "style of the historiographer" is a most significant remark.[9] In all such recordings of events we must therefore suppose that oral and perhaps even written information concerning the circumstances surrounding the recorded event was widely available and that such circumstantial accounts as we later find in works such as the *Tso-chuan* and the "Narratives of the States" (*Kuo-yü*) may indeed furnish us with detailed, if perhaps highly embroidered, accounts of the events in question.

The later commentators emphasized that the keeping of state chronicles had been wholly an official public matter. In Mencius' words, "Strictly speaking, this is the affair of the Son of Heaven."[10] If we assume that Confucius composed the *Spring and Autumn Annals,* this was another striking instance of Confucius the commoner presuming to pass judgments on the weightiest public matters. In the Han period this presumption was indeed taken as proof that Confucius was the man who had been chosen by Heaven as the "uncrowned king" (*su wang*) who had not—for mysterious reasons—actually won the throne. Mencius again quotes Confucius as saying "that I have appropriated the righteous principles of judgment in it," indicating that he was somehow providing his own selected version of the official chronicle.[11] He was daring, as a private person, to submit the actual history of the period to his own "judgment of history." A controversy nevertheless rages over whether the bare text itself is drawn from the official Lu chronicle for which the Master provided an oral commentary or whether Confucius himself wrote these notices. In the latter case, the secret of the meaning of Confucius' message would have to be sought in the very wording of the notices themselves.[12] The use of a particular verb or the presence or absence of a particular title or the use of a formal or informal name might be of the utmost significance. Two of the later commentaries on the work dominant during the Early Han dynasty—the Kung-yang and the Ku-liang commentaries—are composed of question-and-answer discussions in a catechismic form based on the latter assumption. The other great commentary later attached to the text is the exceedingly rich mine of the *Tso-chuan,* which provides colorful and circumstantial accounts of most of the events mentioned and even of events not recorded in the *Annals* text. Here too one finds endless controversies. Was this text composed by persons who were carrying on the oral tradition of Confucius himself, or was it an entirely separate narrative account later imposed on the original text during the Han dynasty? William Hung thinks that it may ultimately be based on a Lu oral tradition and that it is basically Confucian in orientation.

Without attempting to penetrate further the intricate controversies surrounding the text and its three commentaries, one might simply ask whether the issues which the commentaries discuss do indeed relate to the vision of the *Analects*. I would be inclined to answer in the affirmative. If one of the grand themes of the *Analects* is the world's falling away from the normative *tao*, this declination takes place within the stream of history and it is by studying the facts of history that one knows how and why the norms are realized or violated. The treacherous alliances and counteralliances of states recorded in the *Annals*, the accounts of portentous violations of all the norms of role and status relationships, as well as the struggles of some to preserve the norms and ideals in the circumstances of a depraved world, graphically teach us how to judge men in such times of trouble. Confucius' ambivalent attitude in the *Analects* toward Kuan Chung, as we have seen, already involved a complex "weighing of circumstances" (*ch'üan*) and a complex judgment of the man. The concept of "weighing circumstances" occurs quite frequently in the Kung-yang and Ku-liang commentaries on the *Annals* and also in the narratives of the *Tso-chuan*. Here history is indeed held up as a "mirror" which clearly reveals the ugliness or nobility and the wisdom or folly of those who must act in a time of decay. Since noble men must attempt to act in the world as they find it, they cannot avoid history or at the very least they cannot avoid making complex moral judgments about the tangled flow of events.

We cannot be at all sure that our present "three commentaries," which were probably put into written form long after the Master's death, truly reflect his own views or even the version of Confucius' teachings available to Mencius. The vivid accounts in the *Tso-chuan*, while generally Confucian or proto-Confucian in tone, by no means provide judgments of "praise and blame" which reflect a "purist" Confucian ethic. Centuries later, Chu Hsi, who was not an enthusiastic admirer of the "three commentaries" and judged them in terms of his own rigoristic moral standards, finds that the *Tso-chuan* often reflects a morality of pure political expediency and a deplorable concern with "success and failure" rather than with pure moral motivation. While he acknowledges that the other two commentaries do indeed concern themselves with moral judgments, these judgments are in his view often limited and defective.[13]

Yet if the commentaries may not entirely reflect the view of the Master, the *Spring and Autumn Annals* itself was to become a canonical source of the Master's views and the text taken together with its commentaries was thus to exercise a profound influence on Chinese concepts of history in later centuries. What strikes one at first approach is that while the text and commentaries *when viewed as a whole* do provide an overall linear historic account of the entire spring and autumn period, on another level the focus is on human action in an infinite variety of concrete situations which can be treated quite discretely and even, as it were, "ahistorically." The situations themselves involve what might be called perennial and metahistorical principles of ethical and political judgment. It is on this level that the concept of "praise and blame" (*pao-pien*) seems to apply most directly. Here we have an "ahistorical" (in the nineteenth- and twentieth-century sense) attitude to history as a "mirror" which certainly had many counterparts in the premodern West. History is regarded as a kind of reservoir or casebook of universal human behavior in all times and places. While Machiavelli's use of Roman history in the *Discourses* is anything but moralistic, it nevertheless also reflects this casebook approach. In the *Spring and Autumn Annals* as in the *Book of Changes*, the focus is on the "human being in his situation" although the focus is on past events and not on prognostications of the future.

The situation and the human reactions to it are, of course, judged in terms of normative principles. Most later commentators have been struck above all by the particular emphasis on the violations of norms governing sociopolitical roles and statuses and the relations among them. It is often remarked that the *Spring and Autumn Annals* are basically concerned with status obligations (*ming-fen*), and it is indeed this emphasis which underlines the "conservative" side of Confucius' vision. Without question, proper behavior in terms of role and status is one basic aspect of the vision of the *Analects* itself. Yet the focus of attention on the "objective" aspect of things rather than on the "subjective" *jen* aspect does highlight what might be called the more conservative side of Confucius. The three commentaries are, of course, not exclusively concerned with the horrors of regicide and parricide and other modes of flouting legitimate authority. The monstrous behavior and caprices of the occupants of positions of authority are also duly recorded. The central theme is the sinister consequences of the decay of legitimate authority—whether due to subversion from below or to the sins of the holders of authority themselves. Some of the accounts deal with the casuistry surrounding the ethics of authority but the principle of authority itself remains crucial. Consider this example. Chao Tun, a capable minister of Chin, is forced to flee by the monstrous and capricious ruler, Duke Ling. Chao Tun manages to escape but does not manage to cross the state border before the duke is assassinated by Chao's own kinsman. Chao Tun returns to court but fails to punish the assassin. The court historiographer then makes the following entry into the official chronicle, "Chao Tun murdered his ruler." Since he had not left the borders of the state, he had retained his status as minister and it had therefore remained his official duty to punish the murderer of his ruler. Not having done so, he bore the responsibility for the murder. Chao Tun contritely admits his transgression but in the end neither he nor the murderer undergoes further punishment.[14] Here we find a judicious "weighing" of the monstrous behavior of the holder of authority against the need to maintain the principle of authority as such. Yet because of the circumstances, simple admission of transgression by Chao Tun suffices to set things right.

Despite this focus on metahistorical ethicopolitical problems, the *Annals* are not, as indicated, entirely "ahistorical" even in the nineteenth- and twentieth-century Western sense of that term. When one surveys the text as a whole, one in fact perceives the overarching linear movement of a gradual process of historic decline. One proceeds from the relative disarray of the period of "hegemony" to the total breakdown of universal order at the end, and one would imagine that Mencius, who himself seems to have a clear sense of the larger impersonal patterns of history, probably sees the *Spring and Autumn Annals* within this larger framework. The text thus did lend itself to use by that strain of Chinese historical thinking which was to be concerned with overall "patterns of history" as well as by those who were mainly concerned with history as casebook and mirror.

It is thus striking that Tung Chung-shu, who like most of the early Han Confucian thinkers tends to be a specialist in one of the classic "disciplines," actually considers himself above all a student of the *Spring and Autumn Annals* and of the Kung-yang commentary. By using a highly esoteric method of interpretation he even claims to base his entire correlative cosmological system upon it. This is particularly mystifying since neither the text nor the commentary seems to depart very far from its concern with human affairs. Both focus on man's behavior in the human arena. Omens and portents do indeed play a role but not a central one. Nor does Tung Chung-shu himself neglect the purely human ethicopolitical issues which arise in the text. On the contrary, he tends to derive from the texts universal principles of ethicopolitical behavior which transcend all "changes of institutions." While his correlative cosmology provides, as it were, the ontological basis of this Confucian ethic, the *Spring and Autumn Annals* provide him with the ethicopolitical content of his ethic.[15]

On this level of his interpretation of the *Annals,* he is basically concerned with problems of ethicopolitical behavior outlined in the text which seem to transcend all institutional change, just as the perennial political truths of Shakespeare's Macbeth and Julius Caesar seem to transcend all the differences in political systems which mankind has thus far devised. Tung Chung-shu was thus a pioneer in the effort to apply general ethicopolitical principles developed in the age of "feudalism" to the age of more or less centralized bureaucracy. The perennial principles of proper behavior pertaining to role and status were evidently not, in his view, rendered nugatory by the shift in political systems.

The *Annals* tradition is in sharp contrast in this respect to another work of the late Warring States or Early Former Han period—already mentioned above—called *The Rites of Chou (Chou-li),* which did not win high canonical status although it remained on the borderline of such status. This text attempts to provide nothing less than a blueprint of the ideal political structure of the early Chou. The word *li* refers here to an entire institutional structure. Here the perfection of Chou is related to the perfection of its articulated institutional system. In the case of the *Annals* tradition, however, what we are provided with is not an institutional blueprint but a focus on certain normative abiding principles of ethicopolitical behavior. It is no accident that centuries later the famous "radical" statesman of the Northern Sung, Wang An-shih, who was in search of the "blueprint" of an integrated program of reform would exalt the *Chou-li* and make light of the *Annals.*

On another level, however, Tung is also concerned to discern long-range patterns of history in the *Annals.* When viewed on this level, the *Annals* illustrate the gradual decline of the Chou dynasty resulting from its excessive cultural complexity (*wen*). On this level, he places the full sweep of Spring and Autumn history into the Tsou Yen pattern of *yin* and *yang* alternations of periods of complexity and simplicity (*chih*).[16]

The *Annals* can thus be interpreted in ways which will support two dominant Confucian perspectives on history: as a casebook of metahistorical paradigmatic ethicopolitical situations which provide guidance for moral behavior even in a far from ideal world; and as a synoptic view which surveys the larger general patterns of history— patterns which are by no means totally subject to human control.

The two perspectives are by no means mutually exclusive. Both the Confucius of the *Analects* and Mencius see the immanence of Heaven in larger historic patterns which lie, at least in part, beyond human control. The noble man may live in good times or bad and must act accordingly. Yet both cling to the belief that the moral behavior of exemplary men may have an educative and transformative effect which will leave its mark not only on their time but on the future as well. Thus proper ethicopolitical action within concrete circumstances of a given time and place, and proper judgments of the actions of other actors, maintain their lasting and fundamental relevance for all those concerned with the realization of the *tao* within the flux of human affairs.

The *Tso-chuan*, which was in later ages to displace the "New Text" Kung-Yang and Ku-liang commentaries as the main "orthodox" commentary on the *Annals*, provided, of course, an infinitely more interesting and colorful account of events than the sententious, catechismic "New Text" commentaries which do, however, provide clear and decisive ethicopolitical judgments. In the *Tso-chuan*, the storyteller, often swept on by the dramatic flow of his story, is by no means so clear-cut in his moral judgments. The rigoristic Chu Hsi later will charge that "the defect of the Master Tso is that he will discuss right or wrong in terms of success or failure."[17] The moral drawn at times seems to him more a judgment of political success and political prudence rather than of strictly moral "praise and blame." The line between Confucian norms and political sagacity is not always sharply drawn—a fact which was not lost on more "conventional Confucianists" who often read it in this more utilitarian and "practical" spirit. Nevertheless, whatever one's view of the *Annals* tradition as a true expression of Confucian "idealism," its concerns seem to relate directly to fundamental aspects of the vision of Confucius and Mencius if not to the vision as a whole.

## The *Book of Changes*

The *Book of Changes* (*I ching*) presents even more formidable problems than the *Annals*. Here we have a text regarded by many Chinese and some foreigners as well as providing access to the deepest recesses of the "Chinese mind" and embodying the very essence of Chinese culture. It is a text whose core is a particular system of divination and a text closely associated in its present form with a correlative cosmological outlook. It is also a text which achieves canonization as one of the five Confucian classics. With its canonization, no later Confucian thinker can ever entirely ignore it.

When one peruses the vast literature of commentary on this text in later ages, one feels more than in the case of any of the other "classics" that this literature is often used more as a vehicle for expressing the particular preoccupations of particular ages than for revealing the recondite secrets of the text itself. While it is now a fashion of literary criticism to say that all texts simply provide pretexts for the preoccupations of readers, the composite and suggestively enigmatic nature of this text may lend itself particularly easily to this type of "deconstructionist" interpretation. As Irene Eber states in her introduction to the English translation of the famous *Lectures on the I Ching* of Richard Wilhelm, "Its very abstruseness suggests an intriguing richness of multiple meanings."[18]

Without in any way pretending to have mastered the intricacies of the discipline of the *Changes*, I shall say something about some of its more accessible aspects. There is wide agreement that the oldest layer of this highly composite text consists of the symbols of the trigrams and hexagrams and the oracle texts which are attached to them. The basic symbols are the broken (− −) and unbroken (—) lines combined into eight permutations of trigrams (e.g., ☰ , ☱ , ☲ ) and sixty-four sets of hexagrams—each a combination of two trigrams (e.g., ䷀ , ䷁ ).[19] Trigrams and hexagrams each have their assigned names, which presumably represent major aspects of their meaning, and to each hexagram there is attached first a statement providing a general summary of its meaning (*t'uan*) and a text composed of six "attached propositions" (or, in Willard Peterson's translation, "attached verbalizations") (*hsi-tz'u*) which explicate the particular significance of each broken or unbroken line within the context of each hexagram. The latter text reveals a dynamic unfolding process proceeding from the bottom line to the top line, which to the diviner provides an unfolding account of the trajectory of the situation to which the hexagram applies. It is also assumed by most commentators that the present ordering of the sixty-four symbols as one proceeds from one symbol to the next has its own deeper meaning.

While these symbols and their attached "verbalizations" may constitute the oldest stratum of the text, there is no way of knowing when the symbols and texts came together to form a fixed system. Divination by separate hexagrams actually occurs in the *Tso-chuan*, but some scholars regard these accounts as later interpolations. Yet here we find a graphic account of how the system is used as a practical technique of divination.

Since many of the attached propositions clearly contain highly enigmatic and allusive references, Arthur Waley has suggested that imbedded in these texts are what he calls peasant "omen texts," which derive from the hoary lore of diviners based on the significance of bodily states, or occurrences in the natural world—events such as "movements in the great toes" (no. 31) or "wild geese gradually approaching the shore" (no. 53).

The trigrams and hexagrams in our present text have their own fixed names which seem to relate to the most general characteristics of the situation to which the hexagram refers as well as to all the other correlated meanings of the hexagram. Thus hexagram *chien* (no. 53) the text of which contains the reference to the geese *gradually* approaching the shore has the general meaning of "gradualness" or "steady advance" suggesting that the pondering of the diviners on the omen of the geese may have focused mainly on the slow advance of their flight and hence on the idea of gradualness in general. The names of the trigrams and hexagrams refer to categories as utterly diverse as lameness (*chien*, no. 39), litigation or strife (*sung*, no. 6), separation (*li*, no. 30), "intelligence repressed" (*ming i*, no. 36), or duration (*heng*, no. 32). The odd and wildly heterogeneous nature of these categories may not seem so strange when viewed from the point of view of the diviner bent on providing advice concerning the infinitely varied situations of human life.

One aspect of the attached propositions is that they already reflect the strong influence of *yin/yang* cosmology; hence this aspect even of the oracle texts may in fact be quite late. The unbroken line is treated as a *yang* line and the broken line as a *yin* line, while each of the six positions of the hexagram from bottom to top is either a *yang* or *yin* position in alternation. Thus when a *yin* line appears in a *yang* position or vice versa, one has a kind of dislocation—a lack of correspondence which generally seems to represent an unfortunate moment in the relation between the actor and his situation, while a positive correspondence between a *yin* and *yang* line and a *yin* and *yang* position represents a positive state of affairs.

Even among traditional commentators there is a general agreement that the so-called ten wings (*shih i*) or "ten appendices," which constitute the balance of the text and which are sustained treatises on the larger meaning of the oracle texts, emerged later than the oracle texts themselves. Many modern scholars agree that these treatises date from a period no earlier than the third century B.C. and probably no later than the Early Former Han dynasty. Willard Peterson, in his translation of the "Great Appendix," which he calls "The Commentary on the Attached Verbalizations" (*hsi-tz'u chuan*), suggests that "it is not a product of a single act of creation whether by an author or compiler but was accumulated over a certain

period beginning approximately a generation before the Ch'in dynasty and was proclaimed and hardened by the first century B.C."[20]
The assumption is thus warranted that these treatises on the whole
very much reflect the thought of the late Warring States or Early
Han periods.

Any reflection on the text as a whole must begin with a consideration of the implications of the practice of divination. The diviners of
the Shang dynasty, like the diviners of Mesopotamia, directed their
inquiries to gods and spirits. Divination represented an indirect way
of communicating with the divine world concerning the outcomes of
various situations. The augur or diviner depended on the will of the
spirits, and the varied patterns of cracks produced by scorching tortoise shells and shoulder blades of oxen were directly produced by
the decisions of the gods.

It is, however, possible that over time the broodings of the diviners
on the "inner" relations between the patterns of the divinatory signs
they used and the trajectory of the situations led to more abstract
conceptions of the relationship between situations and signs. The
sign perhaps came to "resonate" with the field of the emerging situation, making it not so much a reflection of the wills of the spirits as of
some kind of inner correspondence with the nature of the emerging
situation, just as in the case of the astrologer the conjunctures of the
planet are signs which resonate quite directly with human personal
or political situations. With this development, the emergence of
fixed systems of signs and of methods for relating signs and meanings becomes quite conceivable. It is in this sense that the kind of
thought which one finds in the core of the *Book of Changes* may itself
have been one source of correlative thinking. It is a version of correlative cosmology which focuses in the first instance not so much on
the overall grand patterns and regularities of the natural and
human worlds as on the vastly varied and contingent world of shifting situations and circumstances. The system offers the possibility of
a kind of science of situations which enables the individual or group
to adapt itself correctly to the demands of unfolding situations since
the situations themselves belong to certain general classes of situations. The eight trigrams and sixty-four hexagrams thus provide
symbolic information concerning the principles governing appropriate behavior in given situations.

The "Great Plan" (*hung-fan*) version of cosmology in the *Book of
Documents* provides us with nine sets of categories which are designed
to embrace and control the entire field of individual and sociopolitical experience. Yet one of the categories is the "examination of
doubts." The other general categories, despite their impressive in-

clusiveness do not, it seems, eliminate the factor of contingency and indeterminancy still to be found in concrete life-situations. Here the ruler has recourse to the diviner of tortoise shell and milfoil stock who is prepared to offer guidance even in areas where uncertainty prevails.[21] The author of the treatise who seems to be genuinely Confucian in outlook recommends divination only as one aid to decision-making, alongside the consulting of his own heart and the opinion of officials, nobles, and common people. Yet here we have a clear instance of how the system of divination can be incorporated into a larger system of correlative cosmology.

In the "ten appendices," however, we find a distinct tendency to extend the meaning of the symbols well beyond their specific reference to their divinatory functions. Here we find them associated both with ideas of the highest generality on the one hand and with quite concrete realities such as animals, heavenly bodies, and even human inventions on the other. Thus, if the first and one of the most important hexagrams ch'ien ( ☰ ), composed of six unbroken lines, refers to a situation calling for dynamic, creative, and bold behavior, one can readily understand how it comes to be associated with the principle of yang, with Heaven, the male, the ruler, the father, the symbol of the dragon, and even the abstract idea of the dynamic and the dominant as such, while its opposite (k'un) (☷) comes to be associated with the principle of yin, the earth, the female, the subject, the mother, the mare, and the abstract idea of the passive and the receptive as such. If the first two hexagrams with their universally ramifying meanings seem to embrace the universe between them, all the other hexagrams come to refer to various separate aspects of reality. Thus the "Great Appendix" is grandly able to proclaim that "the tao of Heaven is in it [the book or system of the Changes]; the tao of man is in it; the tao of earth is in it."[22] The Changes can thus be conceived to subsume all the categories of correlative cosmology within its own framework.

As Needham has pointed out, the eight trigrams when taken by themselves refer to familial relations, social categories, natural phenomena such as thunder, wind, lakes, and so on. Given this wealth of associations when the trigrams are combined into sixty-four hexagrams, the room for imaginative association becomes vastly more extensive than anything we find in the ordinary yin/yang and five elements cosmology. While the latter indeed operates only with a limited science of concrete phenomena, the hexagrams provide abstract symbols with possibilities of an indeterminate extension.

Needham has provided a most interesting discussion of how hexagrams acquired meanings of a very high order of abstraction.[23] Thus *chun* (no. 3) is the principle of a process where the beginnings are slow and difficult while the subsequent development is free and un-obstructed, as in a germinating plant. *Chien* ("lameness," no. 39) is the principle of a process where there is constant retardation of movement forward. *Ken* ("limit," no. 52) is the principle of a state of immobility—in terms of situations, a state calling for immobility or quietude on the part of the actor. *Wei-chi* ("not yet ordered," no. 64) is the principle of a process of "disorder potentially capable of con-summation in order."[24] Here we do indeed find what Needham calls a "concept-repository" of unique concepts which never lose their connections to their original function as descriptions of the dynam-ics of situations.

The most ambitious and philosophical interpretations of the sys-tem are to be found in the treatise commonly known as the "Great Appendix" (*hsi-tz'u chuan*). This commentary is not so much con-cerned with the separate abstract meanings of the trigrams and hex-agrams as with claiming for the system the ultimate key to all matters, mystical, metaphysical, and human. The very fact that the book became canonical lends all its statements on ontological mat-ters a peculiar weight for those in later ages who felt impelled to scrutinize the classics in search of an ontological foundation for Confucian values. Thus, statements in the "Great Appendix" which deal with metaphysical principles (principles which move well be-yond the framework of correlative cosmology) became the focus of intense study by Sung Neo-Confucianists such as Chou Tun-i (1017–1073 A.D.) and even Chu Hsi, who otherwise tends to treat the *Book of Changes* as basically a divinatory text.[25] Statements such as the following come to assume a momentous significance: "The alter-nation of *yin* and *yang* [literally one *yin* and one *yang*] is called the *tao*. That which carries the *tao* forward is goodness. That which com-pletes it is the nature [*hsing*]."[26] "That which is above determinate form [*hsing erh-shang*] is the *tao*. That which is within the realm of de-terminate form are the concrete entities [*chi*]."[27] "The ultimate prin-ciple [*T'ai chi*] produces the two basic symbolic forms. The two basic symbolic forms [*i*, — , – –] produce the four figures [*hsiang*, ⚌ , ⚏ , ⚎ , ⚍ ]; the four figures produce the eight trigrams. The eight tri-grams produce fortunate or unfortunate [outcomes]. Fortunate and unfortunate outcomes produce [the need] for great actions [*ta yeh*]."[28]

When we examine these statements we cannot but sense the pow-erful influence of the Taoist vision of the manifold world emerging out of the *tao*. It is true that the early Ch'ing thinker Wang Fu-chih, who rejected what he regarded as the Neo-Confucian "Taoist" dis-tortion of the text, points to the first statement as proof that the *tao* is nothing transcendental apart from the immanent processes of *yin* and *yang* and all the concrete phenomena of the world. Yet the very next statement in the text clearly informs us that the *tao* is "above determinate form." Apart from the above statements, however, the Taoist influence in the "Great Appendix" can be found in many other passages, as Peterson has indicated. The system of the *Changes*, we read, "is without thought and acts by *wu-wei*." "It is still and un-moving."[29] Looming behind all change there is the numinous, mys-terious dimension of reality (*shen*) which is itself beyond change. "That which cannot be fathomed in the *yin* and *yang* is the numinous or divine [*shen*]."[30]

The Taoist dimension of the "Great Appendix" is, however, me-diated through a system of symbols embodied in lines, trigrams, and hexagrams which symbolically mirror and correlate with all the processes and forms of the natural world as well as with the infi-nitely varied circumstances of human life—even circumstances which on the face of it seem indeterminate, doubtful, or laden with contingency. On this level they furnish concrete information con-cerning the "fortunate or unfortunate" trajectory of given situations as well as concerning the mode of behavior appropriate to such situ-ations. Yet while the symbols themselves are in a sense forms, the inner nature of the reality which they symbolize is itself not grasp-able in human language. "That which is written cannot fully ex-haust the meaning of speech. Speech cannot fully exhaust the meaning of ideas. Can we then discern the ideas of the sage? The Master said, 'The sages established the emblematic figures [*hsiang*] in order to give expression to their ideas.' "[31] While the symbols can be visualized, the realities which they symbolize are beyond language even though they provide quite definite information on the level of our ordinary experience. In the words of Peterson, "The technique and text of the 'Changes' include and mediate the known and the unknown."[32]

The ancient sages who established or rather made manifest the system of the *Changes* themselves seem to share the attributes of the Huang-lao Taoist sages, who, through their gnosis of that which is "hidden," are able to establish the symbolic system which mediates between the known and unknown. Because they themselves are fully able to grasp the "inner workings" of the system, their own behavior in all the variegated circumstances of the world constantly conforms to the *tao* by the principle of *wu-wei*. They immediately grasp the principles governing situations and invariably respond appropri-ately. Yet, as Peterson remarks, "We who are not sages can connect up with the non-physical but potent numinous presence through the medium of the 'Changes' which is itself numinous" even when we use the symbols quite mundanely to determine the principles governing the situations in which we are involved.[33]

If the Taoist and correlative cosmological dimensions of the "Great Appendix" are obvious, what are its links to Confucianism? We are after all informed that the *Book of Changes* in whatever form it existed during the Ch'in dynasty was one of the texts exempted by the First Emperor from the general burning of books. As a divination text it was eminently "useful" and he presumably did not associate it with Confucianism. Did the text contain at the time the "ten appendices" as they now exist or did the latter in their full "Confucian" interpretation emerge only in the early Han?

One of the major assumptions of most systems of divination which furnish advice rather than simply predict in a wholly "fatalistic" fashion is that human life may involve doubtful and indeterminate situations in which deliberate decisions must be made. Divination by pointing to the trajectory of a situation can provide information on what type of action is most advisable if success is to be achieved or ill fortune to be minimized. Yet on the face of it, it is hardly obvious that a truly Confucian morality is concerned with hard prudential "practical" advice concerning success or failure. On the contrary, the *Analects,* Mencius, and even Hsün-tzu emphatically reject concern with worldly success or failure. The original oracle texts themselves can easily be read in ways which do not at all suggest Confucian moralism. The resolute firmness (*chen*) which is recommended may have nothing to do with morality and the "cause for regret" referred to in the texts may mean regret for one's lack of acumen. In the *Annals* tradition, an effort is, of course, constantly made to link the "weighing of circumstances" (*ch'üan*) to the question of what ought to be done in terms of Confucian principle. This is by no means obvious in the oracle texts of the *Changes.* The texts often seem to refer to the course of action of a *shih* bent on achieving a career, as is evident from the constant use of the statement, "It will be advantageous [*li*] to see the great man."[34] Much could easily be interpreted wholly in terms of an entirely prudential and "careerist" course of action if the aim were simply success.

In the Confucian reading, however, as in the case of Tung Chung-shu's linkage of his correlative cosmology with Confucian values, what we find is the constant stress on the notion that the sage and noble man is interested only in the proper moral posture required in each situation. If the first hexagram *ch'ien* seems to point to the need for dynamic resolute action, the noble man will eagerly seize the opportunity to serve. It will be advantageous to meet the "great man" (the ruler) presumably because the "great man" is truly great in the highest ethical sense. Thus to be able to predict the trajectory of a situation helps the noble man to act morally in both favorable and unfavorable circumstances. In the appendix entitled "Explanation of the Sentences" (*wen yen*), which is a commentary on the first two most important heaven and earth hexagrams (*ch'ien* and *k'un*), we find one of the most lofty Confucian interpretations of the hexagrams. In describing the noble man as the "dragon lying hidden in the deep" it states, "He will not change to conform to the world nor do anything merely for fame."[35] "He advances in virtue and performs his tasks. He relies on faithfulness and truthfulness in advancing his virtue. He carefully attends to his words and firmly adheres to sincerity in carrying out his tasks."[36] Presumably the hexagrams simply furnish him with useful information on which moral posture to assume in given situations.

It is within this context that the latter two clauses of the statement cited above—"The alternation of *yin* and *yang* is called the *tao;* that which carries it forward is goodness; that which completes it is the nature"—takes on an enormous significance for later thinkers, for here we find a fusion of a metaethical *wu-wei* Taoist-like ontology with the sphere of the ethical and of *yu-wei* human ethical decisions. The system of the *Changes* finds its realization in the human sphere only through the practice of goodness and—as in Mencius—it is only through the constant and deliberate practice of goodness that the nature (*hsing*) can be realized. To figures such as Chou Tun-i or Chu Hsi, who were enormously drawn to a metaethical Taoist mysticism or the Zen vision of enlightenment and yet resolutely committed to a Confucian ethic, this formula seemed to offer a profound solution to their dilemmas.

Yet the fusion of Taoism, correlative cosmology, and Confucianism which we find in the "Great Appendix" seems to reflect common tendencies of the later Warring States period and in different forms can be found in both Hsün-tzu and the "Doctrine of the Mean" (*chung-yung*), which will be briefly considered below. The philosophy we find in the Appendix seems no more "primordially" Chinese than any other tendency of the age. The philosophy itself could indeed be easily detached from the entire apparatus of the book as a divinatory text.

The great Chu Hsi, however, would centuries later insist on maintaining the connection between the two. Chu Hsi treasured Chou Tun-i's interpretation of the "Great Appendix" philosophy, yet in a spirit of stern honesty he rebuked those who refused to recognize that the book as a whole remained a divination text. Without overemphasizing the use of divination and while insisting that the text by no means taught men *how* to achieve moral excellence, he was ready to acknowledge its "practical" usefulness. It could provide men with useful information on how they *ought* to act in the tangled circumstance of what we call in current parlance "the real world."

While Chu Hsi will insist on a rigorously moralistic interpretation of the purposes of divination, one suspects that the pervasive emphasis in the text on fortune and misfortune and success and failure led many "conventional Confucianists" (*su ju*) down through the ages to see in it either a fortune-telling aid to prudential maneuvering in the game of life, a support to the hope that "being good" would lead to tangible worldly success, or a belief that success and good fortune were themselves proof of the presence of virtue.

There is one other mode of interpretation embedded in the vast literature of commentary on the *Book of Changes* which merits consideration. This mode of interpretation concentrates on the abstract meanings associated with the trigrams and hexagrams considered in relation to each other. Since these combinations of symbols are conceived of as being in a constant dynamic relationship with each other, the shift in the arrangement of lines which takes place as one passes from one hexagram to another through proper manipulations can provide opportunities for imaginative reflections and meditations on the relations among the abstract conceptions associated with the hexagrams. Thus, at one point, Richard Wilhelm, a Western interpreter who operates within this Chinese interpretative tradition, relates the hexagram *ching* (䷯) meaning a "well" to the hexagram *hsü* (䷄) meaning "waiting." Note that there is a change only in the bottom line, suggesting a close affinity of the two hexagrams. Wilhelm notes that the idea of the well is associated with the idea of patience, leading him to a disquisition on the relationship between waiting and patience. The waiting involved here is not a waiting involving "bitter resignation" but a "waiting with strength"—the strength not to rush to a desired outcome when this is not advisable.[37] Depending on the user, this medium for the imaginative association of ideas could, of course, lead to arid nonsense, to the expression of great life wisdom, or even to flights of the poetic imagination.

I should say a final word here on Needham's view of the relations of the *Book of Changes* to the question of science in China. After providing a highly interesting account of the text itself, he states that while "the five elements and two force theories were a help rather than inimical to the development of scientific thought in China, the elaborated symbolic system of the *Book of Changes* was almost from the start a mischievous handicap."[38] While sharing the "organismic" orientation which Needham feels will ultimately be affirmed by the image of reality now emerging out of the most recent achievements of modern science, the specific system of the *Book of Changes* is itself simply a sterile filing system—"a concept repository"—to which all the phenomena of nature are "referred back." It generated no new observations of nature, did not encourage the "experimental" manipulation of materials, even though the alchemists were often quite anxious to employ its categories in explaining their experiments; and it had nothing to do with technological innovation despite the claim of the "Great Appendix" that all the great inventions of the past were derived from the hexagrams. Without questioning Needham's assertions concerning the *Book of Changes,* I again question his contrast between the correlative cosmology of Tsou Yen and the system of the *Changes.* Did the five elements and two force theories in themselves generate natural observation, experiment, or technical innovation? Were they not also rather used as categories for classifying and filing? Above all, did not the dominant preoccupations of the correlative cosmologists, like those of the fashioners of the *Book of Changes,* also lie elsewhere? The preoccupation which led to the canonization of the *Book of Changes* as a Confucian classic was based, it would appear, on the continued preoccupation with human destiny and normative behavior in a precarious world full of contingency.

## The "Spirit" of the Five Classics

In dealing with the five classics as canonical books, we are immediately struck by the fact that neither the *Analects* nor the book of Mencius is included despite the fact that Chinese thinkers since the Sung dynasty as well as many modern scholars have been inclined to seek in the *Analects* and in Mencius the very fountainhead of early Confucianism. While the *Analects* are often cited in the early Han and while Mencius finds his first commentator in Chao Ch'i of the latter Han period, neither text became a canonical "classic."

One is thus moved to ask whether the five classics may share common characteristics which account for their elevation to canonical status. The elevation was not evidently due in the first instance to imperial decision. We have seen that at least four of the classics are already mentioned by Hsün-tzu as the foundation of his concept of learning, and the "six classics" are referred to in the "World" chapter of the Chuang-tzu, which is probably a late Warring States or early Han text. It is also quite clear that in the early Han there are a number of *ju* already committed to the status of the *Book of Changes* as a sacred text. Thus when the five disciplines are established as the basic curriculum at the Imperial Academy of Han Wu-ti, they already enjoyed their sacred status among the Confucian scholars despite the highly divergent versions of texts and interpretations.

In seeking common characteristics of these highly divergent texts which achieve canonical status, one first of all notes that they all enjoy a kind of public status. They may not be revelations of God, but they spring from a higher source than the minds of "private" individuals. The poetry of the *Book of Poetry* is conceived of as reflecting the sentiments of the anonymous people or of anonymous noble officials. The *Book of Documents* records the words and deeds of lofty "public" figures such as the ancient sages Yao, Shun, and Yü or kings Wen and Wu and the Duke of Chou, who rightfully proclaim their teachings from their public positions at the pinnacle of the political order. Their words are in fact a kind of transcendental revelation. The *li* preserved in the texts of the *li* were not positive laws proclaimed by human fiat and convention but were firmly rooted in the *tao* itself. These three disciplines belong to that "public tradition" which Confucius transmits to his disciples. The *Spring and Autumn Annals* were supposedly ultimately based on the official chronicle of the state of Lu even if one assumes that Confucius was deeply involved in their selection, editing, and interpretation. By allowing the *Annals* to speak rather than by directly delivering his own private judgments, Confucius is basing himself on the objective, public judgments of history. He is allowing the public facts to speak for themselves. Finally, the entire system of the *Book of Changes* is presented as an evolving revelation extending from the mythic emperor Fu Hsi through King Wen of Chou and the Duke of Chou to Confucius himself, who is credited with the composition of the "Ten Appendices." The sage-kings may be individuals but they are also superhumans who embody public truth. Here, of course, Confucius the "commoner" does emerge as the author of part of a classic. Yet this again probably reflects the early Han effort to elevate Confucius himself to a status of an uncrowned sage who had truly merited the crown of kingship. Here Confucius fundamentally makes manifest the inner meaning of the objective system of the *Changes* rather than simply imparts his own "private" wisdom. He is fundamentally, indeed, a "transmitter" and an explicator of a public truth. Certainly this had indeed been Confucius' own attitude toward the four disciplines of the *Documents,* the *Poetry,* the *li,* and music. The *ju* of the early Han dynasty may have been more anxious than ever to portray themselves to the Han emperors as the custodians of the truly authentic public traditions of the past as opposed to their opponents who, in their view, based their ideas on the aberrant "private

doctrines" of the Warring States period. The latter were the convey-
ors of mere "opinion" in the platonic sense.

The classics seem to be public and "objective" not only in terms of
the basis of their authority but also in their content. They tend, on
the whole, to focus on the "outer" structures of the reality within
which humans operate. This does not mean that the Confucian emphasis on the power of individuals as moral agents (sages and noble
men in particular) is in any way minimized. The sage-kings and
noble ministers of the *Book of Documents* provided paradigms of noble
action in the world but what we witness is the manifestation of their
virtue in the arena of the public world. We are told nothing about
the inner moral processes of moral growth which lead them to their
moral excellence. Indeed, in the case of the sages, the excellence may
be innate.

The commentaries of the *Annals,* to be sure, depict men as moral
agents confronting difficult ethical decisions and involved in difficult objective situations but again one observes them, as it were,
from the "outside" in their public lives. Our view focuses on the historic situations in which they are involved. We learn about the morality or immorality of objective decisions and little about the inner
processes of moral self-cultivation.

The *Book of Changes,* of course, also fixes its attention on the world
in which man acts. It deals with a presumed body of objective
knowledge which helps the noble man to adopt the correct moral
postures in the various external circumstances of life, but it does not
really focus on how the good man achieves his goodness.

The study of *li* in the narrow sense is, of course, preeminently the
study of the objective prescriptions through which the moral man
expresses the nobility of his soul in terms of the established objective
prescriptions of social behavior. It again focuses attention on the
"outer" aspects of the moral life.

Much of the *Book of Poetry,* to be sure, seems to focus on the "inner
life." It is presented even in the *Analects* as being concerned with the
education of the emotional life. It ennobles the affective life. It
teaches men how to elevate the passions of indignation and compassion and how to apply these sentiments appropriately. Hsün-tzu
seems to link the poems, which were of course sung, to the harmonizing effects of music and his view of music very much stresses, as
against Mo-tzu, the power of "classical" music to humanize that
which is beastly in man.[39] Yet while both the *Poetry* and music are
crucial components of Confucius' own conception of learning in the
*Analects,* they still represent external disciplines of training and must
be constantly related back to the student's own subjective effort to

relate these disciplines to his own inner states of mind. Otherwise, like the performance of *li,* the performance or listening to music and the chanting of the poetry may merely become external rituals of social display. In Hsün-tzu's view, to be sure, the training itself can by "proper conditioning" itself create the proper internal states of mind. It must further be pointed out that in the early Han the heavily allegorical interpretation of the *Poetry* as providing ethico-political lessons involving rulers and ministers was a dominant hermeneutic mode.

Thus, if one can indeed speak of a common spirit of the classics it would reside in their focus on the external structures within which human moral action must take place. It is thus by no means accidental that Hsün-tzu, who believes that human nature can only be socialized from without through education, should place a considerable emphasis on the disciplines of the classics (with the notable exception of the *Book of Changes*) as the instruments of moralization. Many scholars indeed see a strong influence of Hsün-tzu in the *Record of Rites* and on the masters of the classics during the early Han—particularly those from the former state of Lu.[40] At the same time, the "cosmological Confucianists," who represent a mode of thought which sharply diverges from that of Hsün-tzu, are equally committed to the five classics.

Correlative cosmology is, after all, also oriented to the objective structures of the world. The patterns of *yin* and *yang* and the five elements, as well as the forces which lie behind the symbolic categories of the *Book of Changes,* are aspects of an external world with which the noble man must constantly be concerned.

Tung Chung-shu's conception of human nature (*hsing*) stresses the primacy of the objective environment. There are, to be sure, resemblances to Mencius. The original substance (*chih*) of the nature may be called good just as the rice seed is good. Yet what is stressed above all is not the presence of the potentiality of internal growth but the essential passivity of the rice seed as such. "Although the nature may be good when it emerges it cannot yet be called good. The full grown rice plant and the good man extend [that which is endowed by] Heaven and are brought to completion by that which is external and not by what Heaven creates as internal. When that which Heaven makes [the seedling] attains [its full formation] it simply stops [*chih*]. The point at which the 'internal' stops is called [that which is endowed] by Heaven. The point at which the 'external' stops is what is achieved by the kingly teachings [*wang-chiao*]. The kingly teachings are external to the nature and the nature must follow them."[41] Unlike Mencius, who stresses the nature's innate power of growth and the "internal" role of the heart and will in fostering this growth (however "weak" this will may be in most humans), here the emphasis is entirely on the inert nature of the *hsing* and the utter dependence on the external role of the political order governed by an elite engrossed in adjusting itself to the objective forces—including the patterns of correlative cosmology—which govern the world. In Tung's case, this objective world would also include the ethico-political lessons of the *Annals*.

The common element in all this is not a rejection of the roles of individual human agents in moralizing the sociopolitical order but a rejection of the inward-looking stress on the individual's power of self-transformation through constant self-examination.

To Mencius, one who knows his own nature knows Heaven even though he by no means denies Heaven's presence in the "objective" patterns of the cosmos and history. To Tung Chung-shu, Heaven is present, above all, in the vast, encompassing normative patterns of the cosmic and sociopolitical order. Indeed, in retrospect, as already suggested, it appears that it was precisely the notion that the source of moral power was to be sought "within" which was the most innovative aspect of the message of the *Analects* and of Mencius, and it was perhaps this introspective aspect of their outlook which was most vulnerable to rejection during the storms and stresses of the Warring States period. The notion that the noble man's *main* channel of access to Heaven or the *tao* was through his own "heart" may have, as suggested, been an important influence in the rise of Taoist mysticism, particularly in its Chuang-tzu interpretation. Here, however, the stress on the "inner" connection with the *tao* becomes completely sundered from Confucian moralism.

The vehement attack on the relevance of Confucius' stress on "inwardness" to the tasks of mastering the "world out there" which begins with Mo-tzu was, however, to spread far beyond the confines of Mohism. In the long run it came to embrace most of the *ju* stratum, many of whom had probably never been deeply affected by the *Analects'* stress on inwardness. When viewed in this context, Mencius must be seen as the beleaguered "theoretical" defender of the Master's stress on the "inner" against a sea of enemies.

There are, however, two texts whose composition may belong to the period from the late Warring States to early Han which seem to carry on the Mencian tradition. They are the two texts which came to be embedded as obscure chapters in the composite classic known as the *Record of Rites*. Legge has translated their titles as the "Great Learning" (*Ta-hsüeh*) and the "Doctrine of the Mean" (*Chung-yung*).[42] Chinese tradition itself attributes the authorship of the latter to Mencius' teacher Tzu-ssu or to the Mencian tradition in general. The "Great Learning" is attributed by Chu Hsi to Confucius' disciple Tseng-tzu, but others regard it as Mencian in spirit. The texts themselves contain many themes, and taken as a whole they by no means neglect the "objective" pole of Confucianism. The fact that both are preserved in the *Record of Rites* even leads Feng Yu-lan to stress passages in the "Great Learning" which, in his view, prove an affinity to Hsün-tzu.[43] In this brief discussion, however, attention will be focused on those passages in both texts which were to lead some Sung Confucianists a millennium later to lift them out of their obscure and neglected place in the *Record of Rites* and elevate them to exalted status as two of the "Four Books" (*ssu-shu*—the *Analects*, *Mencius*, the "Great Learning," and the "Doctrine of the Mean") which were in this mode of Sung thought to supersede the five classics as the ultimate source of Confucian truth.

What is it that Chu Hsi and others will find in these texts? I would suggest that it is precisely support for the focus on inner cultivation—on the task of "making oneself good" through constant self-scrutiny—a focus which they do not find in the five classics taken by themselves. In this view, the entire unhappy history of Confucianism after Mencius had been obscured by the long neglect of the vital core. Thus what is new in the famous sorites of the "Great Learning" is not the assertion that "wishing to order their own states they [the sages and noble men] regulated their own families; wishing to regulate their own families they first cultivated their own persons."[44] Thus far, we have little novelty. Tung Chung-shu had his own prescriptions for cultivating one's own person. What is fresh is what follows: "Wishing to cultivate their persons they first rectified their hearts; wishing to rectify their hearts, they sought to be sincere [true—without self-deception] in their thoughts."[45] Here the focus shifts back dramatically to the moral inner life of the individual.

If the "Great Learning" turns attention back to the inner life of the heart, the "Doctrine of the Mean" seems to provide a strong ontological foundation for the possibility of the achievement of inner self-realization. Thus the word often translated as "sincerity" (*ch'eng*) is here both an ethical and an ontological category. "Sincerity [undivided self-identity] is the *tao* of Heaven. Sincerity is the *tao* of man . . . He who possesses sincerity hits [*chung*] the mark without effort and obtains [perfection] without thought. He who naturally and easily aligns with the *tao* is the sage. He who attains sincerity chooses the good and firmly holds it fast."[46] Here one notes a distinctly Taoist influence together with a Confucian insistence that it is only through a "choice of the good" that the human aligns himself with Heaven. It is, of course, only the superhuman sage who can do this without "effort" or "thought." Yet he remains a Confucian and not a Taoist sage since what he chooses is the good and not a way which is beyond good and evil. The metaethical Taoist disdain for making choices between good and evil is here rejected. It is only the sage who can achieve this without effort or deliberate thought.[47] Yet the non-sages, in whose number Confucius would have included himself, can still hope to attain goodness precisely through *yu-wei* effort and thought. "Heaven and earth," we read in the "Doctrine of the Mean," "is without doubleness [or duplicity?]."[48] The fatal flaw of "doubleness" arises only in the human heart yet the same human heart/mind has the capacity to realign itself with the undivided perfection of Heaven or the *tao* even though the majority of men must rely precisely on conscious effort to achieve this goal.

In the perspective of the variety of Neo-Confucianism (Tao-hsüeh) which was to dominate Chinese elite thought in the southern Sung and Ming dynasties (roughly for some four centuries), the "five classics" Confucianism of the Han had failed to achieve its goal of realizing the *tao,* giving way instead to long centuries in which both ruling elites and the masses sought salvation in Buddhism in all its varieties as well as in "Neo-Taoism" and "religious Taoism" although "five classics" Confucianism had lingered on as an ineffective ghost. Even the "renaissance" of Confucianism in the Northern Sung dynasty had still been largely based on the assumptions of Fan Chung-yen, Ou-yang Hsiu, Wang An-shih, and others that a fresh look at the true meaning of the classics would lead to the true realization of the Confucian vision. Yet this hope was also not fulfilled. May not this entire frustrating history have been due to the neglect of the root problem? In the end the root problem was to be sought where Confucius and Mencius had sought them—in the human heart/mind. It is only the human heart/mind (in the first instance, the mind of the moral vanguard) which possesses the capacity to "make itself sincere" and having made itself sincere to extend this transcendent capacity to realize the *tao* within the structures of human society. When viewed from this perspective, this is the essential gospel of the Four Books. At a deeper level, the Four Books also point to an ontological ground for the belief in this transcendental ethical capacity of the individual in the face of the ongoing challenge of a metaethical Taoist and Buddhist mysticism.

The enormous effort during these centuries to realize this renewed vision of Confucianism was, of course, itself in turn to give rise to its own vast problematique now essentially centered, however, on the interpretation of the "Four Books" themselves.

# POSTSCRIPT

O UR FOCUS throughout this volume has been on modes of thought reflected in the texts of the "high culture" and not on the conscious life of the vast majority who neither read nor wrote.

One obvious justification for such a focus is simply the absence of sources from the period which provide any *direct* testimony concerning popular culture. As one moves forward in time over the following centuries, there does in fact emerge a growing body of material in both official documents and private writings which sheds both direct and indirect light on this area. In the recent past we also have, of course, direct access to the abundant empirical observations of both Chinese and foreign scholars. It would nevertheless be most hazardous to "read back" this later testimony to the circumstances of pre-Ch'in China.

## The Question of Popular Culture

To be sure, the texts of the high culture may themselves throw light on the popular culture, or what might more accurately be called the shared culture. Thus, despite the anti-mythic bias which Henri Maspero and Marcel Granet detect in most of these texts, a large number of twentieth-century Chinese and foreign scholars have attempted to reconstruct themes of ancient Chinese mythology both from these texts and other texts not considered in this volume, such as the "Songs of Ch'u" (*Ch'u tz'u*) and the "Classic of Mountains and Seas" (*Shan hai ching*). Granet, in fact, attempts to reconstruct not a mythology but a total vision of the life and culture of the people in Chou society from his own imaginative reading of the *Book of Poetry*.[1] Here, however, one is inclined to ask with Maurice Freedman whether "this vision relates to much outside Granet's superb sociological imagination."[2]

It might, indeed, be possible to justify our focus on these texts on the cultural-anthropological ground that Chinese culture constitutes an integrated whole embracing the society from top to bottom. Thus whether one is studying ancient texts or carrying on empirical ethnographic field research in contemporary Taiwan, one is simply dealing with variant versions of a common cultural system.

Freedman, in his essay dealing not with the category of culture but with the category of religion (which is, however, very broadly defined), maintains that "elite" religion and peasant religion in China "rest on a common base representing two versions of one religion that we see as idiomatic translations of each other."[3] Elsewhere he uses the term "transformations" to describe the relationship between the two. While he himself obviously preferred empirical field studies at the grass-roots level, he would probably not have denied that the texts we have examined provide valuable access to the elite "transformation" of the common religion of China.

My own inclination, however, would be *not* to justify the focus on these texts in these terms. I would indeed suggest that while the elite culture of China may emerge with the rise of civilization out of the same broad neolithic matrix as the culture of the people, it later diverges in crucial ways from the popular culture. I would also suggest that the subsequent relation of this culture to the popular culture was not that of an unproblematic "parallelism" of two versions of the same culture but that of a constant dynamic interaction involving both mutual influence and mutual tension between two at least partially separate realms.

For good or ill, the emerging ruling stratum of early Chinese civilization would, in the course of its "state-building" activities and in its efforts to find religious foundations for the legitimacy of its authority confront new questions which had not arisen in the experience of the village dwellers. I would, for instance, suggest that the orientation to the notion of a universal, all-embracing sociopolitical order discussed in previous pages was an orientation which necessarily first emerged on the elite culture level and was probably only gradually "internalized" in—and never totally accepted by—the popular culture.

It is, to be sure, an orientation which may have drawn strength from powerful tendencies implicit in earlier shared religious orientations such as ancestor worship, as suggested in Chapter 1. The implications were, however, probably made explicit only on the elite cultural level. The language of this culture thus included new elements which were not at all present in the popular culture.

At this point, however, I should like to draw a further distinction between "elite culture" or "ruling class culture" in general and what

I have here called "high culture." This is a distinction between the culture of the ruling class as a whole and the culture of those groups and individuals who, while they may emerge initially from the ruling stratum and be closely related to it, play something like the role of "intellectuals" in a loose definition of that term. It is impossible to draw such a distinction for the Shang dynasty, where the testimony of the oracle bones basically seems to reflect the outlook of the entire elite culture, although one can certainly speak of cultural experts in Lévi-Strauss's sense. Some evidence for the existence of intellectuals can, however, be discerned in the *Book of Documents* and the *Book of Poetry,* but it is only in the later centuries of the Chou and particularly with the *Analects* and the texts of the Warring States that we become acutely conscious of their presence. What distinguishes them is again their reflective and questioning stance toward both the culture of the people and the culture of the ruling class as a whole. It is essentially the thought of this group which is represented in our texts and to which I shall apply the term "high culture." It is this group which is the Chinese equivalent of the "creative minorities" in the contemporary worlds of India, Israel, and Greece.

The distinction drawn here between intellectuals (in the broadest definition) and ruling class seems, of course, to fly in the face of the textbook generalizations about the unique fusion of "scholar" and "official" in China. To be sure, most of these intellectuals in ancient China may have their origins in the lower levels of a nascent "state service" nobility. Most of them may conceive of "serving in government" as their sole ambition and vocation. A few of them, such as the formidable Lord Shang, actually manage to become extraordinarily tough-minded statesmen, as is often the case with intellectuals in positions of power. What constitutes them as intellectuals in the loose sense here proposed, however, is their conscious preoccupation with large questions involving the problematic relation of the received cultural orientations to the actualities of the world in which they find themselves. It is their reflectiveness and sense of critical distance. They are no longer simply the anthropologist's "cultural experts" who unproblematically expound the "rules of the culture."

When Freedman speaks of "elite" and "peasant" religion as "two versions of one religion," he may, of course, not be referring to the whole range of thought considered in these pages. He may be speaking of religion in a much more restricted and narrow sense. It is, of course, true, as has been emphasized above, that most of the modes of thought we have considered above had indeed been able to incorporate the world of natural and ancestral spirits into their conceptions of order. Their conceptions of order required no "dedivinization" of the world, and one may even agree with Freedman's skepticism of the notion that most of them were "pragmatic agnostics" who simply believed that entities to which sacrifices were performed were simply convenient fictions.[4] By the same token, it seems quite apparent that abstract ideas derived from correlative cosmology became embedded in the course of time in the beliefs and "superstitions" of the popular culture. Here instead of speaking of two versions of the same culture, one can speak both of significant overlaps and of dynamic interactions and tensions between high and popular culture.

Freedman's view may also reflect the fact that in dealing with the high culture his attention focuses particularly on what I would call the religious dimension of the political order. Within the high culture, as we have found, there was indeed the pervasive acceptance of the notion of a universal sociopolitical order, occupying a unique numinous cosmic status between "Heaven" above and *both* the human world and the world of "spirits" below. Since the high culture did not necessarily banish the worlds of natural and ancestral spirits, it also did not reject the notion of the "controlling" role of the sacred political order within the world of subcelestial spirits. One can, if one will, interpret the striking religious claims of the political order as wholly a device of "agnostic" statesmen for using the religion of the masses to control them. The anxiety to control the unpredictable religious life of the people undoubtedly exists. Yet, the anxiety to control the unaccountable activities of the myriad spirits is probably just as much present in the mentality of the majority of the ruling elite. Indeed, they regarded both types of anxiety as intimately related. Thus in its conception of the *religion of the state,* the elite culture may to a point indeed provide a mirror image of the religion of the people. Yet this religious dimension of the state by no means coincides with the entirety of the high culture which figures in the texts discussed above. While most of the modes of thought we have considered tacitly accept the numinous cosmic role of the political order, this acceptance is not relevant to many of the most vital issues considered in these texts—even including issues which might be called religious.

Yet, is the popular religion nothing but a mirror image of this political dimension of elite religion? For the period we have been considering in these pages, the evidence is, of course, extremely scarce. There can be no doubt, however, that during the centuries in which the principle of centralized bureaucracy became firmly entrenched, the bureaucratic metaphor applied to the world of spirits did gain a powerful hold on the religious imagination of the people. Arthur

Wolf, on the basis of his own study of popular religion in contemporary Taiwan, remains impressed with "its firm grip on the popular imagination."[5] I must add, however, that the application of the bureaucratic metaphor to the numinous world did not *necessarily* lead to the view that the divine bureaucracy would invariably support its human counterpart. Indeed, ideas based on the metaphor of a divine bureaucracy might even figure in ideologies of rebellion.

Furthermore, the bureaucratic metaphor applied to the world of gods and spirits must be sharply distinguished from the human political order's claim of jurisdiction over the entire world of spirits— its claim to grant or deny them "legitimacy" by admitting them into the state-sanctioned pantheon of spirits or its claim to promote and demote spirits. One may regard these rather striking claims as simply a cunning rationalization of the ruler's aspiration to maintain a total control of the spiritual lives of the people or as an anxious concern of the rulers themselves to control a spirit world which was as unaccountable and unpredictable to them as the people itself. Indeed, the two modes of unaccountability may have been closely related in the minds of the ruling stratum. I would suggest, however, that if we survey the entire landscape of the diffuse religion of the people over the ages we can also, in fact, find powerful and persistent resistance to all efforts to subordinate the realm of the numinous and divine, either to the claims of the political order or even to some all-embracing conception of cosmic order. Down through the ages shamans, mediums, and other religious specialists who claim direct access to spirits and gods—an access unmediated in any way by the political order—continue to flourish. This direct access, as we have seen, may have even been eagerly sought out by emperors and aristocrats as well as by peasants. Devotional cults and sectarian faiths will later arise which will also seek out direct and unmediated access to the divine realm. New divinities, whether apotheosized human beings or nature spirits unauthorized (at least at first) by official canonization, are likely to emerge at any point from the inexhaustible reservoir of the numinous world. Freedman himself asserts that "prophecy and ecstasy" were phenomena of popular religion which did not find their "transformation" on the high cultural level.[6]

I would suggest that what is never totally eliminated from the popular religious consciousness is not simply "prophecy and ecstasy," but a sense of the divine world as a world of unaccountable forces and spirits not easily contained and constrained by any preestablished system of order, either divine or human. It is a world in which the relations between spirits and humans may not be preordained or totally governed by ritual; a world of contingency, unpredictability, and unanticipated encounters among beings whose behavior is not wholly predetermined by their locus in a structured order.

In dealing with the practice of geomancy, Freedman assigns the abstract correlative cosmological interpretations to the elite version of the common religion and the interpretation in terms of spiritual entities to the popular version.[7] While generally agreeing with Freedman that correlative cosmology as we find it in Tsou Yen and Tung Chung-shu probably originates in the high culture, I remain skeptical of the implication that it does not penetrate the "popular" culture. In the course of time, like the bureaucratic image of the divine world, the categories of correlative cosmology are gradually absorbed into the fabric of popular culture (although most often in a piecemeal fashion), particularly as they affect the life of the family and the individual in such matters as geomancy, medicine, fortune-telling, horoscope reading, and other concerns of daily life. *Yin, yang,* and the five elements are not absent from the discourse of the people and, up to a point, provide the "theory" of many shared elite and popular beliefs. Yet they never seem to have totally displaced the role of spirits which resist incorporation into abstract schemes. In the doctrines of the popular sects and in the "ideologies of rebellion" one can thus find themes of correlative cosmology intricately interwoven with the active intervention of spirits and even with themes drawn from mystical Taoism. Here one finds complex interaction and not simply parallel versions of a unitary religion.

In sum, I would argue that popular culture was not simply a popular version of ideas reflected in the high cultural texts nor were the latter nothing more than the unproblematic elite version of a common Chinese culture. Indeed, many of the ideas in the texts we have considered do not simply mirror the culture of either the masses or of the ruling classes taken as a whole. They are, in effect, the ideas of a conscious minority which stands by dint of its reflectivity at a certain distance from both—like its counterparts in the other civilizations of the time.

A much more basic justification for the focus on these high cultural texts is that the mode of thought reflected in them over time exercised a profound influence—both direct and indirect—on the entire evolution of the culture of the ruling strata and even on the culture of the people. These individuals and groups involved do not merely expound the "rules" of a pregiven culture. They reflect on and wrestle with the meanings of the older cultural orientations even when they remain within the boundaries of these orientations. What they bequeath to posterity is thus not a static, integrated "global" culture but a problematique based on probing questions addressed to the culture from within the culture. Precisely because the high culture and the popular culture are not simply "parallel" versions of one preexistent cultural whole, one can speak of a dynamic, complex, troubled, and never totally resolved interaction between the two over time.

The ultimate justification of this enterprise must, however, be the intrinsic interest of the thought itself in terms of a comparative history of human thought.

## Shared Cultural Assumptions: A Final Retrospective View

The main focus throughout this volume has been on the range of diversity and divergence in ancient Chinese thought. It is, indeed, on this level that we have found some of its most interesting comparabilities with non-Chinese modes of thought. The issues one finds on this level are by no means exclusively Chinese and it is precisely on this level that one seems to reach beyond the boundaries of culture to the possibility of a more universal comparative study of human thought.

Yet in looking back at this entire world of thought in retrospect, one again becomes aware of the presence of shared cultural assumptions (although not equally shared by all modes of thought) through which the universal issues are, as it were, refracted.

In attempting to restate some of these shared orientations, I shall again focus on the following: the idea of a universal, all-embracing sociopolitical order centering on the concept of a cosmically based universal kingship; the more general idea of the primacy of order in both the cosmic and human spheres; and the dominant tendency toward a holistic "immanentist" view of order. All three of these orientations are, of course, related, and I should like to comment briefly on some of the terms used.

The use of the compound term "sociopolitical" throughout this volume has not been accidental. While the "social" emphasis of Chinese thought has been universally recognized, I think it would be misleading to separate the "social" from the "political" in the sense in which the latter word is used in much modern Western social thought.[8] In this particular mode of thought, the "merely political" is often downgraded because it seemingly presupposes a belief in the capacity of the conscious human will to affect human affairs. It is often contrasted in this sense with "social system" or "social forces" which are fundamental and truly causative precisely because they are "independent of the wills of men."

It is interesting to note that many students of India tend to find in

India the overwhelming priority of the social system over the political both in reality and thought. It is a system, in this view, in which the political order is a minor subsystem with a very restricted role. In China, on the contrary, in our very earliest texts we find the dominant notion that the universal king who incarnates the political order and his chosen ministers possess the power to shape or transform the entire nature of society over which they hold sway for good or ill. The word "political" here thus refers to the power of conscious will, whether of kings or political elites, to shape the course of human affairs. From one point of view, this strongly supports what has been called the Chinese optimistic faith in the power of humans to shape human destiny. In Confucianism it even leads to a strong notion of the individual moral autonomy particularly of those who have a vocation to lead society. Yet insofar as the sociopolitical order is conceived of as a total system, there is nevertheless the implication that this power to shape human affairs must at least initially belong to an ethical or intellectual elite. The masses of men, at least initially, are not capable of exercising such initiative. Thus alongside the emphasis on the power of political elites, we have the emergence of what might be called an early "sociological" perspective on the lives of the people whose behavior is massively dependent on the "environment" created by those who occupy the positions of authority in the political order. It is, to be sure, a concept of sociology which seems to have more affinity to certain eighteenth-century enlightenment modes of thought than to the totalistic sociological determinisms of the nineteenth and twentieth centuries. Like the "legislators" of the enlightenment philosophers who are able to transform environments, in China, sages and noble men who somehow have the power to transcend the conditioning power of their own environments are able to transform the lives of those who cannot transcend their environments.

The high confidence in the power of such elites to shape society represents the most exuberantly optimistic interpretation of the idea of sociopolitical order. To some students of Chinese thought it is also one of the most trying. Confucius in the *Analects* expresses enormous confidence in his power to transform contemporary society *if he were only provided the opportunity to influence* the actions of the established rulers. At the opposite pole, Han Fei-tzu has sublime confidence that if he could implement his "method" he could create an entirely new social order. Mo-tzu—while introducing a concept of sociopolitical order which marks a radical departure from the dominant "holistic" assumptions—nevertheless is equally confident that good rulers and men of worth can totally transform the social order. Even

Lao-tzu ascribes mystic powers to the *wu-wei* influence of his sage-rulers.

While it would be wrong to say that Confucianism simply con-cieves of the state as the family writ large, official Confucian rhetoric of later ages abounds in stock references to the king or emperor as the "father-mother" of the people and to magistrates as father-mother officials. The parent-child metaphor bears with it the image of the people as children. This image does not necessarily negate the human potentialities of the people. Given proper environment, the people may, as a result of proper policy and through education, come to achieve an "adult" moral autonomy within their own spheres of life. Even more trying to some than the child side of this metaphor, however, is the parent side, with its image of the ruling elite as caring and all-wise parents rather than as limited humans sharing all the frailties of their "children."

None of this implies that sages, noble, and able men may not rise out of the ranks of the masses. Nor does it at all preclude the con-ception of the equality of all humans *in potentia* as we find this idea expounded in various theories of human nature. It certainly does not imply that those who happen to occupy the loci of authority are thereby automatically endowed with sagehood or virtue. Indeed, one of the most tragic mysteries of human history is that authority seldom coincides with merit. Yet within this dominant outlook it is, in the end, only through the cosmically based structures of the polit-ical order that the society as a whole can be redeemed.

The modalities of this belief could, as we have seen, vary drasti-cally from one school to another. The Confucian metaphor of the people as children does hold out the prospect of their achieving, under proper conditions, a moral autonomy of their own. On the other hand, the Legalist pleasure-pain model of the average man with its emphasis on the need for unceasing conditioning is much more relentlessly sociologistic. The conceptions of the nature of the elites and the proper role of the political order itself within the so-ciety could cover a broad range of possibilities. As we have also found, however, running against the dominant "optimistic" inter-pretation of the role of the sociopolitical order, there are also more somber views. There is the "fatalistic" view that in the end every-thing is determined by the remote and inscrutable operations of Heaven or the *tao*. There is Lao-tzu's radically primitivist critique of the entire project of civilization and the historic Chuang-tzu's utter disdain for the entire notion of the redemptive role of the sociopoliti-cal order. Beyond this there is even in Confucianism, Legalism, and Huang-lao Taoism a vision of a sociopolitical order which will, as it were, in some sense "run itself." Even here, to be sure, the role of the political dimension will not be otiose. Within Confucianism, the spiritual vanguard will still enact its exemplary moral and ceremonial role, and in Legalism the awesome authority of the ruler will still constitute an absolutely essential principle of cohesion. Thus, we find that the idea of the universal sociopolitical produces its own problematique.

The related broader assumption which bears some final scrutiny is what I have called the tendency to a holistic view of both the cosmic and human orders—a tendency which Needham calls China's organismic philosophy. As I have emphasized in my discussion of Mohism, what is at issue here is not so much the idea of the primacy of order but the particular conception of order as holistic and primordial.

While avoiding the word "organismic," I would again agree with Needham that in the evolution of ancient Chinese thought (although by no means obvious in the *Analects* or in the pre-Confucian texts) there emerged a tendency toward the dominance of a holistic, immanentist view of order. One cannot, however, rest here. When we examine closely the concept of holism we find that the entire notion of "wholes and parts" lends itself to the most divergent interpretations depending on the implicit metaphor involved. A biological organism and a work of art may both involve "wholes and parts" but the nature of the relations between the wholes and parts may be radically different in both cases.

In Needham's work, the dominant metaphor seems to be that of the biological organism with its suggestion of total dependence on and inseparability of the parts from the dynamic whole. Although the biological metaphor itself strongly suggests hierarchic subordination, Needham prefers to use "egalitarian" imagery. There is much talk of "cooperation" of parts or "harmony of wills," while avoiding the fact that the image of "cooperation" inevitably suggests the notion of initially separate entities which come together to "cooperate." Yet it is obvious from Needham's discussion that the cooperation and "harmony of wills" is completely determined by the preestablished subordination of the parts to the whole. In the case of mystical Taoism they are not subordinate to a "mind" or a "ruler" but to the ineffable mystery of the *tao* itself, but here too, the initial independence of the parts implied by the word "cooperation" seems entirely inappropriate.

The biological metaphor is not totally absent in Chinese holistic thought. The metaphor of birth and spontaneous growth probably influenced Chinese conceptions of cosmogony and are very much present in the notion of *wu-wei*. Yet much more suggestive, it seems to me, are metaphors of holism based on the family, as suggested by Munro, or even the metaphor of bureaucratic organization, as suggested at one point by Needham himself. Indeed, in Chinese medicine and in the texts of the "Taoist religion," one often finds the bureaucratic metaphor applied to the analysis of the biological organism itself.

The biological element is, of course, itself present in the familial metaphor in terms of the centrality of "ties of blood," although the husband-wife relationship is, of course, not based on "blood." Yet the relation of the family member to the family as a whole is not precisely that of the liver and stomach to the biological organism. The members of the family are conceived of as individuals playing different roles over a lifetime and as bearing autonomous responsibility for the performance of these roles. A family, in this Confucian conception, is not an organism which can dispense with a ruler, and the behavior of the patriarch is, in effect, ethicopolitical. He can determine whether the family will be ordered or disordered and his rulership is never otiose. The individual behavior of other family members is also, of course, crucial. In some sense, the wholeness of the family is maintained only by the behavior of the parts to which one must, after all, assign a degree of autonomy.

The same holds true for the bureaucratic metaphor. A bureaucratic organization is a "whole" insofar as the specialized organs of government all function to serve the whole. Yet most Chinese down through the centuries were acutely aware that those who occupy the offices of ruler and official by no means necessarily conformed to the norms governing their functions. Shen Pu-hai dreamt of a bureaucracy in which behavior would be strictly controlled by the total machinery of rules and procedures, but the main line of later Confucianism—almost in recoil from Shen Pu-hai's image of bureaucracy—was to place its central emphasis on the quality of the human agents who occupied office. Here again, it would be primarily the behavior of the human components that would determine the functioning of the whole.

One has, to be sure, the sense that the holistic order works "as it should" on the "nature" side of the human/nature equation. Yet even here, Needham's insistence that in Chinese "organic naturalism" there is no trace of "world souls" or heavenly rulers as there is even in those strains of "organic naturalism" which arise in the West is simply not so. The principle of the whole in Taoist mysticism, it is true, cannot be called a "world soul" or a "ruler" or even a "process" or a system of "cybernetic control." What is beyond language cannot in the end be described in language. A mystery remains a mystery. Yet the "mind of Heaven" and even attributes which may be called anthropomorphic are to be found at the heart of Tung Chung-shu's "organismic" system, while Heaven's *aspect* as "ruler" does not even totally disappear in the later thought of Chu Hsi. Here again the fact that Heaven's "mind" or Heaven as ruler never departs from the ordered regularities of nature does not in the dominant strains of Chinese thought render the Heavenly mind otiose.

It is, however, in the human sphere that the notion of a preestablished holistic order faces its greatest difficulties, and it is particularly here that the much looser metaphor of the family may be most helpful. Families *ought to* constitute harmonious wholes. They do *not* necessarily do so, and it is on the rock of this ethical reality that the notion of the preestablished, unproblematic, holistic order founders.

There are no concerns more central to Confucianism than the concern with the ethical gap between norms and actualities or the concern with the capacity of human moral agents to bridge the gap. The individual human being must, to this extent, possess at least *in potentia* an autonomous individual life of his own separate from the "whole" of the sociopolitical order which seems to have no inbuilt "holistic" power to preserve its own norms. Here only the individual components can preserve the whole. Even in the Taoism of Lao-tzu and Chuang-tzu, the individual human being possesses the fatal negative power to detach himself from the whole of the *tao*. Chinese holistic thought as a shared cultural assumption—like shared cultural assumptions elsewhere—creates not finished solutions but a vast problematique.

## Ancient Thought and the Later Evolution of Chinese Thought

The range of thought which emerged in China during the period covered in this volume maintained its hold over the entire course of the subsequent intellectual history of China. This fact has in the past led some Western scholars to speak of this period as the only truly "creative" period of Chinese thought. Some twentieth-century Chinese intellectuals have indeed bitterly complained that the later dominance of Confucian orthodoxy led to a disastrous closing off of the rich possibilities to be found in the "hundred schools." In fact, of course, modes of thought such as correlative cosmology, Legalism (often in Confucian disguise), and mystical Taoism continued to influence the later evolution of Chinese thought. Yet Mohism and some of the intriguing explorations which we find in the "logicians," the sophists, and the various lines of thought later assigned by the

Han doxographers to the residual category of the "Eclectics" (*tsa-chia*), were driven to the sidelines—perhaps because they departed so markedly from dominant cultural assumptions. Nevertheless, the struggles within these strains of thought to create a language which could encompass new conceptions will remain of enduring interest to those interested in comparative thought and an enduring cha-lenge to linguistic determinists or believers in a preestablished "Chinese mind."

Does the enormous hold of the thought of this period on the subsequent development of Chinese culture prove that the later thought represents nothing but "uncreative" and inconsequential variations on themes set by ancient thought?

First of all, one notes the obvious fact that for many centuries China was profoundly influenced, both on the level of the high and popular cultures, by the vast world of Mahayana Buddhism which arrived from outside the Chinese cultural orbit. Its reception certainly reflected existing Chinese preoccupations. It was probably accepted because it seemed to provide new answers to questions which had already been posed. This itself would, however, indicate both the transcultural universality of the questions being posed and the openness to new solutions couched in categories not anticipated in the range of thought inherited from the past. One must even be highly suspicious of the facile formula that "Chinese culture finally absorbed Buddhism." Here, too, there lurks the biological image of culture with its implicit image of a digestive process in which foreign substances are completely absorbed into the unchanging identity of the preexistent organism. I would suggest that a more apt image might be that of the simple chemical compound in which the addition of new elements may substantially change the properties of the entire compound. On the level of high culture, Buddhism influenced the entire evolution of later high culture (not least of all in art and literature) and introduced many entirely new themes into the diffuse religion of the people.

If we bracket Buddhism and ask whether there was any originality, novelty, or creativity in a later Chinese thought which still relied so heavily on the agenda of ancient Chinese thought and even on the interpretation of its texts, we confront the question of what we mean by these words. Does creativity necessarily mean *creatio ex nihilo?* Can creativity arise within hermeneutic traditions? How original is originality? The dominant modern Western answer to these questions has more often than not been heavily influenced by the post-Cartesian notion of a mode of thought which, as it were, "begins from scratch" and then relies wholly on the pure and self-sufficient rational "cogito" of the individual thinker. The unprecedented triumph of the natural sciences has, of course, enormously encouraged the idea of absolute novelty as well as the notion of a world of modernity marked by an absolute breach with the entire "traditional" culture of the past. We are led to believe that somehow all modern thought shares the absolute originality and "innovativeness" of the hard sciences. Such a sense of radical break and of *creatio ex nihilo* does not occur in Chinese thought before the twentieth century.

What, then, are we to make of the claims for the creativity of Western medieval thought or even of the thought of the pre-Cartesian Renaissance and Reformation? Medieval thought drew its thematic substance wholly from the matrix of Greco-Roman and biblical thought while the great figures of the Renaissance and Reformation fervently continued to seek truth in the ancient sources. They were all engaged in the hermeneutic reexamination of known ancient texts or the rediscovery of neglected texts. Without claiming a similarity of results, we find in them the same aspiration to reach behind the encrusted misinterpretations of later ages to the uncontaminated truth of the original sources that we will find in Sung and Ch'ing thinkers in China.

The texts of ancient China may or may not have covered as broad a range of possibilities as the texts of the ancient Middle East and the ancient Greco-Roman culture, but like the texts which commanded the attention of medieval Western thinkers, they presented later generations with a range of questions to which these generations felt that the texts furnished answers. Yet the answers were not necessarily conclusive and did not foreclose further interpretation even when they were incorporated as sacred texts into an orthodox tradition. There also remained ample room, as we have seen, for a choice among texts. In the current fashionable discussion concerning the hermeneutics of texts, we are often asked to choose between the notion that the content of texts are either totally transparent and unambiguous in meaning or that they simply serve as pretexts for reading one's own unencumbered thoughts back into them. The view I would here put forth is that the problematique and dominant themes of ancient Chinese thought certainly set their constraints on the thought of later generations. Yet this did not prevent these generations—operating within entirely altered circumstances and with preoccupations of their own—from dealing with this problematique in unanticipated and "creative" ways.

I shall not attempt to assess the validity of the modern Western notion of a total qualitative rupture in the West between modernity and "traditional culture," although one suspects that Descartes owes as much to Plato and the pre-Socratics as he owes to the power of his own "cogito." I would simply suggest that before the presumed rupture in the West had taken place, both Western and Chinese thought operated within the framework of agendas and problematiques created in the ancient world and in both cases one can speak of a significant, creative, and agonizing history of thought.

# NOTES

### INTRODUCTION

1. The term "ancient China" refers roughly to a period from the beginnings of recorded history to the end of the first millennium B.C. (the early part of the former Han dynasty). The main focus, however, will be on texts which belong to the first millennium before the rise of the Ch'in dynasty in 221 B.C.

I use the term "history of thought" rather than "history of ideas" or "intellectual history" precisely because of the indeterminate boundaries of the word "thought." It is a word which may be used to encompass cognition and reasoning as well as intentionality, imagination, sentiment, wonder, puzzlement, and many other aspects of the conscious life which cannot be readily programmed on a computer. There is also the welcome ambiguity of whether the word refers to the process of thinking or to fixed "products" of thought such as ideas, mentalities, or inert attitudes. While my attention in this volume will be mainly focused on the thought of texts which belong to the "high" culture, my concern is not exclusively with "thought" which can be labeled "intellectual" in some narrowly conceived sense of that word.

2. See Karl Jaspers, "Die Achsenzeit," in *Vom Ursprung und Ziel der Geschichte* (Zurich: Artemis Verlag, 1949), chap. 1. For a discussion of Jaspers' observations, see the discussion in the symposium volume "Wisdom, Revelation, and Doubt; Perspectives on the First Millennium B.C." in *Daedalus*, Spring 1974. Eric Weil in his contribution to this symposium suggests that the "Age of Bifurcation" might be a more apt term than axial age, p. 21.

3. It is nevertheless clear that in the ancient Middle East where Mesopotamian, Egyptian, and Minoan civilizations are in constant interaction with each other, they all exercised a complex influence on Greek and Hebrew developments.

4. Joseph Levenson, *Modern China and Its Confucian Past* (Garden City, N.Y.: Doubleday Anchor Books, 1964), p. 212.

5. Clifford Geertz, *Interpretation of Cultures* (New York: Basic Books, 1973), p. 231.

6. In the following pages we will find that the notion of a privileged vantage point of "disinterestedness" can already be discerned in ancient Chinese thought.

7. Geertz, *Interpretation of Cultures*, pp. 196–213.

8. Claude Lévi-Strauss, "Overture to 'le Cru et le cuit,' " in *Structuralism*, ed. Jacques Ehrmann (New Haven: Yale French Studies, no. 36, 1966), p. 56.

9. Geertz, *Interpretation of Cultures*, p. 50.

10. Ibid., p. 363.

11. Ibid., p. 218.

12. For a further discussion of the high culture/popular culture relation, see the Postscript.

13. In Western languages the abstract is often expressed by the use of words without suffixes of abstraction, such as love or "the good" (*to agathon*) of Plato.

14. Chad Hansen, *Language and Logic in Ancient China* (Ann Arbor: University of Michigan Press, 1983), p. 39.

15. Hansen insists that in classical Chinese where explicit devices for expressing the definite and indefinite article or number are absent, words such as "dog" are to be treated as mass nouns such as the English "water" or "paper." See ibid., p. 32.

16. Kwang-chih Chang, *Shang Civilization* (New Haven: Yale University Press, 1980), p. 245.

17. Ibid., pp. 247–248.


## 1. EARLY CULTURAL ORIENTATIONS

1. See David Keightley, ed., *The Origins of Chinese Civilization* (Berkeley: University of California Press, 1983), for a summation of recent thinking in these areas—particularly the "Concluding Remarks" (chap. 17) of Kwang-chih Chang.

2. In much of the current literature on the rise of civilization there seems to be the tacit notion that the rise of civilization and the emergence of the more or less centralized state are synchronous developments. Yet, in fact, both the nature and tempo of state development may have differed markedly from one civilization to another. If one refers to the emergence of a territorially extensive, more or less centralized polity that made universalistic claims, this may be true of ancient Egypt and China. The emergence of the ancient Mesopotamian "universal kingship" from the city-state polities seems to have been a slower development, while the emergence of universal kingship in India is quite late. I need hardly mention the entirely different development of the state in ancient Greece.

3. Kwang-chih Chang, "Sandai Archaeology and the Formation of the State," in Keightley, ed., *Origins*, chap. 16.

4. In the inscriptions the king already refers to himself as "I the one [unique?] man" (*yü i-jen*). On this see Keightley, ed., *Origins*, p. 533; also Hu Hou-hsüan, "Shih yü i-jen," *Li-shih yen-chiu*, no. 1 (1957), 75–78.

5. *T'ien-hsia* (literally the "subcelestial world"). I shall henceforth simply translate this term as "the world" with the understanding that the reference is to the world of human civilization.

6. Chang, *Shang Civilization*, p. 334. In 1977 a large body of fragments of Chou dynasty oracle bone inscriptions was discovered at Chi-shan county in

Shensi province. Two of the inscriptions actually seem to contain references to the founding monarchs of the Chou dynasty, King Wen and King Wu.

7. Keightley, ed., *Origins*, p. 524.

8. Claude Lévi-Strauss, *The Savage Mind* (Chicago: University of Chicago Press, 1966), p. 225.

9. To Lévi-Strauss animal sacrifice, which figures so prominently in the oracle bones, is almost the epitome of religion.

10. Paul Wheatley, *The Pivot of the Four Quarters: A Preliminary Inquiry into the Origins and Character of the Ancient Chinese City* (Chicago: Aldine Press, 1971), passim.

11. Chang, *Shang Civilization*, p. 399. See also Kwang-chih Chang, *The Archaeology of Ancient China* 3d ed. (New Haven: Yale University Press, 1977), p. 103.

12. R. E. Bradbury, "Fathers, Elders, and Ghosts in Edo Religion," in *Anthropological Approaches to Religion*, ed. E. Banton (London: Tavistock Publications, London Association of Social Anthropologists of the Commonwealth, 1969), pp. 131–132.

13. *Mo-tzu hsien ku*, ed. and commentary by Sun I-jang, vol. 4 of *Chu-tzu chi ch'eng* (Peking: Chung-hua shu-chü, 1957), pp. 253–254. Also, Angus Graham, *Later Mohist Logic, Ethics, and Science* (Hong Kong: Chinese University Press, 1978), p. 492.

14. Geertz, *Interpretation of Cultures*, p. 88.

15. Edmund Leach, *Lévi-Strauss*, ed. Frank Kermode (London: Fontana Modern Masters, 1970), p. 96.

16. Claude Lévi-Strauss, *Structural Anthropology* (Garden City, N.Y.: Doubleday Anchor Books, 1969), p. 46.

17. Bradbury, "Fathers, Elders, and Ghosts in Edo Religion," p. 128.

18. For example, Marcel Granet, *Danses et légendes de la Chine ancienne* (Paris: Presses Universitaires de France, 1954), passim. See also Henri Maspero, *La Chine antique*, in *Histoire du monde*, ed. E. De Boccard, vol. 4 (Paris: Boccard Editeurs, 1927), passim.

19. Alexander Heidel, *The Babylonian Genesis* (Chicago: University of Chicago Press, 1963), p. 44.

20. For example, see Emily Ahern, *The Cult of the Dead in a Chinese Village* (Stanford: Stanford University Press, 1973), and Hugh Baker, *Chinese Family and Kinship* (New York: Columbia University Press, 1979).

21. Derk Bodde, *Essays on Chinese Civilization* (Princeton: Princeton University Press, 1981), p. 48.

22. Henri Maspero, "Légendes mythologiques dans le Chou King," *Journal Asiatique*, 154 (1924), 1–100.

23. Chang, *Shang Civilization*, p. 245.

24. Ibid., pp. 163–165.

25. Ibid., p. 227.

26. Kent Flannery, "The Cultural Evolution of Civilization," *Annual Review of Ecology and Systematics*, 3 (1972), 394–426, cited in Chang, *Shang Civilization*, p. 363.

27. Many of Max Weber's "ideal types" are of enormous heuristic value in dealing with China. Yet the experience of other cultures will quite often refuse to

conform to the either/or assumptions lying behind such ideal types, as Max Weber would have been the first to acknowledge. For a full discussion of the issues involved, see Wolfgang Schluchter, ed., *Max Webers Studie über Konfuzianismus und Taoismus: Interpretation und Kritik* (Frankfurt am Main: Suhrkamp-Taschenbuch Wissenschaft, 1983).

28. Miyazaki Ichisada, "Shunshū to Toshi Kokka," *Tōhō Bunka Kōza*, no. 8, (1955), chap. 2.

29. Akatsuka Kiyoshi, *Chūgoku kodai no shūkyō to bunka* (Tokyo: Kadokawa Shoten, 1977).

30. For the difficulties surrounding this word, see Morton Fried, *The Notion of the Tribe* (Menlo Park, Calif.: Cummings Publishing Co., 1975), passim. For a penetrating review of Akatsuka's book, see David Keightley, "Akatsuka Kiyoshi and the Culture of Early China," *Harvard Journal of Asiatic Studies*, 42, no. 1 (June 1982).

31. See Shirakawa Shizuka, *Kōkotsubun no sekai* (Tokyo: Heibonsha, 1972), pp. 71–82.

32. In one inscription we find the inquiry "Shall we perform the *pan* sacrifice to the River and to Shang-chia?" Shang-chia, the reputed son of Wang Hai, is the first king to appear in the ritual calendar. See Shirakawa, *Kōkotsubun*, p. 77.

33. Keightley, "Akatsuka Kiyoshi and the Culture of Early China," p. 295.

34. Kwang-chih Chang, *Early Chinese Civilization: Anthropological Perspectives* (Cambridge: Harvard University Press, 1976), p. 190.

35. Arthur Waley, *The Book of Songs* (London: Allen and Unwin, 1954), no. 253, p. 275. In one version the ancestress of the royal line swallows an egg dropped by the bird. The association of bird symbolism with the Shang has already been noted.

36. Ibid., no. 238, p. 241.

37. David Keightley, *Sources of Shang History* (Berkeley: University of California Press, 1978), p. 33.

38. In Chinese mythic material one also finds the dyadic pair Fu Hsi and Nü-kua represented iconographically as having human upper bodies merging into intertwining serpents' tails. (See Bodde, *Essays*, p. 62.)

39. See G. S. Kirk, *Myth: Its Meaning and Function in Ancient and Other Cultures* (Cambridge: Cambridge University Press, 1970), p. 119.

40. Again what I am here discussing is the image of the state and not the "sufficient" cause of its emergence or its actual nature.

41. James Legge, *The Shoo King*, vol. 3, *The Chinese Classics* (Hong Kong: University of Hong Kong Press, 1960), p. 39.

42. The term for these emissaries, *shih* is depicted by a graph (肯更) which has been described by some scholars as representing a hand holding a pole bearing a container for written documents (probably bamboo slips). According to Shirakawa and others, the documents probably contained royal invocations to the local deities on sacrificial occasions. The term thus came to refer to functionaries who kept records and handled documents and also to functionaries sent to perform various missions. By extension the term came to refer particularly to functionaries concerned with the keeping of chronicles and the records of significant astronomical events relevant to astrological purposes. By further extension,

the graph or modifications of the graph came to refer to recorded history or to significant events as such ( 事 ).

43. For a full summary of these groups see Ch'en Meng-chia, *Yin-hsü p'u-tz'u tsung-shu* (Peking: K'o-hsüeh ch'u-pan she, 1956), pp. 503–522.

44. Keightley, ed., *Origins*, p. 544.

45. Chang, *Shang Civilization*, p. 192.

46. Leo Oppenheim, *Ancient Mesopotamia: Portrait of a Dead Civilization* (Chicago University Press, 1964), pp. 95–109.

47. It is a principle which renders forever suspect the literal application of the religious/secular dichotomy to an analysis of the Chinese political order.

48. See Mircea Eliade, *Shamanism*, Bollingen Series 76 (New York: Pantheon Books, 1964), passim.

49. Maspero, *La Chine antique*, pp. 195–202.

50. For an excellent translation of this work, see David Hawkes, *Ch'u-tz'u: The Songs of the South* (Boston: Beacon Paperbacks, 1962).

51. See Tung Tso-pin, "Yin-tai li-chih ti hsin chiu liang p'ai," *Ta-lu Tsa-chih*, vol. 6 (1953). For an English summation of Tung's hypothesis, see Chang, *Shang Civilization*, pp. 185–186. For a discussion of the annual cycle of sacrifices, see Shirakawa, *Kōkotsubun*, pp. 91–100.

52. Akatsuka, *Chūgoku kodai no shūkyō to bunka*, p. 515.

53. Legge's translation of this passage can be found in *The Shoo King*, p. 457.

## 2. EARLY CHOU THOUGHT

1. The traditional dates of Confucius' (K'ung Fu-tzu) life are 551–479 B.C.

2. For a discussion of this canonical problem that adopts a radical position, see Herrlee Creel, *The Origins of Statecraft in China* (Chicago: University of Chicago Press, 1970), pp. 447–463.

3. David Nivison has recently calculated the date of the Chou conquest at 1045 B.C. See David Nivison, "Dates of Western Chou," *Harvard Journal of Asiatic Studies*, 43, no. 2 (Dec. 1983), 481.

4. Creel, *Origins of Statecraft*, p. 353.

5. Ibid., p. 261.

6. My reference here is to the Western political definition of feudalism and not to the vaguer Marxist uses of the term.

7. Creel, *Origins of Statecraft*, p. 320. The word vassal here should not be thought of in terms of all the legal particularities we associate with medieval Western feudalism.

8. Hu Hou-hsüan has argued that this "feudal" strategy had already been fully applied during the Shang dynasty. Hu Hou-hsüan, "Yin-tai feng-chien chih-tu k'ao," *Chia-ku hsüeh Shang-shih lun ts'ung*, vol. 1 (Ch'eng-tu: Ch'i-lu University, 1944).

9. The Roman Empire had not been truly "bureaucratic" in the Chinese sense.

10. Étienne Balazs, *Chinese Civilization and Bureaucracy*, ed. Arthur Wright (New Haven: Yale University Press, 1964), p. 6.

11. Creel, *Origins of Statecraft,* chap. 6, passim.

12. For a discussion of this term (to be distinguished from the *shih* referring more narrowly to historian/astrologers), see Yü Ying-shih, *Chung-kuo chih-shih chieh-ts'eng shih lun* (Taipei: Lien-ching ch'u-pan shih-yeh kung-ssu, 1980), p. 6, also pp. 102-108.

13. Waley, *Book of Songs,* no. 241, p. 251.

14. Legge, "The Great Announcement" (*Ta kao*), *The Shoo King,* p. 368.

15. Ibid., p. 364.

16. Legge, "The Numerous Officers" (*To shih*), *The Shoo King,* p. 455.

17. Legge, "The Announcement of Duke Shao" (*Shao kao*), *The Shoo King,* p. 426.

18. Legge, "Lord Shih" (*Chün shih*), *The Shoo King,* p. 474.

19. In this he seems to be a prototype of all the legendary rulers who appear in the literature of later centuries such as Yao, Shun, Yü, and the "Yellow Emperor." These are both rulers and culture heroes responsible for most of the arts of civilization.

20. Legge, *The Shoo King,* p. 546.

21. Ibid., p. 577.

22. Waley, *Book of Songs,* no. 199, p. 210.

23. Ibid., no. 199. p. 211.

24. R. C. Zaehner, *Hinduism* (Oxford: Oxford University Press, 1972), p. 211.

25. Legge, *The Shoo King,* pp. 505, 541.

26. Ibid., p. 541.

27. Waley, *Book of Songs,* no. 243, p. 255.

28. James Legge, *The She King,* vol. 4, *The Chinese Classics* (Hong Kong: University of Hong Kong Press, 1960). p. 505.

29. See Joseph Needham, "Human Law and Laws of Nature," *Science and Civilisation in China* (Cambridge: Cambridge University Press, 1956), vol. 2, sec. 18.

30. This suggestion has been made by Donald Munro in an unpublished paper.

31. Waley, *Book of Songs,* no. 276, p. 304.

32. Ibid., no. 267, p. 295.

33. Legge, "The Admonition on Wine" (*Chiu kao*), *The Shoo King,* pp. 399-412.

34. Waley, *Book of Songs,* no. 142, p. 141.

35. Ibid.

### 3. CONFUCIUS

1. The name is derived from the chronicle of the state of Lu, *The Spring and Autumn Annals* (*Ch'un ch'iu*), supposedly edited by Confucius (see Chapter 10). It covers the years 771-481 B.C.

2. See Yü Ying-shih, *Chung-kuo chih-shih chieh-ts'eng shih lun,* p. 6.

3. Arthur Waley, *The Analects of Confucius* (New York: Random House, Vintage Books, 1938), bk. 9, chap. 2, p. 138. *Lun-yü cheng i,* Commentary, Liu Pao-

nan, *Chu-tzu chi-ch'eng,* vol. 1, p. 172. I shall use Waley as a reference text although my own translations will often diverge from his.

4. Yü Ying-shih, *Chung-kuo chih-shih chieh-ts'eng,* p. 2. See also Hsu Cho-yun, *Ancient China in Transition: An Analysis of Social Mobility, 722–222 B.C.* (Stanford: Stanford University Press, 1965). I shall not enter here into a debate on whether the modern Western word "intellectual" is applicable to ancient China.

5. Karl Mannheim, *Essays in Sociology and Social Psychology* (Oxford: Oxford University Press, 1938), p. 255.

6. For two interesting efforts to reconstruct the biography of Confucius, see Herrlee Creel, *Confucius, the Man and the Myth* (New York: J. Day, 1949), and Kaizuka Shigeki, *Confucius,* trans. G. Bownas (London: Allen and Unwin, 1974). The locus classicus of all biographical accounts is to be found in chap. 17 of the *Shih-chi* ("Historical Records"—perhaps translated more accurately by Burton Watson as the "Records of the Grand Historian of China") by China's first "world historian" Ssu-ma Ch'ien (145–90 B.C. circa).

7. Waley, *Analects,* p. 21.

8. Tsuda Sōkichi, *Rongo to Kōshi no shisō* (Tokyo: Iwanami shoten, 1946).

9. Waley, *Analects,* bk. 16, chap. 2, p. 204; *Lun-yü,* p. 354.

10. Waley, *Analects,* bk. 5, chap. 6, p. 108; *Lun-yü,* p. 90.

11. Waley, *Analects,* bk. 5, chap. 12, p. 110; *Lun-yü,* p. 98.

12. A. E. Taylor, *Plato: The Man and His Works* (New York: Meridian Books, 1971), chap. 17; also Eric Voegelin, *Plato* (Baton Rouge: Louisiana State Press, 1966), chaps. 4, 5.

13. Taylor, *Plato,* pp. 393–397.

14. John Spellman, *Political Theory of Ancient India* (Oxford: Oxford University Press, 1964), pp. 3, 4, 14, 22.

15. Louis Dumont, *Homo Hierarchicus* (London: Paladin, 1972), p. 231.

16. Waley, *Analects,* bk. 3, chap. 14, p. 97; *Lun-yü,* p. 56.

17. The famous pre-"Hsia" legendary emperors Yao, Shun, and Yü are mentioned but they are conceived of as culture heroes who initiate the evolution of civilization.

18. Waley, *Analects,* bk. 15, chap. 10, p. 195; *Lun-yü,* p. 33.

19. To traditional commentators these choices symbolize profound ethico-political principles. The Shang coach, we are told, was simple, thus pointing to an emphasis on simplicity in ceremonial matters, while the music of Shao was spiritually elevating. For example, see commentary by Liu Pao-nan in the *Lun-yü cheng i, Chu-tzu chi-ch'eng,* vol. 1, pp. 337–338.

20. The prevailing scholarly view is that the text belongs to the late Warring States period or early Han (third and second centuries B.C.), although it may preserve some authentic details concerning the early Chou period. On the whole it is a schematic utopian construct which very much reflects the zeitgeist of its time.

21. Waley, *Analects,* bk. 7, chap. 1, p. 123; *Lun-yü,* p. 134.

22. See Herbert Fingarette, *Confucius: The Secular as Sacred* (New York: Harper and Row, 1972).

23. Ernest Barker, *The Political Thought of Plato and Aristotle* (New York: Dover Publications, 1959), p. 400; Thorkild Jacobsen, in his "Early Political De-

velopment in Mesopotamia," *Zeitschrift für Assyriologie,* no. 52 (1957), argues that something like "democratic" or oligarchic representative assemblies had already emerged in the city-states of ancient Sumer.

24. Aristotle, *Politics and Poetics* (New York: Compass Books, Viking Press, 1959).

25. Waley, *Analects,* bk. 3, chap. 19, p. 99; *Lun-yü,* p. 62.

26. Waley, *Analects,* bk. 2, chap. 5, p. 89; *Lun-yü,* p. 26.

27. Fingarette, *Confucius,* p. 60.

28. Ibid., p. 7.

29. Ibid., p. 37.

30. Waley, *Analects,* bk. 3, chap. 1, p. 94; *Lun-yü,* p. 41.

31. Waley, *Analects,* bk. 3, chap. 3, p. 94; *Lun-yü,* p. 44.

32. Waley, *Analects,* bk. 3, chap. 26, p. 101; *Lun-yü,* p. 74.

33. Waley, *Analects,* bk. 17, chap. 12, p. 212; *Lun-yü,* p. 375.

34. Fingarette, *Confucius,* p. 8.

35. Ibid., p. 42. Fingarette seems not at all bothered by the Western bias implicit in a philosophy as peculiarly Western as British linguistic philosophy.

36. Ibid., p. 43.

37. Waley, *Analects,* bk. 4, chap. 13, p. 104; *Lun-yü,* p. 80.

38. The term itself (*jang*) can already be found in the *Book of Poetry.* See Legge, *The She King,* p. 405. See also Waley, *Analects,* bk. 14, chap. 2, p. 180; *Lun-yü,* p. 300.

39. Waley, "Introduction," *Analects,* p. 55.

40. Waley, *Analects,* bk. 4, chap. 17, p. 105; *Lun-yü,* p. 83.

41. Fingarette is singularly uninterested in how the early Confucian schools interpreted the Master. He seems supremely confident that he understands the text better than they.

42. Waley, *Analects,* bk. 2, chap. 5. The heart/mind is clearly a center of intention, thought, desires, and emotion.

43. Fingarette, *Confucius,* p. 55.

44. Lin Yü-sheng, "The Evolution of the Pre-Confucian Meaning of *Jen* and the Confucian Conception of Moral Autonomy," *Monumenta Serica,* 31 (1924–1925), 172–204.

45. I need hardly point out that Socrates' conception of the good life must also find full expression in social life.

46. It is noteworthy that many leading modern Chinese scholars in this field very much stress the centrality of the inner virtues. See Feng Yu-lan, *A History of Chinese Philosophy,* trans. Derk Bodde (Princeton: Princeton University Press, 1952–1953), chap. 4.

47. See David Nivison, "Royal 'Virtue' in Shang Oracle Inscriptions," *Early China,* 4 (1978–1979), 52–55.

48. That this royal power may itself contain a "magical" element in Fingarette's sense of magic as a power to influence behavior without recourse to "coercion and physical force" seems quite plausible. See Herbert Fingarette, "Reply to Professor Hansen," *Journal of Chinese Philosophy,* 7, no. 3 (Sept. 1980), 259.

49. I shall use the term "noble man" since it seems to me that our much watered-down "gentleman" hardly captures the lofty pitch of *chün-tzu*.

50. Waley, *Analects*, bk. 16, chap. 2, p. 204; *Lun-yü*, p. 354.

51. Waley, *Analects*, bk. 12, chap. 1, p. 162; *Lun-yü*, p. 262.

52. Fingarette, *Confucius*, p. 4.

53. Barker, *Political Thought*, p. 47.

54. Fingarette, "A Way without Crossroads," in *Confucius*, chap. 2.

55. Waley, *Analects*, bk. 14, chap. 30, p. 188; *Lun-yü*, p. 319.

56. Fingarette, *Confucius*, pp. 188 and 34.

57. Waley, *Analects*, bk. 7, chap. 8, p. 124; *Lun-yü*, p. 139.

58. Waley, *Analects*, bk. 2, chap. 4, p. 88; *Lun-yü*, p. 23. The word "will" seems here to be quite an appropriate translation of the term *chih*.

59. Waley, *Analects*, bk. 14, chap. 45, p. 191; *Lun-yü*, p. 329.

60. Waley, *Analects*, bk. 9, chap. 28, p. 144; *Lun-yü*, p. 193.

61. Waley, *Analects*, bk. 14, chap. 5, p. 180; *Lun-yü*, p. 301.

62. Waley, *Analects*, bk. 1, chap. 1, p. 83; *Lun-yü*, p. 3.

63. Waley, *Analects*, bk. 6, chap. 9, p. 117; *Lun-yü*, p. 121.

64. Waley, *Analects*, bk. 7, chap. 15, p. 126; *Lun-yü*, p. 143.

65. Waley, *Analects*, bk. 7, chap. 18, p. 127; *Lun-yü*, p. 145.

66. Waley, *Analects*, bk. 8, chap. 2, p. 132; *Lun-yü*, p. 155.

67. According to one view, the original graph depicts the pattern of a tattoo on a human body.

68. Waley, *Analects*, bk. 6, chap. 16, p. 119; *Lun-yü*, p. 125.

69. In one passage we find it stated that "Of the saying 'He upon whom neither love of dominance, boastfulness nor petty resentment have any hold can be called *jen*' the Master said, 'He can be said to have done what is difficult but whether he is a man of *jen* I do not know.' " Here we find Confucius' general reluctance to define the ultimate quality of *jen* in limited, particularly negative terms. Yet the vices mentioned along with others are a formidable barrier to its achievement. See Waley, *Analects*, bk. 14, chap. 2, p. 180; *Lun-yü*, p. 300.

70. Waley, *Analects*, bk. 4, chap. 5, p. 102; *Lun-yü*, p. 76.

71. Waley, *Analects*, bk. 3, chap. 4, p. 94; *Lun-yü*, p. 44.

72. Waley, "Introduction," in *Analects*, p. 55.

73. Legge, *Analects*, in *Chinese Classics*, vol. 1, p. 227.

74. Waley, *Analects*, bk. 10, chap. 4, p. 146; *Lun-yü*, p. 201.

75. Waley, *Analects*, bk. 10, chap. 5, p. 147; *Lun-yü*, p. 205.

76. Waley, *Analects*, bk. 10, chap. 6, p. 147; *Lun-yü*, p. 211.

77. Waley, *Analects*, bk. 10, chap. 9, p. 149; *Lun-yü*, p. 225.

78. Waley, *Analects*, bk. 3, chap. 18, p. 98; *Lun-yü*, p. 62.

79. Waley, *Analects*, bk. 3, chap. 9, p. 96; *Lun-yü*, p. 49.

80. The explanation for the emphasis on the "empirical" suggested here is not based on any notion of the "concrete" "nonabstract" nature of the Chinese language. Thus, if by "abstractions" one refers to the use of nouns referring to various moral qualities abstracted from any references to concrete instances, such terms abound in the *Analects*. Words such as "courage" and "faithfulness" are used throughout in a thoroughly "abstract" fashion. When we refer to Confu-

cius' "empirical" study of the ancient literature of the past, such learning itself would include a presumed knowledge of the meanings of the abstract terms found in that literature. "Empirical" does not imply English philosophic empiricism. Again, none of this implies the presence of Platonic or Aristotelian efforts to generalize about the nature of the abstract as such. For a contrary view, see Hansen, *Language and Logic*, pp. 37–42.

81. For example, Liu Pao-nan, "Introduction," *Lun-yü cheng i, chu-tzu chi-ch'eng*, vol. 1, p. 2.

82. Waley, *Analects*, bk. 3, chap. 7, p. 95; *Lun-yü*, p. 47.

83. The origin of the term remains a matter of much debate.

84. Waley, *Analects*, bk. 6, chap. 11, p. 118; *Lun-yü*, p. 122.

85. Waley, *Analects*, bk. 7, chap. 27, p. 128; *Lun-yü*, p. 149.

86. Waley, *Analects*, bk. 17, chap. 9, p. 212; *Lun-yü*, p. 374.

87. Fingarette, *Confucius*, p. 53.

88. Voegelin, *Plato*, p. 133.

89. For the application of such an interpretation, see Waley, *Analects*, bk. 3, chap. 8, p. 95; *Lun-yü*, p. 48.

90. Waley, *Analects*, bk. 16, chap. 9, p. 206; *Lun-yü*, p. 361.

91. Waley, *Analects*, bk. 7, chap. 19, p. 127; *Lun-yü*, p. 146.

92. Waley, *Analects*, bk. 15, chap. 3, p. 193; *Lun-yü*, p. 333.

93. Waley, *Analects*, bk. 5, chap. 8, p. 109; *Lun-yü*, p. 94.

94. Waley, *Analects*, bk. 2, chap. 15, p. 91; *Lun-yü*, p. 31.

95. Waley, *Analects*, bk. 15, chap. 30, p. 199; *Lun-yü*, p. 346.

96. Ibid., "Introduction," p. 45.

97. In bk. 15, chap. 30, p. 199, Waley translates the word *ssu* as "meditation."

98. W. Guthrie, *Socrates* (Cambridge: Cambridge University Press, 1971), p. 38.

99. Ibid., p. 127

100. Ibid., p. 104.

101. Waley, *Analects*, bk. 7, chap. 33, p. 130; *Lun-yü*, p. 152.

102. Waley, "Introduction," *Analects*, p. 22. Waley's claim that there is no evidence of a concern with the "language question" even in Mencius, who lives much later than Confucius, would, I think, now be denied by most scholars. Even the claim that the concern with language in the *Analects* is confined to one particular passage is, I would maintain, incorrect. On this question, see Hansen, *Language and Logic*, p. 181.

103. Hansen, *Language and Logic*, preface, p. vi.

104. Waley, *Analects*, bk. 12, chap. 11, p. 166; *Lun-yü*, p. 271.

105. Waley, *Analects*, bk. 13, chap. 3, p. 171; *Lun-yü*, p. 280.

106. Hansen argues that while Western thought tends to think of the role of language as descriptive, the function of language that preoccupied the Chinese was "regulative." "Words have an impact on people's attitudes and inclinations to act." Hansen, *Language and Logic*, p. 59.

107. Waley, *Analects*, bk. 1, chap. 3, p. 84; *Lun-yü*, p. 5.

108. Waley, *Analects*, bk. 2, chap. 24, p. 159; *Lun-yü*, p. 251.

109. Waley, *Analects*, bk. 2, chap. 24, p. 159; *Lun-yü*, p. 252.

110. Hansen, *Language and Logic*, p. 77.

111. Harry Wolfson, *Philo* (Cambridge, Mass.: Harvard University Press, 1947), vol. 1, chap. 4, passim.

112. Waley, *Analects*, bk. 6, chap. 25, p. 121; *Lun-yü*, p. 130.

113. Waley, *Analects*, bk. 17, chap. 8, p. 211; *Lun-yü*, p. 373.

114. Barker, *Political Thought*, p. 5.

115. Ibid., p. 7.

116. Ibid., p. 244.

117. Waley, *Analects*, bk. 1, chap. 1, p. 84; *Lun-yü*, p. 1.

118. Waley, *Analects*, bk. 5, chap. 27, p. 114; *Lun-yü*, p. 111.

119. Waley, *Analects*, bk. 6, chap. 2, p. 115; *Lun-yü*, p. 113. And Waley, *Analects*, bk. 2, chap. 9, p. 90; *Lun-yü*, p. 28.

120. See Aristotle, *The Ethics of Aristotle: The Nichomacean Ethics* trans. J. A. Thompson (London: Allen and Unwin, Penguin Books, 1973), on intellectual contemplation as the highest pleasure. Here, of course, intellectual life is perhaps not entirely "disinterested," since it is itself a mode of the ethical life.

121. Waley, *Analects*, bk. 1, chap. 2, p. 83; *Lun-yü,,* p. 4.

122. Aristotle, *Ethics*, p. 251.

123. Ibid., p. 26.

124. Legge, *The Great Learning (Ta hsüeh)*, *Chinese Classics* (Shanghai: Shenchou Kuo-kuang she, 1933), vol. 1, p. 357.

125. Waley, *Analects*, bk. 2, chap. 21, p. 92; *Lun-yü*, p. 36.

126. Fingarette, *Confucius*, pp. 69 and 64.

127. Waley, *Analects*, bk. 13, chap. 18, p. 175; *Lun-yü*, p. 291. The Duke of She was a local power-holder in the southern "semibarbarian" state of Ch'u where, in Confucius' view, the older Chou traditions were not deeply rooted.

128. Waley, *Analects*, bk. 3, chap. 3, p. 96; *Lun-yü*, p. 53.

129. Waley, *Analects*, bk. 2, chap. 3, p. 88; *Lun-yü*, p. 22.

130. Waley, *Analects*, bk. 14, chap. 22, p. 186; *Lun-yü*, p. 317. The *Analects* do not refer to the widespread practice of family vendettas or even to the duty to seek private vengeance. Yet the *Spring and Autumn Annals* later attributed to Confucius do refer to the obligation of "righteous" vengeance based on kinship ties. Thus the positive valuation of righteous acts of vengeance by no means disappears in later Confucianism. It is often associated with the cosmic principle of balance based on the cosmic principle of compensation (*pao*).

131. Waley, *Analects*, bk. 12, chap. 7, p. 164; *Lun-yü*, p. 266.

132. Waley, *Analects*, bk. 13, chap. 3, p. 171; *Lun-yü*, p. 283.

133. For this point, see the attitude of Anytus in his dialogue with Socrates in Plato, *Meno*, in *Protagoras and Meno* (London: Penguin Classics, 1974), pp. 144–150. Anytus, when pressed by Socrates to tell him where good men have learned virtue, simply states, "They learned it from their forebears who were gentlemen like themselves" (ibid., p. 148).

134. D. C. Lau, trans., *Mencius* (London: Penguin Classics, 1970), p. 58.

135. Waley, *Analects*, bk. 13, chap. 9, p. 173; *Lun-yü*, p. 287.

136. Waley, *Analects*, bk. 8, chap. 21, p. 137; *Lun-yü*, p. 169.

137. Waley, *Analects*, bk. 1, chap. 5, p. 84; *Lun-yü*, p. 7.

138. One does, to be sure, find statements which might be taken to support the "shame ethic" view of shame. "When the Tao prevails in your land, count it a disgrace to be needy and poor" (Waley, *Analects*, bk. 8, chap. 13, p. 135; *Lun-yü*, p. 163). Since the flat proposition that the "Tao does not prevail" was not readily admitted by most "conventional Confucianists" (*su ju*) in later ages, the "shame" associated with poverty and failure to "make it" was as widely felt among the upwardly mobile in China as in most societies.

139. Waley, *Analects*, bk. 8, chap. 9, p. 134; *Lun-yü*, p. 161.

140. Waley, *Analects*, bk. 14, chap. 13, p. 183; *Lun-yü*, p. 307.

141. Waley, *Analects*, bk. 6, chap. 6, p. 116; *Lun-yü*, p. 118.

142. Waley, *Analects*, bk. 14, chap. 9, p. 181; *Lun-yü*, p. 304.

143. Waley, *Analects*, bk. 11, chap. 2, p. 153; *Lun-yü*, p. 238.

144. Waley, *Analects*, bk. 5, chap. 12, p. 90; *Lun-yü*, p. 30.

145. Legge, *Analects*, in *Chinese Classics*, vol. 1, p. 150.

146. Waley, *Analects*, bk. 14, chap. 13, p. 183; *Lun-yü*, p. 307.

147. Waley, *Analects*, bk. 3, chap. 22, p. 100; *Lun-yü*, p. 69.

148. Waley, *Analects*, bk. 14, chap. 17, p. 185; *Lun-yü*, p. 311.

149. Waley, *Analects*, bk. 14, chap. 18, p. 185; *Lun-yü*, p. 315.

150. Waley, *Analects*, bk. 8, chap. 20, p. 136; *Lun-yü*, p. 168.

151. Waley, *Analects*, bk. 17, chap. 5, p. 210; *Lun-yü*, p. 370.

152. Waley, *Analects*, bk. 9, chap. 8, p. 140; *Lun-yü*, p. 179.

153. Such statements became the basis in a later period for the belief that Confucius regarded himself as the potential sage-founder of a new dynasty. Given his insistence on his commoner state and his disclaimer of sagehood, there is nothing in the Analects which suggests any such notion.

154. Liu Pao-nan's comment appears in *Lun-yü*, p. 315.

155. Waley, *Analects*, bk. 18, chap. 8, p. 221; *Lun-yü*, pp. 396-397.

156. Waley, *Analects*, bk. 13, chap. 10, p. 173; *Lun-yü*, p. 13.

157. It has been suggested that he hoped to persuade Kung-shan to restore the legitimate authority of the Duke of Lu.

158. Waley, *Analects*, bk. 17, chap. 5, p. 210; *Lun-yü*, p. 370.

159. Waley, *Analects*, bk. 17, chap. 1, p. 209; *Lun-yü*, p. 366.

160. And even in their judgments of whether rulers deserve their trust.

161. Waley, *Analects*, bk. 15, chap. 38, p. 201; *Lun-yü*, p. 348; and Waley, *Analects*, bk. 7, chap. 7, p. 124; *Lun-yü*, p. 138.

162. When asked by Tzu-lu how to treat a ruler, Confucius advises him to oppose a ruler to his face without subterfuge.

163. Waley, *Analects*, bk. 16, chap. 1, p. 202; *Lun-yü*, p. 340.

164. Confucius undoubtedly cherishes his own pedigree as the member of a *shih* family. One might nevertheless maintain that as a member of a stratum that had suffered "downward mobility," his real interests lay entirely on the side of mobility and meritocracy.

165. In the following Warring States period, a debate would arise concerning the hereditary nature of the kingship itself (see chap. 7 below).

166. Fingarette, *Confucius*, p. 69.

167. Waley, *Analects*, bk. 5, chap. 12, p. 110; *Lun-yü*, p. 98.

168. There is, in fact, one passage regarded by some as an interpolation in which human nature is discussed. See bk. 17, chap. 2, p. 209; *Lun-yü*, p. 367.

169. Waley, *Analects*, bk. 3, chap. 20, p. 127; *Lun-yü*, p. 146.

170. Guthrie, *Socrates*, p. 99.

171. Waley, *Analects*, bk. 11, chap. 11, p. 155; *Lun-yü*, p. 243.

172. See commentary on *Lun-yü*, p. 243.

173. Waley, *Analects*, bk. 6, chap. 20, p. 120; *Lun-yü*, p. 126.

174. *Hsün-tzu chi chieh, Chu-tzu chi-ch'eng*, vol. 2, p. 236.

175. T'ang Chün-i, *Yüan-tao p'ien, Chung-kuo che-hsüeh yüan-lun* (Taipei: Hsin-ya shu-yüan yen chiu-so, 1973), pp. 135–136.

176. See *Chu-tzu Yü-lei.*

177. Waley, *Analects*, bk. 14, chap. 37, p. 189; *Lun-yü*, p. 321.

178. Waley, *Analects*, bk. 7, chap. 22, p. 127; *Lun-yü*, p. 147.

179. Waley, *Analects*, bk. 9, chap. 5, p. 139; *Lun-yü*, p. 176.

180. Waley, *Analects*, bk. 9, chap. 11, p. 141; *Lun-yü*, p. 184.

181. Waley, *Analects*, bk. 3, chap. 24, p. 100; *Lun-yü*, p. 72.

182. Waley, *Analects*, bk. 17, chap. 19, p. 214; *Lun-yü*, p. 379.

183. Benedict Spinoza, *Ethics*, trans. Andrew Boyle (London: Dent and Sons, Heron Books, 1910), proposition 33, p. 27.

184. Waley, *Analects*, "Introduction," p. 25.

185. Waley, *Analects*, bk. 18, chap. 6, p. 219; *Lun-yü*, p. 391.

186. Waley, *Analects*, bk. 18, chap. 6, p. 220; *Lun-yü*, p. 391.

187. Waley, *Analects*, bk. 18, chap. 7, p. 220; *Lun-yü*, p. 393.

188. Waley, *Analects*, bk. 2, chap. 14, p. 91; *Lun-yü*, p. 31.

189. See the *Cheng-i* commentary on *Lun-yü*, bk. 2, chap. 16, p. 32.

190. Waley, *Analects*, bk. 9, chap. 10, p. 140; *Lun-yü*, p. 182.

191. Waley, *Analects*, bk. 11, chap. 25, p. 159; *Lun-yü*, p. 252.

192. Waley, *Analects*, bk. 11, chap. 25, p. 161; *Lun-yü*, p. 261.

193. Waley, *Analects*, bk. 19, chap. 2, p. 224; *Lun-yü*, p. 401.

194. Waley, *Analects*, bk. 19, chap. 16, p. 227; *Lun-yü*, p. 406.

195. Waley, *Analects*, bk. 11, chap. 2, p. 153; *Lun-yü*, p. 238.

196. Waley, *Analects*, bk. 19, chap. 12, p. 225; *Lun-yü*, p. 402.

197. Waley, *Analects*, bk. 19, chap. 6, p. 225; *Lun-yü*, p. 402.

198. Waley, *Analects*, bk. 11, chap. 15, p. 156; *Lun-yü*, p. 245.

199. Waley, *Analects*, bk. 19, chap. 12, p. 226; *Lun-yü*, p. 404.

200. One classical source is Ssu-ma Ch'ien, "Chung-ni ti-tzu lieh-chüan" (Biographies of disciples of Confucius), *Shih-chi*, chap. 67.

## 4. MO-TZU'S CHALLENGE

1. The question of the degree to which the transition from the Bronze Age to the Iron Age actually affected agricultural production remains a matter of dispute.

2. The ancient state of Chin had been divided into the three new states of Wei[2], Han, and Chao. (This Wei[2] is to be distinguished from the small ancient state of Wei[1].)

3. Ch'ien Mu, *Hsien Ch'in chu-tzu hsi-nien k'ao* (Hong Kong: Hong Kong Uni-

versity Press, 1935), pp. 129-137. Li K'o had presumably been a disciple of Tzu-hsia.

4. Ibid., p. 89.

5. Graham, *Later Mohist Logic*, p. 8.

6. *Huai-nan-tzu,* Kao Yu Commentary, *Chu-tzu chi-ch'eng,* vol. 7, chap. 21, p. 375.

7. *Mo-tzu hsien ku,* commentary by Sun I-jang, *Chu-tzu chi-ch'eng,* vol. 6, chap. 11, p. 45 (hereafter cited as *Mo-tzu*).

8. Ibid., chap. 48, p. 278.

9. There is no evidence in the book of contacts between Mo-tzu and other strains of Confucian thought.

10. *Mo-tzu,* chap. 48, p. 277.

11. Ibid., chap. 48, p. 276.

12. Ibid., chap. 48, p. 274.

13. Ibid.

14. Ibid.

15. Ibid., chap. 48, p. 271.

16. Ibid., chap. 48, p. 272.

17. Ibid.

18. *Mo-tzu,* chap. 11, p. 44. However "theistic" Mo-tzu's Heaven may be, the dominant metaphor of Heaven as a "creative force" remains that of genera-tion or procreation (*sheng*).

19. Hobbes states: "The only way to erect such a Common Power . . . is to conferre all their power and strength upon one man or upon one Assembly of men, that may reduce all their Wills by plurality of voices unto one Will." Thomas Hobbes, *Leviathan* (New York: Dutton and Co., 1950), p. 143. Hobbes, of course, posits the possibility of the sovereignty of an "assembly" but he definitely prefers the sovereignty of a monarch.

20. *Mo-tzu,* chap. 12, p. 46.

21. Ibid., chap. 13, p. 56.

22. Ibid., chap. 12, p. 47.

23. Hobbes, *Leviathan,* p. 101.

24. Ibid., p. 127.

25. *Mo-tzu,* chap. 12, p. 47.

26. Ibid., chap. 4, p. 12.

27. Graham, *Later Mohist Logic,* p. 270, A.8.

28. *Mo-tzu,* chap. 15, p. 64.

29. Graham, *Later Mohist Logic,* pp. 450-451. While leaning heavily on Gra-ham's magisterial work, I shall here allow myself certain departures from his translations.

30. Ibid., p. 451.

31. Ibid., p. 45. Graham points out that the definition of this word in the "logical" chapters has probably been lost.

32. Hobbes, *Leviathan,* p. 105.

33. *Mo-tzu,* chap. 14, p. 63.

34. Ibid., chap. 16, p. 75. "As for mutual love and mutual beneficence, they were practiced by the six ancient sage-kings."

35. Ibid., chap. 14, p. 62.

36. Ibid., chap. 14, p. 63.

37. Ibid.

38. Graham, *Later Mohist Logic*, p. 48.

39. Ibid., p. 256.

40. *Mo-tzu*, chap. 4, p. 12.

41. Ibid., chap. 15, p. 66.

42. Ibid., chap. 35, p. 163.

43. Ibid., chap. 35, p. 165.

44. Graham, *Later Mohist Logic*, p. 275.

45. *Mo-tzu*, chap. 21, pp. 101–102.

46. Graham, *Later Mohist Logic*, p. 270.

47. *Mo-tzu*, chap. 25, pp. 111.

48. Ibid., chap. 32, p. 155.

49. According to the famous commentator Sun I-jang, this may mean "Music is for the sake of joy," since the same graph is used for both. Mo-tzu's simile, however, seems to favor the first translation.

50. *Mo-tzu*, chap. 48, p. 277.

51. Ibid., chap. 32, p. 155.

52. The reasons given for the emphasis on status and wealth are the "three basic principles" (*san pen*): (1) unless their status is high, people will not respect them; (2) unless their income is substantial, people will not trust them; (3) unless they are given decisive power of command, people will not fear them. Ibid., chap. 9, p. 30.

53. Ibid., chap. 6, pp. 17–18.

54. Graham, *Later Mohist Logic*, p. 4.

55. *Mo-tzu*, chap. 39, p. 181.

56. A critical annotated translation of these chapters has recently been completed by Robin Yates of Harvard University.

57. *Mo-tzu*, chap. 48, p. 274.

58. Derk Bodde, *Essays*, p. 80.

59. Graham, *Later Mohist Logic*, p. 15.

60. *Mo-tzu*, chap. 14, p. 62.

61. Ibid., chap. 8, p. 25. The methods (*shu*) would refer to their knowledge of the business of government.

62. Graham, *Later Mohist Logic*, p. 318.

63. Ibid., p. 270, A.8.

64. *Mo-tzu*, chap. 48, pp. 271–272.

65. Ibid., chap. 47, p. 267.

66. John Rawls, *A Theory of Justice* (Cambridge, Mass.: Harvard University Press, 1971), p. 558.

67. Graham, *Later Mohist Logic*, p. 327, A. 80.

68. *Mo-tzu*, chap. 48, p. 280.

69. Ibid., chap. 47, p. 265.

70. Ibid., chap. 9, p. 29.

71. Graham, *Later Mohist Logic*, p. 4. *Lü-shih Ch'un-ch'iu, Chu-tzu chi-ch'eng*, vol. 6, chap. 19, p. 243.

72. Graham, *Later Mohist Logic,* p. 255.

73. One is almost tempted to translate his "uniting opinions" (*i i*) as "creating a general will." See *Mo-tzu,* chap. 13, p. 55.

74. The word used in chap. 35, p. 146, is *piao,* or gnomon, which Graham describes as follows: "a post of standard height; by day the astronomer uses it to estimate the direction and length of the sun's shadow, by night to align with the stars a cord extended from the top of the post to the ground." It thus became metaphorically a method for aligning with the truth. Graham, *Later Mohist Logic,* p. 369.

75. *Mo-tzu,* chap. 35, pp. 163–164.

76. Hansen, *Language and Logic,* p. 86.

77. Hansen again seems to assume in this "pragmatism" an indifference to the question of truth, while Western pragmatism in the philosophic sense is a "pragmatic account of the semantic notions of either truth or meaning" p. 87. It is a particular method of obtaining truth, while Mo-tzu is interested only in satisfactory outcomes. Without maintaining that Mo-tzu is a "philosophic pragmatist" in the manner of Pierce, the fact remains that he makes every effort to base his ethicopolitical language on his image of "how things are."

78. Guthrie, *Socrates,* p. 143.

79. Graham, *Later Mohist Logic,* p. 263.

80. Needham, *Science and Civilisation,* vol. 2, p. 281.

81. Graham, *Later Mohist Logic,* p. 316, A. 70.

82. Ibid.

83. Ibid., p. 307, A. 58.

84. Ibid., p. 36.

85. *Mo-tzu,* chap. 4, p. 12.

86. Graham, *Later Mohist Logic,* pp. 270, 272, and 273.

87. They would hardly seem to fit Hansen's category of mass-nouns.

88. Graham, *Later Mohist Logic,* p. 53.

89. *Mo-tzu,* chap. 4, p. 12.

90. Needham, *Science and Civilisation,* vol. 2, p. 182.

91. Graham, *Later Mohist Logic,* p. 54.

92. Needham, *Science and Civilisation,* vol. 2, p. 182.

93. The book of Han Fei-tzu which belongs at the earliest to the late third century B.C. still states quite flatly that "the most prominent teachings of our generation are those of the Confucianists and Mohists." *Han Fei-tzu chi-chieh, Chu-tzu chi-ch'eng,* vol. 5, p. 351.

94. The replies of Mo-tzu to skeptical questions concerning his personal religion are not very convincing but they nevertheless display a certain stoic faith which would indicate something more profound than his overt arguments.

95. In one of his three "standards" of verification of his religious beliefs, he of course appeals to the experience of the people in the "villages and hamlets." *Mo-tzu,* chap. 31, p. 139.

96. See *Chuang-tzu chi-chieh, Chu-tzu chi-ch'eng,* vol. 3, p. 218; also Burton Watson, *Chuang-tzu* (New York: Columbia University Press, 1968), p. 366.

97. *Chuang-tzu chi-chieh,* p. 217; Watson, *Chuang-tzu,* pp. 365–367.

## 5. THE EMERGENCE OF A COMMON DISCOURSE

1. Among these doxographical sources are the "Essential Principles of the Six Schools" (*liu-chia yao-chih*) of Ssu-ma T'an, the father of the great historian Ssu-ma Ch'ien, and the "Bibliographic Treatise" (*i wen-chih*) of the *History of the Former Han Dynasty* (*Ch'ien Han-shu*).

2. I do not here intend to assign to the word "discourse" the entire weight of meaning assigned to it by Foucault. One is not speaking of a discrete "episteme" qualitatively distinguished from all past and future discourses by "archaeological" breaks, nor do I assume that the shared notions of a period constitutes a total world outlook. The conflicts and tensions *within* a discourse are just as significant as the shared premises.

3. T'ang Chün-i has suggested that the idea of "righteousness" (*i*), with its overwhelming orientation toward action in the world, is at the very heart of Mohism. See *Yüan-tao p'ien*, chaps. 3 and 4.

4. Angus Graham, "The Background of the Mencian Theory of Human Nature," *Tsing Hua Journal of Chinese Studies,* nos. 1 and 2 (Dec. 1967), pp. 215–271. Ch'ien Mu in his *Hsien-Ch'in chu-tzu,* pp. 245–248, calculates the dates of Yang Chu as falling somewhere between 395 and 335 B.C. The whole question of dating, however, remains highly uncertain.

5. Graham, "The Background of the Mencian Theory," p. 215.

6. Legge, *The Shoo King,* p. 429.

7. Hsü Fu-kuan, *Chung-kuo jen-hsing lun shih* (Taichung: Tunghai University Press, 1963), chap. 1.

8. For Waley's version of this poem, see his *Book of Songs,* p. 252.

9. James Legge, *The Ch'un t'sew with the Tso chuen,* vol. 5, *The Chinese Classics* (Hong Kong: University of Hong Kong Press, 1960), p. 708.

10. Ibid. (Duke Chao, Year 25), p. 709.

11. Ibid. (Duke Hsiang, Year 15), p. 467.

12. Graham, "The Background of the Mencian Theory," p. 219.

13. Waley, *Analects,* bk. 5, chap. 12, p. 110; *Lun-yü,* p. 98.

14. Waley, *Analects,* bk. 17, chap. 2, p. 209; *Lun-yü,* p. 367.

15. Graham, *Later Mohist Logic,* p. 245.

16. Ibid., p. 280.

17. A purported dialogue between Yang Chu and Mo-tzu's most prominent disciple Ch'in Ku-li is recorded in the book of *Lieh-tzu, Chu-tzu chi-ch'eng,* vol. 3, chap. 7, p. 83.

18. Graham, "The Background of the Mencian Theory," p. 219.

19. Wang Ch'ung (27–100 A.D.), *Lun Heng, Chu-tzu chi-ch'eng,* vol. 7, chap. 13, p. 28. Ch'ien Mu in *Hsien Ch'in chu-tzu,* p. 615, assigns one of these disciples, Chi Tiao-K'ai, to a date as early as 510–450 B.C.

20. The graph in the oracle bone inscriptions which has often been linked to *ch'i* actually seems to be a verb meaning to request. See Onozawa Seiichi, ed., *Ki no Shisō* (Tokyo: Tokyo University Press, 1981), p. 27.

21. Ibid., p. 21.

22. The terms *ruach* and *neshamah* (wind and breath) in biblical Hebrew both relate to the soullike or spiritlike, as do *pneuma* (wind) and *psyche* in Greek;

*atman* in Sanskrit, *dukh* in Slavic, and *spiritus* in Latin again link breath and soul. See Kurita Naomi, "Jōdai Shina ni mietaru (ki) no kannen," in *Chūgoku jōdai shisō kenkyū* (Tokyo Iwanami, 1948).

23. Onozawa, *Ki no shisō*, p. 34.

24. G. S. Kirk and J. E. Raven in *The Pre-Socratic Philosophers* (Cambridge: Cambridge University Press, 1960), p. 46, point out that the Greek word *aer* in "Homer and sometimes in later Ionic prose meant 'mist'—something visible and obscuring"; see also p. 144.

25. Legge, *The Ch'un Ts'ew* (Duke Chao, Year 1), pp. 580-581.

26. Ibid., p. 573.

27. Werner Jaeger, *The Theology of the Early Greek Philosophers* (Oxford: Oxford University Press, 1967), chap. 2.

28. Kirk and Raven, *The Pre-Socratic Philosophers*, pp. 76-78.

29. F. M. Cornford, *From Religion to Philosophy: A Study in the Origins of Western Speculation* (New York: Harper Torchbooks, 1957), p. 143.

30. Kirk and Raven, *The Pre-Socratic Philosophers*, pp. 8-37.

31. Ibid., p. 113.

32. See Charles Kahn, "Anaximander's Fragment: The Universe Governed by Law," in Alexander Mourelatos, ed., *The Pre-Socratics: A Collection of Critical Essays* (Garden City, N.Y.: Anchor Books, 1974), pp. 97-117.

33. Waley, *Analects*, bk. 10, chap. 4, p. 147; *Lun-yü*, p. 203.

34. Waley, *Analects*, bk. 11, chap. 7, p. 206; *Lun-yü*, p. 359.

35. Waley, *Analects*, bk. 8, chap. 4, p. 133; *Lun-yü*, p. 157.

36. *Mo-tzu*, chap. 21, p. 102.

37. Ibid., chap. 21, p. 104, and chap. 35, p. 117.

38. There is one reference to it in the definition of the term "sincerity" or "whole-heartedness" (*ch'eng*), where it seems to mean something like "zeal." It is thus a disposition of the will. See Graham, *Later Mohist Logic*, p. 273, A. 11.

39. Legge, *The Shoo King*, p. 575.

40. Ibid., p. 451.

41. Waley, *Analects*, bk. 2, chap. 4, p. 88; *Lun-yü*, p. 23.

42. Waley, *Analects*, bk. 6, chap. 5, p. 116; *Lun-yü*, p. 118.

43. Waley, *Analects*, bk. 17, chap. 22, p. 215; *Lun-yü*, p. 383.

## 6. THE WAYS OF TAOISM

1. Ch'ien Mu in *Hsien Ch'in chu-tzu hsi-nien k'ao* estimates the dates of the historic Chuang-tzu as falling somewhere between 365 and 290 B.C.; see pp. 269 and 618.

2. Among scholars who place the emergence of the text after Confucius and Mo-tzu but before Chuang-tzu and the Chi-hsia academicians are Feng Yu-lan, Takeuchi Yoshio in his *Rōshihen, Takeuchi Yoshio Zenshū*, vol. 5 (Tokyo: Kadokawa shoten, 1978), and Lo Ken-tse, *Chu-tzu K'ao-yin* (Peking: Jen-min ch'u-pan she, 1958), pp. 207-281. For the Chi-hsia Academy, see p. 238.

3. Watson, *Chuang-tzu*, chap. 3, p. 66; *Chuang-tzu chi-chieh, Chu-tzu chi-ch'eng*, vol. 3, p. 30.

4. Waley, *Analects*, bk. 15, chap. 4, p. 193; *Lun-yü*, p. 334.

5. Graham, *Later Mohist Logic,* p. 323, A. 76.

6. Ibid., p. 332, A. 85.

7. Ibid., p. 320.

8. *Lao-tzu chu, Chu-tzu chi-ch'eng,* vol. 2, chap. 3, p. 2; I shall here use as a reference the English translation of D. C. Lau, *Lao-tzu; Tao-te ching* (London: Penguin Classics, 1963), p. 59 (hereafter cited as *Lao-tzu*). The term "advancing men of worth" (*Shang-hsien*) is the title of one of the triads of chapters in the *Mo-tzu* (chaps. 8–10).

9. Watson, *Chuang-tzu,* chap. 7, p. 94; *Chuang-tzu chi-chieh,* p. 49.

10. This text, like the *Lü-shih Ch'un-ch'iu* compilation, is considered to be the collective work of a group of literati patronized by the Han Prince Huai-nan (circa first century B.C.). The dominant outlook in the text seems to be a combination of what I call the Lao-tzu and Huang-lao strains of Taoism. See *Huai-nan-tzu, Chu-tzu chi-ch'eng,* vol. 7, chap. 13, p. 218.

11. D. C. Lau, trans., *Mencius* (London: Penguin Classics, 1970), p. 144.

12. Whether mysticism should be defined as "religion" or "philosophy" or either remains a matter of dispute. Certain modern Western definitions of philosophy would hardly admit what has been called the "philosophic Taoism" of Lao-tzu and Chuang-tzu to the category of philosophy while others committed to strictly theistic definitions of religion would not admit them to the category of religion.

13. Gershom Scholem, in his *Major Trends in Jewish Mysticism* (Jerusalem: Schocken Books, 1941), p. 5, denies that mysticism necessarily involves the notion of the "mystical union." "Jews as well as non-Jews have by no means represented the essence of their ecstatic experience, the tremendous uprush and soaring of the soul to its highest plane, as a union with god." I would nevertheless contend that in most outlooks clearly identifiable as mystical, the "ecstatic experience" has been interpreted in terms of the "mystical union."

14. Lau, *Lao-tzu,* chap. 25, p. 82; *Lao-tzu chu,* p. 14.

15. Needham, *Science and Civilisation,* vol. 2, p. 35.

16. Ibid., p. 302.

17. Lau, *Lao-tzu,* chap. 1, p. 57; *Lao-tzu chu,* p. 1.

18. Lau, *Lao-tzu,* chap. 4, p. 60; *Lao-tzu chu,* p. 3.

19. Lau, *Lao-tzu,* chap. 7, p. 63; *Lao-tzu chu,* p. 4.

20. Henrich Zimmer, *Philosophies of India* (New York: Bolling Series, Pantheon Books, 1953), p. 79.

21. Lau, *Lao-tzu,* chap. 1, p. 57; *Lao-tzu chu,* p. 1.

22. Angus Graham, in his article " 'Being' in Western Philosophy Compared with *shih/fei* and *yu/wu* in Chinese Philosophy," *Asia Major,* NS 7, nos. 1–2 (1959), 79–112, stresses the different connotations of Western "being" and Chinese *yu* (which literally means something like "there is"). Whatever may be the case for being and *yu,* it seems to me that *wu* can be translated as "nonbeing" in the sense that both terms refer to the ineffable dimension of reality.

23. Lau, *Lao-tzu,* chap. 25, p. 82; *Lao-tzu chu,* p. 14.

24. Lau, *Lao-tzu,* chap. 14, p. 70; *Lao-tzu chu,* p. 7.

25. Lau, *Lao-tzu,* chap. 51, p. 112; *Lao-tzu chu,* p. 31.

26. Lau, *Lao-tzu,* chap. 34, p. 93; *Lao-tzu chu,* p. 20.

27. Lau, *Lao-tzu,* chap. 39, p. 100; *Lao-tzu chu,* p. 25.

28. Lau, *Lao-tzu,* chap. 56, p. 117; *Lao-tzu chu,* p. 34.

29. Scholem, *Major Trends,* p. 5.

30. Mircea Eliade does not hesitate to use the term "concrete mystical experience" with reference to shamans; see *Shamanism,* p. 265.

31. Vedantic training in Sankara demands both an arduous intellectual discipline and "training of the will" before the disciple is ready for mystical meditation. See Eliot Deutsch, *Advaita Vedanta* (Honolulu: An East-West Center Book, University of Hawaii Press, 1973), chap. 8.

32. Lau, *Lao-tzu,* chap. 1, p. 57, *Lao-tzu chu,* p. 1.

33. Lau, *Lao-tzu,* chap. 6, p. 62; *Lao-tzu chu,* p. 4. There is, however, no indication that this exaltation of the female has any implications for Taoist "social philosophy."

34. Lau, *Lao-tzu,* chap. 61, p. 122; *Lao-tzu chu,* p. 37.

35. Lau, *Lao-tzu,* chap. 5, p. 61; *Lao-tzu chu,* p. 3. According to one interpretation (Lau, *Lao-tzu,* p. 61), "straw dogs," which were used in certain religious sacrifices "were treated with the greatest deference before they were used only to be discarded and trampled on as soon as they served their purposes." According to the great third-century (A.D.) commentator Wang Pi, "The earth does not create straw for the cattle to eat and yet cattle eat it. It does not create dogs for men to eat. Yet men eat them." In both interpretations, Heaven's lack of "providentialism" is quite clear.

36. See David Hume, *A Treatise on Human Nature,* ed. P. Nidditch (Oxford: Clarendon Press, 1983), sec. 6, p. 251.

37. Lau, *Lao-tzu,* chap. 5, p. 61; *Lao-tzu chu,* p. 3.

38. Lau, *Lao-tzu,* chap. 1, p. 37; *Lao-tzu chu,* p. 1.

39. Needham, *Science and Civilisation,* vol. 2, p. 55.

40. D. C. Lau, "The Treatment of Opposites in Lao-tzu," *Bulletin of the Society for Oriental and African Studies,* 21 (1958), 2.

41. So prominent is this association of softness with the Lao-tzu in the minds of those close to the text in time that the *Lü-shih Ch'un-ch'iu* epitomizes his doctrine by the statement that "Lao Tan valued the soft," *Chu-tzu chi-ch'eng,* vol. 6, chap. 17.5, p. 213.

42. Lau, *Lao-tzu,* chap. 76, p. 138; *Lao-tzu chu,* p. 45.

43. Lau, *Lao-tzu,* chap. 48, p. 109; *Lao-tzu chu,* p. 29.

44. Needham, *Science and Civilisation,* vol. 2, p. 33.

45. Lao, *Lao-tzu,* chap. 12, p. 68; *Lao-tzu chu,* p. 6.

46. Ibid.

47. Lau, *Lao-tzu,* chap. 47, p. 108; *Lao-tzu chu,* p. 29.

48. For Chuang-tzu's attitude toward the skills of craftsmen, see Part 2 below.

49. Lau, "The Treatment of Opposites," p. 356.

50. Lau, *Lao-tzu,* chap. 44, p. 105; *Lao-tzu chu,* p. 28.

51. Lau, *Lao-tzu,* chap. 80, p. 142; *Lao-tzu chu,* p. 46.

52. Lau, *Lao-tzu,* chap. 13, p. 69; *Lao-tzu chu,* p. 7.

53. Lau, *Lao-tzu,* introduction, p. 42.

54. Lau, *Lao-tzu,* chap. 3, p. 54; *Lao-tzu chu,* p. 2.

55. Lau, *Lao-tzu,* chap. 57, p. 118; *Lao-tzu chu,* p. 34.

56. Lau, *Lao-tzu,* chap. 18, p. 74; *Lao-tzu chu,* p. 10.

57. Lau, *Lao-tzu,* chap. 2, p. 58; *Lao-tzu chu,* p. 1.

58. Lau, *Lao-tzu,* chap. 38, p. 99; *Lao-tzu chu,* p. 23.

59. Lau, *Lao-tzu,* chap. 38, p. 99; *Lao-tzu chu,* p. 23.

60. Lau, *Lao-tzu,* chap. 38, p. 99; *Lao-tzu chu,* p. 23.

61. Lau, *Lao-tzu,* chap. 19, p. 75; *Lao-tzu chu,* p. 10.

62. Lau, *Lao-tzu,* chap. 75, p. 137; *Lao-tzu chu,* p. 44.

63. Lau, *Lao-tzu,* chap. 53, p. 114; *Lao-tzu chu,* p. 32.

64. Lau, *Lao-tzu,* chap. 30, p. 88; *Lao-tzu chu,* p. 17.

65. Watson, *Chuang-tzu,* chap. 9, p. 105; *Chuang-tzu chi-chieh,* p. 57.

66. Lau, *Lao-tzu,* chap. 25, p. 82; *Lao-tzu chu,* p. 14.

67. Watson, *Chuang-tzu,* chap. 5, p. 72; *Chuang-tzu chi-chieh,* p. 34.

68. Lau, *Lao-tzu,* chap. 57, p. 73; *Lao-tzu chu,* p. 34.

69. Lau, *Lao-tzu,* chap. 17, p. 74; *Lao-tzu chu,* p. 9.

70. Lau, *Lao-tzu,* chap. 61, p. 122; *Lao-tzu chu,* p. 37.

71. Lau, *Lao-tzu,* chap. 80, p. 142; *Lao-tzu chu,* p. 46.

72. Lau, *Lao-tzu,* chap. 36, p. 95; *Lao-tzu chu,* p. 20.

73. Lau, "The Treatment of Opposites," p. 359.

74. Lau, *Lao-tzu,* chap. 30, p. 88; *Lao-tzu chu,* p. 17.

75. Among those who hold this view are Feng Yu-lan, Kuan Feng, Lo Ken-tse, Takeuchi Yoshio, and Angus Graham. Kuan Feng, Lo Ken-tse, and Angus Graham have used stylistic analysis in an effort to define the various strains in this text. Among the Chinese studies of these questions are Lo Ken-tse, "Chuang-tzu che-hsüeh 'wai,' 'tsa' p'ien t'an-yüan," *Chu-tzu K'ao-yin,* pp. 282–312; also, Kuan Feng, ed., *Chuang-tzu che-hsueh t'ao-lun chi* (Peking, 1962), passim.

76. This term has been adopted by many Western scholars. The degree to which these thinkers actually resemble the Greek sophists is a matter I shall not consider at this point.

77. Watson, *Chuang-tzu,* chap. 22, p. 237; *Chuang-tzu chi-chieh,* p. 138.

78. Watson, *Chuang-tzu,* chap. 22, p. 243; *Chuang-tzu chi-chieh,* p. 143.

79. Watson, *Chuang-tzu,* chap. 2, p. 43; *Chuang-tzu chi-chieh,* pp. 12–13.

80. Watson, *Chuang-tzu,* chap. 2, p. 36; *Chuang-tzu chi-chieh,* p. 6.

81. Watson, *Chuang-tzu,* chap. 21, p. 225; *Chuang-tzu chi-chieh,* p. 131.

82. The full context of this passage will be discussed below.

83. Watson, *Chuang-tzu,* chap. 3, p. 23; *Chuang-tzu chi-chieh,* p. 23.

84. Watson, *Chuang-tzu,* chap. 19, p. 200; *Chuang-tzu chi-chieh,* p. 116. In the context, the *ch'i* seems to refer to a cosmic realm of spiritual energy.

85. Needham, *Science and Civilisation,* vol. 2, p. 122.

86. Watson, *Chuang-tzu,* chap. 19, p. 205; *Chuang-tzu chi-chieh,* p. 119.

87. Watson, *Chuang-tzu,* chap. 17, p. 179; *Chuang-tzu chi-chieh,* p. 103.

88. Watson, *Chuang-tzu,* chap. 2, p. 46; *Chuang-tzu chi-chieh,* p. 15.

89. Presumably once these incipient germs crystallize out of the *tao* they have the capacity to engender entirely different forms, depending upon their habitat.

90. Watson, *Chuang-tzu,* chap. 18, p. 196; *Chuang-tzu chi-chieh,* p. 114.

91. Watson, translator's footnote, p. 196.

92. Watson, *Chuang-tzu*, chap. 25, pp. 291–292; *Chuang-tzu chi-chieh*, p. 175. The entire passage ends with the particle phrase *erh-i*, which has a dismissive or deprecatory connotation such as "nothing more than" or "all that."

93. Needham, *Science and Civilisation*, vol. 2, p. 40.

94. Hui Shih was a contemporary of the historic Chuang-tzu and seems to have died before him. Kung-sun Lung's conjectured dates, according to Ch'ien Mu, are between 320 and 245 B.C. His thought may represent a specific reaction against Hui Shih's profound mistrust of language. Others would place his dates earlier.

95. Watson, *Chuang-tzu*, chap. 33, p. 374; *Chuang-tzu chi-chieh*, p. 223.

96. Graham, *Later Mohist Logic*, pp. 26 and 28.

97. Watson, *Chuang-tzu*, chap. 33, p. 374; *Chuang-tzu chi-chieh*, p. 223.

98. *Chuang-tzu chi-chieh*, p. 223.

99. Watson, *Chuang-tzu*, chap. 33, p. 374, *Chuang-tzu chi-chieh*, p. 223.

100. Watson, *Chuang-tzu*, chap. 33, p. 374, and chap. 2, p. 39; *Chuang-tzu chi-chieh*, p. 223 and p. 9.

101. Love presupposes the focus of attention on separate individual entities, thus injuring our relationship with the *tao* as a whole. Hence, "when the *tao* was injured, love became 'complete' " (encapsulated, and closed off from the *tao*). Watson, *Chuang-tzu*, chap. 2, p. 41; *Chuang-tzu chi-chieh*, p. 11.

102. Watson, *Chuang-tzu*, chap. 2, p. 39; *Chuang-tzu chi-chieh*, p. 9.

103. Watson, *Chuang-tzu*, chap. 2, p. 45; *Chuang-tzu chi-chieh*, p. 14.

104. Watson, *Chuang-tzu*, chap. 2, p. 49; *Chuang-tzu chi-chieh*, p. 18.

105. Watson, *Chuang-tzu*, chap. 2, p. 47; *Chuang-tzu chi-chieh*, p. 16.

106. Watson, *Chuang-tzu*, chap. 25, p. 289; *Chuang-tzu chi-chieh*, p. 173.

107. The Chinese term is *ch'iu-li yen*. A *ch'iu*, according to one account, is an administrative unit of ten lineages and a *li* is a unit of twenty lineages.

108. Watson, *Chuang-tzu*, chap. 25, p. 290; *Chuang-tzu chi-chieh*, p. 173.

109. Watson, *Chuang-tzu*, chap. 6, p. 85; *Chuang-tzu chi-chieh*, p. 43.

110. Watson, *Chuang-tzu*, chap. 2, p. 38; *Chuang-tzu chi-chieh*, p. 8.

111. This is the translation of Angus Graham; see "Chuang-tzu's Essay on Seeing Things as Equal," *History of Religions* 9, nos. 2 and 3 (Nov. 1969 and Feb. 1970), 151.

112. Ibid., p. 148.

113. Watson, *Chuang-tzu*, chap. 33, p. 373; *Chuang-tzu chi-chieh*, p. 222.

114. Cited in Graham, *Later Mohist Logic*, p. 324, from *Lü-shih Ch'un-ch'iu*, vol. 6, *Chu-tzu chi-ch'eng*, chap. 14, p. 146.

115. Watson, *Chuang-tzu*, chap. 25, pp. 292–293; *Chuang-tzu chi-chieh*, p. 175.

116. This meaning seems to be older than the meaning of "passions." See Graham, *Later Mohist Logic*, pp. 179–180.

117. Watson, *Chuang-tzu*, chap. 2, p. 38; *Chuang-tzu chi-chieh*, p. 8.

118. Watson, *Chuang-tzu*, chap. 2, p. 41; *Chuang-tzu chi-chieh*, p. 11.

119. Watson, *Chuang-tzu*, chap. 2, p. 42; *Chuang-tzu chi-chieh*, p. 11.

120. Watson, *Chuang-tzu*, chap. 2, p. 38; *Chuang-tzu chi-chieh*, p. 29.

121. Watson, *Chuang-tzu*, chap. 2, p. 39; *Chuang-tzu chi-chieh*, p. 9.

122. Cited in David Wiggins, "Sentence, Meaning, Negation, and Plato's Problem of Non-being," *Plato*, Modern Studies in Philosophy, Metaphysics and Epistemology (New York: Doubleday Anchor Books, 1971), p. 269.

123. Watson, *Chuang-tzu,* chap. 2, p. 48; *Chuang-tzu chi-chieh,* p. 7.

124. Watson, *Chuang-tzu,* chap. 32, p. 353; *Chuang-tzu chi-chieh,* p. 209.

125. Watson, *Chuang-tzu,* chap. 32, p. 353; *Chuang-tzu chi-chieh,* p. 209.

126. In passages which belong to the strain of the historical Chuang-tzu, as indicated above, Confucius often is portrayed either as the protagonist of Chuang-tzu's views (this, of course, may be ironic) or as a man who while still imprisoned in the realm of "little understanding" nevertheless has some glimmerings of the higher truth.

127. Watson, *Chuang-tzu,* chap. 4, p. 54; *Chuang-tzu chi-chieh,* p. 21.

128. Watson, *Chuang-tzu,* chap. 4, p. 57; *Chuang-tzu chi-chieh,* p. 23.

129. Watson, *Chuang-tzu,* chap. 5, p. 69; *Chuang-tzu chi-chieh,* p. 31.

130. Watson, *Chuang-tzu,* chap. 7, p. 94; *Chuang-tzu chi-chieh,* p. 49.

131. Watson, *Chuang-tzu,* chap. 6, p. 82; *Chuang-tzu chi-chieh,* p. 41.

132. Watson, *Chuang-tzu,* chap. 6, p. 77; *Chuang-tzu chi-chieh,* p. 37.

133. Watson, *Chuang-tzu,* chap. 5, p. 75; *Chuang-tzu chi-chieh* p. 36. It is nevertheless true that many of the shadowy allegorical personae who abound in the book are depicted as recluses who are already outside the realm of ordinary existence.

134. Watson, *Chuang-tzu,* chap. 6, p. 84; *Chuang-tzu chi-chieh,* p. 42.

135. Watson, *Chuang-tzu,* chap. 18, pp. 191–192; *Chuang-tzu chi-chieh,* p. 110.

136. They also illustrate the "Yang Chu" theme that their uselessness has helped them to survive.

137. Watson, *Chuang-tzu,* chap. 5, p. 76; *Chuang-tzu chi-chieh,* p. 36.

138. In my own view, this may be true of one variant of Huang-lao Taoism, but the entire recent discussion in China was severely constrained by the fact that the Confucianism/Legalism debate of the early seventies was used as an aesopian political language to refer to very current conflicts between Mao Tse-tung and his opponents.

139. Herrlee Creel, *Shen Pu-hai: A Chinese Political Philosopher of the Fourth Century* (Chicago: University of Chicago Press, 1974), p. 170.

140. Ch'ien Mu, *Hsien Ch'in chu-tzu,* p. 233. He places the date of the founding of the Academy somewhere close to 357 B.C..

141. Ibid., p. 236.

142. Kuo Mo-jo, "Chi-hsia Huang-lao hsüeh-p'ai," in *Shih p'i-p'an shu* (Shanghai: Ch'ün-i ch'u-pan she, 1946), chap. 4, pp. 133–134.

143. Yang K'uan, "Chung-kuo shang-ku shih tao-lun," in *Ku shih-pien,* no. 7, part 1, pp. 195–210.

144. Watson, *Chuang-tzu,* chap. 33, p. 367–368; *Chuang-tzu chi-chieh,* p. 218.

145. "Meng-tzu cheng i," vol. 1, *Chu-tzu chi-ch'eng,* p. 485.

146. Watson, *Chuang-tzu,* chap. 33, p. 368; *Chuang-tzu chi-chieh,* p. 218.

147. "Hsün-tzu chi-chieh," vol. 2, *Chu-tzu chi-ch'eng,* chap. 18, p. 229.

148. Ch'ien Mu, *Hsien Ch'in chu-tzu,* p. 377.

149. Watson, *Chuang-tzu,* chap. 1, p. 31; *Chuang-tzu chi-chieh,* p. 3.

150. Ch'ien Mu calculates the *termini a quo* and *ad quem* of these figures roughly as follows: Sung Hsing, 360–290 B.C.; T'ien P'ien, 350–275 B.C.; Shen Tao, 360–275 B.C.

151. Watson, *Chuang-tzu,* chap. 33, pp. 369–370; *Chuang-tzu chi-chieh,* p. 219.

152. Watson, *Chuang-tzu*, chap. 33, p. 370; *Chuang-tzu chi-chieh*, pp. 219-220. This "knowledge" was obviously not simply Needham's knowledge of the feudal institutions and ideas of the Confucian tradition but seems to have involved deliberative thought as such (*lü*).

153. P. M. Thompson, *The Shen-tzu Fragments* (Oxford: Oxford University Press, 1979).

154. The word *fa* obviously refers here to much more than penal law. It seems to include nothing less than all the procedures, mechanisms, and institutions which govern—or ought to govern—the sociopolitical order.

155. Thompson, *Shen-tzu Fragments*, p. 239, no. 19.

156. The word whose basic meaning seems to be something like power or force is used to refer both to the inertial drift of things (itself a kind of force) and the inertial power of established authority.

157. Thompson, *Shen-tzu Fragments*, p. 234, no. 10.

158. Ibid., p. 235, no. 12.

159. Ibid., p. 236, no. 13.

160. Ibid., p. 267, no. 13. We have a concrete illustration here of the kind of knowledge which Shen Tao rejects. The individual judgments of persons, based simply on individual reasoning and individual experiences, are not only completely subject to private passions but are not based on an understanding of the "whole system."

161. Ibid., p. 238, no. 17.

162. Ibid., p. 260, no. 50.

163. Ibid., p. 249, no. 3.

164. Ibid., p. 295, no. 113.

165. Watson, *Chuang-tzu*, chap. 13, pp. 144-145; *Chuang-tzu chi-chieh*, p. 83.

166. Arthur Lovejoy, *The Great Chain of Being* (Cambridge, Mass.: Harvard University Press, 1971), p. 27.

167. Franklin Edgerton, *The Beginnings of Indian Philosophy* (Cambridge, Mass.: Harvard University Press, 1965), p. 22.

168. For the text and discussion of the texts, see "Ch'ang-sha Ma-wang-tui han-mu ch'u-t'u [Lao-tzu] ti-i pen-chuan ch'ien ku i-shu shih wen" in *Wen Wu*, no. 10 (1974), p. 30; also, T'ang Lan, " 'Huang-ti ssu-ching' ch'u t'an," *Wen Wu*, no. 10, p. 48.

169. *Wen Wu*, no. 10, p. 42.

170. Watson, *Chuang-tzu*, chap. 13, p. 140; *Chuang-tzu chi-chieh*, p. 81.

171. Watson, *Chuang-tzu*, chap. 13, pp. 142-143; *Chuang-tzu chi-chieh*, p. 84.

172. Watson, *Chuang-tzu*, chap. 13, p. 145; *Chuang-tzu chi-chieh*, p. 83.

173. *Wen Wu*, no. 10, p. 30.

174. Watson, *Chuang-tzu*, chap. 13, pp. 147-148; *Chuang-tzu chi-chieh*, p. 84.

175. Watson, *Chuang-tzu*, chap. 33, p. 362; *Chuang-tzu chi-chieh*, p. 215.

176. Watson, *Chuang-tzu*, chap. 33, p. 374; *Chuang-tzu chi-chieh*, p. 222.

177. Watson, *Chuang-tzu*, chap. 33, p. 364; *Chuang-tzu chi-chieh*, p. 216.

178. Ssu-ma Ch'ien, *Shih-chi*, vol. 6, chap. 70, p. 131.

179. Yü Ying-shih, *Li-shih yü ssu-hsiang* (Taipei: Lien-ching ch'u-pan kung-ssu, 1976), p. 19.

180. Watson, *Chuang-tzu*, chap. 13, p. 151; *Chuang-tzu chi-chieh*, p. 87.

181. *Shih-chi*, chap. 70, p. 131.

182. Burton Watson, *Records of the Grand Historian of China*, vol. 2 (New York: Columbia University Press, 1961), chaps. 124 and 129.

183. Watson, *Chuang-tzu*, chap. 6, p. 82; *Chuang-tzu chi-chieh*, p. 41.

184. Anna Seidel, "The Image of the Perfect Ruler in Early Taoist Messianism," *History of Religions* 9, no. 2 (Nov. 1969), 216 and 222.

## 7. THE DEFENSE OF THE CONFUCIAN FAITH

1. *Han Fei-tzu chi-chieh*, in *Chu-tzu chi-ch'eng*, vol. 5, p. 351.

2. Ibid.

3. *Shih-chi*, vol. 5, chap. 14, p. 714.

4. Ch'ien Mu calculates his dates as falling somewhere between 390 and 305 B.C. See *Hsien Ch'in chu-tzu*, pp. 187–188.

5. *Meng-tzu cheng-i, Chu-tzu chi-ch'eng*, vol. 1, p. 423. Lau, *Mencius*, bk. 5, part B, chap. 6, p. 156. I shall here use Lau's translation as the English reference text.

6. Lau, *Mencius*, bk. 5, part B, chap. 7, p. 157; *Meng-tzu* p. 425.

7. Liang is another name of the state of Wei[2].

8. *Shih-chi*, p. 714.

9. Lau, *Mencius*, bk. 3, part B, chap. 9, p. 113; *Meng-tzu*, p. 263.

10. Lau, *Mencius*, bk. 3, part B, chap. 9, p. 113; *Meng-tzu*, p. 264.

11. Lau, *Mencius*, bk. 3, part B, chap. 9, p. 113; *Meng-tzu*, p. 264.

12. Lau, *Mencius*, bk. 3, part B, chap. 9, p. 114; *Meng-tzu*, p. 264.

13. Ch'ien Mu, *Hsien Ch'in chu-tzu*, pp. 245–247.

14. *Lau, Mencius*, bk. 6, part B, chap. 4, p. 173; *Meng-tzu*, p. 486.

15. Lau, *Mencius*, bk. 1, part A, chap. 1, p. 49; *Meng-tzu*, p. 21.

16. Lau, *Mencius*, bk. 1, part A, chap. 1, p. 49; *Meng-tzu*, p. 22.

17. "It is evident then why utilitarians should stress the role of sympathy in moral learning and the central place of benevolence among moral virtues. Their conception of justice is threatened with instability unless sympathy and benevolence can be widely and intensely cultivated." Rawls, *A Theory of Justice*, p. 178.

18. Rawls refers to utilitarianism as a "teleological theory" in that it presumes that "what is right" is determined by some other good to which the right is instrumental. *Theory of Justice*, p. 24.

19. Lau, *Mencius*, bk. 2, part A, chap. 3, p. 80; *Meng-tzu*, p. 130.

20. Lau, *Mencius*, bk. 6, part A, chap. 6, p. 162; *Meng-tzu*, p 441.

21. Lau, *Mencius*, Appendix 5, pp. 235–263.

22. I do not translate it simply as "inborn" since the entire debate involves precisely the question of *what* is inborn. *Sheng*, which also means life, seems to convey the sense of all the properties shared by all living creatures—almost something like our "biological."

23. Lau, *Mencius*, bk. 6, part A, chap. 4, p. 161; *Meng-tzu*, p. 437.

24. Lau, *Mencius*, bk. 6, part A, chap. 4, p. 161; *Meng-tzu*, p. 437.

25. Lau, *Mencius*, bk. 6, part A, chap. 4, p. 161; *Meng-tzu*, p. 438.

26. Geertz, *Interpretation of Cultures*, p. 92.

27. Lau, *Mencius*, bk. 6, part A, chap. 4, p. 161; *Meng-tzu*, pp. 434–435.

28. Lau, *Mencius*, bk. 6, part A, chap. 4, p. 162; *Meng-tzu*, p. 439.

29. The metaphor of plant life is, in fact, used by Mencius. See Lau, *Mencius*, bk. 6, part A, chap. 7, p. 164; *Meng-tzu*, p. 448.

30. Lau, *Mencius*, bk. 2, part A, chap. 6, p. 82; *Meng-tzu*, p. 138.

31. One has a sense that by the time of Mencius the meaning of the term *jen* as a total all-embracing moral excellence has come to be narrowed to its more specific sense as "humanity" towards others. Perhaps the constricted Mohist usage had already influenced the meaning assigned to the word.

32. Lau, *Mencius*, bk. 2, part A, chap. 6, p. 82; *Meng-tzu*, p. 138.

33. Lau, *Mencius*, bk. 6, part A, chap. 8, p. 165; *Meng-tzu*, p. 457.

34. Lau, *Mencius*, bk. 6, part A, chap. 9, p. 165; *Meng-tzu*, p. 459.

35. Lau, *Mencius*, bk. 6, part A, chap. 8, p. 165; *Meng-tzu*, p. 457.

36. Lau, *Mencius*, bk. 3, part A, chap. 4, p. 102; *Meng-tzu*, p. 226.

37. Lau, *Mencius*, bk. 2, part A, chap. 2, pp. 76–78; *Meng-tzu*, pp. 110–125.

38. Lau, *Mencius*, bk. 2, part A, chap. 2, p. 77; *Meng-tzu*, p. 114.

39. Aristotle, *Ethics*, p. 52.

40. Watson, *Chuang-tzu*, ch. 4, p. 58; *Chuang-tzu chi-chieh*, p. 23.

41. Mencius speaks of the "vast flood-like *ch'i* [*hao-jan chih ch'i*] which fills all space between heaven and earth" (Lau, *Mencius*, bk. 2, part A, chap. 2, p. 77; *Meng-tzu*, p. 117). It has been stated that since Mencius is a humanist whose concerns are humanistic rather than "metaphysical," this statement cannot possibly have a metaphysical meaning. In fact, Mencius tends to relate all his "psychological" categories—heart, human nature, and *ch'i*—to their cosmic ground. The sharp antithesis between the "human" and the cosmic seems to be very much our own.

42. Lau, *Mencius*, bk. 2, part A, chap. 2, p. 77; *Meng-tzu*, p. 116. The same phrase can be found in the *Kuan-tzu*, probably an early Han collective work attributed to the famous Kuan Chung which in the view of most scholars contains a great deal of Warring States period material. See *Kuan-tzu chiao-cheng, Chu-tzu chi-ch'eng*, vol. 5, chap. 37, p. 222. Also W. Allyn Rickett, trans., *Kuan-tzu: A Repository of Early Chinese Thought* (Hong Kong: Hong Kong University Press, 1965), p. 169.

43. See Legge, *Ch'un Ts'ew* (Duke Chao, Year 1), pp. 580–581, for an account of the loss of *ch'i* in the *Tso-chuen*.

44. Watson, *Chuang-tzu*, chap. 19, p. 203; *Chuang-tzu chi-chieh*, p. 118.

45. *Huai-nan-tzu*, chap. 7, p. 100.

46. Lau, *Mencius*, bk. 2, part A, chap. 2, p. 77; *Meng-tzu*, p. 114.

47. Lau, *Mencius*, bk. 6, part A, chap. 15, p. 168; *Meng-tzu*, p. 467.

48. Lau, *Mencius*, bk. 6, part A, chap. 15, p. 168; *Meng-tzu*, p. 467.

49. The determination to think itself involves a conative disposition of willing.

50. Chao Ch'i commentary, *Meng-tzu cheng-i*, p. 116.

51. Rickett, *Kuan-tzu*, chap. 49, p. 162; *Kuan-tzu Chiao-chang*, p. 270.

52. Lau, *Mencius*, bk. 2, part A, chap. 2, p. 78; *Meng-tzu*, p. 119.

53. Lau, *Mencius*, bk. 7, part A, chap. 2, p. 182; *Meng-tzu*, p. 517.

54. Lau, *Mencius*, bk. 2, part A, chap. 2, p. 77; *Meng-tzu*, p. 114.

55. Lau, *Mencius*, bk. 2, part A, chap. 2, p. 78; *Meng-tzu*, p. 123.

56. H. Paton, trans., *The Moral Law or Kant's Groundwork of the Metaphysics of Morals* (London: Hutchinson's University Library, 1950), p. 393.

57. Lau, *Mencius*, bk. 7, part A, chap. 15, p. 184; *Meng-tzu*, p. 529.

58. Lau, *Mencius*, bk. 6, part A, chap. 15, p. 168; *Meng-tzu*, p. 467.

59. Lau, *Mencius*, bk. 1, part A, chap. 7, p. 58; *Meng-tzu*, p. 56.

60. Lau, *Mencius*, bk. 6, part A, chap. 7, p. 164; *Meng-tzu*, p. 451.

61. Lau, *Mencius*, bk. 1, part A, chap. 7, p. 58; *Meng-tzu*, p. 55.

62. Lau, *Mencius*, bk. 3, part A, chap. 7, p. 104; *Meng-tzu*, p. 234.

63. Lau, *Mencius*, bk. 1, part B, chap. 4, pp. 61-62; *Meng-tzu*, pp. 63-64.

64. Lau, *Mencius*, bk. 6, part A, chap. 11, p. 169; *Meng-tzu*, p. 470.

65. Lau, *Mencius*, bk. 6, part A, chap. 11, p. 169; *Meng-tzu*, p. 470.

66. Lau, *Mencius*, bk. 7, part B, chap. 35, p. 201; *Meng-tzu*, p. 598.

67. Lau, *Mencius*, bk. 7, part B, chap. 34, p. 201; *Meng-tzu*, p. 596.

68. Lau, *Mencius*, bk. 4, part A, chap. 1, p. 117; *Meng-tzu*, p. 284.

69. The term "well-field" derives from the graph for a well. It provides a map of the layout of the land division.

70. Lau, *Mencius*, bk. 3, part A, chap. 3, p. 99; *Meng-tzu*, p. 211.

71. Lau, *Mencius*, bk. 1, part A, chap. 6, p. 53; *Meng-tzu*, p. 42.

72. Lau, *Mencius*, bk. 1, part B, chap. 8, p. 68; *Meng-tzu*, p. 86.

73. Lau, *Mencius*, bk. 5, part B, chap. 6, p. 144; *Meng-tzu*, p. 381.

74. Lau, *Mencius*, bk. 5, part B, chap. 6, p. 144; *Meng-tzu*, p. 381.

75. Lau, *Mencius*, bk. 5, part A, chap. 6, p. 145; *Meng-tzu*, p. 383.

76. Lau, *Mencius*, bk. 2, part B, chap. 13, p. 94; *Meng-tzu*, p. 183.

77. Lau, *Mencius*, bk. 2, part A, chap. 1, p. 74; *Meng-tzu*, p. 109.

78. Lau, *Mencius*, bk. 1, part A, chap. 7, p. 58; *Meng-tzu*, p. 54.

79. Lau, *Mencius*, bk. 3, part A, chap. 4, p. 101; *Meng-tzu*, p. 219.

80. Lau, *Mencius*, bk. 3, part A, chap. 4, p. 102; *Meng-tzu*, p. 226.

81. Lau, *Mencius*, bk. 3, part A, chap. 4, p. 102; *Meng-tzu*, p. 219.

82. Lau, *Mencius*, bk. 6, part B, chap. 11, p. 179; *Meng-tzu*, p. 507.

83. Lau, *Mencius*, bk. 4, part B, chap. 15, p. 130; *Meng-tzu*, p. 330.

84. Jean-Jacques Rousseau, "Social Contract," in Ernest Barker, ed., *Locke, Hume, and Rousseau* (London: World's Classics, Oxford University Press, 1953), p. 290.

85. Lau, *Mencius*, bk. 7, part A, chap. 1, p. 182; *Meng-tzu*, p. 517.

86. Mencius' first commentator, Chao Ch'i, of the latter Han dynasty, states "Through his thinking he carries out the good and can thus be said to know his nature." *Meng-tzu*, bk. 7, chap. 1, commentary p. 517.

87. Lau, *Mencius*, bk. 7, part A, chap. 1, p. 182; *Meng-tzu*, p. 517.

88. Lau, *Mencius*, bk. 7, part B, chap. 13, p. 196; *Meng-tzu*, p. 472.

89. Ch'ien Mu, *Hsien Ch'in chu-tzu*, p. 143.

90. See, for example, Kanaya Osamu "Junshi no bunkengakuteki kenkyū" in *Nihon Gakushiin Kiyō* (Bulletin of the Japanese Academy) 4, no. 1 (March 1951); Also, Donald Munro, *The Concept of Man in Early China* (Stanford: Stanford University Press, 1969), pp. 77-81. The chapter in question (chap. 23) is found in *Hsün-tzu chi-chieh, Chu-tzu chi-ch'eng*, vol. 2, pp. 289-300.

91. *Hsün-tzu chi-chieh*, chap. 19, p. 231. It is noteworthy that this statement

which epitomizes the very essence of Hsün-tzu's doctrine of evil appears not in chapter 23 but in the chapter on Hsün-tzu's conception of *li*.

92. Ibid., chap. 2, p. 15.

93. The "moral will" in both Mencius and Kant necessarily includes a cognitive component.

94. *Hsün-tzu chi-chieh*, chap. 23, p. 240.

95. Ibid., p. 292. The term *wei* here is a verbal noun referring to discrete deliberate acts of man. The graph used with the explicit "man" classifier emphasizes the notion of *man*-made.

96. I shall nevertheless later note that in Hsün-tzu as well the superior man's "rational" powers somehow also draw on trans-rational sources.

97. *Hsün-tzu chi-chieh*, p. 291.

98. Ibid., chap. 22, p. 286.

99. In *Mo-tzu* the sages realize that they must love and fear Heaven and the spirits and are in the end able to communicate this "religious" message to the people. In the *Hsün-tzu* this particular type of "religious" message is absent.

100. Hobbes, *Leviathan*, pp. 103 and 101.

101. *Hsün-tzu chi-chieh*, chap. 12, p. 151. The word *fa* here seems to be used in its most extended sense and not simply as a term denoting penal law; see chap. 8 below.

102. Ibid., chap 1, p. 1.

103. Ibid.

104. Ibid., chap. 2, p. 12.

105. Ibid., chap. 1, p. 4.

106. Ibid., chap. 23, p. 293.

107. Ibid.

108. Ibid., chap. 23, pp. 295-296.

109. The word *lü* is frequently used by Hsün-tzu. See Graham, *Later Mohist Logic*, pp. 266-267.

110. See particularly chap. 10, "Enriching the State," chap. 16, "Strengthening the State," and chap. 15, "Discussing Military Affairs."

111. *Hsün-tzu chi-chieh*, chap. 19, p. 245. And in chap. 20 (p. 252), "On Music," we find an explicit attack on Mo-tzu and the emphatic assertion that "humans can not live without music."

112. Ibid., chap. 19, p. 250.

113. Ibid.

114. Ibid., chap. 19, p. 236.

115. Ibid., chap. 11 ("On Kingship and Hegemony"), p. 133.

116. Ibid.

117. Ibid.

118. Ibid.

119. Ibid., chap. 11, p. 131.

120. Ibid., chap. 11, p. 133.

121. Ibid.

122. Ibid., chap. 15, p. 176.

123. Leon Vandermeersch, *La Formation du Légisme* (Paris: Publications de l'École Française d'Extreme-orient, 1965), p. 202.

124. Ibid., p. 203.

125. *Hsün-tzu chi-chieh*, chap. 16, p. 202.

126. Ibid., chap. 16, p. 200.

127. Ibid., chap. 9, p. 94.

128. Ibid., chap. 9, p. 96.

129. Ibid.

130. Cited in Barker, *Political Thought*, p. 185.

131. Voegelin, *Plato*, pp. 221 and 223.

132. *Chuang-tzu chi-chieh*, chap. 6, p. 101; Watson, *Chuang-tzu*, p. 77.

133. *Hsün-tzu chi-chieh*, chap. 17, p. 205.

134. Ibid., p. 208.

135. Hsün-tzu attacks the contemporary science of physiognomy based on the principle of a correlation between the physical anatomical structure of the human body and human fortune in chap. 5, "Against Physiognomy" *(fei-hsiang)*.

136. *Hsün-tzu chi-chieh*, chap. 17, p. 205. There is nothing in Hsün-tzu's view of nature which would necessarily preclude strange and "abnormal" phenomena which do not fit ordinary patterns of nature, but he does not regard such phenomena as having implications for human affairs. "Prodigies are possible but not to be feared" (chap. 9, p. 209).

137. Ibid., chap. 17, p. 206.

138. Needham, *Science and Civilisation*, vol. 2, p. 26–29.

139. *Hsün-tzu chi-chieh*, chap. 17, p. 206.

140. Ibid., chap. 17, p. 211.

141. Needham, *Science and Civilisation*, vol. 2, p. 26.

142. *Hsün-tzu chi-chieh*, chap. 22 ("On Correcting Terms"), p. 279.

143. Ibid., chap. 22, p. 278.

144. Ibid., chap. 17, p. 206.

145. Ibid.

146. Ibid., chap. 21, p. 263.

147. Ibid.

148. Ibid., chap. 21, p. 264.

149. Ibid., chap. 21, pp. 264–265.

150. Ibid., chap. 21, p. 264.

151. Ibid., chap. 17, p. 207.

152. Ibid., chap. 18, p. 214.

153. Ibid., chap. 18, pp. 227–228.

154. Ibid., chap. 18, p. 230.

155. Ibid., chap. 6, p. 66.

156. Ibid.

157. Ibid., chap. 23, p. 292.

158. Ibid., chap. 6, p. 57.

159. Ibid., chap. 6, p. 58.

160. Ibid., chap. 21, p. 262.

161. Ibid., chap. 6, p. 59.

162. Ibid., chap. 21, p. 262.

163. Ibid., chap. 6, p. 58.

164. Ibid.

165. Ibid.
166. Ibid., chap. 6, p. 57.
167. Ibid., chap. 32 ("Questions of Yao"), p. 364.
168. Ibid., chap. 15, p. 186.
169. Ibid.

## 8. LEGALISM

1. For a discussion of the term and its many levels of meaning, see Creel, *Shen Pu-hai*, pp. 144–150.

2. The most common specific terms used for this concept of method or *techne* after the fourth century are the graphs *shu*[1] (in the fourth tone) and *shu*[2] (in the third tone), although the word *fa* continues to be used interchangeably with both of these terms.

3. In the famous etymological dictionary of the Latter Han dynasty, the *Shuo-wen* (The explanation of graphs) by Hsü Shen, the early form of the graph seems to refer to punishment or penal law. The initial form of the graph as depicted is extraordinarily complex. It is believed to represent something like a judicial ordeal in which a horned beast is used to test the guilt or innocence of an accused party. See the discussion by Vandermeersch in *La Formation du Légisme*, p. 185.

4. Ibid., p. 186.
5. Lau, *Mencius*, bk. 6, part 1, p. 160; *Meng-tzu*, p. 431.
6. Lau, *Mencius*, bk. 4, part 1, p. 117; *Meng-tzu*, p. 284.
7. Lau, *Mencius*, bk. 4, part 1, p. 118; *Meng-tzu*, p. 284.
8. Creel, *Shen Pu-hai*, p. 32; also pp. 144–148.
9. *Han Fei-tzu chi-chieh* in *Chu-tzu chi-ch'eng*, vol. 5, chap. 54, p. 365.
10. Ibid., chap. 50, p. 356.
11. Legge, *The Shoo King*, p. 392.
12. Ibid., p. 391.
13. The ambivalent attitude of Confucius toward Kuan Chung has already been discussed in chap. 3.
14. Legge, *The Ch'un Ts'ew* (Duke Hsiang, Year 30), p. 558.
15. Ibid. (Duke Chao, year 6), p. 609.
16. Ibid. (Duke Chao, year 29), p. 732.
17. Ibid. (Duke Chao, year 6), p. 609.
18. Ibid. (Duke Chao, year 6), p. 610.
19. Ibid. (Duke Chao, year 29), p. 732
20. *Shang chün-shu, Chu-tzu chi-ch'eng*, vol. 5, chap. 8, p. 18.
21. Called by later doxographers "the school of horizontal and vertical alliances" (*tsung-heng-chia*).
22. A case can be made that the Han Fei-tzu book envisages the achievement of an ultimate state of universal peace and harmony. There can be no doubt, however, that the foreground of its concern is focused on the "science" of wealth and power.
23. Rawls, *Theory of Justice*, p. 178.
24. Vandermeersch, *La Formation du Légisme*, pp. 216–217.

25. The newly conquered territories, where the older local aristocratic lineages had been displaced, were often placed under the direct "bureaucratic" control of the state ruler and came to be administered by state appointed officials.

26. Ch'ien Mu calculates their dates as falling between 455–395 and 440–381, respectively.

27. See Creel, *Shen Pu-hai*, chap. 10.

28. His dates are calculated by Ch'ien Mu as falling between 390 and 338 B.C. See Ch'ien Mu, *Hsien Ch'in chu-tzu hsi-nien*, pp. 227–230.

29. *Shang chün-shu*, vol. 5, p. 1.

30. The details of the program are to be found in Ssu-ma Ch'ien's biography of Lord Shang (*Shih-chi*), chap. 68.

31. Lau, *Mencius*, bk. 6, part A, p. 160; *Meng-tzu*, p. 433.

32. *Shang chün-shu*, chap. 23, p. 38.

33. *Han Fei-tzu chi-chieh, Chu-tzu chi-ch'eng*, vol. 5, chap. 45, p. 330.

34. Michael Crozier, *The Bureaucratic Phenomenon* (Chicago: University of Chicago Press, 1964), p. 177.

35. *Han Fei-tzu chi-chieh*, chap. 49, p. 339; *Shang chün-shu*, chap. 23, p. 38.

36. Ch'ien Mu estimates his dates as somewhere between 400 and 337 B.C., Ch'ien Mu, *Hsien Ch'in chu-tzu*, pp. 237–238. Shen Pu-hai was, however, a native of the old state of Cheng annexed by Han in 375 B.C.

37. See the biography of Shen Pu-hai in *Shih-chi*, chap. 63.

38. Herrlee Creel, "The Beginnings of Bureaucracy in China: The Origins of the *Hsien*," *Journal of Asian Studies*, 23 (1964), 155–184.

39. Max Weber, *The Religion of China*, trans. Hans Gerth (Glencoe, Ill.: Free Press, 1951), chap. 5.

40. Confucian literati in later centuries were, of course, quite aware of Legalistic doctrine concerning these matters.

41. "The sage ruler relies on methods and not on his own knowledge"; Creel, *Shen Pu-hai*, p. 357.

42. See particularly *Han Fei-tzu chi-chieh*, chaps. 30 and 31. Also see Vandermeersch, *La Formation du Légisme*, pp. 230–233.

43. *Han Fei-tzu chi-chieh*, chap. 43, p. 304. I rely here basically on Creel's translation (*Shen Pu-hai*, p. 62).

44. Michael Crozier devotes an entire chapter of his work to the continuing role of power conflict and the need for sanctions in the "rational" world of bureaucracy; see *The Bureaucratic Phenomenon*, chap. 6 ("Power and Uncertainty").

45. *Han Fei-tzu chi-chieh*, chap. 43, p. 304.

46. Ibid., pp. 304–305.

47. Ibid., chap. 51, p. 358.

48. He in fact admits this; see ibid., chap. 40, p. 297.

49. Ibid., chap. 51, p. 358.

50. Ibid., chap. 49, p. 344.

51. Ibid.

52. Ch'ien Mu calculates his dates as lying between 280 and 233 B.C. See Ch'ien Mu, *Hsien Ch'in chu-tzu*, p. 477.

53. Ssu-ma Ch'ien adds the fact most interesting from a psychological point of view, that Han Fei-tzu was a stammerer.

54. *Han Fei-tzu chi-chieh,* chap. 11, p. 55.

55. Ibid., chap. 40, p. 297.

56. Ibid., p. 298.

57. Ibid., p. 300.

58. Ibid., chap. 6, p. 102.

59. Ibid., p. 95.

60. Ibid., p. 101.

61. Ibid., p. 102.

62. See Vandermeersch, *La Formation du Légisme,* p. 68.

63. Jack Dull, in a recent article bent on proving that the leaders of the rebellions against the Ch'in dynasty were not "peasant leaders," emphasizes the degree to which our image of the Ch'in dynasty has been shaped by the distorting propaganda of later Confucian and Taoist sources. While one may readily grant that the leaders of the movements which overthrew the dynasty were not peasants; while one may share Dull's suspicions concerning statistical data used in later accounts, one nevertheless doubts whether he disproves the general picture of the regime's excessive demands on the society's human and material resources and the repressiveness of its penal system on every level of society. See Jack Dull, "Anti-Qin Rebels: No Peasant Leaders Here," *Modern China,* 9, no. 3 (July 1983), 285.

64. Alexander D'Entrèves, *The Notion of the State* (Oxford: Oxford University Press, 1967), p. 39.

65. An English translation is available in Watson's *Records of the Grand Historian,* no. 8, pp. 77–119.

### 9. CORRELATIVE COSMOLOGY

1. I use the word "ontological" here to avoid some of the unending controversies surrounding the words "philosophy" and "metaphysics."

2. Particularly Marcel Granet, *La Pensée Chinoise* (Paris: Albin Michel, 1950).

3. Lévi-Strauss, *The Savage Mind,* p. 9.

4. Ibid., p. 224.

5. K. C. Chang has questioned whether clan emblems or bronze vessel iconography can be interpreted in totemic terms. See *Shang Civilization,* p. 165. The concern with the "four cardinal directions" in the oracle bone inscriptions is taken by some to have some connection to correlative cosmology.

6. Lévi-Strauss, *The Savage Mind,* pp. 225 and 228.

7. See Hsü Fu-kuan, *Yin-yang wu-hsing kuan-nien chih yen-pien chi jo-kan yu-kuan wen-hsien ti ch'eng-li shih-tai yü chieh-shih ti wen-t'i* (Tai pei: Min-chu p'ing-lun she, 1961), chap. 2.

8. Legge, *Ch'un ts'ew* (Duke Chao, year 10), p. 626; also ibid. (Duke Chao, year 17), p. 668.

9. Ibid. (Duke Chao, year 1), p. 581.

10. Ibid. (Duke Chao, year 18), p. 671.

11. Graham, *Later Mohist Logic,* p. 411; also p. 55.

12. Ibid., p. 411.

13. Ch'ien Mu calculates his dates as falling between 305 and 240 B.C.

14. Ssu-ma Ch'ien, *Shih-chi,* chap. 74.

15. Needham, *Science and Civilisation,* vol. 2, p. 325.

16. The currently popular terms "five phases" and "five activities" have their own problems. If the term "five elements" overemphasizes the role of the "static substances," the terms "phases" and "activities" overlook the role of static substances and categories within the entire syndrome of the *wu hsing.* Any translation which dwells on one aspect thus involves metonymy. See John Major, "A Note on the Translation of Two Technical Terms in Chinese," *Early China,* 2 (Fall 1976), 1–3. Also Richard Kunst, "More on *xiu* and *wuxing* with an Addendum on Archaic Reconstruction," *Early China,* 3 (Fall 1977).

17. The same word used above to refer to human spiritual and moral power. Here it is a cosmic power.

18. See Li Te-yung, "Wu-hsing t'an-yüan," *Chung-kuo che-hsüeh* (Peking: Sheng-huo tu-shu hsin-chih, 1980), p. 72.

19. Ibid., p. 72.

20. Vitaly Rubin, "Wu hsing and Yin-yang," *Journal of Chinese Philosophy,* 19, no. 2 (June 1982).

21. Hsü Fu-kuan, *Yin-yang wu-hsing kuan-nien chih yen-pien,* chap. 4; and Li Te-yung, "Wu-hsing t'an-yüan," p. 80.

22. Legge, *The Shoo King* ("The Counsels of the Great Yu"), p. 55. The "six storehouses" are also mentioned in the *Tso-chuan* (Duke Wen, year 7), p. 249.

23. Needham, *Science and Civilisation,* vol. 2, p. 243.

24. W. Heidel, "Qualitative Change in Pre-Socratic Philosophy," in Mourelatos, ed., *The Pre-Socratics,* pp. 86–95.

25. Kirk and Raven, *The Pre-Socratic Philosophers,* p. 329.

26. Kurt von Fritz, "Nous, noein, and their Derivatives," in Mourelatos, ed., *The Pre-Socratics,* pp. 72–79.

27. Kirk and Raven, *The Pre-Socratic Philosophers,* p. 162.

28. Cornford, *From Religion to Philosophy,* p. 143.

29. See Ssu-ma Ch'ien, *Shih-chi,* chap. 74.

30. See Needham, *Science and Civilisation,* vol. 2, pp. 253–261, for a discussion of the various permutations of the five elements theory.

31. These are the same categories used in the *Analects* to refer to simple, untaught native goodness (*chih*) and the complex "objective" prescriptions of behavior embodied in the *li* (*wen*).

32. Watson, *Records,* vol. 2, p. 231.

33. Ssu-ma Ch'ien, *Shih-chi,* chap. 74.

34. Needham, *Science and Civilisation,* vol. 2, p. 247.

35. Ibid.

36. Needham himself points to the natural observations of Tung Chung-shu.

37. Watson, *Records,* vol. 2, p. 25.

38. Nathan Sivin, *Chinese Alchemy: Preliminary Studies* (Cambridge, Mass.: Harvard University Press, 1968), p. 23.

39. Cited in Needham, *Science and Civilisation*, vol. 2, p. 281.

40. Hsü Fu-kuan, *Yin-yang wu-hsing kuan-nien chih yen-pien*, chap. 7.

41. Legge, *The Shoo King*, p. 327.

42. Ibid., pp. 326–327.

43. Ibid., p. 328.

44. Ibid., p. 333.

45. Ibid., p. 334–338.

46. The same calendrical scheme is found in the late Warring States compilation, *Lü-shih Ch'un-ch'iu* (*The Spring and Autumn Annals of Master Lü*).

47. This institution was to play a continuing role in the religico-cosmological framework of the Chinese state. For a Western account, see William Soothill, *The Hall of Light: A Study of Early Chinese Kingship* (New York: Philosophic Library, 1952).

48. See *Hsün-tzu chi-chieh*, chap. 6, p. 59. There has been much debate among Chinese scholars about the meaning of the term *wu hsing* as attributed by Hsün-tzu to Mencius. Since the text of Mencius is barren of any reference to *yin* and *yang* or five-elements cosmology, and since the entire thrust of correlative cosmology seems quite foreign to Mencius' basic outlook, it is difficult to regard him as in any way connected with five-elements theory. Some have surmised that the term *wu hsing,* meaning literally five modes of behavior, may refer to the five cardinal virtues. Is it, however, conceivable that Tsou Yen did indeed attempt to incorporate Mencian ideas on the patterns of history into his own five-elements cosmology and that Hsün-tzu, who was a contemporary of Tsou Yen, knew of Mencius' views through a "Tsou Yen" interpretation? See Hsiung Kung-che, *Hsün-tzu chin-chu chin i* (Taiwan: Shang-wu yin-shu kuan, 1977), pp. 84–85.

49. See Hou Wai-lu, *Chung-kuo, Ku-tai ssu-hsiang t'ung-shih,* vol. 2.

50. *Shih-chi,* chap. 74.

51. Tung Chung-shu, *Ch'un-ch'iu fan-lu* in *Han-Wei Ts'ung-shu,* Ming Wan-li jen chai, 1982, vols. 9–16.

52. Ibid., vol. 12, chaps. 4–6.

53. Ibid., vol. 12, chap. 69, p. 3.

54. Ibid., vol. 12, chap. 70, p. 5.

55. Needham, *Science and Civilisation,* vol. 2, p. 298.

56. Ibid., p. 302.

57. Tung Chung-shu, *Ch'un-ch'iu fan-lu,* vol. 13, chap. 78, p. 3.

58. Needham, *Science and Civilisation,* vol. 2, p. 302.

59. In Ssu-ma Ch'ien's famous treatise "The Feng and Shan Sacrifices" (Watson, *Records,* vol. 2, p. 25), we find references to a "lord of *yang*" and a "lord of *yin.*"

60. Legge, *The Ch'un Ts'ew* (Duke Chao, year 29), p. 731.

61. Needham, *Science and Civilisation,* vol. 2, p. 337.

62. For an excellent English translation, see Watson, *Records,* vol. 2, chap. 28, pp. 13–69.

63. Ibid., pp. 24–25.

64. Ibid., p. 40.

65. The "World" chapter of the Chuang-tzu (chap. 33) ascribes the term to Lao-tzu.

66. Tung Chung-shu, *Ch'un-ch'iu fan-lu,* vol. 12, chap. 67, p. 1.

67. Watson, *Records,* vol. 2, p. 39.

68. Yü Ying-shih, "Life and Immortality in the Mind of Han China," *Harvard Journal of Asiatic Studies,* 25 (1964–1965), 104–105.

69. Watson, *Records,* vol. 2, p. 25.

70. Ibid., p. 38.

71. Ibid., p. 37.

72. Most modern scholars regard the idea as late in origin.

73. Watson, *Records,* vol. 2, p. 13.

74. Ibid., p. 410.

75. For a treatment of some leading Huang-lao figures of the early Han period, see the biographies of Ts'ao Ts'an, Chi An, and Cheng Tang-shih in Watson, *Records.*

76. Ssu-ma Ch'ien, *Shih-chi,* vol. 6, chap. 70, p. 129.

77. Ibid., chaps. 64 and 69; Watson, *Records,* vol. 2, pp. 452–461, and 476–479.

78. Sivin, *Chinese Alchemy,* p. 3.


10. THE FIVE CLASSICS

1. It was, of course, a fusion which may not have been accepted with equal enthusiasm by all Confucianists during the early Han. Takeuchi Yoshio has suggested that some of the most eminent scholars of the former state of Lu continued to represent a tradition closer to that of Hsün-tzu, while the type of cosmological Confucianism represented by Tung Chung-shu was dominant in the Confucian tradition of the former state of Ch'i. See Takeuchi Yoshio, *Chūgoku shisōshi* (Tokyo: Iwanami Zensho, 1957), chap. 11.

2. The "six classics" refer to the six "disciplines" represented by the *Book of Documents,* the *Book of Poetry,* the *Book of Changes,* the *Spring and Autumn Annals,* the *Rites,* and the lost classic of music (*yüeh ching*), the existence of which has been questioned by many scholars.

3. These arts or disciplines are, of course, to be distinguished from the six arts of the ancient aristocracy (*li,* music, archery, chariot-driving, writing, and mathematics).

4. The complex debates concerning the "New Text" and "Old Text" versions of the classics which dominated the development of Confucianism during the Han dynasty lie beyond the scope of this volume. At the risk of oversimplification, I might simply observe that the dominance of "New Text" versions of the classics tended to coincide with the dominance of cosmological Confucianism in the Former Han dynasty.

5. Lau, *Mencius,* bk. 3, part B, chap. 9, p. 114; *Meng-tzu,* p. 267.

6. *Hsün-tzu chi-chieh,* chap. 1, p. 7.

7. Lau, *Mencius,* bk. 3, part B, chap. 9, p. 114; *Meng-tzu,* p. 267.

8. Legge, *Prolegomena, Chinese Classics,* vol. 1, p. 3.

9. Lau, *Mencius,* bk. 4, part B, chap. 21, p. 131; *Meng-tzu,* p. 338.

10. Lau, *Mencius,* bk. 3, part B, chap. 9, p. 114; *Meng-tzu,* p. 267.

11. Lau, *Mencius*, bk. 4, part B, chap. 21, p. 132; *Meng-tzu*, p. 338.

12. For a detailed discussion of these issues, see Hung Yeh's (William Hung) introduction to the Harvard Yenching Index of the *Spring and Autumn Annals. Ch'un-ch'iu ching-chuan yin-te* (Peking: Harvard-Yenching Institute, 1937; supp. no. 11), vol. 1, *hsü* (introduction), pp. ciii-cvi.

13. Ch'ien Mu, *Chu-tzu Hsin hsüeh-an* (Taipei: Ssu-min Shu-chü, 1977), vol. 4, pp. 102-103.

14. Legge, *The Ch'un Ts'ew* (Duke Hsüan, year 3), p. 290.

15. The early chapters of the *Ch'un-ch'iu fan-lu* are, in fact, mainly concerned with ethico-political doctrines derived from the Kung-yang commentary in the *Annals*.

16. Tung Chung-shu, *Ch'un-ch'iu fan-lu*, chap. 12, p. 6.

17. Ch'ien Mu, *Chu-tzu Hsin hsüeh-an*, vol. 4, p. 102.

18. Richard Wilhelm, *Lectures on the I Ching*, trans. Irene Eber (Princeton: Bollingen Series, Princeton University Press, 1979), Introduction, p. xi.

19. The symbolic figures of the trigrams and hexagrams were evidently obtained by manipulating the stalks of milfoil plants and later by other methods.

20. Willard Peterson, "Making Connections: Commentary on the Attached Verbalizations of the Book of Changes," *Harvard Journal of Asiatic Studies*, 42, no. 1 (June 1982), 77.

21. Legge, *The Shoo King*, pp. 334-338.

22. Peterson, "Making Connections," pp. 8-9.

23. Needham, *Science and Civilisation*, vol. 2, pp. 322-325.

24. Ibid., p. 320.

25. Ch'ien Mu, *Chu-tzu Hsin hsüeh-an*, vol. 4, pp. 1-52.

26. Legge, *The I Ching*, Sacred Books of the East, ed. Max Muller (New York: Dover Publications, 1963), p. 355; also, Honda Watari, *Eki, Chūgoku koten-sen* (Tokyo: Asahi Shimbun, 1967), vol. 1, p. 489.

27. Legge, *The I Ching*, p. 377; Honda, *Eki*, p. 519.

28. Legge, *The I Ching*, p. 373; Honda, *Eki*, p. 513.

29. Peterson, "Making Connections," p. 106.

30. Ibid., p. 104.

31. Legge, *The I Ching*, p. 376.

32. Peterson, "Making Connections," p. 109.

33. Ibid., p. 106.

34. For example, this statement occurs in the proposition appended to line 2 of the hexagram no. 1 *(ch'ien)* and recurs constantly throughout the book. See Legge, *The I Ching*, p. 57.

35. Legge, *The I Ching*, p. 409; Honda, *Eki*, p. 13

36. Legge, *The I Ching*, p. 410; Honda, *Eki*, p. 15.

37. Wilhelm, *Lectures*, pp. 98-101. The well as an unceasing source of water is associated in the Chinese texts with the idea of perseverance and by Wilhelm with patience.

38. Needham, *Science and Civilisation*, vol. 2, p. 336.

39. *Hsün-tzu chi-chieh*, chap. 2, p. 7; also chap. 20, passim.

40. For example, see Feng Yu-lan, *Chung-kuo che-hsueh shih,* chap. 14; Also, Derk Bodde, *A History of Chinese Philosophy* (Princeton: Princeton University Press, 1952–1953).

41. Tung Chung-shu, *Ch'un-chiu fan-lu,* chap. 36, p. 6.

42. Legge's translation of the titles of these texts, while generally accepted in the literature, are open to question, but I shall not linger on this question here.

43. Feng Yu-lan, *Chung-kuo che-hsueh shih.*

44. Legge, *The Great Learning, Chinese Classics,* vol. 1, pp. 438–446.

45. Ibid., pp. 357–358.

46. Ibid., p. 413.

47. Ibid., p. 420.

48. Ibid.


## POSTSCRIPT

1. See Marcel Granet, *Chinese Civilization,* trans. Innes and Brailsford (London: Kegan Paul, Trench, Trubner, 1930); also, *Fêtes et chansons anciennes de la Chine,* 2nd ed. (Paris, 1929).

2. Maurice Freedman, "On the Sociological Study of Chinese Religion," in *Religion and Ritual in China,* ed. Arthur Wolf (Stanford: Stanford University Press, 1974), p. 33.

3. Ibid., p. 37.

4. Ibid., p. 39.

5. Arthur Wolf, "Gods, Ghosts, and Ancestors," *Religion and Ritual in China,* p. 145.

6. "With the exception of prophecy and ecstasy, every religious phenomenon to be found among the common people was susceptible of transformation into beliefs and rite among the cultivated elite." Freedman, "On the Sociological Study," p. 39. In fact, it is questionable whether prophecy and ecstasy are not to be found in the texts of the high culture.

7. Ibid., p. 39.

8. I refer here not only to vulgar Marxism but also to a dominant tendency in non-Marxist social scientific literature.

# SELECTED BIBLIOGRAPHY

Ahern, Emily. *The Cult of the Dead in a Chinese Village.* Stanford: Stanford University Press, 1973.

Akatsuka Kiyoshi. 赤塚忠 . *Chūgoku kodai no shūkyō to bunka* 中国古代の宗教と文化 (The ancient religion and culture of China). Tokyo: Kadokawa Shoten, 1977.

Aristotle. *The Ethics of Aristotle: The Nicomachean Ethics,* trans. J. A. Thompson. London: Allen and Unwin, 1953. Reprint. London: Penguin Classics, 1973.

——— *Politics and Poetics.* New York: Compass Books, Viking Press, 1959.

Baker, Hugh. *Chinese Family and Kinship.* New York: Columbia University Press, 1979.

Balazs, Etienne. *Chinese Civilization and Bureaucracy,* ed. Arthur Wright. New Haven: Yale University Press, 1964.

Barker, Ernest. *The Political Thought of Plato and Aristotle,* 3d ed. London: Methuen and Co., 1947. Reprint. New York: Dover Publications, 1959.

Bodde, Derk. *Essays on Chinese Civilization.* Princeton: Princeton University Press, 1981.

Bradbury, R. E. "Fathers, Elders, and Ghosts in Edo Religion." Pp. 127–153 in *Anthropological Approaches to Religion,* ed. E. Banton. London: Tavistock Publications, London Association of Social Anthropologists of the Commonwealth, 1969.

Chang, Kwang-chih. *The Archaeology of Ancient China.* 3d edition. New Haven: Yale University Press, 1977.

——— *Early Chinese Civilization: Anthropological Perspectives.* Cambridge, Mass.: Harvard University Press, 1976.

——— *Shang Civilization.* New Haven: Yale University Press, 1980.

"Ch'ang-sha Ma-wang tui han-mu ch'u-t'u 《Lao-tzu》 ti-i pen-chüan ch'ien ku i-shu shih wen" 长沙马王堆汉墓出土《老子》第一本卷前古佚为书释文 (An explanation of the ancient lost texts preceding the first scroll of the "Lao-tzu" excavated from the Han tomb of in Ma-wang tui in Ch'ang-sha). *Wen Wu* 10 (1974).

Ch'en Meng-chia. 陳夢家 . *Yin-hsü p'u-tz'u tsung-shu* 殷墟卜辭綜書 (A summation of the oracle inscriptions of the Yin wastes). Peking: K'o-hsüeh ch'u-pan she, 1956.

Ch'ien Mu. 錢穆 . *Hsien-Ch'in chu-tzu hsi-nien k'ao* 先秦諸子繫年考 (Chronological studies of the Pre-Ts'in philosophers). Hong Kong: Hong Kong University Press, 1935.

*Chuang-tzu chi-chieh* 莊子集解 (Collected commentaries on Chuang-tzu), vol. 3, *Chu-tzu chi-ch'eng* 諸子集成 . Peking: Chung-hua shu-chü, 1957.

Cornford, F. M. *From Religion to Philosophy: A Study in the Origins of Western Speculation.* New York: Harper Torchbooks, 1957.

Creel, Herrlee. "The Beginnings of Bureaucracy in China: The Origins of the *Hsien.*" *Journal of Asian Studies,* 23 (1964): 155–184.

——— *Confucius, the Man and the Myth.* New York: J. Day, 1949.

——— *The Origins of Statecraft in China.* Chicago: University of Chicago Press, 1970.

——— *Shen Pu-hai: A Chinese Political Philosopher of the Fourth Century B.C.* Chicago: University of Chicago Press, 1974.

Crozier, Michael. *The Bureaucratic Phenomenon.* Chicago: University of Chicago Press, 1964.

D'Entrèves, Alexander. *The Notion of the State.* Oxford: Oxford University Press, 1967.

Deutsch, Eliot. *Advaita Vedanta.* Honolulu: An East-West Center Book, University of Hawaii Press, 1973.

Dull, Jack. "Anti-qin Rebels: No Peasant Leaders Here." *Modern China,* 9, no. 3 (July 1983), 285–317.

Dumont, Louis. *Homo Hierarchicus.* London: Weidenfeld and Nicolson, 1970. Reprint. London: Paladin, 1972.

Edgerton, Franklin. *The Beginnings of Indian Philosophy.* Cambridge, Mass.: Harvard University Press, 1965.

Eliade, Mircea. *Shamanism.* Bollingen Series, vol. 76. New York: Pantheon Books, 1964.

Feng Yu-lan 馮友蘭 . *Chung-kuo che-hsueh shih* 中國哲學史 . Shanghai: Shen-chou kuo-kuang she, 1933. Trans. D. Bodde, *A History of Chinese Philosophy.* Princeton: Princeton University Press, 1952–1953.

Fingarette, Herbert. *Confucius: The Secular as Sacred.* New York: Harper and Row, 1972.

——— "Reply to Professor Hansen." *Journal of Chinese Philosophy* (Dordrecht, Holland), 7, no. 3 (Sept. 1980), 259–266.

Flannery, Kent. "The Cultural Evolution of Civilization." *Annual Review of Ecology and Systematics,* 3 (1972), 394–426.

Freedman, Maurice. "On the Sociological Study of Chinese Religion." Pp. 19–41 in *Religion and Ritual in China,* ed. Arthur Wolf. Stanford: Stanford University Press, 1974.

Fried, Morton. *The Notion of the Tribe.* Menlo Park, Calif.: Cummings Publishing Co., 1975.

Geertz, Clifford. *Interpretation of Cultures.* New York: Basic Books, 1973.

Graham, Angus. "The Background of the Mencian Theory of Human Nature." *Tsing Hua Journal of Chinese Studies,* 1 and 2 (Dec. 1967), 215–271.

——— " 'Being' in Western Philosophy Compared with *shih/fei* and *yu/wu* in Chinese Philosophy," *Asia Major,* NS 7/1-2 (1959), 79–112.

——— *Later Mohist Logic, Ethics, and Science.* Hong Kong: Chinese University Press, 1978.

——— "Chuang-tzu's Essay on Seeing Things as Equal." *History of Religions,* 9, nos. 2 and 3 (Nov. 1969 and Feb. 1970), 137–159.

Granet, Marcel. *Chinese Civilization,* trans. Innes and Brailsford. London: Kegan Paul, Trench, Trubner; New York: Knopf, 1930.

——— *La Pensée Chinoise.* Paris: Editions Albin Michel, 1950.

Guthrie, W. *Socrates*. Cambridge: Cambridge University Press, 1971.

*Han Fei-tzu chi-chieh* 韓非子集解 (Collected interpretations of Han Fei-tzu), vol. 5, *Chu-tzu chi-ch'eng*.

Hansen, Chad. *Language and Logic in Ancient China*. Ann Arbor: University of Michigan Press, 1983.

Hawkes, David. *Ch'u-tz'u: The Songs of the South*. Oxford: Clarendon Press, 1959. Reprint. Boston: Beacon Paperbacks, 1962.

Heidel, Alexander. *The Babylonian Genesis*. Chicago: University of Chicago Press, 1963.

Heidel, W. "Qualitative Change in Pre-Socratic Philosophy." Pp. 86–95 in Mourelatos, ed., *The Pre-Socratics: A Collection of Critical Essays*. Modern Studies in Philosophy. Garden City, N.Y.: Doubleday Anchor Books, 1974.

Hobbes, Thomas. *Leviathan*. New York: Dutton and Co., 1950.

Honda Watari 本田濟. *Eki* 易 (The changes). *Chūgoku kotensen series, 1*. Tokyo: Asahi Simbun, 1967.

Hou Wai-lu 侯外廬. *Chung-kuo ssu-hsiang t'ung-shih* 中国思想通史. Peking: Jen-min ch'u-pan she, 1957.

Hsiao Kung-ch'uan. *A History of Chinese Political Thought*, trans. F. W. Mote. Princeton: Princeton University Press, 1978.

Hsiung Kung-che 熊公哲. *Hsün-tzu chin-chu chin i* 荀子今註今譯. Taipei: Shang-wu yin-shu kuan, 1977.

Hsu, Cho-yun. *Ancient China in Transition: An Analysis of Social Mobility, 722–222 B.C.* Stanford: Stanford University Press, 1965.

Hsü Fu-kuan 徐復觀. *Chung-kuo jen-hsing lun shih* 中国人性論史 (A history of theories of human nature in China). Taichung: Tunghai University Press, 1963.

—— *Yin-yang wu-hsing kuan-nien chih yen-pien chi jo-kan yu-kuan wen-hsien ti ch'eng-li shih-tai yü chieh-shih ti wen-t'i* 陰陽五行觀念之演變及若干有關文献的成立時代與解釋的問題 (The evolution of the concepts of Yin-yang and the Five Elements and the problem of the dating and interpretation of several relevant texts). Taipei: Min-chu p'ing-lun she, 1961.

*Hsün-tzu chi-chieh* 荀子集解 (Collected commentaries on Hsün), vol. 2, *Chu-tzu chi-ch'eng*.

Hu Hou-hsüan 胡厚宣. "Shih 'yü i jen' " 釋《余一人》(Explaining the expression "I, the Unique Man"). *Li-shih yen-chiu*, no. 1 (1957): 75–78.

—— "Yin-tai feng-chien chih-tu k'ao" 殷代封建制度考 (A study of the feudal system in the Yin dynasty) in vol. 1, *Chia-ku hsüeh Shang shih lun-ts'ung* 甲骨学商史論叢 (A collection of articles on the study of Shang history in the oracle inscriptions). Ch'eng-tu: Ch'i-lu University, 1944.

*Huai-nan-tzu* 淮南子. Commentary by Kao Yu 高誘. vol. 7, *Chu-tzu chi-ch'eng*.

Hume, David. *A Treatise on Human Nature*, ed. P. Nidditch. Oxford: Clarendon Press, 1983.

Hung Yeh (William Hung) 洪業. *Introduction to Ch'un-ch'iu ching chuan yin-te* 春秋經傳引得. Harvard-Yenching Institute Sinological Index Series, supplement 11, vol. 1 (Dec. 1937).

Jaeger, Werner. *The Theology of the Early Greek Philosophers*. Oxford: Oxford University Press, 1967.

Jaspers, Karl. *Vom Ursprung und Ziel der Geschichte*, particularly chap. 1 ("Die

Achsenzeit''). Zürich: Artemis Verlag, 1949.

Kahn, Charles. "Anaximander's Fragment: The Universe Governed by Law." In Mourelatos, ed., *The Pre-Socratics: A Collection of Critical Essays*. Modern Studies in Philosophy. Garden City, N.Y.: Doubleday Anchor Books, 1974.

Kaizuka Shigeki. *Confucius*, trans. G. Bownas. London: Allen and Unwin, 1974.

Kanaya Osamu 金谷治. "Junshi no bunkengakuteki kenkyū" 荀子の文献学的研究 (Textual study of Hsün-tzu's work). *Nihon Gakushiin Kiyō* (Bulletin of the Japanese Academy), 4, no. 1 (March 1951).

Keightley, David. "Akatsuka Kiyoshi and the Culture of Early China." *Harvard Journal of Asiatic Studies*, 42, no. 1 (June 1982), 267–320.

—— *Sources of Shang History*. Berkeley: University of California Press, 1978.

Keightley, David, ed. *The Origins of Chinese Civilization*. Berkeley: University of California Press, 1983.

Kirk, G. S. *Myth: Its Meaning and Function in Ancient and Other Cultures*. Cambridge: Cambridge University Press, 1970.

Kirk, G. S., and J. E. Raven. *The Pre-Socratic Philosophers*. Cambridge: Cambridge University Press, 1960.

Kunst, Richard. "More on *xiu* and *wuxing* with an Addendum on Archaic Reconstruction." *Early China*, 3 (Fall 1977), 67–69.

Kuo Mo-jo 郭沫若. "Chi-hsia Huang-lao hsüeh-p'ai *ti p'i p'an*" 稷下黄老学派 (The "Huang-lao" faction at the Chi-hsia Academy). *Shih p'i-p'an shu* 十批判書 Shanghai: Ch'ün-i ch'u-pan she, 1946.

Kurita Naomi 栗田直躬. "Jōdai ni mietaru (ki) no kannen" 上代に見えたる「氣」の觀念 (The Concept of *ch'i* as seen in the Ancient Period). In *Chūgoku jōdai shisō no kenkyū* 中國上代思想の研究 (A study of ancient Chinese thought). Tokyo: Iwanami, 1948.

*Lao-tzu chu* 老子注, vol. 2, *Chu-tzu chi-ch'eng*.

Lau, D. C., trans. *Lao-tzu: Tao te ching*. London: Penguin Classics, 1963.

——, trans. *Mencius*. London: Penguin Classics, 1970.

—— "The Treatment of Opposites in Lao-tzu." *Bulletin of the Society for Oriental and African Studies*, 21 (1958), 344–360.

Leach, Edmund. *Lévi-Strauss*, ed. Frank Kermode. New York: Viking Press, 1970. Reprint. London: Fontana Modern Masters, 1970.

Legge, James. *Analects*, vol. 1, *The Chinese Classics*. Reprinted from the last editions of Oxford University Press, 3d ed.; 5 vols. Hong Kong: University of Hong Kong Press, 1960.

—— *The Ch'un ts'ew with the Tso chuen*, vol. 5, *The Chinese Classics*. Hong Kong: University of Hong Kong Press, 1960.

—— *The I Ching*, Sacred Books of the East, ed. Max Muller. New York: Dover Publications, 1963.

—— *The She King*, vol. 4, *The Chinese Classics*. Hong Kong: University of Hong Kong Press, 1960.

—— *The Shoo King*, vol. 3, *The Chinese Classics*. Hong Kong: University of Hong Kong Press, 1960.

Levenson, Joseph. *Confucian China and Its Modern Fate*. Berkeley: University of California Press, 1965.

—— *Modern China and Its Confucian Past*. Garden City, N.Y.: Doubleday Anchor

Books, 1964.

Lévi-Strauss, Claude. *The Savage Mind.* Chicago: University of Chicago Press, 1966.

——*Structural Anthropology.* Garden City, N. Y.: Basic Books, 1963. Reprint. New York: Doubleday Anchor Books, 1969.

Li Te-yung 李德永 . "Wu-hsing t'an-yüan" 五行探源 (Inquiry into the origins of the five elements). *Chung-kuo che-hsüeh.* Peking: Sheng-huo tu-shu hsin-chih, 1979.

*Lieh-tzu* 列子 , vol. 3, *Chu-tzu chi-ch'eng.*

Lin Yü-sheng. "The Evolution of the Pre-Confucian Meaning of *Jen* and the Confucian Conception of Moral Autonomy." *Monumenta Serica,* 31 (1924–1925), 172–204.

Lo Ken-tse 羅根澤 . "Chuang-tzu che-hsüeh 'wai' 'tsa' p'ien t'an-yüan" 莊子哲学「外」「雜」篇探源 (Investigating the sources of the "Outer" and "Miscellaneous" sections of the philosophy of Chuang-tzu). Pp. 282–312 in *Chu-tzu K'ao-yin.*

——*Chu-tzu K'ao-yin* 諸子考索 . Peking: Jen-min ch'u-pan she, 1958.

Lovejoy, Arthur. *The Great Chain of Being.* Cambridge, Mass.: Harvard University Press, 1971.

*Lü-shih Ch'un-ch'iu* 呂氏春秋 (Spring and Autumn Annals of Master Lü), vol. 6, *Chu-tzu chi-ch'eng.*

*Lun-yü cheng i* 論語正義 (The correct meaning of the Analects). Commentary by Liu Pao-nan 劉寶南 . *Chu-tzu chi-ch'eng.*

Major, John. "A Note on the Translation of Two Technical Terms in Chinese." *Early China,* 2 (Fall 1976), 1–3.

Mannheim, Karl. *Essays in Sociology and Social Psychology.* Oxford: Oxford University Press, 1938.

Maspero, Henri. *La Chine antique* in *Histoire du Monde,* ed. E. De Boccard, vol. 4. Paris: Boccard Editeurs, 1927.

——"Légendes mythologiques dans le Chou King." *Journal Asiatique,* 154 (1924), 1–100.

*Meng-tzu cheng-i,* vol. 1, *Chu-tzu chi-ch'eng.*

Miyazaki Ichisada 宮崎一定 . "Shunshū to Toshi Kokka," 春秋と都市国家 (Spring and Autumn and the City-State). *Tōhō Bunka Kōza* 8, chap. 2, 1955.

*Mo-tzu hsien ku* 墨子閒詁 , ed. and commentary by Sun I-jang 孫詒讓 , vol. 4, *Chu-tzu chi ch'eng.* Peking: Chung-hua shu-chü, 1957.

Munro, Donald. *The Concept of Man in Early China.* Stanford: Stanford University Press, 1969.

Needham, Joseph. *The Grand Titration: Science and Society in East and West.* Toronto: University of Toronto Press, 1969.

——*Science and Civilisation in China.* Cambridge: Cambridge University Press, 1956.

Nivison, David. "Dates of Western Chou." *Harvard Journal of Asiatic Studies,* 43, no. 2 (December 1983), 481–579.

——"Royal 'Virtue' in Shang Oracle Inscriptions." *Early China* (Berkeley), 4 (1978–1979), 52–55.

Onozawa Seiichi 小野沢精一 , ed. *Ki no shisō* 氣の思想 (The idea of *ch'i*). Tokyo: Tokyo University Press, 1981.

Oppenheim, Leo. *Ancient Mesopotamia, Portrait of a Dead Civilization.* Chicago: University of Chicago Press, 1964.

Paton, H. *The Moral Law or Kant's Groundwork of the Metaphysics of Morals.* London:

Hutchinson's University Library, 1950.

Peterson, Willard. "Making Connections: Commentary on the Attached Verbalizations of the Book of Changes." *Harvard Journal of Asiatic Studies*, 42, no. 1 (June 1982), 67–116.

Plato. *Protagoras and Meno*, trans. W. Guthrie. London: Penguin Classics, 1974.

Rawls, John. *A Theory of Justice*. Cambridge, Mass.: Harvard University Press, 1971.

Rhys, David. *The Questions of King Milinda, Sacred Books of the East*, ed. Max Müller, vols. 39–40. Delhi: Motilal Banarsidass, 1969.

Rickett, W. Allyn. *Kuan-tzu: A Repository of Early Chinese Thought*. Hong Kong: Hong Kong University Press, 1965.

Rousseau, Jean-Jacques. *Social Contract*. In *Locke, Hume, and Rousseau*, ed. Lord Lindsay. London: World Classics, Oxford University Press, 1953.

Rubin, Vitaly. "Wu hsing and Yin-yang." *Journal of Chinese Philosophy*, 19, no. 2, (June 1982), 131–155.

Schluchter, Wolfgang, ed. *Max Webers Studie über Konfuzianismus und Taoismus: Interpretation und Kritik*. Frankfurt am Main: Suhrkamp-Taschenbuch Wissenschaft, 1983.

Scholem, Gershom. *Major Trends in Jewish Mysticism*. Jerusalem: Schocken Books, 1941.

Schwartz, Benjamin. "On the Absence of Reductionism in Chinese Thought." *Journal of Chinese Philosophy*, 1, no. 1 (Dec. 1973): 27–43.

Seidel, Anna. "The Image of the Perfect Ruler in Early Taoist Messianism." *History of Religions*, 9, no. 2 (Nov. 1969), 216–247.

Shirakawa, Shizuka 白川靜. *Kōkotsubun no sekai* 甲骨文の世界 (The world of the oracle inscriptions). Tokyo: Heibonsha, 1972.

Sivin, Nathan. *Chinese Alchemy: Preliminary Studies*. Cambridge, Mass.: Harvard University Press, 1968.

Soothill, William. *The Hall of Light: A Study of Early Chinese Kingship*. New York: Philosophical Library, 1952.

Spellman, John. *Political Theory of Ancient India*. Oxford: Oxford University Press, 1964.

Spinoza, Benedict. *Ethics*, trans. Andrew Boyle. London: Dent and Sons, Heron Books, 1910.

Ssu-ma Ch'ien 司馬遷. *Shih-chi* 史記 (Historical records) Fang-chi ku-ko pen 仿汲古閣本

Takeuchi Yoshio 竹内義雄. *Chūgoku shisōshi* 中国思想史 (History of Chinese thought). Tokyo: Iwanami Zensho, 1957.

―― *Rōshihen* 老子篇, vol. 5, *Takeuchi Yoshio Zenshū* 竹内義雄全集. Tokyo: Kadokawa shoten, 1978.

T'ang Chün-i 唐君毅. *Yüan-tao p'ien* 原道篇, vol. 1, *Chung-kuo che-hsüeh yüan-lun* 中国哲学原論. Taipei: Hsin-ya shu-yüan yen chiu-so, 1973.

T'ang Lan 唐兰. "'Huang-ti ssu-ching' ch'u-t'an" 《黄帝四經》初探 (A preliminary study of the four classics of the Yellow Emperor). *Wen Wu*, 10 (1974), 48–52.

*Tao te ching* (A comparison with Ma Wang tui manuscripts), trans. D. C. Lau. Hong Kong: Chinese University Press, 1982.

Taylor, A. E. *Plato, the Man and his Works*. London: Methuen and Co., 1926. Reprint. New York: Meridian Books, 1971.

Thompson, P. M. *The Shen-tzu Fragments*. Oxford: Oxford University Press, 1979.

Tsuda Sōkichi 津田左右吉 . *Rongo to Kōshi no shisō* 論語と孔子の思想 (The Analects and the thought of Confucius). Tokyo: Iwanami shoten, 1946.

Tu Kuo-Hsiang 社国庠 . *Tu Kuo-hsiang wen chi* 社国庠文集 . Peking: Jen-min ch'u-pan she, 1962.

Tung Chung-shu 董仲舒 . *Ch'un-ch'iu fan-lu* 春秋繁露 *Han Wei Ts'ung-shu*, Ming Wan-li jen-chai, 1982.

Tung Tso-pin 董作賓 . "Yin-tai li-chih ti hsin chiu liang p'ai" 殷代禮制的新舊兩派 (The old and new factions in the ritual system of the Yin period). *Ta-lu tsa-chih*, 6 (1953), 1–6.

Voegelin, Eric. *Plato*. Baton Rouge: Louisiana State Press, 1966; originally appeared as part 1 of Voegelin, Eric, *Plato and Aristotle* (Baton Rouge: Louisiana State Press, 1957).

Von Fritz, Kurt. "Nous, Noein, and their Derivatives." Pp. 72–79 in Mourelatos, ed., *The Pre-Socratics: A Collection of Critical Essays*. Modern Studies in Philosophy. Garden City, N.Y.: Doubleday Anchor Books, 1974.

Waley, Arthur. *The Analects of Confucius*. London: Allen and Unwin, 1983. Reprint. New York: Random House, Vintage Books, 1938.

——— *The Book of Songs*. London: Allen and Unwin, 1954.

Wang Ch'ung 王充 . *Lun Heng* 論衡 , vol. 7, *Chu-tzu chi-ch'eng*.

Watson, Burton. *Chuang-tzu*. New York: Columbia University Press, 1968.

——— *Records of the Grand Historian of China*. New York: Columbia University Press, 1961.

Weber, Max. *The Religion of China*, trans. Hans Gerth. Glencoe, Ill.: Free Press, 1951.

Wheatley, Paul. *The Pivot of the Four Quarters: A Preliminary Inquiry into the Origins and Character of the Ancient Chinese City*. Chicago: Aldine Press, 1971.

Wiggins, David. "Sentence, Meaning, Negation, and Plato's Problem of Non-being." Pp. 269–303 in *Plato*. Modern Studies in Philosophy, Metaphysics, and Epistemology. New York: Doubleday Anchor Books, 1971.

Wilhelm, Richard. *The I Ching*, trans. William Baynes. Bollingen Series, vol. 19. New York: Pantheon Books, 1950.

——— *Lectures on the I Ching*, trans. Irene Eber. Bollingen Series. Princeton: Princeton University Press, 1979.

Wolf, Arthur P. "Gods, Ghosts, and Ancestors." Pp. 131–182 in *Religion and Ritual in Chinese Society*. Stanford: Stanford University Press, 1974.

Yang K'uan 楊寬 . "Chung-kuo shang-ku shih t'ao-lun" 中國上古史討論 (An introduction to ancient Chinese history), in *Ku shih-pien* 古史辨 7 (1941), part 1, 195–210.

Yates, Robin, and Katrina McLeod. "Forms of Ch'in Law: An Annotated Translation of the Feng-chen shih." *Harvard Journal of Asiatic Studies*, 41, no. 1 (June 1981), 111–163.

Yü Ying-shih 余英時 . *Chung-kuo chih-shih chieh-ts'eng shih lun* 中国知識階層史論 . Taipei: Lien-ching ch'u-pan shih-yeh kung ssu, 1980.

——— "Life and Immortality in the Mind of Han China." *Harvard Journal of Asiatic Studies*, 25 (1965), 80–122.

——— *Li-shih yü ssu-hsiang* 歷史與思想 (History and thought). Taipei: Lien-ching ch'u-pan kung-ssu, 1976.

Zaehner, R. C. *Hinduism.* Oxford: Oxford University Press, 1972.

Zimmer, Heinrich. *Philosophies of India.* Bollingen Series, vol. 26. New York: Pantheon Books, 1953.

# GLOSSARY

The following is a select glossary of terms mentioned in the text and some lesser known proper names.

ai 愛

Chang I 張義
chen-chün 眞君
chen-jen 眞人
chen-tsai 眞宰
cheng 正 correct
cheng 征 punitive attack
cheng 政 government, punishment
cheng-chiao ho-i 政教合一
ch'eng 成 complete, ''individualized''
ch'eng 誠 sincerity, authenticity
ch'eng su 成俗
chi 幾 incipient germs, impulses
Chi Chen 季眞
Chi-hsia 稷下
chi i 集義
ch'i 氣
Chieh 桀 last ruler of Hsia
Chieh-tzu 接子
chien 漸 hexagram no. 53, ''gradualness''
chien 蹇 hexagram no. 39, ''lameness''
ch'ien 乾 hexagram no. 1, ''dynamic, creative''
Ch'ien Han-shu 前漢書
chih 志 will
chih 指 ''attribute''
chih 質 simple stuff
chih 知 knowledge
ch'ih 恥
ching 經 classic
ching 井 hexagram no. 48, ''well''
ch'ing 情

Chou 紂 last ruler of Shang
Chou-Li 周禮
Chü-tzu 鉅子
chung 中 the ''mean,'' to target
chung 忠 truthfulness
Ch'un Ch'iu 春秋
chün-tzu 君子
Ch'ü Yuan 屈原
ch'üan 權
ch'üan-mou 權謀

fa 法
fa-chia 法家
fa-i 法儀
fang-hsin 放心
fang-shih 方士
feng-chien 封建

hao-jan chih ch'i 浩然之氣
heng 恆 hexagram no. 32, ''duration''
hsi-tz'u 繫辭
hsi-tz'u chuan 繫辭傳
hsiang 象
hsiao-shuo chia 小説家
hsien 仙 immortal
hsien 賢 worthy man
hsin 心 heart
hsin 信 faithfulness
hsing 刑 punishment
hsing 形 form
hsing 性 human nature
hsing-ming 形(刑)名
hsü 虛 empty, emptiness
hsü 需 hexagram no. 5, ''waiting''
hsü-hsin 虛心
Hsü Hsing 許行
hsüeh 学

hsüeh-ch'i 血氣
huang-chi 皇極
Huang-lao 黃老
Huang-lao chün 黃老君
Huang-ti 黃帝 Yellow Emperor
huang-ti 皇帝 emperor
Hui Shih 惠施
Hung-fan 洪範
huo-chih 貨殖
huo-shih 或使

i 義 righteousness
i 異 difference
i 儀 model, form
i 易 "changes"
I ching 易經
i i 一義
i tuan 異端
i wei 以為
i-wen chih 藝文誌
I Yin 伊尹

jang 讓
jen 仁
ju 儒
jūdō 柔道

kan-t'ung 感通
Kao-tzu 告子
ken 根
ko ming 革命
ku 故
Ku-liang 穀梁
Kuan Chung 管仲
Kuan-tzu 管子
kung 公
kung-li 公利
Kung-sun Lung-tzu 公孫龍子
Kung-yang 公羊
kuo 國
kuo-yü 國語

li 禮 ceremony
li 利 interest
li 離 hexagram no. 30 "separation"
li 理 principle
Li-chi 禮記
li i fa tu 禮義法度
Li Ssu 李斯
liang-hsin 良心
liang-i 兩儀
liang-neng 良能

Lieh-tzu 列子
Lin Wu chün 臨武君
ling 令
liu-chia yao chih 六家要指
Liu Hsiang 劉向
Liu Hsin 劉歆
liu i 六藝
lun 倫
lun-lieh 倫列
Lun-yü 論語

mi 米
ming 命 fate
ming 名 name, term
ming-chia 名家 school of names, "logicians"
ming fen 名分
ming-i 明夷 hexagram no. 36 "intelligence
    repressed"
ming-t'ang 明堂
mo wei 莫為

nei 內
nei-ch'eng 內誠
nei-p'ien 內篇
nien-lü 念慮
nung-chia 農家

pa 霸
pa-cheng 八政
pai-shen 百神
pao-pien 褒貶
pien 辯
pu shen 不神

san te 三德
shang-ti 上帝
shao chih 少知
shen 神
Shen Pu-hai 申不害
Shen Tao 慎到
sheng 生
shih 士 "man of service," "intellectual"
shih 史 astrologer, historian
shih 使 emissary, functionary
shih 實 concrete, real
shih 勢 authority, power
shih i 十翼
shih wei 勢位
shu¹ 術
shu² 數
shuo 說
Shuo-wen 說文

ssu 思
Ssu-shu 四書
ssu tuan 四端
Su Ch'in 蘇秦
su ju 俗儒
su wang 素王
Sun-tzu 孫子
sung 訟 hexagram no. 6, "litigation"
Sung Hsing 宋鈃

ta-lun 大倫
ta wei 大偽
ta-yeh 大業
tao-chia 道家
tao-chiao 道教
tao-shu 道術
t'ai-chi 太極
t'ai-i 太一
T'ai Kung-tiao 太公調
T'ai-shang Lao-chün 太上老君
te 德
ti 帝 high god
ti 禘 royal ancestral sacrifice
t'i tao 體道
t'ien-hsia 天下
t'ien-hsia chih li 天下之利
t'ien-hsin 天心
t'ien i 天意
t'ien-jen chih chi 天人之際
T'ien P'ien 田駢
tsa-chia 雜家
tsa p'ien 雜篇
Tsao chün 竈君
tsao hua 造化
tsao wu che 造物者
tse 則
Tsou Yen 鄒衍
Tso chuan 左傳

tsu 祖
ts'un-hsin 存心
Tzu-ch'an 子産
tzu-wei 自為

wai 外
wai-p'ien 外篇
wang 王
wei 為
wei 位 office, position
wei chi 未濟 hexagram no. 64, "not yet completed"
Wei[1] 衛 small state founded by Chou
Wei[2] 魏 one of successor states of Chin
Wei Mou 魏牟
wen 文
wen-yen 文言
wu 無
wu-chi 五紀
Wu Ch'i 吳起
wu-hsing 五行
wu-kuan 五官
wu-ming 無明
wu-shih 五事
wu-wei 無為

yeh 業
yin-tz'u 淫辭
yin-yang chia 陰陽家
Yin Wen-tzu 尹文子
yu 有
yu hsia 遊俠
yu-wei 有為
yü i jen 余一人
yüeh 約 convention
Yüeh Ling 月令

# INDEX

Action, 158, 162, 166, 174, 241

Agriculture, 16, 26, 45, 106, 189; and "private property," 136; and Legalism, 332, 333; and five elements, 358; and correlative cosmology, 367; god of, 372–373. *See also* Labor

Ai T'ai-t'o, 211, 232

Akatsuka Kiyoshi, 19, 28, 29, 30, 35, 180

Alcibiades, 60

*Analects (Lun-yü)*: as text, 61–67; noble men in, 76, 97, 111; and *i,* 79, 145, 174; definition of *jen,* 81, 146, 174, 264; *li,* 84, 383; and history, 86; forms of thought, 90; and language, 91–94, 110; and learning, 96, 98, 276, 315, 402; and politics, 102, 278; and government, 104, 113, 114, 115, 282, 327, 328, 414; ethics, 109, 397; style, 137; and fate, 138–139, 140, 158; "thinking," 157; and organization, 161; and authority, 164; terms, 177, 180, 184, 185, 321; and Taoism, 188, 190, 195, 200, 386, 404; attacks on, 255; compared with book of Mencius, 258, 281, 286, 289, 297; and Hsün-tzu, 297, 304, 318; holism, 353–354; and cosmos, 370, 381; disciplines, 383; commentaries on, 385, 386; and *Spring and Autumn Annals,* 386, 387, 390; and Five Classics, 400, 404; and intellectuals, 409. *See also* Confucius; *jen; li*

Anarchism, 210–213

Anaximander, 183, 203, 360

Anaximenes, 180, 181, 182, 184, 359, 361

Ancestor worship, 16, 20–28, 29, 68; and order, 31, 32, 37; and kingship, 35, 38, 43, 48–49; and family, 69–70, 99, 115; and cultural interactions, 408

Anthropomorphism, 32, 33, 370. *See also* High God; Spirits

Apsu, 31, 182. *See also* High God

Archaeology, 18, 42

Archery, ceremonial, 54, 58, 85

Archivists (*shih*), 34, 58

Arendt, Hannah, 102

Aristotle, 6, 63, 65, 70, 90; and family, 27, 69, 100; compared with Confucius, 83, 84, 100; and goodness, 96; view of "political science," 97; and intellectual curiosity, 99; *Politics,* 101; Hobbes on, 144; and Mo-tzu, 156, 167; orientation, 182, 183; logic, 184; terms, 223–224; and Plato, 231; and Mencius, 267, 270; and Machiavelli, 348; four elements theory, 358; nature philosophy, 362

Artisans, 151, 163, 167, 246, 294

Assyria, high gods, 31

Astrology, 353, 357. *See also* Cosmology

Ataraxy, 202, 242, 243

Athens, 63, 69, 98

Atomism, 182, 184, 359

Authority: and family, 68, 69, 70, 71, 100, 101, 102, 115, 260; and *tao,* 76–77, 344; political, 85, 150, 163–164, 245, 250, 252, 286; hereditary, 110, 114, 115, 116, 161, 163, 283–284, 289, 305, 306, 327; Legalistic view of, 332, 339–348, 349; in *Spring and Autumn Annals,* 387; and merit, 415

Autonomy, 334–335, 337, 417

Babylon, 24, 31

Balazs, Etienne, 43

Barker, Ernest, 69, 78, 96, 97

Behaviorism, Legalistic, 329, 335, 339, 347